volume I

History
of the
CANADIAN
P E O P L E S

Beginnings   to   1867

volume I
History
of the
CANADIAN
P E O P L E S

Beginnings to 1867

Margaret Conrad
Acadia University

Alvin Finkel
Athabasca University

Cornelius Jaenen
University of Ottawa

Copp Clark Pitman Ltd.
A Longman Company
Toronto

ISBN: 0-7730-4843-X

Managing editor: Barbara Tessman
Executive editor: Jeff Miller
Editors: Curtis Fahey, Robert Clarke, Claudia Kutchukian
Photo research: Maral Bablanian
Design: Kyle Gell
Cover illustration: Rocco Baviera
Map illustrations: Allan Moon, David McKay, Valentino Sanna
Typesetting: Carol Magee, Marnie Morrissey
Printing and binding: Best Gagné Book Manufacturers

Canadian Cataloguing in Publication Data

Main entry under title:

History of the Canadian peoples

Includes bibliographical references and index.
Contents: v. 1. Beginnings to 1876 / Margaret Conrad, Alvin Finkel, Cornelius Jaenen. – v. 2. 1867 to the present / Alvin Finkel, Margaret Conrad with Veronica Strong-Boag.
ISBN 0-7730-5346-8 (set)
ISBN 0-7730-4843-X (v.I) 0-7730-5189-9 (v. II)
I. Canada – History. I. Conrad, Margaret. II. Finkel, Alvin, 1947– . III. Jaenen, Cornelius J., 1927– . IV. Strong-Boag, Veronica Jane, 1947– .
FC164.H58 1993   971   C93-093786-4   F1033.H58 1993

Copp Clark Pitman Ltd.
2775 Matheson Blvd. East
Mississauga, Ontario
L4W 4P7

Associated companies:
Longman Group Ltd., London
Longman Inc., New York
Longman Cheshire Pty., Melbourne
Longman Paul Pty., Auckland

Printed and bound in Canada

   2   3   4   5   4843-X   97   96   95   94

For our students past and present.
We hope that this is the kind of text where
they can identify something of their personal past.

CONTENTS

PREFACE   xii

INTRODUCTION Interpreting Canada's Past   xiv

    The New Social History   xiv
    Geography and History   xviii
    Onwards and Upwards   xx

● Part I: Beginnings   1

CHAPTER 1 The First Nations of Canada   5

    The Physical Environment   5
    Writing Native History   9
    First Nations Before 1500   12
    The Atlantic and Gulf Region First Nations   18
    The Great Lakes–St Lawrence Lowlands First Nations   20
    The Canadian Shield First Nations   24
    The Interior Plains First Nations   31
    The Western Cordillera First Nations   34
    The North's First Nations   38
    Conclusion   40

    Native Origins: A Historiographical Debate   42

CHAPTER 2 Second Peoples: The European Background   48

    The European Social Order   49
    Population   52
    Economic Life   58
    Women and the Economy   62
    Role of the State   63
    Religion   65
    Culture and Ideas   69
    Technology   71
    Exploration and Expansion   73
    Conclusion   76

    Cruelty versus Germs: A Historiographical Debate   77

CHAPTER 3 The "Discovery" of Canada: Contact and
            Settlement to 1663   82

    Making Contact: The Role of the Fishery   83
    Early British Colonization: The Newfoundland
        Experience   88
    Early French Colonization: From Cartier to the
        Founding of Acadia   90

The Founding of Quebec, the Fur Trade, and
    European–Native Relations   98
Preaching the Word   102
Women and Religion   106
The Huron–Iroquois Wars   110
Building a Community   113
Conclusion: New France on the Eve of Royal Rule   118

The Destruction of Huronia:
    A Historiographical Debate   120

● Part II: France in America   125

CHAPTER 4 The Emergence of Continental New France,
    1663–1715   129

The Age of Absolutism   130
Absolutism in New France   133
Colonial Administration   139
Law and Order   141
Religious Establishment   145
Mercantilism   151
Seigneurialism   154
Fish, Furs, and Territorial Expansion   158
Wars and Alliances   162

The Status of Women in New France:
    A Historiographical Debate   167

CHAPTER 5 Life in a Strategic Outpost, 1715–60   172
The Imperial Factor   173
A New Strategic Role   174
Louisbourg   177
The Canadian Economy   178
Town Life   190
Canadian Peasant Society   194
The Family Under the French Regime   198
Class and Society   202
Slavery   206
Labour   208
Conclusion   209

Theocratic Tyranny or Benevolent Paternalism?
    A Historiographical Debate   211

CHAPTER 6 Conquest Achieved, Conciliation Attempted,
    1713–91   216

Enemies and Alliances   217

The Beginnings of British Rule in the Atlantic Region   221
The Neutral French   224
Mi'kmaq and Maliseet   226
War of the Austrian Succession, 1744–48   227
The Uneasy Peace, 1749–55   231
The Acadian Deportation   235
The Seven Years' War, 1756–63   238
The Conquest and Native Policy   246
The Conquest and Quebec   249
Civilian Rule   252
The Quebec Act, 1774, and the American Revolution   254

Culture and Conquest: A Historiographical Debate   260

● **Part III: Origins of British North America**   267

CHAPTER 7   The Peopling of British North America, 1750s–1800   271

Nova Scotia   272
St John's Island   279
Newfoundland   281
The Loyalist Interlude, 1775–85   287
Quebec, 1783–91   295
The Constitutional Act, 1791   302
Rupert's Land   305
British North America in 1800   310

The Loyalists: Lessons in Historiography   311

CHAPTER 8   The Atlantic Colonies, 1784–1850s   318

Defining the Atlantic Region   318
Population Growth in the Atlantic Region   321
Economic Adjustment   330
The Domestic Economy   337
Social Relations in Pre-industrial Society   342
Emerging Political Cultures, 1758–1849   343
Religion and Culture   350

The Colonial Economy in Atlantic Canada:
A Historiographical Debate   358

CHAPTER 9   The Canadas, Social and Economic Developments, 1791–1850   365

The Social Landscape, 1791–1812   366

Postwar Migration 375
Family and Work in the Canadas, 1815–50 382
Conclusion 396

Lower Canada's Agricultural Crisis:
    A Historiographical Debate 397

CHAPTER 10   Rebellions and Responsible Government:
    Politics in the Canadas, 1800–1850s 404

Opposition Before 1812 405
The War of 1812 408
The Road to Rebellion 412
The Struggle for Responsible Government 424
Responsible Government in Action 426
Education and the Changing Political Order 430
Conclusion 434

Social Mobility in Canada West:
    A Historiographical Debate 436

CHAPTER 11   The West, 1763–1850s 441

HBC–NWC Rivalry and Native People 442
The Birth of the Métis Nation 451
The Founding of the Red River Settlement 453
The Fur-Trade Monopoly Period, 1821–49 455
British Columbia: The European Phase 462
Visions of the Northwest 472
The Northern Fur Trade 474
Conclusion 475

Native Women and the Fur Trade:
    A Historiographical Debate 476

CHAPTER 12   British North America at Mid-Century 483

Small Worlds 484
Town and Country 490
Gender and Society 493
Class and Culture 495
Race and Racism 497
Contours of Colonial Society 502
Poverty in a Cold Climate 508
Social Control 511
Leisure, Sports, and Creative Arts 514
Conclusion 521

Religion and Culture:
    New Historiographical Approaches 522

● Part IV: Industrializing Canada   531

CHAPTER 13   British North America's Revolutionary Age   535

Industrial Revolution   536
Free Trade, Reciprocity, and Protection   538
Transportation   541
Mobilizing Labour and Capital   545
Law and Industry   549
The Structure of Industrial Capitalism   551
Intellectual Revolutions   554
The Discovery of the Asylum   562
Public and Private Worlds   565

Educational Reform: A Historiographical Debate   572

CHAPTER 14   The Road to Confederation   579

The Nation-State in the Nineteenth Century   580
The Canadas: Economic Success and Political Impasse   582
Great Expectations in the Maritimes   589
The External Pressure for Confederation   591
Planning Confederation   594
The Selling of Confederation   597
Conclusion   606

Economic Elites and Confederation:
    A Historiographical Debate   609

INDEX   614

LIST OF MAPS

Map 1.1	Physiographic Regions of Canada	6
Map 1.2	Aboriginal Cultural Areas	9
Map 1.3	Native Tribes at the Time of Contact	13
Map 1.4	Native Subsistence	15
Map 2.1	Western Europe in 1500	51
Map 3.1	New France in the Seventeenth Century	95
Map 4.1	North America, 1697	134
Map 4.2	North America, 1713	135
Map 6.1	France in America, 1663–1755	220
Map 6.2	Acadia in the Eighteenth Century	223
Map 6.3	North America, 1763	247
Map 6.4	North America, 1783	259
Map 8.1	The Atlantic Region, 1871	349
Map 11.1	The Western Fur Trade in the Nineteenth Century	457
Map 12.1	British North America, 1866	485
Map 13.1	Canals and Railways Before Confederation	546

LIST OF TABLES

Table 2.1	Selected European Population Figures	52
Table 4.1	Immigrants to Canada by Sex and Decade	137
Table 5.1	Fur Exports from Quebec	179
Table 5.2	Value of Ginseng Exports	183
Table 5.3	Occupational Hierarchy of New France	204
Table 9.1	Per Farm Marketable Surpluses and Their Distribution, Ontario, 1861	385
Table 14.1	Population of British North America	582

P R E F A C E

Not so very long ago Canadian history textbooks began at chapter 3 in this text—with the arrival of Europeans on the eastern shores of North America. We start with the origins of the aboriginal peoples and a discussion of their societies in the thousands of years that they occupied the area of present-day Canada. Chapter 2 provides background on the European world that began to export its peoples and cultures around the world in the fifteenth and sixteenth centuries. Together, these opening chapters set the stage for the early encounters between Natives and Europeans that are discussed in chapter 3.

Like most other texts available today, this one surveys the rise of the French empire in North America and the great rivalry between France and Britain for colonial possessions (chapters 4, 5, and 6). We also describe the roles played by aboriginal peoples in these events and the impact of colonial rivalry on their societies. As well as the larger geo-political developments, these and other chapters in the text explore the evolution of colonial communities. A wide range of people usually absent from history texts—women, racial and ethnic minorities, and the poor, among others—helped to create the Canada that we know today, and their stories are included here along with the achievements of the rich and powerful.

Chapter 7 provides an overview of the various colonies in British North America as they had emerged by 1800, while chapters 8 through 11 trace the evolution of these colonies from the late eighteenth century, when their existence depended on the extraction of a few staples, through to 1850, when the impact of the Industrial Revolution began to reverberate throughout colonial British North America. Chapters 12 and 13 examine the social, economic, and intellectual currents that defined British North America in the mid-nineteenth century and provide the context for the confederation movement described in chapter 14.

The authors wish to acknowledge the role of Veronica Strong-Boag, Michael Behiels, and Brian Henderson in formulating the original design of this text, and to thank the many people who read and suggested improvements for some or all of these chapters: Veronica Strong-Boag, Michael Behiels, Jim Pritchard, Brian Young, John Dickinson, Douglas Baldwin, and Barry Moody. Curtis Fahey, our chief editor, suggested a wealth of additions and changes, and copy editor Robert Clarke tried to make our prose as clear as possible. Maral Bablanian provided help with locating various photos and permissions to use them. Without the encouragement, suggestions, and stern reminders from Managing Editor Barbara Tessman, it is unlikely that this text would have survived its difficult birthing process. She more than any other single person involved in the project kept us focussed on the ideal of a readable social history text, and her patience was remarkable throughout. We also gratefully acknowledge secretarial assistance from Myrna Nolan and Claire Gemmell at Athabasca University and Brenda Naugler and Carolyn Bowlby at Acadia. Of course, none of these people bears responsibility for any remaining faults in the text, but each deserves credit for much of what readers may find praiseworthy.

INTRODUCTION

INTERPRETING CANADA'S

PAST

In 1829, Shawnadithit, the last surviving Beothuk, died of tuberculosis in Newfoundland. Several decades later, three British North American colonies united to form the Dominion of Canada. The second of these two events has always had a central place in Canadian history textbooks. The first, until recently, has been ignored. For students of history in the 1990s, it is important to understand why the focus of historical analysis changes and what factors influence historians in their approaches to the past.

The New Social History

In its broadest sense history is the study of the past. In non-literate societies, people passed down oral traditions from one generation to the next, with each generation fashioning the story to meet the needs of the time. When written language was invented, history became fixed in texts. The story was often revised, but earlier texts could be used to show how interpretations of the past had changed over time. Although ordinary people continued to tell their stories, "official" history was embodied in orthodox texts. Some of those texts, such as the Bible and the Koran, were deemed to be divinely inspired.

In Europe and North America, history became an academic discipline in the nineteenth century. Scholars in universities began to compare texts, develop standards of accuracy, and train students to become professional historians. At first professional historians focussed on political and military events, but gradually they broadened their scope to include economic and social developments.

No matter how meticulously researched, most academic histories written before 1970 either ignored, or treated unsympathetically, women, people of colour, and issues relating to private life. For example, a lesbian Native woman reading published historical works would have found only disparaging or condescending remarks about Native people, virtually no information about women's culture, and complete silence on homosexuality. Working-class women and men and members of ethnic groups who were not English, Scottish, or French would have learned little about their forebears from reading Canadian history.

Part of the reason that history was so narrowly focussed lies in the sources of information available to historians. The literate few, and especially the powerful among them—kings, prime ministers, bishops, and the like—have left behind far more written records than the millions of people whose lives they dominated. Our knowledge of medieval Europe, for example, is largely based on the accounts of church officials. Their belief that religious convictions governed the lives of the masses can be neither confirmed nor denied by direct evidence from the serfs, who left no written sources. Although social historians have found indirect evidence suggesting that the clerical interpretation exaggerates the piety and subservience of the majority, the fact remains that serfs, slaves, labourers, and peasants have received far less attention from historians than have the elites who ruled them.

Another reason for the narrow focus is that history was written by a small elite of educated white men to be read by others like themselves. Their interests understandably turned to war and political developments in which they and their peers participated; and their interpretation was usually from the point of view of the people who dominated such events. When women, children of the working class, and minorities began entering universities in larger numbers in the 1960s, they demanded that "their" history also be taken into account. Their questions encouraged a different approach to the past. Instead of seeing history as a sequence of events orchestrated by a small and powerful elite, scholars began to interpret it as an arena in which classes, ethnic groups, and individual men and women struggled to control the values that shaped their collective lives.

When history is approached as a contested terrain, its events must be analysed from a variety of perspectives. For example, when we discuss the rebellions of 1837 in Upper and Lower Canada, we recognize the importance of understanding not only the actions and attitudes of British officials and the ruling cliques within the Canadas, but also those of the ambitious middle classes, the farmers, and the landless poor. The goals of the rebels in Lower Canada varied depending on whether the focus is on a habitante with no bread to feed her children or a wealthy seigneur like the rebel leader Louis-Joseph Papineau. Similarly, the conclusions reached about the significance of events such as the rebellions of 1837 depend upon which actor's—or group of actors'—point of view is being considered.

Because each historian brings individual values and concerns to the study of the past, it is important to know something about the people who write history texts. The region, ethnicity, social class, gender, and political perspective of the historian, as well as the time of writing, are often reflected, consciously or unconsciously, in decisions about what subjects to analyse, what documents to consult, and how to interpret their relative meaning and importance. As historians now realize, documents cannot "speak for themselves." They have to be analysed critically because the context in which they were produced is as complex as the historian's own background.

Over the past two decades, social historians have made a concerted effort to provide a broader view of Canada's past. They have drawn upon other disciplines, such as geography, demography, economics, political science, sociology, anthropology, archaeology, and psychology to fill the gaps in their written sources. By taking an interdisciplinary approach, it is often possible to learn something about the motives of the silent majority who are usually left out of textbooks. Material evidence from archaeological excavations, data from censuses and immigration lists, oral traditions passed down from one generation to the next: these sources have all helped historians to develop a more complex sense of the reality of people's lives in past times. When personal computers became widely available in the 1970s, historians were able to process larger amounts of historical information. The science of demography, which analyses population trends and draws upon vast quantities of data, has proved particularly useful in helping historians to trace changes in family size, life-cycle choices, and migration patterns.

At the same time that new methodologies extended the scope of history, scholars were being influenced by new theoretical perspectives. Historians who studied women, minorities, and the working class brought insights from Marxism, feminism, and postmodernism to bear on historical inquiry. In focussing on issues such as class, race, ethnicity, and gender, and by asking new questions about old texts, historians have revolutionized the way we look at the past.[1]

This two-volume text attempts to integrate the findings of "the new social history" with earlier work on the rich and powerful to produce a more comprehensive portrait of Canadian society. While social history is emphasized, political history is not ignored. Indeed, we make an effort to show the impact on ordinary Canadians of decisions made by elites both inside and outside Canadian geographic boundaries. For example, in our discussion of the complicated class structure within the fur-trading empire of the Hudson's Bay Company in the mid-nineteenth century, we note that decisions made in London as well as those made by Governor Sir George Simpson in Canada helped to put this structure in place. We also show that the men who created the structures could not always control them. The Hudson's Bay Company's ability to focus its profit-making attention on fur trading alone was weakened by Métis resistance to company rules, by changing fashions in European markets, and by changing relations between women and men on the fur-trade frontier. It is this interaction—leading at times to compromises and at times to conflict—that underscores our discussion of Canadian politics.

It would be misleading to suggest that the new social history has produced consensus on historical issues. It is more correct to say that it has widened the debate. At various points in this text we discuss *historiography*; that is, debates about historical interpretation. In a survey text we can only touch upon the range of historiographical discussion, but we want students to consider a few examples of common historical assumptions that recent writings have challenged.

WHAT'S IN A NAME?

Contemporary political movements have forced historians to think about the words they use to describe Canadians. Thirty years ago most textbooks used the term "negroes" to refer to people with black skin. In the 1960s "black" became the politically conscious way to refer to people of African descent. More recently "African Canadian" has become the more popular term. Similarly, the words used to describe aboriginal peoples have changed in recent years. "Savages" was quickly dropped from textbooks in the 1960s, and although the misnomer "Indian" is still widely used today—and has particular applications that as yet seem unavoidable—the preferred terms seem to be "Native peoples" and "First Nations." "Amerindian" is a scholarly term to encompass the wide range of Native peoples and cultures.

Women, too, have insisted on being described in more respectful terms. Feminists objected strongly to the use of the word "girl" when adult women were being discussed, and they dismissed "lady" as being too condescending or elitist. Because "man" was adequate for the male of the species, "woman" seemed the most appropriate term, although some radical feminists have used the spelling "wymyn." Only the most hidebound of scholars still insist that the word "man" can be used to describe the entire human species.

Many scholars complained loudly about being asked to abandon words long established in their vocabularies. A few even argued that "political correctness" restricted freedom of speech. We do not hold such views. Because English is a living language and changes over time, we see no reason why it should not continue to change to reflect the new consciousness of groups in Canadian society. Indeed the importance of language is obvious in the sometimes derisive phrase "politically correct." In our view, the words "politically conscious" more accurately describe the attempts by groups to name their own experience. Language, of course, is not only about naming things but about power. Attempts by oppressed groups to find their own language to fit their experiences should be seen in the context of their struggles for empowerment. In this text we attempt to keep up with the changing times while bearing in mind that people in the past used a different terminology. We are also aware that in the future we may have to revise the words we use as groups continue to reinvent their identities.

Geography and History

Historians have long recognized that geography has played an important role in the understanding of Canada's past, if for no other reason than that we have so much of it. With Canada occupying over 7 percent of the global land mass, it is not surprising that regions figure prominently in the country's historical development, and that an individual's sense of place is defined locally and regionally more often than nationally.

The Canadian nation-state is a human, not a geographical creation. Nevertheless, geography and climate help to define our political boundaries. Ten thousand years ago, most of the area that makes up present-day Canada was covered by ice. The nation's rugged terrain reflects its ice-age origins and explains why the northern half of the North American continent was less attractive to the First Nations and European immigrants than the warmer and more fertile regions to the south.

Canada is a northern nation, dominated by the great Canadian Shield, which makes up two-thirds of its terrain. The east–west thrust of soils, forests, and climate reinforces much of Canada's southern boundary, as does the St Lawrence–Great Lakes heartland. At the same time, north–south divisions of mountain ranges and plains serve as a geographical countervailing force. Most Canadians live within a few hundred kilometres of the American border and have easier access to their southern neighbours by land, air, and water than they have to other parts of their own country.

While twentieth-century developments in transportation and communication have largely eliminated geographical barriers to the movement of people and ideas, the origins of Canada's provinces can be found in an earlier era. The nation's federal system reflects a politics of place that, as we shall see, existed even before the arrival of the Europeans. Despite modern distinctions based on ethnicity, gender, and class, people in the Maritimes, Quebec, and the North, for example, also possess an identity based on geographical location and a shared historical experience in their geographic home.

The reasons why humans react to their environment in certain ways are complex. It is not difficult to understand why the First Nations of Newfoundland in the pre-contact period failed to develop farming practices, while their counterparts in the Great Lakes basin depended on farming for 70 percent of their food supply. There is simply very little good farmland in Newfoundland, while there is excellent potential for agriculture in what is today Ontario and Quebec. But why did the First Nations on the northern Prairies, later the breadbasket of the world, rarely farm? Did they simply lack the imagination? Or did the abundance of game, especially buffalo, make it unnecessary to develop an alternative supply of food? Or were there technological hurdles that had to be overcome before the Prairies could be successfully turned into rich wheatlands? These kinds of questions need to be addressed if we are to fully understand the regional character of the country.

In the past, history texts tended to be written with a Central Canadian bias. Historians, most of them working in Central Canadian universities, focussed on people and events in Ontario and Quebec and saw historical developments from the perspective of this region. They structured their chapters around dates that reflected significant episodes in the St Lawrence–Great Lakes region, such as the conquest or the rebellions, rather than developments in the Atlantic colonies, the Prairies, or the North. In this text we openly acknowledge that the tensions between the St Lawrence–Great Lakes "heartland" and the "peripheral" regions to the east, west, and north play a part in Canadian historical development. We attempt not only to discuss topics relevant to the "peripheral" regions of the nation but also to introduce regional perspectives on national developments, along with time frames that reflect the larger Canadian experience.

Although there is a surprising amount of documentary evidence concerning Canada's changing ecological history, it was only with the growth of the environmental movement in the 1970s that historians began to explore the impact of humans on their natural environment. We can now see new significance in the statements made by New Brunswick historian Peter Fisher in the 1820s to the effect that moose were being indiscriminately slaughtered and lumber companies were stripping the land of trees. In attempting to trace the changes in the environment over the past five hundred years, we offer a historical perspective on the environmental crisis that Canadians face today.

Onwards and Upwards

The questions raised about the relationship of human beings to the planet have also prompted Canadian historians to reevaluate their interpretations of human interaction. In the past, historians simply assumed that the European conquest of Canada represented a step in the upward progress of "Western civilization." They were conditioned to accept notions of European moral superiority over other groups, the value of technological progress, and the right of Europeans to establish dominion over "inferior" peoples. Such views no longer go unchallenged. Aboriginal leaders now reject the Eurocentric view of the contact between Europeans and the aboriginal people of the Americas. They suggest that the First Nations embodied more egalitarian and peaceful values than the technologically superior European societies of the time. They also argue that Native peoples had a more positive relationship with the environment.

There is much evidence to support the Native interpretation of the past. By the time of contact, the Europeans, or at least their elites, had embraced social values that stressed domination: domination of women by men, domination of certain strata of citizens by a relatively tiny ruling group, and domination of the natural world by humankind. By contrast, most Native societies—like many European societies in earlier stages of their development—emphasized harmony among their members and with nature. While European values promoted scientific developments, the Natives of North America avoided the environmental destruction that dogged European "progress."

Many scholars now accept the Native perspective of events relating to the contact period and no longer see the European path of development as having beneficial consequences for the planet. As we shall see in later chapters, there is evidence that Canada's Native peoples had rich cultures that were weakened by European influence. In some cases the contact turned egalitarian, self-sufficient tribes into poverty-stricken groups riddled by disease, drunkenness, and abuse of women and children. This insight developed in part because historians now have a greater appreciation of the devastation wrought by European diseases on the Native peoples of the Americas. Although pre-contact populations are difficult to estimate, it would appear that between 1500 and 1650 the Native populations of the Americas were reduced to a mere 10 percent of their original numbers. In the face of such human devastation it is not difficult to see why the Europeans were able to defeat their aboriginal "enemies." Europeans were not morally or even necessarily technologically superior to the aboriginal peoples; they were only more immune to the diseases they brought with them.

While a positive reevaluation of pre-contact Native life has emerged in recent years, many scholars warn of the danger of romanticizing Native culture. Some aboriginal nations are alleged to have been warlike, others clearly practised slavery, and the evidence regarding the treatment of women in various tribes is, at best, contradictory. The disappearance of various animal species in the pre-contact period and evidence of wasteful hunting practices suggest that small populations, rather than conscious environmentalism, account for the lesser destruction of the environment in the pre-contact period compared to the period of European trade and settlement. We explore aspects of this debate in chapter 1.

The history of Native peoples is only one of many topics that have been fundamentally reevaluated in recent years. The emergence of a large literature on women's history has done more than add women to the picture; it has challenged many of the conclusions reached by historians who examined only the rhetoric and behaviour of male elites. In Canadian history, we now see the winning of responsible government in the mid-nineteenth century as primarily the triumph of middle-class white men. Women had to wait another seventy years for the vote and even longer to exercise significant political power.

Historians of women are quick to point out, however, that women were not merely passive victims of the historical process. Throughout the nineteenth century, for instance, parsons and pundits proclaimed that woman's place was in the home. They also focussed upon motherhood as woman's primary function in society. Despite such admonitions, women entered the work force in increasing numbers and dramatically limited the number of children they produced. So concerned were male legislators about the decline in the birth rate that they passed a law in 1892 denying women access to birth control and making abortion illegal. Nevertheless, the birth rate continued to decline. As is often the case with the powerless in society, women in the nineteenth century left few records to indicate why or how they limited births, but statistical evidence clearly demonstrates that they did so.

The history of the working class has also provided a new perspective on the past. By looking at history "from the bottom up," historians have been able to explain more clearly how power is exercised in Canadian society. Class, of course, is a difficult concept that changes over time. In the eighteenth and early nineteenth centuries, old aristocratic notions of the class structure, emphasizing land and heredity, dominated colonial life. The Industrial Revolution in the mid-nineteenth century increased the power of the middle class and created a landless working class, which was itself highly stratified.

Despite—or more likely because of—the large number of studies conducted on the working class, there is disagreement on a number of important questions. Historians take different views on the extent to which the values of skilled workers differed from those of their employers, and they hotly debate the degree to which skilled workers embraced the cause of the labouring poor. As for the poor themselves, both men and women, their voices remain largely silent in the pages of our history books. Statistical evidence and the views of reformers outside their ranks have been more available to historians than have direct expressions by the poor about their own situation.

Another problem is that documents capture only a moment of reality. As historians, we know that circumstances do not stand still. Values change, people grow older, and new ways of doing things come into practice. It is important, therefore, when studying individuals, to think about where they are in their life cycles. The responses of children to famine migrations or head taxes might well be quite different than the responses of middle-aged adults—and still more different than the responses of people nearing the end of their lives. Only a few documents, such as personal diaries, remind us that individuals are moving through time and that where they are in their own lifetimes is a critical part of understanding their point of view.

The report of the Royal Commission on the Relations between Capital and Labour in 1889 assembled the testimony of child and adult workers from some of Canada's earliest factories. This testimony was influenced not only by the presence of mill owners and supervisors but also by the stage the workers were at in their own lives. Georgina Loiselle, who was beaten with a cigar mould by M. Fortier, her employer, reported the incident with little emotion and no sense of outrage. She may well have been relatively sanguine about the event, not only because Fortier was supposedly acting in place of her parents, but also because she saw her situation as transitory. Like many young women of her generation, she undoubtedly hoped to marry and leave the factory forever. Her testimony in the 1880s must be viewed as one part of an ongoing process, a part that makes only limited sense in isolation.

There is nothing inevitable about historical processes. At times in this text the limitations on an individual's behaviour set by age, class, gender, region, or race may appear to suggest that many, perhaps most, of our ancestors were hopeless victims of forces beyond their control. A closer reading should reveal that people sought in various ways to transcend the limits placed on their lives. Social struggles of every sort changed or at least sought to change the course of history. The American feminist historian Natalie Zemon Davis speaks for many social historians when she observes:

> I want to show how different the past was. I want to show that even when times were hard, people found ways to cope with what was happening and maybe resist it. I want people today to be able to connect with the past by looking at the tragedies and the sufferings of the past, the cruelties and the hatefulness, the hope of the past, the love the people had, and the beating that they had. They sought for power over each other, but they helped each other, too. They did things both out of love and fear—that's my message. Especially I want to show that it could be different, that it was different and that there are alternatives.[2]

As you read this book we hope that you will gain a greater appreciation of how earlier generations of people in what is now called Canada responded to their environment and shaped their own history.

Notes

[1] It should be pointed out, however, that in 1990 more than 85 percent of historians teaching in Canadian universities were white men.

[2] Interview with Natalie Zemon Davis in MARHU, *Visions of History* (New York: Pantheon, 1983), 114–5.

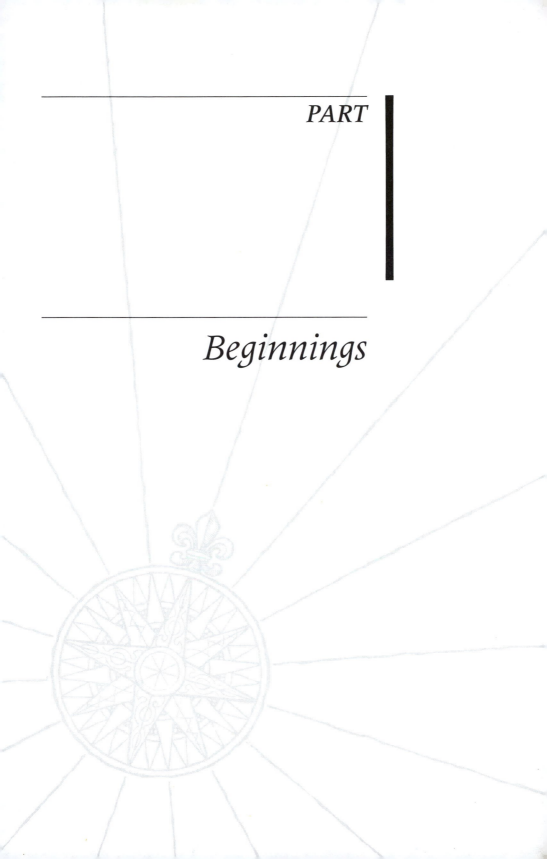

PART

Beginnings

Time Line

30 000–10 000 B.C.	–	Native peoples begin to inhabit North America
10 000 B.C.	–	Native peoples use fluted points (sharpened points on a projectile) to kill giant mammals such as mastodons and mammoths; human remains are deposited near today's towns of Old Crow, Yukon, and Taber, Alberta
9000 B.C.	–	Mastodons and mammoths become extinct
5000 B.C.	–	Natives on southern coast of Labrador build ritual burial mounds; Natives in southern Alberta use buffalo corrals to kill large mammals
4000 B.C.	–	To diversify their food supply, southern Ontario Indians make use of fish nets, weirs, and grinding implements
1200 B.C.	–	Only Siouan speakers are present in the woodlands north and west of the Great Lakes and on the Prairies
1000 B.C.	–	Chiefdoms begin to be established on the northwest coast; agriculture begins in the Atlantic region woodlands; southern Ontario Natives begin making pottery
900 B.C.	–	Algonkian-speaking groups enter the region north and west of the Great Lakes
500 B.C.	–	Trade relations are established between Natives in southern Ontario and the Atlantic region
250	–	Native groups begin using the bow and arrow for hunting
500	–	Horticulture is established in southern Ontario
1000	–	Viking settlements in Newfoundland

1300	–	Iroquoian societies begin building palisaded villages
1337–1453	–	Hundred Years War between England and France
1348	–	Black Death
1444	–	Portugal begins African slave trade
1450	–	Formation of the Iroquois Confederacy
1492	–	First voyage of Columbus to the Americas
1497	–	Vasco da Gama rounds Cape of Good Hope into Indian Ocean; John Cabot "discovers" Newfoundland
1521	–	Hernán Cortés conquers Aztec empire
1532–33	–	Francisco Pizarro conquers Inca empire
1534, 1535, 1541	–	Jacques Cartier voyages along the St Lawrence
1541–43	–	Cartier, followed by Roberval, makes unsuccessful colonization attempt at Quebec
1562–98	–	Religious warfare in France
1605	–	Establishment of Port Royal
1608	–	Establishment of Quebec
1615	–	Recollets arrive in New France
1625	–	Jesuits arrive in New France
1627	–	British seize Acadia; Compagnie de la Nouvelle France established
1629	–	British seize New France
1632	–	Acadia and New France return to French control
1639	–	Ursulines arrive in New France
1642	–	Founding of Montreal
1649	–	Destruction of Huronia
1654	–	British seize Acadia

1

THE FIRST NATIONS
OF CANADA

"I ask for the return of my country to me, and that the reserves be no more. It is not only just now that I came into possession of the country. It has always been mine from the beginning of time." Tsudaike, a chief of the Nackwacto, made this statement in 1914 to a royal commission established to investigate aboriginal land claims in British Columbia. Like many aboriginal leaders over the past five centuries, Tsudaike resented the arrogance of the Europeans who had invaded North America and seized control of the land. "What has been done to me with my country would be the other way," he concluded. "I would have measured pieces [of land] off for the whiteman, instead of the whiteman measuring off pieces for me."[1]

As Canadians approach the twenty-first century, they find the territorial integrity of their nation being increasingly challenged. If all outstanding aboriginal land claims are recognized, Euro-Canadians will suddenly know what it is like to live on delineated "reserves" surrounded by great expanses of territory governed by the first nations. Extensive portions of British Columbia, Quebec, the Atlantic provinces, and the territories have never been ceded by formal treaty. Whose land is it, and what is the nature of the vast territory over which there is so much controversy?

• The Physical Environment

The struggle to adapt to the physical environment has been a continuing theme throughout Canadian history. The mountains, hills, lowlands, the vast plains and forests, the lakes, rivers, and coastal waterways, the rocks and plants, the wildlife and the weather—the cold and the hot, the dry and the wet—have all, in their tremendous varieties, had their part to play in the country's historical record.

Canada is the second-largest nation in the world, covering over 7 percent of the earth's surface. Only Russia is larger. Throughout much of its history, Canada was a cold and inhospitable place, buried under a vast sheet of glacial ice. The last Ice Age reached its maximum extent about twenty thousand years ago. As the ice moved and melted, it created many of the geographical features we associate with present-day Canada.

There are six major physiographic regions—areas with similar landforms—in Canada, and there are several smaller ones (see map 1.1). The typology developed by Statistics Canada and Environment Canada in the 1980s suggests no fewer than fifteen "ecozones"—regions distinguished by similar landforms, climate, and vegetation. There are also eight distinct forest regions, although the boreal (northern) forest region dominated by white and black spruce accounts for the greater part of Canada's wooded areas. East to west, the key physiographic regions are the Atlantic and Gulf region, the Great Lakes–St Lawrence Lowlands, the Canadian Shield, the Interior Plains, the Western Cordillera, and the North.

The Atlantic and Gulf region is the northern portion of a physiographic region usually referred to as Appalachia. Like most other Canadian

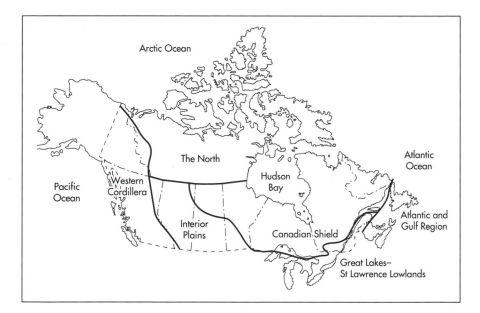

MAP 1.1   *Physiographic Regions of Canada*

regions, Appalachia straddles two national territories, a fact emphasizing the differences between natural regions and historically created boundaries. The Appalachians encompass most of the Atlantic region of Canada (except for Labrador, which is part of the Canadian Shield) as well as the Gaspé Peninsula of Quebec. They consist of ancient rounded hills and plateaus with a few large fertile areas such as the Annapolis–Cornwallis valley in Nova Scotia. Just beyond this region, under water, is the continental shelf, home to once apparently inexhaustible supplies of fish as well as oil and natural gas.

Climate and vegetation vary within this region. Near the coast precipitation is heavy and temperatures are less extreme than in the drier inland areas. The island of Newfoundland forms part of the boreal forest, with few deciduous trees amid the conifers. Most of the Maritime provinces, by contrast, lie within the forest region termed Acadian, which includes both deciduous and evergreen trees. While 80 percent of the Maritimes is forested, only 35 percent of Newfoundland is covered with trees.

In the Atlantic region, population has concentrated in the coastal areas and along the St John River. The sea and the rivers provided much of the food for the first nations peoples, although hunting and plant-gathering also provided important resources for survival. Systematic agriculture developed in the period of European settlement on the flat lowlands of Prince Edward Island and in the fertile valleys and plains of New Brunswick and Nova Scotia. Only a small portion of the land in the Atlantic region is classified as prime farmland—in Prince Edward Island it is 1 percent of the land surface, and in Newfoundland none at all. It is therefore not surprising that the region's first nations lived primarily by hunting and fishing rather than by farming.

The Great Lakes–St Lawrence Lowlands, which includes southern Ontario and southern Quebec, is a region dominated by gentle rolling hills, the product of the last Ice Age that occurred about ten thousand years ago. As it receded the ice ground down the sedimentary rock of the Canadian Shield, leaving an area with several major belts of fertile soil, particularly in southern Ontario. The lakes and rivers of the region provided key transportation routes, which had already led to continent-wide trade links in the period of exclusive occupation by first nations. Before extensive European settlement, deer, rabbits, beavers, bears, fowl, fish, and wild berries abounded, allowing aboriginal populations to increase steadily. Eventually, as population growth necessitated further food sources, some first nations took advantage of areas with good soil and favourable climate to begin planting crops.

If the Great Lakes region was a magnet to both first nations and Europeans, the Canadian Shield, which includes 40 percent of Canada's land mass, was a forbidding obstacle. With its terrain mostly covered by Precambrian rock, this region has proven inhospitable to aspiring farmers. Although its hills are interspersed with areas where the land, soil, and drainage do seem to offer good farming possibilities, the cool summers and limited number of frost-free days restrict agricultural development. But the abundant game within the region's forests supported dispersed Native populations, who faced little competition from European settlers before the nineteenth century when the minerals and trees of the region finally attracted commercial interest. In the twentieth century the hydro-electric potential of the rivers further contributed to industrial development.

In the nineteenth century, farmers began to covet the Interior Plains region, which was earlier only of interest to Europeans involved in fur trading. Over the course of several ice ages, flat layers of sedimentary rock were imposed on Shield rock. Flat clay plains intersected by glacial meltwater produced valleys here and there throughout a region characterized by plains and rolling hills. Good-to-excellent soil for farming marks a large portion of the Interior Plains. One-third of Saskatchewan, for example, consists of quality farmland, but climatic conditions limit yields from this land. Winters are harsh, the growing seasons are short and uncertain, and southwestern Saskatchewan and southeastern Alberta have limited rainfall. The first nations of the region rarely farmed because the abundant game (especially buffalo) and vegetation made a sedentary farming life unnecessary for the relatively small, dispersed populations.

There was a greater concentration of population in the Western Cordillera, a region consisting of a series of six mountain ranges extending through British Columbia and southwestern Alberta. Interspersed with plateaus, rivers, and valleys, the region contains freshwater fish, particularly salmon, as well as mountain sheep, bears, and deer in the coastal mountains. The mountain ranges offered a barrier to contact both among aboriginal nations and, later, between European settlers and Native peoples. The temperate climate on the coast and in the southern interior of the Cordillera provided a marked contrast with the climate of the Interior Plains and especially the North.

The North consists of a variety of subregions. Within the subarctic there are areas that might be seen as somewhat colder and less fertile extensions of the Cordillera and the Interior Plains. Further north is the Arctic, home to the Inuit. It is an area of no trees, little soil, and harsh, long winters. The underground permafrost, literally permanent frost, creates special problems for the construction of buildings. Only small concentrations of people dispersed throughout the region could be supported without depleting the caribou, moose, fish, waterfowl, and fur-bearing animals that the regional populations depended upon for basic survival.

MAP 1.2 *Aboriginal Cultural Areas*

These six regions formed the environment that shaped the experience of Canada's first peoples and challenged European explorers and settlers. In the distant past, major changes in the environment were the result of natural forces. Volcanic eruptions, earthquakes, floods, and falling meteorites were often such dramatic occurrences that they became etched in the folk memory of early peoples. More recently, human intervention has changed the face of the landscape. The first phase of the massive James Bay hydro-electric project, for instance, created a spillway three times higher than Niagara Falls and flooded 10 500 square kilometres of land, equivalent in size to all of Northern Ireland.

•Writing Native History

The role played by the Amerindian peoples in shaping Canada's history has in recent years begun to be recognized by the mainstream of Canadian historians. Before the 1960s, Canadian history texts generally began not with the arrival of the first peoples but with the "discovery" of the "New

World" by European explorers. Arguing that the discipline of history restricted itself to archival sources and therefore to literate peoples, historians relegated the study of pre-contact life to anthropologists and archaeologists. Fortunately, such rigid boundaries between disciplines have now begun to break down.

"Ethnohistorians," scholars whose background may be in one of many fields, study non-literate societies by piecing together evidence from European observations, anthropological studies, archaeological evidence, and relevant data provided by meteorologists, biologists, and other scientists. In short, ethnohistorians consider all the evidence possible to recreate the lives of the earliest inhabitants. Their success in influencing mainstream historical thinking is evidenced in the publication of recent histories of the aboriginal experience that lean heavily on their findings. J.R. Miller's *Skyscrapers Hide the Heavens* (1989) and Olive Dickason's *Canada's First Nations* (1992) reflect this trend.

The rich sources consulted by ethnohistorians often pose problems. The oral tradition of the Native peoples, fur traders' records of their early meetings with the Indians, accounts of priests, travellers, and others who had contact with the Natives, and archaeological evidence may each suggest different conclusions. Furthermore, for the hunting and gathering societies of pre-contact Canada—the groups dominating all regions except southern Ontario, the St Lawrence River valley, and the Pacific coast at the time of European arrival—the archaeological record is, in any case, weak. The archaeological evidence has also produced its share of mysteries. Ritual burial mounds are usually associated with agricultural societies, which have the leisure and labour needed to construct such shrines. Yet three burial mounds, seven thousand years old, have been uncovered on the southern coast of Labrador, where all other evidence suggests only hunters and gatherers ever lived in the pre-contact period. The mounds remind us how little we know and perhaps ever can know about life in the territory of today's Canada in the early periods of Native occupation of the land.

Attempts to reconstruct pre-contact history must obviously rely on the views of that history held by aboriginal peoples themselves. The tradition of handing down the history of a tribe or band orally from generation to generation was firmly established long before the Europeans arrived, and it has continued to thrive. But U.S. historian James Axtell suggests that there are three basic problems with relying on oral traditions to recreate the past. Firstly, one's knowledge of the past is determined by what people are currently talking about, so one has little perception of the past except in terms of the present. The danger, as Axtell says, is that "myth and history tend to merge."[2] Secondly, while oral knowledge is very conservative, it also is subject to "structural amnesia." This means that those elements that no longer have relevance for contemporary society can be forgotten or transformed. Thirdly, oral knowledge depends on human memory, which is, of course, fallible. Information can be lost by simple mistakes or by the death of a member of the community. This is particularly true since many cultures have wise men or women who become the repository for knowledge about the community's history and traditions. The loss of such a person could be devastating to a cultural group.

There is much debate about the impact on the Native oral traditions of massive cultural changes resulting from interaction with Europeans. For example, the oral tradition of the Innu of southern Labrador suggests that land was owned by individuals in the pre-contact period rather than held as common property. Historian A.G. Bailey, commenting on the reliability of oral traditions in this matter, writes: "Damaging to the argument of those who support the more individualized type of tenure as aboriginal is the failure to familiarize themselves sufficiently with the history of the early French fur-trading companies and missionary societies and the force of their impact upon the culture of the Eastern Algonkian peoples in the seventeenth century."[3]

Oral traditions are also limited as a historical source because their interpretation is shaped by the perceptions of the anthropologists who record them. For example, until recently most ethnographers were not only of European descent but also male, and the prevailing gender biases within the discipline of anthropology caused even most female field researchers to restrict their studies of women to women's relationships with men and children. Women's roles in subsistence activities, religion, and warfare were given short shrift by researchers, who concentrated on interviews with men. Writing about the Carrier of British Columbia, anthropologist Joanne Fiske asks:

> What sense do male ethnographers make of the hunting, trapping and fishing that is carried on by native Indian women in subzero temperature? How do they reconcile this with their own sense of manhood and how do they rationalize the fact that this role is not taken up only by women in the absence of men, but is actually sought by women in the presence of men? Moreover, within this situation, how does the male adventurer/ethnographer come to terms with the discovery that strong women assume key political roles through their deft rationalization of themselves as "good providers?"[4]

• First Nations Before 1500

Estimates of the Native population of the Americas at the time of permanent European intrusion toward the close of the fifteenth century have varied greatly, from 30 or 40 million to over 100 million, or about the same as the population of Europe at the time. The territory now called Canada included somewhere between 500 000 and 2 000 000 people. The smaller figure is based on the observations of early European writers, the larger on estimates (difficult to confirm) of the numbers of indigenous people who might have succumbed to European diseases before having direct contact with the invaders. The aboriginal societies in first contact with the Europeans traded the goods they received far and wide, and it is speculated that European germs spread throughout North America faster than the Europeans themselves.

Although the origins of the first nations of the Americas are debated, scholars generally argue that they are of Asiatic origin and arrived in the Americas in various waves of migration from 30 000 to 10 000 years ago. The route these pioneers followed was probably across land bridges that connected Siberia to Alaska during the ice ages. Native peoples themselves often reject the notion that they are descended from people who originated on other continents. Each native group has a creation myth that explains the origins of the world and its creatures, and these stories have in common the view that life began on this continent.

At least fifty distinct cultures encompassing twelve language groupings have been identified among Canada's first peoples. The phrase "language grouping" refers to languages with a common origin, not necessarily mutually understandable languages. The Iroquoian-speaking Huron of southern Ontario and the Five Nations Iroquois of New York, for example, spoke languages as different as the Romance languages of French and Portuguese are from one another.

The types of societies in which the Amerindians lived in the sixteenth century ranged from the scrupulously egalitarian model of the Athapaskan tribes of the subarctic to the slave-owning, highly stratified societies on the west coast. Although contact with the Europeans would bring dramatic and often unwanted changes to aboriginal ways of life, change had always been a feature of their lives.

For instance, when the last Ice Age receded about ten thousand years ago in southern Ontario and northern New York, the region's only residents appear to have been a few aboriginal groups hunting caribou. By 4000 B.C. the region's climate had grown warmer, boreal forest had replaced tundra, and deer had supplanted caribou. The people no longer

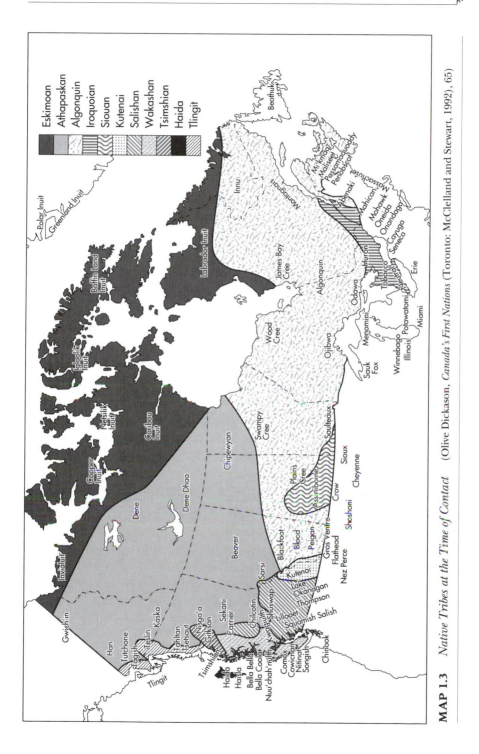

MAP 1.3 *Native Tribes at the Time of Contact* (Olive Dickason, *Canada's First Nations* (Toronto: McClelland and Stewart, 1992), 65)

Legend:
- Eskimoan
- Athapaskan
- Algonquin
- Iroquoian
- Siouan
- Kutenai
- Salishan
- Wakashan
- Tsimshian
- Haida
- Tlingit

Polar Inuit
Greenland Inuit
Baffin Land Inuit
Igloolik Inuit
Netsilik Inuit
Copper Inuit
Caribou Inuit
Labrador Inuit
Innu
Montagnais
Beothuk
Mi'kmaq
Maliseet
Passamaquoddy
Penobscot
Massachuset
Abenaki
Mahican
Mohawk
Oneida
Onondaga
Cayuga
Seneca
Huron
Tobacco
Neutral
Erie
Odawa
Potawatomi
Miami
Illinois
Winnebago
Menomini
Sauk
Fox
Ojibwa
Algonquin
James Bay Cree
Wood Cree
Swampy Cree
Saulteaux
Plains Cree
Sioux
Crow
Cheyenne
Assiniboine
Chipewyan
Dene
Dene Dhaa
Beaver
Blackfoot
Blood
Peigan
Gros Ventre
Shoshoni
Flathead
Nez Perce
Kutenai
Lake
Okanagan
Thompson
Shuswap
Lillooet
Squamish Salish
Sarsi
Chilcotin
Kwaguilth
Nuu'chah'nulth
Comox
Cowichan
Nihinat
Songish
Chinook
Carrier
Sekani
Nisga'a
Gitksan
Tsimshet
Tahltan
Setsaut
Kaska
Tagish
Teslin
Turchone
Han
Gwich'in
Inuvialuit
Haida
Haisla
Bella Bella
Bella Coola
Tlingit

SIZE OF NATIVE POPULATIONS

There has long been a debate about the size of first nations populations in the Americas. Historian Olive Dickason suggests that estimates of pre-Columbian Native populations have been rising throughout the twentieth century as our understanding of Native patterns of subsistence and the impact of European diseases on first nations has deepened. "Archeological evidence is mounting to the point where it can now be argued with growing conviction, if not absolute proof, that the pre-Columbian Americas were inhabited in large part to the carrying capacities of the land for the ways of life that were being followed and the types of food preferred."[5]

No doubt until that absolute proof is presented, skeptics will hesitate to accept that the estimated ten million aboriginals in the Americas at the turn of the eighteenth century represented fewer than 10 percent of those living there three centuries earlier. A recent U.S. demographic history uses the controversial word "holocaust" to describe the impact of contact on the peoples of the Americas: Russell Thornton, *American Indian Holocaust and Survival: A Population History Since 1492* (Norman: University of Oklahoma Press, 1987). The term is controversial because it implies that the decimation of aboriginal populations was not inadvertent but occurred as a result of conscious planning on the part of European invaders, much as Hitler's destruction of the Jews of Europe during World War II was planned.

relied solely on game for survival; they supplemented their food supply by catching fish in nets and weirs and using milling stones and mortars to grind nuts, berries, and roots. As the food supply became more varied and reliable the region's population expanded significantly. By 500 B.C. trade with other more remote nations brought in copper from Lake Superior and marine shells from the Atlantic coast.

Sometime after 500 A.D. in the same region, horticulture was introduced. Small villages of two hundred people or less combining hunting and farming became more common, and life was more sedentary than in earlier periods when the search for game forced frequent relocation. After 1300 the villages grew larger; and when the Europeans made contact with the Iroquoian-speaking peoples of the area in the late sixteenth century, they encountered palisaded settlements of 1500 to 2000 people. By that time confederacies of various nations had been formed in an attempt to bring peace to a region that had long been plagued with warfare. Well-

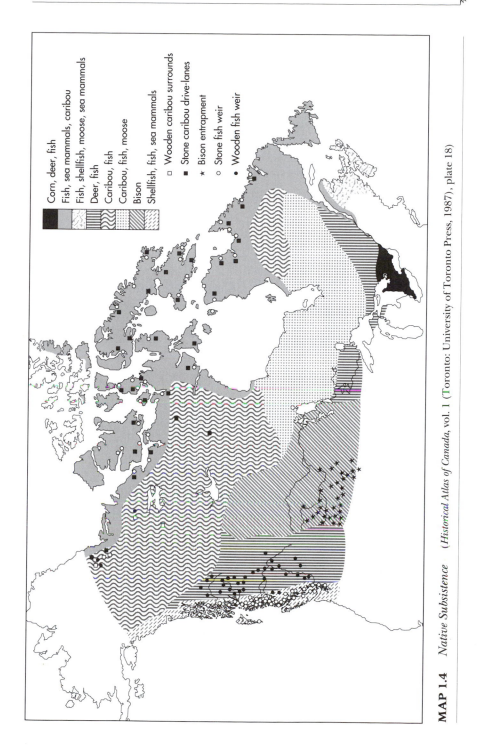

MAP 1.4 *Native Subsistence* (*Historical Atlas of Canada*, vol. 1 (Toronto: University of Toronto Press, 1987), plate 18)

Legend:

- Corn, deer, fish
- Fish, sea mammals, caribou
- Fish, shellfish, moose, sea mammals
- Deer, fish
- Caribou, fish
- Caribou, fish, moose
- Bison
- Shellfish, fish, sea mammals
- □ Wooden caribou surrounds
- ■ Stone caribou drive-lanes
- ★ Bison entrapment
- ○ Stone fish weir
- ● Wooden fish weir

crafted pottery suggests that the people had the wealth and leisure time to indulge in pursuits unrelated to mere survival.

Even in locales where hunting and gathering remained the main means of obtaining food, dramatic changes had occurred. During an estimated twelve thousand years of human habitation on the Prairies, for example, the inventions successively of the spear thrower, the bow and arrow, and the buffalo pound increased the time available for spiritual and leisure activities. The spear thrower allowed for a more forceful and accurate aim of the spear than the unaided hand could provide; the buffalo pound was a giant corral made of brush and hides into which a herd was driven to be systematically killed.

Improved possibilities of subsistence on the Prairies drew newcomers into the region. In 1200 B.C. only Siouan speakers subsisted on the plains of North America, but by the time of European contact the Blackfoot, who were Algonkian speakers, had come to dominate a portion of the region. The Sioux also disappeared from the thickly forested woodlands and the parklands north and west of the Great Lakes, replaced by Algonkian groups, including the Ojibwa and the Cree, who migrated in search of the caribou. By 1600 the Ojibwa and Cree were the chief inhabitants of northern Ontario, with the Sioux having been pushed southward and westward.

While change and diversity characterized Amerindian life in the pre-contact period, the various aboriginal groups shared a number of features. In all Native societies, religion, as much as nature, regulated everyday life. Native religions are characterized by a belief in a divinity residing within all living creatures as well as within all natural objects, a belief that not only reflects Native peoples' traditional closeness to nature but also contrasts with the Judaeo-Christian notions of a natural world in which humans, made in the likeness of God, are considered destined to dominate. Because Native religion was all-encompassing, attempts to analyse pre-contact societies have been limited by an inability to comprehend the intricacies of spiritual practices. As Jennifer Brown and Robert Brightman, writing of two Indian societies, note: "The subjective encounters of Cree and Saulteaux with their guardians in dreams, visions and waking states pose formidable difficulties for cross-cultural understanding, even supposing the willingness of individuals to communicate these often intensely private spiritual events to others."[6]

Another common feature of Native societies was their understanding of the natural world. Millenia of experimentation had unlocked, for example, an extensive botanical knowledge that was evident in an effective use of hundreds of plants for medicinal purposes. A familiarity with the properties of various types of wood and other natural materials was displayed in the successful production of means of transportation, including canoes, snowshoes, and toboggans, as well as homes of varying types, cooking utensils, and weapons. The aboriginal peoples' knowledge of their environment would prove crucial to the Europeans when they turned their attention to the profits available from exploiting the resources of the Americas. Historian Olive Dickason writes:

> Basque whalers availed themselves of Inuit harpooning technology to improve greatly the efficiency of their own techniques; Mi'kmaq . . . sea hunters put their expertise at the service of Europeans to pursue walrus for ivory, hides, and train oil, all much in demand by the latter; and later Amerindians did the same thing in the production of furs, so much sought after for the luxury trade, as status-conscious Europeans used furs (among other items) as symbols of rank. It has been estimated that by 1600 there may have been up to a thousand European ships a year engaged in commercial activities in Canada's northeastern coastal waters. Such activity would not have been possible without the co-operation and participation of the first nations of the land. When it came to penetrating the interior of the continent, Amerindians guided the way for the European "explorers," equipped them with the clothing and transportation facilities they needed, and provided them with food.[7]

The Native willingness to trade with the Europeans reflected the already established lines of trade among different Native groups. In the North, first nations with a local resource not found elsewhere traded for other resources or for manufactured products. Copper, iron, flint, the ivory of walrus, bird feathers, and birchbark canoes all figured in the region's trade. Algonkian hunters in the woodlands traded furs for corn and tobacco grown by Iroquoian-speaking peoples in the Great Lakes region and by the Mandans of the southern plains.

Excavations at Coteau-du-Lac, near the southern point of the present Ontario–Quebec border, indicate that the earliest inhabitants of the upper St Lawrence engaged in extensive trade to meet their needs. Among the materials found there are projectile points originating in northern Labrador, conch shells from the Gulf of Mexico, and copper from the upper Lake Superior region that was heated and annealed to make tools. Evidently, the various nations not only traded extensively with their neighbours but also served as go-betweens for items that moved over long distances along well-established trade and communications networks. When Europeans arrived, Native people introduced them to and often guided them along the established water routes, forest paths, and prairie trails.

Trade was the peaceful side of relations between Native groups, but warfare between neighbours apparently also occurred with some frequency in every region. Although some battles had economic causes or were motivated by cycles of revenge, the major motives for warfare were bound up with Native rituals. Warrior males trained and prayed for opportunities to prove their battle worthiness. Others, particularly women and elders, might attempt to restrain warfare, but it was rarely eliminated for extended periods. The limited technology of warfare in the pre-contact period and the ritualistic motivations for battles reduced the chances of all-out warfare that many European areas experienced in the fifteenth and sixteenth centuries. On both continents, torture or enslavement of captives was common.

Aboriginal peoples also seemed to share a relatively relaxed attitude toward sexual and childrearing practices. According to the early European commentators, premarital sex was widely practised in aboriginal society. Europeans were less shocked by that behaviour, which also occurred in their own societies, than by the fact that Natives expressed their feelings about sex openly and apparently experienced no guilt. By European standards, divorce in Native societies was an all too easy matter for couples who failed to get along with each other. Europeans also criticized the Native peoples' tolerant attitude toward children. The young were subject to little of the discipline, physical punishment, and exploitation that were typically the lot of children in Europe.

Unlike Europeans, who ruthlessly proscribed erotic encounters between members of the same gender, first nations people tolerated homosexual relationships. The term *berdache*, the French word for male prostitute, was used by Europeans to describe aboriginal people who cross-dressed and worked among members of the other gender. Some Native cultures believed that cross-working and cross-dressing women and men actually belonged to a third gender that combined male and female characteristics; but in most cases lesbians and homosexuals simply seem to have assumed the work roles and dress code of the other gender rather than incorporating the behavioural patterns of both men and women.

When Europeans arrived in the Americas in the sixteenth century, they found people hitherto unknown to them. No brief overview can do justice to the complex and diverse societies that existed in pre-contact Canada. The account below deals with only a fraction of the Native nations, and of those nations it provides only a glimpse at a particular moment.

•The Atlantic and Gulf Region First Nations

Several otherwise unrelated Algonkian-speaking cultures inhabited the Atlantic and Gulf region in the fifteenth century. The largest group was the Mi'kmaq, whose territory included parts of all three of today's Maritime provinces, but the region's peoples also included the Beothuk of New-foundland and the Maliseet of what is now southern New Brunswick.

In Newfoundland, geography limited the potential for population growth. Harsh climate, limited floral resources, and limited animal populations restricted the Beothuk to the coastal bays where small, mobile human populations could eke out a subsistence by fishing, hunting, and gathering. In contrast the Mi'kmaq constituted one of the most affluent first nations, living in one of Canada's more favoured geographical areas. Their population has been estimated to have reached as high as 35 000 before 1500, perhaps thirty times the Beothuk population.

Whatever archaeologists may conclude, the Mi'kmaq believed themselves to have been the residents of their territory from time immemorial. They had been placed there by the supreme deity, the Great Spirit. A lesser deity, Glooscap, created the natural features of the land during his stay on earth, and before he departed for the heavens he instructed the Mi'kmaq on how to make tools and weapons. He also foretold the coming of the Europeans.

The Mi'kmaq occupied a territory stretching from the Gaspé Peninsula to Cape Breton Island, taking in present-day Nova Scotia, Prince Edward Island, and northern New Brunswick. Unlike their southern neighbours, they did not establish permanent coastal settlements but lived according to a traditional migratory–subsistence cycle. Their conical wigwams, dress, and diet were much the same at the time of European contact as archaeology suggests they had been 1500 years earlier. Such continuity bespeaks a culture extraordinarily well adjusted and attuned to its natural surroundings, as well as a relatively stable environment capable of regenerating its resources.

Each year, when spring approached the Mi'kmaq would prepare for their fishing season, camping near bays and river mouths and setting up or repairing their fish-weirs in anticipation of the runs of smelt, herring, salmon, and sturgeon. Spring also meant the return of migratory birds in great numbers. Along with the year-round resident ducks and gulls, these birds, as well as their eggs and nestlings, provided an additional source of food. Shellfish, including scallops, clams, mussels, and oysters, were another important dietary item. In summer a variety of seals and walrus basked on the sandy beaches and were eagerly hunted. The Mi'kmaq also caught dolphins and small whales by boat and fished with baited bone-hooks for cod, sea trout, and halibut. As autumn approached they hunted large flocks of migratory birds, and in September they caught eels and dried them for winter use. When the air cooled and the first snow arrived it was time to move inland in search of moose and caribou as well as otter, muskrat, and bear—although the following severe winters often threatened starvation.

The Mi'kmaq greatly impressed the first European observers, who described them as intelligent, self-reliant, honest, and self-confident. Even missionaries, whose professional mandate was to reconstruct aboriginal cultures in the image of their own, admitted that these people were peaceable, hospitable, and charitable, displaying little of the materialistic acquisitiveness of European societies. They appear to have been second in affluence only to the peoples of the Northwest coast, and their wealth was evident in their intricate quillwork. Mi'kmaq society was relatively non-authoritarian. The people possessed neither codified laws nor police, and they exalted individual liberty and permissive childrearing.

Perhaps because of their relative affluence, the Mi'kmaq had produced formal governmental structures that went beyond the level of the band, that is, the face-to-face group of Natives who worked together to guarantee subsistence. Indeed, their structures went beyond the level of the tribe, the collection of bands in a given area, to include the entire Mi'kmaq people. Among the Mi'kmaq, a grand chief presided over all the tribes, and under him were seven district chiefs and a number of local chiefs. The local chiefs were assisted by councils of male elders. Consent rather than coercion kept Mi'kmaq government in place without a state apparatus of courts or police.

The Maliseet shared the Maritime region with the Mi'kmaq, but their subsistence cycle was somewhat different. Inhabiting the southern region of modern-day New Brunswick, they had just begun to cultivate corn and pumpkins at the time of European contact. Evidence is mounting that they built substantial houses near the seacoast and lived there the year round. Their oval, semi-subterranean "pit houses" were conical structures framed with poles, covered with bark and hides, and held in place by stones at the base. In these small buildings, families worked, ate, and slept.

•The Great Lakes–St Lawrence Lowlands First Nations

In pre-contact Canada, along with the societies organized mainly around hunting, gathering, and fishing there were also predominantly horticultural societies. These were mainly Iroquoian-speaking and concentrated in southern Ontario and the St Lawrence River valley, where they grew corn, beans, and squash. Taking advantage of moderate climate and good soils, these nations were less dependent than other groups on an abundance of game or fish to guard against famine. In the sixteenth century most of the

Huron cultivating corn   (Canadian Museum of Civilization J2436, detail)

Iroquois nations, like the Five Nations (later Six Nations) Confederacy in present-day New York state, supplied most of their food by planting crops. The St Lawrence Iroquoians, the Huron (in the Lake Simcoe–Georgian Bay area), and the Huron's neighbours, the Petun and the Neutral, together accounted for perhaps fifty thousand people in 1500. The Huron made up at least half of this group.

The large palisaded villages and the loose political confederacies of some of the Iroquoian groups marked them off culturally from most hunter-gatherer societies. Another distinctive characteristic was the long-house. Built of elm bark and attached to wooden frames, the longhouse was six metres wide and sometimes over thirty metres long, and within it about forty members of an extended family lived and shared responsibilities. A village might contain thirty to fifty of these longhouses, each with a row of fires down the middle and bedrooms on both sides. Underground storage pits, usually about $1^{1/4}$ metres deep and slightly less than a metre in diameter, held part of the harvest to protect it from fire and mice. In some villages chiefs had larger longhouses to accommodate village and war council meetings.

Iroquoian societies were matrilineal—descent was traced through the mother's line—and matrilocal—a man lived with the family of his wife. The women performed all the agricultural work and hence were the main food providers. The men were responsible for supplying the smaller portion of the food supply that came from hunting. A minority of men were also involved in intertribal trade. By the sixteenth century the Huron were extensively involved in barter with a variety of Algonkian groups. Corn, corn meal, and fish nets were traded for animal skins and fish. Only a small number of families controlled the trade, but the wealth they earned from it was redistributed within the Huron confederacy.

Redistribution of wealth within Native societies made it possible for groups to survive without establishing formal policing mechanisms. But it also made it possible for individuals to achieve higher status within the group. As Conrad Heidenreich explains, private property and equal distribution of wealth, mutually exclusive concepts in sixteenth-century Europe, co-existed among the Huron. Self-reliance and status-consciousness, social values that in other contexts produced an unbalanced distribution of wealth, were responsible for the opposite effect within Huronia.

> Land therefore seems to have been individually owned and partially operated by the larger family through mutual aid. The products of the land, however, were shared either with the extended family or with the larger community through gift giving, feasts or other institutionalized methods. The results of such generosity were prestige in the community and any honours such as official appointments that the community might wish to bestow. In a sense, therefore, it was necessary for individuals to own their own fields and produce the surplus necessary for gift-giving in order to gain public standing. Besides prowess in hunting, fishing, and war, a disposable agricultural surplus was the only other means of achieving personal standing in a community, either by giving the surplus away or by trading it for other products that could be redistributed. . . .
>
> It is possible therefore to reconcile individual ownership of land and feelings of communal responsibility.[8]

While village or tribe councils involved all men of the village over a certain age, important decisions required the approval of the women. For example, the men might decide to go to war with another tribe but if the women, who controlled agriculture, refused to supply food for the warriors, there could be no war. Chiefs were men from certain family-lines, but it was the women of the line who chose the chief and who could replace him if he failed to meet their expectations.

There was close contact among the various villages in a given area. Every Huron, for example, belonged to a clan; and any one of them could stay with fellow clan members when passing through a village or could depend upon them for help in a lean crop year. About once a decade the remains of the dead were disinterred in the villages and placed in a common burial ground in a ceremony called the Feast of the Dead. This ceremony was believed to make it possible for the souls of the dead, till then interred with their remains, to travel westward to the land of souls. The Huron's land of souls was thought to be much the same as their earthly home—an indication, perhaps, of their positive view of life in their own lands.

Like all Amerindians and all Europeans, the Iroquoians had creation myths. For the Huron, as for the Five Nations Iroquois, the vast land-area they lived on was an island on the back of a turtle. An Onondaga (the Onondaga were one of the Five Nations) elder explained to a Jesuit missionary that, long ago, beings similar to humans lived in longhouses in the sky. In the centre of their principal village stood the celestial tree blossoming with lights, the symbols of peace and knowledge. One day a curious woman asked her husband to uproot this tree so she could discover the source of its power. As she bent forward to look into the hole where the tree had once been, she fell and tumbled to a lower world. From the light that now shone through the hole into this lower world, the animals saw her plight. The Canada goose flew down to rescue her and then placed her on the back of the turtle. In this way Great Turtle Island, or North America, came into existence.

The confederacies of Great Turtle Island appear to have been a response to a growing cycle of violence in Iroquoian societies, resulting from blood feuds. The Five Nations Confederacy was the earliest. According to Iroquois legend, it owed its origins to the efforts of Dekanawidah, the "Heavenly Messenger," a Five Nations chief, and his disciple, Hiawatha. It proved to be the most effective and enduring of the Iroquoian confederacies, if only because the nations were surrounded by more enemies and their members therefore had more incentive to make it work. The Huron and Neutral confederacies, recent phenomena in the period of first contact with the Europeans, did not develop the cohesion evident in the Five Nations Confederacy.

In the confederacies, men chosen by the women of the villages made decisions on war and peace and tried to settle disputes between villages or clans. They were not always effective. Unanimity was required before a decision could be approved, and even then a tribal council that disagreed with a confederacy-level decision could disavow it. If the women of the tribe opposed the plan and withheld food, the tribal council would have no choice but to restrain from joining planned warfare. The confederacy had no permanent officials, and its decisions required the consent of tribes to be put into effect. It was a loose system of government that made little sense to the recently arrived Europeans.

Iroquoian sexual practices, like sexual practices generally among first nations people, also met with European disapproval. Young women had sexual relations with any man they wished, and although families arranged marriages, a couple slept together for a period before their marriage and had to give their consent to the union. Naked young people would gather in the home of a sick person and perform sexual acts to help heal the sick individual, a practice that particularly offended missionaries who rejected the non-sexual significance that the Native people attached to these events. Divorce was accepted, and the major means of birth control appears to have been sexual abstinence during the two to three years each baby was breast-fed.

While individual freedom and collective sharing of tasks and goods characterized Huron society, the increased warfare of the immediate pre-contact period revealed a different side of the society. Warfare appears to have been on the rise because the young warriors had become more militant in their demands to be allowed to demonstrate their prowess in battle. Often, prisoners were tortured, and sometimes captured warriors were cooked and eaten in ceremonies suggesting that cannibalism, where it involved a captured warrior, had been given religious approval within the culture. Still, casualties in battles between Iroquoian groups were light compared to those experienced in European wars. Women and children taken as prisoners were generally adopted as equals rather than enslaved by the tribe that captured them.

• The Canadian Shield First Nations

The rugged terrain of the Canadian Shield made settlement in large villages impossible in the pre-contact period, but dispersed societies of fewer than four hundred people each could survive by means of co-operative endeavour. While bands in the region were generally self-governing, most had organized contact with other groups whose culture they shared and with whom they intermarried. Informal alliance systems existed for purposes of warfare. Ojibwa bands, for example, co-operated effectively in battles against the Iroquois and others. Although these groupings could not create a formal nation in the European or even Mi'kmaq sense, in modern times many of them have used the term "nation" to describe the bonds that link their members. The nations of the Shield in 1500 included the Montagnais (now known as Innu), the Ojibwa, the Cree, the Nipissing (along Lake Nipissing) and the Algonkin (along the Ottawa River).

The Montagnais, whose home is in northern Quebec and southern Labrador, illustrate an interesting characteristic of pre-contact life among many Algonkian groups: the equal status of women and men. It was a feature that was much commented upon, usually unfavourably, by early missionaries such as the Jesuit Paul Le Jeune, who lived among the Montagnais of northern Quebec in the 1630s. Anthropologist Eleanor Leacock argues that the Montagnais of southern Labrador made decisions by the consensus of those affected by the decision. While such activities were, in part, sex-segregated, the roughly equal participation of the two sexes in economic activity ensured gender equality in decision-making. With respect to the Montagnais, Leacock writes:

> All adults participated in the procuring of food and manufacture of equipment necessary for life in the north. In general, women worked leather and bark, while men worked wood, with each making the tools they needed. For instance, women cut strips of leather and wove them into the snowshoe frames that were made by men, and women covered with birch bark the canoe frames the men made. Women skinned game animals and cured the hides for clothing, moccasins and lodge coverings. Everyone joined in putting up lodges; the women went into the forest to chop down lodge poles, while men cleared the snow from the ground where a lodge was to be erected.[9]

While small groups of Montagnais men hunted big game away from the local camp, women, responsible for childrearing, hunted small game closer to home. Both groups worked together to drive migratory caribou into compounds where they could be speared. Women as well as men became shamans, intermediaries between the people and the spirit world. Yet shamans, while influential, had no formal power. In a society without formal laws and systems of punishment, consensus was needed to prevent disunity, and ridicule served to sway wayward souls from acting against collective decisions. Although each Montagnais band of several hundred people had ties with other Montagnais bands, decisions were usually made at the local rather than the tribal level. Co-operation between bands was also common. A band whose territory became temporarily short of game could hunt within the territory of another Montagnais band or receive food from that band.

Similar to the Montagnais were the Ojibwa, who controlled the northern shores of Lake Huron and Lake Superior from Georgian Bay to the edge of the Prairies. Each Ojibwa band consisted of three to four hundred members living in a village of dome-shaped, birchbark wigwams that served as their permanent homes. Ojibwa men left their village in times of warfare and during the winter hunt, while women remained in the village except when they attended clan feasts or were married to a resident of another village.

Within bands there was a sharing of goods and of work. Tasks were sex-segregated, and chiefs always and shamans usually were male. Men

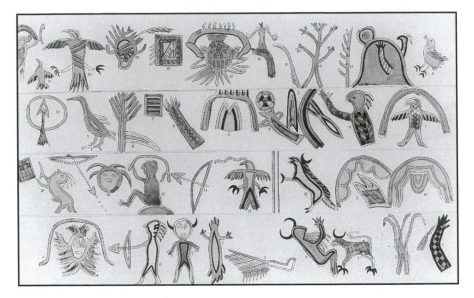

Ojibwa pictographs   (Newberry Library, Chicago)

again were warriors and hunters of big game such as caribou, elk, and deer, as well as fishers and makers of snares, bows, and arrows. They also built the wigwams. Women hunted small game, gathered wild rice and berries, skinned the animals, prepared all the food, made the clothing, blankets, and cooking vessels, kept the wigwams clean and in good repair, and took all responsibility for children. The relative status of the two sexes is harder to determine, but generally it appears that for the Ojibwa sex roles were regarded as complementary rather than based on notions of a superior and an inferior sex.

Before European firearms were available the Ojibwa hunted animals in a number of ways: with snares made of wild hemp, by placing sharp spikes on their path, by using dogs to drive them into water, or by bow and arrow. The bow was made from ironwood or red cedar, the arrows from bone and shell.

Religious ideas were central to Ojibwa life. The spirits were omnipresent in nature, and each person could enlist the aid of guardian spirits to deal with the natural world and other humans. Among the most feared in the human world were sorcerers who might avenge wrongs by driving the soul from the body or enticing game away from a favourite hunting area. Shamans, usually men, acted as intermediaries between individuals and the spirits, prescribing herbs that could heal injuries or cure illnesses and indicating the items a hunter should carry in a medicine bag to enjoy success during the hunt. But most men did not depend solely on the shamans in their relations with the spirit world. They undertook fasts, which were intended to induce visions, and they served as the audience outside "shaking lodges," small barrel-shaped structures where a diviner would sing and drum to attract spirits. Once these spirits arrived, their presence would cause the lodge to shake and the audience would ask them about the location of game or the fate of relatives. It might also entreat them for cures to illnesses.

The Midewiwin, or Grand Medicine Society, played a key role in maintaining and developing the Ojibwa's traditional medical–spiritual practices (the two were usually believed to be related). Years of instruction were required by its members before they reached the highest of its four grades of membership. The annual feast of this society brought together various bands and served as both a social and religious event.

The bands also joined forces on a temporary basis for purposes of warfare. A band chief wanting to send a war party against the Sioux would send an envoy with pipe and tobacco to invite other bands to participate. Warfare was never within the tribe; it occurred only between the Ojibwa and other nations and was designed to establish control over a particular hunting territory. It also provided the warriors with the opportunity to demonstrate their prowess and was accompanied by a great deal of ritual. The limits imposed by the bow and arrow, the major weapon of the pre-contact period, and the relative equality of the contending groups in battle resulted in few casualties in each encounter.

AN OJIBWA BALL GAME

In 1850, Kah-Ge-Gah-Bowh, an Ojibwa who deceptively styled himself as a chief, provided a graphic description of an Ojibwa ball game. His account is reproduced here with the typographical errors that are found in the original printed edition.

> Each man and each woman (women sometimes engage in the sport) is armed with a stick, one end of which bends somewhat like a small hoop, about four inches in circumference, to which is attached a net work of raw-hide, two inches deep, just large enough to admit the ball which is to be used on the occasion. Two poles are driven in the ground at a distance of four hundred paces from each other, which serves as goals for the two parties. It is the endeavour of each to take the ball to his hole. The party which carries the ball and strikes its pole wins the game.

The warriors, very scantily attired, young and brave fantastically painted—and women, decorated with feathers, assemble around their commanders, who are generally men swift on the race. They are to take the ball either by running with it or throwing it in the air. As the ball falls in the crowd the excitement begins.—The clubs swing and roll from side to side, the players run and shout, fall upon and tread upon each other, and in the struggle some get rather rough treatment. When the ball is thrown some distance on each side, the party standing near instantly pick it up, and run at full speed with three or four after him.—The others send their shouts of encouragement to their own party. "Ha! ha! yah" "A-ne-gook!" and these shouts are heard even from the distant lodges, for children and all are deeply interested in the exciting scene. The spoils are not all on which their interest is fixed, but is directed to the falling and rolling of the crowds over and under each other. The loud and merry shouts of the spectators, who crowd the doors of the wigwams, go forth in one continued peal, and testify to their happy state.

The players are clothed in fur. They receive blows whose marks are plainly visible after the scuffle. The hands and feet are unincumbered, and they exercise them to the extent of their power; and with such dexterity do they strike the ball, that it is sent out of sight. Another strikes it on its descent, and for ten minutes at a time the play is so adroitly managed that the ball does not touch the ground.

No one is heard to complain, though he be bruised severely, or his nose come in close communion with a club. If the last-mentioned catastrophe befall him, he is up in a trice, and sends his laugh forth as loud as the rest, though it be floated at first on a tide of blood.[11]

While the Ojibwa bands hunted separately from one another, intermarriage between them was the norm, and clan groupings held annual feasts that linked the bands together. The feasts were an integral part of the entertainment of the Ojibwa, who also played a variety of ball games, including the forerunner of today's lacrosse and a game called "maiden's ball play," a rough game that involved women. Jumping, foot racing, tossing, and gambling were other diversions for a people whose spirituality was never puritanical. Young women were free to engage in premarital sex, but women had no sexual freedom after they married and had little say in the selection of a marriage partner. Rules about marriage, like rules generally, were imposed informally. As Kah-Ge-Gah-Bowh, an Ojibwa writing in 1850, observed: "Fear of the nation's censure acted as a mighty bond, binding all in one social, honourable compact."[10]

North and west of the woodlands Ojibwa lived another Algonkian-speaking nation, the Cree. Almost as populous as the Ojibwa, the Cree had gradually migrated westwards, and some of their bands were west of Lake Winnipeg by the early sixteenth century. Pre-contact populations have been confirmed in the parklands of the Saskatchewan River and the woodlands of Alberta. Because their territory was not as abundant in game as the Ojibwa's, the Cree were more nomadic than their Algonkian neighbours

Cree woman fashioning pottery vessels from clay   (Courtesy Historic Resources Branch/Manitoba Culture, Heritage and Citizenship)

and their bands were smaller. Tipis made of caribou or moose hides, assembled and disassembled by the Cree women, provided them with shelter as they followed the caribou, moose, beaver, and bear, and their sturdy birchbark canoes provided transportation for whole families and their belongings.

The travels of a given band were not boundless, because each band had a relatively limited hunting territory. Yet, as economist Irene Spry notes, the first inhabitants of western Canada had no concept of land ownership. Rather, they believed that a particular group had the right to establish primacy in a particular area, giving it the first right to hunt and gather food there each season. It was also understood that if the area hunted by a band did not provide enough food in a given year, that band would have a right to hunt in the territory of a band that had enjoyed a surplus. Among the Cree, a band that was starving received assistance from a band that was prospering. Large annual Cree tribal gatherings in the summer cemented the bonds that made sharing in times of famine easy to achieve.

Like Cree social organization, Cree religious beliefs and rituals diverged from those of their Ojibwa counterparts in many ways. But the two groups shared a belief in the importance of dreams and vision fasts as means of communicating with the spirit world. Both also venerated the dead. The Cree buried their dead in the ground with great lamentation and held annual feasts in honour of the departed.

DREAMS AND CREE CULTURE

A Plains Cree elder presented a testimony in the 1930s regarding the power of dreams for his people. His emphasis is on the experience of men, but women were equally guided in their lives by the interpretation of dreams.

> The spirit powers may come to you when you are sleeping in your own tipi when you are young. If you want to be still more powerful then you go and fast. The ordinary dreams you have while sleeping are called *pawamuwin*. They are not worth anything although sometimes you dream of things that are going to happen.
>
> You can tell a power dream in this way. You are invited into a painted tipi where there is only one man. The crier, who is the Raven Spirit, calls, and many come. I myself knew right away that they were spirit powers. I sat and thought to myself, "That is Horse, that is Buffalo spirit." The one that invited me said, "That's right."

I was called many times and they always told me the same thing—that I must do more fasting. Each time they invite me to a different painted tipi. Often after I wake up I wonder why they didn't tell me anything. I had nothing to do with girls when I tried to dream.

Finally, they told me that this would be the last time. They want me to go and fast for eight days. One of them said, "Try hard to finish these eight days, for that will be all." I gathered as many offerings as I could. It was during the moon just past [July] and there was plenty of food in camp so I knew the people wouldn't move for a while.

I promised to stand and face the sun all day and to turn with the sun. Only after sunset would I sit down. I had heard that this was the hardest thing to do and that is why I resolved to do it out of my own mind. I thought that I could help myself a little that way. [By making himself suffer more, he would secure greater blessings.] The sun wasn't very high when I got tired. I suffered all day. I tried all kinds of ways to stand, but I was played out. I raised my hands and cried; I could hardly finish. The sun went down and I just fell over. That was the first day.

The next morning I got very thirsty. I was not hungry but was thirsty all the time. On the fourth night my brother came with horses to get me. I told him I would stay. He came again on the sixth night but I said I would remain for two more nights. He said, "From the way you look, I may not find you alive."

All kinds of different spirit powers came to see me every night. Each one who invited me gave me power and songs. Then one gave me the power to make the Sun dance. That is how I got power and how I know many songs. Pretty nearly every night now I sing some of those songs.[12]

•The Interior Plains First Nations

In the pre-contact period a variety of aboriginal groups occupied the territories of the Interior Plains region of North America. Only Siouan-speaking groups lived in the area of present-day prairie Canada a thousand years ago, but by the time of European contact in the eighteenth century, the Blackfoot, an Algonkian people, had achieved dominance on the northern plains of today's Saskatchewan and Alberta. Siouan groups remained in control of the plains of what is now Manitoba, with the Assiniboine constituting the largest Native grouping in that area. The cultures of the Plains peoples of North America were varied, but they also had similarities because of a common dependence on the buffalo.

The Blackfoot were an Algonkian nation whose long separation from their eastern counterparts had produced a variant of Algonkian language not understandable by other Algonkian speakers. The Blackfoot peoples, estimated at about 9000 in number in the early eighteenth century, included three tribal groups: Blackfoot, Peigan, and Blood. They had begun migrating southwards into former Siouan territory before the Europeans arrived, and even before they met any Europeans face to face they had used guns and horses acquired by trade with the Cree to acquire more Sioux territory by force. The Blackfoot tribes first encountered by the Europeans hunted the plentiful buffalo of the Plains and maintained control over their territory by creating a relatively unified armed force under centralized control. They used warfare to expand their tribal hunting grounds and to capture women who could then be adopted by the tribe to ensure its further population expansion.

A SIOUX CREATION MYTH

For the Sioux, who inhabited the Prairies for many centuries before both Europeans and other Native groups challenged their supremacy, humanity had its origins in their corner of the world. A Lakota Sioux elder described the creation of humans:

> Our legends tell us that it was hundreds and perhaps thousands of years ago since the first man sprang from the soil in the midst of the great plains. The story says that one morning long ago a lone man awoke, face to the sun, emerging from the soil. . . . The man looked about, but saw no mountains, no rivers, no forests. There was nothing but soft and quaking mud, for the earth itself was still young. . . . In time the rays of the sun hardened the face of the earth and strengthened the man and he bounded and leaped about, a free and joyous creature. From this man sprang the Lakota nation and, so far as we know, our people have been born and have died upon this plain; and no people have shared it with us until the coming of the European.[13]

As buffalo hunters, the Blackfoot lived a nomadic existence, following the herds and pitching tipis made of buffalo skin. A late-nineteenth-century missionary, John McDougall, aptly summed up the role of the buffalo in Blackfoot life:

> These men were thoroughly buffalo Indians. Without buffalo they would be helpless, and yet the whole nation did not own one. To look at them and to hear them, one would feel as if they were the most independent of all men; yet the fact was they were the most dependent among men. Moccasins, mittens, leggings, shirts and robes—all buffalo. With the sinews of the buffalo they stitched and sewed these. Their lariats, bridle, lines, stirrup-straps and saddles were manufactured out of buffalo hide. Their women made scrapers out of the legbone for fleshing hides. The men fashioned knife handles out of the bones, and the children made toboggans out of the same. The horns served for spoons and powder flasks. In short, they lived and had their physical being in the buffalo.[14]

Most of the men belonged to military societies involving several grades of membership according to experience and achievement. An additional bond was religion. Worshippers of sun and thunder, the Blackfoot attached special importance to sun-dance bundles, which, along with medicine bundles, they kept in rawhide bags. They believed that each object in the bag played a role in assuring good fortune. The transfer of a bundle from one person to another involved an elaborate ceremony lasting several weeks as the new owner was exposed slowly to the significance of each item in the bundle and to the visions and songs that justified the object's inclusion.

The deceptively named Sun Dance was, in fact, an elaborate set of religious ceremonies lasting several days and involving an entire nation. Presided over by a holy woman at a site chosen by a warrior society, it was organized by the extended family of a woman who had promised the Sun Spirit publicly to sponsor the event should the Spirit spare a male relative whose life was in danger. The tribe built a lodge where its various military and secret societies performed dances and rituals in exact sequence. While the Sun Dance was practised before the Blackfoot had direct contact with Europeans, it appears that it did not predate the arrival of the horse, which made Blackfoot hunting easier and left more time for leisure. It is perhaps best viewed as an elaboration of older Blackfoot traditions rather than as a tradition fully in place before the European arrival.

The Blackfoot tribes conferred authority upon male chiefs for purposes both of warfare and the hunt. But, as explorer and fur trader David Thompson observed in the late eighteenth century, the Peigan chiefs "have no power beyond their influence, which would immediately cease by an act of authority and they are all careful not to arrogate any superiority over others."[15]

Blackfoot society was less egalitarian than that of the Ojibwa or Cree. Chiefs and male shamans (but not women) had several spouses and larger tipis than other tribal members. The ceremonial functions performed by these men were thought to require more space and people in the household. Women always outnumbered men, both because of male casualties in warfare and the adoption of female captives into the Blackfoot culture. The status of married women who were not a man's first or second wife was lower than that of earlier wives. In the post-contact period, as some leaders acquired many wives, the number of low-status women increased dramatically.

• The Western Cordillera First Nations

The coastal Native societies of British Columbia stand apart from the other first nations. Of twelve language families that have been identified for pre-contact Canada, six are exclusive to British Columbia. The coastal societies, with a combined population of as many as 200 000 people in the eighteenth century, included the Tsimshian on the northern mainland, the Coast Salish on the southern mainland and Vancouver Island, the Southern Kwakiutl (or the Kwakwaka'wakw, as they prefer to be called) on the east coast of Vancouver Island, the Haida of the Queen Charlotte Islands, and the Nootka (or Nuu'chah'nulth) on Vancouver Island's west coast. These groups constituted the most affluent Native societies of pre-contact Canada, and their social structure is often attributed to this affluence. Although different in many ways, all were chiefdoms characterized by social hierarchies that resembled the ordered patriarchal societies of Europe more than the relatively egalitarian aboriginal societies of the rest of Canada. The chief, always a man, was regarded as a priest who owed his position of power and wealth to the gods. Generally holding his position by virtue of family descent and ruling between one hundred and five hundred people, the chief controlled the distribution of the resources of the community and took disproportionate amounts of the community's goods for his own use. After the chief in the hierarchy came, in descending order, certain members of his family, members of several other wealthy leading families, free men (that is, non-slaves) and their families, and finally slaves.

The potlatch, a feast during which individuals distributed portions of their property in the form of gifts, reduced disparities somewhat and emphasized the connection between all free men and women of the tribe. It demonstrated that property belonged to the community even if custom dictated that its use was not equally shared. Status was indicated by a family's generosity at potlatch time. Ironically, the accumulation of goods for this ceremony encouraged aggressive competition between potlatches, and the elaborate rituals governing gift-giving ensured that the social system reproduced itself.

By redistributing wealth, potlatches legitimized the social structure and served diplomatic roles as well. Within a tribe, by ensuring that no free person was reduced to poverty, the potlatch obviated the need for formal policing mechanisms that might have been required if some members were forced to resort to thievery to survive. Among tribes, potlatches between chiefs allowed one chief to demonstrate his control over an area by granting lavish wealth from the territories in question. They were an indirect means of staking out territory and fending off potential rivals.

Slaves, usually women and children captured in wartime (adult male captives were killed), were almost universally excluded from the potlatches. Slaves worked alongside free people, but their slave status was a badge of shame. Generally, a tribe would pay ransom to free tribal members enslaved by an enemy nation, but slaves captured in forays far from the tribal home of their captors might never be freed; their slave status passed to their children. The treatment of slaves varied. In some villages there was little distinction between the slaves and free people except at potlatch and marriage time. Although in other villages there was mistreatment of slaves, the tendency was exaggerated by European observers, particularly missionaries, who were convinced that slaves were both eaten and used in ceremonial sacrifices. Native oral tradition rejects these claims and insists that cannibalism was taboo and only animal flesh was used in ceremonies.

A favourable geographical location and ingenious use of local resources created wealthy societies on the northwest coast of North America. Plentiful stocks of fish, particularly salmon and halibut, and shellfish provided the staples of the coastal diet. The coastal Indians built weirs, open-work fences, to divert fish so they could be easily harpooned or netted. The men made harpoons of wood with barbs of bone or horn from local animals. While the men fished the women prepared the catch, preserving large quantities by smoke-drying. The women cooked food in pit ovens that they dug in the ground. They started a fire in the pit to heat stones and then placed the food over the hot stones.

Abundant timber allowed the Native peoples of the coast to build large homes for extended families. Among the Tsimshian, for example, homes made of massive timbers from red cedar measured 15 by 16.5 metres. A central pit, 9 by 1.5 metres, served as the main living space,

Curing fish in a Nootka (Nuu'chah'nulth) dwelling   (National Archives of Canada/C3676)

where women cooked and people ate and relaxed. Recreation for coastal nations included wrestling, weight-lifting, tug-of-war, foot races, and gambling.

The free women wove intricate baskets from red and yellow cedar and the flexible roots of the spruce. They also made textiles from mountain-goat wool, dog wool, and the down of ducks and other birds. Crafts, however, were sex-segregated. While the women wove, the men did the woodwork and stonework. The woodwork was particularly impressive, consisting of elaborately decorated totem poles and masks, house facades, feast dishes, canoes, storage boxes, helmets, and even cradles and chamber pots.

The aboriginal societies of the coast had varying resources, religious beliefs, and marriage practices. The Nuu'chah'nulth were whalers while the Haida lived off sea otters, sea lions, and fur seals as well as fish. The Haida and Tsimshian were matrilineal societies: the children inherited their line of descent and thus their position in society from their mothers. Women in these two societies generally enjoyed a higher status than women in the other coastal groups, which traced descent through the father's line. In all coastal societies, pubescent girls were secluded for

West Coast woman painting a hat   (National Archives of Canada/C20848)

lengthy periods, restricting their freedom during a period of life when few restraints existed for males.

The coastal peoples worshipped gods of the forests, mountains, and beaches, but they also believed that sinister forces resided in nature—sea monsters, ferocious birds in caves, ogres in the forest, and thunderbirds on mountains that could swoop down on any prey. To fend off such monsters, a person had, among other things, to carry out periodic fasts, to be continent, and to scrub the body with branches. Shamans, both men and women, were the intermediaries between the Natives and the spirit world. Long years of training taught them how to perform rituals that would cure diseases, which were believed to be the result of souls wandering or the intrusion of foreign objects in the body at the whim of malevolent spirits.

While the coastal societies had developed cultures vastly different from those east of the Rockies, the village-based societies of the Plateau (that is, the southern interior of British Columbia and the mountain regions of southwestern Alberta) were generally characterized by looser, more democratic structures similar to the ones further east. Band-level chiefs in these societies rarely appropriated more of the product from the hunt or salmon fishing than other members of the tribe. Distinctions among families were uncommon, and slavery was not practised. Among both the Carrier and Sekani of east-central British Columbia, hunting grounds and fishing spots were commonly owned by the band. The Carrier women enjoyed a status equal to that of men. Indeed, if recent field research can be accurately projected backwards into the pre-contact period, elder women were regarded as greater repositories of wisdom than elder men. Women participated in key subsistence activities, including salmon fishing, snaring, trapping, and hunting.

• The North's First Nations

In the northern regions of today's four western provinces and in the Northwest Territories, lived a variety of aboriginal societies who spoke Athapaskan languages. Harvesting local resources of the subarctic such as fish, small game, caribou, trees, and berries, these people lived in self-sufficient groups of about twenty or thirty related people. Tribal organization did not exist, and even band-level organization was only temporary: a coming together of people to carry out a specific task.

The lives of members of the Athapaskan groups of the western subarctic were marked by co-operation in the tasks required for eking out a subsistence in a harsh terrain. A group that had experienced a bad year could count on aid if it moved to an area where a local surplus existed. Work was sex-segregated, as it was among the Algonkian groups, but again there is little to suggest that women's work was less valued than men's. While the men hunted big game, women trapped smaller animals and prepared clothing from moose hides and rabbit skins. Both women and men could become shamans.

The Athapaskans believed that, at one time, animals such as the crow and the wolf spoke and behaved like humans. They therefore felt it necessary to know details of the past of these animals as well as of plants so they could understand their nature and how they must be treated. An elaborate mythology detailing this past was passed on from generation to generation.

Elaborate mythologies regarding nature also governed the lives of the most northerly residents of pre-European Canada. By the sixteenth century the Thule people, ancestors of today's Inuit, enjoyed undisputed control of the tundra region beyond the tree line. The Thule, nomadic but originally concentrated in the western Arctic, had gradually followed the caribou to spread their domain as far as the Atlantic. Speaking their own language, Inuktitut, they were alone among the first nations of Canada to have claimed a home on two continents when the Europeans first arrived. Indeed, until political pressures in the nineteenth century forced them to choose to live either in Greenland or Canada, the Inuit moved freely between the Canadian Arctic and Greenland in search of whale, caribou, and seal.

The sealskin-covered kayaks and umiaks of the Thule and Inuit were their main sea transportation; sleds pulled by domesticated dogs provided land transport. With the bow and arrow and the spear thrower they caught their prey and fended off the rare intruder that might dispute their control of the far North. Although they maintained their physical distance from the other Native groups in North America, the Inuit/Thule had religious beliefs and followed cultural practices that had much in common with those of other hunter-gatherer cultures such as the Athapaskans. Like these groups, the Inuit carved out their subsistence in a harsh environment. Their famous igloos, winter homes made of ice and snow, alternated as residences with summer houses that had frames made of whalebone and wood and roofs covered with baleen from whales and then sod.

Although the northern peoples lived in a less favourable environment than other aboriginal peoples, they possessed rich cultures. They developed songs and dances to celebrate their subsistence activities, beating drums made of caribou skins with sticks to accompany the dancers. Gambling, football, archery, and club-throwing were among their leisure activities. They also made every effort to bring beauty into their lives. Author Keith J. Crowe notes:

> They tattooed their bodies and embroidered their clothing with beads of horn or soapstone, with the quills of goose and porcupine, with moosehair or strips of weasel skin. Some made toothmark patterns on birchbark containers. Some people painted their skin tents and shirts with paint made from red ochre or black graphite. Any possession, a wooden bowl, a horn dipper, or a knife, might be decorated in some way. Painting, carving, embroidery, tassels, fringes and beads, dyeing, and bleaching were all used.[16]

Native woman and infant in Labrador   (Angelica Kauffmann/National Archives of
Canada/C95201, detail)

• Conclusion

When Europeans arrived in what is now Canada they encountered a set of
diverse and complex cultures that had evolved over many millenia.
Increasingly it has become clear that throughout those thousands of years
aboriginal peoples not only adapted to various geographical environments
but also carved out rich, dynamic lives and relationships. As part of this
process they defined their earthly existence by developing vibrant spiritual

beliefs, which also no doubt changed over time. While Europeans might envy the aboriginal mastery of regions of endless forests and bodies of water, the first peoples themselves gave credit to the spirits that resided in all animals and throughout nature. Athapaskans in northern British Columbia, for example, were experienced hunters, but they looked to their dreams to find a herd of moose, much as they counted on dreams to help them choose a suitable marriage partner. The people most experienced in unearthing the meaning of dreams were believed able to map the trail to heaven, showing the way a person's life ought to go.

In the fifteenth century, when Europeans began to come regularly to the shores of the Americas, the resident nations started to have dealings with people whose social values, religious beliefs, and cultural practices were at sharp variance with their own. As it turned out, the encounter with those Europeans was bound to be a less than happy one for most of the aboriginal peoples.

• Native Origins:
A Historiographical Debate

Where did Canada's first nations originate? Were their earliest ancestors simply the first immigrants to settle permanently in North America? The first peoples believed they had been present for all time in the places they lived when Europeans first arrived on the continent. Their creation myths suggested a North American origin for all of humanity.

Relatively few people of European origin have ever accepted the Native views. Scholars in the sixteenth century agreed that all human beings had a common origin in the Garden of Eden, as described in the Old Testament. None of them could accept that the Garden was located in the Americas, and so it was assumed that the peoples of the New World had, at some point, emigrated from the Old World, which was the cradle of humanity. Some suggested that the aboriginal peoples of the Americas had originally migrated from Siberia into Alaska. Less widely accepted were claims that the aboriginal peoples were the product of trans-Atlantic crossings by such ancient peoples as the Phoenicians, the Carthaginians, and the ten lost tribes of Israel. Proponents of these views would point to pyramid-like structures in Central America to suggest direct links with ancient Egypt, or they would cite Native customs that resembled those of the lost tribes of Israel.

Archaeologists, anthropologists, and biologists have given scientific respectability to the view that the Native peoples of North America originated in Siberia. Linguistic affinities, common folklore elements, and blood-typing procedures all point to a relationship with Asiatic peoples of eastern Siberia. It is generally believed that the migrations occurred across a land bridge between the continents formed as a consequence of the lowering of the ocean levels. Others argue that there was an ice bridge over which animals and people could migrate. It is also possible that the newcomers could have arrived over water. The Bering Strait is narrow enough to permit a reasonably safe crossing in bark canoes, which have existed in the Amur Valley of Siberia for many millenia.

When did the migrations from Siberia occur? Several widely scattered sites in the Americas seem to indicate that human occupation dates back as far as 30 000 years ago. Some linguists have suggested that at least 50 000 years would have been required to create the diffuse languages of the Americas. But the oldest human remains found so far by archaeologists in Canada, in the diggings near Old Crow in the Yukon and Taber in Alberta, are only 12 000 years old (although it has been argued that debris left by hunters south of Old Crow may be as old as 24 000 years).

Assuming that the Native peoples arrived by migrating from Siberia, it is possible that their migrations occurred over many thousands of years, although it is generally believed that migration ended about ten thousands years ago, after the receding of the ice removed the land bridge between Asia and North America.

The last word on this subject should go to the first nations, whose many stories of how the world began deserve equal consideration with the Judaeo-Christian story of Genesis found in the Old Testament. Both the Inuit of the Arctic and the Dogrib of the sub-Arctic trace their origins to the marriage of a spirit woman with a dog. In the Inuit version, the sea spirit is the mother of all the races of humans and her husband, a dog, is their father. The sea spirit's father, after arguing with this couple, decides to drown the pair. When his daughter clings to the overturned boat, he cuts off her fingers, which then become the mammals of the sea.

Yet another story of the origins of the planet and its creatures is the Cree–Ojibwa tale that suggests that the earth had once been destroyed and was recreated by a culture hero, named Weesakayjac. The story has some similarities with the biblical story of the flood and Noah's ark. It begins when Weesakayjac carries out a revenge killing of the leader of the powerful underwater cats:

> *The remaining underwater cats were very angry when they saw this. They sunk the whole earth. The cats told Weesakayjac they would drown the whole earth and that Weesakayjac would drown too. After this warning, Weesakayjac built a big boat.*

Then he gathered all the animals. Then the rains came. It rained so much the earth was not visible any more. When the rains finally stopped, Weesakayjac called the water animals together. From the big boat, he wanted one of them to swim to the bottom, to reach the earth. The first animal he asked was the otter. He tied a cord to its foot and he told the otter to shake the cord if he was drowning. The otter could not reach the bottom. Next, it was the beaver who tried to swim to the bottom. . . .

Then it was the muskrat's turn. Muskrat went down and down and after a while Weesakayjac felt the cord shaking. He pulled it up. When he got muskrat to the surface, he discovered that muskrat had drowned. But muskrat had something clutched in his hand. It was a piece of moss, so Weesakayjac knew that the muskrat had reached the bottom. . . .

[Later] Weesakayjac asked the wolverine to run around this earth to see how large it was. Wolverine ran out three times and each time he came back and said: "The earth isn't that large yet."

On the fourth trip out, the wolverine did not come back to the boat and Weesakayjac realized that the earth was now as large as before. Weesakayjac then let all the animals out of the boat.

That's how Weesakayjac made the earth again.[17]

•Notes

[1] British Columbia Provincial Museum, McKenna–McBride Commission Report, Hearings, 1913–16, cited in *First People, First Voices,* ed. Penny Petrone (Toronto: University of Toronto Press, 1983), 73.

[2] James Axtell, *The Invasion Within: The Contest of Cultures in Colonial North America* (New York: Oxford University Press, 1985), 14–15.

[3] A.G. Bailey, *The Conflict of European and Eastern Algonkian Cultures 1504–1700: A Study in Canadian Civilization,* 2nd ed. (Toronto: University of Toronto Press, 1969), xxi.

[4] Joanne Fiske, "Ask My Wife: A Feminist Interpretation of Fieldwork Where the Women Are Strong But the Men Are Tough," *Atlantis* 11, 2 (Spring 1986): 68.

[5] Olive Patricia Dickason, *Canada's First Nations: A History of Founding Peoples from Earliest Times* (Toronto: McClelland and Stewart, 1992), 27.

[6] Jennifer S.H. Brown and Robert Brightman, *"The Orders of the Dreamed": George Nelson on Cree and Northern Ojibwa Religion and Myth, 1823* (Winnipeg: University of Manitoba Press, 1988), 139.

[7] Dickason, *Canada's First Nations*, 12.

[8] Conrad Heidenreich, *Huronia: A History and Geography of the Huron Indians 1600–1650* (Toronto: McClelland and Stewart, 1971), 171.

[9] Eleanor Leacock, "Women in Egalitarian Societies," in *Becoming Visible: Women in European History*, 2nd ed., ed. Renate Bridenthal, Claudia Koonz, and Susan Stuard (Boston: Houghton Mifflin, 1987), 22–23.

[10] G. Copway or Kah-Ge-Gah-Bowh, Chief of the Ojibway Nation, *The Traditional History and Characteristic Sketches of the Ojibway Nation* (London, 1850; reprinted Toronto: Coles, 1972), 144.

[11] Ibid., 43–45.

[12] David G. Mandelbaum, *The Plains Cree: An Ethnographic, Historical and Comparative Study* (Regina: Canadian Plains Research Centre, 1979), 160–61.

[13] Quoted in Peggy Brizinski, *Knots in a String: An Introduction to Native Studies in Canada* (Saskatoon: Division of Extension and Community Relations, University of Saskatchewan, 1989), 20.

[14] John McDougall, *Saddle, Sled and Snowshoe* (Toronto: William Biggs, 1896), 261–62.

[15] Quoted in Paul F. Sharp, *Whoop-Up Country: The Canadian–American West, 1865–1885* (Minneapolis: University of Minnesota Press, 1955), 24.

[16] Keith J. Crowe, *A History of the Original Peoples of Northern Canada* (Montreal: McGill-Queen's University Press, 1991), 22.

[17] James R. Stevens and Chief Thomas Fiddler, *Legends from the Forest* (Toronto: Penumbra Press, 1985), 22–23.

• Selected Reading

Useful introductions to Canadian geography include: J. Lewis Robinson, *Concepts and Themes in the Regional Geography of Canada* (Vancouver: Talon, 1989); Lawrence McCann, ed., *Heartland and Hinterland: Canadian Regions in Evolution* (Toronto: Prentice-Hall, 1987); D.F. Putman and R.G. Putnam, *Canada: A Regional Analysis* (Toronto: Dent, 1979); and Geoffrey J. Matthews and Robert Morrow Jr., *Canada and the World* (Scarborough, ON: Prentice-Hall, 1985).

Sections of the following books grapple with general problems involved in studying the history of Native peoples: Olive Patricia Dickason, *Canada's First Nations: A History of Founding Peoples From Earliest Times* (Toronto: McClelland and Stewart, 1992); J.R. Miller, *Skyscrapers Hide the Heavens: A History of Indian–White Relations in Canada* (Toronto: University of Toronto Press, 1989); Olive P. Dickason, *The Myth of the Savage and the Beginnings of French Colonialism in the Americas* (Edmonton: University of Alberta Press, 1984); Bruce G. Trigger, *Natives and Newcomers: Canada's "Heroic Age" Reconsidered* (Montreal: McGill-Queen's University Press, 1985); James Axtell, *The Invasion Within: The Contest of Cultures in Colonial North America* (New York: Oxford University Press, 1985); Calvin Martin, ed., *The American Indian and the Problem of History* (New York: Oxford University Press, 1987); Cornelius Jaenen, *Friend and Foe: Aspects of French–Amerindian Cultural Contact in the Sixteenth and Seventeenth Centuries* (Toronto: McClelland and Stewart, 1976); Eleanor Leacock and Nancy Lurie, eds., *North American Indians in Historical Perspective* (New York: Random House, 1971); and Peggy Brizinski, *Knots in a String: An Introduction to Native Studies in Canada* (Saskatoon: University of Saskatchewan, 1989).

The historical geography of Native settlement is outlined in R.C. Harris, ed., *Historical Atlas of Canada* (Toronto: University of Toronto Press, 1987).

Broad coverage of Indian societies in the eastern half of Canada is found in Bruce Trigger, *Handbook of North American Indians*, Vol. 15, *The Northeast* (Washington: Smithsonian Institute, 1978); and A.G. Bailey, *The Conflict of European and Eastern Algonkian Cultures, 1504–1700* (Toronto: University of Toronto Press, 1969). On Atlantic Canada, see James A. Tuck, *Newfoundland and Labrador Prehistory* (Ottawa: National Museum, 1976); and James A. Tuck, *Maritime Provinces Prehistory* (Ottawa: National Museum, 1984). On the Mi'kmaq, see L.F.S. Upton, *Micmacs and Colonists: Indian–White Relations in the Maritimes, 1713–1867* (Vancouver: University of British Columbia Press, 1979) and Virginia Miller, "The Micmac: A Maritime Woodland Group," in R. Bruce Morrison and C. Roderick Wilson, *Native Peoples: The Canadian Experience* (Toronto: McClelland and Stewart, 1986). On the Innu (Montagnais), see Eleanor Leacock, "The Montagnais-Naskapi of the Labrador Peninsula," in R. Bruce Morrison and C. Roderick Wilson, *Native Peoples: The Canadian Experience* (Toronto: McClelland and Stewart, 1986).

Among important works on the Huron are Bruce Trigger, *The Children of Aatentsic: A History of the Huron People to 1600* (Montreal: McGill-Queen's University Press, 1987) and Conrad Heidenreich, *Huronia: A History and Geography of the Huron Indians, 1600–1650* (Toronto: McClelland and Stewart, 1971). On the Ojibwa, influential works include Charles A. Bishop, *The Northern Ojibwa and the Fur Trade* (Toronto: Holt, Rinehart and Winston, 1974) and Peter S. Schmalz, *The Ojibwa of Southern Ontario* (Toronto: University of Toronto Press, 1991). Two excellent studies of Cree religious and cultural life are Jennifer Brown and Robert Brightman, eds., *The Orders of the Dreamed* (Winnipeg: Manitoba Studies in Native History, 1988) and David G. Mandelbaum, *The Plains Cree: An Ethnographic, Historical and Comparative Study* (Regina: Canadian Plains Research Centre, 1979). Blackfoot life is discussed in Oscar Lewis, *The Effects of White Contact Upon Blackfoot Culture with Special Reference to the Role of the Fur Trade* (Seattle: American Ethnological Society, 1942). See also Irene Spry, "The Great Transformation: The Disappearance of the Commons in Western Canada" in *Man and Nature on the Prairies*, ed. Richard Allan (Regina: Canadian Plains Research Centre, 1976): 21–45.

Philip Drucker, *Cultures of the North Pacific Coast* (Garden City, NY: Harper and Row, 1963), outlines the pre-contact history of Pacific coast Natives. A more focussed study is Helen Coderre, *Fighting with Property: A Study of Kwakiutl Potlatching and Warfare, 1792–1930* (New York: American Ethnological Society Monograph, 1950).

An excellent overview of pre-contact Native life in northern Canada is provided in Keith J. Crowe, *A History of the Original Peoples of Northern Canada* (Montreal: McGill-Queen's University Press, 1991). Also useful are Kenneth Coates, *Canada's Colonies: A History of the Yukon and Northwest Territories* (Toronto: Lorimer, 1985); Kenneth Coates, *Land of the Midnight Sun: A History of the Yukon* (Edmonton: Hurtig, 1988); and the essays in Part 4 of Bruce Morrison and C. Roderick Wilson, *Native Peoples: The Canadian Experience* (Toronto: McClelland and Stewart, 1986).

On Native sexuality, see Gary Kinsman, *The Regulation of Desire: Sexuality in Canada* (Montreal: Black Rose Books, 1987); and Evelyn Blackwood, "Sexuality and Gender in Certain Native American Tribes: The Case of Cross-Gender Females," *Signs* 10, 1 (Autumn 1984): 27–42.

CHAPTER 2

SECOND PEOPLES:

The European Background

They are all, as I said before, unprovided with any sort of iron, and they are destitute of arms, which are entirely unknown to them. . . . No one refuses the asker anything that he possesses, on the contrary, they themselves invite us to ask for it. They manifest the greatest affection toward all of us, exchanging valuable things for trifles, content with the very least thing or nothing at all. . . . I make this promise to our most invincible sovereigns, that if I am supported by some little assistance from them, I will give them as much gold as they have need of, and in addition spices, cotton, and mastic, which is found only in Chios, and as much aloes-wood, and as many heathen slaves as their Majesties may choose to demand.[1]

So, in part, wrote explorer Christopher Columbus to the Spanish king and queen in March 1493. He had just returned from his accidental "discovery" of the Native peoples of the Americas. He viewed these people as pacific and generous and therefore excellent candidates for slaves, and he believed that the resources of their lands could be exploited at will by the Spanish crown.

Columbus was anxious to profit from his discovery: in 1495 he shipped 550 Amerindian slaves to Europe. About 200 of them died on the voyage, and most of the rest died soon after they reached Spain. He had no permission from the Spanish monarchs to engage in the slave trade; indeed he was supposed to be attending to the conversion of these Amerindians to Christianity. But by the standards of his time and continent, Columbus was no monster. In many ways he was simply a typical European, full of the same contradictions as the other people who would come across the sea to conquer the New World's indigenous inhabitants.

And while the societies that the European peoples would establish in the Americas were partly shaped by the quest for wealth as well as the need to survive in a new environment, they were also largely determined by the centuries of cultural baggage that molded the European responses to life in a new frontier amidst the "newly discovered," "Indian" people.

Throughout Western Europe, in the early "modern" age, roughly from 1400 to 1600, societies were in transition from a social order characterized by agricultural self-sufficiency and rigid hierarchies to a new order in which trade and impersonal market-based relationships were becoming increasingly important. Although the traditional landowning elite persisted, in cities and towns new leaders emerged whose wealth came from organizing the trade that linked far-flung territories. This new elite was allied with increasingly powerful monarchs whose attempts to constrain the nobles led to the emergence of nation-states, wherein government bureaucracies rather than individual landlords made the rules that ordinary people were forced to obey. Within the cities, too, lived the intellectuals, whose growing curiosity about how the universe worked led them away from the teachings of the church and toward lines of inquiry that produced both the knowledge and some of the incentive to search for undiscovered lands.

In this age of transition Europe was a complex continent. Not only did incredible opulence sit side by side with grinding poverty, but religious devotion also co-existed with greed and bloody warfare; humanist interest in scientific advance and new forms of artistic and architectural expression co-existed with religious and racial bigotry; and a willingness to accept female monarchs co-existed with the profound oppression of women in society at large. These contradictory tendencies existed as much within European states as between them.

•The European Social Order

In the thirteenth century a minor English baron, the Lord of Eresby, employed "a steward, a wardrober, a wardrober's deputy, a chaplain, an almoner, two friars, a chief buyer, a marshal, two pantrymen and butlers, two cooks and larderers, a saucer, a poulterer, two ushers and chandlers, a baker, a potter, and two furriers, and each had their own boy 'helpers.'"[2] But households of this kind—and it was the household of a *minor* baron— had not always been a feature of European life.

Across Eurasia hunting and gathering societies gave way to agricultural settlements between ten thousand and two thousand years ago as a response to population pressures. The early agricultural societies appear to have been relatively egalitarian, with women and men sharing tasks in the struggle to survive. Gradually religious and military castes formed and society became more rigidly stratified. Slaves captured from other groups usually occupied the bottom rung of the social order, and men generally occupied the new leadership positions. Patriarchal ideology, which stressed female subordination to males, complemented the hierarchical notions that were replacing older egalitarian practices.

Between 900 and 1400, much of European society was stratified along rigid, hereditary lines of social class that had both legal and church sanction. A system of reciprocal, though unequal, obligations, which historians have labelled the feudal system, linked various social strata. For the elites these obligations involved both land and arms. Men of the elite classes had the right to bear arms, and relations among them were formalized through military allegiances secured with religious pledges. At the top of the social pyramid within a region was a king, who granted control over huge estates to a small number of important nobles in return for military allegiance. The higher nobles granted land to lesser lords, who pledged their arms both to the defence of the noble's lands against invaders and to the aid of the noble when he was involved in a king's military campaign.

The vast majority of the people—the "serfs"—were deprived of the right to bear arms and compelled to be the legal subordinates of the military castes. The serfs were also entangled in the system of reciprocal obligations: in return for paying tribute to the lord they received military protection from him and tenure on a small plot within his estate. While tribute was initially paid by working three days a week in the noble's fields, a variety of rental arrangements gradually supplanted this system of forced labour.

Feudalism brought a degree of stability to the women and men who eked out a living from the earth during the Middle Ages (roughly 500–1400). For several centuries after the break-up of the Roman Empire (476), marauding bands of murderous thieves had made life unbearable for the independent small farmer throughout Europe. The nobles who seized control over particular areas brought a measure of social peace and thereby ensured some stability of land tenure—which does not mean that calm descended on the lands of Europe, for warfare between rival claimants to thrones and among the nobility continued.

The gradual growth of towns provided serfs with the possibility of escape from the feudal manor, and from the thirteenth century onwards feudal obligations began to give way to rental obligations. Serfs became tenants who paid fixed rents, whether in money or in kind, to the nobles-become-landlords. As rent-paying peasants, they were often no better off than a serf bound by feudal obligations. In France, where the new rents were usually substantially lower than the old feudal dues, rising taxes imposed by the French monarchy soaked up much of the surplus that a sixteenth-century peasant might have gained relative to a twelfth-century serf. In Eastern Europe nobles refused to commute feudal dues for rents and used repression to hold serfs to the land. The feudal system remained in force in various Eastern European countries into the nineteenth century. In Russia, for example, serfdom was not officially abolished until 1861.

MAP 2.1   *Western Europe in 1500*

•Population

In the sixteenth century, Europe experienced a dramatic population increase. By 1600 the countryside and towns of Europe were home to an estimated one hundred million people, a population comparable to the higher estimates for the pre-contact Americas of a century earlier. Owing to the opening up of new lands to agriculture and to a decline in epidemics, the states that would assemble short-or-long-term empires in the New World counted about thirty-nine million people in 1600, an increase of seven million in a century.

Table 2.1: SELECTED EUROPEAN POPULATION FIGURES (approximate)

Country	circa 1500 (in millions)	circa 1600
Spain and Portugal	9	11
France	16	18
British Isles	5	7
Low Countries	2	3

Source: Carlo M. Cipolla, *Before the Industrial Revolution: European Society and Economy, 1000–1700,* 2nd ed. (New York: Methuen, 1980), 4.

Of all the factors contributing to population changes in Europe, epidemics and warfare were the most important. Epidemics were the by-product of famine. Large stores of grain could often help people weather one year of drought, but two dry years in a row usually brought famine, and weakened populations living in unsanitary conditions became easy prey for germs. Contagious diseases such as diphtheria, typhoid fever, smallpox, whooping cough, and tuberculosis would kill large numbers of people in particular territories before running their course. Maladies without a modern equivalent often cut a deadly swath: in England in 1486, 1507, 1518, 1529, and 1551, "sweating sickness" claimed thousands of lives. Its victims developed fits of shivering and sweated profusely, dying within hours of the onset of symptoms.

But it was the various outbreaks of "plague" that proved the grimmest reaper. Its most spectacular occurrence was the Black Death, or bubonic plague, which was responsible for the death of about twenty-five million Europeans out of a total of approximately eighty million in 1348–49. The germs that infected the European population with such ferocity on this occasion originated in China. Carried by insects on board ships, they were transported to India and then to the West via Constantinople and Egypt.

The famines that led to epidemics were not always the result of crop failure. Warfare often left famine in its wake as plundering soldiers dispossessed unarmed peasants. Wars within Europe were fought for territorial aggrandizement, over questions of honour, and, in the sixteenth and seventeenth centuries, over religion. Once the monopoly of the armed nobility, warfare in the early modern period was generally prosecuted by mercenaries paid by a monarch. Kings and queens aiming to centralize power in their own hands had to disarm the nobility and protect their realm with standing armies of infantrymen, who replaced the noble cavalrymen of the Middle Ages.

Until the second half of the seventeenth century, regal attempts to control soldiers' relations with civilians were limited. Poorly provisioned, soldiers were expected to force peasants to feed and house them, but they often repaid their hosts with massacres, torture, and rape. As people with limited opportunities to practise cleanliness, they sometimes carried epidemics into the lands that they invaded. Their intrusion could be long-term, because wars in Europe often seemed interminable: England and France, for example, were almost constantly at war with each other from 1337 to 1453 (the so-called Hundred Years War). Even when wars ended the peasantry was often harassed by laid-off soldiers who had no source of income and would terrorize local populations to gain tribute.

The Thirty Years War (1618–48), an orgy of religious warfare that embroiled most of the states of Europe, provides a particularly brutal example of the impact of warfare on civilians. The war claimed 350 000 soldiers' lives, but millions of civilians also died. In the areas of heaviest fighting the population declined from 21 million to 13.5 million. Monarchs had proved unable to restrain their rival armies from destroying crops and livestock and raping and murdering innocent farm folk. The extent of the mayhem in that war encouraged monarchs to enforce rules on troops regarding their relations with civilians.

Peasants, though unarmed, sometimes reacted violently to either invaders or their rightful rulers, whose heavy exactions of rents, taxes, and church dues made provision against famine difficult. Peasant revolts were suppressed bloodily where necessary, but still occurred frequently in early modern Europe. Limited possibilities of communication among peasants in various regions made a full-scale peasant rebellion unlikely, but spontaneous local eruptions when famine threatened were frightening to European elites. Usually the peasants had no revolutionary objectives; they merely asked for "just prices" (that is, prices fixed at an affordable level), for the use of grist mills and the like, and for lower rents and taxes.

Perhaps not surprisingly in a society where so many were poor, life expectancy was short—usually about forty-five years for those who got past the first year of life—and death in the first year was common. In seventeenth-century French towns, a third of all children born alive did not celebrate a first birthday; in London, even at the beginning of the eighteenth century, half of all children born alive were dead within a year. Even among the wealthy, death rates for children were high. Well-off women, rather than

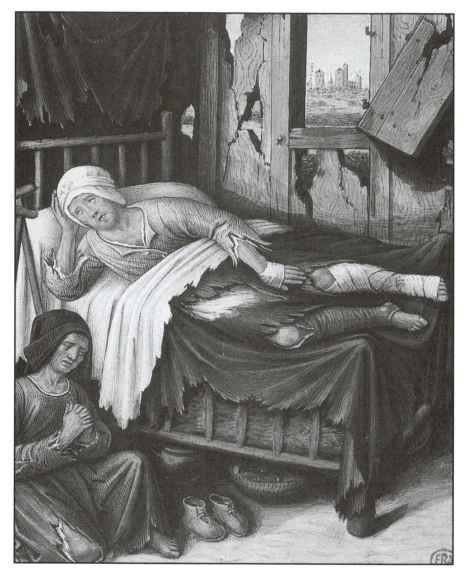

The miniatures on these two pages illustrate the contrast in the living conditions between the poor and wealthy classes in French society.

breastfeeding their own babies, traditionally hired poor women to suckle their young. These ill-fed women thereby suffered the dilemma of being unable to nourish their own child and their employer's at the same time.

(Bourdichon, circa 1490. *L'état de pauvreté*: Masson 91; *L'état de richesse*: Masson 93/École nationale supérieure des beaux-arts, Paris)

FAMILIES AND THE LIFE CYCLE IN EARLY MODERN EUROPE

What was life like for a typical European peasant born about 1600? The birth would take place at home, perhaps with a midwife helping the mother with the birth. For the first year or so the baby would be swaddled and largely unable to explore surroundings, except visually. Because the mother could not leave her field or home duties to take care of a baby—and fathers did not take care of babies—the child would be either cared for by an older sibling or left unsupervised for much of the time. A grandparent might be present in the household, but the nuclear family household had already largely replaced the three-generation and extended-family households once common in Europe.

An older child would accompany mother to the fields. Both mother and father would discipline the child sternly, using physical beatings to enforce warnings that a youngster, who could not always be watched by a working parent, must avoid the fire, the river, the forest, and wild animals. Young children might experience some parental affection; they almost certainly would experience many parental beatings. For the most part children were treated as if they were simply miniature adults.

Girls and boys would receive parental instruction regarding their respective gender-based chores. Formal education in a school was unlikely in 1600. By the age of seven, the girl or boy would be a full-time worker in the household economy: girls cooked, sewed, cleaned, fetched, did field work, and supervised younger siblings; boys joined their fathers in doing the back-breaking work of primitive farming. After work there would be no privacy in the small hut. Everyone slept in one room, and the parents made little effort to copulate out of sight of the children.

In an increasingly commercial economy where families needed cash both to pay rents and taxes and to buy items they did not make for themselves, many children (in England a majority) would leave home between the ages of seven and fourteen to work for a wealthier farmer or a noble, the girls as servants, the boys as labourers. A typical boy and girl would spend their adolescences in households away from home. Even if they stayed at home, the odds were that one or both of their parents would be dead before they left adolescence. So too would perhaps half of their siblings.

While working in service, a girl earned a small wage. She sent most of her income home but kept some of it as a dowry for her marriage. A boy in service would also accumulate some savings. Somewhere between the ages of twenty-four and twenty-eight our typical young adults would be prepared to marry and settle down on a small plot of rented land, often on the estate where the groom's parents had rented property. The marriage-seekers tried to choose a partner who would be an asset in the struggle to eke out a living. Family and friends would be consulted, but anyone who had been separated from parents for a long time would probably be sufficiently independent to make the final choice. As historian Lawrence Stone writes: "Most marriages seem to have been based on a mixture of hard-headed calculation and personal preference. What is clear is that among the poor the individuals made their own choice of persons to be courted, and first met in church, at the alehouse, or at the many village feasts or hiring fairs."[3]

After the marriage ceremony, which was usually performed by a minister but represented a community opportunity for a rowdy party, the young couple would continue to follow an endless round of work activities, except now within their own household. They would also begin to have babies. If both partners managed to live to about the age of forty-five, the woman would bear seven or eight children, with three or four of them surviving to adolescence. Coitus interruptus or sexual abstinence as well as ingestion of plant substances reputed to abort pregnancies were employed to prevent too many births.

Although their economic partnership and their children might cause this couple to feel a strong bond, both spent much of their work-time and leisure time in the company of other members of the community of their own sex. Men might work together in the fields and spend their rare free time at the alehouse, while women would gather around a neighbour's fire, working and talking while their children had an opportunity to play.

If parents lived to an age where they became too frail to farm alone, they might hand over the farm to one of the children in return for bed and board. The chances of living to a ripe old age were, in any case, slim, and most peasants worked the fields until they died.

For an upper-class person there was a greater likelihood of remaining in the parents' home until adulthood. Within that home by 1600, relatively recent notions militated against imitating the peasant treatment of children as miniature adults. Special needs for affection, play, and privacy received some recognition. The parents, not the individual, would have the greatest say in a marriage partner because the goal of marriage was to enhance the wealth and prestige of the family. To avoid division of the family's land, parents prevented their younger sons from marrying and sent them off to the military, church, or state for employment. Women unable or unwilling to find marriage partners would turn to the church or devote themselves to the service of their parents or married siblings.

*A **Country Wedding**, by Bruegel the Elder, circa 1565*   (Kunsthistorisches Museum, Vienna)

•Economic Life

Throughout Europe, including areas where feudalism had disintegrated, the bulk of the population remained on the land. In the sixteenth century, about 75 percent of the people in most countries were dependent for their livelihood on the farming of small and usually rented landholdings. While agriculture was the dominant mode of economic activity it was far from productive, even though crop yields had improved slowly from 1000 to 1600. According to historian Carlo Cipolla, "The land produced little because seeds were not selected, crop rotation and implements were primitive, pesticides were unknown, and last, but not least, manure, the only known fertilizer, was always in very short supply."[4] Animal husbandry practices were also primitive, and peasant diets were low in protein.

Peasant life changed little. The cycle of heavy work in spring, summer, and early autumn was followed by riotous merrymaking after the harvest and preceded by early spring carnivals in what has been called "concentrated effort and exuberant release." Life continued to be punctuated by ravaging wars, pestilential plagues, crop failures, and highway rob-

bery. The church offered some consolation through its sacraments, its liturgical calendar tied to the agricultural cycle, and its sponsorship of pious
practices—although few peasants could go on distant pilgrimages. Peasants
lived in a restricted local community, with money rents and taxes forcing
them to participate reluctantly in the cash economy.

The increased population created another set of problems as more
and more people were forced to leave settled communities for new areas
where infertile land often guaranteed poverty. Average standards of living
fell. Earlier landlords had been concerned that their labour supply might
decrease if they raised rents too high; now they could charge what an overpopulated market would bear.

Unable to both pay their rent and feed themselves, many farm families looked to places other than their fields for income. Farm women
became mainstays in the businesses of many urban textile merchants, who
were looking for cheap labour to replace expensive male workers. The
"putting-out system" involved merchants giving material to women to spin
or weave in their own homes. Farm children, meanwhile, hired out as field
labourers on nobles' estates.

In sixteenth-century France, on the plains and low hills from the
Loire valley northwards, peasants usually farmed less than one hectare.
Cereal grains—wheat and millet—were the staple, although most peasants
grew some peas and beans and root crops and some also had vines and a
few fruit trees. To survive, many men worked as wage labourers on nobles'
estates or as labourers in the woods; the women worked in linen and
woollen manufacture in the farm home. But bare survival was not the rule
in all regions. In the wooded districts of western France—in Brittany and
western Normandy—most peasants had substantial grazing land and could
feed themselves without seeking paid labour.

A worrying side effect of increased population in a society of low-yield
agriculture was that peasants attempted to gain more land by chopping
down forests. During the Middle Ages and the early modern period, there
was large-scale destruction of forests throughout England and Italy, southern France, and central Spain. Governments belatedly passed a variety of
decrees meant to halt or slow down the removal of so many trees and the
inevitable soil erosion that followed. Such legislation was often indifferently
implemented, because alternative short-term solutions to the problems of
peasant hunger eluded authorities bent on preserving the outlines of the
hierarchical social order. A general disinterest in the ecological impact of
economic decisions, born of desperation but consistent with Christian
notions of humanity's right to master nature, would be carried by Europeans into the Americas as well.

While the farm family attempted, by working as a unit, to use its resources to scrape by, many city and town residents lived in a state of permanent desperation by the sixteenth century. In earlier centuries towns had been relatively compact places where guilds—collective organizations of workers involved in particular trades—made rules that ensured good remuneration and limited competition for their members. There were guilds for brewers, weavers, iron-mongers, masons, bakers, and hatmakers, among others. Their main markets were the nobility and the upper echelons of the church, sectors that craved the high-quality products of guild artisans. Gradually, as wealth accumulated in the towns, a merchant class arose that also had considerable disposable income for the purchase of luxuries.

By the sixteenth century, guilds were giving way to workshops organized on capitalist lines. A wage determined by an employer replaced a guild-imposed rate for artisanal work. In the guilds journeymen (and, much less frequently, journeywomen) worked an apprenticeship of seven years to become regular guild members, who were eligible to set up their own shops. Yet masters who controlled the guilds increasingly used their monopoly powers to block or slow down the growth of their numbers. Many journeymen became, in all but name, wage workers who stood little chance of attaining the status of masters. Swelling urban populations, providing the budding capitalists with unemployed potential workers, ensured that the journeymen's resistance to the new order would be ineffectual.

Many who flocked to the cities in hopes of escaping chronic rural poverty found no employment. At the end of the seventeenth century an estimated 10 percent of the French population were beggars. At the same time in England, which had instituted a Poor Law to provide some aid to the "deserving" poor, about one-quarter of the population were chronically poor and underemployed. In Spanish and Italian cities there were constant complaints about the activities of the underworld of thieves, murderers, prostitutes, and con artists who survived as best they could in an environment that offered few prospects of remunerative honest labour. The line between thieves and honest men and women was, in any case, a difficult one to draw in an age in which pirates often enjoyed the support of monarchs and great expeditions of "discovery" were little more than a cover for plunder.

At the bottom of the social order in the towns and the countryside were the slaves, whose numbers were significant even before the Europeans began capturing millions of Africans. In the mid-1300s Tartars, Circassians, Chinese, Jews, Mongols, and Russians were bought and sold in Venice, a crossroads for European commerce in human beings.[5] In Venetian Crete, clergymen of both the Catholic and Orthodox churches as well as officials, professionals, and even some fishermen held slaves. Young males were sold to the Turkish sultan to be used as cannon fodder or to nobles in Crete and Cyprus seeking labour for their fields. Teenage girls, including Christian ones, were sold in Africa, Italy, southern Spain, and southern France as domestic servants or concubines. In 1442 a Venetian gentleman settled his debts to a shipwright by handing him a Russian girl.

A French carpenter's shop   (Bourdichon, *L'état de travail.* Masson 92/École nationale supérieure des beaux-arts, Paris)

All in all, the position of the bulk of the population was deteriorating in the sixteenth century, even though it was an age of overall economic growth. Redistribution of wealth was occurring in favour of the already wealthy, and this development was, from the perspective of many scholars, a prerequisite for an expanding market economy and the colonization and exploitation of "discovered" areas. Summarizing the socio-economic trends of the sixteenth century, historian Ralph Davis observes:

> The growth of population in a society almost wholly dependent on the land caused a sharp worsening in the condition of the masses of the people during the sixteenth century, concentrating a larger share of income in the hands of the well-to-do: the landowners, officials, merchants, lawyers and financiers. It was their demand, for good quality woolen and linen cloths, furs, silks, wine, armour, ornaments and other luxuries, that promoted some concentration in industry and in specialized agriculture, expanded the international market economy, and gave opportunities to economic enterprise, outlets for accumulating capital, and scope for experimenting with new economic institutions.[6]

• Women and the Economy

The expansion of economic specialization and market relations played an important part in changing the position of European women in the fifteenth and sixteenth centuries. While the patriarchal organization of society was long-established in Europe, the degree of subordination of the women of various social classes had fluctuated from era to era. Historian Susan Stuard argues that in the eleventh century women "were equipped with property and inheritance rights and sustained by gender assumptions based on similarities between women and men."[7] While historians disagree about the validity of such a positive evaluation for the eleventh century, they tend to agree that opportunities for townswomen and aristocratic women were declining in the sixteenth century and that intellectuals were propagating a limited sphere of activities for women. In contrast, the position of the great mass of rural women remained much the same. The household economy in which men and women had essentially equal status did not break down, although women who broke social norms were more likely than ever to be punished.

Until the early fifteenth century women were allowed to become members of most guilds. Their presence was especially obvious in areas such as weaving, needlemaking, yarn spinning, and hatmaking, where dexterity rather than strength was a key to success. Women were employed in metallurgical works in France and in the Arsenal of Venice making sails. From 1365 to 1371 relatively equal numbers of men and women were employed in the building yard of Périgord College in Toulouse, France.

Occupational equality between the sexes began to break down when journeymen in guilds, finding themselves less able to become masters, turned on female employees in an attempt to limit competition and improve their chances of advancement. Barring women had the double effect of keeping out competitors and emphasizing the exclusivity of a trade, as did the exclusion of men of illegitimate birth and sons of serfs. So, in 1649, Frankfurt hatmakers kept out not only women but also all journeymen trained in Fulda, because Fulda hatmakers employed women and therefore presumably tainted male employees in the town. Widows of tradesmen had once assumed almost automatically the duties of their husbands, but by the sixteenth century they found themselves increasingly blocked by the guilds. In Frankfurt, in 1624, a widow of a stonemason asked guild permission to keep her late husband's shop in operation; she was rejected on the grounds that women were not proper masters and could effectively control neither a shop nor journeymen.

Kept out of guilds, women worked in hospitals and orphanages, as midwives, in public baths (until these were closed down in the sixteenth century along with brothels), and as domestics. In most cities, 15 to 20 percent of the adult population were in domestic service, with women accounting for most of this number. Poor women sold small items—pretzels, nuts, wooden implements, cookies, candles, herbs, lace, firewood—whatever they could make or gather.

Women were also barred from universities and increasingly unable to use designations, such as "physician," which before the sixteenth century were not reserved for graduates of university schools. With only minor exceptions, women also lacked the capital and connections to become merchant capitalists involved in the expanding global trade of the fifteenth and sixteenth centuries. As historian Merry E. Wiesner suggests, "It was exactly the occupations with formal education, political functions, capital investment, or international connections, such as physicians, merchants, bankers, lawyers, government officials and overseas traders, that were gaining in wealth, power and prestige."[8]

•Role of the State

In feudal times the lords of the manor enjoyed as much or more power over their domains as the monarchs and dispensed justice to their serfs and artisans as they saw fit. The monarch's role was largely limited to arbitrating territorial disputes and leading the nobles in times of war. But as warfare increased and standing armies replaced the army of nobles, kings and queens attempted to limit the powers of the landowners and centralize law-making in their own hands. It was a gradual process, but by the late seventeenth century the notion that kings ruled by "divine right" rather than at the pleasure of the nobility had become a central argument in royal propaganda. After policies had been established by a council of ministers answering to the monarch, a centralized government bureaucracy implemented the rulings across the territory. Courts appointed by the monarch's advisers rather than the nobles enforced royal decrees on everything from commerce to personal morality. Royal prisons, workhouses, and asylums demonstrated the monarch's ability to penalize those whose behaviour fell afoul of the norms established from above. Although many nobles fought rearguard battles to defend their former privileges and even won some concessions, many were simply absorbed into the court as advisers, military specialists, or simply part of the monarch's personal circle.

The increasingly powerful monarchs of France, England, Spain, Portugal, Holland, and other emerging national entities used their armies in attempts to gain control of as much territory as possible. Although most peasants continued to think of themselves solely as part of a local community, the trading classes and intellectuals in the cities increasingly identified themselves as citizens of the larger territory controlled by their monarch. The nation-state was emerging as a conscious entity.

The new economic order represented by the nation-state proved a boon to trade. In the period when nobles and petty princes enjoyed as much or more power as monarchs, trade had been expensive and even dangerous to undertake. A merchant wanting to pass from one town to another would confront armed men and tax collectors at every turn—which at times made relatively short-distance trade as difficult as trade across borders. For those who did try to trade on a larger scale, the presence of pirates, uninhibited by governmental forces, also created endless hazards. The emergence of national monarchies with taxation powers and armies able to humble the princes offered improved conditions for trade.

The role of the emerging nation-state, which created a bond between monarchs and merchants at nobles' expense, went beyond the breaking down of internal and external trade barriers and the provision of protection for merchants. It also played an entrepreneurial role. As historian Fernand Braudel argues with reference to the Mediterranean countries and city-states:

> The state in the sixteenth century was increasingly emerging as the great collector and redistributor of revenue; it derived income from

taxation, the sale of offices, government bonds, and confiscation, an enormous share of the various "national products" . . . whether intentionally or not the state became the principal entrepreneur of the century. It was on the state that modern warfare depended, with its constantly increasing requirements in manpower and money; as did the biggest economic enterprises.[9]

The arsenals at Venice and Galata, the largest manufacturing centres in the sixteenth-century world, were in state hands. The Venice Arsenal, which began operations in the twelfth century, housed a huge shipyard, a fortified naval base, ship repair facilities, and a storehouse of armaments and provisions. By 1423 over sixteen thousand carpenters worked in the Arsenal along with smaller numbers of other tradespeople. Most of Portuguese shipping (though little of Spanish or English) was in state hands along with a considerable portion of Mediterranean banking.

Private-sector growth also owed much to the expansion of the state. The kings and queens, busily making war to expand their territory, convert heathens, and extract new wealth, needed loans from bankers, arms from munitions-makers, and cloth from textile merchants to clothe their armies. The profits made by both private and state entrepreneurs from such ventures were reinvested and permitted greater concentrations of wealth and greater specialization. But in societies where consumer demand was limited to the wealthy, there was a real danger of investment collapsing because of insufficient demand for products. Only continuing state investment prevented such a collapse.

Monarchs and nobles who sponsored trading and exploration ventures hoped that those activities would increase national wealth and make a better life possible for a restive peasantry, as well as provide work for the growing army of unemployed townspeople. For some, the idea of establishing colonies in areas seized from aboriginal inhabitants was appealing partly because of the possibility of unloading surplus people in the new territories. There the new arrivals could both feed themselves and pay taxes to the mother country, while at the same time defending the country's conquered territories from would-be interlopers.

•Religion

The Roman Catholic Church had established its dominance throughout most of Europe during the Middle Ages, ruthlessly suppressing heretics. Led by the pope, regarded as Jesus' earthly representative, the church had

Cathedral of Cologne   (German Tourist Information Office)

received royal recognition of various rights: to dictate the religious beliefs of all the monarch's subjects, to collect tithes to support the church's personnel, and to build and maintain its grandiose edifices. In his efforts to maintain a united Christendom, the pope sometimes feuded with both monarchs and nobles. By 1500 increasingly powerful monarchs asserted their right to control the behaviour of all citizens, including clerics.

The church was a hierarchical and patriarchal organization that mirrored the larger society. Archbishops, bishops, and cardinals, who generally purchased their titles, lived comfortable lives that had little in common with the poverty that faced parish priests and cloistered nuns. The tithes that everyone was forced to pay to the church went disproportionately to the building and upkeep of magnificent cathedrals and the opulent homes of church officials.

In the sixteenth century resentment against the church's corruption and some of its teachings brought a permanent rupture to Western Christendom. The emerging wealthy classes of merchants, industrialists, and professionals remained devout Christians, but they questioned why a considerable amount of their profits should go to maintaining an expensive bureaucracy whose connection with Christian beliefs seemed remote. Ancient church laws against money-lending also offended the new capitalists. While the laws could be circumvented, their very existence seemed to condemn activities that formed the basis of a commercial society. Martin Luther, a priest in the town of Wittenburg, led the challenge against the papacy in 1517. Soon Europe was in a state of religious upheaval. Along with certain monarchs anxious to assert unrivalled authority within their territories, the dissenters created rival "Protestant" churches that disputed the Catholic Church's religious monopoly.

This "Reformation" of Christianity was unacceptable to the Catholic Church, which encouraged its supporters to suppress the dissenters. Wars between Catholics and Protestants sometimes ended with only one variant of Christianity being allowed within a monarch's territory: this was the arrangement, for example, that ended brutal religious wars within and among the German-speaking states in the sixteenth century. In England Henry VIII declared his Church of England to be outside the pope's jurisdiction, and after an initial attempt to suppress the Catholic Church, a degree of official toleration was allowed. In France the battle between Catholics and Protestants (there called Huguenots) resulted in almost constant warfare from 1562 to 1598. A temporary truce between the two faiths occurred in 1598 when King Henri IV created a strong central government and granted toleration to non-Catholics in the Edict of Nantes. But this toleration lasted only until the revocation of the edict in 1685.

Unable to countenance rival versions of Christianity, Western Europeans could hardly be expected to countenance rival religions. Jews were expelled from England in 1290 and from France in 1394. In 1492 Spain expelled Jews as well as the Moslems, who had invaded the Iberian peninsula as early as the eighth century. Venice became a destination for many Jews fleeing these places, but it too began to persecute its Jews in the 1570s. Jews often hid their faith and faked conversions to Christianity in order to stay in countries where their religion had been proscribed. Others resettled in Eastern Europe, in Constantinople, or wherever a temporary welcome might be found.

European intolerance also manifested itself further afield. Christians in Europe regarded Islam as no better than paganism and the Moslem occupation of the Holy Lands of the Middle East as sacrilegious. A series of crusades from the late eleventh century to the mid-thirteenth century left trails of corpses as the outnumbered Christians tried in vain to retake biblical lands. The first crusade, beginning in 1095, was sparked by a call from Pope Urban II to free Jerusalem and other holy lands from the control of the Turks, who, unlike earlier Moslem rulers of the region, attempted to suppress Christianity. Like the following crusades, the first one drew to its ranks representatives in the thousands of all social classes. Motivated by religious fervour, the crusaders seized Jerusalem in 1099 and massacred any Islamic and Jewish inhabitants who failed to escape. But Islamic forces recaptured some of the holy lands in the 1140s and took back Jerusalem in 1187. Jerusalem remained in dispute through several more crusades, until 1244 when a decisive Moslem victory caused the European monarchs to abandon the costly and apparently hopeless objective of regaining the holy lands. Jerusalem would remain under Islamic control until the city fell to the British in 1917.

In the later crusades, religion and plunder often went hand in hand as wealth-seekers, sincerely or insincerely wrapping themselves in the colours of the faith, despoiled the Moslem lands they invaded. The details of Europe's religious feuds or of the crusades need not concern us here, but it is important to understand how rare a commodity religious tolerance proved to be. The Christian conquerors' harsh attitudes toward and treatment of the "infidels" of Africa, Asia, and the Americas were entirely in keeping with their treatment of Jews, Moslems, and Christian heretics in the period before the "discovery" of new territories.

Of course, religion would not likely have commanded the allegiance of the masses if venality and bloody-mindedness had been its only face. Religious orders dedicated to carrying Christ's message of hope to the masses also kept a spirit of sacrifice and missionary zeal alive in a church increasingly implicated in materialist excesses and hopelessly enmeshed in temporal politics. The role of the religious orders was indeed enhanced by the Counter-Reformation, the attempt by the church to correct past abuses that had created a mass base for the Protestant revolt. While asserting the correctness of its doctrines and its liturgical practices, the church accepted that it must now work to maintain the allegiance of the masses rather than simply count on the vigilance of the temporal authorities. Two of the Catholic orders that emerged in this context in the sixteenth century, the Jesuits and the Ursulines, were destined to play an important role in the history of the European occupation of North America.

The militant Society of Jesus, or the Jesuits, was imbued with the mystical devotion of its Spanish founder, Ignatius Loyola, and was organized along quasi-military lines. Fervent in their view that Catholics must be absolutely obedient to the pope, the Jesuits founded schools and universities and became active in foreign missions in an effort to rekindle the Catholic flame that the Reformation had dimmed.

The Ursulines, founded by Angela Merici in Italy in 1535 just as the Jesuits were beginning their work, were devoted to teaching girls. These women took vows of chastity but initially did their teaching uncloistered, in their own homes. The church, believing that girls must be educated in the Catholic faith so they would not become Protestants and pass on heresies to their children, accepted the Ursulines' work but demanded that they perform it within the cloister. After many battles the Ursulines capitulated.

Not all female religious orders followed the example of the Ursulines. In the seventeenth century congregations of uncloistered women proliferated and began to receive grudging acceptance by the church, which needed all the help it could get in its deadly competition with Protestants. In France, for example, the pope gave official recognition to teaching congregations of so-called *dévotes*, women who devoted their lives to the church but remained outside the cloister. Despite its continued patriarchal views, the Catholic hierarchy allowed both its nuns and the *dévotes* to open schools, hospitals, asylums, and orphanages in an attempt to make the church integral to the lives of its adherents. New France would feel the influence of this women's movement in the church, both in its cloistered form (the Ursulines) and its *dévote* form (the Soeurs de la Congrégation and the Grey Nuns).

• Culture and Ideas

Church anxieties about the need to vigorously propagate the faith reflected concerns about the broad questioning of existing knowledge that characterized the period after 1400. Beginning in the Italian city-states, a Renaissance (or rebirth) of interest in the classical scholars and societies of ancient Greece and Rome sparked debates—initially in limited elite intellectual circles—about beliefs that the church held unassailable.

For example, scholars had maintained since ancient times that the earth was the centre of the universe and the sun revolved around it. In 1543 a Polish clergyman-physician named Nicolaus Copernicus dared to suggest that the earth was simply a planet that along with other planets revolved around the sun. Galileo Galilei, a Venetian, built a telescope in

1609 and used it to make observations that corroborated Copernicus's theory. He was forced by the Catholic authorities to recant his discovery, but the die had been cast and a whole new astronomy born.

Other thinkers joined the astronomers in challenging received wisdom about how the universe operated. The French philosopher René Descartes went further than most in his 1637 *Discourse on Method*, which claimed that there were discernible and immutable mechanical laws of nature. The Renaissance thinkers, while nominally accepting the traditional Catholic view that held individuals to be ranked in hierarchical order, with their place in the universe fixed by God, embodied a growing individualism that would soon fracture the traditional social structure. Whether it was a Machiavelli expounding a secular political science or a da Vinci designing machines to make human flight possible, Renaissance intellectuals recognized few boundaries in the topics they explored.

Women were rarely the beneficiaries of the ideas of Renaissance men. The chief male writers and painters of the period, both following and influencing the merchants who sponsored their creative work, revived classical notions of a public sphere exclusive to males and a private, domestic sphere to which women's lives must be devoted. Not surprisingly, women challenged those who tried to restrict their freedom. In 1405 the Italian-born French humanist Christine de Pisan produced a work entitled *The Book of the City of Ladies* in which she exhorted women to refute denigrations of women by following such models as the Virgin Mary; Clotilda, who brought Christianity to the Franks; and Queen Esther, who prevented the genocide of the Assyrian Jews. Among the aristocracy, women courtiers— members of the royal entourage—painted, wrote, and composed, generally resisting attempts to limit their sphere of activity to the household.

Nevertheless, misogynist notions were widespread in European society, and women who were both poor and out of step with the behaviour prescribed for their sex faced fatal consequences. Single women whose babies were stillborn, a common-enough occurrence at a time when infant mortality rates were high, were executed for committing infanticide; the burden of proof for proving innocence was placed on the hapless mother. Older women whose behaviour offended neighbours were often accused of practising witchcraft. Between 1500 and 1750, over 100 000 women in Europe faced this accusation, and about 60 000 were executed. Interestingly, Spain, notorious for an inquisition that hunted down and eliminated religious heretics, was ahead of supposedly more enlightened France and England in abolishing witch trials. Indeed, witchhunts in earlier periods had been conducted by the church against pagan women who practised the ancient worship of goddesses and thereby called into question the patriarchal religion of the Judaeo-Christian tradition.

Painting by Giovanni Boccaccio, circa 1470, shows women gardening, carding, and spinning   (New York Public Library, Spencer collection MS 33, f. 22r)

•Technology

The Renaissance also witnessed a spate of inventions as the curiosity of the age led to a search for solutions to technical problems. To be sure, Europeans had demonstrated a willingness to apply inventions for many centuries before the Renaissance—although many of the new ideas were imported from elsewhere. Between the sixth and eleventh centuries, for example, the Europeans adopted the windmill from Persia, the spinning wheel, gunpowder, and paper from China, and the compass from the Arabs. At the same time, Europeans took ancient inventions that had been little applied and made them crucial to their economy. For example, water mills had been known to the Romans but had been prohibited as labour-saving devices because the Roman authorities regarded employment of citizens as more important than economic efficiency. Europeans of the Middle Ages, by contrast, combined their knowledge of Chinese manual manufacture of paper with their knowledge of water mills and used mills to process pulp.

Historians have debated why Europeans were so willing, compared to other peoples, to search for applications for inventions. The general turmoil in the period after the break-up of the Roman Empire no doubt made its contribution. There were no longer powerful authorities who could join rulers elsewhere in the world to prohibit new inventions. Also, the interminable warfare among land-hungry individuals and groups provided a spur to technological progress as each party dreamed of gaining a military advantage over its rivals. Thus, in China, where emperors held a monopoly over the means of war, gunpowder was used to make firecrackers. In Europe it was used to make deadly weapons.

Military as well as commercial imperatives encouraged improvements in navigation. The introduction of full-rigged ships in the fifteenth century meant that ships could go faster and no longer needed to wait for the most favourable breeze before sailing. In the same century the Portuguese developed greater knowledge of the winds in the Atlantic and invented the quadrant to measure latitude. "The combination of innovation and progress in the techniques of naval construction, navigation, and armament production was at the origin of the overseas expansion of Europe."[10]

Technology was a key to exploration but it does not explain why Europeans in particular ventured to uncharted areas of the globe. Chinese and Arab maritime achievements made those peoples just as likely candidates for such exploration. Economic motives peculiar to Western Europe provided some of the motivation: Islam barred the best land and sea routes to Asia as well as to the grain and timber of south Russia. But Europeans were hardly alone in being partly motivated in their actions by hopes of economic gain. Ultimately the reason for the European quest to explore the globe may rest in the general curiosity of the peoples of that continent—a curiosity exemplified by the Renaissance. Elsewhere powerful rulers sufficiently suppressed such curiosity so that people could not act upon their dream of finding a "new world."

•Exploration and Expansion

Portugal

The leader in European expansion was Portugal. Like Spain, Portugal had been under Moslem control for several centuries and its leaders in the early-modern period were particularly disdainful of "infidels." The desire to liberate the holy lands from Moslem control remained a key component of Portuguese state policy long after the crusading zeal had passed in other European states. As in the earlier crusades, Portugal's religious goals in the East blended with its commercial objectives. Gradually, undermining Moslem control of the Indian spice trade became more clearly the aim of the Portuguese crown than the retaking of Jerusalem from the heathens.

With the monarchy and the merchants allied in search of new territories, it was not long before Portugal had spread its tentacles throughout many parts of the world. Portuguese vessels reached the Gulf of Guinea in 1440 and soon began carrying back gold, slaves, and ivory from Africa. In 1487 Bartolomeu Diaz, a Portuguese navigator, sailed around the Cape of Good Hope. Ten years later his countryman, Vasco da Gama, sailed directly from Africa to India, returning in 1498 to Lisbon with jewels and spices. At its height the Portuguese commercial empire encompassed more people than any previous trading block in recorded history. Fernand Braudel notes:

> The Portuguese had from the start sent their ships to India, then beyond to the East Indies, China and Japan. They also organized the great slave trade between Africa and America, not to mention the clandestine export of silver from Potosi by way of the overland routes of Brazil and, even more, by Buenos Aires and the little boats of the Rio de la Plata. This added up to an immense and complicated system, drawing on the economy of the whole world.[11]

The Portuguese successes left corpses and misery in their wake. The marks of Portugal's seizure of the spice trade were "cities bombarded, ships pillaged and sunk, and appalling cruelties—the slicing off of noses and ears—inflicted on enemies real or imagined."[12] On the Canary Islands the Portuguese wiped out the indigenous peoples, the Guanches, who numbered about 100 000. Those who did not die of diseases or in resistance to Portuguese occupation were enslaved and shipped to places such as Madeira, where they laboured to early deaths on Portuguese sugar plantations. In Brazil the gentle Tupi-Guarani faced much the same fate.

Churchmen, particularly the Jesuits, attempted to prevent the slaughter of the Tupi-Guarani. Amerindians, after all, had souls. While the pope and church scholars insisted that it was proper for these people to be ruled by foreign Christians, they also defended their rights to life and land. But although the Jesuits set up church-controlled villages to protect the Tupi, the slavers still raided the villages for their human resource. In truth, both the Spanish and Portuguese monarchies, while committed in principle to protecting the Native peoples of the territories they conquered, proved unwilling to interfere in practice with the activities of the men they sent to enrich the motherland at the local peoples' expense. The Tupi-Guarani died in scores in hopeless revolts. Others committed suicide while women of childbearing age, seeing the grim future before them, refused to have sex and bear children. Overwork, beatings, and disease killed many more.

The Portuguese slave traders brought African slaves in the millions to the New World, using them to replace the decimated indigenous peoples of Brazil and selling others to British, French, and Spanish plantation owners throughout the Americas. Although the African slaves survived in larger numbers in the Americas than the original inhabitants did, their death rate was high and the treatment they received cruel. Commenting on Iberian attitudes toward Africans, historian G.V. Scammell observes:

> Slavery was to be the Africans' lot since they were of the race that carried, as the Book of Genesis recorded, the burden of Noah's curse on the off-spring of Canaan, son of Ham, and so destined to toil forever in the service of others. They were supposedly captured in what were considered to be "just wars" against societies of evil practices—though in fact most were acquired from pagan or infidel dealers. Their enslavement was accordingly legitimate, and the price they had to pay to become Christians. Crude prejudice reinforced this convenient erudition. Africans looked and smelled differently to Europeans, and were commonly and offensively naked. Above all they were black, the colour that proclaimed the enormity of their ancestors' sins, and the colour popularly identified with evil in a civilization already conscious of the superiority of whiteness.[13]

A similar racism pervaded Europe as a whole.

Spanish Exploration

Spain closely followed its Iberian neighbour in searching for a northwest passage to the East Indies and by the middle of the sixteenth century was the major European power in the New World. Its conquests began modestly with Columbus's short-lived attempts to establish Caribbean colonies in the 1490s. Columbus, a Genoan by birth, won the support of King Ferdinand and Queen Isabella for his plans to find a northwest passage to the Indies. Far off course, he landed on an island that he named Hispaniola (now Haiti and the Dominican Republic). Mistakingly thinking that he had come ashore in India, he called its inhabitants Indians, a misnomer that has survived to this day (although not without controversy) as a description of the first peoples of the Americas.

Permanent Spanish settlement in the Americas occurred when Hernán Cortés conquered Mexico and destroyed the Aztec empire between 1519 and 1521. The Aztecs ruled a vast empire won by conquest, and their architectural and political triumphs impressed Cortés. But their weapons could not match European guns and swords, and the resentment of the peoples they had subjugated ensured that no popular uprising would defend the Aztec military caste against the light-skinned intruders from overseas. Weakened by diseases to which they had no immunity, the Aztecs were soon on the defensive.

The Spanish invasion, with under 1000 soldiers, was made easier by the initial unwillingness of Montezuma, the Aztec ruler, to fight. A prophecy that the Aztec god Quetzalcoatl would return that year coincided with Cortés's arrival, and Montezuma invited the Spaniard to enter his capital, on the site of today's Mexico City, hoping to bribe him into leaving. Instead Cortés took Montezuma prisoner and seized power, incorporating local rulers into his own *conquistador* rule. Spain named Cortés governor and captain-general of New Spain, an area that included most of what is now Mexico, and Cortés lost little time in forcing many of his new subjects to labour in the silver mines to enrich their new masters. Although exploited by the Aztecs, the indigenous peoples of Mexico had achieved a population of some twenty-seven million by 1500. After 150 years of European exploitation and diseases, that number fell to about one million.

Cortés was soon followed by other *conquistadores*, including Francisco Pizarro in Peru and Diego de Almagro and Gonzalo Pizarro in the upper Amazon basin. Initially concerned mainly with the silver and other precious metals of South and Central America, the *conquistadores* quickly found that there was even more money to be earned by harnessing the agricultural abilities of their new subjects. Huge *haciendas* or plantations run by Spanish overlords yielded crops for export and for the feeding of a growing Spanish population. As local populations died out, particularly in the Caribbean, African slaves were imported to replace them. By 1600 the Spanish rule extended over what is now the southwestern United States, Mexico, Central America, the Caribbean islands, Venezuela, Colombia, Ecuador, Peru, Chile, and coastal Argentina and Uruguay.

England and France

Over time other nations followed the lead of Portugal and Spain. In the English port of Bristol, fishing interests active in the North Atlantic where the Vikings had once reigned supreme commissioned Giovanni Caboto

(John Cabot), an Italian navigator with an apparent knowledge of land beyond the "ocean sea," to carry out a voyage of exploration in uncharted territories. It is not surprising that the men of Bristol would engage an Italian seaman: Italy was the heartland of intellectual and cultural activity in Europe, and its navigators were employed by Portugal, Spain, and France as well as England to make pioneering trans-Atlantic voyages.

After Cabot's 1497 "discovery" of "the new isle"—which became known as Newfoundland—French fleets joined the Portuguese and Spanish ships in making regular visits to the Atlantic fishing grounds. England itself at first remained largely content to fish off Iceland but, following the defeat of the Spanish Armada in 1588, became more bold in its overseas ventures. In 1607, a new Virginia colony was established by a joint stock company with a royal charter. Poor people from England were indentured—that is, committed to long-term contracts—by the Virginia Company to farm on their estates. As incentive to servitude, they were promised freedom and land at the end of their contracts. As the tobacco crops raised in Virginia found markets throughout Europe, African slaves were brought in to do most of the plantation work and provide household domestic labour.

The success of Virginia encouraged other colonial ventures. The Puritans, Protestants who regarded the official Church of England as being too close to Catholicism in its rituals and too worldly in its outlook, colonized Massachusetts in 1620; other colonial ventures quickly followed. After its failed attempt in Florida, France was slower to seek colonies. It tended to look on the Americas as a source for resources, mainly fish and furs. Only gradually would rivalries on its home continent convince France that colonial settlements were necessary for global–strategic reasons.

• Conclusion

The decay of the old feudal order and its replacement by a social order characterized by centralized and competing monarchical states, increasing emphasis on trade, and growing intellectual curiosity made Europe the likely candidate for overseas expansion. Population pressures provided monarchs with an incentive to search for new resources and later to support the founding of colonies. The trade-oriented capitalists of the rising cities provided encouragement and finance for such ventures. Finally, the Renaissance intellectuals provided both the theoretical speculations and the technological advances that made the search for new areas of the globe appear possible and desirable. In sum, the interests of nation-building, trade, and science conspired to create an "age of discovery."

• Cruelty versus Germs:
A Historiographical Debate

Historians have noted the extent to which contact with Europeans resulted in the decimation of Amerindian populations. They have also suggested that Europeans treated the indigenous peoples unusually cruelly. But are these two observations linked?

Historian Alfred W. Crosby, while not minimizing the European exploitation of the first nations, suggests that it was the unplanned European biological attack on the Americas that accounted for most deaths. The Amerindians, cut off from the peoples of the rest of the world, had developed no immunities to the epidemic diseases experienced by Eurasians. They were familiar with venereal syphilis, polio, some varieties of tuberculosis, hepatitis, and encephalitis. But they had no experience of and no immunities to smallpox, measles, diphtheria, whooping cough, chicken pox, bubonic plague, malaria, typhoid fever, cholera, yellow fever, influenza, and other infectious diseases the Europeans brought with them. As a result, communities of Native peoples often disappeared or declined precipitously even before Europeans had done much to alter their lifestyles.

Crosby observes that Europeans who wanted to enslave the Indians could not have been happy to see their labourers dying like flies. There were a few diseases that passed the other way—from Amerindians to Europeans—but these were not deadly. Had they been, the ability of the Europeans to conquer the Americas might have been curtailed. The failure of the Crusades, Crosby notes, was in large part attributable to the vast numbers of crusaders who succumbed in the Moslem lands to diseases for which they had as yet no natural protection. Combatants, in any case, were unaware of their biological impact as they intruded on new regions.

> Neo-Europeans did not purposely introduce rats, and they have spent millions and millions of pounds, dollars, pesos and other currencies to halt their spread—usually in vain. The same is true for several other varmints in the Neo-Europes—rabbits, for instance. This seems to indicate that the humans were seldom

> *masters of the biological changes they triggered in the Neo-*
> *Europes. They benefited from the great majority of the changes,*
> *but benefit or not, their role often was less a matter of judgment*
> *and choice than of being downstream of a bursting dam.[14]*

Other historians suggest that while European biological warfare against aboriginal peoples was unfortunate, it was unintentional. In contrast, European labour practices were deliberately cruel. Europeans cared little about the people they found and were happy enough to exploit them ruthlessly, importing African slaves when indigenous labourers were too few or too unwilling to perform the services required. Historian Ralph Davis notes that on the island of Hispaniola, under both Columbus and his successors, the local people were worked to death in gold-placer mining and on building projects. The same tragedy was repeated in Puerto Rico, Cuba, the Leeward Islands, and the Bahamas.

Similarly, in the Aztec empire of Mexico and the Inca empire of Peru, the Spanish *conquistadores* appeared to recognize no bounds to their exactions from the original inhabitants. Both indigenous empires had been rigidly class-stratified, and the conquered peoples were used to paying huge tributes to maintain the military-religious clique that ruled them with an iron hand. Not surprisingly, then, they offered no resistance to the foreigners who deposed their oppressive rulers. Yet their new masters proved even more ruthless. The exactions demanded of the Indians, whose diet was already protein deficient, left them poorly fed and unable to resist diseases.

Uruguayan writer Eduardo Galeano, in a moving if not perfectly documented text, *Open Veins of Latin America*, describes how the Indians were hunted down and forced to work in unbearable conditions far from home; he suggests they died in massive numbers from overwork and hunger. The women were often unable to produce mother's milk, the only possible source of nourishment for infants in a society without cows or goats. Their babies died, and the women who did not commit suicide refused to engage in sexual activity as a way of preventing children from being born into conditions of slavery. In *The World Encompassed* historian G.V. Scammell supports the general lines of this argument.

The germ theory, while important, fails to explain differential death rates among Native groups in contact with Europeans. In regions such as Canada the decline in population, while considerable, was simply not on the same scale as in Mexico, for instance. In most cases a third or more of the indigenous people survived contact with Europeans, while in Mexico fewer than one in twenty-five had similar success.

• Notes

[1] L.S. Stavrianos, *A Global History From Prehistory to the Present*, 5th ed. (Englewood Cliffs, NJ: Prentice-Hall, 1991), 403.

[2] Carlo M. Cipolla, *Before the Industrial Revolution: European Society and Economy, 1000–1700*, 2nd ed. (New York: Methuen, 1980), 78. An "almoner" is an ecclesiastic attached to a noble household.

[3] Lawrence Stone, *The Past and the Present Revisited* (London: Routledge and Kegan Paul, 1987), 334.

[4] Cipolla, *Before the Industrial Revolution*, 125.

[5] G.V. Scammell, *The World Encompassed: The First European Maritime Empires c. 800–1650* (London: Methuen, 1981), 107.

[6] Ralph Davis, *The Rise of the Atlantic Economies* (London: Weidenfeld and Nicolson, 1973), 16.

[7] Susan Stuard, "The Dominion of Gender: Women's Fortunes in the High Middle Ages," in *Becoming Visible: Women in European History*, 2nd ed., ed. Renate Bridenthal, Claudia Koonz, and Susan Stuard (Boston: Houghton Mifflin, 1987), 154–55.

[8] Merry E. Wiesner, "Spinning Out Capital: Women's Work in the Early Modern Economy," in *Becoming Visible*, ed. Bridenthal, Koonz, and Stuard, 245.

[9] Fernand Braudel, *The Mediterranean and the Mediterranean World in the Age of Philip II*, Vol. 1 (New York: Harper Torchbooks, 1975), 449.

[10] Cipolla, *Before the Industrial Revolution*, 177.

[11] Fernand Braudel, *The Mediterranean and the Mediterranean World in the Age of Philip II*, Vol. 1 (New York: Harper Torchbooks, 1975), 227.

[12] Scammell, *World Encompassed*, 236.

[13] Scammell, *World Encompassed*, 257.

[14] Alfred W. Crosby, *Ecological Imperialism: The Biological Expansion of Europe, 900–1900* (Cambridge: Cambridge University Press, 1986), 192.

•Selected Reading

Good overviews of early modern Europe include: Carlo Cipolla, *Before the Industrial Revolution: European Society and Economy, 1000–1700*, 2nd ed. (New York: Methuen, 1980); Fernand Braudel, *Civilization and Capitalism, Fifteenth–Eighteenth Century*, 3 vols. (New York: Harper and Row, 1983–86); and Immanuel Wallerstein, *The Modern World System*, Vol. 1, *Capitalist Agriculture and the Origins of the European World Economy in the Sixteenth Century* (New York: Academic Press, 1974). A critical attempt to explain why Western Europe developed differently than other parts of the world is J.M. Roberts, *The Triumph of the West* (London: BBC Books, 1985).

On the growth of trade and of exploration, see Ralph Davis, *The Rise of the Atlantic Economies* (London: Weidenfeld and Nicolson, 1973); G.V. Scammell, *The World Encompassed: The First European Maritime Empires c. 800–1650* (London: Methuen, 1981); G.V. Scammell, *The First Imperial Age: European Overseas Expansion c. 1400–1715* (London: Unwin and Hyman, 1989); and J.D. Tracy, ed., *The Rise of Merchant Empires: Long-Distance Trade in the Early Modern World, 1350–1750* (Cambridge: Cambridge University Press, 1990). Changes in warfare are detailed in W.H. McNeill, *The Pursuit of Power: Technology, Armed Force and Society Since A.D. 1000* (Chicago: University of Chicago Press, 1984); and Gwynne Dyer, *War* (New York: Crown, 1985). On the Crusades, see Malcolm Billings, *The Cross and the Crescent* (London: BBC Books, 1987). On the *conquistadores*, see Eduardo Galeano, *Open Veins of Latin America: Five Centuries of the Pillage of a Continent* (New York: Monthly Review Press, 1973). See also Alfred W. Crosby, *Ecological Imperialism: The Biological Expansion of Europe, 900–1900* (Cambridge: Cambridge University Press, 1986), and Ronald Wright, *Stolen Continents: The "New World" Since 1492* (Toronto: Viking, 1992).

Important regional studies include Fernand Braudel, *The Mediterranean and the Mediterranean World in the Age of Phillip II*, 2 vols. (New York: Harper Torchbooks, 1975, 1977); Kenneth R. Andrews, *Trade, Plunder and Settlement: Maritime Enterprise and the Genesis of the British Empire 1480–1630* (Cambridge: Cambridge University Press, 1985); C.R. Boxer, *Race Relations in the Portuguese Colonial Empire, 1415–1825* (Westport, CT: Greenwood Press, 1985); Lyle N. McAlister, *Spain and Portugal in the New World, 1492–1700* (Minneapolis: University of Minnesota Press, 1984); and Fernand Braudel, *Identity of France* (London: Collins, 1988).

The literature on social life includes Fernand Braudel, *Civilization and Capitalism, Fifteenth–Eighteenth Century*, Vol. 1, *The Structures of Everyday Life* (London: Collins, 1983); Philippe Aries and Georges Duby, eds., *A History of Private Life*, Vol. 2, *Revelations of the Medieval World* (Cambridge, MA: Harvard University Press, 1988); and Philippe Aries and Georges Duby, eds., *A History of Private Life*, Vol. 3, *Passions of the Renaissance* (Cambridge, MA: Harvard University Press, 1989).

The history of European women of this period is probed in several essays in Renate Bridenthal, Claudia Koonz, and Susan Stuard, eds., *Becoming Visible: Women in European History* (Boston: Houghton Mifflin, 1987); also in Bonnie S. Anderson and Judith P. Zinsser, *A History of Their Own: Women in Europe from Prehistory to the Present*, 2 vols. (New York: Harper and Row, 1989); Merry E. Wiesner, "Guilds, Male Bonding and Women's Work in Early Modern Germany," *Gender and History* 1, 2 (Summer 1989); and Judith M. Bennett, "Feminism and History," *Gender and History* 1, 3 (Autumn 1989). On women in the Catholic Church, see Elizabeth Rapley, *The Dévotes: Women and Church in Seventeenth-Century France* (Montreal: McGill-Queen's University Press, 1990).

On the Renaissance, significant works include Trevor Cairns, *Renaissance and Reformation* (Cambridge: Cambridge University Press, 1987); J.H. Salmon, *Renaissance and Revolt: Essays in the Intellectual and Social History of Early France* (Cambridge: Cambridge University Press, 1987); J. R. Hale, *Renaissance Europe: The Individual and Society* (Berkeley: University of California Press, 1971); Gene Brucker, *Renaissance Florence* (Berkeley: University of California Press, 1983); and Donald R. Kelly, *Renaissance Humanism* (Boston: G.K. Hall, 1991). On the Reformation and counter-Reformation, see DeLamar Jensen, *Reformation Europe: Age of Reform and Revolution* (Lexington, MA: D.C. Heath, 1981); and Simon Schama, *The Embarrassment of Riches: An Interpretation of Dutch Culture in the Golden Age* (New York: Knopf, 1987). The debate on the relationship between religious ideas and the rise of capitalist institutions has sparked several seminal works, including Max Weber, *The Protestant Ethic and the Spirit of Capitalism* (London: Unwin, 1980); R.H. Tawney, *Religion and the Rise of Capitalism* (Magnolia, MA: Peter Smith, 1984); and A.O. Hirschman, *The Passions and the Interests: Political Arguments for Capitalism Before Its Triumph* (Princeton: Princeton University Press, 1977).

CHAPTER 3

THE "DISCOVERY" OF CANADA:
Contact and Settlement to 1663

Montagnais women who summered along the St Lawrence River were accustomed to holding their own councils, and so in 1640 a group of them were surprised to be summoned before a council composed of three male captains. The captains were Christian converts, chosen in a Jesuit-sponsored election. According to the women, who related their experience to the Jesuits: "They treated us so rudely that we were greatly astonished. 'It is you women,' they said to us, 'who keep the Demons among us; you do not urge to be baptized. . . . When you pass before the cross you never salute it, you wish to be independent. Now know that you will obey your husbands and you young people know that you will obey your parents, and our captains, and if any fail to do so, we will give them nothing to eat.'"[1]

One hundred years earlier, if a group of Montagnais men had demanded that the women accept subordinate status and that children be obedient, they would have been dismissed as madmen possessed by evil spirits. Their threat to withhold food would have been meaningless in a society that required its members to take collective responsibility for obtaining and preparing food. Yet after a century of contact with Europeans through the medium of the fur trade, the status of Montagnais women had declined significantly. The Montagnais, like other aboriginal groups, had expected that the fur trade would enhance their traditional culture. Initially it appeared to do so. But European–Amerindian contact provoked challenges to the aboriginal peoples' beliefs and customs and created deep internal divisions in their societies. Europeans too, despite a strong sense of superiority, were influenced in many ways by the encounter of two peoples without a common history.

In Europe, with its societies in a transitional phase between dying feudalism and emergent capitalism, the search for profitable staples as well as the Northwest Passage would spur both exploration and settlement. In the age of exploration, the merchants who led the search for profits were joined by religious enthusiasts, men and women eager to convert pagan souls to Christianity. Despite their conflicting values, the merchants and the apostles of the Counter-Reformation depended upon one another in the attempt to achieve their respective goals. Both merchants and clerics also had their respective, sometimes conflicting, visions of how the farmers, fishers, and small traders of the European colonies should behave. They found that in the frontier environment, the forces of repression that enforced traditional relationships in the metropolis were noticeably weaker.

• Making Contact:
The Role of the Fishery

Intermittent contact between the first peoples of the Americas and various peoples from abroad had most likely occurred for centuries before the European conquest of the New World. There is archaeological, botanical, and linguistic evidence suggesting contacts between the first peoples and ocean-going coastal peoples of Asia, Europe, and Africa. A twelfth-century carving found in southern India has a figure holding a cob of corn, a plant that at the time grew only in the Americas. The peanut, another American native, was planted in southeastern China as early as 3000 B.C., while two varieties of chickens believed to be native to the Orient were being raised in the Americas when the Spanish arrived in the sixteenth century. In Mexico, the Mayans gave their days and months names that some linguists suggest bear a resemblance to their equivalent Chinese names.

One of the more compelling stories of Asian travel in the Americas involves five Buddhist monks reputed to have spent forty years in the Americas in the fifth century A.D. According to the Annals of the Chinese Empire in 499, an official report of events, Hwui Shan, one of the monks, had provided an extensive description to the emperor of lands far to the east of China. His description of indigenous customs accords with later European accounts, and it is believed that Fu-sang, as he called the lands he explored, included today's Mexico and California. Some writers have speculated that the Buddhists, who lived peacefully with their hosts, influenced Native religious traditions.

Irish legends suggest that St Brendan, a sixth-century monk, travelled in the Americas and that an Irish settlement in today's Nova Scotia was established in the ninth century. According to the tradition, the Irish settlers gradually assimilated with the Mi'kmaq. The Irish claim was incorporated in the sagas of the Icelanders—Norsemen who settled in Iceland after slaughtering the Irish hermits who had previously inhabited that island—but so far it lacks archaeological confirmation. The first contact leading to a settlement backed up by archaeological evidence involved Greenlanders and dates from the end of the tenth century. About 986 a Norwegian named Bjarni Herjulfsson was en route from Iceland to newly colonized Greenland when his ship went off course and landed somewhere on the shores of the westerly continent, most likely in what is now Labrador. His reports led Greenlanders to make several attempts to settle in today's Newfoundland and Labrador at the end of the tenth and beginning of the eleventh centuries. The Greenlanders of European extraction were Norsemen or Vikings, kin to the Scandinavians who ruled much of Northern Europe, including most of the British Isles, in the ninth and tenth centuries. An agricultural settlement of these sea-going people had been founded in Iceland about 870, and the Greenland settlement, started about 982, was the brainchild of Eric the Red, a ruffian expelled by the Icelanders. Greenland, unlike Iceland, was also home to Native hunters, and hostile relations developed between the two competitors for resources.

Few details of the Norse attempt to colonize Newfoundland are known, although the site of a Norse village has been uncovered at Anse-aux-Meadows. It is believed to be the settlement founded by Thorvald Ericsson, one of the sons of Eric the Red. An earlier settlement on the same spot had been abandoned by Thorvald's brother, Leif Ericsson. These settlements included women as well as men, and some children were born there, perhaps the first children of European descent to be born in the Americas. Leif called the territory found by the Greenlanders Vinland.

Native people, whom the Vikings called *skraelings*, were present throughout the regions the Norsemen explored and settled. The sagas suggest that while at first the *skraelings* were hospitable and eager to trade for European wares, hostilities soon developed. The Vikings were a people of military prowess, but European weaponry in 1000 was not as superior to its Native equivalents as it would be five hundred years later. Lacking either the numbers or the military might to subdue the local residents, the Vikings apparently stayed in the New World only a short time. The cultures of the Mi'kmaq, Montagnais, and Inuit peoples who came into contact with them were probably not significantly affected by this troublesome interlude. It is possible, however, that memories of this first encounter with

Europeans caused at least one of the groups, the Beothuk, to be wary of the Europeans who came later to their shores.

The peoples of the northeastern parts of the continent saw little more of Europeans until the end of the fifteenth century when, like many other indigenous groups of the Americas, they were inadvertently "discovered" by adventurers searching for sea routes to the Orient. Although small groups of Bristol fishermen may have begun fishing cod off Newfoundland from about 1480, it was John Cabot's reports about a vast cod fishery off the shores of the "new isle" that sparked European-wide interest.

Although Europe's sixteenth-century population had rebounded from the decline brought on by the Black Death, the peasantry remained desperately poor. Their diet was especially deficient in protein, and codfish from the new fishing grounds would be an important addition to their regular fare. In Catholic countries cod was also prized by the better-off members of society who, along with their poorer co-religionists, endured 153 meatless days a year. By 1580 over four hundred Portuguese, Spanish, and French ships with combined crews of about ten thousand were plying the waters off Newfoundland each summer in search of cod. Spaniards and Basques made regular voyages to the Strait of Belle Isle and the Gulf of St

Cod fishing and drying by the French in the eighteenth century   (Elizabeth Melau/National Archives of Canada/C105230)

Lawrence. As late as 1760, shipments of cod bulked larger in France's imports from New France than furs, and the fishery employed far more people than the fur trade.

Conducted exclusively by Europeans for the European market, the cod fishery required neither a slave nor a free Native labour force. Nevertheless, it created the conditions for contact between Europeans and aboriginal peoples. Initially fishermen came ashore only for firewood and drinking water, but it was not long before a "dry fishery" developed, involving the cleaning and salting of the fish on land. The dry fishery required a stay of two or three months in Newfoundland, and by the seventeenth century it was encouraging the modest beginnings of year-round settlement on the island. Although France, Spain, and Portugal continued to use the "green-cure" method of preserving the fish aboard ship, England lacked the ready access to salt that those countries enjoyed. Its fishermen favoured the dry fishery, which required far less salt than green-curing did.

In the sixteenth century, Europeans in Canada, unlike the Spanish *conquistadores*, had no interest in plundering or settling their newly discovered territory, much less enslaving or killing the Native inhabitants. Indeed, friendly trade developed between the fishermen and aboriginal groups throughout Eastern Canada as the fishery gradually moved further inland. The fishermen traded iron pots, kettles, and glass beads, among other items, for the furs that the Native peoples were wearing. The fishermen sold the furs to hatters in Europe. The trade picked up noticeably in the mid-sixteenth century when a rage for broad-brimmed beaver-felted hats took hold among the fashionable set on the continent. As the Baltic sources of fur were exhausted, demand suddenly outstripped supply, leaving North America as the principal source for furs.

Until that time, however, the fur trade in the Americas was simply an extension of the fishery, and Europeans made little contact with the aboriginal peoples outside the hours spent in exchange of furs for iron goods. These goods made life easier for the Natives who acquired them and were held in high regard, as evidenced by their abundance in the burial sites of eastern nations. They were also traded by the Mi'kmaq and other groups in contact with the fishermen to tribes further west: by 1530 iron goods had reached the St Lawrence, and before the end of the century they had penetrated Huron territory.

Scholars have long debated the effect of European trade on Native society. Some anthropologists suggest that the intimate connection between the Amerindians and nature, which permeated not only their social arrangements but also their religion, was undermined by new economic relations. Declining self-sufficiency among tribes intimately involved

SEARCHING FOR ASIA

While fish and furs were the attractions for most of Europe's early venturers to today's Canada, the search for the Northwest Passage—which had alerted Europeans to these resources in the first place—continued to motivate expeditions to the Americas. Most of the European knowledge of the northern territories resulted from the continued search for a sea passage that would link the Atlantic to the Pacific and lead to the wealth of China and the East Indies. In 1576, 1577, and 1578, for example, explorer Martin Frobisher, sailing west from Greenland in search of the elusive passage, "discovered" Frobisher Bay and charted much of the Arctic. Digging for ore in the region, Frobisher found nothing of value but did capture some Inuit, whom he offered to the king of England as evidence of his miraculous explorations.

Like Frobisher, Sir Humphrey Gilbert raised funds from English merchants who believed the passage existed and could guarantee their trading fortunes. In 1583, on his second voyage to the "New World," Gilbert took possession of Newfoundland in the name of Britain and made plans to establish a colony. Within two months, however, Gilbert had drowned at sea and the only ship remaining of the original five that had sailed with him returned home. From 1585 to 1587 another explorer, John Davis, made three voyages along the Arctic coast to search for the passage and wrote sympathetically of the Inuit he encountered. Henry Hudson, working first for the Dutch and later the English, ascended the Hudson River in 1609 before braving the dangers of Hudson Strait the following year and sailing into Hudson Bay. Three centuries would elapse before Norwegian Roald Amundsen's expedition (1903–06) finally traversed the Northwest Passage.

with the European trade, it is argued, created the conditions that allowed the priests and nuns to convince the Native peoples that their religious views were in error.

Apart from the Beothuk, who were gradually annihilated (see chapter 8), the first nations of the Atlantic region enjoyed good relations with the fishermen, although thousands of deaths resulted from the spread of European diseases. Good relations also generally marked another economic activity—the hunting of walrus and whales. Canadian Native peoples were little affected by the walrus and whale hunters who flourished on their coasts in the sixteenth century. The Portuguese on Sable Island and

Spanish Basques on the islands of the Gulf of St Lawrence were the first walrus hunters, joined by the French on Chaleur Bay, Prince Edward Island, and the Magdalen Islands before 1570. A Breton nobleman, Marquis Troilus de la Roche, received a French trading monopoly for all of Canada in 1598 and established a small settlement on Sable Island with forty freed prisoners and ten soldiers. The colonists hunted the walrus, wanted for its ivory and oil, but mutinied when food supplies failed to arrive in 1602. The colony was subsequently abandoned.

One of the earliest and most successful whaling operations in the New World was conducted by the Basques. They established a station at Red Bay in present-day Labrador in the 1540s, and several hundred whalers made use of it annually for about sixty years. The Basques abandoned Atlantic whaling in the wake of damages to their fleet inflicted in the defeat of the Spanish Armada. They were replaced by French, English, and German whalers, searching for the profits from whale oil, which lit most of Europe's lamps, and baleen, the large horny plates that took the place of teeth for whales and bolstered European dresses of the period. Arctic whaling proved even more profitable than Atlantic whaling, and whalers in the northern waters applied Inuit technology for deep-sea whaling.

By the eighteenth century the walrus of Canada had been hunted almost to extinction, much as those of the Baltic had been ten centuries earlier. Whaling, by contrast, remained hugely profitable and was practised on all three coasts in the nineteenth century. But the European hunters gave no thought to conserving whale stocks, and the Arctic supply had lost its commercial viability by World War I. Much later, in December 1972, the Canadian government halted all commercial whaling operations based in Canadian ports, fourteen years before an international moratorium on commercial whaling came into effect.

•Early British Colonization:
The Newfoundland Experience

An English company's vain attempt to capture control of the Newfoundland fishery led to the creation of a settlement at Cupid's Cove in Conception Bay in 1610. The company lured forty fishermen-colonists with the promise that they would have first choice of fishing grounds and get their catch to market before the annual fishing vessels arrived from England. The colonists cleared land, planted gardens, and built homes, surrounding their small settlement with a palisade protected by mounted guns.

Over the next two decades several more settlements were established in Newfoundland. A colony at Renews for Welsh paupers collapsed within a year but was re-established at Trepassey. A small commercial settlement at Ferryland gave refuge to persecuted English Catholics, but it also proved short-lived. The philanthropists behind the founding of these settlements were unable to raise the capital needed to make them successful, and investors saw no reason to support ventures that had little chance of economic success.

The generally poor settlers who had left England, Wales, or Ireland to start a new life in Newfoundland could not afford to return and had little to return to. They survived by fishing, raising a few animals, growing turnips and cabbages, and trading for other essentials with passing ships. In selling their fish they enjoyed little advantage over the English West-Country fishers who came each summer.

The early history of Ferryland illustrates the precarious character of the first Newfoundland settlements. In the late sixteenth century, Ferryland, with its sheltered harbour and good drying areas, became the site of an English fishing station. The London and Bristol Company acquired control over the area early in the seventeenth century and made land grants in the hope of getting settlements started. England's secretary of state for the colonies, George Calvert, whose mercantile interests spanned the Virginia Company and the East India Company, added Ferryland to his commercial interests in 1620. Within a year the foundations of a settlement were laid. Most of the colonists sent to the site were, like Calvert, Catholic.

French privateers and an outbreak of scurvy made the winter of 1628–29 unbearable, causing Calvert to withdraw his active interest in the colony and leave its operation to family agents. All the Catholic settlers in the total population of under 150 people departed, either for Virginia or England. While a small number of Protestant settlers remained, they were soon caught in a crossfire between the Calvert family and the family of David Kirke. Kirke, who had received royal recognition of his claims, forcibly seized Calvert's properties in 1639. Interested mainly in the fishery, Kirke also promoted agriculture and the production of salt. His family was still in charge when a Dutch squadron virtually destroyed the colony in 1673. Two years later the population was estimated at 151; while 11 families lived in Ferryland year-round, 122 residents were fishing servants of the Kirkes. More attacks by Dutch pirates followed in the 1670s and 1680s. After a brief respite attacks began again, this time by France, which captured the colony in 1696 and deported all the settlers.

Although the British reasserted control in the area one year later, they built no adequate fortifications, with the result that the settlement was destroyed repeatedly in the eighteenth century. It was nonetheless rebuilt each time and by 1800 was one of the major West-Country settlements in Newfoundland.

Throughout its early history, Ferryland, like other small colonies in Newfoundland, was faced with the daunting challenge of creating a defensible, agriculturally productive settlement that could provision the dry fishery of the area. In 1622 an optimistic Captain Edward Wynne, appointed commander of the settlement by Calvert, wrote to his superior indicating the steps taken to achieve these objectives:

> After Christmas, we imployed our selves in the woods especially in hard weather, whence we got home as many boord-stocks, afforded us above two hundred boords and above two hundred timber trees besides. We got home as much or as many trees as served us to palizado into the Plantation about foure Acres of ground, for the keeping off of both man & beast, with post and rayle seven foote high, sharpened in the toppe, the trees being pitched upright and fastened with spikes and nayles. We got also together as much fire wood, as will serve us yet these two moneths. Wee also fitted much garden ground for seede, I meane, Barley, Oates, Pease, and Beans. For addition of building, we have at this present a Parlour of fourteene foote besides the chimney, and twelve foote broad, of convenient height, and a lodging chamber over it; to each a chimney of stone worke with staires and a staire case, besides a tenement of two rooms, or a storie and a halfe, which serves for a store house till we are other wise provided. The Forge hath been finished this five weekes: The Salt-worke is now almost ready. . . . We have also broken much ground for a Brew-house roome and other Tenements. We have a wharfe in good forwardnesse towards the Low-watermarke.[2]

• Early French Colonization: From Cartier to the Founding of Acadia

Whereas English settlement in Newfoundland was an outgrowth of the fishery, French colonization in eastern North America was prompted by visions of much greater riches. The successes of Spain and Portugal in finding wealth in the Americas stirred up hopes in the French court of finding similar wealth. While the cod fishery was essentially left to the workings of private entrepreneurs, the state provided funds for expeditions that might lead to conquest of regions rich in gold and other valued resources. In

1534 King Francis I commissioned Jacques Cartier, a sea captain from St Malo, to discover and claim for France the fabled lands where gold and other precious metals were to be found. Cartier undertook three voyages to North America between 1534 and 1541, and the only gold he found was iron pyrite or "fool's gold," which he mistook for the real thing. His attempt at colonization was also a failure, owing in large part to his duplicitous dealings with the aboriginal peoples. Like Columbus, Cartier was a product of European society, which treated all pagan people with disdain. Cartier left a detailed record of his travels that revealed much about both European attitudes to the Indians and first peoples' attitudes toward the intruders.

In 1534, when Cartier entered the Baie des Chaleurs, he met Natives anxious to trade furs for European iron goods and trinkets. The Natives, clearly used to trading with Europeans by that time, exchanged worn beaver-pelt cloaks for hatchets, knives, combs, and glass beads. The Europeans, for their part, prized the pelts obtained in the trade. Because they had been worn by the Natives, the furs had lost their long guard hairs and become glossy and supple through the actions of body oil and perspiration. They were thus ideal for felting by Parisian hatters. Cartier wrote of his early trading encounters with Native people:

> As soon as they saw us they began to run away, making signs to us that they had come to barter with us; and held up some furs of small value, with which they clothe themselves. We likewise made signs to them that we wished them no harm, and sent two men on shore, to offer them some knives and other iron goods, and a red cap to give to their chief. Seeing this, they sent on shore part of their people with some of their furs; and the two parties traded together. The savages showed a marvellously great pleasure in possessing and obtaining these iron wares and other commodities, dancing and going through many ceremonies, and throwing salt water over their heads with their hands. They bartered all they had to such an extent that all went back naked without anything on them; and they made signs to us that they would return on the morrow with more furs.[3]

Cartier believed that what the French gave the Indians for their furs had "small value." Indeed, while this kind of barter might seem to be an unequal exchange, each culture had its own concepts of value and both groups were apparently well satisfied with the trading. The goods the Amerindians had obtained were of either aesthetic or utilitarian value to them, and they must have wondered what the French would do with such quantities of peltries and used clothing.

After leaving the Baie des Chaleurs, Cartier sailed into Gaspé Bay and encountered a hunting party of Iroquoians from the village of Stadacona, located at the present site of Quebec City. Troubles began when he erected a thirty-foot cross in July 1534 only to find that Donnacona, the Stadaconan chief, balked at his boldness. Donnacona, wrote Cartier, "made us a long harangue, making the sign of the cross with two of his fingers, and then he pointed to the land all about, as if he wished to say that all this region belonged to him, and that we ought not to have set up this cross without his permission."[4] Cartier took Donnacona captive and only freed him when he proved more amenable. The chastened chief gave reluctant consent to Cartier's plan to take two of the Native leader's sons to France for a year.

Returning in September 1535, Cartier again showed a lack of tact. The Stadaconans, who were eager to preserve their status as intermediaries between Natives further inland and the Europeans, expressed displeasure

Jacques Cartier at Hochelaga   (C.W. Jefferys/National Archives of Canada/C70257 detail)

at Cartier's wish to travel into Hochelagan country. Cartier ignored their wishes and sailed up the St Lawrence River as far as Hochelaga, where Montreal is now located. Later, wintering with the very people he had offended, the Stadaconans, he and his crew had reason to thank them for saving most of their lives. Twenty-five of the European party of 110 had died of scurvy before Native medicine prevented the rest from succumbing as well. The Stadaconans were aware of the curative powers of a broth and a poultice made from the bark and needles of the *anneda* (possibly white cedar), which is rich in the vitamin C needed to prevent scurvy.

Cartier showed his gratitude by seizing Donnacona, two of his sons, and seven others to accompany his party back to France, where they were paraded in their native dress and accoutrements through the streets of several cities. The kidnapping of Amerindians for this purpose was a common practice among European explorers anxious to convince monarchs and merchants that they had truly discovered new lands full of untold riches. Cartier assured Donnacona that the king of France would handsomely reward him for his visit.

Cartier returned five years later as the leader of an advance party for Jean-François de La Rocque de Roberval, a nobleman from northern France who was commissioned to found a permanent settlement near Stadacona. Nine of the ten Stadaconans had died in France but Cartier, without the survivor along to contradict him, explained to the disbelieving Stadaconans that all ten had become great princes. By this time the Stadaconans were not disposed to aid Cartier's group, who spent a rough winter and then headed home with their diamonds that turned out to be mica chips. Roberval, deserted by his lieutenant, tried nonetheless to re-establish a settlement at the same site during the winter of 1542–43. But the charms of his settlers, most of them ex-convicts, found no favour among the Stadaconans, and after a scurvy-ridden winter they too departed. France would give up on the idea of settlement so far north in the Americas for several generations. Failed attempts at settlement in Florida and Brazil (where the Portuguese and Spanish defended their exclusive claims), followed by forty years of civil religious warfare, absorbed attention that might otherwise have been partially bestowed upon the vast territories of Canada. There was no rationale for settlement in North America as long as the region's only profitable economic activity was the cod fishery; but by 1600 the dramatic increase in demand for furs had changed all that.

After establishing temporary religious peace in France, Henri IV was determined to have his country emulate Spain and Portugal in establishing New World colonies and extracting great wealth. In 1603 he granted Pierre du Gua de Monts, a distinguished Protestant soldier and administrator, a

MARGUERITE DE LA ROQUE

The first French woman to give birth in the Americas was a landowning noblewoman who had been stranded on an uninhabited island in the St Lawrence. Marguerite de La Roque was the niece of Jean-François de Roberval and accompanied him on his voyage to Canada in 1542. Outraged when he discovered that she had been having an affair with a member of his crew, Roberval abandoned her with her lover and her servant on the Isle of Demons. The three castoffs built a log cabin where La Roque gave birth to a child. Her child, lover, and servant all perished before she was rescued by Breton fishers over two years after her abandonment. She told the royal geographer André Thevet that she had survived on her own after her lover's death, which preceded the birth of her child, because she had a gun and could hunt the abundant game of the island. Regarded as a hero by many women in France, La Roque lived the remainder of her life in a convent.

ten-year monopoly of trade in the Atlantic region. In return de Monts promised to settle sixty colonists a year and to promote Catholic missionary work among the Native peoples. In the long run de Monts's attempts to comply would result in the permanent establishment of European settlement in the Maritime region of Canada. But in the short term his colonizing ventures proved disastrous. In 1604 de Monts and seventy-eight colonists, all male, wintered on an island at the mouth of the Ste Croix River on the present border between Maine and New Brunswick. Unlike Roberval's prisoners, de Monts's colonists were mainly gentlemen, artisans, and mariners. Among them was Samuel de Champlain, who would become a towering figure in Canadian exploration and colonization. The rigours of a Canadian winter defeated these men, with thirty-five dying of scurvy. In the spring de Monts decided that the site was not promising for agriculture and moved the remaining group across the Bay of Fundy to the Annapolis Valley. He recruited new colonists for the settlement, which was named Port Royal. The co-operation of the Mi'kmaq, who could show the settlers how to avoid scurvy and survive northern winters, proved invaluable.

De Monts lost his trade monopoly in 1607, but by then the small colony was, however precariously, on its feet. Its forty residents had garden plots, orchards, and small grain fields to sustain themselves. Jean de Poutrincourt, de Monts's lieutenant-governor, received a new monopoly of the fur trade and began to grant formal land titles to settlers. Two Jesuit priests arrived in 1611 to minister to settlers and convert the Natives to

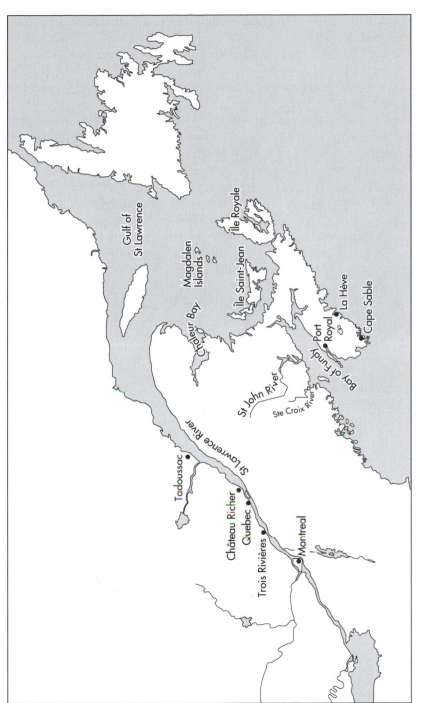

MAP 3.1 *New France in the Seventeenth Century*

Christianity—the first mission by a French religious order in the Americas. Funds for their work were raised by Madame de Guercheville, pious wife of the governor of Paris and chief lady-in-waiting to the queen, the first of several wealthy French women to sponsor religious activities in New France. Acadia, the name France gave to its settlements in the Maritime region, was slowly taking shape.

Yet the colony's initial growth was modest. France was at war with England from 1618 to 1648 and could little afford to pay attention to its North American colonies. Acadia was seized three times by English and New England privateers, first in 1613, then from 1627 to 1632 and again from 1654 to 1667. In between, its settlers had to put up with a ten-year civil war (1635–45) provoked by the rivalry between two claimants to control of the colony. The population had reached about three hundred in 1650 and perhaps four hundred in 1670. At least twenty of the families present in 1650 had been brought from one French seigneury near Loudon by Charles de Menou d'Aulnay, one of the rival contenders for Acadia, whose base was Port Royal. His opponent, Charles de La Tour, brought settlers to the St John River and Cape Sable. As was to be the case in Quebec, many residents of early Acadia were indentured labourers or domestics. Most of them left for France once their indenture was completed, happy to leave a war-torn zone where agriculture was in its pioneer stage and winter's blasts made a spartan living even more unbearable.

The settlers who stayed had mainly been farm labourers in France. Beginning in the 1630s they constructed dikes to reclaim alluvial land from the sea, and they soon became largely self-sufficient. The seizure of Port Royal by New Englanders in 1654 caused the French settlers in the area to move upriver. The Massachusetts merchants in charge of the colony showed no interest in deporting farmers and fishers, and a profitable trade was established between French and English residents. When French rule was restored, Emmanuel Le Borgne, who was then in control of the Port Royal area seigneury, complained that the colonists were resisting his attempts to reassert seigneurial authority. Frequent changes of authority appeared to have incited a spirit of independence among the early Acadians.

European religion first entered the area with the arrival of a secular priest who baptized Membertou, a Mi'kmaq grand chief, and a score of his relatives. Membertou insisted to his people that they be baptized, but his major goal appears to have been to cement good relations with the fur traders by appeasing their religious allies.

Over time, contact with Europeans fundamentally altered many aspects of Mi'kmaq life. Depletion of game occurred early in the Mi'kmaq

MARIE DE LA TOUR

The battle between the d'Aulnays and the de La Tours for control of early Acadia was a complicated affair that pitted two families against one another in a struggle for status and wealth. The wives of Charles de La Tour and Charles de Menou d'Aulnay played important roles in the unfolding of events.

Marie de La Tour arrived in the colony in 1640 and settled at Fort La Tour, across the Bay of Fundy from Port Royal—thus becoming the first European woman to make a home in what is now the province of New Brunswick. Active in defence of the family claim to Acadia, she travelled to France in 1643 to plead—unsuccessfully—her husband's case against charges that he had plotted with the English to place the colony in their control in return for driving d'Aulnay away. When the La Tours refused to surrender their lands, d'Aulnay's forces attacked Fort La Tour in 1645 while Charles was in Boston purchasing arms and supplies. Marie took command of the fort's forty-five or so men and for five days withstood a siege by a larger, better-armed force. She surrendered in return for a promise from d'Aulnay to spare her men—a promise quickly broken. La Tour herself died of causes unknown several weeks later, while still d'Aulnay's captive. Charles de La Tour took refuge in Quebec.

The victorious d'Aulnay drowned in 1650, leaving an estate heavily in debt. His widow battled creditors in the courts and even married Charles de La Tour in a fruitless effort to link two families' claims and thereby convince French officials to reject the case of mere financiers.

territories. By 1663 there had been several famines; moose in Cape Breton had become extinct and so too had elk on Mission Island. Fur-bearing animals, killed in larger numbers to accommodate the traders' demands, became harder to find. The Mi'kmaq were increasingly forced to buy clothes from the Europeans, and as European cottons, woollens, and kettles replaced local manufacture, the women's crucial production roles broke down. The men's skills in crafting items from stone and other indigenous materials also diminished. Resource depletion led the Mi'kmaq to cluster around the settlements, where they began to eat unfamiliar foods such as peas, prunes, and bread. The resulting physical deterioration may have contributed to their vulnerability in the face of European-imported diseases. Kinship groups decayed as disease attacked the population, and while some traditions survived, French missionaries increasingly meddled with familial, sexual, and property arrangements.

By the end of the seventeenth century Mi'kmaq numbers had declined to about 2000 from an estimated 35 000 in 1500. The Mi'kmaq had not been forced by Europeans to change their way of life; they had merely engaged in trade with outsiders whose goods, for a time, seemed to add to the traditional culture. Iron axes, knives, and pots could be shared in gift-giving ceremonies and used to enrich burial sites. But gradually the contact with Europeans had led to dependence. Although the first peoples tended to retain their independence as long as their resource base remained relatively intact, the situation soon changed if those resources were either depleted or simply taken from them. In the St Lawrence River valley and southern Ontario, as in the Maritime region, Native peoples began their trade of furs on a basis of equality with their European customers, only to get caught in a web from which escape proved impossible. Ironically, they helped spin that web, hoping to strengthen their traditional cultures by making use of European goods.

• The Founding of Quebec, the Fur Trade, and European–Native Relations

The fur trade was the initial motor of French expansion throughout North America. It was responsible for the first settlements in Acadia and Quebec and eventually resulted in a series of trading posts that extended westwards to the prairies and southwards to Louisiana. It was a commercial enterprise that required Native participation as trappers, so it ensured that European traders, whatever their prejudices, would treat their aboriginal allies with some respect. Although the objective of traders was profit, the trade was rarely profitable: rivalries, administrative costs, frequent warfare, and eventually an oversupply that depressed prices all frustrated investors' hopes. By the late seventeenth century the trade would become, for France, a means of achieving imperial ends rather than purely a profit-seeking venture, and in fulfillment of this role the trade spread across much of the continent.

The fur trade reached the first nations along the St Lawrence well before more colonization attempts followed the botched efforts of Cartier and Roberval. By 1600, over a thousand Algonkin, Huron, Montagnais, and Maliseet were arriving annually at Tadoussac, where the Saguenay River flows south into the St Lawrence, to trade with Breton and Norman fishermen-traders.

By that time the Iroquoian peoples whom Cartier had met had vanished from the area. Their fate is unknown and much speculated upon. One hypothesis argues that they were dispersed by the Algonkian peoples of the area, while another posits absorption, willingly or by force, into either the Huron or Five Nations Iroquois. It seems unlikely that they left of their own accord. Presumably, the Algonkians in the region, who traded with the Mi'kmaq, would have been in a position with their new hatchets and axes and perhaps a musket or two to chase away peoples minimally involved with European traders. Because some groups traded with Europeans while others were excluded, the relative equality of arms in the past had given way to dramatic imbalances. Yet another possibility is that contact with the Europeans in the Cartier period may have resulted in the spread of mortal diseases, causing the thin ranks of the survivors to flee to other territories to escape a scourge that seemed inexplicable.

The peoples of the first nations were absolutely necessary to fur traders: only they knew the terrain in which beaver could be trapped at just the right time. Beaver-down was thickest in winter when the animals were in remote lakes and streams, their lodges well hidden. European experience with aboriginals elsewhere might have suggested enslaving the Natives to ensure that they became a pliant, reliable, cheap labour force. But unlike plantation workers and mine workers, fur trappers do not work in large numbers in a small area, so the European traders had to treat them with some consideration. The newcomers soon learned that the local peoples could bargain shrewdly, even if the Natives could determine only inexactly the gap between the European resale price of their furs and the traders' costs of acquiring the goods used in the exchange.

Because the fur traders relied upon free aboriginal labour, the trade has often been thought of as a partnership. It should be emphasized, however, that the costs of the partnership for the first nations outweighed the benefits. Although the costs were indirect—disease, increased warfare, an attack on aboriginal religion, and eventually, as the trade declined, European occupation of lands used by Native peoples—they were no less real.

The colony of New France owed its birth to the fur trade. De Monts, having suffered reverses in Acadia, turned his sights to the St Lawrence. His lieutenant, Samuel de Champlain, who had explored the region, chose the site of today's Quebec City as the new base of operation. It had several advantages. In addition to spectacular natural defences, it was also close to the lands of the Native peoples who traded at Tadoussac, where trade continued in violation of de Monts's fur-trading monopoly. Although Champlain soon became obsessed with making Quebec a settled, Christian community on a European model, his goal in 1608 was to monopolize the St Lawrence fur trade with the Indians. Quebec's beginnings were modest and inauspicious. Of twenty-five men who wintered there in 1608–09, only nine were alive the following spring. Again, scurvy had taken its toll.

The credit for the colony's survival belongs in large part to Champlain. We know little about his origins, and most of what we do know comes from his own writings, which are almost void of references to his personal life. What is apparent is that by the time he arrived in Canada he was a devout Catholic and an accomplished navigator and mapmaker. He held no official position in de Monts's initial entourage, receiving the title of lieutenant only in 1608. Three years later, frustrated in his efforts to revive the court promise of a commercial monopoly, de Monts prepared to abandon Quebec. Champlain, as he would several times over the next quarter-century, travelled to France to seek court and financial support for the struggling St Lawrence colony. A robust, ebullient man, he persuaded his French audiences that entrenching a colony in Quebec would soon pay dividends in the form of a Northwest Passage to the Orient as well as mineral discoveries within Canada. A new commercial monopoly was established and Quebec was saved, with Champlain becoming the lieutenant of the new monopolist.

Although Champlain never did become the formal governor of the colony, he had effective charge over its civil administration, enforcing the king's laws and overseeing relations with the Native peoples. He also invested a substantial sum in the colony, using the proceeds from a dowry he received when he married a twelve-year-old French girl, Hélène Boullé, in 1610. Champlain, at about age forty, agreed not to consummate the marriage for two years. His wife joined him in the colony in 1620 but remained only for four years. Champlain was forced out of the colony in 1629 when English raiders seized New France but returned in 1633 after France regained control. He died in the colony in 1635. Having long since given up on the Northwest Passage and mineral finds, Champlain had worked tirelessly to make Quebec a settled agricultural community rather than simply a fur-trading post. Although he had recruited a few farmers and his French patrons had contributed a few more, the colony's total population in 1635 was only about 150. Most of them remained exclusively involved in the fur trade.

The Natives who controlled the territory where Quebec was founded did not reside permanently in the region. Still, their power was very real, and the French needed their consent for the establishment of a settlement. After that consent was obtained, Champlain demonstrated his good will toward his prospective commercial partners by agreeing in 1609 to act as their military ally in an ongoing war with the Five Nations Iroquois. That alliance also led to direct contact with the Algonkians' Huron allies and to a further direct involvement in a battle against the Iroquois in 1615. Within a short time, Indian and European rivalries had intertwined. The Huron became partners with the Algonkin and the Montagnais in a military-commercial alliance with the major French fur-trading interests. The Five Nations Iroquois became fur suppliers to the Dutch at New Amsterdam (New York City) and Albany. This alignment strengthened the French resolve to encourage continued Huron–Iroquois hostility. Otherwise northern nations, for whom the Huron on Georgian Bay and the Algonkin on the upper Ottawa River acted as intermediaries, might barter furs to others who would in turn trade them to European rivals of the French.

Hoping to create a better understanding between the French and their Native allies, Champlain encouraged men in his charge to live among the aboriginals and learn their languages. The first to volunteer was Étienne Brûlé. While still in his teens, Brûlé had been one of the nine survivors of the difficult winter of 1609, and he went on not only to learn the Huron language but also to adopt Huron dress and customs. In turn he was effectively adopted by the Natives, who complained nonetheless that he used the relative sexual freedom of Native society to practise uncontrolled

Champlain in Huronia. The painting shows Champlain and his interpreter, Étienne Brûlé, with a party of Huron on Lake Simcoe in 1615. (Confederation Life Gallery of Canadian History)

lechery. While serving as an interpreter for French traders with the Natives, Brûlé most likely became the first European to see Huronia, Lake Ontario, Lake Superior, and today's state of Pennsylvania. He was also branded a traitor for collaborating with the English after they seized Quebec in 1629. About 1633, for reasons unknown, the Huron turned against him, killing and eating him. This adventurous Frenchman became the prototype for the many young men who would live among the Native peoples later in the century, engaging in the fur trade and adopting, for a time, Native language and ways.

• Preaching the Word

The French did not count on military alliances alone to cement their relations with particular Amerindian societies. For European monarchs, including the French kings, it was important to give the colonizing ventures in newly explored territories a higher purpose than the extraction of filthy lucre. The Christianizing of the Natives became that purpose. Fur traders, leery of imposing representatives of a foreign religion on their trading allies, found that the missionaries could be useful in strengthening relations between the French and particular Native groups as well as instilling European notions of regular work habits. Apart from conversion of the Natives, the church would serve as a cultural link with France within the colony, counselling settlers to obey both divine law and the laws of His Majesty the King. Religious orders, both of women and men, became the exclusive providers of education, health, and charity services to the colonists.

The first group of missionaries in Quebec reaped little success in their conversion efforts. The Récollets began arriving in 1615 and were initially ethnocentric to the point of caricature. They made little secret of their disgust with almost every Native custom and belief. Convinced that the "Savages" must be Europeanized if they were to become Christians, the Récollets, with Champlain's encouragement, promoted their assimilation, but without success.

The Récollets chose the sedentary agricultural Huron villages near Georgian Bay as their chief mission field. The area was a significant location in both commercial and strategic terms: it was the point of exchange between the southern agricultural nations and the northern nomadic hunting groups. From these villages in the Great Lakes basin travellers could have access by waterways and relatively easy portages to the far western plains, the Mississippi River, and even Hudson Bay. It was a logical point from which to start building a Laurentian commercial empire, a missionary network, and later a military chain of forts.

The missionaries found aspects of Native society they could both praise and criticize. While they denounced the relative power of women, the permissive upbringing of children, and sexual freedom among the youth, they did acknowledge Native hospitality and generosity. Brother Gabriel Sagard, writing of the Huron in the 1620s, commented favourably on the skilled craft work of the women and men, particularly their pottery, canoe-making, and weaving. The Huron were sober and healthy; the ravages of European liquor and disease had not yet reached them. Sagard considered them the aristocracy of the Indian peoples because they were sedentary and agricultural, while he likened the roaming Montagnais to the poor of Europe. If the Huron were Christians, Sagard thought, these would be families among whom God would take pleasure to dwell. Their tolerance, a virtue little practised in Europe, caused Sagard's co-religionist, Joseph Le Caron, to conclude: "No one must come here in the hope of suffering martyrdom . . . for we are not in a country where the natives put Christians to death on account of their religion." On the contrary, they "leave everyone to his own belief."[5] Sagard, however, found much to criticize about the Huron. While they were generous to a fault, they were also, in his opinion, unclean, ill-mannered, revenge-seeking, incorrigible liars, and shameless belchers.

All of Sagard's remarks, like those of his fellow missionaries, must be treated with caution. By virtue of their occupation the missionaries were likely to exaggerate the flaws of the culture they wished to destroy; and they tended to overlook the flaws of the culture they wished to impose in its place. Still, they did at times make flattering comparisons of Indian and European customs. Sagard, for example, compared certain Huron warfare practices favourably with European conduct in battle. Huron warriors carried their own food when they went on the warpath, a fact that prompted Sagard to remark: "If Christians were to cultivate the same frugality they might maintain very powerful armies at smaller cost and make war on enemies of the Church and of the Christian name without oppressing the people or ruining the country, and God would not be so greatly offended as He is by the majority of our soldiers who seem, to a good man, rather people without God than Christians born to be raised to heaven."[6]

In general, however, the missionaries believed that they had more to teach the Native peoples than vice versa. In 1625 Jesuits began arriving in Canada, ostensibly to aid the Récollets with their missionary work but in fact to supplant them as the principal missionaries to the Natives. The work of both groups was rudely interrupted by the English takeover of Quebec from 1629 to 1632. By then French political intrigues decreed that only the Jesuits would be allowed to return. After following their predecessors' strategy of maintaining missions in the principal villages, the Jesuits changed course. In 1639 they built a central headquarters called Sainte-Marie to oversee their village missions.

Initially the Jesuits, like the Récollets, sought to transform the aboriginals into Christian farmers and to undermine their existing beliefs and practices. Christian Natives from several tribes were encouraged to move to Sillery, a Jesuit-sponsored Indian reserve outside of Quebec (it lasted from 1638 to 1699) where they would farm under the guidance of the Jesuits and be free of possible contamination by "pagan" influences. The first inhabitants of Sillery failed to adapt to a sedentary agricultural life, and soon alcohol and disease introduced by the European intruders sent the reserve into a steep decline. Huron refugees from the Huron–Iroquois war gave it a more stable existence after 1650. They punished drunks and absentees from mass and proved especially harsh with women who clung to traditional notions of their rights. One young woman, whose parents were converts, was publicly whipped for yielding to advances from a traditionalist, while another woman was chained by one foot for having refused to obey her husband.

Gradually the Jesuits' approach to missionary work changed. By the 1640s, aware that their emphasis on forced assimilation was not working, the Jesuits were showing a new flexibility. They learned Native languages and settled among the peoples, allowing themselves to be adopted by families. They accepted that the fur trade was their lifeline to the Native peoples and that therefore hunting must be combined with, rather than replaced by, farming. Syncretic religious practices, linking Native religious traditions with Christianity, were tolerated. So, for example, the Jesuits acknowledged the practice of resuscitating a dead person by permitting a living relative to adopt the dead person's name and children. In return, Christian Natives were required to recognize Christian notions of death in the speeches that accompanied the resuscitation ceremony.

The Jesuits also encouraged the Native use of rosaries, crucifixes, Christian medals, and rings as good luck charms. Indeed, the Jesuits tried to make use of Native preferences for public-relations purposes. Charles Garnier, writing in 1645 from Huronia to his brother, a monk in France, asked for pictures of a beardless Jesus, including one of him as a youth of eighteen. He stressed that, to make the maximum impression on the Indians, the pictures chosen should have Jesus, Mary, and happy souls in white while others should be dressed in bright red or blue. The agony of man damned in the eyes of God should be portrayed in graphic detail: a huge dragon twisted around him, and two horrible demons jabbing him with an iron harpoon while a third demon scalped him.

The Natives were impressed that Jesuits, with their European technology, could foresee eclipses, and they expected that perhaps the priests could also predict the weather and the appearance of enemies. As preliterates, they were fascinated by the Europeans' books and writing. According to Gabriel Sagard, they found it remarkable that Europeans could make thoughts travel great distances using scribbled notes. Yet, notwithstanding the impression made by the missionaries on the Natives, the extent of real conversions in the early years of Jesuit proselytizing is difficult to determine. Many Natives converted because conversion improved their trading position with the French traders, who regarded christianized Indians as more reliable partners. In Huronia, for example, only the christianized Natives received muskets in their trade with the French.

Jesuit missionaries' persistence and their desire for martyrdom were remarkable. Some were captured by the Iroquois and burned at the stake, while others died less romantically of exposure, drowning, disease, or exhaustion. They were aware that the Natives, at least in the beginning, regarded them as strange and lacking in survival skills; and they knew that the "Savages" were anxious to assert their superiority over Europeans. As Father Jean de Brébeuf, who would become one of the most celebrated "martyrs," indicated in a letter to his superiors in France in 1637: "If you could go naked, and carry the load of a horse upon your back, as they do, then you would be wise according to their doctrine, and would be recognized as a great man, otherwise not."[7]

STE MARIE AMONG THE HURONS

The ambitiousness of the Jesuit objective to establish a permanent presence among the Huron is illustrated by the establishment of Ste Marie Among the Hurons, a fortified centre for the Jesuit mission. Jérôme Lalement, who arrived as the superior of the Jesuit mission in Huronia in 1638, conceived of such a centre as a means both of reducing missionary economic dependency on the Huron and of providing Christian Huron with a place of worship away from their pagan fellows. Founded in 1639, Ste Marie at its height in 1648 boasted eighteen priests and forty-six lay assistants. Among the assistants were four lay brothers, four boys, seven domestics, eight soldiers, and twenty-three *donnés,* that is, men who pledged their lives to the mission's work and received no wages but who took no priestly vows. The lay people included one or more surgeons, pharmacists, master builders, and shoemakers as well as many handymen. The farmers tended pigs and cows and grew crops so that by 1649, although some food was still obtained from the Huron, the diet of Frenchmen in Huronia had become similar to that of their counterparts in Quebec.

Alongside the enclosed compound, reserved for the missionaries, their lay helpers, and a few soldiers, was a Huron compound that included a chapel, a hospital, a cemetery for Christian Natives, and a longhouse for Huron visitors. While Huron converts were encouraged to relocate to Ste Marie, few of them chose to abandon their villages and traditional customs, even as relations between the converts and traditionalists became more strained. For the traditionalists, Ste Marie was a symbol of the Jesuits' attitude of intolerant superiority towards Natives.

Ste Marie was burned to the ground by the Jesuits in 1649 to avoid its desecration by the Iroquois after the dispersal of the Huron. A new Ste Marie started to take shape on Christian Island in Georgian Bay, where the mission relocated, but that centre was also burned down when the Jesuits removed to Quebec in 1650. There is a reconstruction of Ste Marie, close to its original location on the Wye River, east of today's Midland, Ontario, although scholars question its authenticity.

•Women and Religion

Paul Le Jeune, superior of the Canadian Jesuit missions in the 1630s, founded several schools to teach lessons in Christianity to Indian boys, among whom he hoped to find potential priests. Not surprisingly, aboriginal families were not enthusiastic supporters of this endeavour. The Jesuits had to bribe parents to part with their children and then cater to their pupils' whims in order to retain them. Father Le Jeune complained: "They must be well lodged and well fed; and yet these Barbarians imagine that you are under great obligation to them. I add still more: generally, presents must be made to their parents and, if they dwell near you, you must help them to live, part of the time."[8]

The Jesuits did not accept girls in their schools, following the European practice of gender segregation. It was therefore necessary to call on women teachers to found schools for girls in the colony. The call was heeded by Marie de l'Incarnation, an Ursuline in Tours and the first of many remarkable religious women to immigrate to New France. Born Marie Guyart in Tours in 1599, she had a willingness to let her dreams guide her life—much like the Natives whose religion she sought to displace. Dreams led her as a young widow to put her twelve-year-old son in a boarding school and join the cloistered Ursulines. Another dream made her connect her future with the request by Paul Le Jeune for nuns to open a school for Indian girls. Like many of her Ursuline and Jesuit counterparts, she was a religious zealot who tried to mortify her flesh. "She wore a penitential shirt with knots and thorns, slept on a hair mattress that kept her always half awake, and sometimes rose at night to chastise herself, first with thongs, later with a whip of nettles. . . . She ate wormwood with her food, holding the bitterness in her mouth, and sometimes approached the fire to burn her skin."[9]

Marie de l'Incarnation   (National Archives of Canada/C8070)

The founder of Canada's first school for Indian girls was more than an otherworldly self-flagellator. She had managed a large shipping outfit for her brother-in-law for a decade before devoting herself fully to Christ: and the administrative skills she had acquired proved invaluable in her religious endeavours. First she found a wealthy patron, Marie-Madeleine de La Peltrie, who funded and accompanied Marie and two other Ursulines to New France in 1639. Then she supervised the building of one school for Indian and French girls and a convent for the nuns. When the convent burned down in 1650, Marie, seeing herself as the instrument of the Virgin Mary, had a larger convent built to replace it within two years. At the time of her retirement as superior in 1669, her convent housed between fifty and fifty-five people. Of these, twenty-two, including four lay sisters and three novices, were part of the religious community.

The Jesuits encouraged the Indians of Sillery to send their daughters to the Ursulines' school, informing them that the nuns were the daughters of French chiefs. Requiring the girls to board at school so they could be shielded from any non-Christian influences, the Ursulines taught them prayers and simple lessons. Some of the girls were fascinated by the devout women from France and sought to emulate them; but most, at some point or another, tried to run away from their authoritarian European teachers.

Native women were often more hostile than men to missionary attempts to convert their people to European ways. Missionary proscriptions on premarital sex and divorce and the value placed on a family life centred around nuclear, male-headed households threatened women's considerable power within Native societies. Indeed, several Huron men who became Christians were turfed out of their longhouses by their angry mothers-in-law. The women were rejecting, among other things, the Jesuit–European views that lineage must be determined patrilineally and that non-marital sex must be forbidden so men could be certain about the children they had helped to conceive and could thus consider their rightful heirs. Montagnais women knew that the Jesuits were behind the system of electing male captains, who would then attempt to impose Christian morality on the whole group. As a result the women made little secret of their contempt for the new order.

While many Native women continued to assert their traditions, a coterie of women zealots, imitating the nuns, gained notoriety. They whipped each other, wore hair shirts, mixed ashes in their food, stood naked in snowstorms, and put glowing coals between their toes. Some worked to aid the poor and sick, and eventually some of these Native women were allowed to join the French women's religious houses. None, however, survived to enjoy a fruitful religious career.

Native women converts were inspired by the French women who were conspicuous in the religious, educational, and health fields in New France. Apart from Marie de l'Incarnation and her fellow Ursulines, names such as Jeanne Mance and Marguerite Bourgeoys stand out. Both were heirs to the Counter-Reformation creation of non-cloistered religious orders for women. Jeanne Mance was the product of an Ursuline education in her youth. As a member of a society of religious women who devoted their lives to charitable work in her home city of Langres, she learned the nursing skills that would endear her to the sick and to those wounded in the wars with the Iroquois. She had come to Canada in 1641 as a single woman in her thirties. Shortly thereafter she founded the Hôtel Dieu, the first hospital in the planned religious community of Ville Marie. As a member of the Société de Notre Dame, the organization formed by religious enthusiasts to found Montreal, Mance was also able to persuade a wealthy French woman to finance a plan to bring several Soeurs Hospitalières from La Flèche to Ville Marie in 1657. When Ville Marie needed money to hire soldiers for its battles with the Iroquois, Mance repaired to France to persuade her patron of the urgency—even though she had recently fallen on the ice and had to be carried about in France on a stretcher.

Ville Marie in 1642   (W. Decary/National Archives of Canada/C7885)

Marguerite Bourgeoys, founder of the colony's first teaching community, established the Congrégation de Notre Dame, a body of secular teachers who she claimed were guided by the Virgin Mary herself. Modelling her congregation on the non-cloistered Sisters of Charity in France, she concentrated on educating children from poorer families. She appears to have had some success, because illiteracy rates in early New France were far lower than in France. The Congrégation travelled wherever it was needed to educate children because, as Bourgeoys observed, the Virgin was never cloistered and travelled wherever she was needed to do a good deed. The idolization of Mary—a central feature of religious and cultural life in New France—strengthened these pioneer religious women when bishops tried to control their institutions. The Soeurs de la Congrégation de Notre-Dame, for example, successfully resisted efforts of the first bishop, François de Laval, to have their order cloistered and even opened a primary school in the town of Quebec, the seat of his diocese.

• The Huron–Iroquois Wars

Religious interference in the Amerindians' lives, however destructive, was overshadowed by the more devastating impact of European germs and weapons. In the late 1630s, smallpox and measles wrought devastation among the French fur trade allies, particularly the Huron and Montagnais. Huron numbers were probably reduced by somewhere between one-half and two-thirds, leaving only ten thousand Huron in the early 1640s. Death on this scale robbed the Huron of many of their leaders and played havoc with the delicate social arrangements of the four tribes of the loose Huron Confederacy.

Those arrangements had already suffered the strains of quite different responses to the Jesuit teachings and presence. Two of the tribes were receptive to the Jesuits while the other two proved hostile. Opponents of the "black robes" accused the missionaries of practising black magic to unleash deadly diseases among the Natives. Only a threatened cut-off of French trade saved the Jesuits from expulsion from Huronia, underlining the dependence of the evangelical forces on the men of commerce. But the rift between the traditionalists and the Christian minority increased. The converts increasingly refused burials in non-Christian sites and even refused to fight alongside non-Christian Huron in battles against enemies.

Those enemies would destroy Huronia in 1649. The Five Nations Iroquois had become dependent on the fur trade. But they had exhausted fur supplies within their own territory and now sought new sources of supply in the lands to the north. For their part, the Huron and their allies on the Ottawa and St Lawrence Rivers were determined to preserve their monopoly as go-betweens for the trappers and the French.

Iroquois efforts to penetrate the defences of the Huron and their Algonkian allies received a boost when disease decimated the go-between tribes beyond Huronia, forcing the Huron to revise their commercial strategy. Until then the Huron had carried furs only as far as the Ottawa River, leaving the Ottawa nation to ship furs to the French via the Montagnais on the St Lawrence. Now the Huron frequently made the entire 1300-kilometre trip from their own territory to the settlement at Quebec.

In the 1640s, the Five Nations invariably attempted to disrupt the annual flotilla of Huron canoes that made this long journey. In 1642, for example, a Mohawk party massacred Huron returning from Quebec to Huronia. Ignored by priests and ministers, the Five Nations had maintained a cohesiveness that religious rivalries had sapped among the Huron. They were also better armed, because their Dutch allies increasingly traded guns for furs, whereas the French insisted that guns be traded only to the Christian minority among the Huron.

When the attacks on Huron fur convoys proved unsuccessful at forcing the Christianized Huron to bend to their demands for access to furs, the Iroquois launched direct attacks on Huronia itself. An attack in 1648 was repulsed, but not without significant Huron casualties. In 1649 the Iroquois broke through Huron defences. The Huron, caught by surprise, were unable to organize a concerted defence. Terrorized by a hitherto unheard of concentration of enemy warriors, and internally divided, they burned their villages and dispersed. Some traditionalists simply surrendered to the Iroquois, who proved willing to adopt them into their tribes. Most residents of Huronia took the lead of the converts who followed the Jesuits to Christian Island. Even there, they were dogged by disaster. A drought on the desolate island made it impossible to replace the crops abandoned in Huronia. A winter of starvation left five thousand people, half or more of the remaining Huron population, dead.

A majority of the Huron survivors, including many Christians, went south and joined their ancient enemies, the Five Nations Iroquois. The new arrivals introduced Christianity to the Iroquois and had a strong influence: while the Five Nations remained at war with the French, by the end of the seventeenth century a large percentage of their members, particularly from the Mohawk nation, had established themselves on Christian settlements near Montreal. Many of the Huron who did not join the Iroquois in 1650 went to live among the Petun and Neutral Indians, only to face

This wampum belt depicts the formation of the Iroquois League of Five Nations. From left to right, or east to west, are the Mohawk, Oneida, Onondaga, Cayuga, and Seneca. (Courtesy of the Woodland Cultural Centre, Brantford, Ontario)

another Iroquois raid and dispersal later that year. Again the Iroquois absorbed most of the survivors, and many of this expanded Iroquois nation settled in the former territories of the Huron and their allies, as trappers rather than farmers. Not all of the Huron were absorbed by the Five Nations. About six hundred Huron resettled near Quebec, where they were given aid by the religious houses. A small but crucial group moved westwards to live among nations that had once supplied them with furs to sell to the French.

The destruction of Huronia was a pivotal event in the history not only of New France and the fur trade but also of aboriginal culture. For the first nations it demonstrated the extent to which contact with the Europeans had unravelled the delicate fabric of Native societies. War, disease, and forced migrations had never been absent from that fabric, but the scale of these tragedies had been comparatively modest before the introduction of European guns, germs, and religion. First peoples had formed alliances with the newcomers to further their own interests, economic and cultural; but they could not have predicted the consequences of this course of action.

For the Iroquois, the victors in the Huron–Iroquois conflict, the destruction of Huronia meant they could establish settlements in new territories and trap furs to supply to their Dutch and English partners. Algonkian peoples and the remnants of the Huron still gathered furs from the nations in the western Great Lakes area and, with French aid, could still impede Iroquois access to the better fur-bearing territories. The

Ojibwa were also a factor in frustrating Iroquois goals. In the period of Huron dominance of the fur trade they had been exclusively trappers on the parklands and plains. Now they saw an opportunity to become go-betweens. Using French arms, the Ojibwa succeeded in driving the Iroquois out of former Huron territory in the late seventeenth century, and many of them stayed to settle in that territory. Others moved north and west and served as go-betweens for the French traders and the Dakota and Assiniboine, two Siouan-speaking groups, as well as the Cree west of Lake Superior.

For the struggling St Lawrence colony, the loss of Huronia had grave military, commercial, and even agricultural consequences. Before 1649 it had been possible for it to remain a fur depot, with the French receiving furs they could send to Europe without setting foot in the upper country, where the furs originated. Their aboriginal allies had been their chief defence against hostile Natives allied with rival European traders. Now those allies were gone, and their replacements on their own would not become a match for the Iroquois for several decades.

As a result of the collapse of Huronia, the French were forced to send young men of the colony to live in the upper country to help remaining Native allies fend off the Iroquois and to make contact with Native trappers to ensure they were not won over by the aboriginal allies of rival European nations. Frenchmen rather than Native groups would be in charge of the flotillas bringing furs from the interior to the St Lawrence colony. Faced with hostile Iroquois, the colony would require military reinforcements from France on a large scale.

Finally, because the danger of being surrounded by the Iroquois and cut off from the outside world could not be ignored, New France had to become as self-sufficient as possible in foodstuffs, relying on neither Native allies nor France for its sustenance. In brief, the dispersal of the Huron demonstrated that New France could not survive simply as a small fur-trading post. From the 1660s on this reality would prove crucial in French policy-making regarding the colony.

•Building a Community

New France, consisting of Acadia and Canada, grew slowly to 1663. In 1627, when the population of Canada was only 107, Cardinal Richelieu, Louis XIII's chief minister, engineered a new trade monopoly for New France. The monopoly-holders would be required, in return for fur trade profits, to settle at least two hundred Catholic colonists a year for fifteen years and fund missionaries working among the Natives. Richelieu was interested in colonies as sources of wealth and places where the institutions of the mother society could be replicated.

The monopolistic charter company was known as the Compagnie de la Nouvelle France, and its one hundred associates were noblemen. But their venture got off to a poor start when Quebec fell to an English expedition led by David Kirke in 1629. A few French colonists stayed, but Champlain was forced to leave and most of the fur traders departed as well. Champlain returned when England returned the colony to France as part of a treaty in 1632. The company proved an indifferent colonizer interested in fur trade profits. When profits proved elusive in the early 1640s in the face of Iroquois attacks on the Huron fur flotilla, the company sublet the fur trade to the Communauté des Habitants, an organization composed of several leading members of the colony, although it retained administrative control of the colony.

After Champlain's death in 1635, the French court vested authority over civil administration in the colony to a governor, and in 1647 a council was named to direct trade and control justice in consultation with the governor. The governor enjoyed an effective veto over the council and the main battle line for political power lay between the governor and the Compagnie de la Nouvelle France. In 1659 the company obtained a ruling from France that gave it the greatest authority over the administration of justice in the colony, making power arrangements more confused than ever.

A shadowy presence in the emerging colony was the Compagnie du Saint-Sacrement, a secret organization of religious zealots who fought growing secularism in France and saw in the New World a virgin territory that could be consecrated to God. Leading figures in this organization formed the Société de Notre Dame, which established Montreal in 1642 under the leadership of a young army veteran, Paul de Chomedy, Sieur de Maisonneuve. Their influence at court secured the appointment in 1659 of the Jesuit-trained François de Laval-Montigny as New France's first bishop.

Laval was a devoted servant of the sick and poor of the colony, but he was also a domineering individual who expected as the emissary of both pope and king to be obeyed by the civil authorities, the missionaries, and the colonists. Laval's moralistic crusades against blasphemy, gambling, and fornication were of little interest to the civil authorities, and his threat to excommunicate any French colonists who traded liquor with the Natives enraged both the governor and the company. Together they convinced the French authorities that this action could cause France's Native partners to seek new European allies—which would destroy not only the French fur trade but also the central reason for the colony's existence. Even the religious orders, which had for years governed themselves in the colony without aid of a bishop, resented Laval's interference and sometimes defied his orders.

By 1663 two-thirds of the 3035 settlers in the colony resided in the countryside and depended on farming for their livelihood. Land had been granted on the basis of the seigneurial system; the Compagnie de la Nouvelle France granted estates to seigneurs who in turn granted farms freely to *censitaires*, who paid customary feudal dues. Narrow strip farms stretching along the St Lawrence made up a seigneury, with each farm having about the same amount of river frontage. The system differed from the crumbling feudalism of France in that it did not include military obligations, all land was granted without charge, and all obligations between seigneur and *censitaire* were stipulated in a notarized contract. Also, the lands held by individual farmers, who preferred to be called habitants rather than peasants, were far larger than those held by French peasants.

By 1663 sixty-nine seigneuries had been granted, with members of the nobility holding title to 84 percent of the land. The largest seigneury included almost half the land granted, and seven families related by blood held the lion's share of seigneurial land. French politics recognized three "estates": the clergy, the nobles, and the commoners. In Canada the first two estates included seventy-eight and ninety-six members respectively in 1663. This left 94.3 percent of the population in the third estate. Although 68 percent of the population of 3035 were members of farm or labourer households, 796 people were members of bourgeois families, including public servants, merchants, non-noble seigneurs, and master tradespeople.

Although immigrants from thirty provinces lived in Canada in 1663, three western provinces—Normandy, Perche, and Aunis—provided half of the colonists. Most, apart from the clergy and the original residents of Montreal, had come to better their economic circumstances. For the younger sons of nobles this meant the opportunity to become landowners; for habitants, many of whom had been landless labourers in France, it meant a chance to gain a real living from farming. The modest immigration to New France has sometimes been attributed to a French unwillingness to emigrate. But in the sixteenth century about 250 000 French migrated to bullion-rich Spain, where jobs were available at high wages. New France offered no such attraction.

Frontier conditions helped to create a society in which the classes mixed relatively freely during this early period of colonization. The small population was united both by external threats to the colony's survival and by the need to clear land as quickly as possible. Nobles and bourgeois often had black or Native slaves, people who did not benefit from class levelling. Other servants were secured from Europe through indentures of usually three to five years, although enforcement of the contracts sometimes proved difficult. Initially, most indentured servants and labourers returned home at the end of their contracts, but after 1650, as more seigneuries opened up for prospective habitants, a slight majority of immigrants remained permanently in the colony.

Peasants in France eked out a living on a few acres of land and faced execution if they tried to supplement an insufficient diet by hunting or fishing on a noble's land. Settlers in New France, by contrast, were often enticed with large land grants. In 1634, for example, the seigneur Robert Giffard convinced several French families to settle on his seigneury of Beauport near Quebec by offering each family 840 acres of land and part of the harvest of his own farm. In practice, a family could expect to clear only two acres a year, and the work of felling trees and preparing land for crops was backbreaking. The first homes were tiny cabins with board partitions dividing a small area into a set of small rooms. The families had little or no furniture and what did exist was home-made. Oiled paper substituted for glass windows, and the clay chimneys and cold winters often led to destructive fires. Colonists learned quickly to become as self-sufficient as possible, which bred habits of independence, a certain pride in unskilled versatility, and opposition to any trade or artisanal organization and restriction.

A third of the population of Canada lived in the three towns of the colony: Quebec, founded 1608; Trois Rivières, 1617; and Montreal, 1642. In 1633 Quebec, the most highly developed centre, could boast three churches, seven chapels, a college, a convent school for girls, a hospital, nine mills, a brewery, and a bakery. The city was surrounded by five forts that protected area residents.

The Native peoples had a tremendous impact on the crops grown and foods eaten by the early settlers, on the transportation methods they employed, and even on their dress. They also had an impact on the colonists' attitudes to life. Indian corn (maize), pumpkins, beaver flesh, tails, and feet, and the meat of moose, bears, dogs, and feathered game supplemented the colonists' more familiar food items. Tobacco, an indigenous crop that garnered great interest among Europeans, was also grown in New France. The French found Native inventions such as the birchbark canoe, toboggan, and snowshoes to be invaluable. Native medicine helped remedy scurvy and other ailments, although European haughtiness prevented the French from taking advantage of the full cornucopia of Native cures.

A significant minority of colonists in contact with the first peoples familiarized the colony as a whole with Native attitudes. The young men who spent a good part of their lives trading in the bush—a group estimated at 10 percent of the population in the 1680s—were influenced by the Indians' free-spirited behaviour. Most had liaisons with Native women while they lived in the upper country. Some remained in the Great Lakes basin and never returned. Others abandoned their Native wives when they returned to the Laurentian settlements, but a few brought their wives back with them. Champlain and, for a time, the Jesuits, promoted interracial marriages as a means of encouraging assimilation. "Our sons shall marry your daughters and together we shall form one people," Champlain proclaimed. Demographer Jacques Henripin estimates that about 40 percent of today's francophone descendants of the inhabitants of New France have some Native ancestry.

While the men who had lived in the woods among the first nations rarely rejected their own religion in favour of Native religious beliefs, few behaved piously upon their return to the colony. Their drinking, rioting, and gambling, which influenced the activities of other colonists, became the cause of many an unenforceable decree and countless Sunday sermons. Indeed, New France became a society marked by notable excesses of both piety and secular enjoyment.

HISTORICAL NARRATIVE AND THE BORDERLINE BETWEEN HISTORY AND FICTION: THE CASE OF ADAM DOLLARD

At age twenty-five Adam Dollard des Ormeaux, a soldier and recent immigrant to New France, was the leader of a group of seventeen Frenchmen who, with the aid of Algonkin and Huron allies, attempted to ambush a party of Iroquois hunters along the Ottawa River in April 1660. Surprised by a large contingent of Iroquois at the foot of Long Sault rapids, Dollard and his men attempted in vain for a week to fend off their attackers. All seventeen died, with nine of the men being eaten by the Iroquois after undergoing slow, ritual torture. An even larger group of their Native allies suffered the same fate.

The above facts are not in dispute; but historical narratives of the battle of the Long Sault have rarely restricted themselves to the facts. The motivations of Dollard and his men have intrigued historians and shaped their views of the event's significance. For some historians, particularly French-Canadian nationalists, the defenders of the Long Sault were martyrs to the cause of New France, motivated by a desire to free the colony from the Iroquois threat. Other historians, perhaps less sympathetic to the nationalist cause, suggest that the young men were greedy adventurers trying to grab a shipment of Iroquois furs, oblivious to the danger they might thereby create for the colony in the form of Iroquois retribution. Historians focusing on the Native side of the event suggest that the Iroquois target was not the colony but their Native enemies.

All of these viewpoints rely on an imaginative reconstruction of the minds of Dollard and company, on the one hand, and the Iroquois on the other. In the case of the French party, for example, there is simply no reliable way of knowing to what extent altruism and greed motivated the young men. While historians' personal values influence their interpretation of all events, this is particularly so when there are few factual clues regarding an event. In these cases historians cross the borderline between data-based historical conclusions and pure fiction because the facts, rather than speaking for themselves, seem to cry out for interpretation.

•Conclusion: New France on the Eve of Royal Rule

In the early 1660s the future of New France looked bleak. The tiny Acadian colony, with its development impeded by the battles of rival French claimants, was in English hands. Quebec, a product of the fur trade, lay under siege by the Iroquois, whose main demand was the right to control the territories once settled by the Huron and their allies.

The dispersal of Huronia—an event demonstrating the destructive impact of European imperial rivalries and religion on intertribal and intratribal relations—made changes in the organization of both the trade and the colony necessary. If the French wished to retain control of the colony and the western fur trade, they would need more military strength and more population in the colony as well as a direct presence in the west. The growth of the Anglo-American colonies also emphasized the vulnerability of the St Lawrence colony; it was outnumbered by 70 000 to 3000 (counting European settlers only and excluding African slaves and Natives within the territories).

By the 1640s the Roman Catholic Church was a towering presence both in the colony and, through the Jesuit mission, in Huronia. Religious orders of both men and women ran all the schools and hospitals, and one of the three settlements, Montreal, had been the creation of religious zeal.

Huronia's tragic end forced the missionaries to regroup, and the colonists, while respectful toward the church authorities, already demonstrated signs of the free-spiritedness common in frontier societies where authorities lack the structures and personnel to enforce obedience to their will.

Grumbling from within the colony convinced Louis XIV's government in 1663 that the oligarchy controlling the Compagnie de la Nouvelle France was incapable of directing effective colonization. The company's property, administrative, and monopoly trade rights were revoked and replaced with royal government, that is, administration by state officials responsible to the crown. The driving force behind the new regime was Jean-Baptiste Colbert, who shared Cardinal Richelieu's vision of colonial development. It was a vision that had been impossible to implement earlier because of warfare in Europe; but in 1663 France was at peace. Colbert would attempt to fit colonial policy within the framework of his key domestic policies, which were to "increase exports, reduce imports, achieve a favorable balance of trade and a budgetary surplus." France's overseas colonies were "to provide France with raw materials that the kingdom would otherwise have had to import from foreign countries, and with a market for French manufactured goods."[10] This colonial policy, often called mercantilism, was at the root of the politics of modern imperialism as Western European countries competed to create global economic empires.

• The Destruction of Huronia:
A Historiographical Debate

What caused the destruction of Huronia? At one level the answer is simple. The Five Nations Iroquois, with an estimated 500 guns in their possession, dispersed an enemy that could count on only 120 guns. French policy regarding provision of weapons to the Native peoples was inconsistent from region to region, but in Huronia only Christian converts received guns. In 1648 only about 15 percent of the Huron were nominal Christians, and a disproportionate number of those had the job of transporting furs to the French colony. Given the lack of guns, Huronia, including its Christians, became more vulnerable to Iroquois attack.

For historian Cornelius Jaenen there is no conclusive evidence that Iroquois raiders made much use of guns in their attacks on the Huron. They may instead have resorted mainly to the traditional tomahawk and torch to sow terror among their Huron and French enemies. Employing solid military tactics involving concentration of forces, surprise, and sustained attack, they moved quickly from one village to the next before the Huron could assemble and mount a counter-offensive. They also used terror to demoralize their opponents, who were already bitterly divided between Christians and traditionalists.

Some scholars have maintained that arming the Huron would have been unnecessary if European trade rivalries had not promoted Huron–Iroquois hostility. Anthropologist George Hunt argued in 1940 that the Huron and the Five Nations Iroquois, sharing common origins, were unnatural enemies and that the fur trade created new and more intense rivalries between Native groups. While Hunt's general point regarding the impact of the fur trade on the motivations for intertribal conflicts has merit, few researchers accept his claim that the Iroquois and Huron were on good terms in the immediate pre-contact period.

Geographer Conrad Heidenreich suggests that Iroquois desperation and guns alone do not explain their success in vanquishing the Huron. The cohesiveness of the Five Nations

Iroquois, whose contact with Europeans was largely restricted to traders, was in contrast to the disunity of the Huron, whose society had been less integrated than the Five Nations to begin with and became even less so as a result of religious division and the removal of recognized leaders by diseases. Anthropologist Bruce Trigger is still more emphatic in pinpointing Jesuit activities as the cause of the destruction of Huronia. In contrast, Jesuit historian Lucien Campeau argues in the order's defence that the Iroquois destroyed both the Petun and the Neutral; and the Petun had only sporadic contacts with the Jesuits, the Neutral none at all. It was Iroquois guns, Campeau says, not cultural and religious confusion, that destroyed the Huron just as those guns also brought down the other two nations.

A Huron writer suggests an interesting counter-thesis. Georges Sioui argues that the Iroquois understood the Europeans' threat to the Native way of life and so became engaged in a war of liberation against the French. Because they suffered huge losses of life in this war, they could only survive as a people by absorbing new members into their nations, by force if necessary. For Sioui, the large-scale adoption by the Iroquois of the Huron, Petun, and Neutral was not the unintended consequence of the attack on Huronia, but indeed the objective of the attack. Sioui also maintains that historians of European origin have exaggerated the toll of the Iroquois wars on Huron lives to disguise an essential fact: that European diseases, and not Native warfare, were responsible for the sharp decline of Native populations.

•Notes

[1] *The Jesuit Relations and Allied Documents*, ed. Reuben Gold Thwaites, Vol. 28 (Cleveland: Burrows Brothers Co., 1896–01), 105–7.

[2] Joseph R. Smallwood, ed., *Encyclopedia of Newfoundland and Labrador*, Vol. 2 (St John's: Newfoundland Book Publishers, 1984), 53.

[3] *The Voyages of Jacques Cartier*, trans. and ed. H.P. Biggar (Ottawa: King's Printer, 1924), 52–53.

[4] Ibid., 65.

[5] Joseph Le Caron, *Au Roy sur la Nouvelle-France* (Paris: n.p., 1626).

[6] Father Gabriel Sagard, *The Long Journey to the Country of the Huron* (Toronto: Champlain Society, 1939), 153.

[7] *The Jesuit Relations and Allied Documents*, ed. S.R. Mealing (Toronto: McClelland and Stewart, 1963), 50.

[8] *The Jesuit Relations*, ed. Thwaites, Vol. 12, 47.

[9] Joyce Marshall, ed., *Word from New France: The Selected Letters of Marie de l'Incarnation* (Toronto: Oxford University Press, 1967), 5.

[10] W.J. Eccles, *The Canadian Frontier, 1534–1760* (New York: Holt, Rinehart and Winston, 1969), 60.

• Selected Reading

The major survey in English of the history of New France is W.J. Eccles, *The Canadian Frontier, 1534–1760* (New York: Holt, Rinehart and Winston, 1969). A detailed study of New France before 1663 is Marcel Trudel, *The Beginnings of New France 1524–1663*, trans. Patricia Claxton (Toronto: McClelland and Stewart, 1973).

The early history of Acadia is covered in John G. Reid, *Acadia, Maine and New Scotland: Marginal Colonies in the Seventeenth Century* (Toronto: University of Toronto Press, 1981); Elizabeth Jones, *Gentlemen and Jesuits* (Toronto: University of Toronto Press, 1986); Naomi Griffiths, *The Acadians: Creation of a People* (Toronto: McGraw-Hill Ryerson, 1973); and Andrew Hill Clark, *Acadia: The Geography of Early Nova Scotia to 1760* (Madison: University of Wisconsin Press, 1968). Newfoundland in the seventeenth century is discussed in Gillian Cell, *English Enterprises in Newfoundland, 1557–1660* (Toronto: University of Toronto Press, 1969); Gillian Cell, *Newfoundland Discovered* (London: Hakluyt Society, 1982); and H.A. Innis, *The Cod Fisheries: The History of an International Economy* (Toronto: University of Toronto Press, 1978). On whaling, see Daniel Francis, *A History of World Whaling* (Markham, ON: Penguin, 1990).

There is a growing literature on early European–Native relations in Canada; some of these texts are referred to in chapter 1. Additional sources include L.C. Green and Olive P. Dickason, *The Law of Nations and the New World* (Edmonton: University of Alberta Press, 1989) and Cornelius Jaenen, *The French Relationship with the Native People of New France and Acadia* (Ottawa: Indian and Northern Affairs Canada, 1984). On the fate of the Huron, see George T. Hunt, *The Wars of the Iroquois* (Madison:

University of Wisconsin Press, 1967) and Georges Sioui, *For an American Autohistory: An Essay on the Foundations of a Social Ethic* (Montreal: McGill-Queen's University Press, 1992). On the Beothuk, a balanced account is J. Callum Thomson, "Cornered: Cultures in Conflict in Newfoundland and Labrador," in Claire Tkacuzk and Brian C. Vivian, *Cultures in Conflict: Current Archaeological Perspectives* (Calgary: University of Calgary, 1989). Most of this work is ostensibly gender-neutral, and as a result much of it is male-biased, although occasional glimpses emerge of the different impact on men and women of contact with Europeans. More focused in this respect is Eleanor Leacock, "Montagnais Women and the Jesuit Program for Colonization," in *Rethinking Canada: The Promise of Women's History*, 2nd ed., ed. Veronica Strong-Boag and Anita Clair Fellman (Toronto: Copp Clark Pitman, 1991). On education see Jean Barman, Yvonne Hébert, and Don McCaskill, eds., *Indian Education in Canada*, Vol. 1 (Vancouver: University of British Columbia Press, 1986).

Church perspectives both on Native–European relations and conditions in New France are found in S.R. Mealing, ed., *The Jesuit Relations and Allied Documents* (Ottawa: Carleton University Press, 1990); Joyce Marshall, ed., *Word from New France: The Selected Letters of Marie de l'Incarnation* (Toronto: Oxford University Press, 1967); and Father Gabriel Sagard, *The Long Journey to the Country of the Huron* (Toronto: Champlain Society, 1939). A work of synthesis is Cornelius Jaenen, *The Role of the Church in New France* (Toronto: McGraw-Hill Ryerson, 1976).

Apart from the general texts, works with information on the social history of early New France include Louise Dechêne, *Habitants and Merchants in Seventeenth-Century Montreal* (Montreal: McGill-Queen's University Press, 1992); and R. Cole Harris, "The Extension of France into Rural Canada," in *European Settlement and Development in North America: Essays on Geographical Change in Honour and Memory of Andrew Hill Clark*, ed. James R. Gibson (Toronto: University of Toronto Press, 1978). On the society of origin of the first European colonists of Acadia and New France, a lively account is Pierre Goubert, *The Ancien Regime: French Society, 1600–1750* (Paris: Colin, 1969).

On women in early New France, there is good general information in the Clio Collective, *Quebec Women: A History*, trans. Roger Gannon and Rosalind Gill (Toronto: Women's Press, 1987) as well as Isabel Foulché-Delbosc, "Women of Three Rivers: 1651–1663," in *The Neglected Majority : Essays in Women's History*, Vol. 1, ed. Susan Mann Trofimenkoff and Alison Prentice (Toronto: McClelland and Stewart, 1977); and Jan Noel, "New France: Les Femmes Favorisées," in *Rethinking Canada*, ed. Strong-Boag and Fellman.

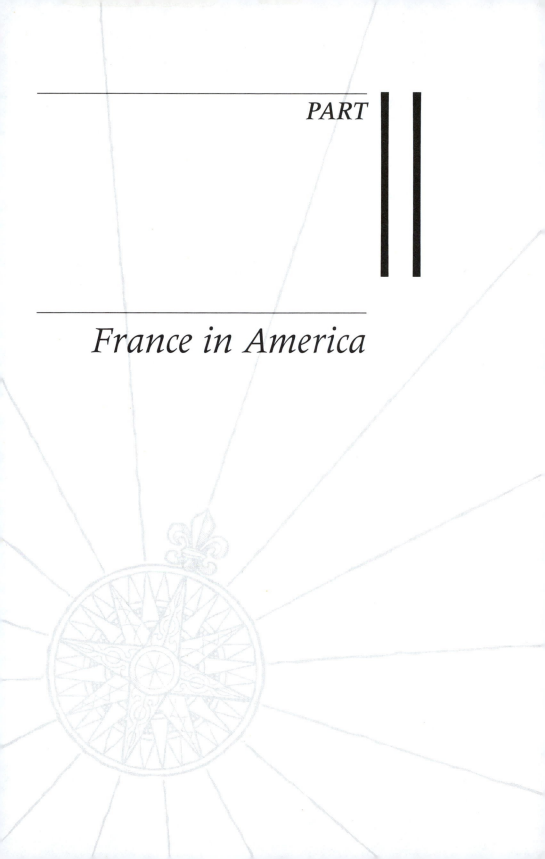

PART II

France in America

Time Line

1661	–	Louis XIV takes control of affairs of state in France
1662	–	France establishes a base at Placentia
1663	–	Royal government established in New France; Bishop Laval establishes a seminary in Quebec
1664	–	English capture New Amsterdam from the Dutch
1665	–	Carignan-Salières regiment arrives in New France; Jean Talon arrives in New France
1666	–	Marquis de Tracy invades Mohawk territory
1669	–	Colonial militia established
1670	–	Governor Grandfontaine arrives at Port Royal; Hudson's Bay Company established by the English
1672–74	–	Joliet and Marquette explore the northern Mississippi
1673	–	La Salle establishes Fort Frontenac at Cataraqui
1682	–	La Salle reaches the Gulf of Mexico
1687	–	Governor Denonville sends an army to quash the Seneca
1689–97	–	War of the League of Augsburg
1690	–	Sir William Phips' unsuccessful expedition against Quebec
1694	–	D'Iberville's forces capture St John's
1697	–	D'Iberville's forces capture Fort York
1701	–	Treaty of Montreal signed by delegates of French and Native allies with Iroquois
1701–13	–	War of the Spanish Succession
1710	–	English capture Port Royal
1711	–	Unsuccessful invasion of Canada by Walker

1713	–	Treaty of Utrecht awards Newfoundland, Acadia, and Hudson Bay territory to the British
1715–74	–	Reign of Louis XV
1720	–	"Mississippi bubble" bursts; construction of Louisbourg begins
1726	–	British sign a treaty with the Mi'kmaq at Annapolis Royal
1744–48	–	War of the Austrian Succession
1745	–	Louisbourg conquered by a British and Anglo-American force
1746	–	D'Anville expedition
1747	–	Battle of Grand Pré
1748	–	Treaty of Aix-la-Chapelle
1755	–	Braddock's defeat; Fort Beauséjour falls to the British
1755–64	–	Explusion of the Acadians
1756–63	–	Seven Years' War
1758	–	Louisbourg captured by the British
1759	–	Conquest of Quebec
1760	–	Articles of Capitulation signed in Montreal
1763	–	Treaty of Paris; Proclamation Act
1763–65	–	Pontiac's Revolt
1774	–	Quebec Act, First Continental Congress
1775–76	–	American invasion of Quebec
1776	–	American Declaration of Independence
1778	–	France enters the war as an ally of the United States
1783	–	Treaty of Versailles

CHAPTER 4

THE EMERGENCE OF CONTINENTAL NEW FRANCE, 1663–1715

It is pleasant to see now almost the entire extent of the shores of our River St Lawrence settled by new colonies, which continue to spread over more than eighty leagues of territory along the shores of this great River, where new hamlets are seen springing up here and there, which facilitate navigation—rendering it more agreeable by the sight of numerous houses, and more convenient by frequent resting places. . . . Fear of the enemy no longer prevents our labours from causing the forests to recede and from sowing their fields with all sorts of grain. . . . The Savages our allies, no longer fearing that they will be surprised on the road, come in quest of us from all directions, from a distance of five or six hundred leagues—either to re-establish their trade interrupted by the wars; or to open new commercial dealings.[1]

This report from the Jesuits in 1668 suggests that the fortunes of New France had changed dramatically in the five years since royal government was proclaimed in 1663. Although the Jesuits were not above exaggerating to make a point, it was clear by 1668 that the French were determined to sink permanent roots on the banks of the St Lawrence. The major problems facing the struggling colony—defence against the Iroquois, the lack of European population, and administrative and economic instability—were all energetically addressed in the 1660s. By the beginning of the eighteenth century, New France was emerging as the heart of a vast colonial empire extending from Hudson Bay to the Gulf of Mexico.

•The Age of Absolutism

The transformation in the fortunes of New France came as a direct result of Louis XIV's decision in 1661 to assume personal charge of state affairs. This was a significant event, not only for France and its colonies but also for Europe as a whole. From the time that nation-states had begun to take shape in the late middle ages, monarchs and nobles had competed for supremacy. Louis XIV effectively brought an end to the competition by creating a complex bureaucracy to administer state affairs and by making royal favour—patronage, privilege, and perquisites—rather than lineage and landowning the chief source of power. The old aristocracy (*noblesse d'épée* or *de sang*) and the new elite created by royal favour (*noblesse de robe*) were drawn to the king's fabulous court at Versailles, the largest and most opulent structure in Europe. There they could be kept under the king's watchful eye.

By centralizing military, legal, and financial administration and domesticating the aristocracy, Louis XIV emerged as an absolute ruler. All power was embodied in the king and passed on to the lower orders—aristocracy, townspeople, and peasants. Even the Roman Catholic Church in France collaborated in this consolidation of power by advancing the theory of the "divine right of kings" to justify the new political order. By this theory the monarch was God's direct representative on earth, which meant that treason was also blasphemy. Few dared to defy the double-barrelled authority of state and church.

So successful was Louis XIV in establishing his absolutist regime that other European monarchs tried to imitate his policies, but no one managed to outshine the "Sun King" and the period of his long reign (1661–1715) is often referred to as "the age of Louis XIV." Despite crippling losses on the battlefield toward the end of his rule, and a society periodically racked by famine and heavy taxation, the Sun King bequeathed one of the most powerful nations on earth to his successor, Louis XV (1715–74).

There were, of course, a number of limitations to the exercise of royal authority under the *ancien régime*. The king was his own first minister, but his policies were only as good as the advice he received from the ministers, secretaries, courtiers, clergy, family members, and mistresses who surrounded him. Although Louis XIV spent long hours reading official correspondence, drafting edicts, and presiding over councils, much was still left to his officials and his burgeoning bureaucracy. As the king became more absorbed by European wars he left colonial affairs to be administered by officials, many of whom literally bought their jobs. This system of purchasing offices, or *venality*, brought money into the government's coffers and attracted a number of men of proven ability to the service of the state. Such a system also permitted members of the bourgeoisie, or upper middle class,

Louis XIV and his heirs, by DeTroy   (Reproduced by the permission of the Trustees of the Wallace Collection, London)

to rise in the social hierarchy, even occasionally to acquire noble titles. But it could also lead to crippling inefficiency and corruption.

Significantly, public offices were not purchased in New France, but were awarded on merit or influence and held "at the king's pleasure." If officials did not perform to the satisfaction of the king (or his minister), dismissal was certain, as two governors, three intendants, and an attorney-general discovered to their chagrin. Thus the colony escaped some of the worst features of the system of venality that prevailed in France. Still, the administrators throughout the French empire did use their positions for personal gain, both for themselves and for members of their families. No conflict-of-interest guidelines existed to prevent public servants from lining their own pockets at the expense of the state or seeking positions for family members. Intendant François Bigot (1748–60), the most notorious of the self-aggrandizing officials in New France, was perceived by many of his contemporaries as a model to be emulated, rather than a crook who should be dismissed from his job.

In the early years of the reign of Louis XIV, one of the most influential royal officials was Jean-Baptiste Colbert. He was controller-general of finances (1662–83) and, after 1669, minister of colonial and maritime affairs as well. Colbert was determined to reform national finances, promote economic self-sufficiency, and build a colonial empire with a navy to defend it. Upon his death in 1683 his office passed to his son, the Marquis de Seignelay, who pursued his father's policies until his own death in 1690.

NEPOTISM IN NEW FRANCE

It is not surprising, given the seventeenth-century system of venality and nepotism (keeping patronage within families), to find that all fifteen intendants who served in New France were related to one, or both, of two powerful clans—the Colberts and the Pontchartrains—who controlled the Ministry of Marine and Colonies under Louis XIV and XV. The Colberts were represented by Jean Talon (1665–68; 1670–72), Claude de Boutroue (1668–70), Jacques Duchesneau (1675–82), Jacques de Meulles (1682–86), and Jean Bochart de Champigny (1686–1702). Champigny was also a member of the second powerful family, the Pontchartrains. They obtained control of the Ministry of Marine and Colonies in 1690 when Louis Phélypeaux de Pontchartrain assumed office. His son, Jérôme, succeeded him in 1715, and he was followed by Jean-Frédéric Phélypeaux, Comte de Maurepas, who held office from 1723 to 1749. The Intendant François de Beauharnois (1702–05), and two important colonial governors, Louis Buade de Frontenac (1672–82; 1689–98) and Charles de Beauharnois (1702–05), were connected to the Pontchartrains. The intendants Jacques and Antoine-Denis Raudot (1705–11) and Michel Bégon (1711–26) were related to both families. At the close of the French regime in Canada, the last intendants, Gilles Hocquart (1728–48) and François Bigot (1748–60), were again members of the Colbert clan.

These close ties between the minister of marine and colonies and the royal intendants in the colony were based on marriage and on common experience in royal financial administration. Although the intendants were clearly clients of these two powerful families, the appointees usually had to prove their ability before being appointed to office. Two exceptions, Jacques de Meulles, a relative of Colbert, and François de Beauharnois, a cousin of Pontchartrain, were cases of outright nepotism.

• Absolutism in New France

The impact on New France of developments in old France was immediate. By 1663 military, bureaucratic, and ecclesiastical elites within the French state were beginning to take up the task of securing the colonial foundations laid by private entrepreneurs, merchant associations, and missionaries. The outburst of royal enthusiasm lasted only a decade before more pressing matters in Europe took up the attention of the king and his ministers. But by the 1670s the structures and policies of absolutism had been firmly implanted and, with only minor changes, would serve the colony for nearly a century.

Because of its distance from the centre of power, New France was not as directly ruled in practice as in theory. Instead, a kind of government by correspondence was established: royal commands and bureaucratic directives were sent to Quebec, and replies from the colony would find their way to the royal court at Versailles each navigational season. The time-lag, which was sometimes more than a year, often meant that state policies were hopelessly outdated by the time they had been formulated and had reached their destination. In many cases the delay had no practical impact because officials in the colony had taken action in response to pressing matters long before they received their obsolete instructions.

The royal government's most immediate problem in the overseas colonies was military security. In 1663 Alexandre de Prouville, Marquis de Tracy, was dispatched with four companies of troops, first to restore order in the West Indies colonies and then to subdue the Iroquois in New France. Tracy and 1200 troops, most of them members of the Carignan-Salières regiment, arrived in the colony in 1665. In the following year two expeditions were launched into Mohawk country. The European-trained army suffered more casualties than it inflicted, but the show of force had the desired effect. All Five Nations sent delegates to Quebec and agreed to keep the peace. Although warfare with the dreaded Iroquois Confederacy would break out again before the end of the century, two decades of relatively good relations gave French authorities the breathing space they needed to transform their St Lawrence colony.

Another matter for the king's immediate attention was the small population of the colony. Recognizing that young families constituted the best method of stimulating sustained population growth, the royal government dispatched over seven hundred women to the colony, where bachelors outnumbered marriageable women six to one. These women were called the *filles du roi* (the king's daughters) because their transport and dowries were paid by the king. Most of them came from the Hôpital-Général in Paris, a state-sponsored institution that looked after the disadvantaged of French society: the poor, sick, insane, and orphaned of all ages and social classes. Officials made an effort to ensure that the women had good health and

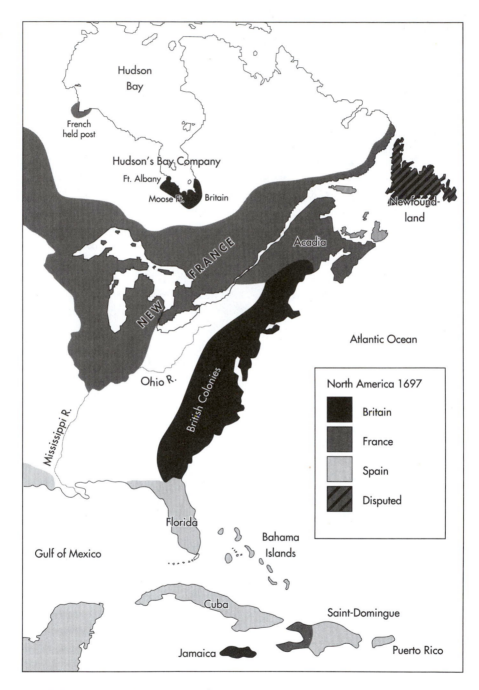

MAP 4.1 *North America, 1697* (W.J. Eccles, *France in America* (East Lansing: Michigan State University Press, 1990), 64)

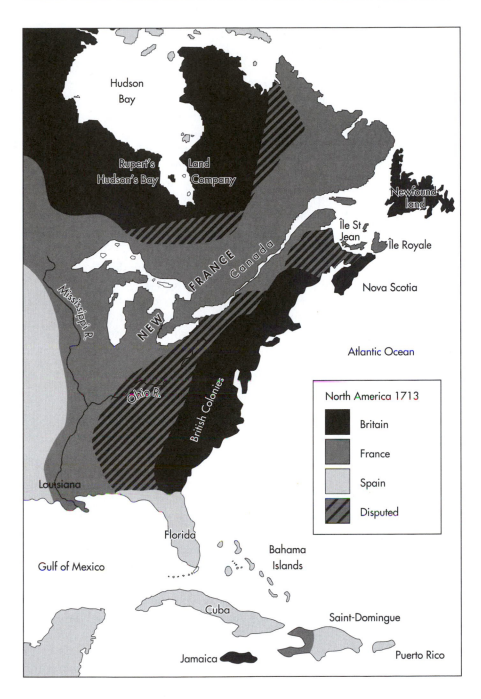

MAP 4.2 *North America, 1713*   (W.J. Eccles, *France in America* (East Lansing: Michigan State University Press, 1990), 122)

morals—although a few Protestants and prostitutes were included—and they were chaperoned by nuns who accompanied them during the long and dangerous sea voyage.

Within a few months of their arrival, most of the women had found husbands, and they seem to have had some say in choosing whom to marry. Men who could offer a place to live were the most likely to be favoured. Any man who was reluctant to take a bride was strongly encouraged to do so by regulations threatening to revoke his fur-trading licence. Despite the short period of courtship, the *filles du roi* had remarkably stable marriages. Only four women formally requested separation from their hastily chosen partners. Most of the thirty-two *filles du roi* who did not marry seem to have eventually returned to France. An exception was Madeleine de Roybon d'Alonne, a notorious adventurer, who remained single until her death in Montreal in 1718 at the age of seventy-two.

Other than the *filles du roi*, most immigrants in the decade following the declaration of royal government were soldiers. The members of the Carignan-Salières regiment, for instance, were encouraged to settle in the colony, and about four hundred of them did so. Indentured servants (*engagés*), in contrast to their counterparts in earlier years, now often chose to stay in New France once they had fulfilled their contractual obligations. Between 1663 and 1673 over two thousand immigrants arrived, nearly doubling the population of the colony and laying the foundations for stable community development.

With the increase in marriages, the peculiar demographic features of New France began to give way to patterns that resembled those of old France. The average age of marriage for women rose, the number of widows increased, and even the times of the year when weddings took place changed. When the immigrant ships dominated marriage practices, ceremonies were held soon after the boats arrived, usually between August and October. By the end of the century marriage customs in New France, as in France, followed the rhythms of agricultural work, with weddings taking place in October (after harvest and before Advent) or in winter before Lent.

The royal government, anxious to increase the population base of New France, was not content to let nature take its course. For a short time it offered bonuses for families of ten or more children and imposed penalties on people outside the church who clung to the single life. Evidence suggests that these "stick and carrot" policies had little impact on family formation. As in France, couples in New France did not practise birth control and on the average had a child every two years. Lower infant mortality rates, a higher standard of nutrition, and a lower incidence of disease than in France seem to account for a rapid population growth, which swelled the population to 15 000 by the end of the century and to 70 000 by 1763.

IMMIGRATION AND SOCIETY

The bureaucratic nature of society under the old regime has had the unintended result of providing historians with excellent sources— parish records, marriage contracts, confirmation lists, indenture agreements, and death certificates—they can use to reconstitute the immigration patterns of New France.

From these sources demographers have determined that immigrant society was not a carbon copy of the European social order. Four times as many men as women, and as many urban as rural people, immigrated to Canada. Nearly all immigrants were single; only one man in twenty and one woman in five were married or widowed. Most were relatively young. Although immigrants came from all provinces of France, the vast majority were from the eastern and northern regions. Paris and the areas immediately surrounding embarkation ports such as Bordeaux, La Rochelle, Rouen, St Malo, and Dieppe contributed a disproportionate number of migrants.

Table 4.1: IMMIGRANTS TO CANADA BY SEX AND DECADE

Period	Men	Women	Total
Pre–1630	15	6	21
1630–39	88	51	139
1640–49	141	86	227
1650–59	403	239	642
1660–69	1075	623	1698
1670–79	429	369	798
1680–89	486	56	542
1690–99	490	32	522
1700–09	283	24	307
1710–19	293	18	311
1720–29	420	14	434
1730–39	483	16	499
1740–49	576	16	592
1750–59	1699	52	1751
Unknown	27	17	44
TOTAL	6908	1619	8527

Source: R. Cole Harris and Geoffrey J. Matthews, *Historical Atlas of Canada*, vol. 1 (Toronto: University of Toronto Press, 1988), plate 45.

People moving to New France also tended to be concentrated into a few specific occupational groups. The overwhelming majority were either *engagés*, committed to a specific term of service, usually three years, or soldiers released from military service. Nearly 1000 were prisoners, many of them salt smugglers. Over 700 were *filles du roi*. Only 500 immigrants came to New France on their own initiative. While most of the immigrants were French citizens, some 350 came from other countries, including black slaves from Africa. In the 150-year period prior to the Conquest, only about 9000 immigrants came to the French colonies in what is now Canada: 8500 to the St Lawrence and another 500 to Acadia.

While French communities were spreading along the banks of the St Lawrence, the aboriginal people adapted as best they could to the aliens in their midst. As early as the 1630s the Montagnais moved to the outskirts of Quebec because the beaver in their territory had been hunted to extinction. Huron and Ottawa valley Algonkin, threatened by the Iroquois, settled near Montreal and Quebec. Abenaki from New England, pushed by war and English immigration, moved into the St Lawrence region in the 1670s, as did some Mohawk and Oneida. Most Native peoples lived apart from French settlements, often in missions directed by Jesuit and Sulpician priests. Over the years their numbers declined as disease and warfare took their toll. By the end of the French regime fewer than four thousand Natives lived in the lower St Lawrence region.

The royal government paid little attention to Acadia, which was held by the English between 1654 and 1670. A governor, subordinate to the governor-general based in Quebec, was finally appointed in 1670. With a motley garrison of fifty soldiers and sixty new settlers to augment the fewer than five hundred people already living there, Governor Hector d'Andigne de Grandfontaine was expected to maintain the king's authority over an area that today roughly corresponds to the Maritime provinces of Canada. The French population moved up the Bay of Fundy to settle at Beaubassin in the 1670s and to the shores of the Minas Basin in the 1680s. Other smaller fishing settlements were maintained along the south shore of Acadia. But as historian W.J. Eccles observes, the French presence was so inconsequential that the real rulers of Acadia were the Abenaki, Mi'kmaq, and Maliseet who roamed freely throughout the area and "who, unwittingly, were to preserve French claims of sovereignty against English encroachment."[2]

In an effort to protect the French fisheries, Colbert established a base at the ice-free port of Placentia, on the west coast of Newfoundland, in 1662. With a governor, a few administrators, a military presence, and missionaries, it soon attracted settlers to its beach property. By the end of the century Placentia consisted of forty resident fishing families and served a fleet of over four hundred vessels, employing an estimated ten thousand men. Like the fishers who could serve on naval vessels in time of war, Placentia also had military potential, a fact that did not go unnoticed by the English based in St John's.

• Colonial Administration

Under royal government, New France was administered in much the same way as a province in France, with modifications adapted to the colonial reality. The chief colonial officer was the governor-general based in Quebec. Always a military man, and usually a member of the old aristocracy (*noblesse d'épée*), the governor-general was responsible for law and order, and he controlled the military forces in the colony. Local governors in Montreal, Trois-Rivières, and Acadia reported to him, and he was responsible for relations with the aboriginal nations. With the arrival of the Troupes de la Marine in the 1680s, New France always had a substantial military force that the governor-general could use to protect the colony from external attack and to quell any civilian unrest. The military establishment was also a significant source of revenue for the colony. In 1712, for example, military expenditures reached 150 000 livres, not including the 25 000 livres invested in fortifications.

The intendant in New France, as in France, was the chief provincial administrator, responsible for finance, economic development, justice, and civil administration. Members of the new aristocracy (*noblesse de robe*), intendants represented the efforts of the king to bring bureaucratic efficiency and centralized control to bear on distant provinces. By the eighteenth century, the intendant, like the governor-general, was assisted by delegates in the main districts as well as a number of minor officials such as royal notaries, road surveyors, and customs officials. The intendant's large staff was based in his "palais" in Quebec, but the influence of his office was felt throughout the colony. In 1686, for instance, Intendant Champigny was instructed to visit the regions between the Gulf of St Lawrence and Montreal to "pay heed to all the complaints and needs of the inhabitants," so that they "enjoy complete tranquility among themselves" and "increase in their numbers." Clearly, an intendant was responsible for what went on in the bedrooms of the colony as well as for matters such as paying the wages of the military and encouraging habitants to grow more hemp.

Both the governor-general and the intendant sat on the Sovereign Council, an appointed body modelled upon the provincial *parlements* in France. Its main functions were to serve as the court of appeal from the lower courts and to register the royal edicts that served as the constitutional framework for the colony. As the population grew, the number of councillors rose from the original five in 1663 to seven in 1675 and twelve in 1703. The Sovereign Council also included the bishop of the Roman Catholic Church and an attorney-general who was trained in law and was a member of the bar at the Parlement of Paris. In 1703, at the behest of the king, the name was changed from Sovereign to Superior Council, reflecting the more modest role that the absolute ruler expected this colonial institution to play.

In the early years of royal government, the powers of the governors and intendants were inadequately defined. The situation was further complicated by the fact that, in 1664, Colbert created another monopoly company—the Compagnie des Indes Occidentales—that controlled the fur trade and shared the right to name public officials. By 1675 the duties of senior officials were clarified, and the company's administrative powers were rescinded. Thereafter, the political structures worked reasonably well, although, of course, personality conflicts were never entirely eliminated. Since the duties of the governor-general and intendant were so hopelessly entwined, any clash between the two senior officials could spell disaster for the administration of the colony. Both men sat on the highest court in the colony; governors-general were responsible for military policy while intendants supplied and paid the troops; intendants often meddled in Native policy because of their interest in advancing the colonial economy; and competition for patronage brought everyone into potential conflict.

The political system in New France reflected the conservative world view that prevailed in France itself. Power in the age of absolutism was to be invested in, and exercised by, the social elite. Any notion of authority emanating from the people was anathema to men such as Louis XIV and Colbert. Indeed, Colbert abolished the system whereby elected syndics from the major towns brought the concerns of the people to the Sovereign Council. According to Colbert, "Each one should speak for himself and none for all." Nor were people allowed to sign petitions. Nevertheless, the habitants were encouraged to take their problems to their superiors, both civilian and spiritual, and, on major issues, colonial authorities were instructed to convene consultative assemblies and report recommendations. While the advice thus rendered need not be acted upon, it was often in the best interest of absolute rulers to listen to the concerns of the people they governed.

Under the old regime, power may have been narrowly focussed, but it was usually exercised with a sense of responsibility toward all classes of society. Such an approach, called *paternalism*, was particularly obvious in New France where special circumstances—pioneer hardships, Iroquois hostility, and colonial rivalries—often elicited a sympathetic response from royal authority. To some extent this sympathy reflected the recognition that frontier conditions made enforcement of edicts difficult. A memorandum dated 1663, for example, explained: "the general spirit of government ought to lean in the direction of gentleness, it being dangerous to employ severity against transplanted peoples, far removed from their prince, and to hazard using an absolute power founded only on their obedience, because having once found a means of resisting they would quickly forget respect and submission."[3] Obviously, a paternalistic approach was more likely to bring positive results than a naked show of force.

Paternalism, as practised in New France, made it possible for the colony to be granted exceptions from the general rules prevailing in the mother country. For instance, the North American colonists were spared the crushing burden of taxation that was levied on the people of France on the grounds that frontier conditions made it difficult for them to pay their share.

Frontier conditions also produced institutional responses that were unique to the New World. In 1669 Louis XIV ordered the governor-general to enrol all male habitants between the ages of sixteen and sixty into militia companies. The Iroquois threat and colonial rivalries made such an innovation necessary for the defence of the colony. With a company in every parish, everyone had easy access to a militia captain, a man chosen from the parish to lead the militia in times of war and to report local concerns to the intendant in times of peace. Ordinances from the civil authorities were also passed down this military hierarchy, in a society where the privileges of the elite were carefully assigned and jealously guarded.

• Law and Order

In 1664 Louis XIV decreed that the Custom of Paris—the legal code used in the Paris region of France—would be the law of the colony. Royal courts were established in Quebec, Trois-Rivières, and Montreal, while the Sovereign Council served as supreme court in the colony. On rare occasions, wealthy colonists appealed their cases to the Conseil des Parties in France. The intendant appointed all court officials, supervised the court system, and had wide legal authority, including judging cases under 100 livres if all parties agreed and intervening in cases where he felt justice was not being done. A few seigneurial and church courts existed in the colonies but, predictably, royal policy worked to erode the rights of these institutions.

It was also in the royal interest to keep legal proceedings cheap and accessible. In France the cost of going to court, driven high by efforts on the part of judges and lawyers to enrich themselves, deterred many people from seeking justice. Legal reforms introduced in New France included the barring of lawyers from the courts. According to one commentator, this policy had the desired effect: "I will in no wise say whether justice is more untainted or disinterested than in France, but at least if it is sold, it is much cheaper. We do not pass through the squeezing of the lawyers, the grasp of attorneys, nor the claws of the clerks; that vermin has not yet affected Canada. Each pleads his own cause, the decision is expeditious and it is not bristling with bribes, costs and expenses."[4]

While judicial officials did not buy their positions in New France and were better paid than their counterparts in France, justice was not free. Nor was it always expeditiously or equally rendered. There was a fixed schedule of court costs as well as fees for bailiffs and witnesses. Access to the system was always easier for the elite. For people in the countryside, there was the added burden of travelling to one of the towns where the cases were heard.

The cases brought before the courts in New France differed considerably from those heard in a provincial court in France. In the colony seigneurial dues and church tithes were carefully stipulated by law and therefore did not often become the subject of extensive legal negotiation. Civil cases relating to debt recovery and disputes over property accounted for most of the cases that came before Quebec's royal court, which was known as the *Prévôté*. Merchants, both retailers and exporters, and artisans resorted most frequently to litigation. The peasantry, which made up about 80 percent of the population, comprised only 18 percent of the litigants. Although wives occasionally brought cases against husbands who had wasted the family fortune or treated them brutally, they rarely won. Unwed mothers or their parents initiated a number of proceedings for damages against fathers who would not acknowledge their offspring or marry the child's mother. Excepting some female servants who had been seduced by their employer or his son and had borne a child out of wedlock, domestic servants, apprentices, and slaves never brought charges against their masters.

Violence, bloodshed, and death were a fact of colonial life, and the criminal law in New France, as in all of Europe in the seventeenth century, was harsh. The Custom of Paris, as it was applied in New France, identified three categories of crimes: crimes against God, such as heresy, blasphemy, and sorcery; crimes against the Crown, such as treason, sedition, rebellion, desertion, duelling, and counterfeiting; and crimes against person or property, such as murder, suicide, rape, slander, libel, theft, and arson. The French inquisitorial system of justice was based on the interrogation of the accused, and the final decision as to guilt or innocence was rendered by the judge, not, as in the British system, by a jury of peers. In this respect French law reflected the political thinking of the time, which emphasized the authority and wisdom of the elite.

When a crime was detected, the attorney-general issued a writ for the arrest of the accused, who was presumed guilty. Once apprehended, the accused was put in irons and, if a man, taken to jail, if a woman, sent to a monastery. The accused was neither informed of what charge had been laid nor allowed legal counsel. Within twenty-four hours after being arrested, the accused was brought before a judge, required to take an oath, and interrogated at length. Then the accused was permitted to confront in person all accusers whose statements had previously been taken by the court. Depending upon the seriousness of the charges, the accused might even be subjected to judicial torture, *la question extraordinaire*, to extract a confession. The royal attorney made a final report on the case, and the judge or judges came to a decision, which was announced to the prisoner in jail. A sentence involving corporal or capital punishment had to be reviewed by the Sovereign Council.

Since the sentences were meant to act as a deterrent to potential criminals, they were conducted in public and with considerable fanfare. There were three categories of punishment, and within each a judge had some latitude. For capital crimes, death could be brought about by beheading, strangulation, burning at the stake, quartering, amputation of the limbs, mutilation, or some combination of these methods. Members of the nobility condemned to death had the privilege of being beheaded rather than hanged. The total number of people executed in Canada during the French regime was eighty-five, six of them broken on the wheel. Infamous punishment included humiliation on a wooden horse, in the stocks, or at the pillory, and might also include exile or loss of civil rights. Pecuniary punishment consisted of fines or confiscation of property.

Although the law set forth brutal punishments for a wide range of offences, the judges in New France were often lenient on appeal. They also showed a marked reluctance to order that an individual have a tongue cut out for blasphemy, be drawn and quartered for passing counterfeit money, or have a fleur-de-lis branded on the cheek for a first offence of selling brandy to Indians. Had they pushed the law to the limit, many more people in New France would have been mutilated than actually was the case. Canadians, as the inhabitants of the Laurentian region gradually came to be known, generally showed an unusual resistance to harsh punishment. It was almost impossible to secure a hangman in the colony, and carpenters often refused to construct pillories. The reason for this attitude, which contrasted sharply with the general European enthusiasm for gruesome public displays, is difficult to determine; but it may be related to the development of a particular sense of community, fostered by the small number of immigrants and the shared frontier experience.

Because there was no municipal government in New France, the royal courts also exercised administrative functions. A series of forty-two by-laws issued by the Sovereign Council in 1676 constituted what today would be

View of Quebec, 1699, from the cartouche on a map by Franquelin   (National Archives of Canada/C15791)

called a municipal code for the colony. Included in this code were ordinances establishing a town market and setting the prices of essential commodities such as meat and bread. Building standards, fire protection, and town planning were also covered in the code. Because human and animal wastes constituted a major health hazard, by-laws were passed to regulate their removal. Poverty, begging, and vagrancy were also subject to regulation. Vagrants, for example, were prohibited from remaining in the town without permission of the authorities, and the town's poor were not allowed to beg without a certificate of poverty signed by a priest or judge.

The growing incidence of prostitution in the port town of Quebec resulted in a 1676 by-law forbidding all citizens to harbour women of dubious morals, as well as pimps and madams. In the previous year, an unusually high number of prostitutes arrived in the colony from France. A judgment handed down in August 1675 sentenced two of these women to banishment and fined their customers 10 livres. Another prostitute, Anne Bauge, was freed by the lieutenant-general of the *Prévôté*, but he was relieved of his duties and Bauge was subsequently banished from Quebec for three years. Jailed in 1678 for violating her banishment, she was released upon the appeal of her husband on the grounds that the couple were soon to leave for France.

•Religious Establishment

Louis XIV kept a tight reign on the institutional church in his realm. Not only did he persecute all non-Catholics, but he also resisted any attempts on the part of the pope to interfere in the functioning of the church on French soil. This relationship of church and state in New France reflected an ideology known as *gallicanism*. In the French context, gallicanism meant that the church was organized on a national scale, with all clergy answering to their superiors up the hierarchy through bishops and archbishops, who, in turn, were responsible to the king, who was advised by an assembly of French clergy. The king, not the pope, nominated all church officials in France and controlled the rules and membership of all religious communities.

As ruler by divine right, Louis XIV claimed to be the supreme protector of the church, and any person or group opposing his claims was ruthlessly persecuted. Protestants, Jews, and Jansenists, the latter a puritanical group within the Catholic Church, bore the brunt of his zeal for spiritual uniformity. With the revocation of the Edict of Nantes in 1685, which had granted Protestants limited toleration in France, one million Huguenots were faced with forced conversion to Catholicism. Many chose instead to leave France, taking their skills and their ambitions with them. Quebec's wealthiest merchant, Gabriel Bernon, was a Protestant and so was obliged to return to France in this new atmosphere of intolerance. He soon escaped and moved to the English colonies, where he continued to trade with his acquaintances in Canada.

The influence of the Roman Catholic Church—so important in the early years of colonization—continued after 1663, but, not surprisingly given the absolutist goals of Louis XIV, the relation of church and state changed. The church in New France emerged as the handmaiden of the state, charged with maintaining schools, hospitals, and charitable institutions, sustaining the social order by preaching obedience and submission, and cementing Native alliances through missionary endeavours. New religious orders, especially those reporting directly to Rome, were discouraged from operating in the colony. While the period before the proclamation of royal government witnessed a veritable explosion of religious orders—Récollets, Jesuits, Soeurs Hospitalières, Ursulines, Soeurs de la Congrégation de Notre-Dame, Sulpicians, and, in Acadia, the Capuchins—only two major new communities appeared in New France in the next century: the Brothers Hospitallers in Montreal and Louisbourg, and the Grey Nuns or Sisters of Charity.

The most notable development after 1663 was the creation of a parish system to serve the needs of the expanding community. Following his arrival in 1659, Bishop Laval began the process of carving out parishes. In 1663 a seminary to train priests was established in Quebec and the tithe was introduced to support the church establishment. Institutions to take care of the poor, orphaned, and indigent—*bureaux des pauvres* and general hospitals—appeared in the colony before the end of the seventeenth century. Although established by the government, they were, like the schools and hospitals, entrusted to the administration of the church.

Despite the church's status in the colony, the parochial system developed slowly, and the bishop won few battles in confrontations with the secular authorities. Colbert was suspicious of clerical officials and even went to the length of sending the Récollets back to the colony in 1670 in an attempt to reduce the power of the Jesuits, who had been influential in the appointment of Laval. The Sulpicians, who became seigneurs of Montreal in 1663 and built their own seminary, also challenged the bishop's authority. When Laval tried to assert his power over the female religious orders, they, too, resisted his efforts. Instructions from France deprived the bishop of his role in appointing and dismissing, jointly with the governor-general, the members of the Sovereign Council, and authorized the intendant to discourage the bishop from attending council meetings. When Laval asked that the tithe be set at one-thirteenth of the produce of the land, parishioners objected and it was set at one-twenty-sixth and on cereals alone, not the entire agricultural output. As a result, the church establishment was dependent upon state subsidies for as much as one-third of its revenue.

By the time that Laval's successor, Jean-Baptiste de la Croix de Saint-Vallier (1685–1727), arrived in Quebec, there were twenty-one priests resident in the parishes, of whom twelve lodged with parishioners because there was as yet no rectory. In only six localities was the tithe sufficient to assure a modest living. Until the eighteenth century, priests were often itinerant, visiting a parish for a few weeks each year rather than residing permanently there. Even at the end of the French regime, with 114 parishes to serve, there were only 169 priests including the seminary, missionary, and chaplaincy personnel.

The church also struggled against the superstitions and questionable religious practices of their often uneducated flock. Bishop Saint-Vallier, sensing the lack of rigour in parish religious life and anxious to please his superiors, published a *Rituel*, or service book, for his priests and a catechism for the instruction of children and Native people. In the eighteenth century, the church faced an even greater challenge in the growing secular orientation of social life.

Despite slow beginnings and seemingly endless obstacles, parish priests gradually became a significant presence in the countryside. They presided over the religious ceremonies that marked every stage of an individual's life. For many of the settlers, religious rituals offered much needed comfort and reassurance in the face of the unfamiliar and often terrifying realities of the New World. The priest also served as a key adviser to the *fabrique*, the board of trustees of the parish. In addition to their religious duties, priests kept parish registers, which today provide us with valuable vital statistics, and they even drew up legal documents. They also provided some of the basic education that country folk received. Ultimately the parish priest, recruited among the local population and trained in the seminary at Quebec, would identify with his parishioners much more than with the bishop, who, with the exception of Laval, spent more time in France than in his diocese.

Although local boys were recruited for the seminary, they were less welcome among the religious orders that drew their members mainly from France. Only three Canadians entered the Jesuit order and before the Conquest none became Sulpicians. Although Canadian-born priests served the rural parishes in increasing numbers, there was always a shortage of clergy. At the end of the French regime, almost one-half of the clergy were still of French origin. No Canadian was appointed bishop or superior of a major religious order during the French regime. Fully 20 percent of the girls in noble families in New France entered the convent, a reflection, in part, of the significantly lower fee for admission than required for a marriage dowry. Church institutions also served as the primary public outlet for the administrative talents of these privileged women who, because of their sex, were denied access to the political structures of the colony.

While the institutional church, both regular and parochial, had its successes and failures in New France, there is no question about the influence that the gallican brand of Roman Catholicism had on the colony. Virtually everyone belonged to the Roman Catholic Church, and those who did not were required by law to conform to its practices. Christian values and prejudices permeated the laws and customs of New France and were imposed, when there was an opportunity to do so, upon the aboriginal peoples. Although Protestants were allowed to return to the colony in the eighteenth century, they posed no threat to the Roman Catholic Church, which remained the only institutional church in the colony throughout the French regime.

By today's standards the culture of New France was spiritual in the extreme. Shrines, many of them dedicated to the Virgin Mary, were erected at the crossroads in most communities, and natural phenomena such as earthquakes and eclipses were interpreted as direct acts of God. Religious holidays punctuated seasonal rituals, while religious processions—with the classes of society all ranked in their proper order—were a popular public spectacle. All formal education, from the elementary parish to the college level, was supervised by the church, and all reading material and cultural activities were carefully scrutinized for heresy and correct morality. In 1694, when a recent immigrant to the colony planned to stage a production of *Tartuffe* by the notoriously anti-clerical playwright, Molière, Saint-Vallier published a *mandement* against the theatre as well as against the unfortunate director, who was forbidden even to enter a church because of his impieties.

Through this close supervision of social life the church maintained a strict religious orthodoxy in the colony. Not surprisingly, Canadian religiosity was a characteristic often remarked upon by visitors. Historians have sometimes argued that the Roman Catholic Church had excessive control over the social and intellectual life of New France, but such claims are exaggerated. While the church did play a vital role in the community, particularly in the administration of educational, health, and charitable institutions, New France was scarcely the "priest-ridden" society that some have claimed. For instance, Bishop Saint-Vallier's moralistic crusades (against low-cut gowns, among other things) led to a reprimand from French authorities for excessive zeal.

Similarly, the failure of the colony to establish printing presses and newspapers—a situation often blamed on the censorship exercised by clerical authorities—must be balanced against the fact that the Roman Catholic Church provided New France with excellent educational institutions. The Jesuits, especially, included men of exceptional learning and talents. The female religious orders produced such women as Mère Sainte-Hélène of the Hôtel Dieu in Quebec, who explored the medical potential of the herbs and Native remedies she found in the colony.

Portrait of Mother Louise Soumande of Saint Augustin by Dessaillant, 1708 (Archives du monastère des Augustines de l'Hôpital-Général de Québec)

WITCHES AND WARLOCKS IN NEW FRANCE

To appreciate the role of the Roman Catholic Church in New France, it is instructive to look at the phenomenon of witchcraft. As we have seen, witchcraft was widely condemned in the European society from which the colonists of New France came. In the Americas, the Protestant community of Salem, Massachusetts, was racked in 1692 by a series of trials against people, most of them women, accused of being witches and warlocks. When the episode finally ended, twenty of the accused had been executed and a hundred were awaiting trial. No such panic occurred in New France, primarily, it seems, because most people in the colony believed fervently in the ability of church authorities to exorcise demons. Nor would the church hierarchy in New France have allowed accusations to get out of hand, as they certainly did in Salem.

Marie de l'Incarnation, writing to her son in 1668, described one case in which a young woman was "possessed by the devil," apparently when a young man, recently arrived from France, was refused permission to marry her. According to Marie de l'Incarnation, the young man "attempted to gain by spite what he could not obtain by fair means," using the offices of "certain magicians and sorcerers that had come from France." She continued:

> To be brief, the girl, who was continually pursued and agitated by demons, was put in a room in the hospital where sick persons are also kept, and, by the order of Monsigneur [Laval], Mother Saint-Augustin was set to watch over her.... The good mother watched over the girl day and night. By day the demon did not appear, but he worked his ravages at night, agitating the girl greatly and from time to time giving her views of the magician, who appeared to her accompanied by many others. But all these hellish flies could never prevail over the girl, since they were always driven away by the one to whom the Church had committed her. Enraged because Mother de Saint-Augustin guarded the girl's purity with such care, the demons appeared to her in hideous forms and beat her outrageously. The wounds and bruises that marked her body were enough to show that they were realities and not illusions.... Finally, the demons and magicians withdrew, through the interces-

> sion of this holy man [Father de Brébeuf], who had spilled
> his blood for the upholding of the Faith in this country.[5]
>
> This incident points to the church's importance in fostering stability in
> a colony where the rigours of frontier life might easily have led to social
> disintegration.

•Mercantilism

Nowhere was the hand of the royal government more visible than in the
economic development of New France. According to mercantile theory,
colonies were meant to enhance the wealth of the mother country, not to
be a drain on the royal coffers. Colbert reasoned that the fur trade had a
detrimental influence on stable colonial development, and he therefore set
out to create a compact colony on the St Lawrence, a place with a diversified economy based on the exploitation of its primary resources of agricultural land, timber, fish, and minerals. The fur trade would be carried on by
a company carefully controlled by the state. Once firmly rooted, the colony
was expected to supply raw materials for France, purchase the output of
French industry, and sustain an expanding merchant fleet. Although mercantilist theory as conceived by Colbert was less successful in practice than
in theory, his efforts to achieve his imperial dream had a profound impact
on New France.

   The chief instrument for executing Colbert's goals for the colony was
the intendant, one of the two most powerful royal officials in the colony.
Jean Talon, the first intendant to arrive in New France, proved equal to the
task defined by Colbert. During his term of office (1665–68; 1670–72), he
worked energetically to establish the colony on a firm economic base and
explored the potential of the local resources. He promoted the development of agriculture, supervising the distribution of imported horses, cattle,
sheep, and goats among the settlers, and encouraged the cultivation of
hemp and flax. In an effort to reduce the dependency on imported wines
and liquor, he ordered that a brewery be built. He laid the foundations for
Canada's first shipyard at Quebec and envisioned the colony's vast timber
resources being transformed into the casks, barrels, tar, potash, and soap

required by the settlers. When he learned of deposits of iron at Saint-Maurice and coal on Île Royale (Cape Breton), he planned their development.

With Colbert's permission—under mercantilist theory colonies were not allowed to trade directly with each other—Talon also explored the possibility of "triangular" trade with France's West Indies possessions of Guadeloupe and Martinique. In 1667 wood, fish, seal oil, and dried peas were sent directly to the West Indies, and the vessel then loaded sugar bound for France, from which metropolitan goods would be shipped back to New France. This trading pattern failed to take root to the same extent as it did for England's empire because Canada was isolated in winter and proved to be a weak link in the system. Other than furs it had no commodities that the other colonies could not get more easily elsewhere. The West Indies, like Acadia, had direct year-round contact with France and easy access to illicit trade with foreign nations. Talon's efforts to provide France with ships and naval stores such as masts, planking, tar, and cordage, also failed because colonial products could not successfully compete with supplies from Northern Europe.

Historians debate the extent to which the mercantile practices of the French state retarded colonial economic development. It was certainly the case that royal policy frowned on colonial economic initiatives, especially if they threatened industries already well established in France. In 1703, for example, when the flax and hemp harvests in Canada had been particularly successful, the royal government refused to send weavers to the colony because metropolitan manufactures might be threatened by a robust textile industry. Three years later royal instructions reiterated restrictions on colonial manufactures that would compete with those of France and expressly prohibited trade with the English colonies and direct intercolonial trade. The only exception that could be made was "in the interest of the poor people."

Despite such injunctions, the exceptions to mercantile restrictions in New France were many and significant. In wartime, Canadians were permitted to trade directly with other French colonies, usually in foodstuffs, and even trade with foreign nations was permitted when the interests of the empire—and the fur trade—dictated it. Because both bureaucrats and merchants in New France supported an economic system based on protection rather than free trade, it was not the case, as it would later become in the British Empire, that there was conflict between the mother country and the colonies over mercantile restrictions. Moreover, France lacked the resources and the will to stop any illicit activities that did occur in North America. Trade along the Montreal–Albany–New York route, for instance, was rarely curtailed. It offered a welcome outlet for an often oversupplied fur market and was an important source of income for Native allies on reserves near Montreal. Similarly, Acadians traded with nearby New Englanders without much interference from metropolitan authorities.

Even the restrictions on textile manufacturing could be circumvented by those with imagination and initiative. In 1705 Montreal businesswoman Agathe de Saint-Père, Madame de Repentigny, ransomed nine English weavers who were being held captive by Native allies and put them to work on looms that she had built for their use. Soon she had turned her home into a workshop, complete with apprentices, making "linen, drugget, twilled and covert-coating serge."

Canadians also showed initiative in overcoming one of the ongoing difficulties of a colonial economy: the chronic shortage of specie, or hard money. Government expenditures were covered by money sent annually from France, but this source proved less than reliable. In 1685 Intendant Jacques de Meulles used playing cards as promissory notes to pay the troops and labourers when the ships failed to arrive from France until late in the season. This ingenious solution also enabled the authorities to carry on normal transactions when money was short during prolonged periods of war. It had its disadvantages. In 1712 the minister of marine and colonies warned the colony's administrators:

> A number of people from Canada have told me this year that it will in future be absolutely impossible to find the means of supporting the troops and meeting ordinary expenses if the treasurers general do not honour the bills of exchange when they fall due, and that the large quantity of cards issued in the country brings them into disrepute, which causes goods to quadruple in price, since [these cards] give the traders nothing but bills of exchange which go dishonoured, which ruins them in interest charges and brings suffering to the entire colony. I accept the truth of all these facts, but the unfortunate state of the kingdom in the past several years has prevented His Majesty from meeting both his expenses and those it was indispensable for him to make, on the other hand, to defend himself against the enemies of the state. . . . The King is not in a position to provide for the colony.[6]

When paper currency was redeemed at less than its face value following the War of the Spanish Succession, those who held playing cards suffered a severe financial loss. France was itself too far in debt to worry about the fortunes of the colonials. A similar and much deeper discounting of paper currency also occurred after the Seven Years' War in the 1760s.

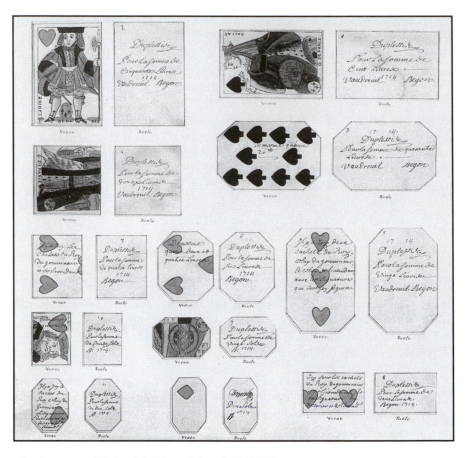

Card money   (National Archives of Canada/C117059)

•Seigneurialism

In pre-industrial Europe agriculture was the mainspring of economic life, and the peasant household was the basic economic unit. The royal government wanted the same stable base for New France and acted quickly to send settlers to the colony. The initial burst of enthusiasm for settlement, which brought the *filles du roi*, soldiers, and *engagés* to the colony, petered out in the early 1670s as Louis XIV turned his attention to European politics. Colbert informed Talon that he had no intention of depopulating France for the benefit of the colonies. It would not be until the last decade of the French regime that immigration would reach the levels achieved between 1663 and 1673. Nevertheless, the roughly 10 000 inhabitants in the colony by 1680 had the experience and institutions to sustain a growing society. Despite a devastating epidemic of smallpox, which took nearly 1000 lives in the early 1680s, the population continued to grow, even without massive immigration.

Seigneurialism was the structure around which peasant agriculture took shape in New France. Introduced by the Compagnie de la Nouvelle France and continued by Colbert, seigneurialism was the typical landholding system in France. According to seigneurial theory, all the land belonged to the Crown, which made grants of estates, or seigneuries, to the privileged orders: the church and the nobility. The seigneur was required to maintain a household on his estate and develop it with the help of peasant farmers, called *censitaires*. This term derived from the annual fees known as *cens et rentes* that the peasants paid for the privilege of working the land for themselves and their seigneur. Notaries in New France called such lots concessions, or *habitations*, and thus the people who lived on them were known as habitants. The seigneur could require his *censitaires* to work a certain number of days on his property, or *demesne*. He could also require that they grind their wheat in his mill for a price (*banalités*) and pay a fee (*lods et ventes*) if the concession changed hands. In these ways the wealth of peasant labour was accumulated by the seigneur in the time-honoured manorial tradition.

The similarity, in formal terms, between the position of the peasantry in France and New France has occasioned much debate. Some historians suggest that, despite feudal forms, the habitant in New France was virtually an independent farmer, paying annual dues to the seigneur, reduced tithes to the church, and token taxes to the state. Others question this characterization, noting that habitants required good fortune to raise a crop that sustained their household needs. Since they rarely produced a surplus, the extractions of the seigneurs, clerics, and state bureaucrats, while not a large percentage of the crop, constituted an oppressive burden. Whatever position is taken on this question, most historians agree that habitants in New France had more land than their French counterparts, a greater likelihood of being able to include fish and meat in the family diet, and, in general, a better chance of being well fed than the chronically oppressed peasantry in many regions of France.

As it developed in the colony, seigneurialism was intended to accomplish a number of objectives: to provide the colony with a basic land-survey system; to perpetuate a traditional class structure; to establish a legal framework for relations between privileged landowners and dependent peasant families; and to develop a system for recruiting and settling immigrants. Not all of these objectives were achieved. Apart from the religious communities that ultimately accounted for about one-quarter of the 185 seigneuries granted (making the church the largest seigneur in the colony), few seigneurs were successful immigrant agents. At the same time, seigneurs and *censitaires* were obliged to bring the land into production or forfeit their grants. In 1711 royal decrees known as the Arrêts de Marly threatened to revoke undeveloped seigneurial grants and tenant concessions.

The traditional survey system quickly adapted to the geography of the Laurentian lowlands. Instead of a three-field system encircling a village, which was typical in France, the grants conformed to the river, becoming long, narrow trapezoids fronting along the St Lawrence River and other waterways. Talon experimented with circular-shaped seigneuries near Quebec, but this style failed to catch on. Seigneurial grants were on the average ten times longer than they were wide, and tenant grants were similarly strip-like. When the first line of farms, or *côte*, was full, a second line, or *rang*, was opened along a road running behind the first settlements.

For a pioneer community there were many advantages to this type of survey. In addition to being inexpensive to run, it permitted farmers to live near their own fields and to each other. It gave them access to fish and other marine life, and to the best transportation route in the colony. By cutting across the ecological boundaries that tended to run parallel to the river, it gave each farmer access to a variety of soils and vegetations: marshlands for fodder near the river, rich heavy soils for cereals, upland meadows for grazing, woodlots for fuel, and lumber at the upper reaches of the property. One disadvantage was that villages were slow to develop under such a system, and services, both commercial and religious, were often underdeveloped in the rural countryside.

Although the seigneurial system succeeded in reflecting the conservative class structure favoured in the age of absolutism, social distinctions and upper-class privileges were somewhat blunted in New France. Especially in the early years of settlement, some seigneurs were almost as poor as their *censitaires*. As a result they were unable to provide such customary services as a grist mill and church. Once a seigneury had thirty or forty well-established *censitaires*, it became profitable, and traditional privileges—such as hunting and fishing rights, ownership of ferries and common pastures, and the reservation of building stone or wood supply—were carefully guarded.

Social custom reinforced the status of the seigneur. The front pew of the parish church was reserved for the use of the seigneur and his family, the family received communion before all others, and if the seigneur was also a patron founder of the parish church he would be mentioned in the

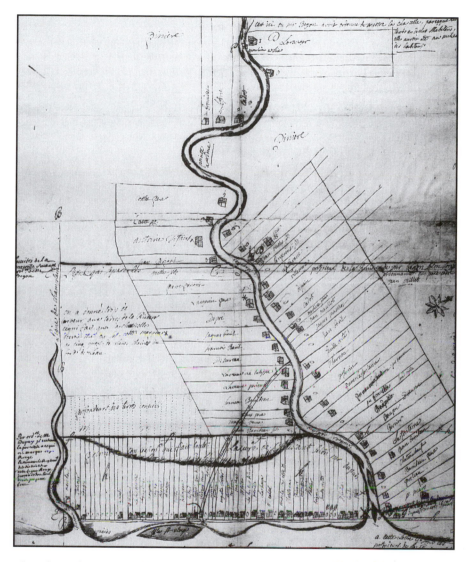

A cadastral survey of Batiscan, a seigneury belonging to the Jesuits   (Archives nationales, Paris: Section Outre-Mer, Colonies)

weekly prayers. Nevertheless, the foundation of the old nobility was never allowed to take root in New France. Seigneurs had no official military role, as they did under the feudal regimes of Europe. Indeed, in New France seigneurs were not always nobles; and even if they were ennobled, most could not claim hereditary privileges from time immemorial. They, like the new nobility in France, owed their status to the kind offices of the king.

In New France, the bulk of the seigneur's income came from trade, military service, and government positions, not from the rents extracted from tenants. So significant was commercial activity to the social structure of the colony that a special ordinance, issued in 1685, made it possible for the colonial nobility to engage in trade. In France such involvement in pursuits "beneath one's station" usually led to the loss of noble status. Thus, especially in the early years, the elite in New France was a fusion of noble and middle-class elements, and the *bourgeois-gentilhomme* was a typical member of the colonial upper class.

• Fish, Furs, and Territorial Expansion

Cod proved economically more important to France than beaver. In 1664 the bank fishery, based in Le Havre, Honfleur, and Les Sables-d'Olonne, accounted for about a third of the French fleet. It supplied green fish to the huge market in and around Paris and along the Loire. Ships from the other major fishing ports produced dried cod for the southern European market. Appreciating the value of cod to the French economy, Colbert was quick to commission a study of the fisheries and to impose regulation on it. By a 1670 ordinance, boys under twelve could not be hired on fishing crews, and fishers who had completed five or six seasons were made liable for service in the royal navy. An ordinance in 1681 required a surgeon on every vessel with a crew of twenty or more, and another ordinance in 1694 called for a chaplain as well. Few surgeons or chaplains seemed to be attracted to such a demanding calling, but the sons of peasants from western France did enter the lucrative industry, becoming fishers, sailors, and, in a few cases—most notably in Placentia in Newfoundland—pioneer settlers in the New World.

While the fisheries led to limited territorial claims, the fur trade encouraged expansion. In 1663 New France extended westward only a short distance beyond Montreal. By 1715 the French had not only explored and laid claim to more than half of the North American continent, but had also cemented their New World empire by forging alliances with the Native nations. The fur trade alone would not have justified such dramatic imperial ambitions. There were, after all, limits to the numbers of furs required to adorn France's fashionable elite. But when the fur trade became the vehicle for advancing French power at the expense of English and Dutch rivals, the potential for growth was limited only by the will of the French state to foot the bill.

When the Iroquois threat was reduced in 1666, furs again began moving through Montreal. The profits from the trade, kept artificially high by fixed prices, encouraged others to become involved. With dreams of vast wealth, young men made the hazardous journey into the *pays d'en haut*, the area around the Great Lakes, to contact distant tribes and secure the best furs. By the end of the 1660s, Michilimackinac, on the north shore of Lake Superior, had became the focus of the fur trade in the interior, but it was only a short time before the drive for better furs and higher profits pushed French traders farther west. Missionaries and explorers also traded in furs to finance their costly activities. Even Talon justified fur trading on these grounds, assuring Colbert that the explorers he sent to find minerals and the rumoured western sea would be self-financing.

Talon's interest in what lay in the interior was further stimulated in 1670 when the English established the Hudson's Bay Company, which was granted a monopoly to trade furs in all the territories drained by rivers flowing into Hudson Bay. Because the English had also recently taken control of New York from the Dutch, they seemed poised to restrict the French to a narrow band on the St Lawrence.

The efforts of French officials to control the fur trade inadvertently gave the king of England an excuse to award a charter to the Hudson's Bay Company. In 1660 two St Lawrence-based traders, Pierre-Esprit Radisson and his brother-in-law Médard Chouart, Sieur des Groseilliers, returned from a trading expedition north of Lake Superior with a plan to ship furs to Europe through Hudson Bay. French officials refused to countenance such a proposal, and added insult to injury by accusing Radisson and Groseilliers of illegal trading. The pair took their idea to New England and eventually to England where a group of merchants agreed to finance an expedition to Hudson Bay. The intrepid *Nonsuch* and its crew spent the winter of 1668–69 at the mouth of the Rupert River on James Bay, and returned to England the following summer with a cargo of high-quality furs. By 1670 investors had created a company and applied for a charter from King Charles giving them a monopoly of all the territory drained by rivers flowing into Hudson Bay. The area, called Rupert's Land in honour of Prince Rupert, a cousin of the king and the company's first governor, included nearly one-third of the territory of present-day Canada.

Throughout most of the seventeenth century, the Baymen confined themselves to posts on the shores of Hudson Bay, while French traders based on the St Lawrence moved steadily westward in their search of furs. Indeed, in a curious twist of fate, Radisson and Groseilliers, who had reverted to their earlier allegiance, attacked and captured the English posts in a seaborne expedition launched by the French in 1682–83. Since England and France were technically at peace, Louis XIV was obliged to return both the trading posts and Radisson to the English. The contest between the St Lawrence and Hudson Bay traders remained a feature of North American history for nearly 150 years. In 1690–91, Bayman Henry Kelsey became the first European to reach what are today the plains of Saskatchewan. It would be another half century, however, before competition from the St Lawrence traders forced reluctant Hudson's Bay Company officials to build posts in the interior of the continent.

In 1671 Talon sent an expedition, which included the Jesuit Charles Albanel, into the Hudson Bay region and another under fur trader Daumont de Saint-Lusson into Lake Superior country in search of a route leading to the Pacific. Louis Jolliet, another experienced fur trader, was commissioned in 1672 to follow up on earlier efforts by Sulpician priests François Dollier de Casson and René de Bréhant de Galinée to find the rumoured river that flowed into the Gulf of Mexico. Jolliet was joined at Michilimackinac by Father Jacques Marquette, and together they explored the Mississippi as far as the mouth of the Arkansas River.

Talon returned to France in 1672, two years before Jolliet found his way back to the colony. By that time the initiative for territorial expansion had been seized by Louis de Buade, Comte de Frontenac, the new governor-general of New France. A military man of great personal ambition, Frontenac defied Colbert's instructions. In 1673 he had a fortified trading post built at Cataraqui (present-day Kingston) and obtained rights for his friend René-Robert Cavalier de La Salle to build posts and to trade in the valley of the Mississippi River. La Salle maintained that his goal was to follow up the explorations of Jolliet and Marquette, and he did finally reach the Gulf of Mexico in 1682, but he spent most of his time constructing fur-trading posts. He had also disturbed Native and European fur traders with his irascible behaviour and aggressive trading activities. The Iroquois, in particular, were alarmed by La Salle's alliances with their enemies, the Illinois. Governor La Barre felt obliged to send soldiers into the interior to protect the posts from attack, and they, too, became deeply involved in the fur trade. In 1687 La Salle was murdered, apparently by his own men.

By the 1680s, then, France was well on the way to claiming the whole of the North American continent, but it was an empire with a difference. The French did not occupy the land that they claimed. Except for a few poorly defended trading posts, the land was inhabited by the first nations, who took advantage of the territorial ambitions of the French or any of the other Europeans invading their homelands. Nevertheless, the European presence would gradually transform the culture of the Native nations and embroil them in new political alliances. The magnetic attraction of the hinterland would also change the Europeans who succumbed to it and bring pressure upon the struggling colony on the St Lawrence.

Colbert introduced a number of policies designed to control what were considered the two biggest problems created by the fur trade: the use

Des castors du Canada. Vignette from a map by Nicolas de Fer, 1698 (National Archives of Canada/NMC16825, detail)

of alcohol as a major trade item and the loss to the colony of so many young men who entered the trade, often in defiance of the law. By the 1670s it was plain for all to see that alcohol had become a principal commodity in the fur trade. The church, in particular, complained about the deleterious effects that the brandy trade had upon the Natives. In 1678 the intendant was ordered to convene a consultative assembly of leading laymen to advise on the matter. Significantly, no churchmen were invited, and although the evils of the traffic in liquor were deplored, those assembled recommended against major restrictions on the trade. If the French curtailed the trade in alcohol, it was reasoned, the Natives would simply turn to the English for their supply, and the French fur trade would collapse. A royal edict issued the following year forbade carrying brandy to Native dwellings but otherwise respected the wishes of the fur traders.

The problem of the *coureurs de bois*, as the unlicensed fur traders were called, was equally contentious. By 1680 over six hundred *coureurs de bois* were trading in the interior in defiance of repeated ordinances. Attempts to have the Natives bring their furs to Montreal had failed miserably. Again the church was involved in the debate over how to handle the problem, this time expressing concern about the impact of the fur trade on the moral fibre of young men in the colony. *Coureurs de bois,* by definition outlaws, often became too fond of the brandy they traded and occasionally had sexual relations with Native women without benefit of marriage. Both religious and civic authorities also fretted about the effect on the colony of the absence of so many of its young men. Farms and families were being neglected, church attendance and tithes ignored, and the fabric of community life weakened by men who failed to return promptly to the colony when ordered repeatedly to do so.

Admitting failure in the attempts to control the interior trade, Louis XIV issued two edicts on the matter in 1681: one granted amnesty to all *coureurs de bois* if they would return immediately to the colony; the other set up a system of trading permits, called *congés*, each of which initially permitted one canoe and three men to engage in the upcountry trade. The illicit traders paid little attention to the edicts, and the *congés* soon became little more than a source of revenue for the governor and intendant who sold them to the colonists. Meanwhile, trade continued, more posts were built in the interior, and the Iroquois began to menace the French and their new Native allies who were encircling their territory.

The glut of furs on the European market and the prospect of an Iroquois war were not calculated to advance French interests. In 1696 orders came from Versailles that no more *congés* were to be issued and that all western trading posts except St Louis in the Illinois country were to be closed down. Yet within five years Louis XIV had commissioned Pierre Le Moyne d'Iberville to establish a base at the mouth of the Mississippi and the system of *congés* had been restored—a dramatic shift in colonial policy closely related to France's relations with foreign powers, both Native and European.

• Wars and Alliances

Until the late 1680s French expansion into the interior had been largely determined by the ambitions of fur traders and officials in New France itself. This expansion inevitably incurred the wrath of the Iroquois, who took offence at any attempt by the French to claim or occupy more territory. Although preoccupied by developments on their southern and eastern flanks through much of the decade after 1666, the Iroquois would not let France outmanoeuvre them. The fact that the Iroquois were now in alliance with the English, who were beginning to send trading expeditions into the interior, made the situation even more complicated.

The Seneca attacked La Salle's fort at St Louis in 1684. Governor La Barre, as deeply involved in the fur trade as Frontenac had been, sent an expedition to intimidate the Iroquois but was forced to accept a humiliating peace. La Barre was recalled for his failure and his successor, the Marquis de Denonville, sent another expedition in 1687. This time the troops—832 regulars, 900 militiamen, and 400 Indian allies—had more success. English fur traders sent by Governor Thomas Dongan of New York were intercepted, the Seneca were subjected to a "scorched earth" policy, and a blockhouse with a garrison of a hundred soldiers was built at the mouth of the Niagara River to guard French access to the Illinois country. Nevertheless, the Iroquois were still in control of the southern interior and posed a real threat to the colony. In August 1688, 1500 Iroquois descended on Lachine, putting fifty-six homes to the torch and killing their captives, sometimes after torturing them. The tactics of the Iroquois were no better or worse than those of the French in this period of history. Before the 1687 expedition Louis XIV had instructed Denonville to eliminate the Iroquois "barbarians" and ordered that captured warriors be sent to France, where they would become slaves for the Mediterranean fleet. Some thirty-six prisoners were seized for this purpose in 1687.

While the frontier echoed with battle cries of *la petite guerre*—what is today called guerrilla warfare—Louis XIV had become embroiled in *la grande guerre* in Europe. Throughout the 1670s he harassed the Dutch, and then began asserting his right to occupy the territory on the northeast border of France. Finally a defensive coalition, the League of Augsburg, was formed, which included England and Holland. War in Europe, declared in 1689, made it easier for Governor Frontenac, who had returned to the colony in the same year for a second tour of duty, to launch retaliatory raids against the English in New England and New York in an effort to convince them to abandon their alliance with the Iroquois. Although the border raids had the desired effect—the English trading base at Albany was temporarily rendered ineffective—they also brought a direct attack on Quebec itself.

The expedition against New France by land and sea was the idea of the feisty New Englanders who in the previous year had attacked and looted Port Royal in Acadia. While the force sent overland soon collapsed, Sir William Phips, with his armada of thirty-four ships and two thousand men, appeared below the walls of Quebec in the middle of October 1690. With winter approaching and smallpox ravaging his troops, Phips was forced to withdraw without achieving his objective, but it was an indication of the scale of military and naval effort that the English were prepared to mount.

The French were also capable of daring feats. In 1694 the Canadian-born naval captain Pierre Le Moyne d'Iberville captured and burned St John's as well as a large number of fishing bases along the coast of Newfoundland. He then proceeded to Hudson Bay where he captured Fort York from the Bay Company one week before peace was negotiated in

Europe. In the colony itself, civilians, including women such as Madeleine de Verchères, distinguished themselves by showing exceptional initiative in the face of Iroqouis attacks. The War of the League of Augsburg ended in 1697 by the Treaty of Ryswick without any territorial losses to the French empire in North America.

Ironically, French successes in the war almost destroyed the colony. The war made it easier for Frontenac and his ambitious fur-trading friends to justify building more fortified posts in the interior. By 1695 French traders had made direct contact with the Sioux and the Assiniboine, traditional enemies of France's allies, the Ottawa. For a time it seemed as if the Iroquois would become allied with the aggrieved Ottawa, and together the groups would force the French out of the interior and even North America. But Frontenac realized his strategic blunder soon enough to launch a blow to the heart of Iroquois territory. In 1696 an expedition destroyed the villages of the Onondaga and the Oneida.

The French decision in 1696 to abandon the western interior had come at the end of this series of disasters and near-disasters in the Americas. Not surprisingly, such a policy was strongly resisted in the colony and, like the edicts of 1681, was ultimately doomed to fail. *Coureurs de bois* would go to the English on Hudson Bay and New York rather than abandon the lucrative trade. Similarly, officials such as Frontenac would continue to cloak their commercial objectives in arguments about the strategic interests of the French empire. And Natives, whether friend or foe, were now more dependent than ever upon European manufactures. They would insist on making alliances with any nation that would meet their needs. If the Native nations became hostile toward New France, the colony's days could be numbered. The colonists had been brought to their knees by Iroquois raids conducted sporadically during the war. More than anything, they wanted stable and friendly relations with the nations that surrounded them.

Fortunately for the Canadians, the near century of warfare between and among Natives and newcomers in North America prompted a general desire for peaceful relations. In September 1700, delegates from four Iroquois tribes (the Mohawk stayed away) made peace at Montreal with the Huron, Abenaki, and Ottawa who lived on reserves in the colony. In July of the following year, over 1300 Natives from thirty-two nations assembled near Montreal to negotiate peace among themselves and renew their alliances with the French. By the Treaty of Montreal the French recognized the Iroquois as an independent nation and in return the Iroquois promised to remain neutral in any war between France and Britain.

As people in North America were sorting out their relations, France became embroiled in another war. This time, Louis XIV hoped to establish his grandson on the throne of Spain, thus uniting two of Europe's great empires. As a pre-emptive move, d'Iberville was dispatched in 1698 to the mouth of the Mississippi to lay claim to the region for France. Three years later he was ordered to establish a colony there. Louisiana was to become the final link in a chain of posts reaching from the St Lawrence to the Spanish empire in Mexico. Lamothe Cadillac, another prominent member of the beaver aristocracy, also convinced the minister of marine and colonies to move the western base from Michilimackinac to Detroit as part of the strategy to intimidate the Iroquois and contain the English.

In this rapidly developing scenario the economic aspects of the fur trade were superseded by military considerations. The posts that France had planned to abandon in 1696 were now to be maintained; and new ones were to be established. The fur trade would help cement Native alliances, while the *coureurs de bois*, with their skills in Indian relations and guerrilla warfare, would become agents of the Crown. This turn of events, driven by developments in Europe, put the final nail in the coffin of Colbert's dream of a compact colony on the St Lawrence.

The War of the Spanish Succession broke out in 1702 with England and France ranged on opposing sides. Although unwilling to antagonize anew the recently subdued Iroquois, Governor Vaudreuil had no hesitation in attacking settlements on the New England frontier. Raiding expeditions conducted by the Canadian militia and their Native allies in 1703 and 1704 wrought havoc in outlying settlements and flooded New France with prisoners, many of them slaves of their Native captors. From the Deerfield raid alone over one hundred hostages were taken. Once again, the New Englanders struck back by sea. In 1703, 1704, and 1707 they attacked the outlying settlements in Acadia but achieved no strategic objective. Finally, in 1710, a combined force of 1900 British and colonial troops captured Port Royal, which was defended by Governor Daniel d'Auger de Subercase with a garrison of 258 soldiers. The English launched an ambitious attack led by Sir Hovenden Walker on Quebec in 1711 but they were forced to abandon their invasion following heavy losses of men and ships in the treacherous currents and shoals of the lower St Lawrence River.

With the exception of Port Royal, the French suffered few losses in North America and inflicted considerable damage on English settlements and posts in New England, Newfoundland, and the Hudson Bay area. But European considerations dictated the terms of the peace. To secure the Bourbon dynasty on the Spanish throne, Louis XIV was forced to make concessions in the Treaty of Utrecht, which ended the war. Colonial territory was thrown into the balance. France agreed to abandon Hudson Bay, Acadia, and Newfoundland to the British and to recognize British authority over the Iroquois Confederacy. France retained fishing rights on the north coast of Newfoundland as well as two islands protecting the entrance to the

Gulf of St Lawrence: Île du Cap-Breton (soon to be rechristened Île Royale) and Île St Jean (Prince Edward Island). On the surface, the losses seemed inconsequential. France had invested little energy into developing these lost outposts of its emerging continental empire, and they had brought in little or no direct wealth. For New France, however, the signs were ominous: European interests alone seemed to determine the fate of colonies in the Americas. For the over two thousand Acadians in New France, it was the final conquest.

Madame de Guercheville (Bibliothèque nationale de France, Paris)

• The Status of Women in New France:
A Historiographical Debate

Historians disagree about how to interpret the status of women in New France. Jan Noel has argued that the unusual conjunction of cultural heritage, demographic features, and economic conditions combined to make women in the colony "femmes favorisées."[7] She cites examples of twenty outstanding women in business, church, and politics who made their mark on the colony's history, and she comments on the level of education— usually better than that of men in the colony—and the range and freedom of action that colonial women enjoyed. Such examples, Noel maintains, suggest that women in New France had more opportunities than did their contemporaries in New England and Europe, and more even than women in the nineteenth century.

There is considerable evidence to back up Noel's position. In particular, the female religious orders produced women of outstanding intellectual achievements and administrative abilities. Marie de l'Incarnation, Jeanne Mance, and Marguerite Bourgeoys stand shoulder to shoulder with Champlain, Maisonneuve, and Laval for their pioneering activities in the New World. Moreover, because they held dower rights to property and wealth, women were often critical to raising the capital needed for commercial and religious ventures in the New World. For example, Hélène Boullé, who married Champlain at the age of twelve, was a wealthy heiress whose dowry financed her husband's early expeditions. Another woman, Madame de Guercheville, never came to the New World but used her wealth to finance Jesuit activities in Acadia. When she became suspicious of the motives of the fur traders in charge of developing Port Royal, she purchased (with her husband's permission) de Monts's rights in New France. She held title to Acadia until she relinquished her claims to the Compagne de la Nouvelle France in 1627.

Micheline Dumont, one of the authors of a collective history of Quebec women, takes issue with Noel's perspective. She maintains that women in the seventeenth century may have played a unique role because of the exceptional circumstances prevailing in the infant colony, but that by the eighteenth century their status had become more like that of their sisters in France.[8] And while it is true that women in New France were sometimes forced to do the tasks traditionally assigned to men, they saw their fate as an aberration, not a step toward some ideal of liberation. Madeleine de Verchères, for instance, who organized the defence of her village against an Iroquois attack in 1692, argued for a pension on the grounds that she was an unusual woman with "feelings which lead me to glory, just like many men." Most women, she implied, would not aspire to such acts of heroism.

Dumont also cautions historians not to confuse privileges based on class with the experience of all women. As in France, elite women in New France had considerable scope for action under the laws of the *ancien régime*, especially when they acted on behalf of their husbands or in segregated religious orders. Marie de La Tour fought to the death to defend her absent husband's fort in Acadia in 1645, but such leadership was expected of wives in this period. In New France women may have stretched the boundaries of the limitations placed upon them, but at no time were those boundaries ever erased. Others have added that no woman ever served as a governor, a priest, an intendant, a military commander, a notary, a sovereign councillor, or a judge, and as far as we can tell no one ever argued that they should have done so.

Finally, by emphasizing exceptional women, Dumont argues, historians often overlook the significant contribution that women made to colonial society through their productive and reproductive work within the family. In pre-industrial European and colonial society, the family was the fundamental unit of economic life. The bearing and rearing of children, the growing and preparing of food, the making of cloth and warm clothing, and the nursing and nurturing of family and friends—all carried on almost exclusively within the domestic setting—were fundamental to the survival of the family, the community, and the colony.

Even if Dumont's cautions are correct, it remains the case that women in New France functioned in a different environment than the one that prevailed in France or even in nearby New England. The important institutional roles played by the church and state, the significance of the fur trade and the military establishment, the absence of deeply rooted traditions, the influence of first nations, and perhaps even the particular cultural practices brought by the few thousand immigrants selected from French society to settle in the New World: all these elements combined to produce, if not a totally new society, at least a considerably altered one.

Perhaps women in New France were not so much *favorisées* as challenged to adapt their traditional notions of gender roles to the colonial environment. The same could be said for men, whose roles were also reshaped by the colonizing experience. Together in the New World, French women and men became *Canadiennes* and *Canadiens*, whose differences from their counterparts in old France became the cause for comment, and sometimes conflict, during the course of the eighteenth century.

• Notes

[1] *The Jesuit Relations and Allied Documents*, ed. Reuben Gold Thwaites, 73 vols. (Cleveland: Burrows Brothers Co., 1896–1901), 51: 167–77.

[2] W.J. Eccles, *France in America* (New York: Harper and Row, 1972), 66.

[3] National Archives of Canada, MG1, Series CIIA, Anonymous memorandum on colonization [1663], 2: 48.

[4] Cited in André Vachon, "Le Notaire en Nouvelle-France," *Revue de l'Université Laval* 10, 3 (1955–56): 235.

[5] *Word from New France: The Selected Letters of Marie de l'Incarnation*, trans. and ed. Joyce Marshall (Toronto: Oxford University Press, 1967), 343–44.

[6] Cited in Guy Fregault, "La colonisation du Canada au XVIIIe siècle," *Cahiers de l'Academie canadienne-française* 2 (1957): 53–81.

[7] Jan Noel, "New France: Les Femmes Favorisées," in *Rethinking Canada: The Promise of Women's History*, 2nd ed., ed. Veronica Strong-Boag and Anita Clair Fellman (Toronto: Copp Clark Pitman, 1991), 28–50.

[8] Micheline Dumont, "Les femmes de la Nouvelle-France: Etaient-Elles Favorisées?" *Atlantis* 8, 1 (Fall 1982): 118–24; see also the Clio Collective, *Quebec Women: A History* (Toronto: Women's Press, 1987).

•Selected Reading

The age of Louis XIV is described in Pierre Goubert, *Louis XIV and Twenty Million Frenchmen* (New York: Random House, 1970), and Roger Mettam, *Power and Faction in Louis XIV's France* (Oxford: Basil Blackwell, 1988). The standard biography of the Sun King is J.B. Wolf, *Louis XIV* (New York: Norton, 1968). The age of absolutism in New France is summarized in W.J. Eccles, *The Canadian Frontier, 1534–1760* (New York: Holt, Rinehart and Winston, 1969), and *France in America*, rev. ed. (Toronto: Fitzhenry and Whiteside, 1990); and in Eccles's earlier *Canada Under Louis XIV 1663–1701* (Toronto: McClelland and Stewart, 1964) and *The Government of New France* (Ottawa: Canadian Historical Association, 1965). Some of Eccles's articles are collected in *Essays on New France* (Toronto: Oxford University Press, 1987). See also Marcel Trudel, *An Introduction to New France* (Toronto: Holt, Reinhart and Winston, 1968), and André Vachon, "The Administration of New France," *Dictionary of Canadian Biography* (Toronto: University of Toronto Press, 1969), 2: xv–xxv.

Aspects of social and institutional developments in New France are summarized in R. Cole Harris and John Warkentin, *Canada Before Confederation* (Toronto: Oxford University Press, 1974), ch. 2, and Brian Young and John A. Dickinson, *A Short History of Quebec* (Toronto: Copp Clark Pitman, 1987), chs. 2 and 3. Volume 1 of R. Cole Harris and Geoffrey J. Matthews, *Historical Atlas of Canada* (Toronto: University of Toronto Press, 1988), provides a wealth of information on Native and European society under the French regime, as do volumes 1–4 of *The Dictionary of Canadian Biography* (Toronto: University of Toronto Press, 1966–79).

Studies of social and institutional life in New France include Marcel Trudel, *The Seigneurial Regime* (Ottawa: Canadian Historical Association, 1956), and R. Cole Harris, *The Seigneurial System in Canada: A Geographical Study* (Madison: University of Wisconsin Press, 1966); Cornelius Jaenen, *The Role of the Church in New France* (Toronto: McGraw-Hill Ryerson, 1976); Roger Magnuson, *A Brief History of Quebec Education* (Montreal: Harvest House, 1980); Louise Dechêne, *Habitants et marchands de Montréal au XVIIe siècle* (Paris: Plon, 1974); André Lachance, *Crimes et criminels en Nouvelle-France* (Montreal: Boréal Express, 1984); Jean-Charles Farlandeau, "The Seventeenth Century Parish in French Canada," in *French Canadian Society*, ed. Marcel Rioux and Yves Martin (Toronto: McClelland and Stewart, 1964); Jonathan Pearl, "Witchcraft in New France in the Seventeenth Century: The Social Aspect," *Historical Reflections* 4 (1977).

On women, see the Clio Collective, *Quebec Women: A History* (Toronto: Women's Press, 1987); Alison Prentice, Paula Bourne, Gail Cuthbert Brandt, Beth Light, Wendy Mitchinson, and Naomi Black, *Canadian Women: A History* (Toronto: Harcourt Brace Jovanovich, 1988); Jan Noel, "New France: Les femmes favorisées," in *Rethinking Canada: The Promise of Women's History*, 2nd ed., ed. Veronica Strong-Boag and Anita Clair Fellman (Toronto: Copp Clark Pitman, 1991), 28–50; and Yves Landry, "Gender Imbalance, les Filles du Roi, and Choice of a Spouse in New France," *Canadian Family History: Selected Readings*, ed. Bettina Bradbury (Toronto: Copp Clark Pitman, 1992), 14–32.

CHAPTER 5

LIFE IN A STRATEGIC OUTPOST, 1715–60

The common man in Canada is more civilized and clever than in any other place in the world that I have visited. On entering one of the peasant's houses, no matter where, and on beginning to talk with the men and women, one is quite amazed at the good breeding and courteous answers which are received, no matter what the question is. . . .

I travelled in various places during my stay in this country. I frequently happened to take up my abode for several days at the homes of peasants where I had never been before, and who had never heard of or seen me, and to whom I had no letters of introduction. Nevertheless they showed me wherever I came a devotion paid ordinarily to a native or a relative. Often when I offered them money they would not accept it. Frenchmen who were born in Paris said themselves that one never finds in France among the country people the courtesy and good breeding which one observes everywhere in this land. I have heard many native Frenchmen assert this.[1]

When Peter Kalm, a European scientist and university professor, visited the English and French colonies in 1749–50, he was especially impressed by New France. He found productive farms, happy peasants, and a sophisticated governor: the Marquis de La Galissonnière regaled Kalm with his theories on "ways of employing natural history to the purposes of politics, the science of government." These conditions represented everything that an enlightened eighteenth-century gentleman found desirable. Kalm's judgments also reflected a view held by many visitors to the colony: that a distinctive Canadian culture was emerging on the banks of the St Lawrence. Although it was definitely French in tone and structure, New France differed from a province of old France, just as the regions of France differed from each other.

• The Imperial Factor

Between the death of Louis XIV in 1715 and the outbreak of the French Revolution in 1789, Europe entered a new era of social and material development. Economic expansion, population growth, and cultural brilliance characterized the age. Sometimes called the age of enlightenment, the eighteenth century was also the period in which European nation-states matured and were tested in economic and military rivalries. As in the previous century, developments taking place across the Atlantic would profoundly affect life in the colonial society of New France.

The death of Louis XIV brought a five-year-old child, Louis XV, to the throne of France. During the minority period (1715–23), Philip, Duc d'Orléans, directed state policy as regent. As a tool for an aristocracy anxious to regain its power, the duke restored the authority of the *parlements* and replaced bureaucrats on the councils with eminent aristocrats who pursued their own supposedly enlightened policies. Even Protestants and Jews would be tolerated as long as they kept silent in public. On one issue, however, the duke carried on the Sun King's tradition. Colonies remained low on the royal priority list. They were important only insofar as they enhanced the wealth of France and restrained the growth of rivals to French imperial power.

The problem of finding enough money to carry out the wishes of an absolute ruler always loomed large. Nobles and the clergy were reluctant to pay taxes, and there was a limit to what the overtaxed peasantry could bear. In an effort to pay off the massive debt that Louis XIV had accumulated, the Duc d'Orléans cut in half the army of over 400 000 and reduced the navy's allocation by two-thirds. Consideration was also given to making New France pay its share of taxes. Since its founding, colonials had been spared the direct taxes levied in France: the *taille*, the *capitation*, the *vingtième*, and the dreaded *gabelle*, or salt tax.

Both the governor-general and intendant warned authorities in France that Canadians would resist taxation because they, too, had suffered during the war. Moreover, they argued, colonists had contributed to the empire directly through military service, capturing English vessels, holding forts on Hudson Bay, and conducting border raids. Given these compelling arguments and the difficulty of forcing compliance in a frontier colony, the matter of a direct tax was dropped.

The nagging debt crisis induced the Duc d'Orléans to support a disastrous scheme put to him by the clever Scottish financier John Law. Law proposed to establish a government-sponsored central bank that would issue paper notes, expand credit, and encourage investment in a new trading company for the French colonies. By tying the bank to the Compagnie des Indes—another monopoly company with control over colonial enterprises, including the trade in furs, tropical produce, and slaves—and predicting vast profits from Louisiana, Law encouraged speculative investment in his project. The "Mississippi bubble" burst in 1720, as did the pocketbooks of many investors, undermining confidence in new colonial ventures.

Fortunately, the Regency ushered in a period of peace in the colonies that was not disrupted until a dispute about the succession to the Austrian throne led to a formal declaration of war in 1744. The War of the Austrian Succession (1744–48) and the Seven Years' War (1756–63) spelled disaster for French imperial dreams in North America, but the society that had been planted along the St Lawrence had expanded and matured in the first half of the eighteenth century to the point where it could withstand the most debilitating shocks.

• A New Strategic Role

In the thirty years following the Treaty of Utrecht in 1713, France moved to consolidate its North American empire. The forts along the Mississippi route between Louisiana and Canada were reoccupied and garrisoned, and the fur trade was subsidized to help sustain Native alliances. In the northwest, Canadian traders outflanked the Bay traders and set up trading networks with new nations in the far west. On Île Royale the fortified town of Louisbourg—the likes of which had never been seen before in North America—rose to prominence. The British would have much to reckon with when they faced France again on the battlefield.

In 1717 the Illinois country was attached administratively to Louisiana, and in the following year a base was established at Fort de Chartres. Posts were also maintained at Kaskaskia and Cahokia. Between 1716 and 1735 successive governors in New France pursued a sporadic military campaign against the Fox nation, which had resisted incursions into their territory. The Fox wars slowed development, but by 1731 there were 108 families, most of them originally from the Montreal area, as well as 44 soldiers, several missionaries, and scores of traders in Illinois country. Twenty years later the population had reached over 3000, including 1536 French and 890 African and Amerindian slaves. By that time large slave-worked estates were shipping wheat, flour, corn, cattle, and swine to Louisiana and the French West Indies.

In the years immediately following the Treaty of Utrecht, Louisiana was in desperate straits. Officially a regional jurisdiction, subordinate to officials in Quebec, Louisiana was in practice directly administered from

France, often with the help of Canadian-born officials. Even the seasoned Canadians found Louisiana a difficult challenge. In the first two decades of its existence, a high death rate from disease and famine conditions gave the colony a bad name and caused surviving troops and settlers to desert to nearby Spanish or English colonies. When John Law's Compagnie des Indes resorted to sending foreigners, felons, prostitutes, and even Protestants to the colony, and when they too succumbed to the rigours of the colonization process, it became virtually impossible to persuade people to go to Louisiana of their own free will. Freehold land tenure, offered as an inducement, brought little response. The colony produced no needed raw materials for the mother country; indeed, ships had trouble reaching the colony through the treacherous Gulf of Mexico and the swampy, mosquito-infested Mississippi Delta.

Despite the odds, Louisiana survived, but only because the French state willed it so. In 1722 the seat of government was moved from Mobile to New Orleans, considered a healthier site. Between 1719 and 1729, six thousand African slaves were brought to the colony. By 1739 only four thousand blacks could be counted; two-thirds of them were born in the colony, proving that Africans had no better chances of survival in the region than Europeans. Nevertheless, the colony began to produce for subsistence and export. The exports included pitch, tar, furs, hides, and eventually tobacco, silk, indigo, cotton, and rice. Troupes de la Marine were sent to defend the colony, and Ursuline, Jesuit, Carmelite, and Capuchin orders ministered to the spiritual and social needs of the settlers. By 1746 there was a white population of over four thousand, one-fifth of them soldiers. The cost to the crown of this ambitious colonization project was staggering: 20 million livres by 1731 and 800 000 livres a year thereafter to sustain the strategic outpost.

On the northwest frontier the French aggressively pursued trading alliances with the Natives in the Abitibi–Temiscaming region, along the north shore of Lake Superior, and into the Prairies. By the 1730s La Vérendrye and his sons were building posts around Lake Winnipeg and forging alliances with the Ojibwa, Cree, and Assiniboine. The English might well claim sovereignty over their posts on Hudson Bay, but they would have considerable difficulty controlling their inland supply routes. So aggressively did the French pursue their trading enterprises that the Bay men were forced to fight fire with fire, sending their own traders into the interior. In 1754 Anthony Henday set out on a journey that took him to the site of what is today Edmonton, Alberta, in an effort to persuade the Natives to bring their pelts to the Hudson's Bay Company posts.

By the mid-eighteenth century Canada's commercial hinterland consisted of most of the interior of the continent. Two main entrepôts, Detroit and Michilimackinac, served as headquarters for merchants, traders, and Jesuit missionaries as well as transhipment points. Detroit also had a garrison of troops and a summer population of over four hundred people. Outside the fort, five hundred settlers made a good living supplying the fur trade network from their productive farms. The Jesuit mission at Detroit served a resident population of 2600 primarily Ottawa, Petun, and Potawatomi, the largest aboriginal concentration in the Great Lakes basin.

LA VÉRENDRYE

The man who played the biggest role in establishing the French presence on the Prairies was Pierre Gautier de Varennes et de La Vérendrye. While serving as commander of a fur-trading post at the mouth of the Nipigon River, La Vérendrye heard from a variety of aboriginal sources about a "muddy lake" and a "great river" to the west. In the spring of 1730, a chief of the Kenisteno, called La Martleblanche by the French, promised to guide La Vérendrye to these mysterious bodies of water, which he hoped would lead to the Pacific. La Vérendrye sought and secured from Louis XV a commission to find the Pacific Ocean and a monopoly of the trade in the territories claimed by the Hudson's Bay Company. In the summer of 1732 La Vérendrye, two of his sons, a priest, and at least sixteen voyageurs joined an aboriginal war party of fifty canoes on a journey into the interior.

Over the next ten years La Vérendrye established a chain of trading posts stretching from the western end of Lake Superior (Grand Portage) to the Lake of the Woods (Fort Saint Charles), Lake Winnipeg (Fort Maurepas and Fort Rouge), the Assiniboine River (Fort La Reine), and Lake Winnipegosis (Fort Dauphin). The success of his effort depended upon alliances with the Cree and Assiniboine and their longstanding rivals, the Ojibwa and the Dakota. Anxious to maintain good relations with the Native nations, he chose several young men from each post to live with the local tribes. He even permitted two of his sons to be adopted by the Cree.

Although La Vérendrye's party never found the Pacific, one of his sons reached the foothills of the Rockies. La Vérendrye himself lost his fur-trade monopoly and died a poor man in 1744. Nevertheless, he left a significant legacy. French trading posts in the interior were a more convenient source of supplies for Native peoples than the distant posts on Hudson Bay. Only the limited capacity of canoes, the principal vehicle of inland trade, restricted the ability of the French to totally undermine the commercial activities of the Bay traders.

•Louisbourg

France's purposes in building a fortress at Louisbourg were to protect the St Lawrence entrance to its continental empire and provide a North American base for the lucrative fisheries. Like Louisiana, Louisbourg was an expensive venture, costing nearly 20 million livres to establish. But it was a top priority for the minister of marine, Jérôme Phélypeaux de Pont-chartrain, who was determined to maintain French pre-eminence in the fisheries. Construction of the fortified town began in 1720. Although it fell both times it was attacked and was never very effective in protecting the St Lawrence, Louisbourg soon became a major fishing port and a thriving entrepôt for the North Atlantic trade.

Even before the ink was dry on the Treaty of Utrecht, Louisbourg had a population of 116 men, 10 women, and 23 children, all of whom had moved from Placentia, Newfoundland, in 1713. The remainder of the evacuees arrived the following year. It proved more difficult to persuade the Acadians to leave their prosperous farms on the diked marshlands of the Bay of Fundy for the rocky soil and damp climate of Île Royale. The prospect of freehold land tenure—there would be no seigneuries on Île Royale—was no boon to the Acadians, who had enjoyed the benefits of, if not official title to, free land for nearly a century. Only sixty-seven Acadian families (some five hundred people representing less than one-quarter of the Acadian population) immigrated to Île Royale between 1713 and 1734. Most of them lived in areas outside the town where they could farm and fish for their subsistence.

For most of Louisbourg's short history under French rule, the majority of people who lived there came directly from France. French fishers and sailors often wintered in the town, some of them marrying local women and setting down roots. As in other French colonial possessions, the military were well represented, making up one-quarter to one-half of the population. The Récollets, Frères Hospitaliers, and Soeurs de la Congrégation de Notre-Dame located in the community. Although most of the residents were Roman Catholics, Louisbourg attracted people from a variety of ethnic and religious backgrounds. A significant proportion of the fishing community was drawn from the Basque-speaking region of southern France, and between 1722 and 1745 about 20 percent of the garrison consisted of German and Swiss soldiers of the Karrer regiment. Louisbourg's inhabitants included black and Native "servants," a few Irish, Scots, and Spanish sojourners, and even a Jew.

By the 1740s there were over two thousand residents in the town, and the population of the island had grown to over five thousand. Historian Kenneth Donovan has tabulated the origins of individuals married in Louisbourg between 1722 and 1745. His figures confirm the heterogeneous profile of the population and the tendency of European-born men to take colonial wives.

Not surprisingly, it was the primarily Newfoundland-born settlers from Placentia, the first people on the spot, who got the choice beach lots and the best land grants in and around Louisbourg. These fishing proprietors (*habitant-pêcheurs*) dominated the island's economy and helped to maintain a spirit of independence and nativism in the town. They also controlled the Superior Council until 1745, holding four of the five council positions. As in Canada, the leading officials in Louisbourg (a lieutenant-governor and *commissaire-ordonnateur*) were from France.

Louisbourg was a cosmopolitan place. Open to sea traffic for much of the year—fogs permitting—it was the single most productive fishing port on the North Atlantic, harvesting some 150 000 quintals of fish annually by 1720. An average of 154 ships a year called at the port, a number exceeded in North America only by Boston, New York, and Philadelphia. Although fish and fish oil were the only locally generated exports, the wharves in Louisbourg harbour were awash with manufactured goods, fishing supplies, and foodstuffs from France; molasses, sugar, and rum from the West Indies; foodstuffs and building supplies illegally shipped from New England, and foodstuffs and forest products from Canada. There was a sixfold increase in French seaborne commerce in the years between 1710 and 1740, and Louisbourg was one of the major beneficiaries of this growth.

French authorities also made efforts to entice the Acadians to move to Île Saint-Jean, but with no better results than they had on Île Royale. In 1719 the islands of Saint-Jean, Miscou, and Magdalen were granted to the Comte de Saint-Pierre with the stipulation that he settle the territory. Like most private colonization efforts, this one also failed. In 1726 the governor of Louisbourg was ordered to send over an armed detachment—all of thirty men—to confirm French sovereignty by occupying Saint-Pierre's dilapidated buildings at Port La Joie. By the 1730s the Parisian merchant Jean-Pierre Roma had some success developing the cod fisheries from his base at Trois-Rivières on the east end of the island. According to a census taken in 1735 there were 432 colonists on Île Saint-Jean, about a third of them of Acadian origin.

• The Canadian Economy

By the eighteenth century most of Canada's population was colonial-born but the economy of the St Lawrence colony was still largely being shaped by the interests of the mother country. Canada's strategic importance to the French empire in North America accounted for two of the three main sources of investment in the colony: the fur trade and the military. The third pillar of the St Lawrence economy, agriculture, also benefited from the need to supply the troops stationed in the colony and at the interior posts.

Fur remained Canada's chief export and was the focus for white–Native relations. Although the supply of beaver continued to decline from

***Buffalo**, a watercolour by Mark Catesby, 1724, is an example of a European painting that details the flora and fauna of the colony.*   (Windsor Castle, Royal Library. © 1992 Her Majesty Queen Elizabeth II, RE 26090, detail)

overtrapping in the eighteenth century, other fur-bearing animals more than took up the slack. The slaughter in the wilderness netted over 250 000 pelts a year in 1728, rising to over 400 000 by the 1750s, and the trade was worth about three-quarters to a million livres annually.

Table 5.1: FUR EXPORTS FROM QUEBEC (Number of pelts)

Year	Beaver	Other pelts	Total
1728	101 840	157 234	259 074
1732	106 929	176 078	283 007
1733	147 235	163 178	310 413
1735	118 353	187 035	305 388
1736	123 372	183 042	306 414
1737	82 524	273 609	356 133
1739	88 751	236 539	408 628
1754	88 301	320 327	408 628
1755	99 332	315 973	415 305

Source: H.A. Innis, *The Fur Trade in Canada: An Introduction to Canadian Economic History* (Toronto: University of Toronto Press, 1927), 153–54.

In 1700 a group of Canadians tried to gain control of the fur trade from their metropolitan creditors. The Compagnie de la Colonie went bankrupt six years later and the monopoly reverted to French interests. However, some of the profits from the trade, perhaps as much as 28 percent, remained in the colony. By the 1740s over forty *congés*, or licences, were granted each year, translating into seventy canoes used by four hundred *engagés*. Equipping these expeditions cost about 350 000 livres a season, of which about 150 000 was spent in the colony; *engagés* made another 100 000 livres in wages. A tax on the export of beaver pelts and moosehides, amounting to about 5 percent of the value of the trade, was collected at Quebec as a source of administrative revenue.

Montreal was the pivot of the trade, which reached far to the interior of the continent and back across the Atlantic to La Rochelle in France. Each year the convoys of canoes set out from Montreal for the *pays d'en haut* laden with items for the fur trade and supplies for the long journey and the interior posts. In the upper country the trade developed on a three-tier system. Forts Frontenac and Niagara operated as king's posts in direct competition with British interlopers and their agents at Oswego. To ensure its success, the trade was heavily subsidized by the state. At Detroit and Michilimackinac and other garrisoned posts the trade was controlled through *congés*, often held by officers, but there were still unlicensed *coureurs de bois* operating in their own interests or on behalf of unnamed merchants and royal officials. At Green Bay and posts west of Sault Ste Marie—the *mer de l'ouest* region where the trade was now the most lucrative—monopolies were leased by the crown to military officers and a few merchants.

La Rochelle *by Joseph Vernet*   (Louvre—dépôt du Musée de la Marine, © La Réunion des musées nationaux, Paris, detail)

As a result of this arrangement, by the 1750s the trade was controlled by thirty nobles and military officers. In 1751 royal instructions warned Governor La Jonquière that such a situation threatened the livelihood of the smaller merchants and might even undermine Native alliances:

> It would be wrong to leave you in the dark as to the complaints that have been reaching the King on the situation of the trade in Canada. It is said that the management of the posts has been arranged in such a way that the entire trade is in the hands of a private association made up of a handful of individuals among whom are the officers of the posts. Few business opportunities remain consequently for the colonial businessmen acting for those in France who normally send ships across. It is added that apart from the disreputability of the manoeuvring that thus occurs, the resulting abuses do great damage to the colony and its trade and even to our control over the Natives.

The appointment in 1748 of Intendant François Bigot only made a bad situation worse. By the mid-1750s Bigot and his corrupt friends were bilking the colony of millions of livres siphoned from the spiralling appropriations for the fur trade and military operations in the colony.

These were not the only abuses. To avoid customs duties and export controls, furs shipped on the accounts of colonial officials were loaded onto fishing vessels at Kamouraska or the Gaspé or unloaded clandestinely in France before reaching La Rochelle. Other traders bypassed Quebec by shipping out of New Orleans, or even New York via Oswego and Albany. The trade through New York was officially condemned but unofficially winked at because of its many advantages. These included sizable profits, immediate payments, and access to English trade commodities, which were eagerly sought by Canadians and Natives alike.

The necessity of satisfying their Native allies was acknowledged in an official memorandum as early as 1717:

> The Trade with the Natives is a necessary commerce; and even if the Colonists could get along without it, the State is, as it were, forced to maintain it, if it wishes to hold on to the country. . . . There is no middle course; one must have the native as either friend or foe; and whoever wants to have him as a friend must furnish him with his necessities at conditions which allow him to procure them.[2]

Manufacturers at Montpellier, Montauban, Carcassonne, and Rochefort in France made goods specifically for the fur trade. Far from being blindly exploited, taken in by inferior quality and short measure, the Native traders were discriminating in taste and value, and they commanded and received goods of acceptable standards.

THE CHINA CONNECTION

Although the fur trade was the golden goose of the Canadian economy, the colonists briefly made fortunes on ginseng, a plant that grew wild in the St Lawrence valley. The ginseng root was much prized in Asia for its reputed medicinal, restorative, and aphrodisiac properties. It came to the attention of the Jesuits through correspondence with their counterparts in Manchuria, where the root was harvested by the peasants. Father Joseph-François Lafitau at the Caughnawaga (Kahnawaké) reserve, near Montreal, identified the plant in the neighbouring woods. By 1721 Canadian ginseng shipped to France was being sold in Canton, China. The market boomed in the late 1740s when a regular trade was established through the Compagnie des Indes, which obtained the exclusive right to sell ginseng in the Orient.

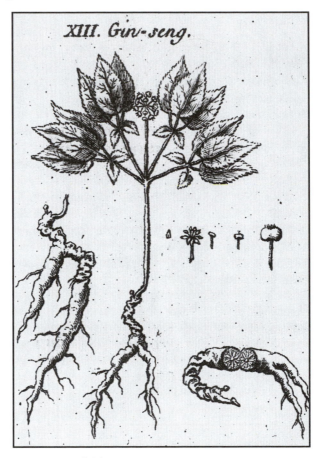

Etching of ginseng, 1744   (National Archives of Canada/C103993)

With the value of the trade at La Rochelle approaching 20 percent of the revenues from the fur trade, ginseng fever struck the colony. The governor reported:

> In 1751, the merchants learning of the popularity that ginseng enjoyed in France, besides the great shipments sent to China, entered into agreements with the habitants to furnish them with certain quantities. Some even equipped canoes to go off to the ginseng hunt among the Natives and others who picked it. The latter perceiving the favour this root enjoyed and the little heed that was paid to its quality and if it had been prepared well or not, had it dried precipitously in ovens and sold it for up to 20 [livres] a pound. The merchants took it at the price asked, delighted to find an outlet for their wares.

Even the religious communities sent their domestic servants and slaves to gather the precious root. When preparing his report on colonial agriculture, the engineer Louis Franquet remarked that the Canadian farmers were neglecting their harvests and could not find Natives willing to help them because everyone seemed bent on making quick money by gathering ginseng.

As with so many colonial ventures, the ginseng boom was a short one. In 1751 the Compagnie des Indes refused to purchase the stocks accumulating in La Rochelle, and by 1752 ginseng was selling for only 9 livres a pound in Canton. Because of its inferior quality, the Chinese refused to purchase the Canadian product. Thereafter the Compagnie des Indes would buy only properly harvested and treated roots. A very modest trade continued until the conquest, by which time the plant had been hunted virtually to extinction. Abbé Raynal, who frequently commented on colonial affairs, noted, "The colonists were severely punished for their excessive rapaciousness by the total loss of a branch of commerce, which if rightly managed, might have proved a source of opulence."

TABLE 5.2: VALUE OF GINSENG EXPORTS

Year	Value in Livres
1747	12 900
1748	10 125
1749	76 300
1750	65 562
1751	152 100
1752	484 120
1753	33 000

Source: Brian Evans, "Ginseng: Root of Chinese-Canadian Relations," *Canadian Historical Review* 61, 1 (March 1985): 1–26.

An ancillary activity associated with the strategic role of the colony and the fur trade was the military establishment. Although it is impossible to separate the exact amounts that were spent maintaining troops and fortifications from the general crown expenditures in New France, most years the military had the lion's share of the appropriations. Between 1715 and 1744 the cost of military and administrative activities in Canada ranged from around 500 000 to 600 000 livres. When the colony was put on a wartime footing in 1744, the annual budget soared to over a million livres and stayed in that range until the conquest. The French government also spent large sums on arming and equipping the Canadian militia, which was of direct benefit to the colonists, and on presents to their aboriginal allies. In wartime the crown provided subsistence for the families of the Native auxiliaries, who fought side by side with the colonial militia and the regular troops.

Other than furs, few colonial resources proved successful as exports. Although sawmills became a familiar site on the Canadian landscape— there were fifty-two in operation by 1752—they produced squared timber and lumber primarily for local use. Shipbuilding proved more successful. By the 1730s colonists were building 150-ton and 200-ton vessels. A royal bounty of three livres per ton stimulated investment, and in most years Canadians completed eight to ten vessels that qualified for the subsidy. With the expansion of the West Indies trade, ships were built in the colony specifically to carry flour, wood products, and stoves to the Antilles.

Military needs proved to be a vital stimulus to shipbuilding. In 1731 the navy placed orders for the construction of ships-of-the-line at the royal shipyards on the St Charles River near Quebec. Ten warships were built for the French navy in the 1740s and two more in the 1750s before the project was dropped. Appropriately, the first warship launched was christened *Le Canada*, but the pride of the shipyards was *Le Caribou*, a 700-ton man-of-war. In the 1750s, four naval vessels were built to patrol Lake Ontario.

Comparing the experience with that of nearby English colonies, contemporaries and later historians judge New France's shipbuilding industry a failure. Admittedly, there were problems. In 1741 imported skilled workers brought to the colony under contract resented the Canadians who were hired seasonally by the day, bringing construction activities to a halt. The imported workers complained that they had poor housing and unfair working conditions compared to the Canadians, who were sometimes better paid and given leave during inclement weather. Intendant Gilles Hocquart "found it necessary to repress in the beginning, and once only, by imprisonment and irons, their mutiny which went to the point of resisting the orders of their commandant." The official report of the incident concluded that the mutinous workers "recognized their error and are now very docile." Constituted authority was prepared to deal harshly with insubordination from the lower orders, and in pre-industrial society there was little working-class consciousness that might have induced the Canadian workers to co-operate with their metropolitan brothers to protect their collective economic interests.

The ships built in the colony also cost too much. In part this was because of the corruption that characterized state activities in New France. One commentator noted tersely, "Many expenses which have no relation-ship to construction are put on the account." An even bigger problem was the quality of the final product, which rotted quickly. Without proper facili-ties for drying and storing the lumber, it was exposed to the elements and soon deteriorated. Moreover, colonists rapidly depleted the supply of hard oak and pine in the St Lawrence lowlands and were forced to use less sturdy timbers, which led to an inferior product. While the colonials lacked the resources and skills to construct the huge 500-ton ships required by the navy, they had no difficulty producing the thousands of fishing boats, coastal vessels, and bateaux that served their local needs.

In the eighteenth century, mining got underway in Île Royale, where coal reserves near the ground surface were easily exploited. With the age of steam still a century away, coal was used primarily as a source for heat and could not as yet form the basis of a booming industry. Denys La Ronde spent 25 000 livres bringing equipment and two German experts to explore the possibilities of exploiting the copper deposits in the Lake Superior region, but little came of the venture.

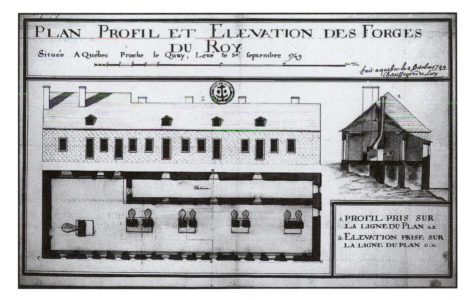

Plan of forges at Quebec, 1749   (Archives nationales, Paris: Section Outre-Mer)

Iron was a basic commodity for people in pre-industrial Europe, and Canada had an excellent source on the banks of the St Maurice River about twelve kilometres from Trois-Rivières. In 1730 a Montreal merchant, François Poulin de Francheville, opened a bog-iron plant there to provide the colony with forged iron for stoves, cauldrons, pots, axeheads, and the small tools and implements required in the colony. After his death in 1735 the ironworks were taken over by François-Étienne Cugnet. With a royal subsidy of 100 000 livres, Cugnet began full-scale production, but within five years the company was bankrupt and the state assumed full management of the forges. As a state enterprise, the company occasionally made a profit. In 1747 the ironworks began experimenting with steel-making and cannon founding with a view to supplying the military, but such efforts had barely got off the ground before the conquest.

Like the shipyards, the St Maurice ironworks were less than a complete success as an economic venture, and for some of the same reasons. Skilled workers had to be imported and mistakes were made in the construction and layout of the plant. One investigation also revealed "a great number of useless People employed there . . . at large salaries." Clearly, capitalist notions of efficiency were not always uppermost in the minds of those pioneering such enterprises. In any case, industrial capitalism had yet to transform the way that people worked and planned their manufacturing ventures. What is significant is that the French state supported these new efforts in its colonies and that a new way of thinking about economic activities was beginning to take shape in the North Atlantic world.

Artisan production was one area where European traditions were allowed to lapse in the French (and other) North American colonies. In France, guilds controlled the progression from apprentice to journeyman and master craftsman, and they exercised the right of inspection over a trade. But in the colonies, the crown restricted the operation of guilds and reserved the supervision of all manual trades to itself. When master roofers in Quebec asked for *la jurande*, or the right to control the standards of their trade, the Superior Council rejected their request on the grounds that "There are in this town neither master craftsmen nor jurandes, nor the exclusive right to pursue a particular craft or trade."

In the absence of guilds the state regulated, as corporate bodies, the bakers, butchers, surgeons, midwives, and notaries and permitted the church to exercise regulatory authority over the activities of itinerant schoolmasters and private tutors. The state also encouraged the religious activities of these corporate groups. Within each trade *confréries*, or religious fraternities, organized annual religious observances in honour of the craft's patron saint. While such organizations had the potential for collective political action, they remained essentially religious and social institutions.

The guild system in Europe was already breaking down by the time that colonists began moving to North America. In New France it was scarcely allowed to get a foot in the door. Nor would Canadians have reacted well to guild regulations. The ideal in the colony—as it was throughout much of European-settled North America—was to be a "Jacques of all trades," free to work as needs determined. A few colonists entered partnerships to learn a trade, and apprenticeship was still common, but these arrangements were often short-lived and less regulated than in France. Journeymen, those who had served their apprenticeship and were required to practise their trade as a wage earner for a period (usually six years) before becoming a master craftsman, virtually disappeared in New France. Most shops were small family affairs consisting of a master who worked with the help of his wife and older children, and perhaps one or two apprentices. They produced goods on order, not in large quantities, striving for honest subsistence and, if possible, an easy living, rather than ever-increasing wealth.

There was, to be sure, money to be made in commerce in New France for anyone with ambition and connections. All colonists, including the nobility after 1685, had the right to engage in trade. In 1706 foreign merchants were permitted to set up shop in the colony. With its failure to develop industrially, the colony relied on France for a number of crucial commodities: cloth and clothing, wines and brandies, guns, powder and lead, utensils, salt, and a variety of luxury goods. A score of importers in Montreal and Quebec did a comfortable business bringing in merchandise from France and selling it to the one hundred or more *négociants*—traders, outfitters, and shopkeepers—whom Intendant Hocquart believed to be double the number the colony could support. The degree of competition can be imagined when one considers Intendant Bigot's exaggerated claim in 1754 that the fourteen Protestant firms in Quebec controlled three-quarters of the commerce of the capital.

Merchants in Quebec were also active in organizing their own interests. In 1708 they established a *bourse*, an organization similar to a board of trade, and rented a house for its activities. A royal decree of 1717 authorized the merchants in Montreal and Quebec to meet every day in a suitable place to carry out their business and to make representations to the king on matters of policy that would benefit their trading activities. In a 1719 communication to the king, this tightly knit community of Canadian merchants made specific reference to their colonial origins, claiming to "have had great-great-grandfathers, great-grandfathers, grandfathers, their fathers, in this colony, or they came to settle there, that they have their families there, most of which are large, that they were the first to contribute to establishing it, that they have opened up and farmed lands in it, built churches . . . had fine homes built, contributed to fortifying the towns, supported the war."[3]

Women played a significant and direct role in the commercial life of New France. They worked with their husbands in commercial and artisan establishments and operated businesses as diverse as taverns and sawmills. Some women became active in trade when their husbands were away on business or died prematurely. Marie-Anne Barbel, for instance, took over her husband's business interests when he died in 1745, continuing his partnership in a fishing concession and his fur trade operations. Just as any man would do in similar circumstances, she traded properties, established new businesses, and took her adversaries to court. She continued to make a comfortable living for herself and her unmarried children until her death at the age of ninety.

By the 1740s François Havy and Jean Lefebvre, representing the firm of Dugard in Rouen, were the most powerful merchants in Canada. They retailed goods in both Quebec and Montreal, invested in sealing expeditions along the Labrador coast, and exported wheat to Louisbourg. Smaller merchants in the towns, and eventually a few pedlars who travelled the seigneuries along the river, stocked imported items and made their living by retailing. Like the first nations, Canadians were becoming discriminating consumers and could not be sold inferior products, a trait that earned them the accusation of being vain.

Canadian merchants were dependent upon their metropolitan suppliers and appear to have been perpetually indebted to them. The Chamber of Commerce of La Rochelle observed in a memorandum of 1734: "It is also well-known that the merchants of Quebec as well as Montreal, convinced that they could not extend their business except through credit obtainable in France, were convinced since time immemorial to pay eight percent per year for the advances made to them, so that this arrangement became a common usage which may be said to be as old as the colony itself." Such long-term credit arrangements were typical of the pre-industrial world in which banks, accounting structures, corporate values, and rapid transportation networks were still in their infancy.

In addition to the private trade, which occupied at least fifteen vessels each year out of La Rochelle, the crown shipped supplies to the colony to support its military establishment and related state activities. This was a highly profitable trade for the metropolitan merchants and their Canadian contacts. Supplies for colonial troops were brought at cheaper prices and the crown bore the risks of the voyage—shipwreck, piracy, spoilage, and capture in wartime. Even if the ship were lost at sea or the cargo spoiled, the contractor would receive his commission. In some cases contractors could also draw upon naval stores and sailors to outfit their ship. Bordeaux emerged as the major port in this trade. By the late 1750s merchants there were sending an average of twenty-seven vessels each summer to Canada, and they accounted for half the total imports of the colony.

During the 1750s, the Bordeaux connection in the supply trade took on a special significance. Intendant François Bigot organized a ring with Bordeaux merchants and Canadian collaborators to monopolize the lucrative supply trade. Members of this *grande société* amassed large personal fortunes by mismanaging military appropriations and defrauding the colonists. In addition to Bigot, the principal culprits were Governor Vaudreuil the younger and Joseph Cadet, *munitionnaire* (supplier of the Ministry of War). In all, twenty-two millionaires emerged from this operation. Bigot headed the list with a fortune of 29 million livres followed by Governor Vaudreuil with 23 million and Cadet with 15 million. The military elite in the colony generally accounted for 35 million livres, the bureaucrats attached to the intendant's office for 79 million, and those in charge of the stores for another 20 million—although they were millionaires in paper money only. When the war ended and the bills of exchange were discounted to the tune of 85 percent, the wealth of these rascals was greatly deflated. Nevertheless, excessive profiteering did little to advance the French cause in the Seven Years' War or the colonial economy.

Bigot had developed his skills while stationed at Louisbourg, which was also a place where officials found easy opportunities for lining their pockets. In this busy entrepôt, clandestine trade was particularly lucrative. Port registers indicate that the greatest number of vessels clearing the harbour were from the English colonies and the West Indies. Even the vessels owned by Louisbourg residents were often of New England origin.

THE FATE OF FRANÇOIS BIGOT

François Bigot was born in 1703 in the Bordeaux region of France. The Bigot family had risen to prominence over three generations, and young François was probably attracted to the marine department because his cousin had briefly served as its chief minister. Known for his passion for gambling and pretty women, as well as for his ambition, Bigot was appointed financial commissary to Louisbourg in 1739 and intendant to Canada in 1748. Bigot had no great desire to live in the colonies, but he saw service there as an opportunity to make his fortune. In taking advantage of his posting, he was no different than other colonial officials. He nevertheless differed from most of them because he was brought to trial for his corrupt administrative practices.

Following the surrender of Canada, Bigot and many of his former business associates were arrested. The state needed a scapegoat for the loss of the colony, and the activities of the *grande société* were so outrageous that they had reached the ears of the highest authorities in France. By exposing Bigot the king could also justify the decision to default on the colonial debts that had been accumulated during the war. Bigot spent nearly two years in the infamous Bastille before being brought to trial in 1763. A tribunal of twenty-seven magistrates handed down a seventy-eight-page indictment, announcing Bigot's banishment for ever and the confiscation of all of his property. Several of Bigot's close associates were also heavily fined.

Shortly before the judgment was delivered, Bigot moved to Switzerland, where he lived under an assumed name. Although not destitute, he lived less elegantly than he had planned, and he suffered from poor health. He died on 12 January 1778 at Neuchatel. As requested in his will, he received a modest burial: "I desire that my body be buried in the cemetery at Cressier without any pomp, just as the poorest person in the parish would be."4

• Town Life

The administrative, commercial, and religious activities in Canada guaranteed a limited but vibrant urban life. In 1757 the French commander Montcalm judged Quebec to be the equal of most French towns. As the port and capital of Canada, located on one of the most imposing sites in North America, Quebec had grown from a population of five hundred in 1660 to ten times the size a century later. Importers and artisans mixed in Lower Town, while administrative and religious services were concentrated in Upper Town. Dominating all was the Château Saint-Louis, the residence of the governor-general. At the rear of the town stood the intendant's palace, which served as his official residence and the meeting place for the Superior Council, the Quebec Prévôté, and the Admiralty Court. Stone fortifications ran behind the town from the St Lawrence to the St Charles River.

Quebec was a busy place, especially in the spring when ships began arriving from France. Then, once the mails were delivered, dignitaries suitably entertained, supplies placed in the storehouses, and the crews rejuvenated in the local taverns, the fur brigades began moving down from Montreal with their winter harvest—at least the part of it that was being legally shipped back to La Rochelle. During religious holidays, which marked a large number of days on the Roman Catholic calendar, Quebec could mount the most impressive processions, with all ranks of society well

The intendant's palace at Quebec, 1761   (Richard Short/National Archives of Canada/C360)

accounted for. The town was home to the highest ranking officials in church and state as well as over 350 skilled artisans representing more than thirty different crafts.

Quebec's narrow streets were crowded with people and animals. Market day brought people from the countryside and leisure activities were conducted in public. "The lower class people of both sexes meet right under my windows after supper," Bishop Dosquet complained to the minister of marine in 1731. "They sing and engage in very free talk. . . . That is where the drunks come to sober up. . . . On feast days and Sundays the noise that the people make there playing ninepins and bowls is head-splitting."[5]

Montreal was Canada's second-largest town, with over four thousand inhabitants in the mid-eighteenth century. By that time it had lost much of its earlier religious tone and taken on the trappings of a frontier garrison town, dominated by soldiers and men of the fur trade rather than the Sulpicians. Dominated by Mount Royal and protected by a stone wall, Montreal, like Quebec, made an impressive site. Its island location was surrounded by prosperous farms and flanked by Native communities. During the summer Natives from the interior were also frequent visitors. Rich and rowdy, especially when brigades were assembling for, or arriving from, the *pays d'en haut*, Montreal may have been less dignified than Quebec, but it was certainly a more lively place.

LIFE IN QUEBEC

Many of the houses in Quebec were built of stone, especially in Lower Town, where merchant houses, some of them three or four storeys high, were crowded together to take advantage of the waterfront location. Following a disastrous fire in Montreal in 1721 and another in Quebec in 1726, Intendant Claude-Thomas Dupuy reissued a ban on wooden buildings in towns, forbade the construction of mansard roofs, and decreed that roofs be built of overlapping boards or slates. He also required that houses have cellars and that frames be built of lighter timbers so they could be easily dismantled in case of fire. Chimneys were to be set in firewalls projecting above roofs. In the case of semi-detached houses, a fire wall was mandatory between the two dwellings. Such regulations, coupled with the limited skills of colonial carpenters and masons, meant that towns in New France soon developed a standardized architecture.

By the middle of the eighteenth century Quebec was a tenant's town, with over half of the town's population renting rather than owning their dwelling places. The mobility of the population and the competitive economic climate made it difficult for labourers and artisans to earn enough money to purchase a home. While widows in Quebec had the highest rate of home ownership, they were also the most likely people to rent out rooms. The favourite time for moving to new lodgings, then as now, was in the first week in May, when spring encouraged new beginnings.

In backyards throughout Quebec, but especially in the expanding precincts of Upper Town, people grew gardens, kept live animals, and built their privies. Pigs and cattle commonly wandered the streets unattended. When the citizens wanted to discard refuse, they simply spread it on the unpaved streets, thus adding new odours to those already wafting from the open sewers that carried the town's liquid sludge to the river's edge. Butchers and fishmongers were required by law to carry their wastes to the river and wash away the blood and refuse from their shops and market stalls. Apparently they obeyed the edict: when Peter Kalm visited Lower Town he remarked that it was built on a promontory of rubbish. Within a year of his visit in 1749, inhabitants of Quebec were being asked to discard their garbage at the north end of Saint-Pierre Street where "ships did not land too often."[6]

By the 1740s Louisbourg was a handsome town, reflecting the most advanced thinking in urban planning and defensive strategy. On top of the town's highest hill stood the major public buildings, all constructed in stone. The royal fleur-de-lis graced the elegant bell tower that topped the imposing citadel. A thick stone and mortar rampart, with outer rings of ditches and earthworks, encircled the town. Around the harbour, gun batteries were mounted with heavy cannon to ward off enemy attack. With a population of over four thousand, and even more in the summer when the fishing fleets and merchant traders were in port, Louisbourg hummed with activity.

The people of colonial towns were remarkably law-abiding. Tavern brawls and the occasional duel between officers were de rigueur, but the presence of the Troupes de la Marine made law and order a relatively easy matter for authorities. As the size and complexity of town life increased, so too did the number of vagabonds and foundlings. In the 1730s the state's cost of maintaining *enfants bâtards* in Canada became a cause for concern: nearly 5000 livres for Quebec, nearly 8000 livres in Montreal, and slightly over 1000 livres in Trois-Rivières. The crown responded by reducing the stipend for the care of the infants, but it was clear from their numbers and the proliferation of other proscribed activities—including maintaining mistresses, drinking, gambling, and prostitution—that colonial society reflected the relaxed moral values that also characterized French society in this period. Later, when an air of fatalism seized the colony during the Seven Years' War, public and private morality, as defined by the church, would reach a low ebb.

The care of foundlings became one of the prime concerns of the Soeurs Grises, or Grey Nuns, a religious community in Montreal that received official sanction from the king in 1753. Founded by Marie-Marguerite d'Youville, the Soeurs Grises devoted their energies to the care of the sick and poor. The problem of abandoned infants led them to take in about twenty babies a year. A death rate among the unfortunate foundlings of 80 percent—typical of such institutions in Europe—underscored the fragility of life in institutional settings in the pre-industrial world.

The towns were also the centre of the intellectual life in New France. In addition to the religious orders that had long provided the colonies with a high standard of education and social services, there developed a class of civilian intellectuals, both French and colonial-born, whose interests reflected the preoccupations of the enlightenment philosophers of France. Two eighteenth-century medical doctors, Michael Sarrazin and Jean-François Gauthier, for instance, sent reports on the natural history of Canada to the Academie Royale des Sciences in Paris. Marie-Élisabeth Bégon, a resident of Montreal, excelled in the eighteenth-century art of letter writing. With

Ex-voto of three shipwrecked persons from Lévis. Ex-votos often commemorated miraculous events.   (Musée, Basilique de Sainte-Anne de Beaupré)

France on the cutting edge of European intellectual life in the eighteenth century, the colonial elites relied heavily upon their mother country for the ideas that animated their dinner conversations. They neither produced their own newspaper nor bothered to import a printing press.

Painting, sculpture, and architecture were stimulated in New France by the demands of the growing urban elite, as well as by church and state. While much of the fine furnishings that graced the elegant homes and public buildings of the towns came from France, local artisans also practised their skills in fine crafts. Surviving *ex-votos* (paintings commemorating miraculous events), portraits of notable citizens, beautifully carved pine furniture, and locally crafted silver plate all testify to the rich level of material culture that was produced in eighteenth-century New France.

•Canadian Peasant Society

Trade, services, and artisan production in the towns engaged only a small proportion of the Canadian population. By the mid-eighteenth century over 80 percent of Canadians lived in the rural countryside, where they farmed the soil. Most of these habitants were Canadian-born. Although the fur trade still attracted the young and unmarried men, most of them came from the towns of Montreal and Trois-Rivières, not from the seigneuries. Meanwhile, many of the common immigrants to the colony, whether *engagés*, salt smugglers, soldiers, or free pioneers, gradually found themselves absorbed into the countryside where a peasant culture had taken root.

In the early years of settlement the process of creating a farm from the tree-covered banks of the St Lawrence was backbreaking and soul-destroying work. At best a peasant family could clear two *arpents*—roughly one hectare—a year, and a farm of thirty to forty arable *arpents* was the most that could be expected from a lifetime of labour. The children of the first generation had an easier task. Not only were they used to the hard work involved, but they could also live at home while starting their new farms.

By the mid-eighteenth century seigneurial farms had spread along both sides of the St Lawrence, down the Richelieu River, and up the Ottawa. A second and sometimes even a third *rang* of seigneuries was being carved out behind original grants. Parish churches, a few seigneurial manors, and many small habitant houses dotted the landscape. The houses of the habitants were usually constructed of squared logs, whitewashed and topped with a thatched or cedar roof. Their ground floors, averaging eight by six metres, were divided into two or three rooms. Manor houses tended to be more imposing and often built in stone. Besides the main house, a manor would usually include a wooden barn with a central threshing floor and bays for storing hay and grain, stables for horses and cattle, a shed, an outdoor oven, and perhaps other small structures for specific functions.

A typical peasant farm might consist of a hundred arpents, about ten times the size of a peasant holding in France—although not all of this land was cleared or arable. The farm would produce heavy yields for the first decade and then drop well below the metropolitan level of production. Rapid soil depletion necessitated the clearing of more forest land on the upper reaches of the river-front farm. Wheat was the chief cereal crop, but Canadians also grew flax, oats, barley, and peas. At the interior posts the colonists learned to grow corn, the staple crop of the Iroquois nations. Almost every farm in the St Lawrence valley had kitchen gardens planted with onions, cabbage, beans, carrots, lettuce, radish, beets, parsnips, and a variety of herbs. Around Montreal, which had more fertile soils and a longer growing season than Quebec, apple, pear, and plum trees, as well as melons and pumpkins, did particularly well. Tobacco was harvested in the sandy soils around Trois-Rivières, but most kitchen gardens throughout the colony included some tobacco among their plantings. By the end of the French regime, horses, cattle, and sheep grazed on the marshes and uplands, and pigs and poultry roamed the farmyards. A 1709 ordinance

Street Scene, Quebec at Night, *by Clarence Gagnon. The painting shows an old* *habitant house.*   (National Gallery of Canada/1449)

stipulating that no person was to keep more than two horses and a foal seems to have been ignored. Canadians raised horses for farm work and transportation and even for racing.

Despite injunctions from intendants that crop rotation, fertilization, and selective breeding be practised, most peasants engaged in extensive, rather than intensive, agriculture. Habitants produced mixed crops for their own subsistence and not for a specialized market. Only near Quebec and Montreal was there any obvious attempt to respond to market demands. Although there were usually surpluses to be sold in the nearby towns, peasant agriculture rarely managed to produce enough for export. One of the biggest difficulties facing the peasant farmers was the fact that wheat was not ideally suited to the soil and climate of the St Lawrence low-land. Early frosts, smut, rust, drought, or infestations of grasshoppers and caterpillars reduced wheat yields. In years of poor harvest—seventeen times between 1700 and 1760—flour had to be imported. In 1749 hungry peasants congregated in the towns. Intendant Bigot, reminded of the periodic bread riots in France, quickly opened the storehouses and enacted regulations to prohibit begging and vagrancy.

By the third generation of settlement, the problem of excessive subdivision of the holdings loomed large. This process was encouraged by the Custom of Paris, which required that all children in non-noble families share equally in inheritance—whereas in noble families a larger portion of the estate was bestowed upon one heir. The habitants responded to the problem in a variety of ways. One strategy involved an arrangement whereby one or two children acquired the family farm; the others took their inheritance in cash or kind and could then move to outlying regions individually or in groups. This process brought people from different seigneuries together in a new settlement. Yet another approach was to send the older children to other seigneuries with their moveable inheritance while the parents entered into a contract, usually with the youngest son still under the parental roof, requiring him to care for his parents in their old age in return for the farm. This *donation* among the living heirs enabled the family to avoid inheritance laws.

Finally, in areas where farms had become too small to ensure subsistence, habitants made attempts to supplement farm income by gaining winter employment on government construction projects, in the fur trade, or in the timber trade. It was usually the more prosperous habitant families whose sons turned to wage labour. A few even managed to take up trades permanently and set up shop in the villages that had begun to develop in the rural countryside. The most prosperous habitants bought farms from their poorer neighbours for their children, while the original owners moved to new settlements. Although undeveloped concessions were free, no one could enter farming without money to buy the tools, animals, and seeds needed to get started and enough provisions to last until the first crops were harvested.

Most of the peasants in New France lived better than their European counterparts, rarely facing the famine and levels of taxation that still oppressed the peasantry in France. Although they remained near the bottom of the social hierarchy in the colony and had much lower literacy rates than their immigrant ancestors, they enjoyed a relatively high level of material culture. They were notorious for their lack of discipline and defiance of authority. "The ordinary habitants would be scandalized to be called peasants," one contemporary commentator observed. "In fact, they are of better stuff, have more wit, more education, than those of France. This comes from their paying no taxes, that they have the right to hunt and fish, and that they live in a sort of independence."

By the mid-eighteenth century, the habitants had become the solid base of the colony that Colbert had once hoped for. Soon the influence of France would be eliminated, the fur trade frontier would be taken over by the Hudson's Bay Company traders, the military establishment would be staffed by foreigners, and the towns would be transformed by an influx of English-speaking administrators, soldiers, and merchants. But the farming communities along both sides of the St Lawrence would remain intact and largely French in culture—just as they are today.

• The Family Under the French Regime

Among all the people of European origin—whether they were on the peasant farm, in the artisan shop, or in the governor's mansion—the family in New France was the fundamental social unit. It was in the family that most of the colony's production took place, where services were administered, and where pain and pleasure alike were experienced. Even on the frontier, families thrived. Commandants, for instance, often took their wives and children with them to the interior posts or formed close relationships with aboriginal women.

Canadians married young and often. In France in the eighteenth century the average age of marriage for women was twenty-five; in New France it was twenty-two. Men in both places were usually three or four years older. In New France men remarried within a year or two after losing a wife; women after three years of widowhood. In New France *coureurs de bois* often took Native companions and produced Métis children. No doubt owing to the influence of the church and the relatively young age of marriage, illegitimacy rates were low, only ten or twelve per thousand compared to much higher rates in the twentieth century. Sex was officially for procreation, not pleasure, although prostitution was practised in the larger towns, where a population of unmarried soldiers and labourers provided a ready market.

Canadian families were large. Because of the younger age of marriage, Canadian women had more children on the average than women in France. A woman who survived her childbearing years in the eighteenth century could expect to give birth to about seven or eight children. In Acadia, where the age of marriage was lower than on the St Lawrence, the average family was even larger. Families provided most of the social services that were taken up by the state in the twentieth century. Children were born at home with the assistance of an experienced midwife, and much of the education in practical and productive skills took place under the watchful eye of parents. When people were sick or injured they were treated in their homes. Without a family, an individual was forced to rely on the church-operated public institutions.

MADAME BÉGON

Marie-Élisabeth Rocbert was the eldest daughter of the king's storekeeper in Montreal. In 1712 Claude-Michel Bégon de La Cour, a sublieutenant suffering from a variety of war wounds, including a missing eye, became a boarder in the Rocbert home. When the young people fell in love, their marriage was opposed by Bégon's older brother, Intendant Michel Bégon, on the grounds that Marie-Élisabeth was of lower rank. Because military men could not marry without the consent of the governor, the intendant was in a position to put a stop to the wedding plans for several years. The

Madame Bégon (Photographie Giraudon, Paris/Archives nationales du Québec)

lovers responded by marrying *à la gaumine*. Since common-law marriages were vigorously condemned by the church, the intendant finally relented and permitted the relationship to be regularized on 19 December 1718.

Madame Bégon gave birth to five children, only one of whom survived her. A daughter had died in 1740, leaving two young children to be raised by their grandmother. Her husband, who rose to the position of governor of Trois-Rivières, died in 1748. Following his death Bégon started a lengthy correspondence with her widowed son-in-law, Michel de La Rouvillière, a man almost her own age who had become the financial commissary of Louisiana. These thinly disguised love letters described public and private events in New France. Since Bégon was well connected to important people in the colony—the acting governor of the period, La Galissonière, was her nephew by marriage—she had many important visitors and was well informed. In 1749 Bégon moved to Rochefort, France, where she apparently hoped to attract her elusive son-in-law. She continued to keep in touch with her native land through letters and visits from people returning to France, and she passed on this information to La Rouvillière. He died in 1752 and Bégon died three years later. Her letters provide a unique perspective on the political and social history of the final years of the French regime in Canada.

Weddings were social events, surrounded by Christian and pagan customs. The rituals included the *charivari*, a noisy gathering of young people in the community under the window of a recently married couple. If the marriage were socially questionable—a widow who had remarried too soon after the death of her husband, or a couple of too unequal age—the affair could take a menacing tone. Occasionally couples married *à la gaumine*, without the benefit of clergy, and common-law relationships were even more likely to take place on the fur trade frontier where marriage *à la façon du pays* reflected Native customs and the absence, or defiance, of priestly injunctions. The church frowned on all such unions. It also discouraged marriages with Protestants or non-Christians, or of a couple too closely related, and it proscribed all homosexual relations.

Death was a frequent visitor to families in pre-industrial society. Urban areas were particularly dangerous places to live, with their high vulnerability to the epidemics that periodically ravaged the colony. In 1702–03 an outbreak of smallpox in Quebec took the lives of 350 people—nearly 20 percent of the town's population. Because of the high death rate, marriage partners could expect their unions to last only fifteen or twenty years or so before the grim reaper took one of them away. Women and children were the most vulnerable. On average one in four children died in the first year of life, and childhood diseases prevented a good many of the rest from reaching the age of fifteen. It was a relatively common occurrence for women to die in childbirth, which meant the death rate for women between the ages of fifteen and forty-nine was higher than the rate for men in the same age group.

In pre-industrial society, families were important economic units, with everyone working together to ensure collective survival. No peasant farm could thrive without the work of all members: father, mother, and children. Property was most commonly received through inheritance, not purchase. For elite families, *protection*, or patronage, first went to members of the family—as exemplified by the adeptness of the Colberts and Pontchartrains at finding positions for their relatives within the Ministry of Marine. In 1704 Governor Vaudreuil wrote to the minister on behalf of his own children: "I have eight boys and a girl who need the honour of your protection. Three of them are ready for service. I entered the musketeers when I was as young as my oldest. I hope you will have the goodness to grant to me for him the company of the Sieur de Maricourt who has died."[7]

Marriage was also a business partnership to which a woman brought a dowry in return for her husband's patronage. Dowries varied in amount according to class and, especially among the peasantry, might be largely in kind—household linen, items of furniture, clothes, or livestock. When her husband died, a woman was expected to continue living in the manner to which she had become accustomed in marriage. The law of dower was an attempt to ensure that this was the case. Marriage contracts sometimes stated that a wife would receive a fixed dower no matter what outstanding debts were held against her deceased husband's estate. A woman without a fixed dower was entitled to the "customary dower," that is, "the enjoyment" for life of one-half the husband's estate, but she was obliged to pay the outstanding debts and the dues on the land, as she was required to maintain the real property so it could pass intact to her husband's heirs.

Like society as a whole, families in New France were hierarchical, with the father at the top. Unless a wife made a special contract, all of her possessions were controlled by her husband. Children belonged first to their fathers, and they could not marry without his consent until the age of twenty-five for daughters and thirty for sons. Because marriage was so critical to the family's economic well-being and social status, it was an event that could not be entrusted to the wishes of consenting partners alone.

The colony's approaches to childrearing and education were transplanted from France. Because so many children died in infancy, parents tried to avoid strong emotional attachments to their babies, and grieving parents found consolation in the popular belief that their deceased infants became angels who interceded on their behalf in heaven. Particularly in elite families, swaddling, wetnursing, and early toilet-training were part of infant regime. To inculcate respect for authority, obedience, and discipline, corporal punishment was liberally administered. One of the views commonly held in New France was that the Native peoples' permissiveness with their children and the lack of formal schooling accounted for their "uncivilized" behaviour. The religious orientation of French education reinforced authoritarian practices. Children were taught to emulate their teachers in their devotion to self-discipline, abstention, and fasting. When children were disobedient, they were threatened with the fiery hell and terrifying demons of eternal damnation.

Despite the seemingly harsh discipline, most families enjoyed a reasonable level of domestic harmony. The need for habitant families to function as a unit of production coupled with religious teachings encouraged co-operative behaviour. In the eighteenth century, the cults of the infant Jesus and the Virgin Mary introduced a less rigorous approach toward those in subordinate positions within the family. Gradually, too, the examples of Native childrearing practices may also have made an impact. Joseph-François Lafitau remarked that, despite the lack of discipline, Native children were "quite docile, show sufficient respect to those in their cabin, and to their Elders." They never seemed to wish to be emancipated from their obligations to their kinfolk, as did European children. Indeed, he concluded, "In the matter of raising children, kindness is often more effective than punishment, especially than violent punishment."

Lafitau's remarks may well reflect the tendency of educated people in the eighteenth century to see aboriginal culture in a more positive light. The idea of the "noble savage" appealed to those who perceived with increasing clarity the flaws in the social system of the *ancien régime*. According to several intendants, Canadian youth showed a remarkable lack of discipline and were prone to an independent spirit. Freedom and independence would soon become the watchwords for revolutionary groups throughout Europe and North America. Perhaps the authorities were reading things into the behaviour of Canadians that reflected their own growing concerns.

•Class and Society

On the evening of 3 July 1744, Angélique Butel, wife of Quentin Le Lievre, a small job merchant, was beating her child for having disobeyed her. Servanne Bonnier, wife of the butcher Pierre Santier, was passing by the house and interceded on the child's behalf, claiming that Butel was a "whore" and that she did not like her children. . . .

Butel and Bonnier exchanged insults and accusations on several occasions that evening and Butel eventually took Bonnier to court, accusing her of slander. During the trial, one witness testified that Butel claimed that Bonnier was "not of the same rank. . . ." Apparently, the wife of a butcher had no right to tell the wife of a small job merchant, who assumed she had a more prestigious social position in the community, how to discipline her children.[8]

This case, heard before the Louisbourg courts and described by historian Kenneth Donovan, tells us more than the fact that some eighteenth-century mothers beat their children and that there were others who obviously disapproved of such behaviour. Angélique Butel's presumption of superiority reveals the significance of rank and status even among the lower classes of colonial society.

There is no indication that New France in the eighteenth century had become more egalitarian than society in Europe, or that social distinctions had become less pronounced. Indeed, quite the reverse seems to be true. As the population grew and as communication across the Atlantic became more reliable, the values of Europe seem to have taken root more firmly than ever. The emphasis on class and rank under the *ancien régime*, and the privileges that went with such distinctions, eventually led to violent revolution in France in 1789. In New France, before a revolution could occur the conquest intervened, neatly removing the top echelons of the French ruling elite and substituting English conquerors.

Social structure in New France was not built on economic differences alone. Rather, social rank dictated economic behaviour. Social position, achieved by birth or influence, demanded a particular way of life, and people in New France, whether they could afford to or not, lived on a scale deemed appropriate to their rank. Those who did otherwise were widely scorned. Governor Jean de Lauson, for example, was criticized by his contemporaries because he lived without a personal servant and ate only pork and peas, like a common artisan or peasant, while peasants who used their horses for racing rather than farm work earned disapproving comments from authorities.

For many members of the colonial elite, maintaining the outward show of their status often kept them on the edge of bankruptcy. Those below them, in contrast, could live simply while accumulating wealth. One tanner in Quebec, for example, possessed only 82 livres of clothing and furniture when he died but held promissory notes to the amount of 4312 livres. Wealth, of course, usually went hand in hand with rank. Those higher up on the social ladder had access to more forms of wealth, including seigneurial grants, military appointments, and commercial opportunities.

While a great gulf existed between the nobility and the common folk, there was a precisely defined pecking order among the members of the middle classes. Fine craftsmen, for example, distinguished themselves from those who practised more common trades, and royal officers had more status than municipal officials. Rituals and ceremonies observed throughout the colony reinforced this hierarchy. In a church the benches were assigned so that the elite sat closest to the front, with the middle classes behind them. The lower orders sat or even stood at the back. People dressed, lived in homes, and behaved in public in ways that "befitted their station."

Women usually derived their status from their husbands' positions. By examining the conventional dowers stipulated in forty-five marriage contracts, historian Peter Moogk uncovered a class structure that accurately reflects what other historical sources tell us about rank in New France (see table 5.3).

Table 5.3: OCCUPATIONAL HIERARCHY OF NEW FRANCE BASED ON CONVENTIONAL DOWER

Ranking by Average Dower	Other Occupations
I. The Elite (2000–8000 livres per annum)	
Commissioned military officers	Senior clergy and nuns
Senior judicial and administrative officers	
II. Honourable Employments (800–1500 livres)	
Architects	Minor clergy
Master builders in stone	Wholesale merchants
Silversmiths	Royal notaries
Non-commissioned officers	
III. Good Trades (600–750 livres)	
Hatmakers	Land surveyors
Surgeons	*Hussiers*
Shoemakers	
IV. Modest Occupations (425–500 livres)	
Metalworkers	
Woodworkers	
Private soldiers	
V. Base Occupations (400 livres or less)	
Stonemasons	Food retailers
Tenant farmers	Carters
Tailors	Sailors
	Hired servants

Source: Peter Moogk, "Rank in New France: Restructuring a Society from Notarial Documents," *Historie sociale/Social History* 7, 15 (May 1975): 43.

At the top of the social hierarchy in New France was the *noblesse*, a class of military officers, administrators, and the highest ranking church officials holding letters patent of nobility. The *noblesse* in New France had its own special features. Nobles in the colonies—unlike those in France—were allowed to engage in trade without being stripped of their titles. It was also possible, by combining seigneurial, military, commercial, and administrative functions in a way that would draw the attention of the king, for an ambitious young commoner to achieve noble status. As individuals rose up the social scale, they also often managed to "marry up," especially in a second or third marriage—although upward mobility was easier in the seventeenth than in the eighteenth century. It was also easier in the early years of settlement for individuals to claim noble status that they did not have. In 1684 those who used the title *écuyer* (esquire) in legal documents were ordered to give proof of their pretensions. They were fined if they made false claims.

Because they had large families, the nobility was more than able to perpetuate itself, even though few colonials were ennobled in the eighteenth century. The restrictions on upward mobility did not, however, stop those in the upper echelons of the middle class from seeking the trappings of noble life. By 1760 nearly 50 percent of the seigneurs in the colony were members of the middle class. The middle class also sought places in the Troupes de la Marine for their sons, but these, too, dried up over the course of the eighteenth century. With only 112 positions in the officer corps and fifty-six cadetships, commissions in the Troupes were the objects

CHARLES LE MOYNE: A SELF-MADE NOBLEMAN

The son of a French innkeeper, Charles Le Moyne arrived in New France in 1641, at the age of fifteen. He worked for the Jesuits for a time and then became a fur trader, interpreter, and soldier. In 1654 he married a commoner, Catherine Thierry, and together they had twelve sons and two daughters. Le Moyne, who became one of the most successful merchants in Montreal, distinguished himself in the wars against the Iroquois and received small seigneuries before being raised to noble status in 1668. Four years later he was granted the seigneury of Longueuil. As members of a noble family, Le Moyne's sons easily found commissions in the military. His eldest son, Charles, was named Baron de Longueuil in 1700 and received the coveted *Croix de St-Louis* in 1703. Another son, Pierre Le Moyne d'Iberville, had a distinguished military career. Yet another, Jean-Baptiste, usually known by his noble title Bienville, was a long-time governor of Louisiana.

of bitter competition among the leading families of the colony. Historian W.J. Eccles argues that by 1753 these positions were reserved almost exclusively for the sons of Canadian officers.[9]

The church also reflected the rigid class system that prevailed in Canada in the eighteenth century. While the Quebec seminary recruited most of its students from the colony, it was not an institution that advanced the careers of peasant boys. Most recruits came from the noble and wealthier middle-class families. Toward the end of the French regime there was a marked increase in sons of artisans entering the priesthood, but only two of the 195 ordained colonial-born priests between 1611 and 1760 were sons of common farmers.

Its aristocratic ethos and military flavour made New France distinct from its English neighbours. The colony came by its snobbish image honestly. After all, the court of Versailles was the centre of diplomatic life in Europe, French was the common language of the European elite, and the French army was the envy of absolute rulers everywhere. The strategic role defined for the colony, with its garrisoned towns and interior fur trading posts, enhanced the values of superiority. Bigot and his friends perhaps best exemplified the objectives of both the Canadian-born and the transient French elite in the colony during the *ancien régime*. They puffed up their fortunes so they could do what all self-respecting nobles aspired to: build a fashionable château and enjoy the good life.

The elite were not the only ones inspired by the aristocratic ideal. Peasants had virtually no chance of moving up the social scale in eighteenth-century New France. They nevertheless aped the values of their social superiors and had a better standard of living than most of their counterparts in France. They melted down coin to fashion decorative ornaments as a way of saving their wealth and remained largely immune from the market opportunities that awaited them. They, too, enjoyed being lords of their domaines, even if they were only seigneurial concessions. Nor were they excluded, as were most Europeans in this period, from military conscription. With the colony at war or under the threat of hostilities for much of the eighteenth century, the military ethos penetrated deeply into the social fabric of New France.

• Slavery

In pre-industrial society the problem of securing a reliable labour force had resulted in a variety of work-inducing institutions, including seigneurialism, indentured labour, and slavery. All of these forms of labour took root in New France, albeit under somewhat modified circumstances. Although they would come under assault as the industrial revolution made wages the primary incentive for making people work, they remained integral features of colonial society under the *ancien régime.*

Slavery was typical of many aboriginal societies around the world, including North America, but it became a very different institution when it was transplanted to the commercial colonies of the New World. Black slavery, in particular, developed insidious characteristics. As slavery became equated with skin colour, racial stereotyping soon followed. Eventually it became difficult for any black person to be other than a slave, and the distinction between servant and slave, once narrow, widened precipitously.

Records show that there were at least 4000 slaves in the colony between 1680 and 1800. About 1500 of these slaves were black and another 2500 were aboriginal. The first black "servants" to arrive in the French colonies came with de Monts and Champlain to Acadia. It is highly likely that Mathieu d'Acosta, a black man who knew "Acadian tongues," served as an interpreter on at least one of these early voyages to the region. Another black "servant" is recorded as having died of scurvy at Port Royal. Aboriginal slaves began arriving in the colony in the late 1680s when Pawnee from the Mississippi region were sold to French explorers and fur traders. The French called all slaves of Native origin *panis* (Pawnee), but they took slaves from a number of first nations. Slave owners were uncertain of the status of their chattels, especially Native slaves, until 1709 when Intendant Jacques Raudot proclaimed slavery to be legal.

Slaves throughout the French empire were governed by the Code Noir. Under its provisions slaves could be bought and sold as property, but their owners were obliged to house, feed, and clothe them properly and care for the aged and infirm. Slaves were to be encouraged to marry, and all of them were to be instructed and baptized in the Roman Catholic religion. Although masters could whip their slaves, they could not imprison or execute them without recourse to the courts. Women were not to be sexually exploited, nor children sold separately from their parents before reaching adolescence.

During the French regime, Canadians on several occasions asked the crown to dispatch African slaves to the colony to help relieve the perpetual labour shortage. Such shipments never came to Canada, in part because of the curious belief of the period that Africans were especially ill-suited to northern climates. African slaves were, however, common in Louisiana, the Illinois country, and the French West Indies. Most of the African slaves who came to Canada were purchased from one of these colonies or picked up as "prizes" in raids on the English colonies. In Canada slaves did the same work as common labourers.

Slaves, whether black or aboriginal, were expensive. The price of a black slave ranged between 200 and 2400 livres and averaged about 900 livres. Native slaves were worth less, about 400 livres, no doubt because of the greater supply and the likelihood of them running away. Because of their cost, slaves were purchased only by the wealthier colonials. Governor Charles de Beauharnois owned twenty-seven. Marguerite d'Youville, founder of the Soeurs Grises, owned several slaves, as did Bishop Laval. Institutions operated by the church often relied heavily on the labour of their unhappy chattels. Like all moveable property, slaves could be passed on by inheritance. Charles Le Moyne, the first Baron de Longueuil, left seven slaves when he died—a mother and father and their five children. He instructed that they be divided among his two sons.

Both black and Native slaves had an appallingly short life expectancy: 17.7 years for Natives and 25.2 for Africans, compared to nearly 50 for white colonials. Slaves could marry only with the permission of their owners, and their children became the master's property too. Baptismal records usually record only the master's name, not that of the mother. Nearly 60 percent of slave children were born out of wedlock, sometimes fathered by other slaves, more likely by the master or the master's son, who often had no compunction about exercising the *droit de seigneur* on a chattel slave. As a result, Métis and mulatto children were relatively common in the elite families who owned slaves. Blacks and Natives were encouraged to marry each other, and forty-five of these "mixed" marriages were recorded.

Nearly 80 percent of the slaves in Canada were baptized into the Roman Catholic Church, over 12 percent of them just before death. Baptism, among other things, meant that they received a Christian burial and a Christian name, most commonly Marie, Joseph, Jean, and Pierre. Slave owners very likely had mixed feelings about the conversion of their slaves. Although the Code Noir required that slaves be instructed in the Roman Catholic religion, conversion might well put the morality of slavery in doubt.

Few records have survived of slave resistance to their treatment. An exception is the case of Marie-Joseph Angélique who, when threatened with sale, set fire to her owner's house and ran away. She was caught and condemned to death for defying her master. A more positive case is recorded in 1753 in Louisbourg, where Jean-Baptiste Cupidon, a free black servant, purchased the freedom of his future bride.

•Labour

Much of the work in New France conducted outside the family context was done within the structure of feudal obligations. Seigneurs could extract dues from their *censitaires*, who were also required to work a stipulated number of days on the seigneur's *demesne*. In addition, the crown imposed the *corvée*, a requirement to work a certain number of days on public works. These obligations remained an important feature of the work world in New France and, indeed, would be carried on for many years after the conquest.

Merchants or administrators requiring a fully committed work force commonly used indentured labour, contracted for a specific period of time. The fur trade's *engagés*, or voyageurs, were usually recruited in the colony, as many as four hundred a year. Perhaps because of the profits to be made and the adventure associated with the trade, it seems there was little difficulty finding enough young men willing to take the backbreaking trip into the interior. However, it then became impossible to find the extra hands required at harvest time or to help build the roads that were becoming increasingly necessary as the population moved inland. Because of the shortage of labourers, the crown permitted soldiers in the colony to work for wages when they were not needed for military duties.

The shortage of labour led to the arrival of the largest single source of French immigrants to Canada in the eighteenth century, other than soldiers: men who had been condemned as salt smugglers. During the Regency period, Governor Vaudreuil had asked the Duc d'Orléans to have his officials send out poachers, counterfeiters, and salt smugglers as a source of labour for the colony. In the 1730s these unfortunates, who had often committed no more serious crime than to attempt to circumvent the *gabelle*, were still being rounded up and sent to Quebec.

Available records indicate that nearly nine hundred salt smugglers arrived in New France between 1730 and 1745. They do not seem to have been treated much differently from *engagés*. A dispatch from the minister of marine in 1739 announced that, of eighty-one salt smugglers sent to Canada, all had either been incorporated into the troops or distributed to individuals or communities offering good contracts. They were not hardened criminals and were regarded in the colony as individuals possessing a great deal of initiative, creativeness, and independence of mind, all qualities admired and useful in a society itself in creation.

• Conclusion

By the mid-eighteenth century French institutions and culture had made a major impact on the North American environment. Europeans who owed their allegiance to France lived in communities stretching from Île Royale through the St Lawrence–Great Lakes heartland to the mouth of the

Mississippi. Although their numbers were small—some sixty thousand in total in Canada and Acadia in 1750—the French had set down permanent roots.

Meanwhile, aboriginal populations had been reduced through epidemics. The numbers of beaver and other fur-bearing animals had also been drastically reduced. Only the European population, supported by its metropolitan homeland, continued to show remarkable capacity for expansion, its numbers doubling every twenty-five to thirty years.

Indeed, most of the people in New France in 1750 had been born in North America and were beginning to call themselves "Canadians" and "Acadians." With little more than a century of colonial settlement behind them, they had succeeded in adapting to a new climate, in creating an uneasy alliance with their aboriginal neighbours, and making North America their home. They may have been subjects of the French king, but they had also become citizens of their own new world.

•Theocratic Tyranny or Benevolent Paternalism?
A Historiographical Debate

The noted American historian Francis Parkman, writing in the late nineteenth century, portrayed the inhabitants of New France as ignorant, superstitious, downtrodden colonials crushed under the heavy weight of stifling mercantilist restrictions, metropolitan intervention, an oppressive and despotic monarchy, and an even more powerful and fanatical church. He asserted that the "fault" of the absolutist monarchy and authoritarian church "was not that they exercised authority, but that they exercised too much of it, and, instead of weaning the child to go alone, kept him in perpetual leading strings, making him, if possible, more and more dependent, and less and less fit for freedom."[10]

Similar views of colonial rule were perpetuated by both British imperial and English-Canadian historians until quite recently. Among the French-Canadian historians, Canon Lionel Groulx, in formulating his views of the dominant role of the church in colonial life, came closest to the Parkman interpretation. However, Groulx celebrated rather than criticized New France's authoritarianism. He described a "proper subordination" of the state to the church in the laying down of "the foundations of the social and political order" of his future Quebec.

At the opposite pole of the debate came Guy Frégault's interpretation of French rule as benevolent paternalism. According to Frégault, colonial administration concerned itself with poor relief, hospitalization and medical care, welfare provisions, building regulations, price controls, and the supervision of the church's charitable and educational institutions. Land was free and there was no direct taxation. Although New France was not Utopia, it could stand favourable comparison with New England.

It was William J. Eccles who documented and refined this interpretation, to the point that New France emerged as an embryonic welfare state in which the health, safety, security, and contentment of the population was a major concern of the governing class. As Eccles stated, "The basic premise, not merely of royal policy, but of all social institutions—indeed the basic premise upon which society in New France rested—was individual and collective responsibility for the needs of all."[11]

This concern for the welfare of the community should not be confused with democracy: in France the Estates-General had not met since 1614, and there were no elected assemblies in the French colonies. Still, the people of New France were not completely powerless. Royal edicts contrary to the interests of the colonists were never implemented; the council at Quebec did not register and proclaim them, but delayed action by asking for further instructions and suggesting amendments in the time-consuming process of government through annual correspondence. There were also avenues for the expression of popular will in the colony in the form of consultative assemblies, *fabriques*, and *bourses*. Moreover, several historians have noted that the colonists did not seem entirely submissive or as respectful of their social superiors as convention required. Eccles attributes this to the relative independence of the colonial farmer, to the influence of the Native peoples and fur traders, and also to the slow implantation of social distinctions.

Cornelius Jaenen concludes, in his study of the role of the church in Canada, as does Charles O'Neill for Louisiana, that the clergy was frustrated in its attempts to dominate either socially or politically: "The colonists were far from docile, subservient, downtrodden, inarticulate, priest-ridden peasants. Contemporary documentation shows them to be remarkably independent, aggressive, self-assertive, freedom-loving and outspoken individuals."[12] Terence Crowley, in examining popular disturbances in the colony, found that people demonstrated against what they considered to be unfair impositions, or against government inaction to remedy perceived injustices such as hoarding or profiteering. They protested the abuse of power but did not rebel against constituted authority.

New France, then, appears to have been neither a theocracy nor a tyranny. The clergy may have wielded great power in the period before 1663, but royal authority would soon assert itself in line with Gallican principles of the mother country. As for royal power, it was attenuated by a wide ocean, a cumbersome bureaucracy, and the relative unimportance of the colony. It was also more successful than private enterprise in populating and sustaining the colony in a difficult northern climate. The social legislation that Eccles underscores flowed not only from what Frégault and others called paternalism, but also from Catholic social teaching regarding the responsibilities of elites, just price, and charity. According to the prevailing views of the period, the common good should have priority over individual interest and advantage. The coming of British rule would introduce a different philosophy while providing an element of continuity.

•Notes

[1] *Peter Kalm's Travels in North America*, Vol. 2, ed. Aldolph B. Benson (New York: Dover Publications, 1966), 558.

[2] National Archives of Canada, MG7, A–2, I, Fonds français, Ms. 12105, memorandum of le Maire [1717], 83.

[3] Cited in André Vachon et al., *Taking Root: Canada from 1700 to 1760* (Ottawa: Public Archives of Canada, 1985), 235.

[4] See J.F. Bosher and J.-C. Dubé, "Bigot, François," in *Dictionary of Canadian Biography*, Vol. 4, *1771 to 1800* (Toronto: University of Toronto Press, 1979), 59–70.

[5] Cited in Vachon, *Taking Root*, 242.

[6] See Yvon Desloges, *A Tenant's Town: Quebec in the Eighteenth Century* (Ottawa: National Historic Sites Parks Service, Environment Canada, 1991), 106.

[7] John F. Bosher, "The Family in New France," in *Readings in Canadian History: Pre-Confederation*, 3rd ed., ed. R. Douglas Francis and Donald B. Smith (Toronto: Holt, Rinehart and Winston, 1990), 117.

[8] Kenneth Donovan, "Tattered Clothes and Powdered Wigs: Case Studies of the Poor and Well-To-Do in Eighteenth-Century Louisbourg," in *Cape Breton at 200: Historical Essays in Honour of the Island's Bicentennial, 1785–1985*, ed. Kenneth Donovan (Sydney, NS: University College of Cape Breton Press, 1985), 5.

[9] W.J. Eccles, "The Social, Economic and Political Significance of the Military Establishment in New France," *Canadian Historical Review* 52, 1 (March 1971): 1–22.

[10] Francis Parkman, *The Old Régime in Canada*, Vol. 1 (Toronto, 1899), 199.

[11] W.J. Eccles, *Essays on New France* (Toronto: Oxford University Press, 1987), 39.

[12] Cornelius Jaenen, *The Role of the Church in New France* (Toronto: McGraw-Hill Ryerson, 1976), 155.

•Selected Reading

In addition to the works cited in the previous chapter, see Dale Miquelon, *New France, 1701–1744: "A Supplement to Europe"* (Toronto: McClelland and Stewart, 1987), and André Vachon et al., *Taking Root: Canada From 1700 to 1760* (Ottawa: Public Archives of Canada, 1985), for excellent surveys of developments in New France in the eighteenth century. On the history of Louisbourg, see Christopher Moore, *Louisbourg Portraits: Life in an Eighteenth Century Garrison Town* (Toronto: Macmillan, 1982), A.J.B. Johnson, *Religion in Life at Louisbourg* (Montreal: McGill-Queen's University Press, 1984), and Kenneth Donovan, "Tattered Clothes and Powdered Wigs: Case Studies of the Poor and Well-To-Do in Eighteenth Century Louisbourg," in *Cape Breton at 200: Historical Essays in Honour of the Island's Bicentennial, 1785–1985*, ed. Kenneth Donovan (Sydney: University College of Cape Breton Press, 1985), 1–20. See Georges Arsenault, *The Island Acadians, 1720–1980* (Charlottetown: Ragweed, 1989), for information on the early history of Île Saint-Jean. On the "upper country," two recent studies deserve attention: Charles J. Balesi, *The Time of the French in the Heart of North America, 1673–1818* (Chicago: Alliance Française, 1992); Joseph L. Peyser, *Letters from New France: The Upper Country, 1686–1783* (Urbana: University of Illinois Press, 1992).

Specialized studies include Harold Innis, *The Fur Trade in Canada: An Introduction to Canadian Economic History* (Toronto: University of Toronto Press, 1927); André Lachance, *La vie urbaine en Nouvelle-France* (Montreal: Boréal Express, 1987); Hubert Charbonneau, *Vie et Mort de Nos Ancêtres* (Montreal: Les Presses de l'Université de Montréal, 1973); Allen Greer, *Peasant, Lord and Merchant: Rural Society in Three Quebec Parishes, 1740–1840* (Toronto: University of Toronto Press, 1985); Jacques Mathieu, *La Construction navale royale à Québec, 1739–1759* (Quebec: Société historique de Québec, 1971); Brigitte Caulier, "Les confréries de dévotion à Montréal du 17e au 19e siècles" (PhD thesis, Université de Montréal, 1986); Paul Lemieux, "Le clergé catholique de la Vallée du Saint-Laurent, 1756–1810" (MA thesis, University of Ottawa, 1986).

Articles that explore specific topics include John F. Bosher, "The Family in New France," in *Readings in Canadian History: Pre-Confederation*, 3rd ed., ed. R. Douglas Francis and Donald B. Smith (Toronto: Holt, Rinehart and Winston, 1990); Brian Evans, "Ginseng: Root of Chinese–Canadian Relations," *Canadian Historical Review* 61, 1 (March 1985): 1–26; James Pritchard, "The Pattern of French Colonial Shipping to Canada before 1760," *Revue française d'histoire d'outre-mer* 63, 231 (1976); Allan Greer, "The Patterns of Literacy in Quebec, 1745–1899," *Histoire sociale/Social History* 11, 22 (Nov. 1978); Terence Crowley, "'Thunder Gusts': Popular Disturbances in Early French Canada," *Historical Papers/Communications historiques* (1979); John Dickinson, "Reflexions sur la police en Nouvelle-France," *McGill Law Review* 32, 2 (1987); Peter Moogk, "Les Petits Sauvages," in *Childhood and Family in Canadian History*, ed. Joy Parr (Toronto: McClelland and Stewart, 1982), and "Rank in New France: Restructuring a Society from Notarial Documents," *Histoire sociale/Social History* 8, 15 (May 1975); Lilianne Plamondon, "A Businesswoman in New France: Marie-Anne Barbel, The Widow Fornel" in *Rethinking Canada: The Promise of Women's History*, ed. Veronica Strong-Boag and Anita Clair Fellman (Toronto: Copp Clark Pitman, 1986); Gratien Allaire, "Fur Trade Engagés, 1701–1745" in *Rendezvous: Selected Papers of the North American Fur Trade Conference 1981*, ed. Thomas C. Buckley (St Paul, MN: Minnesota Historical Society, 1984), and "Officiers et marchands: les sociétés de commerce des fourrures, 1715–1760," *Revue d'histoire de l'Amérique française* 40, 3 (1987); Louise Dechêne, "L'Évolution du régime seigneuriale au Canada: le cas de Montréal aux XVIIe et XVIIIe siècles," *Recherches sociographiques* 12, 2 (1971); Yves Zoltvany, "Esquisse de la Coutume de Paris," *Revue d'histoire de l'Amérique française* 25, 3 (1971). On slavery in New France, see Marcel Trudel, "Ties That Bind," *Horizon Canada* (1985).

On historiographical questions, see Serge Gagnon, *Quebec and Its Historians: The Twentieth Century* (Montreal: Harvest House, 1984); Dale Miquelon, *Society and Conquest: The Debate on the Bourgeoisie and Social Change in French Canada, 1700–1850* (Toronto: Copp Clark Pitman, 1977); Paul Bennett and Cornelius Jaenen, eds., *Emerging Identities* (Scarborough, ON: Prentice-Hall, 1986); Roberta Hamilton, *Feudal Society and Colonization: The Historiography of New France* (Gananoque, ON: Langdale Press, 1988).

CHAPTER

CONQUEST ACHIEVED, CONCILIATION ATTEMPTED, 1713–91

6

> Why do you suffer the white men to dwell among you? . . . Why do you not clothe yourselves in skins, as your ancestors did, and use the bows and arrows, and the stone-pointed lances, which they used? . . . You have bought guns, knives, kettles, and blankets, from the white men, until you can no longer do without them; and what is worse, you have drunk the poison firewater, which turns you into fools. Fling all these things away . . . and as for these English . . . you must lift the hatchet against them.

So spoke Pontiac, the Ottawa chief in the Detroit region who led an armed uprising against the British in 1763. Pontiac's insights came too late to save his people or himself. Although the first nations living along the Anglo-American frontier scored spectacular successes against the hated British, they were soon forced to surrender the posts they had captured. Their dependence on European guns, ammunition, and even food made it difficult for them to sustain a prolonged campaign now that their French allies could no longer help them.

After more than a century of interaction with European traders, soldiers, and missionaries, the primarily Algonkian-speaking nations in the *pays d'en haut* had adopted new cultural practices that were threatened by the victory of the British in the Seven Years' War. No longer able to play one empire off against the other, the Native peoples fought among themselves for supremacy and turned to new chiefs and prophets for reassurance in the face of famine and poverty. Pontiac himself became a victim of the confusion and desperation of his people, who resented the fact that he finally agreed to peaceful relations with the British and monopolized all the attention of the white authorities. In 1769 he was assassinated by the nephew of a Peoria chief in Cahokia. His death, according to historian Richard White, was "a monument to the limits of chieftainship."[1]

•Enemies and Alliances

The eighteenth century was a time of intermittent warfare as European powers struggled for supremacy and first nations fought to secure their own advantage in a rapidly changing North American environment. It was also a century in which liberal ideologies inspired people to challenge the authority of absolute rulers. Between 1744 and 1791 two European wars—the War of the Austrian Succession and the Seven Years' War—and two revolutions—the American and the French—transformed politics and society in the North Atlantic world. These struggles also sealed the fate of France in North America and profoundly altered the relationships between Natives and newcomers.

The long period of relatively peaceful relations between 1713 and 1744 gave Britain and France a chance to position themselves for another contest. On the surface the British had the upper hand in North America. Their colonies had grown in population and wealth, while the French holdings remained sparsely settled and economically dependent upon their mother country. In theory, when the British colonies conscripted human resources for war they could draw upon a population base of nearly one million people; French possessions, including Louisbourg and Louisiana, had less than one-tenth that number.

Balanced against this demographic reality was the Amerindian population of North America. The Treaty of Utrecht in 1713 gave Britain control over Iroquois territory and the Hudson Bay region, but it had been slow to develop formal policy with respect to the people living in these areas. France, in contrast, had been aggressive in pursuing Native alliances. By the 1740s most of the interior of the continent, as well as the Atlantic frontier, was occupied by first nations loosely allied with France.

The success of the French in developing alliances with the first nations was a result, in part, of Louis XIV's decision to use the fur trade as a diplomatic tool. By supplying the Natives with manufactured items, including the weapons they needed for hunting and fighting, the French became the preferred trading partners of many aboriginal nations. The French abandoned the goals of direct sovereignty and settled for exercising protective rights over the territory occupied by their Native allies.

The French had learned early in their colonization experience that aboriginal peoples would accept neither European claims to land ownership and sovereignty nor French laws and taxes. If alliances were to succeed, the French were obliged to recognize the original inhabitants of North America as "free and independent people" with title to their ancestral lands. Alliances embodying such provisions were signed with much pomp and ceremony, and were reinforced by the annual distribution of "King's presents." These agreements remained secure only as long as the French were willing to accept the fact that they were partners and protective patriarchs, not overlords. Just as they shared the air and water, the French and aboriginal peoples could share the land and its resources, which were in theory given by the creator for the common good of all people.

ABORIGINAL RIGHTS AND NATIVE SELF-GOVERNMENT

When Roberval attempted the first settlement in 1542–43 near Stadacona, in the region inhabited by the Laurentian Iroquois, his commission instructed him to "enter these lands and put them in our possession, by means of friendship and amicable agreements, if that can be done, or by force of arms, strong handed and all other hostile means." Over the next two centuries, the French took formal possession, asserting their sovereignty over a vast portion of the continent, but in terms of appropriating land for European settlement in both Acadia and Canada, they never found it necessary to displace Native inhabitants. On the contrary, in Canada, they succeeded in attracting Native people to abandon inland regions and relocate near French settlements on reserves.

Governor Rémy de Courcelles was instructed in 1665 by Louis XIV to see that all colonial officials and settlers "treat the Natives with kindness, justice and equity, without causing them any harm or violence; that the lands they live on never be usurped on the pretext it would be better if they were in French possession." The policy thereafter was the restriction of French settlement to a narrow belt along the lower St Lawrence River, thus leaving the hinterland to the self-governing and independent Native nations.

Although the French never entered into treaties of land surrenders with Native inhabitants, as did the Anglo-Americans, they were forced to come to terms with Native claims to self-government. The clearest statement of Native claims came from the Ministry of War in a memorandum to serving officers in the colony in 1755. It said, "The Native peoples are jealous of their liberty, and one could not without committing an injustice take away from them the primitive right of property to the Lands in which Providence has given them birth and placed them." The French saw no contradiction between their own assertion of sovereignty against British and Spanish claimants, and the recognition of Native nationhood, self-government, and occupancy rights. Aboriginal peoples spoke of their kinship relation with the French, wherein Native warriors fought alongside the French as allies, and Native producers and traders bartered as equal partners with the settlers.

It was this concept that the French sought to protect in the Articles of Capitulation of 1760, stating that the Native peoples "shall be maintained in the Lands they inhabit." The Royal Proclamation of 1763 firmly entrenched the concept of Native title to the hinterland under British sovereignty. It is, therefore, rightly regarded as a great charter of Native rights, although it also provided the vehicle for the alienation of Native lands to the Crown for redistribution to newcomers. In the court case *Connolly v. Woolrich et al.* (1867), the judge observed that "neither the French Government, nor any of its colonists or their trading associations, ever attempted, during an intercourse of over two hundred years, to subvert or modify the laws and usages of the aboriginal tribes, except where they had established colonies and permanent settlements, and, then, only by persuasion."

Despite the devastating impact of European diseases on aboriginal society, Natives had their own reasons for entering into alliances with the foreigners in their midst. They enjoyed the increased material wealth that resulted from trade, and they used European alliances to enhance their power in relation to other Native nations. After many years of contact, aboriginal peoples found their cultural practices gradually transformed. Many Natives, especially in the eastern regions of North America, had been drawn into family relationships with Europeans and converted to Christian beliefs. Even had they wished to do so, they would have found it difficult to disentangle themselves from the Europeans who had made North America their home. They also recognized that wars among European nations were often waged on their ancestral lands, making it impossible for them to remain neutral. This reality was most obvious in the Atlantic region and the Ohio territory, where the settlement frontier was fast encroaching on a "middle ground" of joint European–Native occupation.

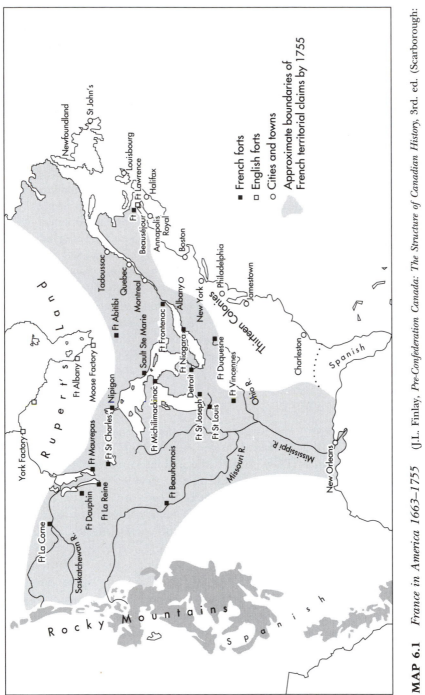

MAP 6.1 *France in America 1663–1755*   (J.L. Finlay, *Pre-Confederation Canada: The Structure of Canadian History*, 3rd. ed. (Scarborough: Prentice-Hall), 68)

Like the European nations, the first nations were not uniform in their response to military alliances. The Iroquois initially tried to remain neutral and profit from European rivalries. Their strategic geographical location between the French and British colonies, and the hard lessons learned in the wars of the seventeenth century, made this the logical approach to take. In Acadia and the Ohio–Mississippi region the Natives tended to form alliances with the French because of the threat that expanding Anglo-American settlement posed to their territorial claims. The Iroquois who sought sanctuary in the French missions understood this reality when they stated in 1754:

> Brethren, are you ignorant of the difference between our Father [the French] and the English? Go see the forts our Father has erected, and you will see that the land beneath his walls is still hunting ground, having fixed himself in those places we frequent, only to supply our wants; whilst the English, on the contrary, no sooner get possession of a country than the game is forced to leave it; the trees fall down before them, the earth becomes bare, and we find among them hardly wherewithal to shelter us when the night falls.[2]

For the Natives as much as for the French in North America, the rise of the British empire and the birth of the United States of America in the second half of the eighteenth century would force major adjustments.

• The Beginnings of British Rule in the Atlantic Region

Nowhere was the three-way struggle for power more intense than in the Atlantic region. According to the Treaty of Utrecht, the French ceded "All Nova Scotia or Accadie, comprehending its ancient boundaries," to Britain. Those "ancient boundaries" soon became the subject of dispute. France tried to make the best out of a bad bargain by claiming that Acadia meant only the Nova Scotia peninsula. The British argued that the traditional French definition of Acadia included the area north of the Bay of Fundy. The dispute was eventually submitted to arbitration, but in the meantime Britain and France jockeyed for control over the borderland region, which was a critical territorial link in both colonial empires.

At first it was not clear that Britain was prepared to take much initiative in governing its Atlantic colonies. Following the 1710 capture of Port Royal, renamed Annapolis Royal in honour of Queen Anne, a garrison of fewer than five hundred British and colonial soldiers was stationed in Nova Scotia. British fishing fleets returned to St John's, which had been sacked by a French force in 1709, but the official policy remained one of discouraging settlement in Newfoundland. With only a few British settlers and servants in Newfoundland—less than three thousand year-round residents in 1713—a population of less than two thousand Roman Catholic Acadians in Nova Scotia, and hostile Beothuk, Mi'kmaq, and Maliseet throughout the region, there was little incentive to establish an apparatus of colonial administration.

In 1717 the British made a feeble attempt to mould the region into a coherent administrative unit by appointing Colonel Richard Philipps governor of Placentia and Nova Scotia. He lost his authority over Placentia when Captain Henry Osborn became governor of Newfoundland in 1729, but Philipps retained his Nova Scotia posting until 1749. Neither official was permanently resident in the colony he governed. Philipps spent only six of his thirty-two-year tenure in Nova Scotia and Osborn made only seasonal visits to Newfoundland. In the three decades following the Treaty of Utrecht, British settlement in the Atlantic region remained unimpressive, consisting of a few soldiers, merchants, and officials at military outposts and several hundred fishing families scattered along a vast coastline. The most obvious British presence was a seasonal one: fleets of fishing vessels based from May to October off Canso and the eastern coast of Newfoundland.

This "phantom" British rule was reflected in the near absence of public institutions. Following the Treaty of Utrecht, no representative assemblies of the sort that existed in the other British North American colonies were introduced in either Nova Scotia or Newfoundland. Orders from the Board of Trade and Plantations, sitting in London, served as legislation for the region and sanctioned the actions of officials on the spot, who coped as best they could when crises arose. Justice was crudely meted out by untrained officials, including appointed justices of the peace in administrative centres and self-appointed fishing admirals in the outports of Newfoundland. If baptisms or weddings needed clerical sanction in Nova Scotia, it was easier to find a Roman Catholic priest than an Anglican clergyman. The Church of England, the established church of Britain, was conspicuously absent in the colony, although Roman Catholic priests, under the terms of the Treaty of Utrecht, ministered to their Acadian and Native flocks.

In the Atlantic region potential difficulties over land claims remaining from the French regime were avoided by abolishing seigneurial tenure. Only one claimant, Agathe Campbell, formerly Agathe Saint-Étienne de La Tour, received compensation for the seigneurial lands held by her family, who had been prominent in the founding of Acadia. In Newfoundland the

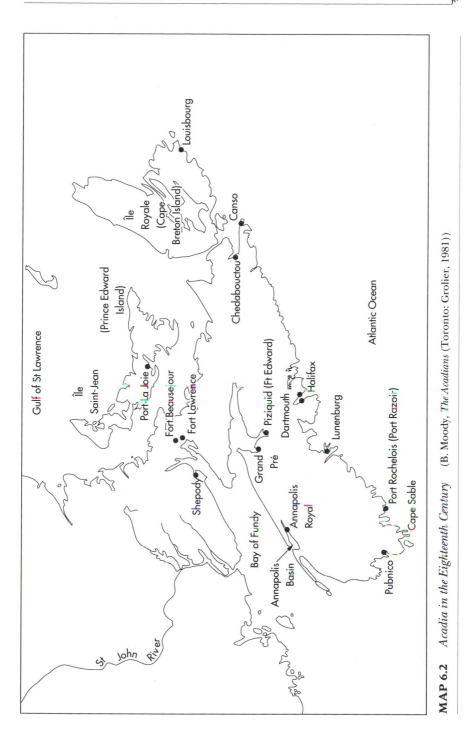

MAP 6.2 *Acadia in the Eighteenth Century* (B. Moody, *The Acadians* (Toronto: Grolier, 1981))

granting of fishing rights to the French on the north coast prevented conflict with British fishermen who were still concentrated mainly on the "Old English Shore" from Trepassey to Cape Bonavista. The British quickly occupied the south coast following the departure of the French, but the number of permanent residents on the island grew slowly for one obvious reason: there were few women.

British immigrants were reluctant to settle in Nova Scotia because the status of the colony was still in doubt. Another war or even the stroke of a diplomatic pen could reverse the decision made at Utrecht in 1713. Given the meteoric rise of the Acadian population in the post-conquest period and the growing French presence on Île Royale and Île Saint-Jean, there is little doubt that the Atlantic region, Newfoundland excepted, was more French in 1744 than it had been in 1713.

• The Neutral French

By the Treaty of Utrecht the Acadians were granted the liberty "to remove themselves within a year to any other place, as they shall think fit, together with their moveable effects." Those who decided to remain were to be "subject to the Kingdom of Great Britain" and permitted "to enjoy the free exercise of their religion, according to the usage of the church of Rome, as far as the laws of Great Britain allow the same." Most of the Acadians opted to remain on their farms in the Bay of Fundy region. Acadia had changed hands several times during the previous century, and it must have seemed distinctly possible that their homeland could once again be returned to France.

When the British assumed control of Acadia they already had experience governing conquered peoples with different cultural traditions. In the previous two hundred years the English had absorbed the Welsh and Scots into their greater British empire and made every effort to subdue the Roman Catholics in Ireland. Britain had also assumed control of the Dutch colony of New Amsterdam (renamed New York) and the Swedish settlements in Delaware—in addition to having held title to Acadia for a fifteen-year interlude between 1654 and 1670.

With these experiences in mind, British officials tried to persuade the Acadians to take an oath of allegiance, but through delegates their new subjects made it clear that any oath of loyalty must include explicit guarantees that they not be required to take up arms against the French and Mi'kmaq. Such a provision was the only practical alternative to becoming the victims in the crossfire between the British and the French and their

Native allies. By the 1730s the determination of the Acadians to stay clear of imperial entanglements had earned them the sneering title of the "neutral French," and British authorities were forced to admit defeat in their efforts to secure an unqualified oath of allegiance.

For Acadians, the thirty years following the conquest of 1713 must have seemed, in retrospect, a golden age. Family life flourished, population grew, economic opportunities beckoned, and the hand of authority was light. Settlement expanded up the Shepody, Petitcodiac, and Memramcook estuaries, and along the eastern shore from Baie Verte to the Baie des Chaleurs. With the establishment of Louisbourg, the Acadians had an alternative to the Boston market for surplus products from their farms and fisheries. Hard work and a healthy climate gave them a better than average chance of reaching old age surrounded by an expanding network of kin. By 1750 there were over nine thousand Acadians in "Nova Scotia or Accadie" and perhaps three thousand more scattered throughout the rest of the region.

Although most of the Acadians stayed well out of the way of their new masters, a few ambitious families made the most of the situation. Marie Madeleine Maisonnat, for example, married Huguenot officer William

*Detail of **William Shirley*** (National Portrait Gallery, Smithsonian Institution)

Winniett, who soon became prominent in the economic and political life of Nova Scotia. Their large family of seven sons and six daughters extended the influence of the Winnietts throughout the colony. Similarly, Agathe Saint-Étienne de La Tour married, in succession, two British officers stationed in Annapolis Royal. Her sons from the first marriage, Simon and John (baptized Jean-Baptiste) Bradstreet, both secured commissions in the British army. As a young officer John Bradstreet was stationed in Canso and became engaged in smuggling goods to Louisbourg. He was captured by the French when Canso was attacked in 1744. Upon his release he turned his knowledge of Louisbourg to his advantage by advising Governor William Shirley of Massachusetts about conditions at the French fortress, and he participated in its capture in 1745.

• Mi'kmaq and Maliseet

The biggest problem facing the British in their recently acquired Atlantic colonies was the hostility of the Mi'kmaq and Maliseet. Allied with the Abenaki, who comprised the first line of defence against the New England settlers moving up the Atlantic seaboard, the Mi'kmaq and Maliseet fought both on land and sea to preserve their traditional territorial rights, and they remained steadfast in their French alliances. After nearly one hundred and fifty years of French missionary activity, most of them were practising Roman Catholics, and some had intermarried with the Acadians. They preferred not to enter political alliances with the British, whose religion and language were foreign to them.

The Treaty of Utrecht made no mention of any territorial rights of Natives in the Atlantic region. The British assumed that the Mi'kmaq and Maliseet were allied to the French and would therefore share their defeat. Following the transfer of the colony, authorities tried to insist that the Natives in the region, like the Acadians, swear an oath of allegiance to the British crown. In return they were offered the same privileges that the Acadians enjoyed in religious matters and government-sponsored trading posts called "truck-houses." The Mi'kmaq and Maliseet were less than impressed with the proposal. They had never sworn allegiance to the French, and they had no intention of doing so to the British. Acadia was their land, which they called Megumaage. Moreover, they had little need of trading posts, because they usually obtained better prices from the ships that arrived in their inshore waters every spring.

When the French learned that the British were attempting to exert control over the Natives in the Atlantic region, they moved quickly. Pontchartrain, as minister of marine, sent Canadian-born missionary

Antoine Gaulin to convince the Mi'kmaq to move to Île Royale. Like the Acadians, the Mi'kmaq were reluctant to do so, except on a seasonal basis to receive their "presents" from the French. Thus the French were thrown back on subsidized trade, annual gifts, and the good offices of the Roman Catholic missionaries to maintain their Native alliances.

In the period between 1713 and 1744 three political priests proved particularly effective in their missions. Gaulin served the region from 1689 to 1731. After 1735, Pierre-Antoine-Simon Maillard orchestrated French–Mi'kmaq relations from his base on Chapel Island, Île Royale. Jean-Louis Le Loutre, whose missions included the Acadians as well as Mi'kmaq from 1737 to 1755, was so effective in his political activities that the British finally put a price on his head. During his early years in Nova Scotia, Le Loutre was based at Shubenacadie, some fifty kilometres northeast of Halifax, but by 1750 he had relocated to the Isthmus of Chignecto. The budget for "presents" in Acadia rose from around 200 livres a year in the 1710s to 37 000 livres in 1756. By the mid-eighteenth century, Mi'kmaq and Maliseet from the Atlantic region ranged from Louisbourg to Quebec to take advantage of French "hospitality."

Adept warriors and seafarers, the Mi'kmaq were particularly effective in harassing the British. They drove the New England fishermen out of Canso in 1720, justifying their act as protecting the land that God had given them. During the summer of 1722 Mi'kmaq mariners were reported to have captured thirty-six trading vessels in the waters off Nova Scotia. The New Englanders and the British authorities in Nova Scotia were quick to retaliate. For the next three years the New England–Nova Scotia frontier was embroiled in a bloody "Indian War." In the summer of 1724 the Mi'kmaq even attacked Annapolis Royal, burning part of the town and killing several British soldiers. Finally, in December 1725, peace treaties were concluded in Boston and Falmouth (in present-day Maine); they were ratified at Annapolis Royal the following year. These agreements included recognition of British sovereignty over "Nova Scotia or Accadie" as well as of the traditional hunting and fishing rights of the Natives. It was the classic stand-off, with both sides interpreting the agreement in ways that the other failed, or refused, to understand.

• War of the Austrian Succession, 1744–48

The test of Acadian neutrality and Native alliances came in 1744, when the lack of a male heir in the Hapsburg line provoked a general European war over the succession to the Austrian throne. Britain and Holland supported the claims of the Archduchess Maria Theresa while France and Prussia opposed her right to rule. In Europe the French and Prussian armies, the mightiest in the world, were successful, but in the colonies the results were mixed.

Three weeks before the news reached Annapolis Royal and Boston, Governor Le Prévost Duquesnel at Louisbourg learned that war had been officially declared. Following his instructions from France, Duquesnel authorized privateers to attack New England shipping and dispatched a force under Captain François Du Pont Duvivier to capture Canso. Caught off guard, the eighty-seven British soldiers at Canso surrendered almost immediately, in May 1744. Encouraged by this success, Duquesnel instructed Abbé Le Loutre to take an advance force of Mi'kmaq and sympathetic Acadians to Annapolis Royal where they would join with reinforcements sent from Louisbourg to lay siege to the colonial capital.

Le Loutre led about three hundred Mi'kmaq and a few Acadians to Annapolis Royal, but they withdrew in disgust when reinforcements from Boston arrived instead of the promised French naval squadron. Duvivier, who had been born in Port Royal, eventually laid siege to Fort Anne, which protected the town, with a small force including both Mi'kmaq and Maliseet. Because of the poor Acadian support, the failure of Louisbourg to send reinforcements, and the timely arrival of troops from Boston, Duvivier retreated after four weeks. The British commander at Annapolis Royal, Paul Mascarene, was able to report that "The inhabitants tho French . . . have however kept in their Fidelity much beyond what was expected notwithstanding all the entreaties of the French officers from Louisbourg who could not prevail on them to take up arms against them."

Inevitably, the New Englanders were alarmed by these developments on their northeastern frontier. Under the direction of Governor Shirley of Massachusetts, a volunteer militia of 4300 men led by William Pepperell was organized to attack Louisbourg. A squadron from the West Indies under the command of Commodore Peter Warren provided naval support. In the spring of 1745 the New Englanders managed to land two thousand men at Gabarus Bay, about three kilometres behind Louisbourg. From there they dragged heavy cannon through marshlands, captured the Royal Battery on the north shore of the harbour, and pounded the mighty fortress for seven weeks. On 17 June Governor Louis Du Pont Duchambon, his supplies dwindling and his town in ruins, surrendered.

Stung by the loss of their lucrative fishing base, the French began almost immediately to plan for its recapture. In June 1746 a squadron of fifty-four ships carrying seven thousand men sailed from France, but the expedition was dogged with bad luck. Because of contrary winds the fleet took nearly three months to reach North America. One violent gale scattered the ships, destroying a number of them. While waiting for reinforcements in Chebucto Bay (now Halifax), the commander of the expedition, the Duc d'Anville, died and his successor tried to commit suicide. By the end of the summer nearly half the men had been laid low by disease. Still, the fleet made plans to attack Annapolis Royal, but was hampered by heavy winds and fog. In October the tattered remnants of the squadron retreated without having fired a shot at their enemies in Louisbourg.

The expedition was testimony to the decline of the French navy, which no longer had the ships or the experienced commanders needed to protect its North American empire. After the 1746 fiasco French seapower was devastated. The British easily won two resounding naval victories against the French in the West Indies and destroyed the Spanish fleet off Havana. With communications between France and its North American colonies at the mercy of the British, the French colonials were left to pursue their own wartime strategies.

The loss of Louisbourg galvanized the Canadians into action. They launched border raids against New York and Massachusetts and strengthened fortifications protecting the heart of the colony. Fortunately for the Canadians, only the Mohawk used the occasion to launch a few attacks on outlying settlements. Otherwise they escaped the ravages of warfare on their territory. They were not, however, immune to the economic impact of the war. The fall of Louisbourg had disrupted trade with France, while border raids put an end to clandestine exchanges through Albany and New York.

LIFE IN THE COLONIAL MILITIA

The feats of bravery and endurance of Canadian militiamen have become the stuff of legend. In the eyes of their enemies, the Canadians possessed superhuman abilities. They were capable of travelling hundreds of kilometres in the dead of winter, their knowledge of the terrain equalled that of their Native allies, and they were crack shots with their flintlock muskets.

They were also noted for their cunning and cruelty. In the early years of settlement they commonly attacked their enemies at night, sometimes burned their captives in their homes, and spared neither women nor children. Although the cruelty of border raids abated considerably in the eighteenth century, the Canadian militia remained widely respected and feared.

The French authorities made every effort to keep their militia in top fighting condition. After 1669 every Canadian male between the ages of sixteen and sixty capable of bearing arms was subject to conscription and monthly military training. In 1752, when Governor Ange de Menneville Duquesne discovered that the militia was not up to scratch, he ordered weekly exercises and required that each soldier have a rifle, a full powder horn, and at least twenty bullets. Militiamen wore civilian clothes and were thus spared the expense of buying a costly uniform. The young men who cut their teeth on the gruelling fur trade expeditions into the *pays d'en haut* clearly had the advantage over their farm-based cousins in the militia, but most men in the colony were accustomed to hunting and knew the basics of frontier survival.

Few men, it seems, tried to shirk their military responsibilities, and many men aspired to the social and political rewards that went with the unpaid position of militia captain. During the siege of Quebec, even the students at the seminary formed their own company, which was nick-named "Royal Syntax." The old feudal emphasis on military loyalties cou-pled with the desperate attempt to save the cherished homeland meant that almost all male colonists were willing to serve.

Following the conquest of 1760, British commanders and British traditions dulled the Canadian enthusiasm for military exploits, but during the French regime the Canadian militia was the best fighting force on the continent.[3]

A Canadian militiaman going into battle on showshoes　(National Archives of Canada/C1854)

Annoyed by the poor quality and high prices prevailing at the French posts, Native allies began turning to Anglo-American traders for the commodities they needed. By 1747 bands of former allies were attacking French *voyageurs* in the interior, and reports from the posts suggested that a general uprising against the French was being planned. In defiance of royal instructions, colonial governors and commandants increased the volume of trade and present-giving. Alliances were preserved and even strengthened, but it was clear that they would last only as long as they served Native interests.

Quebec also sent militia to reinforce the Acadian frontier. In 1746 Governor Charles de Beauharnois organized a force of 680 men under the Sieur de Ramezay to assist the hapless d'Anville expedition. Ramezay stationed his men at Beaubassin on the Isthmus of Chignecto and made plans to launch an assault on Annapolis Royal. When d'Anville's force failed to appear, Ramezay dispatched Captain Louis Coulon de Villiers with three hundred men on a classic guerrilla campaign. They made their way through heavy winter snows to Grand Pré, where they encountered five hundred New England troops quartered in Acadian homes. Alerted by several Acadians, de Villiers and his men surrounded the houses where the New Englanders were sleeping, killed seventy of them, including their leader Colonel Arthur Noble, and forced the rest to surrender.

The "Massacre of Grand Pré," as the English called it, put the Acadian strategy of neutrality in serious jeopardy. While it was clear that some of the Acadians had warned Noble about the French presence in the area, he had not believed them. After the event, when the English discussed Acadian policy, it would be the "treacherous informers" and "traitors," not those who had maintained a desperate neutrality, who would be remembered.

Further reprisals were temporarily averted when the two sides agreed to a negotiated peace. By the Treaty of Aix-la-Chapelle in 1748 Britain and France agreed to restore their captured possessions, which meant that France gave up its conquests in the Netherlands and India in return for Louisbourg. The New Englanders were appalled by Britain's apparent lack of concern for their safety and well-being. If this was the thanks they got for shedding blood on behalf of the empire, they would insist that Britain end its phantom rule on their northeastern frontier.

•The Uneasy Peace, 1749–55

All sides—French, British, and Native—moved immediately to strengthen their positions for the war that was certain to come very soon. Again the activity was particularly intense in the Atlantic region. In 1749 the French reoccupied Louisbourg, which had been badly looted by the triumphant New Englanders. The British, aware of resentment in their colonies, decided to build a fortified base on the Nova Scotia peninsula to counter the threat posed by Louisbourg. In the spring of 1749, Edward Cornwallis arrived in Chebucto Bay with three thousand servants, settlers, and disbanded soldiers to found Halifax. Between 1750 and 1753 over 2500 German and French-speaking Protestants were recruited from Europe to increase the numbers of "loyal" settlers in the colony.

Since the Treaty of Aix-la-Chapelle had failed to mention the Natives, the British claimed that it was necessary for the first nations that had fought with the French to sign separate peace treaties. While the Maliseet and Passamaquoddy on the north shore of the Bay of Fundy were prepared to reconfirm the treaty of 1725–26 with Cornwallis and his emissaries, the Mi'kmaq were defiant. The expansion of British interests in Nova Scotia posed a direct threat to their survival. They resumed their attacks against the British on land and sea and harassed the British base at Halifax, which was located on one of the Mi'kmaq's favourite summer encampments.

Cornwallis responded with an order for all British subjects to "take or destroy the savage commonly called Micmacks wherever they are found," offering a reward of ten guineas for every "savage taken or his scalp." The Mi'kmaq in turn declared war on the British in September 1749 for having settled their lands without permission and for undertaking to exterminate them. A formal declaration of war was drawn up with the help of Abbé Maillard and Abbé Le Loutre.

The Mi'kmaq war gave the French the opportunity they were looking for to extend their influence in the region. Since 1713 they had claimed possession of the area north of the Bay of Fundy, and now it was more critical than ever to establish a military presence there. In 1750 they built Fort Beauséjour north of the Missaquash River on the Isthmus of Chignecto. The plan, as conceived by French officials and fleshed out by Le Loutre, was to encourage the Acadians to move north of the Missaguash or to Île St-Jean where they would establish their agricultural communities, add numbers to the militia, and give substance to French claims to the region. Le Loutre also assumed that the Mi'kmaq at Shubenacadie, whom he referred to as "my Indians," would fall into line with this strategy.

Cornwallis reacted quickly, dispatching Lieutenant-Colonel Charles Lawrence and two regiments with orders to construct a fort within sight of Beauséjour. Despite Mi'kmaq and Acadian opposition, Fort Lawrence was constructed in 1750 as planned. Raids, skirmishes, and treachery continued for the next five years as the adversaries sat facing each other across the wind-swept Tantramar marshes.

The Mi'kmaq also kept up their attacks in other regions of the colony. In 1751 they even conducted a successful raid on the new community of Dartmouth across the harbour from Halifax. Cornwallis's successor, Peregrine Hobson, managed to get a few Mi'kmaq to sign his treaty of peace and friendship in 1752, but this did not prevent Le Loutre from proceeding with his grand plan. With more than a thousand Acadian men within two days' march of Fort Beauséjour, and four hundred Natives encamped at nearby Baie Verte, the French had proved once again that they were masters of war in time of peace.

In Canada, Governor Roland-Michel Barrin de La Galissonière made impressive plans for defending French interests in North America. He sent a detachment to the mouth of the St John River, strengthened the forts in the Lake Champlain region, and sent a military expedition under Pierre-Joseph Céloron de Blainville into the Ohio Valley. As Blainville's force of two hundred French and thirty Iroquois and Abenaki advanced through the interior, it became increasingly clear that the alliances in the region were disintegrating. New leaders had emerged who owed no allegiance to the French, and old chiefs had difficulty keeping rebel warriors in line. Although the Ohio "republics" were not necessarily hostile to the French, they were developing their own agenda in the face of growing European encroachment.

From the point of view of French authorities, there was no question about the cause of the new independence among the Native communities of the Ohio: increased British activity in the region had undermined the old alliances. The scope of Anglo-American ambitions was revealed by the creation of the Ohio Company in 1748. With capital invested by London merchants and such powerful Virginia families as the Lees, Fairfaxes, and Washingtons, the Ohio Company planned to make vast profits by selling half a million acres to land-hungry settlers.

By the 1750s the growing European presence in the Ohio region had prompted a shift in perception among the Natives living there. The Europeans, whether British or French, were encroaching on their land and using it as a battleground. As a Delaware chief explained to a British emissary: "We have great reason to believe you intend to drive us away and settle the country, or else why do you come to fight in the Land that God has given us. . . . Why don't you and the French fight in the old Country, and on the Sea? Why do you come to fight on our Land? This makes everybody believe you want to take our land from us by force and settle it."[4]

The French moved quickly to maintain their ascendancy in the interior of the continent. Friendly Iroquois were gathered at La Présentation (Odgensburg, N.Y.) by Sulpician priest Abbé Picquet to serve as a buffer between New France and New York. In an effort to protect their communications from Fort Frontenac to Fort Niagara, the French put a small fleet on Lake Ontario. Fort Rouillé was built at present-day Toronto, site of a strategic portage. In 1752, a new governor, the Marquis de Duquesne, arrived at Quebec with orders to drive the British out of the Ohio.

Duquesne dispatched three hundred Troupes de la Marine, seventeen hundred Canadian militia, and two hundred allied Natives into the Lake Erie region to construct a road to the headwaters of the Ohio and establish forts at strategic locations. The commander of the expedition, Pierre-Paul de Marin, drove his men as hard as he did himself. Marin and over four hundred of the two thousand men under his command died. The rest were weakened by the bad food provided by Intendant Bigot and his *grande société*. There was little assistance from the Natives in the region because they no longer grew surplus food.

Despite these difficulties, the French were initially successful in undermining British control over the Ohio area. In 1753 Governor Robert Dinwiddie of Virginia sent George Washington to the region to officially protest French activities there, but the delegation received a polite rebuff from French commander Jacques Saint-Pierre at Fort Le Boeuf (present-day Waterford, Pennsylvania). In an attempt to strengthen the French position, Duquesne dispatched a winter expedition into Ohio country to build a fort at the junction of the Monongahela and Allegheny rivers. The few British in the region were driven out and the local Miami, Iroquois, and Shawnee were encouraged in the usual manner to side with the victorious French. Fort Duquesne, built on the site of present-day Pittsburgh, stood as a symbol of French control over the region.

Washington returned in the spring of 1754 with a small detachment of militia to order the French out of the Ohio territory. When they encountered a French scouting party, led by Ensign Joseph de Jumonville, they attacked it, killing Jumonville and nine of his men. Such an attack at a time when the British and French were officially at peace brought a swift reaction. On 3 July a force from Fort Duquesne, led by Jumonville's brother, Louis, caught up with Washington's party, which had taken refuge in a crude shelter aptly named Fort Necessity. After a bruising assault that lasted nine hours, Washington surrendered. He and his surviving men were granted the "honours of war" and allowed to retreat in safety, but by the terms of the capitulation agreement the Virginians promised to abandon all claims to the disputed Ohio territory.

The success of the French on the frontier forced the Anglo-American colonies into co-operation. Although the colonial legislatures rejected plans for political union, their delegates did agree to form a common military strategy against the French and their Native allies. They decided to launch a four-pronged attack against the outer defences of New France: Fort Beauséjour in Acadia, Fort Fréderic on Lake Champlain, Fort Niagara in the Great Lakes region, and Fort Duquesne. Major-General Edward Braddock and two regiments of regulars were sent by Britain to assist the colonial effort.

France in the meantime had sent out Jean-Armand, Baron de Dieskau, with three thousand Troupes de Terre, regular French soldiers normally under the control of the Ministry of War. During their sojourn in Canada, they, like the Troupes de la Marine, were placed under the governor, who in 1755 was Pierre de Rigaud de Vaudreuil. The son of an earlier governor of the colony, he was the first Canadian-born appointee to the highest position in the colonial administration. Vaudreuil's strategy was to launch surprise attacks at various points along the American frontier. Guerrilla raids would keep the colonists terrorized, unnerve the British soldiers, and put the enemy on the defensive. Such a strategy would also take advantage of one of France's major assets: its Native alliances.

Major-General Braddock himself led the force that was organized to capture Fort Duquesne. Unused to frontier conditions, he failed miserably. A detachment of 108 colonial regulars, 146 Canadian militia, and 600 Indians defeated Braddock's army with little difficulty. Two-thirds of Braddock's 2200 men, and Braddock himself, were killed or wounded, while the French and their allies left the field with only 43 casualties. Among the equipment abandoned by the British was Braddock's papers, which revealed the plans for the other campaigns.

Governor Shirley of Massachusetts led the expedition against Fort Niagara, but his force of 2400 colonial militia was dissolved by disease and desertion before it reached its objective. The thrust toward Lake Champlain was blunted by a force led by Dieskau. Only on the Nova Scotia frontier were the British successful. A colonial militia of nearly 2500 men under the command of Lieutenant-Colonel Robert Monckton captured Fort Beauséjour on 12 June 1755 after a brief siege. With only 160 regular soldiers, and 300 militia and hastily conscripted Acadians, the French commander's position was hopeless. It was not helped by the presence of the traitor Thomas Pichon, who kept the British informed of conditions within the fort and who favoured an early surrender. Only Le Loutre was prepared to hold out longer, no doubt concerned about his own fate if he became a prisoner of the British.

• The Acadian Deportation

On 1 May, even before the fall of Beauséjour, British authorities had decided to expel the Acadians living north of the Missaquash River. New Englanders would be placed in this borderland district to serve as a barrier between the remaining Acadians in peninsular Nova Scotia and the Canadians on the St Lawrence. On 25 June, this policy was approved by the governing council in Halifax.

The fate of the remaining Acadians was still to be decided, but it was unlikely that they would continue to live as they had since 1713. When Fort Beauséjour surrendered, some two hundred Acadians were discovered within its walls. They protested that they had been forced to fight against their will, and the articles of capitulation had granted them pardon, but the authorities were no longer disposed to give them the benefit of the doubt. With rumours circulating in the colony that the French were preparing to launch a counter-attack, Lieutenant-Governor Charles Lawrence decided to act immediately to force the Acadians to do his bidding or face the consequences.

In July delegates from the Acadian communities in peninsular Nova Scotia were summoned to Halifax and ordered to take an unqualified oath of allegiance. They refused to do so, promising only to remain neutral. Told that deportation would be the consequence of their refusal to take an

The Expulsion of the Acadians at Fort Amherst   (Artist: Lewis Parker/Courtesy: Canadian Parks Service, Atlantic Region)

unqualified oath, they stuck stubbornly to their position, even when given another chance to reconsider. Unfortunately for the Acadians, the strategies they had pursued in the past would no longer work. While these negotiations were taking place, word of Braddock's defeat reached Halifax and panic spread throughout the town. The decision to deport the remaining Acadians was taken by Lawrence and his council on 28 July. It was a military decision, made by colonial authorities faced with the responsibility of defending a frontier colony. Although it clearly lacked humanity, it would solve the problem of the "neutral French" once and for all.

Lawrence moved quickly. Orders were sent to the military commanders at Chignecto, Piziquid, and Annapolis Royal instructing them to seize the men and boys as well as the boats, so that the women and children would not try to escape. As soon as it could be arranged, transports from Boston would take them away. All Acadian land and livestock became the property of the crown. The deportees could take only the goods they could carry with them. Their destination would be other British colonies in North America where they would be scattered like leaves before the wind.

Terror swept through the Acadian communities as the awful reality dawned. At Chignecto the men were summoned to Fort Cumberland (formerly Fort Beauséjour) to be told of their fate and held in captivity; eighty of them escaped by digging a tunnel and fleeing with their families into the nearby woods. The Acadians near Piziquid were imprisoned in Fort Edward. At Grand Pré the parish church served as a makeshift prison until the transports arrived. Annapolis Royal was a different story. There the Acadians had prior warning, and many managed to escape before the authorities issued their fatal order. Whether free or captive, no Acadian was spared the horror of what followed. The British soldiers put Acadian homes, barns, and churches to the torch and rounded up their cattle. In a few hectic days in the late summer of 1755 the golden age of Acadian life came to a tragic end.

The departure brought more heartbreak as extended families and neighbours were separated and the land they so loved was left behind. In his diary Colonel Edward Winslow, who was in charge of the deportation at Grand Pré, described the pitiful scene as men "went off Praying, Singing & Crying, being Met by the women & Children all the way . . . with Great Lamentations upon their Knees praying, etc." For Winslow, who had seen much during his military career, it was "the worst peace of Service that Ever I was in."

The horrors of the deportation did not end there. Authorities in the British colonies, with no idea that they were expected to receive hundreds of refugees, offered them little assistance. A few colonies even refused to accept their quota of "boat people" and sent them on their way. For many Acadians, their deportation from Nova Scotia marked the beginning of a lifetime of wandering that took some of them the length of North America and others to the West Indies, to Britain, or back to France. Nowhere did they feel at home. Even in France they felt like strangers and begged to be returned to the "New World" where they had been born.

Nor were the heart-rending events of 1755 the end of the deportations. In 1756, Lawrence seized some two hundred people in the Pubnico area of peninsula Nova Scotia and shipped them off to Boston. In 1758, after the fall of Louisbourg, the 3500 Acadians on Île Royale and Île Saint-Jean were sent to France. Three years later another 300 Acadians in the Miramichi area were exiled. By 1764, when the last deportees arrived in the southern colonies, about 11 000 of an estimated 13 000 Acadians had been removed from their native land. Many had died, including those drowned when their boats capsized during their endless wanderings. Some 2000 of them escaped to Canada and were among the most determined defenders of the colony during its siege in 1759–60. Many of those who were dumped in the southern colonies made their way to Louisiana where their descendants, called Cajuns, still live. Those who remained in Nova Scotia survived by hiding out in the woods and living with the Mi'kmaq. A few were rounded up and used as prison labour in the colony during the war.

The lesson of the deportation was not lost on the Canadians and their Native allies. They could now expect the worst from the British, who, it was clear, would take whatever measures were necessary to gain the upper hand in North America. Although the Acadian deportation had not been authorized by Lawrence's superiors in Britain, they had little difficulty in sanctioning it. Lawrence was not reprimanded for his controversial action; on the contrary, he was promoted from lieutenant-governor to governor of Nova Scotia in July 1756.

The departure of the Acadians made the Mi'kmaq more vulnerable to Lawrence's efforts to conquer them. In May 1756 he authorized both military forces and civilians to "annoy, distress, take and destroy the Indians inhabiting different Parts of this Province" and offered rewards for the capture of men, women, and children. The final battle for the control of the border colony had begun in earnest.

•The Seven Years' War, 1756–63

In 1756 the "French and Indian" wars finally merged into a larger contest, known as the Seven Years' War. It was essentially a continuation of the War of the Austrian Succession, this time with France and Austria pitted against

Britain and Prussia. Fought both in Europe and its colonies, this war would profoundly alter the balance of power in North America and open the way for a dramatic confrontation between Britain and its American colonies.

When war was declared the Canadians moved quickly to secure the approaches to their colony. In 1756, Dieskau's successor, Louis-Joseph, the Marquis de Montcalm, led a successful expedition against Oswego, thus blocking British entry to the Great Lakes. In the following year another campaign down the Lake Champlain route resulted in the capture of Fort William Henry. After the surrender, Montcalm's Native allies fell on the retreating British forces, killing twenty-nine and taking over one hundred prisoner. This incident added fuel to the fire of intense hatred that was building in the Thirteen Colonies against their adversaries. On the frontier, French and Native raiding parties had made life intolerable. Governor Vaudreuil informed his superiors in 1756 that one of his commanders had been "occupied more than eight days merely in receiving scalps; that there is not an English party but loses some men, and that it was out of his power to render me an exact report of all the attacks our Natives have made."

Oswego and Fort William Henry were important victories for Montcalm, but they brought criticism from Vaudreuil, who felt that the European style of warfare was too formal for frontier conditions. As commander of the Troupes de la Marine, the militia, and Native forces, Vaudreuil championed the flexible guerrilla tactics of his army and was afraid that the conventional European fighting techniques used by Montcalm and his Troupes de Terre would lead to disaster. He criticized Montcalm for not taking Fort Edward following the victory at Fort William Henry and complained to a friend, "At present war is waged in Canada as in France, with the usual panoply and baggage." Montcalm, in turn, was aghast at the notion that France defend its North American territories by relying on undignified bush-fighting strategies, contrary to accepted "rules of war."

During the first year of the war Britain was slow to mobilize its forces, but William Pitt's accession as prime minister in 1757 brought new energy to the British cause. Pitt focussed military strategy on the colonies, directing British troops in large numbers—at least 23 000—and naval resources to the conquest of New France. While the Canadians were experts in frontier wars, they were more vulnerable to the formal campaigns envisioned by Pitt. If the British blockaded the northern coastline the colonials would be required to provision their military and civilian population without help from France. Withstanding a prolonged siege would be virtually impossible.

As the British converged on the colony in 1758 the conflict between Montcalm and Vaudreuil intensified. Montcalm, with a force of 3600 men, won another major victory at Carillon (Ticonderoga) against a massive British army of 15 000 men, but he remained convinced that the best strategy

The Marquis of Montcalm   (National Archives of Canada/C27665)

was to abandon outlying defences and concentrate all available manpower on the St Lawrence heartland. With the British using concentrated forces and siege tactics, Montcalm had apparently adopted the correct military strategy. Vaudreuil, however, continued to insist that the outlying forts be defended and that guerrilla tactics were the best way of keeping the British troops divided and defeated. If the British were forced to fight for every foot of territory on the North American frontier, he reasoned, they would eventually give up the struggle.

Montcalm was so discouraged by the situation in North America that he asked to be recalled. Instead, he was promoted to lieutenant-general, a rank that made him supreme commander of all French forces in North America. Vaudreuil was now required to submit to the dictates of his superior officer and watch his Canadian forces become secondary to the Troupes de Terre from France. "It is no longer a matter of making a raid," Bougainville asserted, "but of conquering or being conquered. What a revolution! What a change!"

While Vaudreuil and Montcalm were quarrelling over strategy, Louisbourg had been captured for the second time by the British. Jeffrey Amherst led a force of eight thousand men who took the fortress on 26 July

1758 after a seven-week siege. With the British navy under Admiral Edward Boscawen preventing the French from receiving provisions or reinforcements, there was little people in Louisbourg could do other than keep the British engaged long enough to prevent a campaign against Quebec that summer.

It was clear that the British were circling ever closer on their prey. The small force on Île Saint-Jean surrendered following the capture of Louisbourg. In August Colonel Bradstreet took Fort Frontenac, effectively cutting the French supply line to the Ohio region. The French were forced to blow up Fort Duquesne to prevent it from falling into British hands. During the winter of 1758–59 the French made plans to strengthen their western flank and pursue a counter-offensive in the Ohio region. This activity came to an abrupt halt in June 1759 when the Royal Navy under Vice-Admiral Charles Saunders appeared on the St Lawrence with 8500 seasoned British troops under the command of General James Wolfe. By capturing river pilots, the British had managed to navigate the difficult river entrance. The siege of Quebec had begun.

The arrival of the British on the St Lawrence made it impossible to hold the interior. On 25 July Fort Niagara surrendered after a siege of three weeks. Fort Carillon and Fort Fréderic were blown up in the face of an advancing army led by Jeffrey Amherst, now chief of the British forces in North America. The French commander Bourlamaque entrenched his

A view of Louisbourg as seen from the lighthouse during the seige of 1758 (P. Ince/ National Archives of Canada/C5907)

troops at Île-aux-Noix on the Richelieu River, his last line of defence against the capture of Montreal.

Conditions in Quebec had become desperate even before British ships appeared on the St Lawrence. While Montcalm, Bigot, and their friends indulged themselves in the good times of the casino, ballroom, and banquet hall, the ordinary people faced rationing and even starvation. The presence of nearly sixteen thousand regular, militia, and Native soldiers added pressure to the limited supplies of food available in the colony. Prices had risen dramatically for any commodities that were still available, and even horses were being slaughtered to feed hungry mouths. Crop failure and an outbreak of typhus added to the misery. Only the arrival of twenty-two supply ships from France in May 1759 made it possible to feed the soldiers and civilians in the town until the fall harvest.

The British reasoned correctly that the capture of Quebec would ensure the eventual surrender of the entire colony, but success would not come easily. Although the British succeeded in taking Pointe Lévis across the river from Quebec, they failed to land on the left flank of the town. Nor could they cut communications to the main supply base at Batiscan, eighty kilometres upstream from Quebec. Wolfe's forces launched an artillery bombardment from their base on Point Lévis, ultimately reducing four-fifths of the buildings in Quebec to rubble, but the walled town remained invincible. Repeated landing attempts were driven back by a combined force of 4000 regular French troops, up to 10 000 Canadian militiamen, and 1000 Native warriors. In each encounter the British suffered heavy casualties.

Wolfe, suffering from a severe illness, became increasingly irritated by his inability to penetrate Quebec's defences. In desperation he sent a detachment of 1600 soldiers to lay waste to the parishes along the south shore of the St Lawrence. Their orders were to burn all buildings and ships, destroy all crops, and slaughter the animals. In the process several civilians were killed and six women and five children, who failed to escape, were held as hostages. This scorched-earth policy set off a great fear of further British atrocities. Although the practice was not unusual behaviour in eighteenth-century warfare, it did little to reassure Canadians about their fate in the event of a conquest.

By early September the town of Quebec, but not its walls, lay in ruins, and what remained of its frightened population was threatened by starvation. Montcalm made plans for an eventual retreat to distant Louisiana. But the British were in an even worse state. A thousand men had been laid low with dysentery in an unsanitary base hospital, General Amherst's forces were stalled at Lake Champlain, and Wolfe's staff officers were becoming more and more discouraged as their commander became more ill and agitated. With fall rapidly approaching, Vice-Admiral Saunders was afraid his fleet would be caught in the ice of an early winter. Unless something happened soon, the Canadian climate would dictate the outcome of the battle of Quebec.

Good luck rather than good management determined victory. On the night of 12 September Wolfe managed to land nearly 4500 men at Anse-au-Foulon, a cove about three kilometres above Quebec. They scrambled up a steep cliff to the Plains of Abraham, where they stood in battle array on the morning of 13 September. From a tactical point of view the Battle of the Plains of Abraham was a blundering fiasco for both the French and the British. With few rations, no reserves, and only one field gun, Wolfe ordered his men to form two lines below a crest of higher ground to await the French army, which arrived breathless from Beauport. Montcalm could have waited for the British to charge uphill against his winded troops, or he could have remained within the stout walls of the town until reinforcements under Bougainville arrived from Batiscan with cannon to attack the British from the rear. He did neither. Instead, he lined up his troops outside the town walls and ordered them to charge in three columns. This strategy severely limited the number of men who could fire at any one time and resulted in the breaking of the charge under a withering British volley. As the French retreated in disarray to the protection of the town, Montcalm was mortally wounded and Wolfe lay dead on the battlefield.

Casualties were heavy on both sides—658 for the British and 644 for the French—and despite their success on the field, the British still held only the Plains of Abraham. Nevertheless, the war-weary inhabitants of the town, as well as the jaded Troupes de Terre, were anxious to surrender. On 19 September the French troops left the fortress of Quebec, their flags unfurled, torches lit, drums beating, and fifes playing. The British navy returned home, and a garrison under Brigadier James Murray was left behind in the shambles of the old capital. They faced a cold winter, short rations, and a devastating outbreak of scurvy. Whenever they ventured outside the walls of the town for food or firewood, the British were attacked by Canadian militiamen and their Native allies, who also harassed anyone caught collaborating with the conqueror.

In the spring a contingent of seven thousand men under the Chevalier de Lévis, who had succeeded Montcalm, attempted to retake Quebec. Murray then made the same tactical blunder as Montcalm. Instead of waiting for an assault on the walled fortress, he ordered his troops to meet the French at Sainte-Foy. The British charged without success, were routed by a bayonet charge, and fled in disarray to Quebec. The arrival of the British navy with reinforcements prevented Lévis from following up his victory. Sainte-Foy was the last major engagement of the war. Although the French won that battle, they lost the war and the colony.

Governor Vaudreuil surrendered New France to General Amherst on 8 September 1760. Although Amherst refused to grant the honours of war to the French troops, he responded in a practical way to Vaudreuil's pleas for leniency in dealing with the conquered Canadians. Under the Articles of Capitulation, everyone who wished to do so could leave the colony and take their possessions with them. Those who remained were granted security of property and person. Canadians were granted freedom to practise their Roman Catholic faith, but the status of enforced tithing remained in doubt. Amherst refused Vaudreuil's request to permit the king of France to name the Roman Catholic bishop of the colony, and he reserved decision on the rights of the Jesuits, Récollets, and Sulpicians to continue their ministries. In contrast, the female religious orders were granted their customary privileges.

The Acadians who had sought refuge in Canada were mentioned several times in the document. While they were given permission to go to France, they were specifically excluded from the guarantees against deportation that were given to the French and Canadians. Afraid that the British would deprive the conquered people of their valuable human property, Vaudreuil also secured guarantees for the continuance of black and aboriginal slavery and the right of owners to bring up their slaves "in the Roman Religion." Vaudreuil also attempted to protect his Native allies from the wrath of the conqueror. Article XL provided that "Indian allies" of the French were to be "maintained in the lands they inhabit" and were not to be "molested" for having fought against the British.

Until the peace treaty was signed in Paris on 10 February 1763, New France was ruled by martial law. Although the British gave some thought to exchanging their conquered territory for Guadaloupe, the Treaty of Paris confirmed British possession of all of New France, except for Saint-Pierre and Miquelon. Louisiana, which was not a theatre of war during the hostilities, was divided along the Mississippi, with Britain receiving the eastern section and navigational rights to the mighty river. France ceded the area west of the Mississippi to its ally Spain in a separate treaty.

During the negotiations France showed surprisingly little interest in regaining Canada, which philosopher Voltaire sneeringly referred to as "a few acres of snow." As well, the French took some pleasure in the prospect of a full-scale confrontation erupting between Britain and its Thirteen Colonies, now that the French threat on the continent had been eliminated.

In all of these negotiations the Natives were not represented, and their homelands were parcelled out to European powers as if North America were an empty frontier ripe for exploitation.

Cartoon of Wolfe at Quebec. Drawing by George Townsend (McCord Museum of Canadian History/M1791)

•The Conquest and Native Policy

Britain emerged from the Seven Years' War as the dominant imperial power in North America, but its efforts to administer the colonial possessions and impose order and economic efficiency met with failure on all sides. Not only did the British find themselves fighting an Indian war on the frontier, but they also faced a rebellion in their colonies. The attempt to impose British political and legal institutions in Quebec failed and had to be abandoned. As the British responded to these troublesome colonial realities, their policies increasingly resembled those of their French predecessors. Like the French, the British found themselves fighting the Thirteen Colonies, forging Native alliances, and resorting to aristocratic paternalism in a desperate attempt to maintain their North American empire.

The transfer of New France to British control was as traumatic for the aboriginal peoples of North America as it was for the Canadians. With the rivalry of the British and French removed, the Amerindians could no longer play one side against the other to their advantage. The price of furs plummeted, the quality and quantity of European trade goods declined, and the custom of giving annual presents in recognition of military alliances was abandoned. The aboriginal peoples were now at the mercy of Anglo-American speculators and land-hungry settlers; their very survival was at stake.

Aware of the potential for disaster in their Native policy, the British developed a new approach to relations with the first nations, drawing upon lessons learned from their French rivals. They had observed, for example, the necessity of respecting Native self-government and the value of trading alliances. In addition they saw how important it was to maintain a unified approach. They knew that by permitting each colony to pursue its own Native policy they had nearly lost their strategic advantage to the French. In 1755 Britain established an Indian Department, the initial step in its attempt to impose a co-ordinated imperial policy on aboriginal people.

Britain's new Native policy was first implemented in Nova Scotia. The fall of Louisbourg and Quebec signalled the end of aboriginal ascendancy in the region. Without a source of supply for arms and ammunition, Natives could neither hunt for food nor fight the British. The Maliseet and Passamaquoddy made peace in 1760 and the Mi'kmaq did likewise in 1761.

Following French practices, the authorities in Halifax used the signing of peace treaties as an occasion for considerable pomp and ceremony. Representatives of "the several Districts of the general Mickmack Nation of Indians" were invited by Lieutenant-Governor Jonathan Belcher to his farm near Halifax on 25 June 1761. The members of the provincial council were there, as well as officers of the British military and the leading citizens of Halifax. Abbé Maillard, who had moved from Île Royale to Halifax to help his Christian flock, served as an interpreter for this important diplomatic event. Belcher addressed the chiefs: "Brothers . . . I assure myself that you Submit . . . with hearts of Duty and Gratitude, as to your merciful Conqueror." He then led them to a pillar in a field where he received their public vows of obedience. Following a ceremonial burying of the hatchet, the chiefs signed treaties, one for each band, renewing the peace agreements made in 1726. The Mi'kmaq were now, as Belcher put it, "in full possession of English protection and Liberty."[5] What Belcher really meant was that

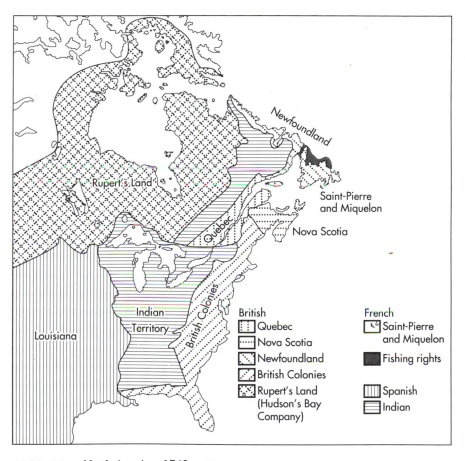

MAP 6.3   *North America, 1763*   (*Historical Atlas of Canada*, vol. 1 (Toronto: University of Toronto Press, 1987), plate 42)

they were subjects of the British king and bound by British laws. In the following year Belcher issued a proclamation ordering the removal of all people settled on Native lands and reserved the northeastern coast from Musquodoboit River to the Baie des Chaleurs as Mi'kmaq hunting grounds.

The Royal Proclamation of October 1763 was a further manifestation of Britain's new Native policy. A decree of the Crown, not a law of Parliament, the proclamation set out the policy for governing the newly acquired territories and for relations with Native people in North America. Canada was reduced in size (see map 6.3) and renamed Quebec. The eastern part of the colony was placed under the jurisdiction of Newfoundland, while the interior region west of the Allegheny Mountains was declared to be Indian territory.

According to the proclamation, any lands that had "not been ceded to or purchased" by Britain were reserved for "the said Indians." The British "strictly" forbade, "on Pain of our Displeasure, all our loving Subjects from making any Purchases or Settlements whatever, or taking Possession of any of the Lands above reserved, without our especial leave and Licence for that Purpose first obtained." In other words, individuals were not permitted to purchase Native land. If Indians wished to sell their land, they could do so only through the British Crown "at some public Meeting or assembly of the said Indians, to be held for the Purpose by the Governor or Commander in Chief of our Colony." Only those who held a licence from the governor could trade with the Native people.

The provisions of the Royal Proclamation of 1763 were of little immediate consequence to the Native nations on the frontier who were facing deprivation and even starvation. Under Britain's streamlined policy, trade was confined to a limited number of designated posts, and annual gift giving was abandoned. The policy proved a dismal failure. The new shortage of guns and ammunition brought particular hardship to the aboriginal nations that had come to depend upon them. Encouraged by French traders still resident in the interior, the first nations prepared to strike at the hated British in their midst. During the summer of 1762 a war belt and hatchet circulated among the disaffected peoples. By the following spring a border war had erupted.

One of the principal leaders of the uprising was the Ottawa chief Pontiac, who hoped for the return of French forces to aid his people and appealed to his fellow warriors to wipe the "dogs dressed in red" from "the face of the earth." They had come, he warned his listeners, "to rob you of your hunting grounds, and drive away the game." Always ingenious guerrilla fighters, the Natives captured most of the posts in the upper Mississippi and Ohio River basins and killed over two thousand settlers.

Detroit held out because the commander had been warned of the attack. It took the British nearly two years to regain control of the frontier. In desperation, Amherst even considered resorting to biological warfare. He suggested that his commanders might use smallpox-infected blankets "to extirpate this execrable race," and at least one officer, Captain Ecuyer at Fort Pitt, acted on this suggestion.

The sequel to Pontiac's revolt was mounting pressure on the British to resume the fur trade out of Montreal as a means of maintaining Native goodwill. Through the mediation of William Johnson, the superintendent of Indian affairs in the Mohawk valley, efforts were made to define a boundary for Indian territory. More than three thousand Natives, mostly Iroquois and their allies, met with Johnson at Fort Stanwix in 1768 to establish a permanent boundary between white settlements and Indian hunting grounds. The Iroquois abandoned much of the Ohio country to white settlement. Since neither the Iroquois nor the British could control the people they claimed to bargain for, the new boundary line was widely ignored. As independent traders and settlers clashed with Native communities, the Anglo-American frontier dissolved into chaos. William Johnson's nephew, Guy Johnson, was instrumental in convincing the British to exert more control over the region by placing the Ohio territory under the jurisdiction of Quebec in 1774.

• The Conquest and Quebec

The controversy surrounding the meaning of the conquest of Quebec makes it difficult to sort out what actually took place in the years immediately after the British assumed control. Undoubtedly, the destruction caused by a victorious foreign army, followed by the imposition of the conqueror's rule, constituted a traumatic series of events. But while the conquest brought changes, it could not prevent continuity. As the British experimented with various administrative policies, groups within the new British colony of Quebec began to assert themselves, and developments in the larger North Atlantic world continued to influence the course of events. It was by no means the conquest alone that determined the fate of the *Canadiens* in subsequent years.

In the aftermath of the conquest, between two and three thousand people moved to France—mostly administrators, merchants, and military leaders—but the bulk of the colonists remained. Most of the seventy thousand people living in Canada had been born in the colony; some of them traced their ancestors back several generations. They had little choice but to accept the fact that they were now British subjects by conquest. Required to take an oath of allegiance to the British king, they did so with little resistance. Their conquerors had taken the precaution of disarming them, and the fate of the Acadians was still fresh in their minds.

The colony remained under military rule and military occupation until 1764. James Murray maintained a strict discipline among his occupying forces and a lenient policy toward the conquered people. A fiery Scot with twenty years of military service behind him, he was still only thirty-nine years old when he became the most powerful man in the colony. His decisions respecting colonial policy would have a major impact on how the conquered colony developed under British rule.

Murray introduced a form of military rule that resembled the political system under the French regime. He governed with an appointed council and subordinates in the three jurisdictions of Quebec, Trois-Rivières, and Montreal. Since the chief military officers all spoke French and French laws were respected, the transition to British authority was eased considerably. Murray granted new commissions to former militia captains, and most of them adequately performed the required duties.

Like most Protestants, Murray distrusted the Roman Catholics, particularly the Jesuits, who were notorious around the world for their political intrigues. The capitulation agreement reflected this distrust by stipulating that only the parish priests and female religious orders could continue their activities. Male religious communities were forbidden to recruit new members and would gradually die out. If they had wished to do so, the British could have crippled the Roman Catholic Church by refusing to appoint a successor to Bishop Pontbriand, who had died in 1760. Without an official head of the church, no priests could be consecrated, and in short order the whole structure of the institutional church would crumble.

Murray quickly recognized the critical role played by the church in the social and spiritual life of the colony. Accordingly, he provided monetary assistance to the parish priests and the various women's orders. He also collaborated in having Abbé Jean-Olivier Briand whisked off to France to be consecrated by French bishops in 1764. As "Superintendent of the Romish Religion," Briand had full episcopal powers. For the time being at least, the institutional structure of the church remained intact.

Like the French administrators before him, Murray relied upon the church to perform necessary social services. He also expected the priests to counsel their flocks to submit to their new masters. Briand and most of those who served under him proved obedient, motivated not only by their fundamental respect for authority but also by the knowledge that the fate of the church would be determined by the good will of the conquerors.

The economic crisis induced by a generation of warfare and profiteering was perhaps the biggest problem facing the conquered colony. Not surprisingly, the merchants who had made the biggest profits were among those who quickly decided to leave. Those who stayed found themselves unable to compete with the British and New England merchants who arrived in the wake of Wolfe's army. Although there were not many of them—the immigrant British population remained under one thousand in the decade following the conquest—they had the connections, the capital, and the competitive edge over their French rivals in the British mercantile system. Because the rules of mercantilism required that colonial trade be confined solely to the mother country, the Canadians' contacts in France, which once counted for everything, were now worthless.

Not all the problems of the merchant class could be blamed on the British. Most of the remaining Canadian merchants faced bankruptcy as a result of the economic crisis that had developed during the long years of warfare. Under the French regime, paper money had replaced hard currency and prices had skyrocketed. The British brought hard currency, imposed price controls, and regulated the supply of necessities. Paper money was registered and, although heavily discounted, gradually disappeared from circulation. While the conquered people were apparently impressed by the British efficiency in these matters, they paid a heavy price for the colony's discounted currency.

In the early years of the occupation the sympathy shown by Murray and his army surprised the Canadians, who had been encouraged to expect the worst from their conquerors. The military paid in hard cash for the supplies it commandeered, and when there was a shortage of essential supplies in the colony the British made military stores available to civilians. Even Murray felt compelled to comment to his superiors on the "uncommon generosity" displayed by his men toward "these poor deluded people."

> I must here, in justice to those under my command in this government, observe to Your Lordship, that in the winter which immediately followed the reduction of this Province, when from the Calamaties of War, and a bad harvest, the inhabitants of these lower parts were exposed to all the horrors of a famine, the Officers of every rank, even in the lowest, generously contributed towards alleviating the distress of the unfortunate Canadians by a large subscription. The British Merchants and Traders readily and cheerfully assisted in this good work, even the poor Soldiers threw in their mite, and gave a day's provisions, or a days pay in a month, towards the fund. By this means a quantity of provisions was purchased and distributed with great care and assiduity to numbers of poor families, who, without this charitable support, must have inevitably perished.[6]

Soon after the conquest, orders had to be issued to stop the soldiers from marrying Canadian women without permission from their commanders. Clearly, the attitudes of at least some of the conquered people were softening toward the conqueror.

•Civilian Rule

With the Treaty of Paris signed, British officials began to make plans to incorporate New France into the British colonial empire. James Murray was appointed governor of the new, compact British colony of Quebec and his commission, dated 10 August 1764, together with the Royal Proclamation of 1763, served as the foundation of civilian government. Under these regulations Britain made little attempt to accommodate the cultural differences of its new subjects. Quebec was to become a colony like most of the others in North America, ruled by a governor advised by an appointed council and an elected assembly. British law would be introduced and justices of the peace appointed at the local level. Roman Catholics were denied political rights under British law, so only the few hundred Protestants in the colony would be eligible to vote and hold public office. The thinking behind such policy—if there was any thinking at all—seems to have been that the conquered subjects would be quickly assimilated into the language and religion of the conquering people.

Both Murray and his successor, Sir Guy Carleton, quickly realized that British institutions were not suited to the newly conquered colony. The Canadians complained about the cost and complexity of the British legal system as well as the harsh penalties it imposed for minor offences. Because only Protestants could serve as lawyers, jurors, justices of the peace, and judges, cultural antagonism soon coloured the judicial process. Murray eased the tension by permitting Roman Catholics to practise law and serve on juries, but it was clear that the conquered people longed for a return to the French civil code.

As British institutions began to take root, the whole structure of Canadian society was put in jeopardy. The seigneurs, for instance, found themselves in a precarious position. Although they retained ownership of their estates, their seigneurial privileges were less secure under British law. Even more damaging to their status was the loss of income derived from their military and political offices, which had previously supplemented their seigneurial dues.

Canadian merchants also faced predictable difficulties in their attempts to adjust to the British mercantile system. While a few of them made a successful switch from French to British suppliers, the British merchants usually had the upper hand in securing military contracts, credit, and cargo space. British merchants in Montreal also quickly gained primacy in the fur trade, and like the French before them they emerged as the chief rivals of the Hudson's Bay Company traders. Canadian personnel proved valuable as guides, interpreters, and labour in the fur trade, but they no longer commanded the posts or determined trade policy.

For the majority of people, the problems facing the privileged classes were manifested only indirectly. A few habitants endured exorbitant increases in their seigneurial dues as seigneurs desperately tried to shore up their declining incomes, but the worst abuses in exacting rents would come only after the seigneurial regime was sanctioned by law in 1774. In the years following the conquest, agricultural production increased and the population grew at a rapid rate. These were not the best of times for Canadian peasants, but they were certainly not the worst.

The old aristocratic ideal as reflected in the seigneuries appealed to British administrators. For Murray, the system stood in sharp contrast to the grasping commercialism typical of the small knot of British and New England merchants in the urban centres. Murray informed the Board of Trade in London:

> Little, very little, will content the New subjects; but nothing will satisfy the licentious fanatics trading here but the expulsion of the Canadians, who are perhaps the bravest and the best race upon the face of the globe, a race, who could they be indulged with a few privileges which the laws of England deny to Roman Catholics at home, would soon get the better of every national antipathy to their conquerors, and become the most faithful and most useful set of men in this American empire.

In an effort to prevent the British minority from using its power to exploit the Canadians, Murray postponed calling an assembly. The English merchants were outraged. They were also annoyed both by the restrictions on the fur trade that Murray enforced and by his obvious attempts to conciliate the conquered Canadians. In 1765 their criticisms of the governor led to his recall.

Sir Guy Carleton arrived in Quebec in 1766 prepared to address the concerns of the small British community in the colony, but he soon adopted the views of his predecessor. Both men were influenced to a considerable degree by the larger political forces emerging on the North American continent. With France no longer a threat to their development, the Anglo-American colonists were less willing to accept colonial policies defined exclusively with British interests in mind. Like Charles Lawrence, the official in Nova Scotia responsible for the Acadian explusion, Murray and Carleton were military men charged with protecting their colony in the event of war. Yet the strategic factor coupled with their own aristocratic values caused them to reach a different conclusion than that of the governor of Nova Scotia. The conquered Canadians would make better patriots, they reasoned, than the rebellious, republican-minded Anglo-American colonists.

•The Quebec Act, 1774, and the American Revolution

Carleton's views were reflected in the Quebec Act, passed by the British Parliament in 1774. Designed to strengthen the traditional elites in the colony, the act was based on the mistaken belief that those elites would ensure the loyalty of the masses in time of war. To that end the tithes of the church were guaranteed, the seigneurial system was legally recognized, and French civil law was reintroduced in the colony. English criminal law would remain in force. The status of the colonial elite was also enhanced by the decision to permit Roman Catholics to participate in colonial government. Under the Quebec Act, the colony was to be ruled with the advice of an appointed council rather than an elected assembly. Canadians could be appointed to the council, but all councillors would serve at the pleasure of the governor. No rabble-rousing assembly like the ones that existed in the colonies of Massachusetts and Virginia would stir up problems for imperial authorities in Quebec.

The Quebec Act also dramatically increased the size of the colony. Quebec's boundaries were extended southwest into the Ohio territory, eastward to include Labrador, and north to the borders of Rupert's Land. Here, too, strategic interests seem to have dominated the thinking of British authorities. What better way to forestall the greedy Anglo-American settlers eyeing the fertile lands of the Ohio frontier than to attach the region to the fur trade interests of Montreal? If anyone could establish some semblance of order in the region, it was the Montreal traders. Similarly, Quebec was the nearest administrative centre to Labrador and the northern fur trade frontier. These areas were virtually empty of permanent European settlement and Britain hoped to keep them that way. By Palliser's Act of 1775, Newfoundland was also barred to settlement and North American-based fishing interests. Not surprisingly, many Anglo-Americans saw both the Quebec Act and Palliser's Act as deliberate attempts on the part of the mother country to restrict their access to the rich resources of the North American continent.

By 1774 the British had virtually reestablished the old regime in Quebec. Their reasons for doing so were practical. With another war in North America a virtual certainty, it was important to ensure the security of this strategically located and potentially rebellious colony. Secret instructions to Carleton indicated that, in the long run, the British authorities hoped to whittle away the legal and clerical concessions of the Quebec Act, but in the meantime those concessions would serve to placate the Canadian elite. There is little doubt that the seigneurs and clerical leaders were pleased by the restoration of their traditional privileges, but other segments of Quebec society were less enthusiastic. Although delighted with the extension of the boundaries of their fur trade empire, the Protestant merchants resented the loss of their democratic right to an elected assembly they could dominate. The habitants also had mixed feelings about an act that left them more beholden than ever before to the seigneurs and clergy. Would not an elected assembly work for the ordinary people in a colony where there were fewer than a thousand British immigrants and a Canadian elite that survived only through the intervention of the conqueror?

Although the Canadians may have reserved judgment on the Quebec Act, people in the rebellious Anglo-American colonies knew exactly what they thought about it. By granting the Ohio country to a despotic and Roman Catholic colony, Britain had clearly gone too far. Such a policy seemed to be of a piece with other "intolerable" acts passed by the British Parliament.

Anxious to make the colonies cover the enormous costs of their defence and administration, King George III and his chief ministers introduced a series of unpopular measures without the approval of the elected colonial legislatures. Anglo-Americans, especially in Massachusetts, erupted in riotous indignation when taxes on sugar, paper, and tea were imposed upon them without their consent. Britain's decision to enforce its mercantile regulations restricting colonial trade and to billet soldiers in private homes brought further howls of protest and outright defiance. In 1774, unwilling to back down in the face of colonial opposition, British authorities closed the port of Boston, suspended democratic government in Massachusetts, and subjected the colony to an army of occupation. A number of the British colonies responded by uniting in angry indignation against what they viewed as their despotic mother country.

In September 1774, delegates from twelve colonies—all except for Newfoundland, St John's Island, Nova Scotia, Quebec, and Georgia—met in Philadelphia to co-ordinate a response to Britain's arbitrary colonial policy. The First Continental Congress condemned the coercive acts and demanded their repeal. When Britain refused to back down and instead sent more troops to North America to enforce its will, colonial militia were placed on alert. Clashes between the two sides occurred at Lexington and Concord in Massachusetts in the spring of 1775. A second Continental Congress in May voted to raise an army under George Washington to defend "American liberty." After driving the British out of Boston, they planned to march on Quebec.

This decision to invade Quebec was based on a number of assumptions. There was every reason to expect that the Canadians would be eager to throw off the yoke of their recent conquerors, and a few of the English-speaking merchants were sympathetic to the republican cause. If there were spontaneous uprisings in support of their invading armies, all to the good. Nova Scotia was also home to a sympathetic population, but was impossible to attack without supporting seapower. The British forces in Quebec, however, might succumb during a winter siege.

Prior to invasion, the Americans flooded the colony with propaganda designed to convince the Canadians to join their cause. One of the broadsides made a dramatic call to arms:

> Seize the opportunity presented to you by Providence itself! . . . You are a small people compared to those who with open arms invite you into fellowship. A moment's reflection should convince you which will be most for your interest and happiness, to have all the rest of North America your unalterable friends, or your inveterate enemies. The injuries of Boston have roused and associated every colony, from Nova Scotia to Georgia. Your province is the only link that is wanting to complete the bright strong chain of union. Nature has joined your country to theirs. Do you join your political interests? For their own sakes they will never desert or betray you. Be assured that the happiness of a people inevitably depends on their liberty, and their spirit to assert it.

It is difficult to assess the impact of such stirring sentiments on the common people. What is clear is that one of the issues fuelling this war was democratic idealism, which contrasted sharply with the values of European monarchies.

In September 1775 an army of two thousand men led by Richard Montgomery moved down the Lake Champlain–Richelieu River route toward Montreal. The plan was to take Montreal and proceed to Quebec, where they would meet another army under Benedict Arnold, which was marching overland along the Kennebec and Chaudière rivers. Because

Carleton had sent half of his garrison to assist General Gage in Boston, he was left with only six hundred regulars for the defence of his colony. The fate of Quebec hung on the reaction of the colonists to the invading forces.

To the surprise and dismay of Carleton, who had been so certain of the loyalty of his "new subjects," Montgomery's troops met little resistance and considerable support as they moved toward Montreal. The citizens of the city capitulated without a fight, and Carleton himself narrowly escaped capture as he fled to Quebec. In Quebec Carleton found the people anxious to repel the invading forces, whose popularity had dwindled. The Americans had begun commandeering supplies when their money ran out, and their hostility toward the Roman Catholic Church was manifested in vandalism against shrines and churches. By the time winter had set in, few Canadians saw the Anglo-Americans as their liberators.

Like Wolfe before him, Montgomery found it difficult to breach the natural defences that surrounded Quebec. A desperate attack launched on the evening of 31 December failed. Montgomery was killed during the encounter and Arnold was wounded. In May 1776 the Americans beat a hasty retreat when British ships arrived bearing ten thousand troops. The large military force also guaranteed the good behaviour of the civilian population.

During the nine-month occupation by the Americans, Carleton found little to criticize about the behaviour of the seigneurs and clerical officials. They had supported his efforts to raise a colonial militia among the habitants and behaved as Carleton felt leaders should in times of crisis. Bishop Briand had even threatened to withhold the sacraments from those who refused to take up arms in defence of their homeland. Although less enthusiastic than the seigneurs, the French-speaking merchant class also leaned toward the British.

The habitants, however, showed no inclination to follow the example of their superiors. What had happened to the fighting spirit of the Canadians? Carleton and the Canadian elite were appealing to a generation that had already fought a difficult war. They were not enthusiastic about taking up arms again. Moreover, both sides were led by English-speaking Protestants whose goals had little to do with the needs of the war-weary Canadians. A few people voluntarily participated in the fighting on both sides, but most habitants waited out the conflict, selling supplies to those who offered hard cash, and preserving their neutrality as long as possible. After the arrival of the British army in 1776, the possibility of resistance was considerably reduced. Carleton's successor, Sir Frederick Haldimand, handed out stiff sentences to those who resisted the hated military *corvée* and kept a close watch on anyone suspected of disloyalty.

The British element in the colony was no more reliable than the habitants. Some of the merchants actually acted as informers for Montgomery. As the war dragged on, fur traders such as Peter Pond found it a convenient time to make a trip into the interior to discover new customers and communication routes. In Nova Scotia the majority of the population showed a similar disinclination to shoulder a musket in the cause of British imperialism. Indeed, many people in the frontier colonies often found it difficult to see why they should become involved in a war that they played no part in causing and that could bring disaster to their dependent colonial economies.

Like the Canadians, the Iroquois were also encouraged to take sides in the conflict, and, again like the Canadians, they were divided about what to do. Joseph Brant convinced his Mohawk followers and some Seneca to fight with the British, while Guy Johnson helped to enlist the support of the Iroquois of the Caughnawaga and St Regis reserves. The Oneida and Tuscarora, perhaps influenced by their ties with Congregational ministers, leaned toward the Americans. The Onondaga and Cayuga remained neutral until 1779, when American troops invaded their territory. This provoked them into retaliatory raids on American settlements. As the struggle continued, guerrilla fighting gripped the whole Anglo-American frontier. With their homelands at stake, the Natives proved to be among Britain's most effective combatants, although they were fighting for themselves, not for any European power.

Carleton's failure to pursue the retreating militiamen meant that the Americans lived to fight another day. On 4 July 1776 the Thirteen Colonies declared independence from Britain. When Britain's forces were defeated in the battle of Saratoga in 1777, its European enemies could not resist the chance to strike a mortal blow. France joined the fray in 1778, followed by Spain the next year. With France as an ally of the Americans, another invasion of Quebec was planned. However, the French were reluctant to see the new United States control too much of the continent, while the Americans preferred even the hated British over the French on their northern flank. Because neither side could agree on who should rule the colony if it were captured, Quebec was spared a second invasion.

For the aboriginal peoples and Canadians, the American Revolution had brought another devastating war to their homelands, followed by an equally disruptive peace treaty. The Atlantic colonies had remained largely outside of the theatre of war, although in the end they would also be profoundly influenced by the conflict. After the right of the Thirteen Colonies to independence was recognized by the Treaty of Versailles, signed in 1783, British North America was confined to the northern half of the continent and included only those areas that had been ceded by France to Britain in 1713 and 1763.

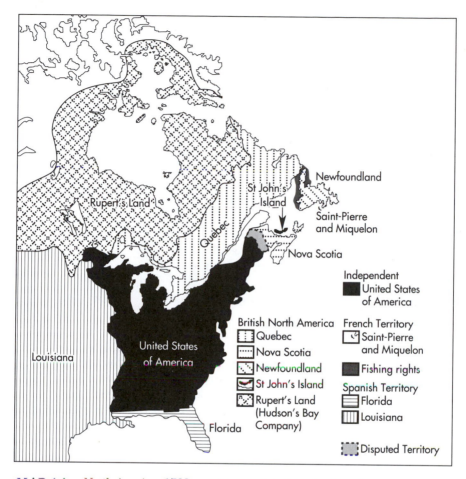

MAP 6.4   *North America, 1783*   (*Historical Atlas of Canada*, vol. 1 (Toronto: University of Toronto Press, 1987), plate 44)

After the conflict, an invasion of ten thousand Loyalists brought new pressures on the British administrators in Quebec. The refugees demanded British institutions such as an elected assembly, common law, and freehold tenure. Like the English-speaking merchants of Quebec, they complained bitterly about the provisions of the Quebec Act that denied them their rights as British subjects. The stage was set for another attempt on the part of British authorities to devise a constitution for its bicultural North American colony.

• Culture and Conquest:
A Historiographical Debate

Historians have little difficulty agreeing upon the immediate impact of the conquest on the Canadians. As stated most bluntly by Susan Mann Trofimenkoff, "Conquest is like rape."[7] Scholars are less likely to agree upon the long-term impact of such a traumatic event.[8] As with most historical debates, events in the present very often shape the way historians view this critical moment in Quebec's history. There were other conquests in Canadian history—for instance, that of Acadia in 1710–13 and the centuries-long subordination of the first nations—but the conquest of Quebec has generated the most comment because many historians see it as a causal factor in the problems facing the Québécois in the nineteenth and twentieth centuries.

Early French-Canadian historians were inclined to see the conquest as a tragedy that blunted the colony's cultural and institutional development. Conservative in their political philosophy, they argued that New France was devastated when the leading citizens departed for France following the conquest and French political structures were replaced by "barbaric" British institutions. In the words of one of French Canada's first historians, François-Xavier Garneau, "The evils they had previously endured seemed light to them compared to the sufferings and humiliations which were in preparation, they feared, for them and their posterity."[9]

A contrasting view, popular among nineteenth-century clerics, saw the hand of God in a conquest that spared Quebec the evils—in particular the liberalism and atheism—of the French Revolution. Only a few liberal French-Canadian historians, such as Benjamin Sulte, saw virtue in the conquest *because* Britain replaced absolute rule with constitutional government. This view had been typically argued by anglophone historians, most notably Francis Parkman, who maintained, "A happier calamity never befell a people than the conquest of Canada by British arms."[10] For Parkman, the most important theme in history was the broadening of liberty as represented in the Protestant Reformation, representative institutions, and laissez-faire economic policies. New France, with its Roman Catholic hierarchy, authoritarian political institutions, and mercantile economy, clearly had, in his view, little to offer to the progress of Western civilization.

As the Industrial Revolution began drawing more and more *Canadiens* into the ranks of the urban working class, conservative historians in Quebec gradually made the habitant farmer the hero of New France. It was in the countryside that the seeds of French-Canadian nationalism were well and truly planted, they argued, and where Christian virtues remained uncorrupted. Abbé Lionel Groulx, writing in the inter-war years, even claimed that the French Canadians were a superior race, purified by the fires of the conquest and guided throughout by the steady influence of the Roman Catholic Church. In Groulx's estimation, the Québécois were "perhaps the purest race on the whole continent," a characteristic not easy to verify by demographic evidence but one that clearly meant much to him.[11]

As Quebec entered a period of rapid social and economic transformation following the Second World War, "la survivance" in the countryside was no longer enough, and the interpretations of the conservative school were squarely challenged. Maurice Séguin, an influential historian at the Université de Montréal, called upon *Canadiens* to lift themselves from the paralyzing hold of the "agrarian retreat." For Séguin, Canada under the *ancien régime* was "colonization in the full sense of the term," while the conquest was a "catastrophe" forcing the *Canadiens* back on an ever declining agricultural economy. "The solution to Quebec's problems," he maintained, "would be a return to the kind of integral colonization we had before 1760." His call to action inspired many of the students who attended his classes: "Let us take the land, but also the forest, the mines, the watercourses, the fisheries; in a word; all the resources of our country, their processing and their trade, if we want to save our nationality by ensuring its unrestricted economic life."[12]

Two of Séguin's colleagues at the Université de Montréal, Guy Frégault and Michel Brunet, were the most articulate advocates of what became known as the "Montreal School." Frégault concluded that New France was, like all colonies, dependent upon imperial investment, but its evolution was "normal" within the context of North American colonial development. The Canadian community in 1763, however, was "conquered, impoverished, socially decapitated, and politically in bonds," while "French colonization, more vital than ever, was conclusively halted."[13]

Michel Brunet went even further. Drawing directly upon Marxist theory, which held that the bourgeoisie was the dynamic class in capitalist society, he explored the impact of the conquest on the Canadian middle class in the thirty years following the conquest. "The Conquest forced them to compete with unequal weapons," he concluded. "This fact dominates the whole of the economic history of French Canada after the Conquest." For Brunet, the excessive emphasis on agriculture, the domination of social and intellectual life by the Roman Catholic Church, and the distrust of democracy all stemmed from the "decapitation" of the Canadian society in 1763.

The Montreal School's position reflected contemporary concerns over the English domination of the Quebec economy. By the 1960s they were politically linked with the *nationalistes* who were seeking independence for Quebec. Historians at Université Laval in Quebec City, who were branded as "federalists" for their historical interpretations, challenged the views put forward by the Montrealers. Jean Hamelin led the way, calling into question the notion that there was a dynamic middle class in pre-conquest New France. "The essential fact on this subject that emerges from the intendants' correspondence," he maintained in 1960, "is the poverty of merchants and traders as a group throughout the period of French rule." For Hamelin, "The absence in 1800 of a vigorous French-Canadian bourgeoisie . . . emerges not as a result of the Conquest but as the culmination of the French regime."[14]

Hamelin's views were echoed by Fernand Ouellet, who accepted the finding that there was a weak middle class in the pre-conquest period. Unlike Hamelin, however, Ouellet concluded that this fact was irrelevant to the economic condition of French Canadians in the post-conquest period. For Ouellet, the profound changes wrought by the Industrial Revolution were reasons enough for the economic underdevelopment that characterized Quebec in the nineteenth and twentieth centuries. In recent years, most historians have followed Ouellet's lead in moving away from overly deterministic interpretations of the conquest. While welcoming the rich historical evidence marshalled for the debate, they resist seeing it as having value except in revealing more about life as it was lived in the eighteenth century.

•Notes

[1] Richard White, *The Middle Ground: Indians, Empires, and Republics in the Great Lakes Region, 1650–1815* (Cambridge: Cambridge University Press, 1991), 313.

[2] W.J. Eccles, *The Canadian Frontier, 1534–1760* (New York: Holt, Rinehart and Winston, 1969), 158.

[3] See René Chartrand, "Death Walks on Snowshoes," *Horizon Canada*, 260–74.

[4] White, *Middle Ground*, 252.

[5] L.S.F. Upton, *Micmacs and Colonists: Indian–White Relations in the Maritimes, 1713–1867* (Vancouver: University of British Columbia Press, 1979), 58.

[6] Cited in W.J. Eccles, *The Ordeal of New France* (Montreal: Canadian Broadcasting Corporation, 1966), 139.

[7] Susan Mann Trofimenkoff, *The Dream of Nation: A Social and Intellectual History of Quebec* (Toronto: Gage, 1982), 31.

[8] For a summary of the debate, see Dale Miquelon, ed., *Society and Conquest: The Debate on the Bourgeoisie and Social Change in French Canada, 1700–1850* (Toronto: Copp Clark Pitman, 1977); "The Conquest of 1760: Were Its Consequences Traumatic?" in *Emerging Identities: Selected Problems and Interpretations in Canadian History*, ed. Paul Bennett and Cornelius Jaenen (Scarborough, ON: Prentice Hall, 1986), 76–105; and Serge Gagnon, *Quebec and Its Historians: The Twentieth Century* (Montreal: Harvest House, 1985), 53–89.

[9] François-Xavier Garneau, *History of Canada, from the Time of Its Discovery till the Union Year (1840–41)*, Vol. 2, trans. Andrew Bell (Montreal, 1860), 84–6.

[10] Francis Parkman, *The Old Regime in Canada*, Vol. 2 (Toronto, 1899), 205.

[11] Lionel Groulx, *Lendemains de conquête* (Montreal, 1920), 234–5, cited in *Emerging Identities*, ed. Bennett and Jaenen, 90.

[12] Maurice Séguin, "La Conquête et la vie économique des Canadiens," *Action nationale* 28 (1947), cited in Miquelon, *Society and Conquest*, 78.

[13] Guy Frégault, "La colonisation du Canada au XVIIe siècle," *Cahiers de l'Académie canadienne-française* 2 (1957), 53–81.

[14] Jean Hamelin, *Économie et société en Nouvelle-France* (Quebec, 1960) cited in Miquelon, *Society and Conquest*, 105, 114.

•Selected Reading

As for earlier chapters, R. Cole Harris and Geoffrey J. Matthews, *Historical Atlas of Canada*, Vol. 1 (Toronto: University of Toronto Press, 1987), and the pertinent volumes of the *Dictionary of Canadian Biography* (Toronto: University of Toronto Press, 1966–90) offer a wealth of information on this period of Canadian history.

On Native relations in the eighteenth century, see J.R. Miller, *Skyscrapers Hide the Heavens: A History of Indian–White Relations in Canada* (Toronto: University of Toronto Press, 1989); L.S.F. Upton, *Micmacs and Colonists: Indian–White Relations in the Maritimes, 1713–1867* (Vancouver: University of British Columbia Press, 1979); Richard White, *The Middle Ground: Indians, Empires, and Republics in the Great Lakes Region, 1650–1815* (Cambridge: Cambridge University Press, 1991); Howard H. Peckham, *Pontiac and the Indian Uprising* (Chicago: Russell, 1971); Barbara Graymont, *The Iroquois in the American Revolution* (Syracuse, NY: Syracuse University Press, 1972); Cornelius J. Jaenen, "French Sovereignty and Native Nationhood during the French Regime, *Native Studies Review* 2, 1 (1986); Olive Dickason, "Amerindians Between French and English in Nova Scotia, 1713–1763," *American Indian Culture and Research Journal* 10, 4 (1986): 31–56, and "Louisbourg and the Indians: A Study in Imperial Race Relations," *History and Archaeology* 6 (1976): 1–206.

On the military history of the eighteenth century, see I.K. Steele, *Guerrillas and Grenadiers: The Struggle for Canada, 1689–1760* (Toronto: Ryerson Press, 1969); George F.G. Stanley, *New France: The Last Phase, 1744–1760* (Toronto: McClelland and Stewart, 1968), and *Canada Invaded, 1775–1776* (Toronto: Hakkert, 1973); C.P. Stacey, *Quebec, 1759: The Siege and the Battle* (New York: St Martin's Press, 1959); Guy Frégault, *Canada: The War of the Conquest*, trans. Margaret M. Cameron (Toronto: Oxford University Press, 1969); Robert McConnell Hatch, *Thrust for Canada: The American Attempt on Quebec in 1775–1776* (Boston: Houghton Mifflin, 1979).

On the Acadians, see Naomi Griffiths, *The Acadians: Creation of a People* (Toronto: McGraw Hill-Ryerson, 1973), and *The Contexts of Acadian History, 1686–1784* (Montreal: McGill-Queen's University Press, 1992); Andrew Hill Clark, *Acadia: The Geography of Early Nova Scotia to 1760* (Madison: University of Wisconsin Press, 1968). Jean Daigle, ed., *The Acadians of the Maritimes* (Moncton: Centre d'études acadiennes, 1982) brings the Acadian odyssey up to the twentieth century. J.B. Brebner, *New England's Outpost: Acadia Before the Conquest of Canada* (New York: Columbia University Press, 1927), and George A. Rawlyk, *Nova Scotia's Massachusetts: A Study of Massachusetts–Nova Scotia Relations, 1630–1784* (Montreal: McGill-Queen's University Press, 1973) offer valuable insights on geopolitical developments in the Atlantic region in the early eighteenth century.

On Quebec following the conquest, see A.L. Burt, *The Old Province of Quebec* (Ottawa: Carleton University Press, 1933; reprt. 1968); Hilda Neatby, *Quebec: The Revolutionary Age, 1760–1791* (Toronto: McClelland and Stewart, 1966); Fernand

Ouellet, *Social and Economic History of Quebec*, trans. Robert Mandron (Toronto: Gage Publishing, 1980); Cameron Nish, ed., *The French Canadians, 1759–1766: Conquered? Half Conquered? Liberated?* (Toronto: Copp Clark Pitman, 1966); Dale Miquelon, ed., *Society and Conquest: The Debate on the Bourgeoisie and Social Change in French Canada, 1700–1850* (Toronto: Copp Clark Pitman, 1977); and José Iguartua, "A Change in Climate: The Conquest and the *Marchands* of Montreal," Canadian Historical Association Papers (1974): 115–43.

PART III

Origins of British North America

Time Line

1741	–	Bering and Chirikov explore the North Pacific
1749	–	Founding of Halifax
1752	–	*Halifax Gazette* begins publication
1758	–	Elected assembly established in Nova Scotia
1759–67	–	New England Planters arrive in Nova Scotia
1764	–	Acadians permitted to settle in Nova Scotia
1767	–	St John's Island granted by lottery to British proprietors
1769	–	St John's Island given colonial status; *History of Emily Montague* published in London
1772	–	Samuel Hearne reaches Arctic Ocean
1774	–	Juan Pérez sights the Queen Charlotte Islands; Cumberland House established
1775	–	Palliser's Act
1775–85	–	Arrival of the Loyalists
1776	–	Eddy Rebellion
1776–83	–	American Revolutionary War
1778	–	The Nuu'chah'nulth (Nootka) of Vancouver Island encounter Captain Cook
1783	–	North West Company formed
1784	–	New Brunswick and Cape Breton established as separate colonial jurisdictions
1789	–	King's College founded; French Revolution begins
1790	–	Nootka Sound Convention
1791	–	Constitutional Act
1792	–	Simcoe becomes lieutenant-governor of Upper Canada; Black Loyalists depart for Sierra Leone
1793	–	Alexander Mackenzie reaches the Pacific by an overland route; Upper Canada Act against slavery
1793–1815	–	French Revolutionary and Napoleonic wars
1794	–	Spanish give up their claims to the North Pacific coast
1799	–	St John's Island renamed Prince Edward Island
1809	–	Labrador placed under jurisdiction of Newfoundland
1811	–	David Thompson descends the Columbia to its mouth
1812	–	Establishment of Red River settlement
1812–14	–	War of 1812
1815	–	Election of Louis-Joseph Papineau as speaker in Lower Canadian Assembly
1817	–	Arrest of Robert Gourlay
1819, 1825, 1845	–	Franklin expeditions

1820	–	Cape Breton annexed to Nova Scotia
1821	–	Merger of Hudson's Bay Company and North West Company
1826	–	George Simpson becomes North American governor-in-chief of Hudson's Bay Company
1829	–	Death of Shawnadithit; Upper Canada College founded; Catholic emancipation
1832	–	Newfoundland granted an elected assembly; first cholera outbreak in the Canadas
1833	–	Major crop failure in Lower Canada
1834	–	92 Resolutions passed in Lower Canadian Assembly; Upper Canadian Assembly endorses Report of Committee on Grievances; second cholera outbreak; York incorporated as City of Toronto
1835	–	Slavery abolished in British Empire; Kingston Penitentiary opened
1836	–	Controversial Conservative win in Upper Canadian Assembly elections; *Backwoods of Canada* published
1837	–	Russell's Ten Resolutions; crop failure in Lower Canada for second consecutive year
1837–38	–	Rebellions in Lower and Upper Canada
1839	–	Lord Durham's report
1840	–	Act of Union
1842	–	Montreal Board of Trade established; Dawn community founded; Webster-Ashburton Treaty
1845–51	–	Famine in Cape Breton
1845–52	–	Garneau's *Histoire du Canada* published
1848	–	Responsible government in Nova Scotia and United Canadas
1849	–	Rebellion Losses bill; ten-year lease of Vancouver Island to Hudson's Bay Company
1850	–	Fugitive Slave Law passed in United States
1851	–	James Douglas becomes governor of Vancouver Island; first coalition government of elected conservatives
1854	–	Abolition of seigneurial system and clergy reserves
1855–66	–	Reciprocity Treaty
1858	–	Gold rush on Fraser and Thompson rivers; mainland British Columbia becomes Crown colony
1860	–	Report of Hind expedition
1862	–	Report of Palliser expedition
1863	–	London bankers buy Hudson's Bay Company

CHAPTER 7

THE PEOPLING OF BRITISH
NORTH AMERICA, 1750s–1800

In 1783 Filer Diblee, a lawyer from Connecticut, arrived on the north shore of the Bay of Fundy with his wife and children. They were part of the movement of thousands of Loyalist refugees from the newly created United States of America to an area that remained under British control. Arriving destitute in Nova Scotia, the Diblee family spent their first rough winter in a log cabin, and very quickly Filer's "fortitude gave way" at the prospect of imprisonment for debt. He subsequently "grew Melancholy, which soon deprived him of his Reason, and for months he could not be left by himself." Finally, in March 1784, "whilst the Family were at Tea, Mr. Diblee walked back and forth in the Room, seemingly much composed: but unobserved took a Razor from the Closet, threw himself on the bed, drew the Curtains, and cut his own throat."[1]

Not all Loyalists experienced such despair at being cast adrift by the exigencies of war, but for a professional person used to city life, the frontier experience was overwhelming. Diblee's family bore the brunt of his premature death. When their crude cabin caught fire twice in one year, Filer's widow, Polly, was forced to depend upon the mercy of neighbours and relatives for survival. "I assure you, my dear Billy," Polly informed her brother in England in the fall of 1787, "that many have been the Days since my arrival in this inhospitipal Country, that I should have thought myself and family truly happy could we have 'had Potatoes alone,' but this mighty boon was denied us."

During the second half of the eighteenth century, 75 000 people—many of them, like the Diblees, with tragic tales to tell—arrived in the territories that had been ceded by France to Britain in 1713 and 1763. These immigrants would have a dramatic impact on the areas where they settled.

In 1750 people of aboriginal and French origins dominated the northern half of the North American continent. Some fifty years later, English-speaking settlers made up the majority of the population in the Atlantic colonies and were a growing presence in the St Lawrence–Great Lakes region. By the end of the century, too, British fur traders and explorers had mapped the extent of Rupert's Land and had dotted the interior of the continent with trading posts.

By 1800 the "old regime" that had characterized European nations and their colonies had been swept away. The so-called "modern" world, based upon democratic political systems and industrial capitalism, was still in its infancy, but there was little doubt about which nation would dominate the new world order. Despite its embarrassing loss of thirteen American colonies, Great Britain was well on the way to establishing a global empire based on seapower and industrial capacity.

•Nova Scotia

Britain's first serious attempt to colonize the French possessions acquired by the Treaty of Utrecht came in 1749. In May of that year, Colonel Edward Cornwallis sailed into Chebucto Bay with the aim of establishing a naval and military base to counter the French presence at Louisbourg. Named after the chief officer of the Board of Trade and Plantations, the town of Halifax was to attract a curious mix of immigrants. Cornwallis was accompanied by three thousand settlers, including artisans from London and soldiers and sailors discharged from the recent war. Soon after they arrived many of the military men disappeared on vessels bound for Boston, but in their place came New Englanders attempting to escape debt or indenture and merchants anxious to profit from the vast sums of money being invested in the frontier colony.

Halifax represented the latest thinking in urban planning. The town was laid out according to a rigidly symmetrical model plan, with rectangular streets moving up the steep slope from the waterfront. In the centre was the Grand Parade, which served as the focus of community life. An Anglican and a Presbyterian church were located facing the parade grounds alongside storehouses for munitions and powder. On the landward side, the town was protected by a palisade and five forts, while water approaches were secured by three batteries. A common burial ground was located just outside the palisade.

In year-round communication with the North Atlantic world, Haligonians were kept informed about the latest developments by their local newspaper, the *Halifax Gazette*, founded in 1752. The paper, with its four pages of cramped print, bore little resemblance to today's bulky illustrated dailies. Nor was it the principal vehicle of communication in Halifax. Gossip travelled quickly through the compact community's streets, helped along by an abundance of taverns—estimated at as many as one hundred by 1760—where merchants, administrators, military men, and civilians mingled regularly.

In the first decade after its founding, Halifax was a divided and unhappy community. Old and New Englanders nurtured ancient grudges and spawned new grievances. Merchants and government officials clashed over contracts and public policy. Into this fractious community stepped a Jersey-born merchant, Joshua Mauger, who took advantage of the chaos to gain ascendancy over both the economy and political institutions of the colony. Using his vast wealth gained from the West Indies trade and smuggling with Louisbourg, he advanced credit to the merchants in Halifax and soon became their indispensable patron.

Mauger's influence in London and Louisbourg made him a major player in administrative circles. Moreover, his monopoly of the manufacture of rum, protected from imports by a high customs duty, ensured that his wealth and influence would both continue to increase. By the 1760s Mauger was so powerful in London that he could secure the dismissal of governors and other officials who challenged his authority. Many citizens found little reason to stay in Halifax. In 1755 the town's population was less than it had been in 1749. The outbreak of war brought welcome relief from the economic doldrums, but a pattern of boom-and-bust cycles based on imperial favour was already deeply rooted in the rocky Halifax soil.

Between 1750 and 1753 nearly 2500 German- and French-speaking immigrants from Protestant states of the old Holy Roman Empire were brought to Nova Scotia under contract by John Dick. Part of a much larger continental European migration to North America, these "foreign Protestants" were recruited to balance the Acadian presence in the colony. Cornwallis had intended to locate them in Acadian settlements, but he soon realized that the plan would not work. The continuing hostility of the Acadians and Mi'kmaq made it impossible to guarantee the safety of the settlers. To the consternation of the authorities, some of the French-speaking among them deserted to the enemy and those who remained had no more liking for their military overlords than did the Acadians. After spending as many as three unhappy years in makeshift camps in Halifax, some 1600 of the immigrants were moved to Lunenburg on the south shore of Nova Scotia. Despite several difficult years, the Lunenburg "Deutsche" sank permanent roots. Those who remained in Halifax left evidence of their early settlement along Dutch Village Road.

After the expulsion of the Acadians and the capture of Île Royale and Île Saint-Jean, British officials renewed their attempts to attract settlers to the region. A ready source of immigrants was near at hand. For decades New Englanders had used the Atlantic shores of Nova Scotia as a base for their summer fisheries and had coveted the rich dyked farmlands of the Annapolis valley and Chignecto. Only one obstacle stood in their way. Over the years since the British conquest of 1713, Nova Scotia had developed a well-deserved reputation for despotic government. Liberty-loving New Englanders were not prepared to come to Nova Scotia without their cherished "rights as Englishmen" being fully protected.

Although Cornwallis was authorized to establish British administrative and judicial institutions, he and his immediate successors continued to keep power in the hands of appointed officials. The commissioners on the Board of Trade and Plantations finally forced a reluctant Governor Lawrence to call an elected assembly in 1758. In the same year Lawrence issued a proclamation, widely circulated in New England, inviting prospective immigrants to Nova Scotia. A second proclamation in 1759 outlined the rights guaranteed in the new Nova Scotia: two elected assembly members for each settled township, a judicial system like the one in New England, and freedom of religion except for Roman Catholics. Under British law, Catholics were permitted to worship as they wished but were denied political rights.

With these important matters seemingly settled, New Englanders began to see Nova Scotia in a new light. The offer of land, free of charge and exempt of taxes for ten years, was one few people could resist. A head of household could claim one hundred acres as an individual and fifty acres for each family member. Even servants could be included in the count to increase the size of the grant. Since some of the land was already cleared and surveyed, it compared favourably with the tree-covered wilderness that usually faced immigrants on the settlement frontier. Many New Englanders, including Benjamin Franklin, tried to get their names on petitions for land grants submitted to the Nova Scotia authorities—although Franklin and other speculators had no intention of moving to Nova Scotia. They simply hoped to lay claim to the land and later earn a profit by selling it.

For once the British authorities guarded against the worst excesses of land speculation by issuing title only to bona fide settlers. Over eight thousand New Englanders responded to Lawrence's call. Known as "Planters" the old English term for settlers, they created a new New England in the western portions of the old colony of Nova Scotia. Fishing families from Massachusetts moved into the sheltered bays and harbours of Nova Scotia's south shore; farming families from Connecticut, Rhode Island, and Massachusetts filled up the townships located in the Annapolis valley and around the Isthmus of Chignecto. James Simonds, James White, and William Hazen, New England merchants associated with Joshua Mauger, established trading operations at Portland Point, near the mouth of the St John River. Their influence was soon paramount in the region. When a party of farmers from Essex County, Massachusetts, squatted further up the river on land that was occupied by Acadians and Maliseet and reserved for disbanded soldiers, the newcomers prevailed. Helped by Mauger's intervention, the New Englanders received title to the land and promptly named their settlement Maugerville in honour of their champion.

By the end of the 1760s the New England migration had slowed to a trickle. Land speculation contributed to the decline: in one seventeen-day period in 1765 some 1.2 million hectares of land had been granted, leaving little arable land for potential settlers. The opening of the western territories by the Treaty of Fort Stanwix in 1768 also pulled New England settlement in a westerly rather than a northerly direction. By that time well over half the 14 000 people in Nova Scotia could trace their origins to New England.

The Planters brought a distinctly "Yankee" culture to the shores of Nova Scotia. Dissenting religious views, close-knit families, a penchant for trading, and a fierce individualism were typical New England traits. Since the settlers were so close to their original homeland they had little difficulty drawing upon its resources to sustain their values and institutions. Congregational ministers were recruited from New England and aspiring Planter parsons returned home to be ordained. Whole buildings were disassembled in New England, loaded on sailing vessels, and reassembled in Nova Scotia. Although it took time for the Planters to develop their own educational institutions, the more affluent families sent their offspring to live with Boston relatives so the children could attend the best schools in North America. The surplus from farm and fishing operations was sold in the Boston market as often as in Halifax. Despite the return of a few disgruntled immigrants to New England, the Planter townships quickly established themselves. In less than one generation these resourceful Yankees had reached a level of subsistence and institutional development rare in the annals of North American settlement.

The New England Planters were only the largest of several immigrant groups to locate in Nova Scotia in the two decades following the expulsion of the Acadians. Indeed, the Acadians themselves maintained a precarious presence in the region. As many as two thousand of them managed to hide in the outlying regions of Nova Scotia and St John's Island (formerly Île Saint-Jean), while others were held as prisoners. The prisoners were employed by their captors in repairing the dykes in the Annapolis valley and served as domestics and labourers in the Halifax area.

In 1764 the British agreed to permit the Acadians to stay in Nova Scotia on condition that they take an oath of allegiance. This decision served as a signal for those in hiding to lay claim to land and for those in exile to return to their beloved "Accadie." Concentrating in the areas where many of them had waited out the expulsion, they carved out homes in Argyle and Clare in southwestern Nova Scotia, Canso, and Cape Breton in eastern Nova Scotia, the northeastern shore of what would become New Brunswick, and the western side of St John's Island. Scratching a miserable existence from the stubborn soil that characterized their grants, they soon turned to the sea to supplement their subsistence. The establishment of Jersey-based fishing operations in the Gaspé and Cape Breton regions encouraged this seaward orientation and also attracted Jersey immigrants to Acadian communities.

ELIZABETH AND EDMUND DOANE

Elizabeth and Edmund Doane were enterprising New England Planters who settled in Barrington, Nova Scotia. According to family tradition, the Doanes dismantled their two-storey house in the Cape Cod community of Eastham and loaded it, together with their seven children, livestock, and provisions, for the journey to Nova Scotia. Bad weather and shipwreck dogged their journey northward in the fall of 1761, but they finally reached Barrington the following spring.

In addition to running their own farm, they kept a shop that held accounts for fifty of the community's families. Elizabeth Doane also served as doctor and midwife for her neighbours.

When the Doanes began to think of returning to New England because of hard times in the pioneer community, their neighbours encouraged them to stay by suggesting that Elizabeth Doane submit a petition for a land grant in her own name. Her petition, dated 13 May 1770, stated: "Elizabeth Done Being Destitute of Accomdation of Land to Set a House upon But am Nevertheless free and willing to Exert my facilities and Skil [in physic and surgery and midwifery] and having a Love for the People . . . Request the favour of . . . a Small tract of Land." Thirty-eight proprietors of the Township of Barrington—all men—signed her petition, and her grant was approved. Elizabeth Doane continued to provide medical care for her Barrington neighbours for many years, and when she became too old to make house calls by foot, two men carried her in a basket suspended by a pole across their shoulders. She died in 1798 at the age of eighty-two.[2]

Mi'kmaq   (National Gallery of Canada/6663)

Following the defeat of their French allies, the Mi'kmaq and Maliseet had little hope of retaining their hunting grounds and fishing bases. In the Atlantic region, Natives were expected to petition the British Crown for land in the same way as whites, and they had to forfeit any uncultivated holdings. Although some land was periodically reserved for Natives, it remained unprotected from the encroachment of immigrants and never formed the basis of the extensive reserve system that existed in other British North American colonies.

The plight of the Mi'kmaq is revealed in an 1823 petition from Jean Baptist and Joseph Elexey, Mi'kmaq in southwestern Nova Scotia:

> Your petitioners were formerly settled at Eel Brook in this Township and was drove off by the Lands being granted and since that have set-tled on three different tracts of Land and have also been removed in the same manner at last your petitioners settled on a Tract of Land up the Tusket River Twenty Miles from Salt Water the Last season we built

one House and a number of Hutts and raised one hundred Bushel of potatoes, Some Indian Corn and considerable garden Stuff last [fall] three men came on the Land with the intention of taking possession your petitioners having been so often removd, beg your Excellency will take the [case] into your consideration and grant them the Land they now occupy or such other Lands as your Excellency may think proper.[3]

The Mi'kmaq and Maliseet were handicapped by their linguistic and religious differences: they spoke very little English and were Roman Catholics. When British authorities refused to continue the French practice of annual gift giving and the services of a Roman Catholic priest, a few Mi'kmaq made their way to Newfoundland to contact the French based at Saint-Pierre. They inevitably incurred the hostility of the Beothuk, who were fighting a losing battle for existence. It is impossible to estimate the number of Natives who survived the final struggle for ascendancy in the Atlantic colonies, but after 1763 their fate was never seriously in doubt. They were pushed to the margins of society, at best the objects of charity, at worst easy targets for exploitation by rapacious immigrants. Only their Roman Catholic faith and the folk memory of an earlier golden age when they were a proud race of farmers, fishers, hunters, and gatherers sustained them through the long winter of defeat and dispossession.

Under British rule Nova Scotia also supported a growing black population, both slave and free. Over half of the more than one hundred "Negroes" enumerated in the Nova Scotia census of 1767 lived in Halifax, where they were used as slave labour by the military and more affluent settlers. A few Planters brought their slaves with them, and a few free black Planters received land grants from the Crown in the 1760s. Whether slave or free, African-Americans were the victims of unrelenting racial prejudice. In a diary entry for 28 August 1767 Simeon Perkins, a merchant and magistrate living in the south shore Planter community of Liverpool, described how an unnamed black man came to experience punishment at the town's newly acquired whipping post: "The negro Sailor was brought before Elisha Freeman, Esq and me. He was found guilty of taking fish out of Snow's yard, valued at one shilling (petite larceny). He was ordered to be stripped, whipped 20 stripes, set in stocks one hour, pay treble damage, and cost of prosecution. He was whipped at the new whipping post and stocks. He was the first to suffer such punishment."[4] Blacks would often find themselves before colonial magistrates, victims of poverty, dependence, and discrimination in a society dominated by whites.

Irish of both Protestant and Roman Catholic backgrounds became part of Nova Scotia's cultural mosaic. The Irish were prominent among the settlers accompanying Cornwallis in 1749 and afterwards continued to trickle into Halifax. Soldiers, indentured servants, tenant farmers, and shipwrecked sailors escaped from the narrow opportunities of the Emerald Isle to try their luck in Nova Scotia. Land speculator Alexander McNutt spun ambitious schemes for planting thousands of Ulster Protestants in Nova Scotia on the one million hectares he claimed for the purpose. He enticed fifty families of Protestant Irish from Londonderry, New Hampshire, to settle on land around the Cobequid arm of the Bay of Fundy in 1761. He also brought several hundred immigrants directly from Ulster to Cobequid and the township of New Dublin on the south shore of Nova Scotia. But most of McNutt's proprietorial plans came to naught, frustrated by his own lack of capital and Britain's firm refusal to sanction mass emigration from Ulster.

Between 1772 and 1776 some one thousand Yorkshire English settled in the Chignecto area of Nova Scotia. Encouraged by Lieutenant-Governor Michael Francklin and pushed out of Yorkshire by high rents, land enclosures, and their own ambitions, they brought with them commercial and farming skills typical of the emergent industrial heartland of Britain from whence they came. They had a low opinion of the New Englanders among whom they settled, criticizing them for their sloppy farming methods and their reliance on barter rather than money in their trading activities. The Methodist faith of the Yorkshire settlers also served to set them apart from their New England neighbours.

In the mid-eighteenth century there was little evidence of a Scottish presence in New Scotland. Although as many as 25 000 Scots emigrated between 1763 and 1776, most of them moved to colonies further south along the Atlantic seaboard. In Nova Scotia outside of Halifax, the first focus for Scottish settlement was the Philadelphia plantation on the Northumberland Strait. Granted to fourteen Scots proprietors in 1765, it received its first direct shipload of Highland settlers in September 1773, when the *Hector* sailed into Pictou harbour. Less than half of the 178 people on board the *Hector* remained in the settlement a year later, but the occasion marked the beginning of a migration that by 1830 would make the Scots the largest ethnic group in Nova Scotia.

• St John's Island

Scots made up a significant portion of the British pioneers on St John's Island (Prince Edward Island). Of great interest to land speculators once it was confirmed as a British possession in 1763, the island was surveyed into sixty-seven townships by Captain Samuel Holland in 1764. Three years later, in one of the most spectacular lotteries in Canadian history, the British government gave sixty-four of the lots to favourites of the king and court in London.

According to the conditions of the grants, the proprietors were required to bring out Protestant settlers, improve their properties, and sustain early colonial administration through the payment of quitrent. Such stipulations were similar to those of the seigneurial system in New France. As in New France, there was a twofold purpose in resorting to this method of planting colonies. One was to maintain a conservative social structure that placed power and wealth in the hands of a colonial elite. The other, and more important, consideration was to have private initiative bear the cost of colonial settlement. Theoretically there was little risk involved in delegating authority in this way. If the proprietors failed to fulfil the conditions of their grants, their titles could be escheated, or cancelled, and the ownership of the land would revert to the Crown.

Unfortunately for St John's Island, the proprietors did not fulfil the conditions of their grants, nor did the normal processes of escheat prevail. The proprietors used their influence to have a separate administration for the island proclaimed in 1769. In 1770 Governor Walter Patterson arrived in the colonial capital, named Charlottetown in honour of the queen, and by 1773 the first assembly was elected. Thereafter any policy for land reform had to be approved by the colonial legislature as well as by British authorities. Since proprietorial interests had strong supporters both on the island and in Britain, movements to improve the land system were easily frustrated. The lottery of 1767 thus marked the beginning of the great "land question" that would bedevil island society until the proprietorial system was abolished in the 1870s.

In their initial flush of enthusiasm, several proprietors did make serious efforts to fulfil their settlement obligations. By the terms of the grant, proprietors were forbidden to recruit immigrants directly from Britain, but these restrictions failed to deter them. Many of the proprietors were Scots and they were in a good position to know the social conditions among the Highland crofters. A disintegrating clan structure, a declining kelp industry, overcrowding on meagre tenant properties, and rising rents made emigration an obvious option for many Highlanders.

The first settlers, some eighty Scots recruited by Captain Robert Stewart for Lot 18, arrived on the *Annabella* in 1770. James Montgomery, the lord advocate for Scotland from 1766 to 1775, planted Scots on his extensive holdings, while the Scottish Catholic Church sent out a group of Highlanders under the direction of John MacDonald of Glenaladale in

1773. Tenants from Ulster were tempted by what seemed like reasonable terms for leasing land, and a colony of London Quakers established a base at Elizabethtown. Lack of provisions, social conflict, and crop failures—plagues of mice were a recurring menace—threatened survival in the first years of settlement. Many who could afford to do so left their farms for better opportunities elsewhere. Nevertheless, St John's Island had nearly 1500 residents by 1775 and, in the words of historian J.M. Bumsted, "appeared to be teetering on the brink of success."[5]

• Newfoundland

Unlike Nova Scotia, Newfoundland did not attract a wide range of immigrants, nor was the island the object of government-sponsored settlement schemes. The British authorities continued to oppose settlement in Newfoundland for political and strategic reasons. The fishermen in the western counties of England were a powerful lobby group determined to keep a tight control over their lucrative fishing banks. They wanted no competition from free agents based in North America. In this policy they were supported by the Crown because fishermen were the chief source of recruits for the British navy in times of war. It was much more convenient for the British Admiralty to send press gangs to the ports of Cornwall and Devon than to the outports of Newfoundland.

Notwithstanding official policy and tough laws discouraging settlement, Newfoundland drew a steady stream of immigrants from the home ports of the British fleet and the south coast of Ireland where crews were recruited for the fishing season. The advantages of wintering in Newfoundland were obvious to the fishermen. They could get a head start on the fishery in the spring, protect their shore bases from interlopers, and live without tax or trouble on a sheltered patch of the coastline. By 1775 over twelve thousand people called themselves "Newfoundlanders," a term apparently used as early as the 1760s.

In the eighteenth century the shore-based fishery grew steadily, while the catch of the migratory fleet declined. Recognizing the obvious, British merchants sent an increasing number of "sack ships"—the large ocean carriers of the eighteenth century—to purchase the product of the resident fisheries for their European markets. By the 1750s, New Englanders were competing with British merchants in supplying Newfoundlanders with manufactured goods, provisions, and rum in return for fish, which they sold in the West Indies. Yankee traders also carried fishermen to New

England, where labour was often in short supply. This activity contravened the British navigation acts that governed colonial trade, but as long as the acts were not enforced in Newfoundland waters, New England and foreign vessels could trade with impunity.

Following the Seven Years' War Britain took steps to establish tighter control over the Newfoundland fishery. In 1764 laws were passed giving British authorities more power to arrest smugglers. A customs house was built at St John's to collect duties on imports, followed by a Court of Vice-Admiralty to handle disputes relating to trade. Between 1762 and 1770 Captain James Cook and his successor Michael Lane carried out a survey of Newfoundland (including the islands of Saint-Pierre and Miquelon, which had been ceded to the French by the Treaty of Paris in 1763), providing British authorities with a more accurate picture of the colony over which they officially had control.

The imperial thrust was epitomized in the person of Captain Hugh Palliser, who became governor of Newfoundland in 1764. He expelled as many as five thousand fugitives during his four-year tenure, challenged the rights of "owners" of shoreline property, and, in his well-meaning efforts to protect Native people, even seized the bases of the Labrador seal fisher-

A Moravian missionary with the Natives at Nain, Labrador   (Maria Spilsbury/ National Archives of Canada/C124432)

men. In 1775 the British government confirmed imperial control over the fisheries in an act of Parliament, commonly named after the governor who so persuasively argued the narrow mercantile perspective.

Palliser's Act issued strict regulations against permanent settlement, provided bounties to increase the competitive edge of the British-based fishing fleet, and imposed fines on captains who failed to return with their full complement of crew. In short, Newfoundland was to remain a great wharf moored in the North Atlantic for the benefit of the West Country fishermen. Under no circumstances was it to become a colony like the others in North America, with its own political and social institutions. Indeed, it was to have no permanent settlers other than the Beothuk. Like many of Britain's imperial policies in this period, Palliser's Act flew in the face of colonial reality and only consolidated the growing resentment within the older British North American possessions. Nevertheless, it served as the basis for colonial policy for nearly fifty years.

European settlers, for good reasons, earned the fear and enmity of the Beothuk. In Labrador, the Inuit, Naskapi, and Montagnais populations survived the impact of European contact. In 1770 George Cartwright built a fur-trading and fishing base at Cape Charles and later moved to Sandwich Bay. He was followed by other British-based companies, but it was not until 1834 that the Hudson's Bay Company built its first trading post at Rigolet. Over sixty years earlier, in 1763, Jens Haven, a Moravian missionary in Greenland, established a mission in Nain, the first of several operated by the United Brethren. They established schools, taught practical skills, provided medical services, and kept close control over the trade of the region. It was perhaps because of the missionary presence that the Native peoples in Labrador were able to survive the disease, intertribal warfare, and European greed that led to the total destruction of the Beothuk.

ARTISTS IN A NEW WORLD

Native artists in British North America produced intricate carving, beading, baskets, and painted skins. The first non-Native artists in the colony were soldiers, draftsmen, and natural scientists who had received some training in drawing. Because drawing was the only method of creating a visual record before the introduction of photography in the mid-nineteenth century, it was a valuable skill taught in many professions.

Eighteenth-century European-born artists were trained to impose a rigid order on their subject matter, omitting any details that might offend

European sensibilities. The idealized North American environment can be seen in the work of Moses Harris, an entomologist and engraver who arrived in Halifax in 1749, and Richard Short, a purser with James Wolfe's expedition.

Joseph Frederick Wallet DesBarres was a Swiss-born army officer who, together with Samuel Holland and James Cook, surveyed most of the Atlantic region in the period following the Seven Years' War. DesBarres included landscape views in his much-praised *Atlantic Neptune*, a four-volume guide to navigation in the region. In their detail and colour, the paintings of Thomas Davies represent a departure from the topographic watercolours done by students of the military academy. Davies was posted in the British colonies from 1755 to 1790, and his work, such as *View of the River La Puce*, offers an exceptional visual record of the eighteenth-century landscape.

By the eighteenth century it had become fashionable among the middle class in Europe and North America to have their portraits painted. It was difficult to make a living solely as a portrait artist in British North America, in part because members of the colonial elite often travelled either to Britain or the United States to have their portraits done by the most widely acclaimed artists of the period. The first colonial-born portrait artist in the Atlantic region was Joseph Brown Comingo, from Lunenburg, Nova Scotia. Although little is known about his artistic training, he worked extensively throughout Nova Scotia and New Brunswick, painting both portraits and landscapes. His miniatures, such as the one of Jane Harbel Drake, were particularly popular in the eighteenth and early nineteenth centuries.

One of British North America's most accomplished artists was William Berczy. Born in Wallerstein (Germany), in 1744, Berczy arrived in 1794 in Upper Canada, where he was involved in various colonization schemes. During his sojourn in the colony he supplemented his income by painting miniatures and portraits. His portrait of Joseph Brant is considered an accurate portrayal of the Mohawk chief, and art historian Dennis Reid argues that Berczy's *The Woolsey Family* is "one of the few exceptional Canadian paintings" of the early nineteenth century.

In the private schools that flourished following the arrival of the Loyalists, young ladies received training in the "polite" accomplishments of drawing and watercolour painting. Women were also occasionally taught to draw by their formally trained fathers and brothers. Because they had few practical outlets for their work, women rarely earned a living from their artistic endeavours, and very few signed pieces of their work have survived the ravages of time and neglect.

The Woolsey Family, 1809, by William Berczy   (National Gallery of Canada/5875)

A painted robe, Sioux type   (Canadian Museum of Civilization/74-7928)

View of the River La Puce Near Quebec in Canada, 1792, *by Thomas Davies* (National Gallery of Canada/6274)

Miniature of Jane Harbel Drake by Joseph Brown Comingo   (New Brunswick Museum/ 989.13.1)

•The Loyalist Interlude, 1775–85

The impact of the American Revolutionary War was as great on the North American colonies that remained in the British Empire as those that joined the new United States of America. A flood of immigrants, a reorganized colonial administration, and a new boundary line followed in the wake of the war. In one crucial decade, the British Empire in North America was reduced to a shadow of its former self, and the foundations of a second transcontinental nation on the North American continent were tentatively laid.

There is no easy answer as to why Quebec, Newfoundland, Nova Scotia, and St John's Island did not join with the other British North American colonies in shaking off the yoke of British imperialism. Certainly, the failure of the invasion of 1775–76, the presence of British troops, and the caution of the population combined to keep Quebec within the British sphere of influence during the American Revolutionary War. For a variety of reasons the Atlantic colonies also remained under British control.

Newfoundland's situation was perhaps the most clear cut. Its fisheries were part of the great triangular trade dominated by Britain, so it would have been economic suicide to cut the ties that bound that trade together. Even if Newfoundlanders had chosen to take the side of the Thirteen Colonies, they would have had difficulty doing so in any formal way. There were no local institutions on the island that could respond to an invitation from the Continental Congress to join in the crusade for liberty.

Halifax was similarly a creation of the imperial system, and the people there, unlike Bostonians, considered British soldiers an economic boon rather than a social irritant. In the outlying regions of the colony there was much sympathy for the rebel position but little enthusiasm for battle. A religious revival led by Henry Alline in the Planter townships attracted as much, if not more, attention than the secular battles raging around them. On St John's Island the inhabitants were too busy putting down roots to participate in a war for independence. In short, the Atlantic colonies were at such an early stage of economic and social development that revolution was low on the list of priorities.

Still, for most people in the Atlantic region, the issues fuelling the conflict were sharply drawn. To take up with the wrong side could result in the loss of property, position, and even life itself. Seizure of rebel property by British soldiers or attacks by New England privateers could wipe out a generation of hard-earned subsistence. Few of the pioneer colonists could risk such a fate, and as a result behaved cautiously.

The presence of a British fleet in the North Atlantic during much of the war discouraged George Washington from any serious thought of invading the region. There was, however, a brief flurry of rebel activity in the fall of 1776 when Jonathan Eddy, a member of the Nova Scotia assembly for Cumberland, and John Allan, a Scottish-born resident in the area, led a force of nearly 180 men against the British garrison at Fort Cumberland (formerly Fort Beauséjour). As in many other colonies, class and cultural conflict as much as colonial liberation motivated the resort to violence. Eddy's ranks included some nineteen Natives from the St John River area and perhaps forty Acadians prepared to use the occasion to strike at their British conquerors. Over sixty of the rebels came from Machias and Maugerville, where identification with the Massachusetts cause was strongest. The rest were mostly New England-born settlers in the Cumberland–Cobequid region of Nova Scotia. While the Fort Cumberland attack was easily repulsed by soldiers sent from Halifax, the aftermath had a devastating impact on the people in the area. The tension among Planters, Yorkshire settlers, and British soldiers resulted in bloodshed, looting, and litigation that continued for over a decade.

HENRY ALLINE AND NOVA SCOTIA'S GREAT AWAKENING

The New Englanders living in Nova Scotia probably had more difficulty than other settlers in the colony deciding where their loyalties lay during the Revolutionary War. As the people of Yarmouth noted in a petition to the British authorities asking not to be conscripted, "almost all" of them were "born in New England" and had "Fathers, Brothers & Sisters in that Country." As they stated: "Divided betwixt natural affection to our nearest relations, and good Faith and Friendship to our King and country, we want to know, if we may be permitted at this time to live in a peaceable State, as we look on that to be the only situation in which we, with our Wives and Children, can be in any tolerable degree safe."[6]

For most ordinary people war is a troubling experience, and Nova Scotians were not alone in seeking to avoid participation in the armed conflict. As members of dissenting churches, many New England Planters in the colony could advance religious reasons for a neutral stance. Spiritual salvation, they argued, not worldly concerns, was the goal of committed Christians. During the war a charismatic advocate of this position emerged in the person of Henry Alline.

Born in New England in 1748, Alline moved to Falmouth, Nova Scotia, with his parents in 1760. He experienced a dramatic religious conversion in 1775 and thereafter travelled the Maritime region preaching his "New Light" message. He was well received by New England Planters, many of whom had witnessed similar "awakenings" in their former homeland. Others, especially those of the Church of England and Roman Catholic persuasion, found the rhetoric and emotional style of Alline's preaching unappealing. They may also have had difficulty accepting Alline's argument that the New England Planters were "a people highly favoured of God" in being called to the safe haven of Nova Scotia before the outbreak of war. In fact, few of Alline's followers probably held such a view of their migration experience. They responded instead to the message of liberation at the heart of Alline's teachings and to his inspiring hymns, many of which he wrote himself.

When the war ended Alline carried his free will message back to New England, where he died of tuberculosis in February 1784. Most, though not all, Allinites in the Maritimes became members of the Baptist churches, which still maintain a strong following in the region. Alline's journals were published by his followers, and along with his hymns they represent some of the earliest prose and poetry produced in British North America.

Privateering raids were a feature of the war for most people living in the seabound Atlantic colonies. In November 1775, for example, privateers landed in Charlottetown, plundering homes, seizing provisions, and carrying away the colony's leading officials, including the acting governor, Phillips Callbeck. Most raids were similarly selective, leaving all but targeted victims unmolested, but such activities did little to endear pioneer settlers to the revolutionary cause. Virtually every outport settlement from Yarmouth Township to Labrador was visited by privateers, an indication that republican forces perceived the northern colonies as an extension of the British frontier of influence in North America rather than as allies in the cause.

After the defeat of British forces at Saratoga in 1777 the scene of fighting moved to the middle and southern American colonies. Thereafter the North Atlantic colonies became even more British in orientation. The increased military presence in colonial capitals, the profit to be gained by supplying British troops, and the influx of Loyalists fleeing from rebel-held strongholds sealed the fate of Nova Scotia and St John's Island.

When the war ended, the Atlantic region became a homeland for the losers of the revolution. Branded as "Tories" or "Royalists" by the triumphant American patriots, 70 000 self-styled "Loyalists" left the United States to start their lives over again. Half of them went to Nova Scotia. Some of them eventually moved on to other destinations such as Britain or the West Indies, but most had little alternative but to remain in this nearest British-controlled territory.

Although the Loyalists had few good words for "Nova Scarcity," and their suffering during the first years was genuine, they were luckier than many refugee peoples. They were given provisions and temporary shelter, and a few eventually received compensation from the British government for their losses. Governor John Parr in Halifax quickly escheated unoccupied lands in his jurisdiction and had his surveyor, Charles Morris, carve out townships in the still unsettled regions of the colony. In a remarkably short time cities sprang up at Port Roseway (Shelburne) and Parrtown (Saint John), and dozens of villages—Guysborough, Ship Harbour, Rawden, Aylesford, Digby, Sussex Vale, Gagetown—emerged from the forest-covered wilderness.

When Loyalists on the St John River complained that Halifax was too remote from their concerns, the British government responded by reorganizing colonial administration. In 1784 the old province of Nova Scotia was reduced in size and two new colonies were created: New Brunswick and Cape Breton, with capitals at Fredericton and Sydney respectively. Governor Patterson of St John's Island tried to lure Loyalists to his estates there, but few wanted to begin their new lives as tenant farmers. Over half of the five hundred Loyalists on the island were disbanded soldiers who had been stationed there during the hostilities.

While historians often discuss the Loyalists as if they were a homogeneous group, they were, in reality, as socially and culturally diverse as the society they came from. Perhaps as many as 40 percent of the Loyalist grantees in the Atlantic colonies were soldiers disbanded from volunteer and regular regiments. Many of the rest were refugees who had burned their bridges behind them when they sided with the British. Although these refugees might have preferred to return to their homes after the war ended, hostility against the hated "Royalists" was such that their property had been seized and their lives were still in danger. Other migrants were attracted by the British promise of free land and provisions for three years and saw the possibility of creating a better homeland on the northeast frontier of American settlement.

Ominously for a frontier region, a disproportionate number of the Nova Scotia Loyalists came from urban centres, such as Boston, New York, and Charleston, where British armies had been stationed at various times during the war. Such people were not always well suited to the hardships of pioneer life and, like many of the soldiers, were tempted to leave once they had received their grants. Shelburne was perhaps the most extreme example of Loyalist mobility; its population of nearly ten thousand in 1783 had dwindled to less than one thousand a decade later.

The greatest number of Loyalists who came to the Atlantic colonies were drawn from the lower and middle classes of labourers, farmers, artisans, and merchants. Although a few highly placed colonial officials and Harvard-trained professionals came to the region, most of the wealthy Loyalist elite went to Britain or the West Indies rather than to the northern colonies. Nor were the pretensions of a few Loyalists well received by the mass of refugees. When fifty-five prominent Loyalists petitioned for estates of five thousand acres rather than the basic allowance of a hundred acres for each head of household and fifty for each family member, there was such a hue and cry that British officials were forced to bow to the wishes of the majority. Clearly, loyalism did not include acceptance of the aristocratic ideal that prevailed among British officialdom and those who aspired to it.

Culture as well as class divided the Loyalists. While most of the migrants were colonial-born, 10 percent were recent immigrants from Britain and elsewhere. Ethnic and religious minorities were particularly visible among the refugees. Dutch and Scots, Huguenot and Quaker, for various reasons, swelled the Loyalist ranks. Slaveholding Loyalists brought their "property" with them, and over three thousand free black Loyalists chose to

BLACK LOYALIST PREACHERS IN NOVA SCOTIA AND SIERRA LEONE

Shelburne, Nova Scotia, was the initial destination of nearly half of the free black Loyalists. Pushed to the opposite shore of the harbour, they founded a community they called Birchtown in honour of the British commander in New York who had signed their embarkation certificates. Religious leaders played an important role in the African-American community. Many of the Birchtown settlers were under the pastoral care of the Methodist minister Moses Wilkinson, a former slave. Blind from birth, he was a fiery and persuasive preacher who inspired Boston King, another black Loyalist, to take up the ministry. King was appointed to the Methodist society in Preston, near Halifax, in 1791. Another member of Wilkinson's congregation, John Ball, became an itinerant Methodist preacher in the colony.

After the arrival of the Loyalists, one-quarter of the Methodists in Nova Scotia were African-Americans, a fact that did not go unnoticed by the denomination's founder, John Wesley. In a letter to the white Methodist Loyalist James Barry in July 1784, Wesley noted: "The work of God among the blacks in your neighbourhood is a wonderful instance of the power of God; and the little town they have built is, I suppose, the only town of negroes that has been built in America—nay perhaps in any part of the world, except only in Africa."[7] Wesley vowed to keep his black followers supplied with religious books and encouraged white Methodists to "give them all the assistance you can in every possible way."

Not all the citizens of Birchtown were Methodists. The Reverend John Murrant attracted about forty families to the evangelical Anglican sect known as the Huntingdonians after Countess Huntingdon who funded their missions. When Murrant left Nova Scotia in 1791, his successor as chief pastor to the black Huntingdonians was Birchtown resident Cato Perkins.

By far the most controversial and successful of the black Loyalist preachers in the Shelburne area was David George. Converted to the Baptist faith while still a slave in Georgia, George was a founding member, in 1773, of North America's first African-American church, Silver Bluff Baptist, in South Carolina, and the first slave to serve as its pastor. When the Revolutionary War broke out he escaped to the British lines and came to Shelburne in 1784. His meetings were attended by both black and white settlers, but rioting soldiers tore down his house and drove him out of the town. Birchtown residents, it seems, also found his message too radical and forced him to return to Shelburne.

In addition to their emphasis on salvation through faith rather than good works, Baptists also insisted on adult rather than infant baptism and baptism by immersion rather than by sprinkling. By adopting these beliefs and practices, Baptists defied the teachings of established churches and were widely perceived as encouraging opposition to law and order.

Gradually George's following grew and his fame spread. Like Henry Alline, he preached in many communities in Nova Scotia and New Brunswick, founding churches and appointing elders. He also resembled Alline in his passionate oratory, enthusiastic hymn singing, and emphasis on free will. Not surprisingly, he incurred the hostility of people who liked neither his message nor the colour of his skin. In New Brunswick the lieutenant-governor insisted that he preach only to black people. Riots broke out when he baptized a white couple in Shelburne.

The dream of a "promised land," where they could escape prejudice, own property, and live independently, had inspired black Loyalists to move to Nova Scotia. This dream also led nearly 1200 of them to emigrate to Sierra Leone in 1792. Assisted by philanthropists in Britain who believed that blacks would have a better life in their African homeland, they were also encouraged by their religious leaders to make this last pilgrimage. Over one-third of the blacks in Shelburne, including virtually all of David George's congregation as well as most of Moses Wilkinson's Methodists and Cato Perkins's Huntingdonians, accepted the challenge. The members of Boston King's Methodist chapel in Preston also joined the exodus.

Despite their short sojourn in Nova Scotia, the black Loyalist ministers and their followers had a significant impact on the colony. They left a legacy of literacy, religious conviction, and self-help in both of their adopted homelands, and to this day in Sierra Leone the descendants of the black Loyalists are identified by their Nova Scotia heritage.

settle in Nova Scotia. During the war the British had encouraged slaves to leave their rebel masters by promising them their freedom if they fought in British regiments. Black Loyalists, thus freed, were offered land in Nova Scotia, but were given smaller grants in less desirable areas and became the objects of hostility and violence during the tension-ridden early years of settlement. Not surprisingly, nearly 1200 black Loyalists chose to leave the region in 1792 when offered passage to the new colony of Sierra Leone in Africa.

Over half of the Loyalists who came to the Atlantic region were women and children whose fortunes were dictated by family decisions to support the British cause. A number of widows whose husbands had served in the war were included in the land grants. Even before the arrival of the Loyalists, women and children formed the majority of people in the Atlantic colonies. The Nova Scotia census of 1767 indicated that over

40 percent of the population was female and nearly half of the population was under sixteen. With the family producing most of the goods and services needed for survival in pre-industrial society, and serving as the vehicle for training children in practical skills and moral values, pioneer settlements had little likelihood of success if they were not built upon a solid foundation of productive family units.

Like most pioneer women, Loyalist women were forced to adjust to the circumstances thrust upon them. Sarah Frost, for example, was pregnant when she, her husband, and their two small children boarded the *Two Sisters* in New York harbour in the spring of 1783. The vessel contained 250 passengers, and six families shared a cabin with the Frosts—causing considerable "confusion" below deck. "We bear it pretty well through the day," Sarah confided in her diary, "but as it grows towards night, one child cries in one place and one in another, whilst we are getting them to bed. I think sometimes I shall be crazy." Sarah's parents had supported the revolution and therefore remained in their Connecticut home. Leave-taking was, for many Loyalists, the last time that they would see close family members. When they arrived at the mouth of the St John River on 29 June, Sarah's apprehension clearly showed through in this brief entry in her diary: "It is, I think, the roughest land I ever saw."[8]

The family was not the only institution successfully transplanted by the incoming Loyalists. Because many Loyalists had enjoyed the amenities of urban life, they were impatient to establish churches, schools, and newspapers in their new homeland. Only a minority of them belonged to the Church of England, but the structure of the established church of Britain was strengthened by the Loyalist presence. In 1787 Charles Inglis, the Loyalist rector of Trinity Church in New York, was consecrated the first Church of England bishop of Nova Scotia, with jurisdiction over all the British North American colonies. The first overseas bishop in the British empire, Inglis was anxious to enhance the status of Anglicanism in the colonies. He supported the founding of King's Collegiate Academy and King's College in Windsor, Nova Scotia, as exclusive institutions for sons of the Anglican elite, and he backed various missionary efforts—most of them futile—to draw the mass of the population from their dissenting religious views. In New Brunswick the Loyalists were instrumental in founding the Provincial Academy of Arts and Sciences, which received its charter as the College of New Brunswick in 1800.

As a "consolation to their distress," many educated Loyalists turned to literature. They produced poems, essays, and sermons and were avid readers of British fiction and advice books. In 1789 John Howe, a Loyalist from Massachusetts, and William Cochran, an Anglican clergyman and classical scholar, attempted to provide a forum for colonial writers. Although their

Nova Scotia Magazine lasted less than two years, it ranks as the first literary journal in the British North American colonies.

The pens of Loyalist women were also active. Deborah Howe Cottnam, a teacher and poet, established schools in Halifax and Saint John for the daughters of the Loyalist elite, many of whom wrote poetry and fiction for the amusement of family and friends. Rebecca Byles, a member of a distinguished clerical and literary family forced to flee from Boston in 1775, attended Cottnam's school, read extensively, and wrote verse. She believed that eighteenth-century advances in formal education would result in an improvement in the status of women. "In a few years I expect to see women fill the most important offices in Church and State," she declared.

With the Loyalists came the full range of eighteenth-century political ideologies, which not only raised the level of political debate in the region but also heightened political tensions. The Loyalist elite was unable to cut back on the democratic tendencies taking root in the era of the American and French revolutions, but they added weight to the conservative side of the political spectrum. Loyalists stood for political office in Nova Scotia and St John's Island and dominated the government of New Brunswick. When New Hampshire-born Sir John Wentworth became lieutenant-governor of Nova Scotia in 1792, the Loyalists had one of their own at the helm. They revelled in the courtlike atmosphere of Halifax social life, which included the king's son, Prince Edward, Duke of Kent, and his mistress, Madame de St Laurent. Outside Halifax and Fredericton, however, the pioneer experience had a levelling effect on everyone, and the Loyalist heritage counted for little in a region where after 1783 nearly everyone claimed to have supported the British cause.

•Quebec, 1783–91

The 10 000–12 000 Loyalists who arrived in Quebec increased the influence of the English element in the colony. Most of them were refugees from up-state New York and the back country of Pennsylvania and New England. As in Nova Scotia, the Loyalists who came to Quebec were a diverse lot. A few were prominent officials such as William Smith from New York, who became chief justice of the colony. Others were members of disbanded Loyalist regiments or pacifists whose loyalty had been called into question because they refused to fight. For many of the immigrants, Britain's offer of free land and provisions was a powerful inducement to loyalty. Quebec had a frontier ripe for exploitation, and few people were more aware of the potential of the *pays d'en haut* than the frontier settlers of Pennsylvania and New York.

JOSEPH AND MOLLY BRANT

Mary Brant—generally known as Molly—and her brother Joseph were members of a powerful Mohawk family who allied themselves with the British during the Seven Years' War. In 1758, as a young man of fifteen, Joseph Brant took part in Abercrombie's campaign to invade Canada. He subsequently joined Indian superintendent Sir William Johnson in the capture of Niagara in 1759 and participated in the seige of Montreal the following year. It was around this time that Molly Brant attracted Johnson's attention. Their first child was born in 1759, and before Johnson's death in 1774 they had seven more children who survived infancy. Molly Brant presided over Johnson's household in the Mohawk valley and proved a valuable partner in his fur trade and diplomatic activities. In his will Johnson left his estate to his white son, John, and gave Molly Brant a good portion of land, a black female slave, and £200. With her legacy she opened a store, which sold rum and other trade items to her people.

When the American Revolutionary War broke out, Joseph and Molly Brant allied themselves with the British. Joseph Brant was made official "Interpreter for the Six Nations Language" with an annual salary of £85. In 1775–76 he travelled to Britain to discuss the terms of the alliance. Dressed in the colourful regalia of a Mohawk chief, he was the talk of Londoners, who inducted him into the Freemasons and convinced him to have his portrait painted. Back in North America, Joseph Brant led a force of Native and white soldiers in frontier battles, which included campaigns against the Oneida and Tuscarora, who had sided with the United States. Like white Americans, the Six Nations experienced the American Revolution as a civil war.

Meanwhile, Molly Brant helped to provision the Loyalist forces and kept them informed about rebel activities. In 1777 the victorious Oneida took revenge on the Mohawk. Brant's home was looted and she took refuge at Onondaga (near Syracuse, New York) and later at Niagara. As head of the Six Nations matrons, she exercised her considerable influence to prevent the Mohawk from wavering in their support of the British. During the darkest days of the war, she went to Carleton Island, New York, to convince her discouraged people there to continue the fight. According to Alexander Fraser, the commander in the region, Molly Brant was instrumental in keeping the warriors in line. Their "uncommonly good behaviour is in great measure to be ascribed to Miss Molly Brants Influence over them, which is far superior to that of all their Chiefs put together," he concluded.

When the war ended, Molly Brant moved to Kingston, where Governor Haldimand had a house built for her use. She was also awarded an annual pension of £100, the highest paid to an aboriginal ally. Joseph Brant, embittered by Britain's decision to relinquish sovereignty over all the territory west of the Mississippi to the Americans, tried in vain to forge a confederacy that would, by war or diplomacy, produce a better deal for his people. Fearing another frontier war like the one that had erupted in 1763, Haldimand quickly made arrangements for a tract of land in the Bay of Quinte area to be provided for the Mohawk and other members of the Six Nations and their allies who wanted to move to British-held territory. When the Seneca complained that the proposed site of their new settlement would disperse the Six Nations over too wide an area, Haldimand issued a grant further west along the Grand River, which the Mississauga Ojibwa had recently relinquished. A census taken in 1785 indicates that 1843 aboriginal Loyalists moved to Quebec, including 400 Mohawk, several hundred Cayuga and Onondaga, and smaller groups of Seneca, Tuscarora, Delaware, Nanticoke, Tutelo, Creek, and Cherokee.[9]

Included among the Loyalists were Joseph Brant and his Mohawk followers, who as allies of the British were eligible for land grants. Other Natives living along the North American settlement frontier were not so fortunate. They had been neither consulted nor involved in the negotiations ending the war. By the Treaty of Versailles in 1783, all British territorial claims south of the Great Lakes had been ceded to the Americans. Within a short time the citizens of the United States of America, no longer bound by the paternalistic regulations of the British, pushed their settlement frontier into the heart of the North American continent, trampling the aboriginal population in the process.

Pressured by their desperate Native allies and the merchant community of Montreal, the British decided not to abandon the western posts south of the Great Lakes for the immediate future and granted 300 000 hectares of land in the Grand River valley to the Mohawk. The reserve was part of a much larger land purchase arranged by Governor Frederick Haldimand with an Ojibwa group known as the Mississauga, who occupied the north shore of Lake Ontario. Many Loyalists had their hearts set on settling the fertile lands now known as the Eastern Townships, but Haldimand felt that the territory was too close to the United States for Loyalist settlement. Another war might come at any time, and it would be difficult for British forces to protect such an exposed frontier.

Until the 1780s, the present-day southern Ontario peninsula was the homeland of the Ojibwa, Ottawa, and Algonkin, collectively called the "Anishinabeg," a word meaning "true human beings." These nations had a history of nearly two hundred years of contact with Europeans. When approached by Haldimand, they relinquished control over some of the best agricultural land in British North America, often for seemingly little in return. The Mississauga, for instance, exchanged a strip of land near Fort Niagara for "three hundred suits of clothing" in 1781. By 1788 most of the rest of the land north of Lake Ontario had been ceded in return for guns, ammunition, clothing, and other material items.

While the British believed they were engaging in real-estate deals, the first nations saw the transactions differently. They had a small population and practised collective ownership of the land and its resources. If the British needed the land, the first nations were prepared to share it—for a price. They relied upon manufactured goods and saw the arrival of the Loyalists as an opportunity to enhance their material wealth. It was difficult for them to foresee that in less than a century millions of white settlers would claim the land as their own and deny access to the territories that the first nations had expected to share with the invaders.

In 1784 surveyors began laying out townships for the Loyalists. The fourteen townships in the St Lawrence–Bay of Quinte area were numbered rather than named, because Haldimand had been instructed to incorporate them as fiefs into the seigneurial system. By July 1784 Sir John Johnson, who supervised settlement in the region, reported that 1568 men, 626 women, 1492 children, and 90 servants had arrived. Five of the townships went to Johnson's Royal Yorkers, who arranged themselves in cultural groupings: Catholic Highlanders, Scottish Presbyterians, German Calvinists, German Lutherans, and Anglicans. Other townships in the region were allotted to Major Edward Jessup's corps, Robert Rogers's corps, and refugees from New York organized under Captain Michael Grass and Major Peter Van Alstine. Loyalists also settled in established communities in the colony: Saint-Jean, Chambly, Yamachiche, Pointe-Claire, Sorel, Gaspé, St Armand, Foucault, and Montreal.

Loyalists arriving from the frontier districts of New York and Pennsylvania settled around Fort Niagara. Others located at Sandwich (present-day Windsor) and across the river at Amherstburg, where they mingled with French settlers already long established near Fort Detroit. When the British finally agreed to evacuate the western posts by Jay's Treaty in 1794, settlers moved from Detroit to British-controlled territory; technically, these were the last "real" Loyalists. By that time, Upper Canada had also become the destination of a wave of Americans moving along the settlement frontier. Known as "late Loyalists," they were attracted by the generous terms under which they could take up land rather than by the prospect of living under the British Crown.

Rue Notre-Dame, Montreal, 1786   (Molson Archives/National Archives of Canada, detail)

Like their counterparts in the Atlantic region, the Loyalists who moved to Quebec were given food, shelter, and equipment to get them started in their new homeland. The frontier experience of many of the Loyalists served them well. Within a few years they were producing subsistence crops, and their makeshift shelters were giving way to frame homes. Drought and crop failures resulted in hardships, especially in the "hungry year" of 1789 when some families were forced to rely on their wilderness skills and the sympathy of their aboriginal neighbours for survival; but, overall, the success of their efforts pointed to the potential of the Great Lakes heartland for agricultural settlement. In 1783 Haldimand predicted, "The Loyalists may be the happiest people in America by settling this country." Subsequent events proved him correct.

Although they were only about 10 percent of the population of the colony, the Loyalists brought powerful pressures to bear on authorities in Quebec and London to address their needs. They wanted an elected assembly, common law, freehold tenure, and all the other "rights of Englishmen." In 1785 Johnson and a group of officers petitioned the king on behalf of the Loyalists. They complained of the "rigorous Rules, Homages, and reservations, and Restrictions of the French Laws and Customs, which are so different from the mild Tenures to which they had ever been accustomed." They requested a separate colonial jurisdiction in which a "liberal system of Tenure, Law and Government" would prevail.

As in Nova Scotia, there was also tension among the Loyalists. Many of the settlers resented the pretensions of their former military officers, who received larger land grants and attempted to establish themselves in positions of authority. In addition, the 84th regiment had received especially generous grants, a preferential treatment that piqued the jealousy of those less favoured. Carleton, who had been knighted for his service during the American Revolution and returned as governor of Quebec in 1786, reduced dissatisfaction by increasing land grants all around, but the pressure for constitutional reform would not go away.

Among the most vocal critics of the status quo in British North America were the English merchants in Quebec. They remained stoutly opposed to the provisions of the Quebec Act, which denied them access to the full range of British legal and political institutions. For a time it looked as if Chief Justice William Smith would become a spokesman for this disgruntled group, but his first concern was for the Loyalists in the colony, and he alienated many members of the middle class with his elitist notions of a land-based aristocracy in the Canadian wilderness.

Smith's thinking moved well beyond the limited legal and political concerns of the English merchants. Proposing a federated British North America under a "governor-general" to serve as a "showcase of the continent," he argued for "the admission of all, whether French or English, to office, honour and popular suffrage and trust without any contracted preference or religious discrimination." His "grand design" for the British colonies in North America was a little premature, but it had merits that would soon be recognized by colonial politicians.

In the years during and following the American Revolutionary War, the numbers of English-speaking settlers in Quebec had risen steadily. Most of the English lived in Montreal and Quebec City, near the mercantile and administrative operations they controlled. Despite their small numbers in the countryside, they were rapidly assuming a dominant position in the colony. By 1784 the English owned 26 percent of the seigneuries and received 43 percent of the wealth derived from them. Four of the five most lucrative seigneuries, all worth a thousand pounds or more a year, were in the hands of people with the names of Jacob Jordan, James Cuthbert, Alexander Grant, and Henry Caldwell. In the fur trade, men with names such as McGill, McTavish, Mackenzie, McLeod, Frobisher, and Ross had become prominent. Stiff competition with each other and the Hudson's Bay Company traders pushed the weak to the wall and resulted in the partners in the North West Company—the Bay Company's principal rival—gradually achieving a monopoly over the Montreal-based trade. Few French merchants were included among the North West Company's directors.

Private clubs, such as the Masonic Lodge and Veterans' Club, were established, and informal literary salons, popular in Britain, became a feature of polite society. Between 1763 and 1768 Frances Brooke, one of Britain's leading literary figures, lived in Quebec and produced the first novel written in what would become Canada. *The History of Emily Montague,* published in London in 1769, described the rich social life that prevailed in administrative and military circles in Quebec. As the wife of the Reverend John Brooke, who served as garrison chaplain, Frances Brooke was in a

Portrait of Frances Brooke, circa 1771 (Catherine Read/National Archives of Canada/C117373)

good position to observe the behaviour of her social set. The rapid rise in literacy in the English-speaking world in the second half of the eighteenth century meant that there was a larger audience for written material designed to entertain as well as educate.

By the late 1780s there were also two newspapers, the Quebec *Gazette* and the Montreal *Gazette*, which were bilingual but reflected the views of the English middle class in Quebec. The Montreal *Gazette*, the more radical of the two, advocated greater social equality, public education, and restrictions on the powers of the church. In the summer of 1791 a debating club christened the Robin Hood Society—its name was later changed to the Montreal Society—was formed. Among the topics of debate were the "duty of electors" and the relative merits of marriage and celibacy. Clearly, enlightenment thought had invaded the precincts of the English community in Quebec.

The French middle class of merchants and professionals in Quebec also found liberal values appealing. Many of them were eager to establish an elected assembly in the colony, as long as Roman Catholics retained political rights. Since the conquest the French-Canadian population had doubled, reaching over 160 000 by 1790. It could easily dominate any elected assembly. In contrast the seigneurs and clergy, fearing the loss of their privileges, were suspicious of elected assemblies and argued for the retention of the appointed councils that were authorized by the Quebec Act. Although tensions between English and French were never far from the surface of life in Quebec, class interests often cut across ethnic lines. The radical message of the Montreal *Gazette* reflected the values of both the English and the French middle class in the colony.

Petitions from both sides in the debate over the future of Quebec were sent to the authorities in London, who were now more disposed to listen to their disaffected colonists. In the aftermath of the American Revolution, support for democratic ideals had grown quickly in Europe. Even France, the supreme symbol of absolute government, was awash with debates about the power of the people. When a popular revolution broke out in France in 1789, colonial officials in London moved quickly to try to find a safe middle ground between unbridled democracy and despotic government.

•The Constitutional Act, 1791

In 1791 the British Parliament passed the Constitutional Act, the third attempt to establish institutions for Quebec in as many decades. William Grenville, the secretary of state for the colonies, drafted the bill, which authorized the division of the colony into Upper and Lower Canada. In Upper Canada—the basis for the future province of Ontario—the English-speaking Loyalists made up the majority of the population. Upper Canada would be governed by British laws, including freehold land tenure. Lower Canada with its overwhelmingly French-speaking population would retain the seigneurial system and French civil law. As a compensation to the English settlers in Lower Canada, provision was made for freehold tenure outside of seigneurial tracts, and the Eastern Townships were opened for settlement.

The Constitutional Act represented an attempt on the part of British authorities to stem the tide of democratic sentiment sweeping the North Atlantic world. From their point of view, the American and French revolutions had been caused by an excess of democracy. A British system, it was argued, must retain a balance among monarchical, aristocratic, and democratic principles. In Grenville's own words, the act was designed to prevent "the growth of republican or independent spirit" as inspired by the excessively democratic constitutions of the Thirteen Colonies.

The sole concession to democracy in the Constitutional Act was a House of Assembly in both Upper and Lower Canada to be elected by all qualified voters every four years. Assemblies had already been firmly established in the Maritime colonies and were now difficult to deny to any British colony because of policies developed during the American Revolution. In an attempt to conciliate the Thirteen Colonies, the British Parliament had passed an act in 1778 conceding the principle of "no taxation without representation." Any internal taxes levied in a British colony now had to be approved by the elected representatives of the people bearing the burden of the tax. By granting assemblies to Upper and Lower Canada, the British authorities hoped that colonists would tax themselves for the programs that they supported and thus reduce the burden on the imperial treasury.

Voting privileges followed the British practice. Anyone with a forty-shilling freehold in rural areas or who owned property with a yearly value of at least five pounds, or paid rent for at least a year at the rate of ten pounds per annum, was qualified to vote. Because of the availability of land in North America, a larger proportion of the men in the colonies could vote than in Britain. Women rarely held property in their own name, and even if they did, they seldom exercised the franchise, which was considered a male prerogative. A special oath of allegiance was devised to permit Roman Catholics to vote and hold public office, thus extending the civil rights guaranteed to French Canadians and other Roman Catholics by the Quebec Act. This was an important concession, not only for Quebec but for the whole British Empire. Once granted in the colonies, political rights for Roman Catholics in Britain could not long be denied. Similar concessions were soon granted in Nova Scotia, and by 1829 Roman Catholics throughout the empire had achieved political rights.

Under the Constitutional Act, the powers of the assemblies in the new colonies were constrained by the institutions representing the monarchy and the aristocracy. The monarchy was embodied in the person of a governor in Lower Canada and a lieutenant-governor in Upper Canada. Each colony had a bicameral legislature, with a legislative council to supplement the assembly. The governor (or lieutenant-governor), acting on behalf of the Crown, appointed individuals to the legislative council, which could introduce its own bills and veto all bills originating in the assembly. Because the members of the legislative councils held office for life, were granted huge tracts of land, and under the Constitutional Act were even eligible for titles, they were clearly meant to become the nucleus of a colonial aristocracy. No titles were ever granted in Upper and Lower Canada, but the appointed legislative councillors aspired to special status, especially when it came to land grants and government patronage.

The powers of the governor, the king's representative in the colonies, added even more control over the activities of the assemblies. A governor could withhold consent from a bill passed by the colonial legislature; or he could reserve it for consideration by British authorities, who could disallow the bill within two years of its passage. He could also dismiss an assembly whose policies he found not to his liking.

The governor was also authorized to appoint executive councils to advise him on colonial matters. As was the case with the legislative councils, the men chosen to serve on the executive councils tended to hold office for life. Although the responsibilities of the executive councils were not defined in the Constitutional Act, executive councillors acted as advisers to successive governors and were consequently in a position to exert an enormous influence on colonial policy. They often named friends and relatives to government positions and enhanced their own status by persuading the governor to support their self-serving policies.

Other aspects of the act also strengthened the appointed authorities at the expense of the elected assemblies. Under the Constitutional Act, one-seventh of the land granted in every township was reserved for "the Support and Maintenance of a Protestant Clergy." The wording was vague and would soon be subject to much debate, but the intent was clear. In Upper Canada there would be an established church, presumably the Church of England, to add strength to the monarchical principle. The separation of church and state, a policy now favoured by democrats everywhere, was still too radical a concept for British colonial policy makers.

Like the Quebec Act before it, the Constitutional Act was an attempt to accommodate a variety of interests and conditions. It had barely been passed before war in Europe once again greatly changed the political context. The triumphant republicans in France set out in 1792 to export their revolutionary ideals to the rest of Europe. Britain and other European monarchies tried to stop them. When Napoleon seized control of his war-ravaged country in 1799, he, too, took on his European rivals. It was not until 1815 that Europe finally settled down to an uneasy peace. By that time the weaknesses of the Constitutional Act had become all too apparent.

• Rupert's Land

By far the largest British possession in North America had no formal political institutions whatsoever. Indeed, in 1750 Rupert's Land was still a vaguely defined area. According to the charter granted by King Charles II in 1670, the Hudson's Bay Company had exclusive trading privileges in the area drained by rivers flowing into Hudson Bay. The Bay traders confined their posts to the shores of Hudson Bay—Moose Factory, Albany, York Factory, and Churchill—but soon found their hinterland invaded by their French rivals. By the 1750s the French on the St Lawrence operated a network of posts that extended as far as the forks of the Saskatchewan River.

Competition from the French and the growing instability among Native communities gradually forced employees of the Bay Company to venture inland. In 1754 Anthony Henday, a labourer and netmaker at York Fort on Hudson Bay, volunteered to explore the interior. He was possibly the first European to reach the foothills of the Rocky Mountains. Travelling in the company of a group of Cree, he made contact with the plains nations and returned in 1755 with not only detailed maps but also a rich supply of furs. His original journal was severely edited because in it he chronicled his sexual relationship with his "Indian wife," which offended the sensibilities of some Bay Company officials. He nevertheless proved the profitability of making contact with distant tribes and of using Native guides and interpreters as partners. After his initial foray, Bay Company traders made annual visits to the plains and parkland regions of Rupert's Land in pursuit of furs.

Although there were few Europeans in Rupert's Land by the mid-eighteenth century, their impact on aboriginal society was already significant. For example, most of the Natives living on the Prairies had never set eyes on anyone of European descent, but they used horses, which had been introduced by the Spanish in the early seventeenth century and which had spread rapidly northward through trade networks. The plains Indians found the horse easy to adapt to their hunting and fighting needs. Even without European guns and ammunition, the Natives were more effective hunters and warriors mounted on horseback. When European weapons became available through trade networks in the eighteenth century, the nations of the plains and parklands became the most feared of Native military forces.

The arrival of British and French fur traders in the seventeenth century dramatically altered the ways of life of Native peoples in the interior and their relationships with each other. As in the eastern regions, a clear differentiation soon emerged between Native peoples who trapped and prepared fur-bearing animals for market and the intermediaries who transported the product and traded it with Europeans. After the Huron were forced out of their role as go-betweens, the Ojibwa took their place, and by the eighteenth century some Ojibwa had moved north and west from their traditional homelands to the parklands and plains. In the eighteenth century, the Cree, Assiniboine, and Chipewyan also established themselves as intermediaries in the fur trade.

The conquest of New France only intensified the rivalry between the St Lawrence and Hudson Bay for supremacy in the fur trade. Even before the Treaty of Paris was signed, traders from New York, New England, and Scotland moved to Montreal and began to occupy French posts in the interior. The skilled labour of the *Canadien* voyageurs, guides, and interpreters gave the Montreal traders an edge over their Bay Company rivals. Pushing aggressively north and west, they extended their range to the outer reaches of the continent. During the American Revolutionary War, Montreal-based trader Peter Pond established a post in the Lake Athabaska region. Montreal traders were soon tapping the main fur-producing areas along the Athabaska, Peace, and Mackenzie rivers. In 1789 Alexander Mackenzie, exploring on behalf of the North West Company of Montreal, reached the Arctic Ocean along the river that bears his name.

Not to be outdone, the Hudson's Bay Company opened its first interior post in 1774, at Cumberland House some eight hundred kilometres from Hudson Bay. By that time Bay men were crisscrossing the west in their efforts to outdistance their rivals based in Montreal. Like their Montreal counterparts, the Bay traders explored areas new to Europeans. In 1772, for example, Samuel Hearne reached the Arctic Ocean by way of the Coppermine River and put an end to speculation about a water passage from Hudson Bay to the Pacific.

Competition between the river and the bay led to the proliferation of trading posts. In 1774 there were only seventeen posts in the Northwest, seven of them belonging to the Hudson's Bay Company and ten to the St Lawrence traders. Of the ninety new posts by 1789, sixty-five belonged to the Montreal-based merchants. The competition grew even fiercer in the following fifteen years, when no less than 323 new posts were built in Rupert's Land. By the end of the century there was scarcely a Native living in the Northwest who was more than two hundred kilometres from a trading post. The fierce rivalry led to the merger of the North West Company and the rival XY Company in 1804, and this firm in turn merged with the Hudson's Bay Company in 1821. In the meantime the foundations for European settlement in the great Northwest had been firmly laid. Although most of the early trading posts were temporary shelters, they were often built on strategic sites where twentieth-century cities would flourish.

By the end of the eighteenth century as many as 1500 European traders were wintering in Rupert's Land. The majority were either French Canadians or Scots from the Orkney Isles. They usually planned to work for their allotted time in the fur trade and then retire to their homelands, and most of them did just that. But a few succumbed to the lure of the west and remained in Rupert's Land for the rest of their lives. Others left behind children borne to Native companions, offspring who would form the basis of a French Métis and English half-breed population in the region.

The growing numbers of the Europeans had a predictable impact on the Natives in the region. In 1781 an epidemic of smallpox swept through the Assiniboine, Ojibwa, Cree, and Blackfoot nations, reducing their numbers by half. The explosion of posts in the interior eliminated the carrying trade for the Cree and Assiniboine, but provided them with alternative employment in the form of provisioning the posts. In the Great Lakes and Hudson Bay regions the fur trade rivalry had depleted both the smaller fur-bearing animals and deer and moose, making a return to a pre-contact hunting and gathering economy impractical. The result was a widespread migration of Assiniboine, Cree, and eventually Ojibwa to the northern plains. Although they clashed with the Blackfoot, Mandan, and Sioux in their efforts to claim hunting territories, the Cree and Assiniboine quickly adjusted to plains life. They became skilled buffalo hunters who learned the many ways of using buffalo to provide food, clothing, and ceremonial items. For a time the new plains peoples became less dependent on the fur traders' goods.

West of the Rockies, European contact came later and under different conditions. The coastline was *terra incognita* for the British until 1778, when Captain James Cook surveyed the northwest coast in his search for the elusive Northwest Passage from Hudson Bay to the Pacific. Before that time Russian and Spanish explorers had approached the region from opposite directions. In separate expeditions the Russians Vitus Bering and Aleksei Chirikov explored the Alaska coast in 1741. A growing Russian presence on the Pacific coast led the Spanish to send expeditions from San Blas, their naval base in Mexico, to search for interlopers and establish a Spanish claim to the region. In 1774 Juan Pérez sighted what would become known as the Queen Charlotte Islands and traded with the Haida, who sailed out to meet his ship. The coastal Natives had traded among themselves for at least three millennia and needed no coaxing to make exchanges with newcomers bearing products made of metal. The following year Juan Francisco de la Bodega y Quadra officially claimed the North Pacific coast for King Carlos III of Spain.

In 1789 the Spanish sent Captain Esteban José Martínez to establish a fortified base at Nootka Sound, on Vancouver Island, the very place where Cook had landed the previous year. For a few tense months it seemed that Britain and Spain were prepared to go to war over the North Pacific coast, but saner heads prevailed. The Nootka Sound Convention of 1790 permitted joint occupation of the Pacific coast north of San Francisco. In a subsequent agreement negotiated by British captain George Vancouver and Bodega y Quadra, in 1794, the Spanish agreed to abandon their fortified base on Nootka Sound. When the troops sailed away in March 1795, their departure marked the end of a Spanish military presence on the north Pacific coast.

By that time Europeans and aboriginal peoples had taken stock of each other and found a common ground of interest in the exchange of material goods. During his four-week stay with the Nuu'chah'nulth (Nootka) in 1778, Cook and his crew traded a variety of goods for sea-otter pelts, food, and artifacts. Cook reported that the Native demand for European products was insatiable:

> Hardly a bit of it [brass] was left in the ships except what belonged to our necessary instruments. Whole suits of clothes were stripped of every button; bureaus of their furniture; and copper kettles, tin cannisters, candlesticks, and the like, all went to wreck; so that our American friends got a greater medley and variety of things from us, than any other nation whom we had visited.[10]

The profits that Cook gained from the sale of sea-otter skins in China opened a thriving trade for the Nuu'chah'nulth. Between the 1780s and the 1820s they and other coastal nations traded with ships from Spain and the United States as well as with fur trade companies based in British North America.

Callicum and Maquinna, Nuu'chah'nulth leaders, 1789 (National Archives of Canada/C27699)

The maritime fur trade was not conducted without conflict. In 1802, for instance, Maquinna, the successor of the man of the same name who had first greeted Captain Cook, ordered the capture of an American ship, the *Boston,* when its captain called him a liar. The Nuu'chah'nulth killed twenty-five of the twenty-seven crew members and held the remaining two as prisoners. Years of insults, assaults, and murders at the hands of American traders produced a power keg of resentment that, on this occasion, exploded.

•British North America in 1800

By the end of the eighteenth century, British North America consisted of seven formal colonies and a vast stretch of territory exploited by British-financed fur trade companies. Only the Inuit of the far north still lived outside direct European contact. Over 500 000 people made their home in British North America, about one-third (approximately 175 000) of them Amerindians living in the western regions. In the eastern colonies fewer than 20 000 Natives had survived the first three centuries of European contact. Only the 2000 Mohawk Loyalists living in the Grand valley of Upper Canada had reached levels of subsistence comparable to those of most of their white neighbours.

The largest European population was concentrated in the St Lawrence region. There, by 1800, 215 000 people, including 190 000 of French descent, lived primarily by subsistence farming. In Lower Canada the 25 000 English-speaking settlers were concentrated in Quebec, Montreal, and the Eastern Townships. In Upper Canada the primarily Loyalist population, supplemented by later pioneers, had reached nearly 35 000. The numbers in the Atlantic colonies were approaching 100 000.

Halifax and Quebec were the largest towns, each boasting a population approaching 8000 people, but fewer than 10 percent of British North Americans lived in cities. With fur and fish still serving as the principal exports, the colonial economy remained essentially on the course established in the sixteenth century. Most people survived by practising subsistence agriculture and fishing. For great numbers of people life tended to be nasty, brutish, and short, but no more so than in Europe at the time. Life expectancy was still less than fifty years for both women and men, and the infant mortality rate remained at roughly one in five live births. During the winter months the vitamin intake was often dangerously reduced, leading to disease and death for all classes and cultures.

Separated by great distances of rock and trees, most British North Americans, whether Natives or newcomers, had relatively little contact with each other or with the outside world. This isolation perhaps suited many of them who were British neither by origin nor by choice. Although they were technically British subjects, most people living in the settled colonies had little or nothing to do with their political masters or their elected representatives. The seasonal round of farm life and the hunt by land or sea structured their daily existence, while religious beliefs, often practised without benefit of priest or parson, defined the boundaries of socially acceptable behaviour.

In the first half of the nineteenth century British North Americans would come to share an increasing array of values and institutions. Advances in transportation and communication, increased European immigration, and dreams of economic development would bring colonial elites together mentally as well as physically. Within the second half of the century a nation called Canada, still an integral part of the British Empire, would span the continent.

• The Loyalists:
Lessons in Historiography

No immigrant group in the history of Canada has attracted more historical controversy than the Loyalists, who represented a thick slice of North American society: white, black, and Native, rich and poor, liberal and conservative. Most Loyalists were ordinary people who happened, for a variety of reasons, to become refugees during the American Revolution, but this was not the dominant historical interpretation for most of the two centuries following the revolution.

Indeed, the Loyalists were so useful in providing English Canadians with a sense of identity that historians now talk about a Loyalist "myth." A myth is an instrument for self-identification, drawing its justification from an ideological interpretation of events. The search for a "usable past" is not unique to Canada, but the case of the Loyalists offers an excellent example of how a nation's history can become distorted when historians set out to create a past rather than to analyse it.

Writing in 1898, Henry Coyne, a fellow of the Royal Society of Canada, offers one of the more extreme claims for his subjects: "The Loyalists, to a considerable extent, were the very cream of the population of the Thirteen Colonies. They represented in very large measure the learning, the piety, the gentle birth, the wealth and good citizenship of the British race in America, as well as the devotion to law and order, British institutions, and the unity of the Empire." This passage includes some of the essential elements of the Loyalist tradition as defined by historian Murray Barkley: the elite origins of the refugees, their loyalty to the British Crown, their suffering and sacrifice in the face of hostile conditions, their consistent anti-Americanism, and their divinely inspired sense of mission.[11] Historians could emphasize any aspect of this cluster of attributes as the need arose. Thus, during the period when Loyalists were claiming compensation for what they had left behind when they fled the revolution, historians focussed on loss and suffering. In the late nineteenth century, when Loyalist centennial celebrations coincided with a revival in British imperial sentiment, historians singled out their sense of mission. By the twentieth century the Loyalist tradition had become a full-blown myth. The Loyalist experience explained why Canada, unlike the United States, had maintained a continuing colonial association with Britain, while at the same time sustaining liberal political values and institutions.

As with most traditions, many of these claims contain a grain of truth. A few Loyalists were members of the colonial elite, and a good number of the refugees developed an unshakable loyalty to all things British. A few suffered unspeakable violence and hardship. Many of them were committed to liberal political principles. But other aspects of the tradition are harder to justify. Research suggests that immigrants from Britain were just as loyal as the refugees of the American revolution. The records also show that many Loyalists—probably up to 20 percent—returned to the United States once it was safe to do so. Other Loyalists actually participated in the War of 1812 on the side of the United States: so much for their loyalty and committed anti-Americanism.

In using their history to justify claims to superiority, descendants of the Loyalists abused the truth and actually diminished their status in the eyes of their non-Loyalist neighbours. At the same time, the definition of Loyalist descent became so broad that by the twentieth century most Anglo-Canadians who bothered to do so could find a Loyalist ancestor somewhere in their family tree. In New Brunswick, where for obvious reasons the Loyalist myth was particularly pervasive, even descendants of Irish immigrants passed themselves off as Loyalists.

While those aspiring to Loyalist roots may be forgiven for exaggerating aspects of their family past, historians should not be judged so lightly. Many textbooks still present the Loyalists as the first anglophone immigrants to present-day Canada, conveniently ignoring more than 50 000 English settlers already living in the British colonies by 1783. The scholars who argue that the Loyalists planted the seeds of Canadian liberalism or conservatism in British North America usually fail to take into account not only the larger context of political discussion that prevailed throughout the North Atlantic world but also the political values brought to British North America by immigrants of every class and culture in the second half of the eighteenth century.

There are important lessons to be learned from the Loyalist myth. In any historical inquiry, researchers must constantly question received truths and unsubstantiated assumptions. Nothing can substitute for hard work in the archives and the careful reading of primary sources. Historians also have to ask basic questions about their subjects, even if those questions may be difficult to answer. Are all classes, cultures, and genders accounted for? Do we know what values and beliefs motivated the people whose documents we are analysing? Can this source have a different meaning than it appears to have upon first reading? It is also important to put a subject in historical context, so the claims made for any individual, group, or event can be measured against the claims of other individuals, groups, and events. It is difficult for historians to stand outside of the cultural biases that shape their interpretation, but the difficulty of the enterprise should not discourage them from trying.

•Notes

[1] Wallace Brown, *The Good Americans: The Loyalists in the American Revolution* (New York: William Morrow, 1969), 141, 206.

[2] Phyllis Blakeley, "And Having a Love for the People," *Nova Scotia Historical Quarterly* 5, 2 (June 1975): 172–73.

[3] Bill Wicken, "Mi'kmaq Land in Southwestern Nova Scotia, 1771–1823," *Making Adjustments: Change and Continuity in Planter Nova Scotia, 1759–1800*, ed. Margaret Conrad (Fredericton: Acadiensis Press 1991), 114.

[4] *The Diary of Simeon Perkins*, Vol. 1, ed. H.A. Innis et al. (Toronto: Champlain Society, 1948).

[5] J.M. Bumsted, *Land, Settlement, and Politics on Eighteenth Century Prince Edward Island* (Montreal: McGill-Queen's University Press, 1987), 64.

[6] National Archives of Canada, Nova Scotia Series A, Vol. 94, memorial of the inhabitants of Yarmouth, 8 December 1775.

[7] James W. St. G. Walker, *The Black Loyalists: The Search for a Promised Land in Nova Scotia and Sierra Leone, 1783–1870* (New York: Longman, 1976), 73.

[8] Sarah Frost's diary is cited in Walter Bates, *Kingston and the Loyalists of the "Spring Fleet" of A.D. 1783* (1899; rprt. ed. W.O. Raymond, Woodstock, NB: Non-Entity Press, 1980), 28–30.

[9] See Barbara Graymont, "Koñwatsi?tsiaienni," in *Dictionary of Canadian Biography*, Vol. 4, *1771 to 1800* (Toronto: University of Toronto Press, 1979), 416–18; and Barbara Graymont, "Thayendanegea," in *Dictionary of Canadian Biography*, Vol. 5, *1801 to 1820* (Toronto: University of Toronto Press, 1983), 803–12.

[10] John Douglas, ed., *A Voyage to the Pacific Ocean in the Years 1776, 1777, 1778, 1779 and 1780 . . .*, Vol. 2, by Captain J. Cook, cited in J.C.H. King, "The Nootka of Vancouver Island," in Hugh Cobbe, ed., *Cook's Voyages and Peoples of the Pacific* (London: British Museum Publications, 1979), 102.

[11] Murray Barkley, "The Loyalist Tradition in New Brunswick," *Acadiensis* 4, 2 (Spring 1975): 3–45.

• Selected Reading

The best overviews of British North America in the eighteenth century can be found in R. Cole Harris and Geoffrey J. Matthews, *Historical Atlas of Canada*, Vol. 1, *From the Beginning to 1800* (Toronto: University of Toronto Press, 1987) and R. Cole Harris and John Warkentin, *Canada Before Confederation*, (Toronto: Oxford University Press, 1974). For the larger context see J.B. Brebner, *The North Atlantic Triangle* (Ottawa: Carleton University Press, 1968 c. 1945); John J. McCusker and Russell R. Menard, *The Economy of British North America 1600 to 1798* (Chapel Hill, NC: Duke University Press, 1985); D.W. Meinig, *The Shaping of America: Atlantic America, 1492–1800* (New Haven, CT: Yale University Press, 1986); and Bernard Bailyn, *Voyagers to the West: A Passage in the Peopling of America on the Eve of the Revolution* (New York: Knopf, 1986). Graeme Wynn draws upon the insights from this literature in "A Region of Scattered Settlements and Bounded Possibilities: Northeastern America, 1775–1800," *The Canadian Geographer* 31, 2 (1987): 319–38.

Although written nearly three decades ago, the best general survey of this period for all four Atlantic colonies is still W.S. MacNutt, *The Atlantic Provinces: The Emergence of Colonial Society, 1713–1857* (Toronto: McClelland and Stewart, 1965). Specialized studies include Andrew Hill Clark, *Three Centuries and the Island: A Historical Geography of Settlement and Agriculture in Prince Edward Island* (Toronto: University of Toronto Press, 1959); J.M. Bumsted, *Land, Settlement and Politics on Eighteenth Century Prince Edward Island* (Montreal: McGill-Queen's University Press, 1987); Frederick W. Rowe, *History of Newfoundland and Labrador* (Toronto: McGraw-Hill Ryerson, 1980). The post-expulsion Acadian odyssey is described by Naomi Griffiths, *The Acadians: Creation of a People* (Toronto: McGraw-Hill Ryerson, 1973), and Jean Daigle, ed., *The Acadians of the Maritimes: Thematic Studies* (Moncton: Centre d'Études Acadiennes, 1982). The Native experience in the region is described in L.S.F. Upton, *Micmacs and Colonists: Indian–White Relations in the Maritimes, 1713–1867* (Vancouver: University of British Columbia Press, 1979).

New England's influence on the Maritime region is comprehensively explored in two classic volumes by J. B. Brebner: *New England's Outpost: Acadia Before the Conquest of Canada* (New York: Columbia University Press, 1927) and *The Neutral Yankees of Nova Scotia* (New Haven: Yale University Press, 1937). George A. Rawlyk, *Nova Scotia's Massachusetts: A Study of Massachusetts–Nova Scotia Relations, 1630–1784* (Montreal: McGill-Queen's University Press, 1973), also offers useful insights. Articles in *They Planted Well: New England Planters in Maritime Canada* (Fredericton: Acadiensis Press, 1988) and *Making Adjustments: Change and Continuity in Planter Nova Scotia, 1759–1800* (Fredericton: Acadiensis Press, 1991), both edited by Margaret Conrad, offer wide-ranging perspectives on this early wave of anglophone immigrants. These people are also the focus of George A. Rawlyk and Gordon Stewart, *A People Highly Favoured of God: The Nova Scotia Yankees and the American Revolution* (Hamdon, CT: Archon Books, 1972), and J.M. Bumsted, *Henry Alline* (Toronto: University of Toronto Press, 1971).

The Yorkshire settlers are the subject of James D. Snowdon, "Footprints in the Marsh Mud: Politics and Land Settlement in the Township of Sackville, 1760–1800," MA thesis, University of New Brunswick, 1975. The Scots in the region are well served by Donald MacKay, *The People of the Hector* (Toronto: McGraw-Hill Ryerson, 1980); and J.M. Bumsted, *The People's Clearance: Highland Emigration to British North America, 1770–1815* (Winnipeg: University of Manitoba Press, 1982). The German and French Protestants who were transported to Nova Scotia between 1750 and 1753 have received detailed treatment in Winthrop Bell, *The "Foreign Protestants" and the Settlement of Nova Scotia* (Toronto: University of Toronto Press, 1961), republished in 1991 by Acadiensis Press. For insights on women's experience, see

Margaret Conrad, Toni Laidlaw, and Donna Smyth, *No Place Like Home: The Diaries and Letters of Nova Scotia Women, 1771–1939* (Halifax: Formac, 1988), and Gwen Davies, "Consolation to Distress: Loyalist Literary Activity in The Maritimes," in *Studies in Maritime Literary History* (Fredericton: Acadiensis Press, 1991), 30–47.

On Quebec in this period, see Hilda.Neatby, *Quebec: The Revolutionary Age, 1760–1791* (Toronto: McClelland and Stewart, 1966). Fernand Ouellet offers an excellent synthesis in the chapter "Lower Canada in 1791" in his *Lower Canada, 1791–1840: Social Change and Nationalism* (Toronto: McClelland and Stewart, 1980), 1–27; his *Economic and Social History of Quebec* (Toronto: Macmillan, 1981) is also valuable. On Upper Canada, see Gerald M. Craig, *Upper Canada: The Formative Years, 1784–1841* (Toronto: McClelland and Stewart, 1984); Curtis Fahey, *In His Name: The Anglican Experience in Upper Canada, 1791–1854* (Ottawa: Carleton University Press, 1990); Isabel Thompson Kelsay, *Joseph Brant, 1743–1807: Man of Two Worlds* (Syracuse, NY: Syracuse University Press, 1984); and Richard White, *The Middle Ground: Indians, Empires, and Republics in the Great Lakes Region, 1650–1815* (Cambridge: Cambridge University Press, 1991).

There is an extensive literature on the Loyalists. In *The United Empire Loyalists: Men and Myths* (Toronto: Copp Clark Pitman, 1967), L.S.F. Upton discusses the historiographical issues that haunt the topic. Specialized studies that avoid most of the historiographical traps include Esther Clark Wright's *The Loyalists of New Brunswick* (Wolfville, NS: Wright, 1955); Neil MacKinnon, *This Unfriendly Soil: The Loyalist Experience in Nova Scotia 1783–1791* (Montreal: McGill-Queen's University Press, 1989); Marion Robertson, *King's Bounty: A History of Early Shelburne* (Halifax: Nova Scotia Museum, 1983); David Bell, *Early Loyalist Saint John: The Origins of New Brunswick Politics* (Fredericton: New Ireland Press, 1983); Ann Gorman Condon, *The Envy of the American States: The Loyalists of New Brunswick* (Fredericton: New Ireland Press, 1984); Phyllis R. Blakeley and John N. Grant, eds., *Eleven Exiles: Accounts of Loyalists of the American Revolution* (Toronto: Dundurn, 1982); Robert S. Allen, *The Loyal Americans: The Military Role of the Loyalist Provincial Corps and Their Settlement in British North America, 1775–1784* (Ottawa: National Museums, 1983); Bruce Wilson, *As She Began: An Illustrated Introduction to Loyalist Ontario* (Toronto: Dundurn, 1981); James J. Talman, ed., *Loyalist Narratives from Upper Canada* (Toronto: Champlain Society, 1946). The black Loyalist experience is described in James Walker, *The Black Loyalists: The Search for a Promised Land in Nova Scotia and Sierra Leone, 1783–1870* (New York: Longman, 1976), and in William Spray, *The Blacks in New Brunswick* (Fredericton: Brunswick Press, 1972). On Loyalist women, see Mary Beth Norton's pioneering article, "Eighteenth Century American Women in Peace and War: The Case of the Loyalists," *William and Mary Quarterly* 3, 33 (1976): 386–409; Janice Potter, "Patriarchy and Paternalism: The Case of the Eastern Ontario Loyalist Women," *Ontario History* 81, 1 (March 1989): 3–24; and

Katherine M.J. McKenna, "Treading the Hard Road: Some Loyalist Women and the American Revolution," MA thesis, Queen's University, 1979. Overviews are provided by Christopher Moore in *The Loyalists: Revolution, Exile and Settlement* (Toronto: Macmillan, 1984); Wallace Brown and Hereward Senior, *Victorious in Defeat: The Loyalists in Canada* (Toronto: Methuen, 1984).

On Rupert's Land, see chapters 1 to 4 of Gerald Friesen, *The Canadian Prairies: A History* (Toronto: University of Toronto Press, 1984); E.E. Rich, *The Fur Trade and the Northwest to 1857* (Toronto: McClelland and Stewart, 1967); Arthur J. Ray, *Indians in the Fur Trade: Their Role as Hunters, Trappers and Middlemen in the Lands Southwest of Hudson Bay, 1660–1860* (Toronto: University of Toronto Press, 1974). On the Pacific coast, see Robin Fisher, *Contact and Conflict: Indian–European Relations in British Columbia, 1774–1890* (Vancouver: University of British Columbia Press, 1977).

CHAPTER

THE ATLANTIC COLONIES,

1784–1850s

8

In 1823 three Beothuk women were seized by fur traders and brought to St John's. The Reverend William Wilson saw them in the street. "The ladies had dressed them in English garb," he observed, "but over their dresses they all had on their indispensable deer-skin shawls." The youngest, Shawnadithit, renamed Nancy by her captors, attracted particular attention. She decorated her forehead and arms with tinsel and coloured paper, chased onlookers, and was amused by the townsfolk's material possessions. When pencil and paper were placed at her disposal, Wilson reported, "She was in raptures . . . in one flourish she drew a deer perfectly."[1]

By the nineteenth century, after more than three centuries of continuous European contact, the Beothuk in Newfoundland were nearly extinct. Hounded from their coastal locations by Europeans, their numbers drastically reduced by diseases and impossible living conditions, they shunned any contact with the white invaders. Of the three women taken to St John's, the two older ones died within a few years of their forced visit. Shawnadithit was eventually taken under the care of the Beothuk Institution at Twillingate, an island settlement in northeast Newfoundland. There she helped Newfoundland scholar William Epps Cormack develop a Beothuk vocabulary, and she drew pictures representing the history and culture of her people as she knew them. When Shawnadithit died of consumption in 1829, at the age of twenty-three, she was the last of the Beothuk.

•Defining the Atlantic Region

After the American Revolution the Atlantic region began to take on the features still in place today. The geographical boundaries, population patterns, and cultural practices established by the mid-nineteenth century

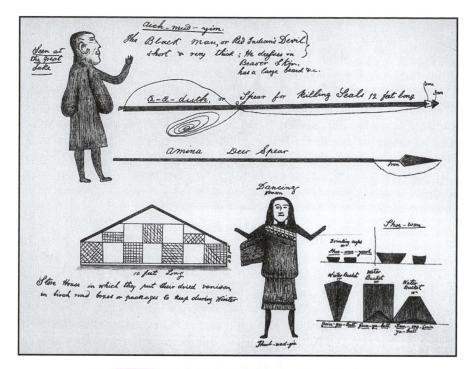

Demasduwit, renamed Mary March, one of the Beothuk women taken to St John's in 1818. This portrait was painted by Lady Hamilton, wife of the governor of Newfoundland. Above are drawings by Shawnadithit, the niece of Demasduwit (National Archives of Canada/C87698, C28544)

proved to be remarkably enduring. For Shawnadithit and her people the new century marked the end of an era, but for European immigrants and their descendants it was a period of economic growth and social development, the prelude to a "golden age."

Then as now, the Atlantic region consisted of a miscellaneous group of islands, peninsulas, and northeastern fringes of the North American continent exposed to the North Atlantic. A political as much as a geographical region, it included four British colonies: Nova Scotia, New Brunswick, Newfoundland, and St John's Island. In 1799 St John's Island was renamed Prince Edward Island, not just to honour the royal prince but also to avoid the confusion resulting from having so many places of the same name in the region. Between 1784 and 1820 Cape Breton functioned as a separate colonial jurisdiction, but it was returned to Nova Scotia in 1820.

During the negotiations ending the American Revolution, the Ste Croix River and some vaguely defined "highlands" separating the St Lawrence watershed from the waters draining into the Bay of Fundy became the boundary line between British and American territory. Unfortunately, the map used by the negotiators was woefully inadequate, and it took over half a century to determine the international boundary between New Brunswick and the part of Massachusetts that became the state of Maine in 1830. Even the identity of the Ste Croix River, which had been cited as part of the boundary in 1783, remained in doubt. A boundary commission determined the location of the Ste Croix in 1798, but it was not until 1842 that the Webster-Ashburton Treaty, named after the principal negotiators, finally put an end to the confusion. The division of the disputed territory, which left a hump of land between New Brunswick and the Eastern Townships, came as a disappointment to New Brunswickers, who had hoped for a more direct link to the Canadas.

The Magdalen Islands in the Gulf of St Lawrence were lost permanently to the region in 1787, when they were awarded to Captain Isaac Coffin under seigneurial tenure administered from Quebec. Between 1774 and 1809 Labrador was also briefly under the jurisdiction of Quebec/Lower Canada. A territory inhabited by Montagnais, Naskapi, and Inuit, Labrador in the eighteenth century hosted a growing migratory fishery. Europeans and North Americans fished the Labrador waters, their numbers rising to as many as 30 000 by the middle of the nineteenth century. Because of the growth of a Newfoundland-based fishery in Labrador waters and naval considerations during the Napoleonic Wars, Labrador was returned to Newfoundland's jurisdiction in 1809. The interior boundary between Labrador and Lower Canada, which had never been surveyed by Europeans, remained undefined until the twentieth century.

•Population Growth in the Atlantic Region

Following the American Revolutionary War, the Atlantic colonies caught the advance wave of British immigration that washed up on the shores of North America. Although the majority of the over one million British immigrants who came to British North America between 1785 and 1850 went to the Canadas or passed on to the United States, a good many stayed in the Atlantic colonies, supplying the labour required to develop the region's growing port cities, its fish and timber frontiers, and the still unsettled portions of the countryside.

The forces prompting people to leave their British homeland can be classified into two general categories: those pushing people out and those pulling people to their new destinations. By the end of the eighteenth century, economic conditions were pushing many Britons out of their customary social arrangements. The new factory system had ended the "putting out" system in the textile industry, reducing many families to destitution. In their efforts to bolster their own declining social positions, landlords increased rents, converted common lands to sheep pastures, and tried to improve the commercial viability of their estates. Tenant families bore the brunt of these reforms and became the source of cheap labour for the growing industrial cities and for overseas settlement frontiers.

The most dramatic collapse of social organization took place in recently conquered regions of the British Isles. Following their defeat by the British army at Culloden in 1746, clan chieftains in the Scottish Highlands became oppressive landlords, forcing their dependants to either emigrate or be reduced to penury. Since most of the Highlanders were Roman Catholic, they were excluded from the political processes that governed their lives. Religious discrimination also plagued the Irish, who had become reluctant British subjects by the Act of Union in 1801. For the Roman Catholic peasantry in Ireland, the combination of a growing population, periodic famines, and political oppression was a powerful stimulus to emigration.

Initially artisans did well in the transformation from commercial to industrial production. As raw materials became cheaper and money more plentiful, the demand for commodities such as shoes, clothing, and furniture increased. However, artisans, in turn, became vulnerable as the products of the factory system rendered their crafts obsolete. In desperation many rural artisans moved to larger urban centres, but like factory workers they soon became the victims of cutthroat competition and lack of work, especially in periods of economic recession.

Ultimately the new social order also had its impact on the rural gentry and the military elite. Many of them found themselves sliding down the social scale in the industrial age, when capital rather than land was emerging as the basis of wealth. Families who found themselves land-rich and cash-poor could no longer sustain their upper-class way of life. For the younger children of the upper class the prospects were particularly bleak, as fathers passed all their land and wealth on to the eldest son in an effort to maintain the family name. Similar pressures were being felt by military officers, whose services were less in demand following the Napoleonic Wars. Forced to rely on their inadequate pensions, they searched for ways of supplementing their income and shoring up their crumbling status.

North America seemed to offer a refuge for those who were faring badly in the uncertain economic climate of postwar Britain. Land on easy terms was an attractive prospect for tenant farmers, unemployed artisans, and younger sons of the rural gentry with no prospect of inheriting land in Britain. Wages were higher in North America than in Europe. Labourers who could not afford the cost of an overseas passage could sign on a timber ship or find a sponsor to provide passage money in return for an agreement to work. Even people who had excellent prospects in Europe were often pulled by the opportunities that the Americas seemed to offer. Merchants eager to expand their operations, farmers with visions of being gentlemen, young families anxious to make a better life for their children, and any number of adventurers and ne'er-do-wells, all hoping that providence would smile on them in a new location, turned their sights on North America.

The Atlantic region attracted immigrants from areas linked with the fisheries and the timber trade, and it also drew in Scottish Highlanders looking for the nearest available land. Merchants and military families also found the region attractive. Many immigrants brought traditional values with them, spurred by the desire for "independence" economically and spiritually as much as by a thirst for wealth. Others were converts to the values of industrial capitalism, more anxious to "get ahead" than to reestablish a way of life rapidly disappearing in Britain.

By the end of the eighteenth century the forces gaining momentum during the previous fifty years had come together to increase the tide of emigration from Scotland. The Scots took up land throughout the region, but their presence was particularly concentrated in eastern Nova Scotia, Cape Breton, and Prince Edward Island. Between 1785 and 1849 nearly 40 000 Scots arrived in Nova Scotia, which finally became home to a population reflecting its seventeenth-century name. The most ambitious Scottish settlement scheme on Prince Edward Island was sponsored by Thomas Douglas, Earl of Selkirk, who in 1803 brought eight hundred Highlanders to the Orwell–Point Prim area.

Scots were also prominent in mercantile circles throughout the region. In major port cities such as St John's, Halifax, Saint John, and St Andrews, Scottish merchants operating out of Greenock, Glasgow, and Edinburgh handled both the legal and covert import-export trade. Their early presence was documented by the founding of the North British Society in Halifax in 1768 and the Saint Andrews Society in Saint John in 1796. Scots dominated the timber trade and were counted among the major shipbuilders in the region. Fraser and Thom on the Miramichi was one of the most successful Scottish timber and shipbuilding firms, with its operations attracting labour from the old country to a region hitherto dominated by Mi'kmaq and Acadians.

In addition to a strong attachment to the land, the Scots brought their religious values, including the Roman Catholic traditions of the Highlanders and Presbyterian beliefs that flourished mainly in the Lowlands. They also planted the Scottish reverence for education in the Atlantic region. Thomas McCulloch, a Presbyterian minister who settled in Pictou, founded Pictou Academy, one of the most respected schools in British North America. A widely acclaimed natural scientist, McCulloch also wrote *The Stepsure Letters*, one of the first works of fiction produced in British North America.

ORAL HISTORY

One of the most valuable sources for information about ordinary people is oral history. Family lore, ballads, and superstitions, passed down through generations, can often open a window on how people in the past thought about themselves. But as with written documents, historians must be careful about how they interpret oral sources. The ballads produced by the Highland Scottish immigrants who came to the Atlantic region provide a useful case study for students of history.

The Scots, especially the Gaelic-speaking Highlanders, drew upon a rich and complex cultural heritage. As they moved to new locations around the world they composed poems and songs to commemorate the often difficult and painful emigrant experience. Historians who consult only one or two of these ballads might make the mistake of assuming that there was only one point of view on the migration process. As the work of Margaret MacDonell illustrates, nothing could be further from the truth.[2] While many bards lamented that they ever came to North America, others found in the New World the freedom to reestablish a way of life that was fast being swept away in Britain. A person's point of view, it seems, depended upon his or her political perspective and motivation in coming to the New World.

Among the Selkirk settlers on Prince Edward Island was Calum Bàn MacMhannain (1758–1829) from the Isle of Skye. The extortions of the "balie," or bailiff, and intermittent plague among his cattle induced him to immigrate with his wife and six children. For MacMhannain the island was a haven from the oppressive conditions of his native Scotland:

> By Mary, for a very long time
> we remained in that land;
> although we could raise sufficient there,
> many a calamity and loss
> plagued these at times,
> so that they vanished into the mists on the mountain.
> Although we might go to market
> and sell our herd,
> for which we got a fair price
> the bailie would come around
> with the cruel summons
> and extort the entire sum from us. . . .
>
> But if you ever go
> over the sea
> bring my greetings to my friends.
> Urge them without delay
> to flee the rents
> and come out as soon as opportune for them.
> If they could find a time
> and means to come over
> they would not be beholden to MacDonald.
> They would get land
> in which to sow crops,
> and potatoes and barley would grow very well there.
>
> This is the isle of contentment
> where we are now.
> Our seed is fruitful here;
> oats grow
> and wheat, in full bloom,
> turnip, cabbage, and peas.
> Sugar from trees
> may be had free here;
> we have it in large chunks.
> There is fresh red rum

in every dwelling and shop,
abundant as the stream, being imbibed here.

In contrast, another bard, known only as a MacLean from Raasay, had a different perspective on the Prince Edward Island experience. With the entrepreneur Samuel Cunard as his landlord and one Peters as his rent collector, conditions were as oppressive in North America as in Scotland.

I am lonely here
in Murray Harbour not knowing English
it is not what I have been accustomed to,
for I always spoke Gaelic.
My neighbours and I
used to chat at length together;
here I see only scoundrels,
and I do not understand their language.

I am offended at my relatives
who came before me;
they did not tell me about this place
and how it has tried them.
Going through the wilderness
there is nothing but a blazed trail
this is truly a lonesome place
for one who lives by himself.

A matter of grave concern,
as you may surmise,
is the want of footwear and clothing
for each one who needs them.
No one can procure anything
unless he wrests it from the forest.
The length of winter is depressing;
it is fully half one's lifetime. . . .

We left there
and came out here
thinking we would receive consideration,
and that the rent would not be so exacting.
But Peters is oppressing us,
and, if he doesn't die,
we must leave this place
and Cunnard, himself a beast.

Ireland continued to pour forth its population in the first half of the nineteenth century. Following the end of the Napoleonic Wars, young men escaping the poverty and oppression of their native island jumped on fishing vessels bound for Newfoundland and made their way to other Atlantic colonies. The expansion of the timber trade in New Brunswick offered direct passage in one of the empty timber vessels sailing to the Miramichi or Saint John. When periodic famines raged in Ireland, the worst occurring in the mid-1840s, port cities in the Atlantic colonies were clogged with destitute Irish families.

FAMINE IN IRELAND

The Irish were the largest single ethnic group to immigrate to the Atlantic colonies—and to North America generally—in the first half of the nineteenth century. Presbyterian Irish, the majority in the northern area of Ireland known as Ulster, were among the first to leave in large numbers after the French Revolutionary and Napoleonic wars. Anglican small farmers and Roman Catholic tenants soon joined the exodus. Until 1829 Roman Catholics in Ireland possessed few civil rights. Agitation for "Catholic emancipation" finally ended in victory in 1829 when Roman Catholics throughout the British Empire were granted the right to vote and hold public office, but the hated Act of Union of 1801 was still in effect and most Roman Catholic Irish remained tenant farmers on land owned by Protestant landlords.

The potato, a North American import, had become the staple crop of tenant families, and it sustained them well in good years. Between 1780 and 1840 the population of Ireland nearly doubled, from four to eight million. Unfortunately, overdependence on one food source made life precarious when blight or bad weather destroyed the crop. Famine years in 1817, 1821, 1825, 1829, and much of the 1830s offered incontrovertible evidence that the rapidly expanding Irish population could no longer be sustained through traditional agricultural methods and feudal class relations. Between 1825 and 1845 at least 450 000 Irish landed in British North America, about one-third of them moving on to the United States.

These emigrants were the lucky ones. Tragedy finally struck in 1845 when a new strain of blight invaded Ireland. By 1848 over 800 000 people had died of starvation and disease. Another million had moved overseas and still more had migrated to other areas of Great Britain. Nearly half of the five million who remained in Ireland were living on soup and meal provided by the British authorities. At the height of the famine one officer wrote an account that appeared in the London *Times*:

Fever, dissentry, and starvation stare you in the face every-where—children of ten and nine years old I have mistaken for decrepit old women, their faces wrinkled, their bodies bent and distorted in pain, the eyes looking like those of a corpse. Bodies are found lifeless, lying on their mothers' bosoms. I tell you one thing which struck me as particularly horrible: a dead woman was found lying on the road with a dead infant on her breast, the child having bitten the nipple of the mother right through in trying to derive nourishment from the wretched body. Dogs feed on the half-buried dead, and the rats are commonly known to tear people to pieces who, though still alive, are too weak to cry out. . . . Instead of following us, beggars throw themselves on their knees before us, holding up their dead infants to our sight.[3]

Few events in British and North American history had such immediate and widespread consequences as the Great Famine. In 1846, in an effort to alleviate the human misery, British prime minister Sir Robert Peel abolished the Corn Laws, which imposed duties on imported wheat. This policy not only permitted grains to be purchased at cheaper prices to feed the destitute Irish, but it also set in motion the forces that dismantled the old British mercantile system.

The outpouring of Ireland's starving and disease-ridden masses created short-term problems for the communities that received them. Over 300 000 Irish refugees came to British North America between 1845 and 1850, most of them entering through quarantine stations at Grosse Île, in the St Lawrence, and Partridge Island, near Saint John, New Brunswick. They were subject to resentment, discrimination, and exploitation. By their simple presence they intensified ethnic, class, and religious tensions throughout North America. They also carried a particularly virulent strain of fever that decimated both their own numbers and the people they came in contact with.

The Irish understandably reciprocated the hatred expressed against them, and soon the "anglophobia" that characterized the slums of Dublin and the devastated Irish countryside appeared full blown in the greater Ireland overseas. In the 1850s the disaffected Irish spawned an organization that was determined to lift the yoke of British oppression by any means possible. Known popularly as the Fenians, the Irish Republican Brotherhood and Clan-na-Gael had supporters on both sides of the Atlantic. They were a force to be reckoned with in American and British political life and even played a role in the confederation movement in Canada.

While the Irish Protestants were quickly assimilated into the dominant culture of the Atlantic colonies, the Roman Catholic Irish remained distinct, separated by their religion, history, and, for many, Gaelic language. The Irish swelled the population of Newfoundland outports, became tenant farmers on Prince Edward Island, harvested New Brunswick forests, and worked as domestic servants. By mid-century they had penetrated virtually every corner of the Atlantic region and constituted more than half the population of such cities as Saint John, Fredericton, and St John's.

The rapidly growing numbers of Irish immigrants prompted the founding of Roman Catholic churches and diocese and sparked clashes with the Scottish and Acadian Catholics who were already deeply rooted in the region. The desperate condition of many Irish immigrants inspired philanthropic efforts among their compatriots. In 1776 a Charitable Irish Society was founded by Irish naval officers in Halifax, and similar organizations were founded in Saint John (1806), Charlottetown (1825), and Fredericton (1830).

The Irish gradually emerged as an important factor in the political life of all the colonies. In Prince Edward Island, Irish tenant farmers resorted to tactics learned in their homeland to resist hated Protestant proprietors. Issues defined in Ireland, such as Catholic rights and repeal of the 1801 Act of Union, were commonly debated in colonial settings. Institutions organized around Irish concerns quickly made their appearance and were forces to be reckoned with in pre-industrial communities where issues of religion and culture played an important part in defining status and power. By the 1840s in most colonial jurisdictions, Orange Orders and Protestant Alliances could be found aligned against Roman Catholic organizations with names such as Ribbon, Repeal, and St Patrick's.

Between 1817 and 1822 ships carrying Welsh settlers also arrived in the three Maritime provinces. Like the Scots and Irish, the Welsh were pushed from their homes by population pressures and pulled by the prospects of a better life in North America. Although never a large portion of the incoming tide of immigrants, they were easily singled out for their distinctive costumes, Welsh tongue, and, for many, a dissenting Baptist heritage. In 1818 Nova Scotia's lieutenant-governor George Ramsay Dalhousie located several Welsh families at New Cambria near Shelburne and in the following year 180 Welsh immigrants from Cardigan were placed on land sixteen kilometres north of Fredericton. Like all immigrant groups they experienced hardships in the first years of settlement. The early Welsh settlers did not inspire chain migration to the Atlantic colonies, and, notwithstanding a few miners sent to the Maritime colonies later in the century, their numbers remained small.

A distinctly English presence was most obvious in Newfoundland, which attracted settlers from the west and south coasts of England. English immigrants were also present in most colonial capitals but could be found as well in rural areas throughout the region. Following the Napoleonic Wars, half-pay officers drawn from all ethnic groups in the British Isles found their way to the Atlantic colonies. Many were granted land on the upper reaches of the St John River and along a road built through the interior of Nova Scotia from Halifax to Annapolis Royal. Nineteenth-century censuses show that the Atlantic colonies also received immigrants from mainland Europe, Africa, and Asia—people who, as crew members, occasionally disembarked from ships in one of the many ports in the region. These individuals were usually quickly absorbed into the larger society through marriage and left only their names and perhaps a court case or two as evidence of their presence.

The largest migration from the United States in this period resulted from British policy during the War of 1812. In this war, as in the American Revolutionary War, the British received runaway slaves as free individuals. During and following the conflict, over two thousand blacks were sent to Nova Scotia. They were received on Melville Island, on the Northwest Arm of Halifax Harbour. There they spent a difficult winter in 1815 before being settled in communities outside the city. Preston and Hammonds Plains absorbed most of the immigrants and another five hundred settled at Loch Lomond in New Brunswick. As in earlier settlement programs, blacks received small grants in less fertile areas of the colonies. Although slavery continued into the nineteenth century in the Atlantic colonies, it was not upheld by the courts and gradually died out after the abolition of the slave trade in the British Empire in 1807. Thus the black refugees were, like other blacks in the region, free to fend for themselves, but in a context defined by a tradition of bigotry and discrimination.

As a society of immigrants, the Atlantic colonies in the early nineteenth century were characterized by cultural diversity. In certain areas, German, French, and Gaelic were spoken almost exclusively; in the port towns, whites, blacks, and aboriginals intermingled. In some communities women worked outside the home; in others they confined their productive labours exclusively to the household. The Scots tended to marry late and have small families; Acadians and New Englanders married young and raised large broods. Although political creeds reflected class interests, religion and ethnicity often dictated political affiliation. Irish Roman Catholics tended to be liberal or reformist in their politics while Anglicans tended to be conservative. There were exceptions to all of these generalizations, but they were often exceptions that proved the rule.

Thomas Chandler Haliburton   (Webster Canadiana Collection/W647/New Brunswick Museum)

By the mid-nineteenth century the four Atlantic colonies, with a population of over 650 000, had reached their limits of pre-industrial settlement. Most of Europe's emigrating millions would thereafter by-pass the region for western frontiers. Indeed, people from the Atlantic colonies joined the exodus, lured by the notion of richer land, warmer climates, and better opportunities. The region was also losing population to the new industrial frontier centred in New England. Thomas Chandler Haliburton, the Nova Scotia-born author of *The Clockmaker* and *The Old Judge*, observed in the 1840s that his province was a land of "comers and goers." While artisans, sailors, farmers, and "factory ladies" departed the scene, paupers, professors, and officeholders continued to arrive. Haliburton had little use for the wanderlust of his compatriots—he felt they should be developing the resources of their homeland rather than seeking greener pastures elsewhere. Nevertheless, the pattern of "coming and going" had been set in the Atlantic colonies, where year-round access to both the European and North American frontiers of opportunity made people a major export in an evolving colonial economy.

• Economic Adjustment

In the years between 1785 and 1849 there were two Atlantic economies, a formal one subject to the dictates of British mercantile policy and a less formal one serving the basic needs of a pioneer society. The two economies often intersected. British ships embarking for cargoes of colonial fish and timber usually carried trade items such as salt, tea, textiles, and hardware. To supplement their meagre subsistence, colonists sold their farm, fish, and forest products to British markets. A local merchant class emerged to encourage and handle the exchange process. Gradually, too, colonists began processing their primary resources for sale in Britain's far-flung empire—dried fish, barrels, and staves for the West Indies market; masts, squared timber, deals, and wooden ships for the British market—and became involved in the carrying trade. They also produced a wider range of the commodities required in the colonies, and they established banking institutions to accumulate capital for larger enterprises. By the 1840s, when the last vestiges of the old mercantile system were finally swept away, the Atlantic colonies had developed thriving commercial economies of their own that for a time could withstand the loss of imperial protection.

From a mercantile perspective, the Atlantic colonies were valuable for their vast resources of fish and timber and, to a lesser extent, their minerals and agricultural land. Such primary resources, or staples, were jealously guarded in an age when closed commercial systems regulated global trading patterns. British authorities tried to keep tight control over the bank fishery. The Crown also reserved white pine and great expanses of timber for the Royal Navy and retained rights over valuable minerals such as Cape Breton coal. Under the Navigation Acts of the seventeenth century, staple products could be exported only to Britain or designated markets in the British Empire and could be transported only in British ships. To keep manufacturing jobs in the mother country, the processing of raw resources in the colonies was actively discouraged. Further, as the policies in Prince Edward Island and Newfoundland attest, land in the colonies was granted under laws made in Britain. In 1790 free land grants were temporarily terminated in Nova Scotia and New Brunswick by a British administration hoping to recoup some of the money spent in transplanting the Loyalists.

During the negotiations leading to the Treaty of Versailles in 1783, the British seriously considered abandoning the old mercantile system. In 1776 political economist Adam Smith had written *An Inquiry into the Nature and Causes of the Wealth of Nations*, persuasively arguing that a policy of free trade would best serve British economic interests. Many British merchants anxious to expand the markets for their trade agreed with him. Although there was considerable pressure to give the newly independent United States access to the West Indies market, this concession was not immediately granted. British mercantilists were still strong enough in 1783 to prevent such a revolution in economic policy.

The decision to exclude the United States from Britain's imperial trade had a significant impact on the Atlantic colonies. Among the last

Loyalist arrivals in the region were colonial merchants reluctant to abandon their lucrative place in the triangular trade that linked Britain and the West Indies. British firms, excluded from American cities, turned their attention to the remnants of empire in North America. Rich in natural resources and still largely dependent on British capital, labour, and markets, the Atlantic colonies were ideal frontiers for mercantile endeavour. In their pioneer state of development, they remained importers of the necessities of life, and their towns served primarily as distributing centres for British products. If properly developed, their port towns might well replace Boston and New York as the commercial centres of Britain's North Atlantic trade.

In the half century following the American Revolutionary War, economic growth in the Atlantic colonies exceeded even the most optimistic expectations. Between 1785 and 1815 the Newfoundland fisheries doubled in volume. The timber trade, centred in New Brunswick, reached boom proportions, and shipbuilding and the carrying trade made promising beginnings. There were even signs that the region could become a major player in the lucrative West Indies trade.

These developments parallelled the first stages of the Industrial Revolution in Britain and were accelerated by two decades of war with France. With the introduction of the factory system in the late eighteenth century, Britain's productive capacity outstripped that of its competitors, and the country's need for resources and markets grew accordingly. The wars with France increased the demand for ship timber and caused deteriorating relations with the United States, which finally led to war in 1812. In 1807, when Napoleon declared his continental system and attempted to prevent the products of Europe from reaching Britain, the Atlantic colonies, already thriving on the wartime economy, entered a period of unprecedented economic growth.

During the French and Napoleonic Wars, which raged between 1793 and 1815, the number of West Country vessels sent to the Grand Banks and inshore fishery declined precipitously. Saint-Pierre and Miquelon were occupied by British troops, bringing the French fishery to a standstill. In an effort to escape wartime restrictions and impressment, British merchants and fishers took refuge in Newfoundland. By 1815 the population of the colony had reached 40 000 and the migratory fishery had entered a period of continuous decline. St John's emerged as the commercial capital of the North Atlantic fisheries, with a population of over seven thousand.

The shift in balance of power was dramatic. In 1784 Newfoundlanders produced 212 616 of the 437 316 quintals of cod harvested; by 1816 their share was 739 977 out of 819 200. They would henceforth dominate the British salt-fish trade as well as the lucrative seal fishery that had developed during the long years of war. In the same period a local shipbuilding industry had emerged and Britain even relented, ever so slightly, on its prohibition of land grants. As historian Shannon Ryan put it, Newfoundland "had always been a fishery based around an island." Now, with the French and Napoleonic Wars serving as a catalyst, it "would finally become a colony based on the fishery."[4]

The wars also provided the stimulus for the timber trade in the region. Equivalent in importance to oil in the twentieth century, timber was essential to the successful prosecution of overseas trade and global wars. The huge stands of forests in the Atlantic colonies represented the British Empire's most accessible source of masts and ship timber. By the 1790s New Brunswick masts had already found a British market, but the navy still relied primarily on Baltic suppliers for timber. This source was seriously restricted when Napoleon entered into alliances with Russia, Prussia, Sweden, and Denmark in 1807. Britain moved quickly to raise duties on foreign timber, thereby offering some guarantee of long-term protection for capitalists prepared to invest in colonial production. Between 1805 and 1812 the fir and pine timber reaching Britain from New Brunswick increased more than twenty-fold. Nova Scotia and Cape Breton also expanded timber production, although never reaching the levels achieved by New Brunswick. With its vast reserves of Crown land, New Brunswick quickly developed into a "timber colony."

The effects of the timber trade on the New Brunswick economy were spectacular and immediate. Businessmen, many of them based in the Scottish port city of Greenock, brought their capital, labour, and technology to the shores of the Miramichi and St John rivers. Farmers left their fields and took to the woods, where wages were good and work plentiful. Shipbuilding emerged as a major sideline of the industry. By 1815 the New Brunswick economy was dominated by the products of its forests, which accounted for nearly two-thirds of the colony's exports. Control over Crown lands and the revenue of the timber trade became issues that would dominate New Brunswick's social and political life long after the wars that prompted the timber boom had come to an end.

In the decade following the American Revolutionary War, it looked as if the Atlantic colonies would fail miserably in their attempt to pre-empt New England in the West Indies trade. Indeed, the Atlantic colonies seemed unable to supply even their own needs. Foodstuffs, livestock, and even lumber were imported from the United States. Trading took place under a warrant from the lieutenant-governor or a special act of Parliament if possible, by smuggling if necessary. Vessels plying the West Indies trade out of Halifax, Liverpool, St Andrews, and Saint John stopped at American ports to pick up their cargoes, and American produce was smuggled into the British West Indies through French-controlled islands. Making a virtue out of necessity, Britain gave American ships access to markets in the British West Indies by a clause in Jay's Treaty of 1794. Within a short time colonial fleets had been devastated and the future of the carrying trade looked hopeless.

Yet the tables were soon turned. During the second phase of the Napoleonic Wars (1803–15), the United States became embroiled with Britain over the rights of neutral countries to trade with belligerents. The Atlantic colonies benefited from the trade war leading up to the outbreak of hostilities in 1812. Legislation was passed giving preference to colonial shipments to the West Indies, and Halifax emerged as the great entrepôt for produce shipped under convoy to the Caribbean. When President Thomas Jefferson imposed an embargo on British trade in 1808, Britain declared Halifax, Shelburne, Saint John, and St Andrews to be "free ports." This designation allowed trade to be conducted without the imposition of customs duties—a clever manoeuvre that effectively undermined Jefferson's embargo. New England shippers, angered by the restrictions placed upon them, sold their produce—mostly flour, pork, tobacco, and naval stores—through Maritime ports and bought British manufactures and colonial fish, gypsum, and grindstones for the return voyage.

For those unwilling to use the free ports, there were other tried and true methods of avoiding legislative restrictions on trade. Smuggling flourished "on the lines" around the Passamaquoddy Islands and anywhere else that proved convenient along the hundreds of kilometres of coastline in the region. Although official figures showed that American trade with Britain dropped by 50 percent, British exports to the United States in real terms fell only by 7 percent. The free ports obviously served their purpose of sustaining British commerce while also keeping the army and navy fed; and they emerged as important commercial centres in an expanding regional economy.

When war was officially declared between Britain and the United States in 1812, the Atlantic colonies, buffered by a neutral New England, were spared military invasion. In 1814 Maritime pride and purses swelled when Sir John Sherbrooke's forces occupied part of the coast of present-day Maine. Under the cover of occupation, trade between the Maritimes and New England flourished. Many New Englanders welcomed the British flag and a few even considered applying for reentry into the British Empire as a way of legitimizing their clandestine trade. Wartime conditions in Halifax were summed up by a local writer who declared in 1814: "Happy state of Nova Scotia! amongst all this tumult we have lived in peace and security: invaded only by a numerous host of American doubloons and dollars, which have swept away the contents of our stores and shops like a torrent."[5]

The War of 1812 also expanded the potential for privateering, which had been carried on against French shipping, with more or less success, throughout the Napoleonic Wars. Thirty-seven vessels from the Atlantic colonies engaged in privateering activities during the conflict, recording 207 captures. The *Liverpool Packet* was the champion of the privateering fleet, taking fifty "prizes," most of them from Massachusetts. These captures helped to line the pockets of ambitious Halifax and St John's merchants who bought the vessels at prize courts and sold them at a profit. In the port cities a carnivallike atmosphere prevailed as luxury cargoes found their way to consumers. According to historian W.S. MacNutt, on one occasion residents of St John's witnessed the spectacle of thirty American prize ships roped together in the harbour, and "The clerks of the great mercantile establishments used champagne bottles for target practice on Sunday afternoons."[6] Haligonians shared a fine moment on 19 March 1813, when twelve full-rigged ships, eight brigs, and nineteen schooners were sold to the highest bidder.

When the wars came to an end in 1814–15 the demand for staples declined and prices fell, but the contours of the Atlantic regional economy had been set. Newfoundland remained dominated by the fisheries, and timber continued to fuel the New Brunswick economy. In Prince Edward Island farmers began to produce a surplus of wheat, root crops, and cattle

Market Wharf and Ferry Landing, Halifax. Painting by William H. Eagar (Royal Ontario Museum. Canadiana/955.218.4)

for markets in New Brunswick, Newfoundland, and farther afield. Nova Scotians farmed, fished, and built ships and were prominent in the West Indies trade. In 1826 the General Mining Association began developing the colony's extensive coal resources under a monopoly granted by the Crown.

Shipbuilding, financed by British and colonial capitalists, emerged as the region's most important manufacturing endeavour. By 1825 there were four brokers in Greenock and others in Liverpool and Glasgow who specialized in colonial-built vessels. Saint John alone had twenty-five shipyards, and more were scattered along the region's ample coastline. Over the next twenty-five years the region became a major producer of ocean-going vessels for sale in Britain and elsewhere. Smaller coastal and fishing vessels were built by the thousands. Between 1815 and 1860 more than two million tonnes of shipping were built in the Maritime provinces. This was nearly three times the shipping produced in the Canadas and almost 40 percent of Britain's output in the same period.

In addition to building and selling vessels, merchants in the Atlantic region became involved in shipping. Initially most of their vessels carried local staples such as timber or fish. When shipping capacity outstripped the resources of the region, the merchants found cargoes elsewhere. By mid-century, sailing ships from the Maritimes were plying the seven seas, full participants in the rapid expansion of the carrying trade that accompanied the Industrial Revolution.

The founding of banking institutions testifies to the attempts of the region's mercantile elite to organize their wealth for systematic investment. In Saint John, the Bank of New Brunswick (1820) and the Commercial Bank (1834) dominated financial activities. Halifax supported two banks, the Halifax Banking Company (1825) and the Bank of Nova Scotia (1832). Smaller communities in the region also began mobilizing their capital, sometimes in branches of already established banks, more often in locally incorporated operations.

While much of the region's economic growth was tied to the fortunes of Great Britain, the colonies could not always rely on imperial policy to protect them from foreign competition. Americans lost the "liberty" to fish in the region's inshore waters following the War of 1812, but by the Anglo-American Convention of 1818 they were given access to the fisheries of Newfoundland and Labrador. In 1822 American vessels were permitted to trade directly with the British West Indies, thus reducing the importance of Halifax and Saint John as transshipment ports for American products. By 1830 colonial ships had been granted access to ports in the United States. The end result of these complex trade manoeuvres was that commercial interests in the Atlantic colonies were largely free of British mercantile restrictions by the 1830s. Fish, timber, and ships still benefited from protective tariffs that gave them preference in British markets, but colonial products were becoming competitive enough to hold their own in the international marketplace.

The British mercantile system was finally eclipsed in the wake of the Irish famine of 1845. In order to import foodstuffs as cheaply as possible, the British Parliament suspended its longstanding preferential duties on grain, precipitating a revolution in British economic policy. Between 1846 and 1849, the entire system of colonial preference was dismantled and the Navigation Acts were abolished. Although cries of gloom and doom prevailed in merchant circles—and especially among those whose fortunes were tied to the timber trade—the free trade "crisis" did not immediately change the structure of the colonial economies. Timber, fish, and sailing ships continued to find markets in Britain's informal economic empire.

• The Domestic Economy

Although the world of staple trade and colonial shipping touched the lives of Atlantic Canadians both directly and indirectly, the seasonal rhythms of domestic production determined most people's general well-being prior to 1850. Pre-industrial families engaged in a variety of activities that included farming, fishing and hunting, building houses and barns, spinning and weaving wool, making and repairing clothing, preparing and preserving food, and bearing and rearing children. Pioneers made their own furniture and crafted shoes, harnesses, and even carriages for their horses. Travellers in the region, most of them accustomed to more sophisticated settings, often remarked on the relative self-sufficiency of the "bluenoses," who were "jacks of all trades and masters of none."

Clearing the land was a daunting task for most pioneer settlers. They assaulted the forests as if trees were an enemy to be conquered. Despite the lessons learned in Britain, where most of the productive forests were gone and hunting had become a sport reserved for the aristocracy, immigrants showed little interest in conservation. They found it difficult to believe that the great quantities of forest land and wildlife could ever become exhausted. In their haste to establish themselves they cut down giant hardwood stands and burned the stumps, a process often leading to runaway fires that destroyed both the forests and those who inhabited them. Walter Johnstone, a Scottish visitor to Prince Edward Island, remarked in 1820, "Burnt woods are to be seen in the neighbourhood of almost every settlement, some of them of considerable magnitude."[7] The greatest disaster of this kind took place on the Miramichi in 1825, when fire consumed over two million hectares of forests and took the lives of 160 people and countless animals.

Clearing the town plot, Stanley, New Brunswick, 1834   (W.P. Kay/National Archives of Canada/C17)

The speed with which European immigrants killed off wild animals is one of the most remarkable features of the colonization process. As early as 1794 the Nova Scotia government felt compelled to pass a law to protect grouse and black duck, both facing extinction. Moose had virtually disappeared from New Brunswick by the 1820s. According to Peter Fisher, they "were found in great abundance when the loyalists first came to the province" but "were wantonly destroyed, being hunted for the skin, while their carcasses were left in the woods, a few only being used for food." Although laws had been enacted for the preservation of moose, they were not enforced. The great auk, a shorebird easily caught and much favoured as a tasty morsel by fishers, was another victim of European greed. When Cartier visited the shores of Newfoundland in the sixteenth century he remarked upon the abundance of the fat, flightless birds. By 1844 there were no more great auks on the face of the earth.

It was not only the mercantile system that encouraged many immigrants to put less energy into their farming activities than they might otherwise have done. Nature's bounty in the region made subsistence survival a real alternative to the "get ahead" mentality that characterized the age. With a plot of land and the bountiful sea at one's doorstep, why work so hard? Why not, if one could do so, live like the gentry, who seemed to have plenty of time for the good life? Colonial officials, anxious for the "labouring class" to take a more commercial approach to farming, were understandably appalled by the lack of discipline displayed by many colonists. Writing in 1817, Nova Scotia's lieutenant-governor Dalhousie used typical language: "The people are very poor & indolent; fond of rum, they appear generally half drunk & wasting their time; they loiter about their houses & field work & seem content in raising a sufficiency for winter. But the country is capable of great improvement, & were proper encouragement held out, much good might result."[8]

The wars had highlighted a fatal flaw in the colonial economy: an inability to produce an adequate amount of foodstuffs, especially wheat. As late as 1845 Frances Beavan noted in her book *Life in the Backwoods of New Brunswick* that most farmers in the colony were still unable to "bread themselves," thus necessitating the importation of wheat from the United States and the Canadas. The failure to produce enough wheat partly reflected the ease with which it could be imported into the region and the difficulty of producing wheat in the Maritime climate. Nevertheless, many farmers in Atlantic Canada, especially in the Annapolis and Saint John valleys and on Prince Edward Island, managed to produce livestock, coarse grains, and root crops for export. They also supplied much of the huge demand for food created by the timber trade and the fisheries. A busy coastal trade in the Gulf of St Lawrence and the Bay of Fundy bore witness to a highly integrated primary economy based on farm, forest, and fisheries.

Women's work in pre-industrial society was largely confined to the domestic realm, where most of the food and clothing was produced. Yorkshire farmers John Robinson and Thomas Ripsin, travelling through the Annapolis valley in 1774, remarked on the intensive labour carried out in the home:

> The women are very industrious house-wives, and spin the flax, the growth of their own farms, and weave both their linen and woollen cloth; they also bleach their linen and dye their yarn themselves. Though they will not descend to work out of doors, either in time of hay or harvest, yet they are exceedingly diligent in every domestic employment. The candles, soap and starch, which are used in their families, are of their own manufacturing. They also make their own yeast, and make a kind of liquor, by boiling the branches of the spruce tree, to which they add molasses, and cause it to ferment in the manner we do treacle beer in England.[9]

By the mid-nineteenth century, colonial census takers were examining home-based production, noting, for example, that over 1.5 million kilograms of butter, 296 000 kilograms of cheese, and over 50 000 pounds of maple sugar as well as over a million yards of cloth and flannels were produced in Nova Scotia in 1851. Not surprisingly, women's paid labour in the pre-industrial colonies usually took the form of domestic service in the homes of other women where they learned and practised the skills of "the industrious house-wife."

European class distinctions still prevailed in the Atlantic colonies and in some cases were actually enhanced by colonial conditions. This was particularly the case for skilled artisans, whose status was rapidly declining in Europe under the impact of the Industrial Revolution. In the colonies the demand for the products and services of an artisan class was actually expanding. Women in colonial cities could eke out a living making hats and dresses for the local elite, while the services of blacksmiths, carpenters, and millers were widely used. As T.W. Acheson has shown in the context of Saint John, the artisan class rose to prominence in the first half of the nineteenth century, and a few of their number would be in a position to transcend their class when new techniques of production and capital accumulation made it possible to turn their shops into industrial enterprises.[10]

The colonies also supported an administrative and professional class of doctors, lawyers, clergy, politicians, and soldiers. Together with the great wholesale and export merchants, these people made up the elite of colonial society. In the early years of settlement this class consisted almost exclusively of immigrants from Britain and the United States, but colonial elites soon asserted themselves. As citizens of the British Empire, young

Trotting Match on the Ice—Prince Edward Island, by Henry Buckton Laurence (Confederation Centre Art Gallery and Museum)

men in the colonies had a broad scope for their career ambitions. For example, native son Provo Wallis entered the Royal Navy, eventually becoming an admiral. His assumption of command of the *Shannon*, which captured the American warship *Chesapeake* on 6 June 1813 after a thirteen-minute battle near Boston, brought him instant acclaim throughout the empire. Colonial-born entrepreneur Samuel Cunard rose from relative obscurity to become a timber merchant, Prince Edward Island proprietor, shipbuilder, and, in 1840, instigator of the first transatlantic steamship service between Britain and North America.

ENOS COLLINS

One of Nova Scotia's most successful businessmen, Enos Collins (1774–1871), got his start during the French Revolutionary and Napoleonic wars. The second of twenty-six children born to a Liverpool, Nova Scotia, merchant and his three successive wives, Enos was captain of a schooner at the age of twenty. In 1799 he turned from trade to privateering, serving on the famed *Charles Mary Wentworth*. Investing his capital in vessels trading out of Liverpool, he made a handsome profit running the French blockade to supply the British army on the Iberian peninsula.

In 1811 Collins moved to Halifax, where he engaged in shipping and privateering. Collins was part-owner of the *Liverpool Packet* and, with his partner Joseph Allison, did well in the prize courts. After the war Collins diversified his activities into everything from currency trading to whaling. His public and private activities consolidated his growing status. In 1822 he was appointed to a seat on the colony's Council, which gave him considerable political influence. He married Margaret Halliburton, the eldest daughter of a member of the Council, and lived in Gorsebrook, a fine estate in the south end of the city. Collins was prominent among the founders of Halifax Banking Company, which became known as "Collins' Bank."

His influence in the political and economic life of the colony and his conservative opposition to the democratic tendencies of the age soon drew criticism from the reform movement led by Joseph Howe. In 1840 Collins retired from the Council and retreated into his private life of family and business. The confederation movement caused the aging Collins to break with the Conservatives and publicly support the anti-confederates. Like many other merchants in the region, he saw the union as the death-knell to the commercial empire that had financed his fortune. When he died in 1871, Collins left an estate worth over $6 million and was reputed to be one of the richest men in British North America.

On the other side of the social scale were unemployed landless labourers, many of them recent immigrants, and the dependent poor, including the very old and very young as well as the mentally challenged and physically disabled. Fires, crop failures, economic cycles, and seasonal hardships increased the number of dependent poor in the colonies. Even those who owned land often lived in stark conditions that barely yielded subsistence. An outbreak of potato blight in the 1840s reduced many people to the level of starvation. For those dependent on seasonal labour, the onset of winter was little short of tragic. Although these unfortunate members of colonial society were the objects of charity and could claim limited assistance from the government in times of extreme crisis, they had little hope of rising out of their poverty. Cases of death in remote cabins or in the streets of the major port cities stood as a stark reminder to those in more comfortable conditions of the fate that awaited any people who stumbled on the path of life.

The dangers inherent in the colonial economy were perhaps most obvious in Newfoundland, where the mercantile and domestic economies both revolved around the fishery. Following the Napoleonic Wars, a major drop in fish prices and renewed competition from France and the United States threw many fishers out of work. St John's attracted most of the desperate unemployed. When the city experienced a series of fires and an unusually cold winter in 1816–17, only relief from outside sources and mass deportation averted wholesale starvation and death from exposure.

• Social Relations in Pre-industrial Society

In colonial society all its members—men and women, rich and poor, immigrant and native-born—were bound together by the mercantile and domestic economies, which functioned on barter and mutual dependence as much as on hard currency. Women's work was performed within the context of the family, where, by law, the male head of the household controlled the wealth of his wife and children. Both the fisheries and timber trade nurtured the infamous "truck system" in which merchants provided their labourers with the equipment and provisions they needed for the season's work in return for the product of their labour. Many workers never saw their wages and were perpetually bound to their merchant-supplier by a web of debt. The same system often prevailed in farming communities, where merchants held mortgages on indebted farms. In Prince Edward Island rents to proprietors were notoriously in arrears, and tenants could be—though they rarely were—forcibly ejected from their lands. The region's aboriginal population, having incorporated European society into traditional seasonal rhythms, was now part of the network of dependency. Each spring Native women emerged from their winter retreats with quill boxes and woven baskets to sell in the urban markets, while Native men made axe handles and brooms and found work during the peak season as guides, loggers, and dock workers.

What is most obvious about these economic relationships is a fundamental inequality. Patriarchy, the belief that men should have power over women and children, and paternalism, the practice by which people in authority rule benevolently but intrusively over those below them on the social scale, encouraged duty and deference in colonial society. Women and children were socialized to obey the male head of the household, and members of the labouring class deferred to their social superiors. Both patriarchy and social inequality came under strong attack in the nineteenth century, and the more recent British immigrants often complained that colonials failed to show proper respect for those above them on the social scale. Nevertheless, unequal social relations had sunk strong roots in the Atlantic colonies and would not yield easily to new notions of democratic equality.

The values of industrial capitalism, which were rapidly gaining ascendancy in Britain and the United States, required new economic and social relationships. In the nineteenth century individualism, monetary exchange, capital accumulation, wage labour, and rigid work schedules gradually replaced subsistence production, seasonal rhythms, and client–patron relationships as the framework of economic life. Thomas Chandler Haliburton used his fictional character, Yankee clock pedlar Sam Slick, to chide colonials for their unprogressive ways. Nova Scotians were wanting only three things, Slick opined: industry, enterprise, and economy. *An owl should be their emblem, and the motto, 'He sleeps all the days of his life.'* The whole country is like this night; beautiful to look at, but silent as the grave—still as death, asleep, becalmed."[11]

•Emerging Political Cultures, 1758–1849

The same could not be said for colonial politics, which was often a noisy and ugly affair. At the formal level the colonies moved along the continuum from imperial dependency to representative and responsible government in the century after 1749. This was not always an easy or uniform process. Nor was it necessarily the democratic triumph that is often portrayed. Only a relatively small number of men emerged as the power brokers under responsible government, and their values were revealed in the laws they imposed on the society they governed.

Colonial politics evolved within the larger framework of Western political thought. In Europe the divine right of kings and the concentration of power in the hands of a small hereditary landed elite, which was bolstered by a state-supported church and a standing army, were crumbling in the face of a rising middle class. Its demand that power be shared among all men with a stake in society—usually defined as those possessing property or wealth—was a popular rallying cry in both the American and French revolutions. By the end of the eighteenth century, wider concepts of democracy were being advanced by a few people. Why not give every man—and even women—an equal political voice? Indeed, why not create a society in which equality of condition, not just equality of opportunity, prevailed? In the Atlantic colonies, as in much of the North Atlantic world, these political discussions were informed by three perspectives: conservatism, liberalism, and socialism.

When calling for political reforms, colonial politicians could draw upon the practical experience of an evolving parliamentary democracy in Britain and a full-fledged republican system in the United States. Colonials who lamented the erosion of traditional institutions looked to European conservatism for their inspiration. Tories were still a force to be reckoned with in Britain, and the papacy, emerging from a century of retreat, sounded the clarion call to all Roman Catholics to resist the "sins" of liberalism and socialism. Those more remote from the formal political process also took lessons from their American and European counterparts. The Irish movement for repeal of the Union of 1801 became a model for mobilizing mass support for a political cause and was closely watched by Irish Catholics in the Atlantic colonies. The British labour movement, still in its infancy, also offered practical ideas about how ordinary people could exert influence.

Representative government in the Atlantic colonies first came in 1758 with the calling of an elected House of Assembly in Nova Scotia. Although the Assembly theoretically had a position analogous to that of the British House of Commons, in practice the apparatus of colonial administration was weighted in favour of appointed officials. The lieutenant-governor was appointed by the Crown and so, too, were his colonial advisers, who sat on a council that performed both legislative and executive functions. A miniature British court system ranging from justices of the peace at the local level to a supreme court was put in place in Nova Scotia before 1775. Judges, as well, were appointed rather than elected to office. Because councillors and magistrates usually held their positions for life, they exercised considerable influence over colonial lieutenant-governors, whose terms of office were much shorter. The lieutenant-governor and his Council were responsible not to the Assembly but to the Board of Trade and Plantations (after 1801 to the Secretary of State for War and Colonies), which in turn was responsible to the British Parliament.

When St John's Island and New Brunswick became separate colonies they received political structures similar to those of Nova Scotia. Newfoundlanders did not have a resident governor until 1825 and were granted a House of Assembly only in 1832. William Carson, a Scottish-born surgeon, had waged a one-man battle against the despotic system, but to no avail. It was only when the British Parliament began formulating its own Reform Bill, which passed in 1832, that the injustice done to Britons in Newfoundland stood out in bold relief. Because representative government was so late in coming, Newfoundland became the first among the Atlantic colonies where legislative and executive councils were separated.

Appointed councils brought little stability to Newfoundland politics. By the time that the first Newfoundland election was called, political conflict in the colony had already found extra-parliamentary forms of expression, many of them based on military and mob violence. Tensions between Catholic and Protestant, fisher and merchant, outport and St John's, liberal and conservative, immediately engulfed island politics. In an effort to establish control over the political process, Britain amalgamated the Assembly and the appointed Council in 1842, thereby making Newfoundland the only Atlantic colony to temporarily surrender its assembly after it had been granted.

On Prince Edward Island, the land question was the animating force of political life. During the first decade of the nineteenth century Irish lawyer James Palmer and Rhode Island Loyalist William Haszard led a society known as the Loyal Electors, which criticized the corruption of the official coterie around Lieutenant-Governor J.F.W. DesBarres (1805–13). Local authorities and absentee proprietors used their influence to have Palmer dismissed from his public offices. Postwar efforts to make the proprietorial system work ended in failure and frustration for both proprietors and tenants.

In 1831 William Cooper, a former land agent for absentee proprietor Lord James Townsend, won a hard-fought election for a seat in the island legislature on a platform of "our country's freedom and farmers' rights." He soon emerged as leader of the Escheat Movement, which won an overwhelming victory in the 1838 election. When Cooper travelled to London to plead his case for a general escheat or cancellation of the proprietary grants, he was refused even a hearing from Colonial Secretary Lord John Russell. Thereafter, reform on the island was focussed on responsible government as the only means of achieving a satisfactory conclusion to the interminable land question.

In New Brunswick the timber trade dominated the political process. The revenues from the sale, leasing, and licensing of Crown lands, spent at the lieutenant-governor's prerogative, became the object of the assembly's reform efforts and were a prize worth fighting for. The issue became more contentious with the appointment of Thomas Baillie as commissioner of Crown lands in 1824. Charged with bringing bureaucratic efficiency to the administration of Crown lands, Baillie alienated virtually everyone in the colony while chalking up vast surpluses in the colonial treasury. In 1833, when the Colonial Office decided to divide the Council into legislative and executive branches, Thomas Baillie headed the list of appointments to the new Executive Council.

Charles Simonds of Saint John led opposition to the "placemen" in government, and in 1837 the Assembly agreed to a compromise worked out the previous year with the Colonial Office. In return for a "civil list" guaranteeing the salaries of civil servants, including the hated Thomas Baillie, the revenues from Crown lands would be turned over to the Assembly's disposal. Moreover, the new Executive Council in New Brunswick was relieved of the dead weight of lifetime appointments by Colonial Secretary Lord Glenelg's injunction to Lieutenant-Governor Sir John Harvey to choose councillors who had the confidence of the Assembly. With Simonds now the chief adviser to the lieutenant-governor, New Brunswick had achieved one of the most important conditions for the operation of responsible government: executive responsibility to the majority in the Assembly.

Resentment against appointed colonial officials was also a cause of complaint in Nova Scotia. Customs officers, magistrates, and councillors, their positions emanating from the Crown, could be impervious to the popular will. In 1835 Joseph Howe successfully defended himself against a charge of libel when he published a letter criticizing the colony's magistrates in his newspaper the *Novascotian*. Riding on his popular acclaim, he won a seat in the Assembly and used it to continue his battle for political reform. Perhaps more than any other colonial politician, Howe knew what he wanted: the same constitutional rights for British subjects in the colonies as they enjoyed at home.

This was an audacious request and one that seemed incompatible with imperial control of the colonies. Nevertheless, Howe pressed his case in London and applauded the recommendations of Lord Durham, who had been sent to report on the British North American colonies following the 1837 rebellions in the Canadas. In 1839, when Lord John Russell stubbornly refused to concede the principle of responsible government as recommended by Durham, Howe expounded his position in a series of public letters to the colonial secretary. "Every poor boy in Nova Scotia . . . knows that he has the same rights to the honours and emoluments of office as he would have if he lived in Britain or the United States," Howe concluded. "And he feels, that while the great honours of the empire are almost beyond his reach, he ought to have a chance of dispensing the patronage and guiding the administration of his native country without any sacrifice of principle or diminution of self-respect."[12]

By the time Howe was writing his letters to Lord John Russell, Britain had split the old Council into executive and legislative councils, and the principle of permanent executive appointments had been abandoned. However, before responsible government could become a reality, two more changes were required. First, it was necessary, as a general principle, for members of the Executive Council to have the support of the majority party in the Assembly and to resign when they had lost the Assembly's confidence by a vote in the house or in a general election. Secondly, it was necessary for the lieutenant-governor to defer to the recommendations of his cabinet advisers and, like the monarch in Britain, withdraw from the daily routine of political life.

For these principles to be accepted, changes had to occur both in Britain and the colonies. The party system in the colonies was rudimentary at best, as was the system of cabinet responsibility in the Executive Council. Both the party system and bureaucratic processes began to take shape in the turbulent political atmosphere of the 1840s. Meanwhile, imperial reluctance to cut the colonial apron strings was reduced by the adoption of free trade in 1846. Although political reform was not tied directly to economic reform—British colonies inhabited primarily by people of colour were actually stripped of representative government in this period—free trade undermined one of the major rationales for maintaining control over colonies where white settlers were in the majority.

In 1847 Sir John Harvey, who had assumed the position of lieutenant-governor of Nova Scotia in 1846, was instructed by Colonial Secretary Lord Grey to choose his advisers from the party that commanded a majority in the assembly. In an election that year the Reformers were victorious and stood firm in their resolve to take exclusive control of the reins of power. Early in 1848 a Liberal government under the leadership of James Boyle Uniacke became the first "responsible" administration in the British Empire.

The process by which political institutions evolved was different in each of the Atlantic colonies, but the end result was the same. Responsible government, by which the executive authority was drawn from and responsible to an elected colonial assembly, was introduced in all the Atlantic colonies between 1848 and 1855. This did not mean that the colonies were politically independent. The Colonial Office still kept a watchful administrative eye over colonial politics; the British Parliament continued to legislate on matters relating to defence, foreign policy, and constitutional amendment; and the Privy Council in Britain remained the final court of appeal for the colonies. Another century would pass before these ties of empire would be fully dissolved in "British" North America.

Responsible government represented the official transfer of power from the British to the colonial middle class. In some ways it was a clever tactical move binding the colonies ever closer to Britain, which was steadily extending the boundaries of its informal empire based on trade and naval power. Although responsible government did not immediately alter the power structure in the Atlantic colonies, it coincided with a debate over who could participate in the democratic process.

Under representative government the Atlantic colonies had adopted a broad franchise that extended the vote to all "freeholders." In Prince Edward Island leaseholders were included on election lists, and in Newfoundland all adult males who had resided in a house for one year were eligible to vote. In the 1850s the Atlantic colonies extended the franchise to include most ratepayers, whether they owned or rented property. Meanwhile, women, whether they were property owners or not, were disfranchised by law in all the colonies between 1832 and 1851. Although aboriginal peoples were in effect disqualified by virtue of their poverty, the Nova Scotia government specifically denied the franchise to Natives and paupers in 1854. Responsible government was thus a victory for that propertied portion of colonial society that was male, white, and twenty-one years of age and older. In practice, less than a quarter of the population in the Atlantic colonies was legally entitled to vote in the mid-nineteenth century, and even fewer people were eligible to run for public office.

The people who were denied the franchise still found ways to exert political pressure. Organized demonstrations could spur colonial administrations to action, even if only to bring in troops to quell actual or potential violence. Women signed petitions supporting reforms such as temperance and petitioned on their own behalf for pensions and relief. The first nations had early learned that imperial authorities were usually more sympathetic to their concerns than were colonial politicians and often appealed directly to the monarch for redress of grievances. Mi'kmaq chief Paussamigh Pemmeenauweet, tired of seeing his people pushed out of their traditional territory by greedy whites, petitioned Queen Victoria in 1840:

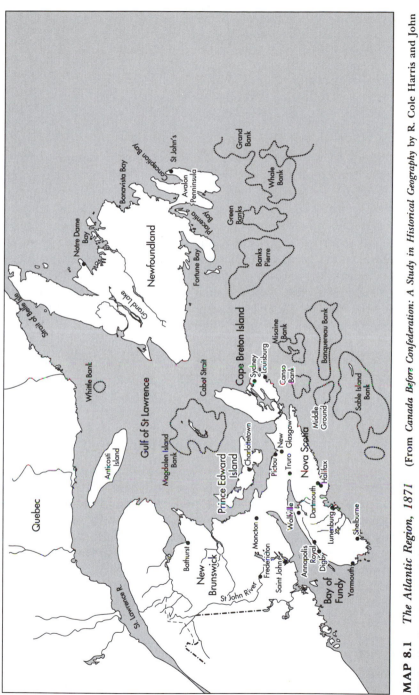

MAP 8.1   *The Atlantic Region, 1871*   (From *Canada Before Confederation: A Study in Historical Geography* by R. Cole Harris and John Warkentin. Copyright © 1974 by Oxford University Press Inc. Reprinted by permission.)

I cannot cross the great Lake to talk to you for my Canoe is too small, and I am old and weak. I cannot look upon you for my eyes not see so far. You cannot hear my voice across the Great Waters. I therefore send this Wampum and paper talk to tell the Queen I am in trouble. My people are in trouble. . . . No hunting Grounds—No Beaver—no Otter . . . poor for ever. . . . All these Woods once ours. Our Fathers possessed them all. . . . White man has taken all that was ours. . . . Let us not perish.[13]

Five days after Queen Victoria received the petition, the Colonial Office sent a dispatch to Lieutenant-Governor Falkland in Nova Scotia, ordering him to investigate the problems facing aboriginal peoples in the colony. In the mid-nineteenth century, control over Native policy was transferred to colonial legislatures, an ominous development for the region's first nations.

On the less formal level, power and status in colonial society were as often determined by violence as by bureaucratic processes. Indeed, violence was never far from the surface of colonial life. Elections could result in cracked heads, mutilated bodies, and even death as contending voters battled at the polls. If women or children stepped out of line, they could expect to be physically punished. Despite laws forbidding it, men fought duels to defend their honour. Any mass action was considered suspect and usually put down by the military. For many people on the margins of the political process, the threat of violence was enough to keep them in their place.

• Religion and Culture

In 1827, nineteen-year-old Eliza Chipman of Cornwallis, Nova Scotia, married her cousin William Chipman, a widower, twenty-six years her senior. Two of William's eight children were older than Eliza and one was opposed to the marriage. Eliza and William had twelve children, eight of whom survived infancy. Eliza herself died in 1853 at the age of forty-six. Given the realities of married life, it is little wonder that Eliza Chipman was apprehensive about her wedding day. "My case [is] extraordinary," she remarked in her diary. "How can I perform the part of a mother to these orphan children on account of my youth and inexperience?" As a practising Baptist she accepted her fate as God's will and turned to religion for strength to live up to her "calling." She concluded, "But I can only say, if God has called me thereto, he is able to qualify me for the task."

Perhaps no single source of identity in colonial society was more important than organized religion. Although eighteenth-century pioneers in the Atlantic colonies often lived without the services of resident clergy, by the nineteenth century churches were sprouting like mushrooms across the Atlantic landscape. Religious affiliation, of course, had been a vital political issue in Western society since the Reformation, but in the nineteenth century both the Protestant and Roman Catholic churches became more aggressive in their pursuit of converts and in their attempts to mould the values of their adherents. In the Atlantic colonies this new religious energy was, for some communities, an integrative force, but just as often it spawned divisions that were reflected in every aspect of colonial life.

The single most important feature of the religious history of pre-Confederation Atlantic Canada was the rise of evangelicalism, a movement that swept Europe and North America in the eighteenth and early nineteenth centuries. Those, like Eliza Chipman, who embraced evangelicalism emphasized individual piety, personal "conversion," and direct communication with God. Such views defied the notions of hierarchy and social order advocated by the "established" Anglican, Presbyterian, and Roman Catholic churches and parallelled the secular demand for greater personal freedom and democratic consent that had found expression in the American and French revolutions.

In Atlantic Canada evangelicalism was rooted in the ministries of two eighteenth-century evangelical preachers, Henry Alline and William Black. Alline's ministry coincided with the American revolution and was most successful among the New England Planters. William Black came from Britain, where Methodism was emerging as the supreme expression of evangelicalism. Like Alline, Black initially had the greatest appeal among his own countrypeople, including the Yorkshire settlers and members of the Halifax merchant class.

In the first half of the nineteenth century, Baptist and Methodist churches grew more rapidly than any other denominations in the region. Itinerent evangelical preachers carried the message to remote corners of the colonies, and periodic revivals brought dramatic numbers of new converts. Although Anglican bishop John Inglis railed against the "illiterate rambling preachers," his ministers sent out by the Society for the Propagation of the Gospel could not match their success. Even the Halifax elite, and especially the young women among them, were attracted by the message preached by the Baptists. St Paul's Anglican Church was split in two by religious controversy in the 1820s, with the result that some of the city's leading families became Baptists.

Evangelicalism appealed to a broad spectrum of the colonial population because it tapped into the ideological currents of the age. In today's terms, it was a movement of "empowerment." William Black reported after one of his meetings in Liverpool, Nova Scotia, that the people were "set at liberty" after "an astonishing outpouring of the spirit" that led to the manners of the people being "entirely changed." Alline, whose hymns remained popular well into the nineteenth century, defined the essence of evangelicalism in one of them: "'Tis not a zeal for modes and forms/That spreads the gospel-truths abroad;/But he whose inward mien reforms,/And loves the saints, and loves the Lord."[14] In his study of the "Second Great Awakening," historian George Rawlyk found that women, children, servants, and minorities often played a role in revival meetings.[15] After a particularly successful revival meeting, for instance, one observer noted that religious enthusiasts went from door to door in the community, led by "Many small Boys and Girls, Some telling the goodness of God, others in distress."

The public expression of the evangelical spirit was a transformed personal life. Although salvation could not be bought through good works, "saved" individuals were expected to show outward manifestations of their reformed spiritual state. It was not long before evangelicals also turned their reforming zeal on society. Largely in self-defence, Anglicans, Presbyterians, and Roman Catholics were also caught up in the reforming spirit of the age. Not surprisingly, the areas traditionally dominated by the church—education, charity, and personal behaviour—became arenas for public controversy.

For people of evangelical persuasion, formal education was more than a vehicle for teaching "the basics" of reading, writing, and cyphering. It offered a structured way of imparting morality and civic virtues. In the early nineteenth century, education in the Atlantic region was offered in a hodge-podge of institutions, many of them sponsored by colonial churches, both Protestant and Catholic. The Madras school system, so called because it was developed in India, used older students as tutors to younger ones, and was promoted by the Church of England in the region. The Sunday school movement became popular in the 1830s, particularly among Methodists, Presbyterians, and Baptists. Although educational reformers were eager to establish a uniform state-supported education system like the ones that existed in Ireland and Massachusetts, their efforts were frustrated by opposition from those who feared the cultural and financial costs of such a move. Most politicians preferred to provide grants to locally generated schools rather than to attempt to impose a single, centralized system upon their reluctant constituents.

In the area of higher education the churches emerged triumphant. Between 1838 and 1855 the foundations of no less than seven universities were laid in the Maritime colonies: Prince of Wales and St Dunstan's in Prince Edward Island; Acadia, St Mary's, Mount St Vincent, and St Francis Xavier in Nova Scotia; and Mount Allison in New Brunswick. Each was associated with a religious denomination, as had been the earlier Anglican institutions, King's College in Windsor, Nova Scotia, and the College of New Brunswick in Fredericton. Dalhousie College, founded in 1818 by Lieutenant-Governor Dalhousie as a non-denominational institution, became narrowly Presbyterian in its faculty-hiring practices and drew fire from the outlying regions for its Halifax location. Joseph Howe tried to forestall the fragmentation of higher education in Nova Scotia by introducing a bill for one state-supported university in Halifax; but he earned only the antipathy of his opponents, who resented his assertion that supporters of small denominational colleges were "four-eyed lawyers," "eloquent wiseacres," and "sap-headed shingle merchants."

Churches in the colonial period also emerged as important dispensers of charity in a society characterized by rampant poverty and disaster. In more rooted societies families and municipal institutions played larger roles in caring for the needy, but in the highly mobile and economically unstable colonies the church was often the only refuge for people facing destitution. In urban centres, churches occasionally sponsored institutions in the form of orphanages, hospitals, and shelters. The Protestant churches in Saint John, for example, co-operated in the 1834 founding of a Female House of Industry, which offered work for destitute women as well as nursery and educational facilities for their children. Such institutions were financed by the more affluent church members and often administered by the women of the church, for whom charitable acts were among the few public roles considered appropriate for them to perform.

In addition to educational and charitable activities, the church served as the focus for various reform movements in colonial society. The most successful by far was the temperance movement, which from its beginnings in the late 1820s soon engulfed the region. Even the Anglican and Roman Catholic churches encouraged temperance among their followers, although they were much less likely than their evangelical counterparts to countenance total prohibition of alcoholic beverages as a solution to society's ills. If the comments of contemporaries can be believed, temperance was an idea whose time had come. The availability of cheap rum in the colonies encouraged excessive drinking and undermined the family-based brewing industry. For those wanting to "get ahead" in life, alcohol was both a waste of money and a detriment to hard work.

Because of their role in defining social values, churches moved quickly to exert their influence through newspapers, the most important source of information in colonial society. By the 1840s most of the religious denominations in the region sponsored their own newspapers, which debated global and local political events as well as religious questions. Nova Scotia newspapers—including the *Christian Messenger* (Baptist), the *Cross*

(Roman Catholic), and the *Guardian* (Church of Scotland)—were often as widely read as the newspapers sponsored by political parties. In St John's, where religion was always a potent political factor, the *Public Ledger* represented the Protestant perspective; the *Newfoundlander* represented Roman Catholic thinking.

The church was the one institution in colonial society where men and women, rich and poor, old and young met together. Nevertheless, churches revealed the status of their members in many ways. In many colonial churches the renting of pews still permitted the rich to sit closer to the pulpit. Women were sometimes relegated to a separate section of the church. People of colour were almost always set apart. The black Baptists of Nova Scotia, never fully accepted by their white co-religionists, formed separate churches and associations under the leadership of such men as the Reverend Richard Preston, an emigrant from the United States who studied for the ministry in Britain.

In the early nineteenth century the gulf separating Protestant and Roman Catholic was nearly as wide as that separating the races. Particularly

Richard Preston   (Black Cultural Centre)

in Newfoundland and Prince Edward Island, both with populations largely British in origin and numbers of Protestants and Catholics equally matched, the religious battles of Europe were easily transported to the colonies. In 1800 several of the Irish soldiers in the locally recruited Newfoundland regiment were involved in a conspiracy to murder English merchants and their associates in St John's. The plot was discovered and foiled by Bishop James Louis O'Donel, and five men were hanged for their treachery. But Prince Edward Augustus, the Duke of Kent, who was then in charge of British forces in the region, felt it wise to transfer the Newfoundland regiment to Halifax, where he could keep a closer eye on the potentially mutinous Irish Catholics.

Harmony did not always prevail within Protestant and Roman Catholic ranks. In the early years of settlement evangelical ministers did not have the privilege of performing legally recognized marriage ceremonies, which added to the dissenting Protestant sects' resentment of Anglicans. Presbyterianism was racked by divisions between the established Church of Scotland and various secessionist groups. So deeply did these divisions go that in 1845 the sheriff erected a barrier over two metres high across Pictou's main street to keep the warring factions apart. Roman Catholics were also divided among themselves, usually along ethnic lines. With Natives, Acadians, Scots, and Irish all practising Roman Catholicism, there was little hope for unity either in language or administration.

As in Upper and Lower Canada, Roman Catholics in the Atlantic colonies gradually gained civil rights. In Nova Scotia, laws preventing them from voting and acquiring land were abolished late in the eighteenth century. The ban on Roman Catholics holding public office was lifted for Lawrence Kavanagh, a merchant elected to a Cape Breton Assembly seat in 1822. In 1829 Roman Catholics throughout the region acquired civil rights as part of the larger policy of imperial reform.

At the same time, the number of Roman Catholics was growing dramatically, and the missionary nature of their church was giving way to more formal structures. In 1784 the Reverend James Louis O'Donel was sent to Newfoundland where he assumed the title of bishop in 1794. The Maritime provinces remained under the jurisdiction of the bishop of Quebec until 1817, when Edmund Burke was named bishop of Nova Scotia. In 1829 a separate bishop was appointed for New Brunswick and Prince Edward Island. These administrative changes marked the beginning of a reinvigorated Roman Catholicism in the Atlantic colonies.

By the middle of the nineteenth century competition with the Roman Catholic Church forced the fractured Protestant churches to co-operate to achieve political and social goals. Protestant alliances sometimes came together to fight Roman Catholics at election time and to develop a common position on controversial issues such as education and temperance. The degree of Protestant consensus varied depending on the colony and never reached the level found in Canada West. Nevertheless, the impact of denominational rivalry on the colonies was clear. Organized religion now played a key role in the lives of most people, serving as a lens through which they interpreted personal growth and public developments.

The rise of evangelicalism and the growth of religious institutions were only two of the symptoms of the reform spirit sweeping Western society in the early years of the nineteenth century. Perched on the margins of the North Atlantic world, colonial citizens were full participants in debates over social change. Their newspapers, college professors, and urban literati were alive to the intellectual currents of the age. It was often only a matter of a few years or even a few months before movements in Britain or the United States had their impact and their imitators in the Atlantic colonies. Travelling lecturers, speaking on a wide range of subjects, were enthusiastically received. Ambitious young men from the colonies travelled to Britain and the United States to be educated as doctors, scientists, and philosophers, and many of them returned home to practise and teach their new-found knowledge in the local colleges.

One of the most influential organizations to be transplanted from Britain was the Mechanics' Institute. Founded in Scotland in 1823 as a vehicle for scientific education among the artisan class, mechanics' institutes took root in the Atlantic region in the 1830s. Patronized by the upwardly mobile professional class in cities such as Saint John and Halifax, they helped to spread the doctrine of self-help and encouraged a growing interest in literary and scientific pursuits.

The first half of the nineteenth century witnessed a growing readership for both regional and international literature. Libraries and bookstores could be found in most urban centres, and literacy was widely prized among the middle classes. Julia Catherine Beckwith of Fredericton became the first native-born British North American novelist in 1824 with the publication of *St. Ursula's Convent*, written when she was seventeen years old. Following publication of his two-volume history of Nova Scotia in 1829, Judge Thomas Chandler Haliburton turned to satire in his Sam Slick series, which won him international acclaim. Halifax-based journals such as the *Acadian* (1826–28), the *Halifax Monthly Magazine* (1830–31), the *Pearl* (1837–40), and the *Olive Branch* (1844) were short-lived but indicative of the general interest in creative literature.

Colonial newspapers also carried British and North American authors in serial form, making Walter Scott, Frances Trollope, and Charles Dickens as well as local authors easily accessible to colonials. It has been estimated that Anthony Henry Holland's *Acadian Recorder* and Joseph Howe's *Novascotian,* both of which carried literary as well as political items, had from 12 000 to 15 000 readers. Cheap pirated reprints of popular fiction also flourished briefly in the early 1840s but were quickly put out of business by copyright laws.

The intellectual awakening in the region was often practical in its manifestations. In 1818 John Young, a Scottish merchant in Halifax, wrote a series of letters under the pen name of "Agricola" in which he encouraged scientific methods in agriculture. As a result of his efforts and financial assistance from the government, agricultural societies were established throughout the colony in the 1820s. Farmers experimented with new varieties of crops and breeds of livestock. Colonial scientists such as Charles Fenerty and Abraham Gesner devised methods of making paper out of wood and kerosene oil from coal. Since both men failed to establish a patent on their processes, they failed to reap commercial rewards from their discoveries and perhaps betrayed a lack of professional savvy that was increasingly necessary in the age of industry.

As in economic and political life, the Atlantic colonies by the middle of the nineteenth century were on the brink of a new age of cultural maturity. Nearly three-quarters of the inhabitants in the region were native-born, and the sense of colonial identity was strong. This was especially so on the three major islands, which bred their own special sense of place. Even in Nova Scotia, the most culturally diverse of all the Atlantic colonies, there was a growing patriotism that transcended narrow identities. For Joseph Howe, one of the colony's most enthusiastic patriots, time was all that was required to solve the problems posed by limited cultural identities: "You who owe your origins to other lands cannot resist the conviction that, as you loved them, so will your children love this: and though the second place in their hearts may be filled by merry England, romantic Scotland or the verdant fields of Erin, the first and highest will be occupied by the little province where they drew their earliest breath, and which claims from them filial reverence and care."

Howe perhaps underestimated the tenacity of cultural identities and what Sigmund Freud called the "narcissism of small differences." But the optimism of Howe and men such as him was in some measure understandable. Like the British Isles, the Atlantic colonies were poised on the edge of a great continent. They had an abundance of coal and iron, the basic resources of modern industry. What could possibly stop them from developing a commercial empire to rival even that of Britain itself?

•The Colonial Economy in Atlantic Canada:
A Historiographical Debate

The legacy of mercantilism in the Atlantic region was a mixed one. As early as 1825 New Brunswick historian Peter Fisher, author of the *First History of New Brunswick*, offered a scathing attack on the exploitative nature of mercantilism:

> *The persons principally engaged in shipping the timber have been strangers who have taken no interest in the welfare of the country; but have merely occupied a spot to make what they could in the shortest possible time. Some have done well, and others have had to quit the trade: but whether they won or lost the capital of the country has been wasted, and no improvement of any consequence made to compensate for it, or to secure a source of trade for the inhabitants, when the lumber shall fail. Instead of seeing towns built, farms improved, and the country cleared and stocked with the reasonable returns of so great a trade; the forests are stripped and nothing left in prospect, but the gloomy apprehension when the timber is gone of sinking into insignificance and poverty. . . . These are some of the causes that have and still do operate against the prosperity of the country. Men who take no interest in the welfare of the province, continue to sap and prey on its resources.[16]*

Other contemporary observers remarked upon the negative impact of the timber trade on colonial agriculture. Lieutenant-Colonel Joseph Gubbins, inspecting the New Brunswick militia in 1811, noted: "The labouring class devote much time to this lucrative employment which would be much better bestowed on their farms."

Following the collapse of the Atlantic region's industrial economy in the twentieth century, scholars began to see the mercantile era in a somewhat different light. Political economist Harold Innis, perhaps reflecting the general nostalgia for the "age of sail" in the Maritimes, wrote in 1930: "Nothing . . . has been a more serious blow to the development of that section of the Dominion than the decay of the industry of shipbuilding. . . . The competition of iron and steel destroyed a magnificent achievement, an integration of capital and labour, of lumbering, fishing and agriculture, on which rested a progressive community life."[17]

Although there is little doubt that staples exploitation stimulated economic growth of a specific kind, most historians agree with Fisher and Gubbins that the timber trade and the shipbuilding industry helped to retard agricultural and industrial development in the Atlantic colonies. In their recent study of the shipping industry in Atlantic Canada, for instance, historians Eric W. Sager and Gerald Panting argue persuasively that the economic and social structures inherited from the region's mercantile past contributed to the unequal integration of the Atlantic region into the North American industrial economy following Confederation.[18]

To a considerable extent, the sheer success of shipbuilding prior to the 1870s diverted the attention of merchants in the region from other avenues of industrial investment. Moreover, staples exploitation, shipbuilding, and shipping reinforced pre-industrial modes of production and seasonal rhythms, making a full-scale transition to a modern industrial economy difficult. In many parts of the Atlantic region, people worked part of the year in mercantile industries and then retreated to the family farm, where a subsistence existence was always an alternative to wage labour. Without a landless working class driven by desperation to take low wages and poor working conditions, it was difficult for the region to compete in the race for industrial ascendancy.

Colonial dependency also remained long after the Navigation Acts had been swept away. Shipbuilders and timber merchants, many of them representing British-based companies, used their influence to import the tools of their trade and the cargoes for their vessels rather than supporting legislation that would encourage the growth of local industries. The Maritimes thus failed to develop what economists call the "backward linkages" of their activities. Sails, metal fittings, and engines were imported, as were cheap foodstuffs to feed the crews employed on the ships and in the lumber woods. When wood gave way to iron as the preferred fabric of ship construction, the Atlantic colonies had relatively few industries that would survive the transition.

The question, of course, remains: Why did Maritime entrepreneurs not invest in the iron ships that were beginning to dominate their trade? Evidence suggests that they, like other business leaders in the period, were attracted to investment frontiers elsewhere, or shifted their interest to textiles, transportation, and iron rails. As the mercantile era gave way to industrialization, the activities of staple exploitation, shipbuilding, and shipping remained linked, and they all collapsed together, leaving the Atlantic region trapped in a "great coastal nation with a small merchant navy."[19]

In the final analysis, of course, all of the British North American colonies produced staples—fish, fur, timber, and wheat—for export and functioned as a resource frontier for a rapidly developing British Empire. Harold Innis, in pondering the larger meaning of staples exports, concluded that the British North American colonies remained within the British sphere of influence largely because of the ties binding staples economies to the mother country.[20] It was the continuing British connection that ultimately led to the creation of a second nation-state in North America.

• Notes

[1] L.S.F. Upton, "The Extermination of the Beothuk of Newfoundland," *Canadian Historical Review* 58, 2 (1977): 133–53.

[2] Margaret MacDonell, *The Emigrant Experience: Songs of Highland Emigrants in North America* (Toronto: University of Toronto Press, 1982), 105–12, 118–25.

[3] Cited in Donald Mackay, *Flight from Famine: The Coming of the Irish to Canada* (Toronto: McClelland and Stewart, 1990), 245.

[4] Shannon Ryan, "Fishery to Colony: A Newfoundland Watershed, 1793–1815," *Acadiensis* 12, 2 (Spring 1983): 52.

[5] David Sutherland, "Halifax Merchants and the Pursuit of Development, 1783–1850," *Canadian Historical Review* 59, 1 (March 1978): 4.

[6] W.S. MacNutt, *The Atlantic Provinces: The Emergence of Colonial Society, 1712–1857* (Toronto: McClelland and Stewart, 1965), 122.

[7] D.C. Harvey, ed., *Journeys to the Island of St. John or Prince Edward Island, 1775–1832* (Toronto: Macmillan, 1955), 104.

[8] *The Dalhousie Journals*, ed. Marjorie Whitelaw (Ottawa: Oberon Press, 1978), 73.

[9] John Robinson and Thomas Ripsin, *Journey through Nova Scotia* (1774; rprt. Sackville, NB: Mount Allison University, 1981), 19.

[10] T.W. Acheson, *Saint John: The Making of a Colonial Urban Community* (Toronto: University of Toronto Press, 1985).

[11] Thomas Chandler Haliburton, *The Clockmaker or the Sayings and Doings of Samuel Slick of Slickville* (Halifax, 1836 rprt. Toronto: McClelland and Stewart, 1958), 49.

[12] Howe's fourth Letter to Lord John Russell, 1839, cited in *The Speeches and Letters of Joseph Howe*, ed. J.A. Chisholm (Halifax: n.p., 1909), 266.

[13] Quoted in L.F.S. Upton, *Micmacs and Colonists: Indian–White Relations in the Maritimes, 1713–1867* (Vancouver: University of British Columbia, 1979), 89.

[14] Cited in Nancy Christie, "'In These Times of Democratic Rage and Delusion': Popular Religion and the Challenge to the Established Order, 1760–1815," in *The Canadian Protestant Experience, 1760–1990*, ed. George A. Rawlyk (Burlington, ON: Welch Publishing Company, 1990), 37.

[15] G.A. Rawlyk, *Ravished by the Spirit: Religious Revivals, Baptists and Henry Alline* (Montreal: McGill-Queen's University Press, 1984).

[16] Peter Fisher, *The First History of New Brunswick* (1825; rprt. Woodstock, NB: Non-Entity Press, 1980), 73.

[17] C.R. Fay and H.A. Innis, "The Maritime Provinces," *The Cambridge History of the British Empire*, Vol. 6 (New York: Macmillan, 1930), 663.

[18] Eric W. Sager with Gerald E. Panting, *Maritime Capital: The Shipping Industry in Atlantic Canada, 1820–1914* (Montreal: McGill-Queen's University Press, 1990), 7.

[19] Ibid., 210.

[20] Harold Innis, *The Cod Fishery: The History of An International Economy* (rev. ed., Toronto: University of Toronto Press, 1954); *The Fur Trade in Canada* (New Haven, CT: Yale University Press, 1962).

•Selected Reading

The best general survey of this period for all four Atlantic colonies is still W.S. MacNutt, *The Atlantic Provinces: The Emergence of Colonial Society, 1712–1857* (Toronto: McClelland and Stewart, 1965). George A. Rawlyk, ed., *Historical Essays on the Atlantic Provinces* (Ottawa: Carleton University Press, 1967) includes many of the now "classic" essays on the region. P.A. Buckner and David Frank, eds., *The*

Acadiensis Reader: Atlantic Canada before Confederation, 2nd ed., Vol. 1 (Fredericton: Acadiensis Press, 1988), offers a sample of more recent scholarship on the pre-Confederation period. The chapter on "The Atlantic Region," in R. Cole Harris and John Warkentin, *Canada Before Confederation* (Toronto: Oxford University Press, 1974) provides a useful overview.

Provincial histories include: W.S. MacNutt, *New Brunswick: A History, 1784–1867* (Toronto: Macmillan, 1984); Graeme Wynn, *Timber Colony: A Historical Geography of Early Nineteenth Century New Brunswick* (Toronto: University of Toronto Press, 1981); Andrew Hill Clark, *Three Centuries and the Island* (Toronto: University of Toronto Press, 1959); J.M. Bumsted, *Land, Settlement and Politics on Eighteenth Century Prince Edward Island* (Montreal: McGill-Queen's University Press, 1987); Frederick W. Rowe, *History of Newfoundland and Labrador* (Toronto: McGraw-Hill Ryerson, 1980); James Hiller and Peter Neary, eds., *Newfoundland in the Nineteenth and Twentieth Centuries: Essays in Interpretation* (Toronto: University of Toronto Press, 1980). On Cape Breton, see Donald Macgillivray and Brian Tennyson, eds., *Cape Breton Historical Essays* (Sydney, NS: University College of Cape Breton Press, 1980) and Stephen Hornsby, *Nineteenth-Century Cape Breton: A Historical Geography* (Montreal: McGill-Queen's University Press, 1992); and two books edited by Kenneth Donovan: *Cape Breton at 200: Historical Essays in Honour of the Island's Bicentennial, 1785–1985* (Sydney, NS: University College of Cape Breton Press, 1985) and *The Island: New Perspectives on Cape Breton's History, 1713–1975* (Fredericton: Acadiensis Press, 1990).

The impact of sea-based industries on the Atlantic region has been extensively explored by the Maritime History Group, based at Memorial University in St John's. In addition to five books of published proceedings, several monographs have appeared, including two by Eric Sager: *Seafaring Labour: The Merchant Marine in Atlantic Canada* (Montreal: McGill-Queen's University Press, 1989), and *Maritime Capital: The Shipping Industry in Atlantic Canada, 1820–1914* (Montreal: McGill-Queen's University Press, 1990); and two by Rosemary Ommer: *Merchant Credit and Labour Strategies in Historical Perspective* (Fredericton: Acadiensis Press, 1990) and *From Outpost to Outport: A Structural Analysis of the Jersey–Gaspé Cod Fishery, 1767–1886* (Montreal: McGill-Queen's University Press, 1991). A Canadian Historical Association booklet by Eric W. Sager and Lewis R. Fischer, *Shipping and Shipbuilding in Atlantic Canada, 1820–1914* (Ottawa: Canadian Historical Association, 1986), offers a convenient summary of general trends relating to shipbuilding. On the nineteenth-century marine labour force, see also Judith Fingard's richly textured *Jack in Port: Sailortowns of Eastern Canada* (Toronto: University of Toronto Press, 1982). The best study of the salt-fish trade in this period can be found in Shannon Ryan, *Fish Out of Water: The Newfoundland Saltfish Trade, 1814–1914* (St. John's: Breakwater, 1986). Two articles that help to round out the contours of economic life in the region are David Sutherland, "Halifax Merchants and the Pursuit of Development, 1783–1850," *Canadian Historical Review* 59, 1 (March 1978), and Julian Gwyn, "Economic Fluctuations in Wartime Nova Scotia, 1775–1815," in *Making Adjustments: Change and Continuity in Planter Nova Scotia, 1759–1800*, ed. Margaret Conrad (Fredericton: Acadiensis Press, 1991), 60–88. Urban studies include T.W. Acheson, *Saint John: The Making of a Colonial Urban Community* (Toronto: University of Toronto Press, 1985), Thomas H. Raddall, *Halifax: Warden of North* (Toronto: McClelland and Stewart, 1974), and Patrick O'Neill, *The Story of St. John's, Newfoundland* (Erin, ON: Boston Mills Press, 1975).

The politics of pre-Confederation Nova Scotia have been described in J. Murray Beck, *Politics of Nova Scotia*, Vol. 1, *1710–1896* (Tantallon, NS: Four East Publications, 1985). Beck's earlier work, *The Government of Nova Scotia* (Toronto: University of Toronto Press, 1957), offers detailed information on the structures of colonial government, and his two-volume biography, *Joseph Howe* (Kingston: McGill-Queen's University Press, 1982, 1984), is by far the most thorough study undertaken of a Maritime politician in this period. On Newfoundland politics in the mid-nineteenth century, see Gertrude Gunn, *The Political History of Newfoundland, 1832–1864* (Toronto: University of Toronto Press, 1966). The political implications of the land question in Prince Edward Island are summarized in Ian Ross Robertson's introduction to *The Prince Edward Island Land Commission of 1860* (Fredericton: Acadiensis Press, 1988). The Maritime context of imperial developments is clearly outlined in P.A. Buckner, *The Transition to Responsible Government: British Policy in British North America, 1815–1850* (Westport, CT: Greenwood, 1985).

Social and cultural developments in the Atlantic colonies have yet to be fully explored. J.M. Bumsted, *Henry Alline* (Toronto: University of Toronto Press, 1971), and George Rawlyk, *Ravaged by the Spirit: Religious Revivals, Baptists and Henry Alline* (Montreal: McGill-Queen's University Press, 1984), trace the roots of religious revivalism in the region. Judith Fingard, "The Relief of the Unemployed Poor in Saint John, Halifax, and St. John's, 1815–1860," *Acadiensis* 1, 5 (Autumn 1975): 32–53 explores local aspects of a larger reality in pre-industrial society. The same subject is described in Fingard's "The Winter's Tale: The Seasonal Contours of Pre-industrial Poverty in British North America," Canadian Historical Association, *Historical Papers*, 1974, 65–94. On the Irish, see Thomas P. Power, ed., *The Irish in Atlantic Canada, 1780–1900* (Fredericton: New Ireland Press, 1991). For the Beothuk, see Ralph Pastore, "The Collapse of the Beothuk World," *Acadiensis* 19, 1 (Autumn 1989): 52–71.

A good place to start looking for an understanding of literary development in the region is Fred Cogswell, "Literary Activity in the Maritime Provinces, 1815–1880," in *Literary History of Canada: Canadian Literature in English*, ed. Carl Klinck (Toronto: University of Toronto Press, 1976). Thomas Vincent and Gwendolyn Davies have added greatly to our knowledge of the region's literary heritage. See, for instance, Thomas B. Vincent, *Narrative Verse Satire in Maritime Canada, 1779–1814* (Ottawa: Tecumseh, 1978), and Gwendolyn Davies, *Studies in Maritime Literary History* (Fredericton: Acadiensis Press, 1991). An interesting perspective on the European vision of Nova Scotia can be found in Mary Sparling, *Great Expectations: The European Vision of Nova Scotia, 1749–1848* (Halifax: Mount Saint Vincent University, 1980). Early architectural development is described in Allen Penney, *Nova Scotia Houses: A Field Guide* (Halifax: Formac, 1989), and Neil V. Rosenberg and Shane O'Dae, *Interiors: Cultural Patterns in the Atlantic Canadian Home*, Material History Bulletin, no. 15, Ottawa, 1982. Ruth Holmes Whitehead, *Micmac Quillwork* (Halifax: Nova Scotia Museum, 1982) offers a detailed analysis of an important feature of Mi'kmaq economic and material life.

CHAPTER 9

THE CANADAS: Social and Economic Development, 1791–1850

George Forbes, son of an Aberdeenshire tenant farmer, wrote his brothers in 1856 urging them to come to Upper Canada: "We in Canada have this glorious privilege that the ground where on we tread is our own and our children's after us. . . . No dangers of the leases expiring and the laird saying pay me so much more rent, or bundle and go, for here we are laird ourselves. I may thank my stars that I am out of such a place."[1]

While George Forbes clearly felt he had improved his social status by moving to a new home across the sea, good fortune was not always so readily available. Many farmers in both Canadas were poor, and many did not own the land they farmed. In 1838 the Church of Scotland magazine in Upper Canada provided a glimpse of the other side to a settler's life in Canada, noting there were "thousands upon thousands in this vast uncultivated territory, struggling with the hardships and penury of new settlements, and with whom years of constant toil must pass away, ere they can hope to attain any thing beyond the merest necessities of life."[2]

Contrasts of this kind abounded throughout the Canadas from the 1790s to the 1850s. Before 1840, political leaders asserted the need for a hierarchical society structured roughly along the lines of British society, but their vision for Canada failed to take root. The differences were evident in the franchise: a minimal property qualification was all it took to disfranchise 95 percent of the adult population in Britain, including 100 percent of women and 90 percent of men. In the Canadas women also rarely voted (although the Constitutional Act was silent on their civic rights), but a majority of men met the property qualification.

The seigneurial system, which remained in force in the Lower Canadian territories settled before the conquest, mirrored the British landholding system rather imperfectly: in Britain most of the people who farmed the land were wage-earning farm labourers; in Lower Canada's seigneurial belt most farmers were self-sufficient, if often poor, tenants. Landownership patterns in both Upper Canada and the new settlements in Lower Canada resembled the British system even less. While a small number of landowners held vast tracts of territory, a majority of the residents were independent farmers. In the minds of many immigrants, independence would mean prosperity; but many farm families learned that it could also mean endless work and threadbare survival.

In the Canadas, as this period unfolded, growing towns and cities were homes to ever-expanding commercial and manufacturing activities. The distribution of the proceeds from these ventures provided a stark contrast between wealth and poverty. While many entrepreneurs and professionals lived in brick mansions with servants at their beck and call, labourers lived in hovels and required charity during periods of unemployment. Filth, disease, crime, and poverty were rampant in the urban areas, and by the 1840s these conditions had called into being a myriad of organizations promoting social reform. Still, for all the urban growth, the Canadas remained largely rural in the period from the Constitutional Act of 1791, which created the provinces of Lower Canada and Upper Canada, to the 1840s and 1850s, when the Act of Union of 1840 created an uneasy political entity, the United Canadas, with two increasingly different societies called Canada East and Canada West.

• The Social Landscape, 1791–1812

Upper Canada

In the years 1791 to 1812 the population of Upper Canada increased by over 500 percent, from 14 000 to 75 000, with most of the new residents coming from the United States. The immigration had been encouraged by John Graves Simcoe, the colony's first lieutenant-governor (1792–98), who offered free land to anyone willing to settle the frontier colony. Simcoe pursued two goals of questionable compatibility. On one hand he wanted Upper Canada to be a Britain-in-miniature; on the other he wanted to rapidly build up its population so that local defence forces could replace the costly British troops that guarded the colony against the expansion-minded United States. In Simcoe's estimation, the Americans who came to farm would again become loyal subjects of the king if Britain took care to cultivate British institutions in the colony.

"The utmost attention should be paid," wrote Simcoe, "that British Customs, Manners and Principles in the most trivial as well as serious mat-

John Graves Simcoe   (Law Society of Upper Canada Archives/Art Collection #34)

ters should be promoted and inculcated to obtain their due ascendancy to assimilate the colony with the parent state."[3] In Simcoe's view such customs included the establishment of a landed aristocracy and a hierarchical social structure, state support for the Church of England, and the provision of education for the elite. These anti-democratic notions could hardly be expected to gain favour with American immigrants who assumed that equality of opportunity and separation of church and state were civic virtues.

Indeed, the Duke of Portland, the colonial secretary in the 1790s, believed that re-creation of the British landholding system in which a few thousand men owned the land that millions farmed was sheer fantasy in the North American environment. He ordered the lieutenant-governor to make land available to new arrivals—but as landowners, not as tenants. Simcoe granted the land as directed, but he followed former governor Frederick Haldimand's practice of ensuring that not all landowners were equal. Simcoe, a career officer who had commanded a Loyalist unit, the Queen's Rangers, during the American Revolution, appointed officials with backgrounds and views similar to his own. In return for their services he granted them land, of which Upper Canada had plenty. Thereafter, it was common practice for governors in both Upper Canada and Lower Canada to reward officials, contractors, and military officers with vast tracts of land. Most of this land would then sit uncultivated for years, held by its owners for speculative purposes. Along with the clergy and Crown reserves, these speculators' grants constituted a major grievance for early immigrants. New settlements, instead of being compact, were generally widely dispersed, making the provision of local services such as roads and schools costly and separating neighbours by inconvenient distances. The keen interest in speculation and land sales demonstrated the folly of Simcoe's dream of re-creating the British landholding system in Upper Canada: neither settlers nor landowners had much interest in creating a pyramid of aristocrats, tenants, and farm labourers.

In 1839, when Lord Durham reviewed the state of surveyed land in Upper Canada, he found that over half of it had either been granted to "classes of grantees whose station would preclude them from settling in the wilderness" or set aside as clergy reserves.[4] Less than a tenth of the surveyed land had even been occupied, let alone cultivated. Loyalists and their heirs had received 8 million hectares; militiamen 1 825 000 hectares; discharged soldiers and sailors 1 125 000 hectares; magistrates and barristers 625 000 hectares; executive councillors 340 000 hectares; legislative councillors 125 000 hectares; clergymen 92 220 hectares; and army and navy officers 230 640 hectares. One grant alone gave 120 620 hectares to Colonel Thomas Talbot in Essex and Elgin counties on Lake Erie.

In the early years of Upper Canada, the land-rich political elite was concentrated in York (renamed Toronto in 1834), a site selected as the capital in 1793 because it was less vulnerable to American attack than other centres. At the time the colony was almost wholly rural: perhaps 95 percent of the pre-1812 population lived in the countryside. Kingston, the largest town, boasted fifty homes. While York itself, cut out of the wilderness, developed slowly, the lieutenant-governor's power of patronage swelled the ranks of a local elite. The badges of elite membership were a land grant along with a government post and membership in the Law Society of Upper Canada, which controlled entry into the legal profession in the colony. The elite built large, comfortable homes, hired servants, and educated their children in private schools. Their male children generally also joined the elite. William Jarvis, for example, owed his appointment by Simcoe as provincial secretary and registrar to his rank as an officer in the Queen's Rangers. A generation later his son Samuel was deputy provincial secretary and chief superintendent of Indian affairs, while his other son, William, became sheriff of Gore District.

Women in elite families lived more restricted lives. Following the injunctions of an emerging cult of domesticity in the British middle class, women of means in Upper Canada were expected to marry and make motherhood and household work their *raison d'être*. The lives of three daughters of Chief Justice William Powell illustrate the limited options for elite women. Mary, the eldest daughter, married into another elite family in 1818 and gave birth to ten children. Her letters told of a life preoccupied with care of children and household chores, despite the presence of domestic help. Her sister Elizabeth never married. Sustained by family money, she spent her days engaged in charity activities and in helping out her female relatives. Anne, the third sister, also never married. She wanted to open a school but was discouraged in this by her parents, who asserted that teaching would be beneath her social status. Rebellious and without employment, Anne Powell became mentally ill. Her father planned to place her in a convent in France well away from the family and polite society in Upper Canada, but a shipwreck in 1822 took her life.

Among the largely rural population, the early pioneer farm families were mainly preoccupied with the arduous tasks of clearing forest and planting crops. With few entertainments available, Methodist circuit riders from the United States found a ready audience when they ventured into the Upper Canadian bush. They won many adherents, including Egerton Ryerson and his two brothers, the sons of Anglican Loyalists in Vittoria, a few miles inland from Lake Erie. It was to head off such "fanatic preachers," whom he regarded as potential sowers of political subversion, that Simcoe wholeheartedly supported efforts to create a strong Church of England presence in the colony. By 1841 disputes among the Methodists had fractured their organization and reduced their popular appeal.

In 1841, the four Methodist sects combined could claim the adhesion of about 17 percent of the Canadian population against 22 percent identifying with the Church of England, 20 percent with the Church of Scotland and dissenting Presbyterian sects, and 12 percent with Roman Catholicism. Baptists, Quakers, Lutherans, Congregationalists, Mennonites, and Tunkers (a pacifist sect with origins similar to the Mennonites) all had their followings, along with several smaller sects. About 10 percent of the population either failed to describe their religion to the census taker or indicated no affiliation with a particular religious group.

Religion was important in the lives of most Upper Canadians. Splits within Methodism and Presbyterianism over beliefs and rituals indicated that church attendance was more than a mere social formality for many people. Belief systems promoted by various churches were the principles by which many people lived their lives. Churches were also important social institutions. In an age when the state offered little or no help, networks among co-religionists assured families of a helping hand when illness or tragedy struck. Co-operation among members of different Protestant denominations in the establishment of schools, charities, and, later, temperance societies suggested a degree of religious toleration—although intolerance was also evident. For instance, Church of England leaders in the colony campaigned for establishment of their church to the exclusion of all others. This policy was consistent with British practice but was rejected by other denominations whose members refused to accept that their institutions were inferior in rights and privileges to the "established" church.

Although many colonists resisted the British system in religious matters, they enjoyed some benefit from the British connection. The British government provided the funds for military roads that became commercial routes as well, and Lieutenant-Governor Simcoe established a system of local government along British lines that provided a framework for services. Upper Canada was divided into districts, which were in turn divided into townships. The township was the locus of local administration, and its property-owners elected the men who assessed property values for tax purposes, collected these taxes, and oversaw the highways. As in England, these unpaid officials were less important than the justices of the peace, appointed in Upper Canada by the lieutenant-governor. The justices of the peace levied local taxes, appointed district treasurers, and superintended the building of jails and highways and the sale of liquor licences. Everywhere, government jobs and contracts were the prerogatives of officials beholden to the lieutenant-governor. This created local oligarchies loyal to the government throughout Upper Canada.

Lower Canada

In Lower Canada, governors used patronage to sustain the power of an English-speaking elite despite the overwhelming preponderance of French-speaking people in the province. Some members of the elite were merchants or merchant-industrialists who had made their fortunes in the fur trade. After 1800 this wealth was often increased by investments in local industries such as brewing and distilling. In the new century, huge fortunes were made by investment in the timber trade. In 1807 Napoleon blockaded the Baltic, the source of timber for the British fleet, and Britain turned to its colonies as a source of timber. By 1810, 74 percent of exports from Lower Canada were forest products. Furs, which accounted for 76 percent of exports in 1770 and 51 percent in 1788, made up only 9.2 percent of export receipts in 1810.

Commercial connections in Britain gave English-speaking merchants an advantage over their French counterparts in the new timber trade.

PHILEMON WRIGHT: AN EARLY CAPITALIST

While the backgrounds and successes of Lower Canada's capitalists varied, the career of Philemon Wright provides a glimpse of how fortunes were made—and solidified.

Wright, born in Massachusetts, owned several pieces of land in Vermont before he began to purchase lands in Lower Canada in 1796. In 1797 he was granted land in Hull Township on the Ottawa River under the leader and associate program. Three years later he founded the first European settlement in the area, at a place called Wrightstown (later renamed Hull). The original settlers included thirty-seven men, five women, and twenty-one children. Wright's main interest initially was agricultural development, and by 1835 his family controlled 145 000 hectares of Hull Township. In 1806 he began floating his first rafts of squared timber from Hull to Quebec, and timbering was responsible for most of the large fortune he left his family at his death in 1839.

Wright employed a large pool of cheap seasonal labour to operate his lumber camps, transport his wood to Quebec, and run his mills. In 1820 he employed 164 men and 11 women in these operations. A year earlier he had built a steamship to tow his rafts on the Ottawa River. His enterprises ranged beyond agriculture and timbering to most of the economic activities in the township, including its retail trade, innkeeping, and such industrial endeavours as a distillery, tannery, hemp and carding mill, iron ore mine, brickworks, and cement factory. Although he was not particularly religious, he gradually came to favour the Church of England because of its forthright defence of his social class. Wright's financial support made possible the construction of an Anglican church in Wrightstown in 1832.

British demands for squared timber also encouraged other ventures, such as John Molson's steamboat service on the St Lawrence and the beginnings of a Quebec shipbuilding industry. Capitalists who had made money in the fur trade bought seigneuries both to gain access to timberlands and to earn income from habitants' dues. By 1812 an estimated two-thirds of the seigneuries were in the hands of English-speaking merchants.

The predominantly English-speaking merchant group of Montreal also accumulated about 2.5 million hectares of land outside the seigneurial belt, granted by the Crown under the "leader and associate" system. A leader received 2500 hectares for every farmer he settled on a 500-hectare farm; the leader's grant supposedly repaid his costs of both recruiting and transporting settlers and provisioning them until they could grow their first crop. In practice the leaders, many of them wealthy merchants, provided the government with inflated lists of alleged settlers and generally provided few services to the real settlers.

The new settlers were mainly Americans from the New England area. By 1812 about 20 000 of them had been enticed by promises of free land in the Eastern Townships south and east of Montreal. Because they received their lands in freehold tenure, the settlers did not have to contend with the seigneurial system, but they did have to cope with rocky soil, poor transportation, and huge areas of wilderness held aside for clergy reserves, Crown reserves, and speculative purposes. The modest lives of these former New Englanders underscore the fact that only a small proportion of the English-speaking residents of Lower Canada, who in 1812 numbered 50 000 or about 15 percent of the population, were wealthy. Apart from the Yankee farmers and the merchant elite, they included large numbers of artisans and small shopkeepers in the two main cities and some smaller towns.

The French-speaking majority included only a small number of wealthy capitalists and seigneurs. The socially ambitious continued to look to the purchase of a seigneury as a badge of their success. Louis-Joseph Papineau, who became the leader of the opponents of the government after 1815, was the son of a notary who purchased a seigneury called Petite Nation on the Ottawa River in 1801.

There was a dramatic growth in the number of French-speaking professionals in the early nineteenth century. The leaders of the Roman Catholic Church, unwilling to look to a revolution-engulfed France for future priests, opened a number of classical colleges with the aim of training potential clerics within the colony. About 50 percent of the classical-college graduates sought employment in secular areas, using their academic talents to become notaries, lawyers, journalists, and clerks. Frustrated by their failure to enter the government bureaucracy, the French-speaking middle class became increasingly nationalistic. Its members saw themselves as the natural leaders of French Canada and, through their newly formed Parti canadien, focussed upon the elected House of Assembly as a forum for demanding greater popular control over government. Supportive of the seigneurial system, and initially favourable to church control over education and social services, most members of the Parti canadien saw democracy as a tactic that could be used to protect French Canada's language and culture, limit the power of the merchants, and ensure that economic development was not controlled from abroad.

The secret instructions to the governor accompanying the Constitutional Act forbade the expansion of the seigneurial system beyond the boundaries

Making maple sugar, Lower Canada, circa 1837   (P.J. Bainbrigge/National Archives of Canada/C131921)

established in 1791. New areas to be opened for settlement, such as the Eastern Townships, would be granted in freehold tenure only. But few habitants had the capital required to buy land. As a result the seigneuries could not contain the burgeoning habitant population and an agrarian crisis ensued. At times lands were subdivided to the point where farm units were unproductive; more frequently, younger sons were forced to leave the land and seek waged employment. Indeed, to make ends meet even the men who remained on the land often required off-farm work in the winter in the lumber camps, on canal construction, or in shipbuilding. For many farmers the family economy was a modified subsistence agriculture, with the women mainly responsible for farm management and the men requiring off-farm wages to buy goods and foodstuffs not readily available from the land.

Historians are generally agreed that after 1815 there was a widespread rural crisis of overpopulation combined with poor crop yields. But there is debate about whether a crisis existed before 1812. Almost a million bushels of wheat were exported annually from the colony to Britain at the turn of the century; so, clearly, many farmers had surpluses and were not purely engaged in subsistence farming. On the fertile Montreal plains and in the area around Quebec City, farmers continued to prosper in the early nineteenth century. Elsewhere there were clear signs of an agricultural crisis. In Sorel, along the Richelieu River, at least one-third of the adult male population in the 1790s contracted with the North West Company to work in the western fur trade. Some two-thirds of these went west during the growing season. Wheat, the exportable crop, would not grow well in this area. When the NWC merged with the Hudson's Bay Company in 1821 and implemented large layoffs, Sorel was thrust into poverty. Similarly, in the Gaspé in 1800, over five thousand individuals depended for most of their income on the Robins and other Channel Island families who bought their fish for resale in Britain. Unable to subsist on agriculture, *Gaspésiens* depended for their survival on merchants who paid them not in cash but in credits, which could be redeemed only at the merchants' stores. Above all, in Lower Canada after 1806 it was seasonal work for lumberjacks, teamsters, drivers, and raftsmen in the timber trade that added cash to hard-pressed subsistence-agriculture households.

Overpopulation and outdated agricultural practices were not the only problems facing the habitants. While the impact of seigneurial dues on the habitants is much debated for the post-conquest period, one estimate is that habitants on the lower Richelieu yielded over half their agricultural surpluses to the upper classes. This left little possibility of saving for the poor crop years that, because of wheat-fly infestations, became more frequent in Lower Canada after 1800; and it left little for investment in machinery and new farming practices revolutionizing agriculture in other areas of North America and Europe. In any case, as historian Allan Greer notes, the small surpluses remaining increasingly fell into the hands of British rum merchants. In contrast to researchers who describe an increasing agricultural-commodity trade, Greer writes: "The general pattern found in much of the world, rural Quebec included, is one of commercial capital introducing a worthless or harmful habit of consumption as a means of initiating or increasing trade with a population whose life is not already organized around buying and selling."[5]

While men who could not be supported on the farms might find employment in the timber trade, fisheries, or fur trade, women had fewer options. Many women became domestic workers in the cities; others became prostitutes. In the city of Quebec, with a population of only about fourteen thousand in 1810, four to six hundred prostitutes, native-born and immigrant, tried to earn a living off their bodies, relying particularly on the members of a local British garrison that averaged 2425 men from 1810 to 1816.

The British officials tended to dismiss poverty in Quebec as the fault of its allegedly unprogressive victims. This was a distortion of reality. Both before and after the conquest the *Canadiens* demonstrated an ability to take advantage of market opportunities. Furthermore, whatever the anti-materialist ideology of their church, the *Canadiens* were far from other-worldly. Rather, their problems were rooted in the failure of the British either to fix rents—which had been done before 1760 to prevent gouging—or to grant free lands to capital-short farmers. British policies—or the lack thereof—on these fronts stymied the *Canadiens* economically and stimulated their desire for political reforms.

•Postwar Migration

After the end of Europe's Napoleonic Wars in 1815, "as was usually the case after a long and protracted war, fought without regard for expense, peace brought a general economic collapse at the same time that it flooded the labour market with thousands of disbanded soldiers and sailors."[6] Britain's depressed economy resulted in political unrest, with demands from artisans and labourers for greater democracy. The authorities responded with repression, most notably in 1819 in Manchester, when cavalry broke up a meeting of 80 000 people addressed by a "radical" (which in nineteenth-century parlance tended to refer to those who called for universal suffrage or, more often, universal "manhood" suffrage). Eleven people were killed and four hundred injured in the so-called Peterloo Massacre.

The post-war crisis in Britain had a direct impact on the British North American colonies. Faced with massive unemployment and political agitation, British officials were inclined to accept the conclusions of economist Thomas Malthus who maintained that Britain was overpopulated. Since the British Isles could not sustain the growing number of citizens, they reasoned, the obvious solution was emigration to the colonies. Emigration would act as a safety valve, easing the pressure on the British authorities from disenchanted common folk who regarded themselves as victims of capitalist landlords and factory owners. It might also encourage paupers to give up their lazy and intemperate ways and become productive citizens of Britain's growing overseas empire.

Most of the people who migrated to Canada were not paupers but small landowners or tenants—people anxious about their future in a new capitalist order in which market forces rather than custom were dictating economic relations between social classes and among individuals. Wealthy enough to purchase their sea passage and to pay for the initial costs of establishing themselves in British North America, many of them also bene-fited from the monetary assistance Britain provided sporadically to emi-grants willing to go to the colonies. Recent research has also established that, contrary to earlier beliefs, the migrants did not come to North America as individuals, abandoning relatives and friends in their search for a better life. Rather, as a study of Protestant Irish migrants from north Tipperary demonstrates, many emigrated in extended-family and commu-nity groups and were often joined by kin from the old land. Only the filling up of most of the good farmland of Ontario by the mid-1850s caused the breaking of this migratory chain.

When the British government offered assisted passage to a group of Scots wishing to settle in Glengarry County, Upper Canada, in 1815, four Highland parishes provided about half of the total group of eight hundred émigrés. Most of the other passengers were from the Glasgow area, where people were most likely to see advertisements for assisted emigration. The emigrants, rather than being unattached individuals or members of nuclear families, constituted large parish groups who had decided that col-lective resettlement in the New World was an alternative to impoverish-ment at home. Some 80 percent of the Highland Glengarry group were farmers; only 20 percent were labourers. The weak representation of the landless is not surprising, because settlers were required to repay some of the costs of their transport, and a mandatory deposit was enough to weed out the poor.

There were, nonetheless, poor immigrants to Canada from Britain, people who managed to scrape up the cost of an uncomfortable passage in the steerage of a transatlantic vessel but who lacked the capital, connec-tions, and sometimes skills necessary to prosper in their new home. Irish Catholics figured largely in this group. Some of the Irish poor did eventu-ally escape poverty in the countryside of Upper Canada. In Montague Township, Lanark County, Irish newcomers in the 1840s were mainly squat-ters. In 1852 fully 30 percent of them lived in shanties. By 1861, however, as a result of families and neighbours working close together, only 1 percent lived in shanties and a majority owned the land they occupied.

In the cities and the lumber camps, poverty was more commonplace. While the authorities and British upper-class writers who commented on the Canadas believed that any industrious "head of family" would quickly be able to buy land if he chose, many could never afford this luxury. As in the countryside, a disproportionate number of the urban and industrial poor were Irish Catholics who—even though they were not of the poorest class at home—often arrived penniless after they had paid the costs of pas-sage to Canada. In Leeds Township the successful Irish-Catholic farmers disdained the poor Irish-Catholic workers in Gananoque and maintained their own church rather than associate with their poor compatriots in the parish church in town.

British government promotion of emigration also resulted in rural horror stories. In 1832 a large group of military pensioners was persuaded to trade their pensions for a lump sum and land in the Canadian bush. Anna Brownell Jameson, an upper-class British woman whose husband was Upper Canada's attorney-general, was shocked in 1836 to find a hamlet at Penetanguishene peopled with old, sick veterans, many unable to farm. The area had no roads to take produce to market for those who could farm, and Jameson was appalled that "men who fought our battles in Egypt, Spain, and France" were living in shacks, often reduced to begging in order to survive.[7]

Immigrant Reception

Immigration from Britain helped to swell the Upper Canadian population from 90 000 in 1812 to 237 000 in 1831, 487 000 in 1842, and 952 000 in 1851. In 1842 one-third of the Upper Canadian population had been born in the British Isles. Of these, one-half came from Ireland, one-quarter from Scotland, and one-quarter from England and Wales. Only about 50 000 immigrants from Britain settled in Lower Canada from 1815 to 1850, and the large francophone birth rate in that province prevented the new arrivals from reducing the French-speaking proportion of the population by more than a few percentage points. The arrival of immigrants created social tension, because the newcomers were rivals for land and jobs. Many settled in the Eastern Townships, whose lands the Parti canadien leaders vainly hoped to make the site of farms for habitants crowded out of existing seigneuries. In the Ottawa valley, Irish labourers pursued the jobs in the timber trade previously monopolized by the French and used violence to force employers to hire them, although the *Canadiens* were generally regarded as more skilful and industrious. In the late 1830s and early 1840s wealthy timber merchant Peter Aylen, seeking personal control of the valley, led the Irish in open warfare against the French-speaking lumbermen. The so-called Shiners' War continued until Aylen unleashed his troops on the respectable middle-class Protestant citizens of Bytown (now Ottawa), who then used state authority to stop the armed Irish–French confrontations.

The *Canadiens* particularly resented the new arrivals because many were carriers of disease. A cholera epidemic swept through Britain in 1831 and arrived in British North America with infected immigrants the following year. The cramped, unsanitary conditions on the ships spread cholera among the passengers and, on shore, poor water systems and urban filth resulted in rapid contamination of a terrified population. The four major years of the cholera epidemic—1832, 1834, 1849, 1854—witnessed far more deaths in Lower Canada than in Upper Canada because Quebec City was the first port of entry for immigrants to the Canadas. In 1832 health officials reported 5820 cholera deaths in Lower Canada and 504 in Upper Canada. The immigrants leaving the ships and *Canadiens* in Quebec and Montreal accounted for most deaths in Lower Canada. In 1834, 2358 Lower Canadians died of cholera, compared to 555 in Upper Canada and 320 in Nova Scotia. The 1849 epidemic left 1638 reported dead in Lower Canada and 638 in Upper Canada. In addition a typhus epidemic among Irish arrivals in 1847 resulted in thousands of deaths, mainly among the immigrants themselves.

After the epidemic was recognized, new arrivals in 1832 were taken immediately to an improvised quarantine station down river from Quebec City at Grosse Île. Only those not infected with the deadly disease were allowed to go on to their destinations. The spread of cholera caused city residents in particular to despise new arrivals. Communities in both Lower Canada and Upper Canada often blocked off their roads to keep out possibly infected immigrants. Furthermore, there were far too many arrivals at the port of Quebec for the quarantine to prove effective: from 1828 to 1832 an average of 31 541 immigrants per year landed there, and the average dropped only to 22 444 annually over the next five years.

While disease and economic rivalries fuelled tension between immigrants and the settled population, and particularly tension between the *Canadiens* and other groups, old-country hatreds afflicted the immigrants themselves. This was particularly the case among the Irish. Ogle R. Gowan, an Irish Protestant immigrant to Brockville, Upper Canada, in 1829, was a major figure in transplanting Irish religious feuds to British North American soil. A younger son of the gentry, he had not inherited any land and had earned his living in Dublin as a writer of anti-Catholic tracts. In 1830 Gowan established the Grand Orange Lodge of British North America, with himself as head. The Orangemen in Ireland were Protestant bigots, and although the Canadian Orange Order would eventually serve its members as a social club and even insurance company, its anti-Catholic roots permeated its being. By 1833 there were ninety-one lodges in Upper Canada and eight in Lower Canada, with a combined membership of 10 000. By 1860 the order claimed 100 000 members in British North America. Orange employers and union members associated with their own group and favoured Protestants over Catholics for jobs and for political and community offices. Clashes between the Orange and the Green on

CHOLERA AND UPPER CANADA

Upper Canada's distance from the immigrant landing point of Quebec City spared the colony from cholera deaths on the scale of the lower province. But conditions in towns in Upper Canada were just as hospitable to the spread of infection. In 1832, for example, York lost about five hundred of its five thousand residents to an outbreak of cholera. The town quickly established a Board of Health to prepare reports on conditions in various neighbourhoods that might be conducive to the spread of disease. The inspection report for the 7th ward gives a vivid description of the town's living conditions:

> New Street . . . yard rather dirty dung &c wants removing . . . Barns & under them . . . stagnant water which might be easily drawn off . . . Tavern Keepers house in bad order very dirty wants white washing & repairs very much, yard & premises in a most shameful condition . . . Tenant complains that his landlord will not make any repairs . . . Duchess Street . . . a privy shelter overflowing & causes much offence & inconvenience to the neighbours . . . Water course on both sides of the Street wanted repairs . . . Duke Street: House owned by George Duggan in a very dirty state, no less than 5 families in the House, yard of which is in a dirty state Dung &c about it . . . In Duke Street from Bank to New Street the water courses want repairs . . . stagnant water, a dung heap, & draining running across pathway into street . . . yard in a very dirty state a large quantity of dung stagnant water &c &c.[8]

James Lesslie, a stationer and apothecary in York, kept a diary of his thoughts and observations during the cholera epidemic. Like many Upper Canadians, he believed that the epidemic was "a fearful visitation of heaven upon mankind" and that it was "calculated to rouse them from their apathy to the solemnities of futurity." The speed of the disease's attack was underscored in Lesslie's diary entries. He noted, for example: "This day Seely the Jailor dies of the Cholera—took ill this morning at 6 and was a corpse in the afternoon!—a rapid and solemn transition!"[9]

days of importance to the two Irish religious groups were frequent throughout the second half of the nineteenth century, although compared to the hostilities in Ireland the level of Protestant–Catholic conflict in Canada was relatively mild.

Immigrants aboard ship in the 1820s   (Charles William Jefferys/National Archives of Canada/C73435)

REGULATING MORALITY

Communities in both Lower and Upper Canada attempted to impose their particular brand of morality on anyone in the vicinity. The popular classes did not always resort to law to enforce conformity; sometimes they utilized social practices such as the charivari to convey their disapproval or give pause to people who might consider offending community norms.

In the 1830s, quoting a neighbour's report, author Susanna Moodie provided a detailed description of a charivari:

When an old man marries a young wife, or an old woman a young husband, or two old people, who ought to be thinking of their graves, enter for the second or third time into the holy estate of wedlock, as the priest calls it, all the idle young fellows in the neighbourhood meet together to charivari them. For this purpose they disguise themselves, blackening their faces, putting their clothes on hind part before, and wearing horrible masks, with grotesque caps on their heads, adorned with cocks' feathers and bells. They then form in a regular body, and proceed to the bridegroom's house, to the sound of tin kettles, horns and drums, cracked fiddles, and all the discordant instruments they can collect together. Thus equipped, they surround the house where the wedding is held, just at the hour when the happy couple are supposed to be about to retire to rest—beating upon the door with clubs and staves, and demanding of the bridegroom admittance to drink the bride's health, or in lieu thereof to receive a certain sum of money to treat the band at the nearest tavern.

If the bridegroom refuses to appear and grant their request, they commence the horrible din you heard, firing guns charged with peas against the doors and windows, rattling old pots and kettles, and abusing him for his stinginess in no measured terms. Sometimes they break open the doors, and seize upon the bridegroom. . . . I have known many fatal accidents arise out of an imprudent refusal to satisfy the demands of the assailants.

Mrs Moodie's neighbour observed that mob justice sometimes had an ugly side. In one instance a mob, seeking to penalize a black barber for marrying a local Irishwoman, dragged him nearly naked from his wedding bed and rode him upon a rail. The ordeal resulted in the death of the victim, but no one was brought to trial.

The state also played a role in attempting to force individuals to conform to community moral standards. Homosexuality was a capital crime under British law, but the records of court cases in Upper Canada suggest that gay males in the army, the elite, and the middle class had secret networks. Those caught faced the loss of their careers or long jail sentences, although it seems that the death sentence was not used. In 1842 Samuel Moore, lance corporal, and Patrick Kelly, private, of the 89th regiment of Foot, were discovered making love and were tried and sentenced to hang for "sodomy." They did not hang, but they both spent a decade or so in Kingston Penitentiary.

•Family and Work in the Canadas, 1815–50

Upper Canada: The Countryside

Historians have increasingly recognized the importance of religious and national ties for immigrants, as well as the importance of the family economy in shaping the lives of individuals. In the case of Upper Canada, political economist Marjorie Griffin Cohen notes, "The private nature of production, the isolation of female labour, and a rigid division of labour by gender were common features of the pre-industrial period."[10]

Conventional economic analysis, with its concentration on the production of commodities and their sale in markets, provides a limited picture of the workings of the economy in Upper Canada. Certainly, from an early period surpluses were sold in local markets and export markets; but it took years until a farm family cleared enough land to allow it to have surpluses, and it was not until the second half of the nineteenth century that a large export market was tapped.

Only the household production of women ensured that farm families could get by without marketable surpluses. While the men cleared the land and took charge of production for markets, women produced the goods for household consumption that allowed the family to meet its basic needs. The men's labour, then, was the key less to subsistence for the pioneer family than to the provision of luxuries or at least extras, an ironic reversal of the "pin money" thesis that bedevils discussion of women's labour in later periods. Writer W.H. Graham itemizes the various tasks that women performed:

> They grew their own hops to make their own rising to make their own bread. They saved ashes to make their own lye to boil with collected fat to make their own soap. They made their own candles. They spun wool, they made clothes, cutting up old garments for patterns. They had complete responsibility for the dairy, the milking, the butter-making and the cheese-making. . . . They took part in the butchering of the beasts, in the making of sausages, the smoking of hams, the salting of pork. They did great laundries, which they finished, in spite of protective bandages, with bleeding wrists. They stood through the long nights keeping the fire going under the huge potash pots and stirring the hardening mass. In the cold spring nights they tended the fires under the maple syrup. . . .
>
> The vegetable garden too was the woman's care, as well as the putting down of berries, pickles, fruits and preserves; the making of substitutes for tea and coffee from dandelion roots, sumach leaves and parched grain; the dyeing of wool and knitting; the care of the poultry;

the dressing and curing of fish and game. And, of course, there were three meals a day to prepare.[11]

The number of tasks a farm woman could undertake was limited by the resources available to her, by the time required for each of the jobs, and by her total responsibility for the upbringing of children. With the prosperity of the farm household so dependent upon the farm wife, it is not surprising that—as a contemporary commentator reported—a woman was "prized in this country according to her usefulness; and a thriving young settler will marry a clever industrious girl, who has a reputation for being a good spinner and knitter, than one who has nothing but a pretty face to recommend her."[12]

Despite her crucial economic role, a woman was legally subordinate to the husband, father, or even brother for whom she performed labour. The husband's right to dispose of the family property was limited only by a widow's legal claim to one-third of it, and most men willed their farm homes to a son or grandson or son-in-law. In Peel County, at mid-century, only one-quarter of the widowed wives received a separate inheritance from their husbands. The others became boarders in the homes of a male heir. The wills generally indicated what provisions the heir was to make for the widow, and over 20 percent of the documents explicitly forbade the widow to remarry, on pain of being forced to surrender the property her labour had helped to create. From 1845 to 1855 the inheritances of farms in Peel County were divided as follows: 32.1 percent to one heir, 28.6 percent to more than one heir, and 39.3 percent to one heir but with detailed provisions for other members of the family. After 1855 this "Canadian" system of inheritance, which gave the heir to the land responsibility for implementing the provisions of the will for other family members, became the norm, accounting for 71.2 percent of all wills from 1856 to 1865 and 79.7 percent of wills from 1866 to 1873.

In law the labour of married women and children held no monetary value. For instance, in 1844 one woman sued her father's estate after receiving nothing from it despite having served as a virtual slave to her father. Chief Justice John Beverly Robinson dismissed her claim, commenting: "This young woman could not be living any where else more properly than with her aged and infirm parent; and if she did acts of service, instead of living idly, it is no more than she ought to have done in return for her clothes and board, to say nothing of the claims of natural affection which usually lead children to render such service."[13]

Women's inferior position made divorce or separation a bold gamble even in cases where they were abused by their husbands. Before mid-century a woman who left her husband received no property settlement, and custody of the children went to the father except in rare cases. A divorce could be granted only by a special act of the legislature in cases where the husband was proved to be guilty of incest, rape, sodomy, bestiality, or bigamy. Before 1900 cruelty was not a legal justification for a divorce in British North America, with the exception of Nova Scotia; and as the head of the family a man was considered to have the right to beat his wife and children provided he did not use excessive force. The law also did not question a husband's right to his wife's sexual favours on demand: a wife could seek a divorce from a husband found guilty of raping another woman, but she had no recourse in law if she was the victim of her husband's sexual assaults.

Most women remained with their husbands until one or the other died. In 1851 two of every ten women who died between the ages of fifteen and fifty died in childbirth. Before mid-century the average Upper Canadian woman bore six children and women tended to have children at home with them for most of their lives. The Peel County records show that 40 percent of the women starting families there in the 1850s were dead before all their children had reached adulthood.

Small children may have been a burden to their mother, but older children were put to work both inside the farm home and outside in the fields. Boys or girls around the age of ten could expect to spend much of their day looking after younger siblings or helping mother with tasks, from cleaning house to gardening. A fifteen-year-old girl would join her mother in a full range of tasks, while a fifteen-year-old boy worked in the fields with his father. Infancy, then, was followed not by a long period of playful childhood but by an apprenticeship to farm work. The unpaid labour of older children was an essential element in a household economy that left little room for hiring farm labourers or house servants.

Upper Canadian farm families gave education a low priority, at least before the 1840s. After 1816 a community that built a school and hired a teacher could obtain provincial subsidies, but it had to assess fees to make up the shortfall between school-operating costs and the government grant. In the 1830s the fee was two or three dollars per quarter, plus firewood in winter months. Often farmers did not have the money to pay these fees and did not feel they could spare their children's time on education—much less their own time in transporting children to and from a central location where a school might be located. As late as 1851, Prescott County reported only 7 and 17 percent of French-speaking and English-speaking children respectively, aged five to sixteen, attending school; by contrast, 39 percent of children in that age group in Hamilton attended school that same year. The main goal of the family economy was the acquisition and improvement of land, and education seemed to contribute little to this endeavour. A farmer working on his own could, on average, clear only four hectares per year. A large family all working the land could clear ten hectares in a year.

While mere ownership of land struck men and women who had been tenants or farm labourers in Britain as an achievement, many families failed to accumulate the capital to buy land or, where land was free, the implements and seed to clear land and start a farm. In Peel County, for example, in 1835 a quarter of all householders were tenants or squatters. In the rural areas of Home District in 1851, 67.8 percent of the men of labouring age were landless. Without roots, the landless folk ranged far and wide in search of often-elusive opportunities. Those who did own land took years to prosper, with at best modest surpluses as a source of income for purchasing off-farm goods. Wheat, the major exportable crop, provided an average income per household of only about $25 in 1830, although, in fact, some farms sold a great deal of wheat and others none at all. Only in the 1840s, when wheat exports increased about 500 percent, were many farm families able to rise above subsistence. At best an Upper Canadian farm household produced a surplus that met the needs of two other families.

Table 9.1: PER FARM MARKETABLE SURPLUSES AND THEIR DISTRIBUTION, ONTARIO, 1861

	Value of Marketable Surplus
Average for all farms in sample	$210
Average for farms with positive surplus only	$280
First quartile: value exceeded by 75 percent of farms	$ 20
Median	$149
Third quartile: value exceeded by 25 percent of farms	$324
Value exceeded by 10 percent of farms	$639
Value exceeded by 5 percent of farms	$830
Percent of farms with deficit	16
Percent of farms with surplus in excess of consumption requirements of 3 households	16

Source: Marvin McInnis, "Marketable Surpluses in Ontario Farming," in *Perspectives on Canadian Economic History*, ed. Douglas McCalla (Toronto: Copp Clark Pitman, 1987), 45.

About half of the cash income on the farms before 1850 came not from exported wheat but from other products sold in local markets. Farmers on Lake Ontario raised pigs to satisfy local markets for pork; western Upper Canada farmers produced rye, tobacco, and barley; farmers in eastern Upper Canada sold ashes and lumber; women everywhere sold surpluses of milk, butter, and eggs.

Upper Canada: The Cities and Towns

In 1851 only 15 percent of Upper Canadians lived in urban communities of a thousand people or more. Five towns contained half of this population, with the rest spread out between thirty-three centres. York was a government centre, Kingston the site of an important military garrison, and Bytown the heart of a thriving timber industry. Most towns served the needs of the rural population and moved rural surpluses to export markets. The relatively small urban population reflected the modest purchasing power of the farmers, the limited impact of exports and imports, and the insignificance of the urban economy in pre-industrial society.

York—which became incorporated as the city of Toronto in 1834—was the fastest-growing centre because of its location in the Home District, the colony's most prosperous rural area because of the good roads that led to the capital. From only 2235 people in 1828, Toronto's population grew to 12 571 in 1838 and over 30 000 in 1851. By that time perhaps one in four persons employed outside the home worked in manufacturing or processing. The existence of factories producing ginger, syrup, glue, oil cloth, and patent leather indicated that the increased wheat sales of the 1840s were creating a domestic market for a wider array of products. By contrast Kingston, the largest town before the 1830s, was centre to a relatively poor agricultural area and failed to develop an important manufacturing sector despite its relatively large population (over 10 000 in 1851).

Kingston, from Barriefield   (Metropolitan Toronto Reference Library/J. Ross Robertson Collection/T15304)

Hamilton's population, meanwhile, grew from 1400 in 1833 to 4300 in 1842 and 14 000 in 1851 as its agricultural hinterland expanded. The city's reputation as a centre for iron products was established with the opening of the Gurney stove-works in 1843 and of several other foundries in the early 1850s. A Hamilton carriage factory employing 131 workers in 1851 was one of Upper Canada's largest industrial plants. A cloth factory in Cobourg with 175 workers and a Dundas foundry with 120 completed the list of factories in the province in 1851 employing over 100 persons. In addition, London was already establishing itself as a brewing centre: both Thomas Carling and John K. Labatt launched businesses there in the 1840s.

In the countryside, where few were wealthy, the sharpest social division was between landowners and labourers. The landless workers were generally forced to be transient in search of employment or of cheap available land. In towns, particularly the larger ones, a more complex social class structure asserted itself early on. Towns were home not only to the wealthy, who received land grants, government jobs, and contracts, but also to the poor who could not afford to obtain land and so took whatever labouring jobs they could find. In between were small shopkeepers, artisans, carters, professionals, and, by 1850, an increasing number of skilled tradesmen who worked in the small plants of the nascent manufacturing sector.

The wealthy lived in substantial brick homes. The poor lived in rented wooden shacks densely packed together—places that burned like matchsticks when a fire started. In all families the women participated in household duties, but the wealthy hired servants, usually young immigrant women. The rich, groaning about the general insubordination of servants in the New World relative to their British counterparts, paid the help poorly and housed them in tiny rooms. Women in poor families and widows in particular often worked as charwomen, washerwomen, or pedlars. Children broke stones for roads, took labouring and servant jobs, or worked with their parents as pedlars, cleaners, or beggars.

Canal construction provided perhaps eight or nine thousand men with seasonal work annually, but the wages were low and working conditions unsafe. According to John Mactaggart, a British engineer who was clerk of the works on the Rideau Canal from 1826 to 1828, "One tenth of all the poor Irish emigrants who come to Canada perish during the first two years they are in the country."[14] In Bytown, reported Mactaggart, the Irish labourers "burrow into the sand-hills; smoke is seen to issue out of holes which are opened to answer the purpose of chimneys." Without blankets, many of the workers suffered from frostbite. Many of them also contracted malaria from drinking swamp waters. And many of them were injured or even killed in explosions when tree stumps were blasted.

Rideau Canal　(Metropolitan Toronto Library Board)

Mactaggart, reflecting the ethnic prejudices of the time, blamed the Irish for their own problems, saying that they did not properly learn how to do their jobs and that they knew little about sanitation. In practice, as historian William Wylie observes, immigrant workers were the victims of ruthless exploitation as subcontractors competed for jobs by setting aside the least money possible for pay, training, and supervision of workers. Challenging the standard view that anyone who wanted to start a farm or small business could do so, Wylie writes: "The economic future of the workers was bleak. The evidence suggests that few wage-earners on the Rideau were able to save much from their earnings. While some may have become struggling farmers, artisans, or shopkeepers, the majority had to continue competing for jobs with successive annual waves of immigrants."[15]

It was this competition for jobs that produced the Shiners' War of the 1830s and the battles between Irish workers from Munster and Connaught on canal construction in the 1840s. Since the wages of the Irish workers could barely sustain life, there were times when they co-operated among themselves in strikes for higher wages or for payment of overdue wages. Troops were often used to quash these strikes. The authorities, defending the employers, argued that the strikes were the result of an Irish proclivity to violence rather than a justifiable attempt to seek redress of grievances.

Lasting unions of labourers were unthinkable in an economic climate in which jobs were short-term and workers easily replaced by new immigrants. Skilled workers such as printers and moulders did form trade unions, but at mid-century these organizations were small and served more as co-operative insurance companies for members' families in case of illness or death than as organizations to negotiate contracts with recalcitrant employers. Only fifty-six strikes were recorded in the Canadas from 1815 to 1849, an indication that few workers were organized and that those who were could rarely challenge their employers directly.

By the 1840s there was begrudging recognition from the authorities that at least some of the poor were victims of circumstance rather than creatures of sloth and intemperance. Houses of industry, providing shelter and food to the "deserving poor," opened in cities. Unless they were too old, very young, or infirm, most of the inmates of these institutions were required to work for their supper and bed. The Toronto House of Industry, for example, apprenticed children to respectable country folk in hopes that the youngsters would become sober and industrious. In its first year of operation, this institution provided relief to one-twelfth of the city's residents and one-seventh of its children. Kingston's House of Industry opened in December 1847 and admitted 183 persons the first month, 175 of them Irish. Of the total of 183, 47 were widows and 63 were children under ten.

In Upper Canada the temperance movement was gaining popular support. Toronto's temperance society, founded in 1839, had 1300 members by 1841. Members took a pledge to abstain from alcohol and worked to convince others of the moral ruin that strong drink left in its wake. In Lower Canada, Roman Catholic *curés* sponsored a similar movement.

Some historians suggest that the reforming zeal in Canada West was directed towards integrating citizens into the emerging new industrial order. Writing about educational reformers in the province at mid-century, Susan Houston and Alison Prentice suggest that the reformers formed "part of a team of mid-19th century moral missionaries that included, among others, temperance crusaders, volunteer charity workers, and urban officers, to name only the most obvious." The "shared objective" of this team, Houston and Prentice conclude, was "to instil a work ethic and moral discipline appropriate to the new society."[16]

Lower Canada: The Countryside

While the farming population in Upper Canada was gradually being drawn into the emerging international capitalist economy, where they sold their farm surpluses, in Lower Canada members of the rural population were increasingly becoming part of the larger economy as sellers of their labour, particularly to the timber companies. As a group of feminist historians in Quebec observe: "In rural Quebec in 1851, there were almost as many agricultural labourers (63,365) as farmers (78,437), and a woman was considered lucky if she married someone who would inherit land."[17] The rural districts of Montreal, with 38 percent of householders landless in 1844, told the same story. As the seigneuries filled, and because new lands were usually opened up only in freehold, landlessness spread. The French-Canadian population of Quebec increased by 250 000 from 1815 to 1840. Habitants resisted subdivision of small plots of land among their children, aware that the land would not support anyone if a holding fell much below 125 hectares. Older sons tended to become the only heirs to land, and younger brothers were forced either to move elsewhere in search of land or find work as agricultural labourers, forestry workers, or fishers. Daughters could marry a landholder, become domestics, or move away from home. In the 1830s many habitants moved to the Eastern Townships, and the French-Canadian component of the population of this once English-only area increased from 23 percent in 1831 to 30 percent in 1844. Settlement also occurred in places once considered too poor agriculturally for colonization. The Saguenay, the Mauricie, and the Ottawa River regions were settled as "agro-forestry" areas, where, it was hoped, forestry income would allow families to survive on marginal agricultural land. New seigneuries opened in Malbaie, but the land there was hilly and farmers survived by fishing and working for forestry companies.

After 1830 the expanding textile mills of New England offered an escape to landless men and women unable to find remunerative employment within Lower Canada. By 1850 what had begun as a trickle became a flood of émigrés, and by 1900 an estimated 700 000 French Canadians had left for the United States. Their willingness to leave raises questions about popular notions that French Canadians in the nineteenth century were poor because they lacked a capacity for risk-taking. In fact, what they lacked was capital and good land. The soils of Lower Canada were generally poorer than the land in Upper Canada, especially western Upper Canada, and had become exhausted from years of questionable agricultural practices, particularly the lack of crop rotation. The situation in Lower Canada was not unique: soil-exhausting agriculture was practised everywhere in North America and had, for example, turned the farmers of the Atlantic seaboard of the United States into net importers of wheat. But in the United States the usual solution to lowered productivity from agricultural land was to move west to new areas where the same poor practices could be followed anew. Such an option was unavailable to the *Canadiens*, who were not encouraged to take up lands in the upper province and were therefore forced to live with the consequences of their poor agricultural practices.

Changes in crops reflected the agricultural crisis. Wheat had accounted for 60 to 70 percent of agricultural production in Lower Canada in 1800, and a record export of one million bushels in 1802 indicated the crop's economic importance to the province. By 1831 wheat accounted for 21 percent of agricultural production, and Lower Canada was a large importer of wheat. Wheat-fly infestations ravaged crops in the 1830s, and by 1844 wheat provided only 4.4 percent of total agricultural revenue.

Oats and potatoes replaced wheat in both the farmers' diet and their off-farm sales. These products were sold mainly in local markets rather than internationally and provided less revenue than wheat had once done. But wheat yields were too low to make its continued cultivation outside a few areas profitable. Habitants also raised more sheep, pigs, and cows than before, but limited capital and small farms restricted the potential of the livestock industry in Lower Canada. Capital was required to buy high-quality livestock and supplies of feed and to build better winter shelter for animals.

Instead of capital, the habitants had debts. Unable to achieve self-sufficiency on their small plots of land, they bought goods, seeds, and animal feed on credit from local merchants, both English-speaking and French-speaking. The merchants bought the habitants' crop surpluses as partial payment for debts incurred, paying low prices for products in good crop years and then holding on to them to sell dearly in poor crop years. Repayment of debts to merchants as well as dues to seigneurs and the various levies of the church created a treadmill of debt throughout the entire seigneurial belt. In Petite Nation, the seigneury presided over by Louis-Joseph Papineau, most habitants at any given time were indebted both to local merchants and to their seigneur. In the political arena the seigneurs castigated heartless landlords, but in their own affairs they forgave no debtors. Habitants without cash paid seigneurs back in kind, whether by working on their buildings, roads, and manors, in upkeep of their sawmills and dikes, or by supplying construction materials, animals, and furs.

Life on credit also characterized the agro-forestry frontier. In the 1840s in the Saguenay, the William Price company controlled the local forestry sector and paid workers in credits at a company store rather than in cash. The farmers were dependent on the company for employment because its forest reserves were large enough to block agricultural expansion. When Jean-Baptiste Honorat came to the Saguenay in 1844, sent by the archbishop of Quebec to be the superior of an Oblate mission, he denounced company subordination of the settlers to a capitalist enterprise and of agriculture to forestry. The archbishop responded by removing him from the region in 1849.

Feudal exploitation by seigneurs and clergy, along with capitalist exploitation by merchants and lumber companies, left habitants vulnerable to bankruptcy when crops failed, as they did in 1813, 1816, 1826, 1833, 1836, and 1837. The *Journals* of the Legislative Assembly in 1833 claimed that in the Quebec district a third of the population had nothing to eat and another third could not afford to buy enough food to tide themselves over until the next harvest. While further credit allowed most people to scrape through, many left the land to escape an endless debt cycle. By the 1830s the habitant diet had potatoes rather than bread at its centre and was neither as varied nor as nutritious as it had been a generation earlier. Potatoes, peas, maple sugar, and pork were the basic staples.

When the overcrowding, poor crops, and debt caused habitant men to seek off-farm work, habitant women stayed on the land, doing all the farm work as well as caring for the children and looking after the home. Women born in 1825 would, on average, bear eight children, as had women in the *ancien régime*; but women born in 1845 would reduce this average to six, as birth-control knowledge spread by word of mouth despite the church's efforts to suppress it.

A View of the Château-Richer, Cape Torment, and the Lower End of the Isle of Orleans near Quebec, 1787. Painting by Thomas Davies   (National Gallery of Canada/6275)

As in Upper Canada, to reduce the household's dependence on markets and credit women tried to produce items the family needed for survival. Families raised sheep so their women could make the family's clothing, and they raised pigs so they did not have to purchase meat. These activities improved the farm family's economic situation; but they could not solve all the problems created when neither the land base nor other resources for total self-sufficiency were available.

The people who decided to stay in the rural areas in Lower Canada depended to a large extent on the continued British demand for squared timber. The forest industry at least created seasonal employment, albeit at low wages. There were 727 sawmills in operation in the province in 1831 and 911 in 1844. Farmers produced staves, hoops, and barrel ends for local and export markets. For the most part, however, they simply hired out their labour as loggers and raftsmen, and the families attempted to eke out a living from the men's wages and women's household and farm production.

In general therefore, while the period from 1815 to 1850 witnessed a gradual improvement in living conditions in Upper Canada for its hardworking farmers, it also saw a significant deterioration in living standards for rural *Canadiens*. In 1851 the average farm in Upper Canada could boast a net value of production twice that of a Lower Canadian farm and sold about four times as much in the market.

Lower Canada: The Cities

In 1851 in Lower Canada (or Canada East as it was called after 1840), as in Upper Canada (Canada West), only 15 percent of the population lived in towns and cities with over one thousand residents. But in Lower Canada, unlike Upper Canada, two centres accounted for three-quarters of this population, and there were only thirteen other towns with over one thousand persons.

Montreal, with 57 715 residents in 1851, was British North America's largest city. After 1815 Irish and Scottish immigrants bolstered the Anglo-American component of the population enough that from 1835 to 1865 the majority of Montreal's population were English speakers. The city benefited from British mercantilist policies that ended only in the late 1840s, when free trade became the new British economic religion. Before then, Americans shipping wheat to Britain would ship from Montreal to avoid paying the high tariffs on goods arriving on non-British ships. Wheat from Upper Canada also passed through Montreal, more than making up for declining shipments of wheat from the rural sections of Lower Canada. Montreal was also headquarters of the Grand Trunk Railway, which played a key role in American–Canadian trade beginning in the late 1850s.

The bourgeoisie of Montreal formed a committee of trade in 1821 and a board of trade in 1842. They were a society apart, living in huge mansions in exclusive neighbourhoods. Its members rubbed elbows at curling, hunt, cricket, and racquet clubs, the Horticultural Society and the Mercantile Library, the Anglican and Presbyterian churches, and Tory political meetings. Their English-language newspapers, *The Gazette* (unilingual after 1816), *The Canadian Courant and Montreal Advertiser* (1807–34), the *Montreal Herald* (1811–1957), and the *Daily Advertiser* (1833–34), among others, extolled capitalist values and scoffed at the peasant mentality of legislators unwilling to raise taxes to pay for canals and roads that would ignite commerce. French Canadians were poor cousins within Montreal's bourgeoisie, but their presence among property owners was noticeable. One of the biggest landowners was Denis-Benjamin Viger, cousin to Louis-Joseph Papineau and himself a Parti canadien politician. Viger rented commercial properties and in 1825 was the second biggest property renter in Montreal after Pierre Berthelet, who let twenty-three properties to sixty-one tenants and also rented out three hundred cast-iron stoves in the winter.

French speakers were also a minority of the bourgeoisie of Quebec. That city's population had grown steadily from 8449 in 1795 to 17 880 in 1818, 27 632 in 1831, and 42 052 in 1851. Much of its growth was the result of the expansion of port facilities to handle increased timber exports. It was the lack of return cargoes for the timber ships that led their owners to rent space to British immigrants for the return journey. The consequence was that Quebec was the first stopover for most British immigrants to the Canadas. The timber trade and shipping also stimulated the construction of shipyards: in 1851 seven shipyards employed 1338 persons. Men of Scottish origin dominated the shipyards and the timber trade.

English-speaking merchants also dominated civic administration in the two cities. Their main concern was to maintain low property taxes, the source of civic revenues, and they neglected streets and drains, disease, and fire. Saint Roch, the working-class area of Quebec City, had mud roads, wooden drains that easily broke, and wooden homes crowded close together. Poor drainage meant contaminated water, and death rates were higher in the poor areas than in the prosperous ones. In 1845 two huge fires left 20 000 people, or half the population, in Quebec City homeless. A major fire in Montreal in 1852 razed 1100 homes, leaving one-sixth of the population without shelter.

In both Quebec City and Montreal people were beginning to band together in a variety of associations. In the 1830s and 1840s tailors, shoemakers, bakers, carpenters, printers, mechanics, firefighters, painters, stonecutters, and milkmen all organized for mutual protection and very occasionally went on strike. French-speaking professionals and small businessmen also organized, especially in Montreal. In the 1830s, apart from the Parti patriote (the name for the Parti canadien after 1826), there were nationalist societies such as La Société Saint-Jean Baptiste and the Société aide-toi et ciel t'aidera. The Irish formed the St Patrick's Society. In the 1840s the Instituts Canadiens became centres for intellectual exchange, their offices serving as libraries, newsrooms, and conference halls all rolled into one.

Before the rebellions of 1837 and 1838 the influence of the Roman Catholic Church was waning, both in the urban and rural areas. From one cleric for every 355 residents in 1760, the priest-to-population ratio was one for every 1375 in 1810 and one for every 1834 in 1830. In Montreal only 36 percent of parishioners took Easter communion, and regular attendance was far smaller.

In the 1840s, however, the church made a comeback, with a priest-to-faithful ratio of one for every 1080. As well, recruitment in France contributed to a doubling of numbers in female religious communities, and by the 1860s attendance of parishioners at Easter communion was nearly universal. The church established newspapers and associations, and organized processions, to reassert its influence and counter the liberalizing tendencies of the Instituts Canadiens. Led by energetic bishops such as Jean-Jacques Lartigue and his successor, Ignace Bourget, in Montreal, the church successfully marginalized political-nationalist reform elements that had once dominated the province's political discourse.

Even before the church achieved its influential political role, its pre-eminence in social welfare for Catholics, established before 1760, was largely unchallenged. Social welfare services and hospitals continued to be the responsibility of the religious orders, especially the female ones, and services expanded as their numbers swelled. The Soeurs de la Charité de l'Hôpital-Général of Montreal, for example, cared for the sick and poor as well as foundlings. Priests were also involved in charitable services through the St Vincent de Paul societies, which collected donations in the parishes to be used to aid the destitute.

In the English-speaking community women also came to dominate social services, which were all operated by private charity organizations rather than the state before the 1840s. In 1817 upper-class women in Montreal organized the Female Benevolent Society, which established the Montreal General Hospital four years later; the Female Compassionate Society, to assist married women in childbirth, in 1822; the Montreal Protestant Orphan Asylum in 1822; and the Ladies' Benevolent Society, which aided destitute women, in 1824. While well-off women often felt genuine compassion for those they aided, this attitude was often mixed with contempt. After all, their husbands insisted that these needy people were profligate and intemperate rather than victims of poor pay and seasonal work.

The poor took help from whatever quarter offered it. Every winter people struggled to find enough money to buy food and firewood and hoped they would be spared the smallpox, diphtheria, and measles that killed off many of the youngest and oldest members of the population. Maria Louisa Beleau was not spared during the severe winter of 1816–17. The daughter of a single mother, she died in a home that was described by a witness at her inquest:

> The hovel in which the deceased had lived, with her mother, and two sisters, is not fit for a stable. It is open in many parts of the roof and on all sides. There is no other floor than the bare earth. It is a mere wooden stall: it has no window nor any chimney. In the middle is a shallow hole made in the earth, in which there are marks of a fire having been made; and the smoke escaped through the open parts of the roof and sides. When I was there on Tuesday last, there was no fire in the hole.[18]

• Conclusion

Superficially, the societies of the Canadas in 1791 and 1851 were similar: most people farmed, and trade activity centred around a few exportable natural products. Beneath the surface, however, much had changed. In the 1790s the farm families of both Upper Canada and Lower Canada depended on their collective labours to provide the necessities of life; market exchanges provided only a small percentage of the goods they consumed. By the 1850s, in contrast, most farmers in both Canada West and Canada East depended on market exchanges for a growing portion of the products they used.

In Upper Canada this typically meant that a farm family sold about two-thirds of what it produced, using the proceeds to buy farm equipment and household items. In Lower Canada it meant that farmers without saleable surpluses had to supplement their farm income with off-farm waged work, usually in the timbering trade. Towns and cities in the Canadas grew because of increased foreign demand for Canadian staples and increased domestic demand for manufactures. The towns and cities in both provinces were increasingly class-divided and included growing numbers of poor people dependent on private charities for at least part of their survival. These social divisions within the countryside and the cities would create political divisions—manifested most dramatically in the rebellions of the late 1830s.

Lower Canada's Agricultural Crisis:
A Historiographical Debate

Two views of Lower Canada's French-speaking majority underlie the debate on the causes and the timing of the colony's agricultural crisis in the nineteenth century. One view, associated particularly with Fernand Ouellet, regards the *Canadiens* as the authors of their own doom, victims of traditional peasant social values: conservative and unenterprising, they were otherworldly rather than materialistic. The second view, associated most closely with Gilles Paquet and Jean-Pierre Wallot, paints the French Canadians as rational participants in the marketplace, uninhibited by the peasant cultural values that Ouellet attributes to them.

According to Ouellet, the habitants benefited from increased market demand from Britain for Canadian wheat in the 1790s. Afterwards, although demand grew, the *Canadiens* proved unable to take advantage of it because of an unwillingness to re-examine their agricultural practices: extensive, soil-exhausting monoculture. Agriculture was already in crisis in the first decade of the nineteenth century, Ouellet suggests. He concludes: "The wheat crisis then did not have its source in the greater or lesser opportunity offered by the Imperial markets, it resulted essentially from the techniques and agricultural methods employed by the mass of agricultural producers."[19]

While Ouellet maintains that subsistence agriculture was the chief characteristic of the Lower Canadian economy, Paquet and Wallot state, "The economy of Lower Canada, at the turn of the nineteenth century, was dynamized rather by circulation and commerce in the Atlantic System."[20] These historians agree with Ouellet that the imperial market for wheat was growing in the nineteenth century, but they disagree that a habitant indifference to market forces prevented them from meeting this demand. Rather, they argue that an analysis of fluctuations in wheat prices demonstrates that farmers sold grain abroad in years when it was profitable to do so and avoided producing surpluses for the British market in years when prices failed to match costs of production. Paquet and Wallot indicate that the habitants were able to influence the direction of wheat prices by limiting production in certain years and that such shrewd manipulation of the market lasted until 1815 and perhaps 1820; there was no agricultural crisis before that period, in their opinion. There was a crisis, they agree, after 1820, but they attribute it to climatic changes (a large number of unseasonably cold growing seasons) and invasions by parasites such as the Hessian wheat-fly rather than to peasant conservatism.

Historian T.J.A. LeGoff argues that habitant production of wheat by 1812 often failed to meet domestic demand, let alone foreign demand. He rejects Paquet and Wallot's notion that the habitants simply responded to price fluctuations and says that there was indeed an agricultural crisis in the first decade of the nineteenth century. But, unlike Ouellet, who relies on a psychological explanation—habitant conservatism—to explain the crisis, LeGoff focusses on the effective limits of the land to meet demand.[21] Economist John McCallum agrees with LeGoff, suggesting that the lower quality of farmland in Canada East relative to Canada West, rather than cultural values, explains both the lesser productivity of the land in the lower province and its industrial lag: while farmers of Canada West were able to produce surpluses and use the proceeds to buy manufactured goods, the farmers of Canada East were in too weak a position to provide a stimulus to industrialists.[22]

Historian Allan Greer, on the basis of several regional studies of Lower Canada, argues that there is no evidence of market-oriented behaviour on the part of habitants. Instead, he says there was a "constant orientation toward use-value rather than any market-oriented specialization."[23] But Greer rejects the view implicit in both Ouellet and Paquet/Wallot that what requires explanation is whether farmers responded to market demands. He suggests that both in Upper Canada and Lower Canada farm families aimed at self-sufficiency, and he says that a useful analytical focus is the "factors contributing to the destruction of the independence of petty producers and the construction, under the leadership of the owners of capital, of a new social formation where the wage nexus reigned supreme."[24] For Greer, the agricultural crisis that affected various regions of Lower Canada cannot be understood solely in terms of either ethnic cultural values or climate and soil considerations, although both of these are important. Instead, he suggests, in each region the interaction between seigneurs, merchants, and habitants and the presence or absence of seasonal-labour possibilities played as significant a role as cultural and geographical factors in shaping the pace of the habitants' transition from self-sufficiency to domination by market forces.

Historian Ronald Rudin has placed the debate pitting Ouellet versus Paquet and Wallot within a context of the changes in Quebec society from the time Ouellet began writing to the time that the other two produced their collaborations. Ouellet, in this view, is a product of Quebec society before 1960, in which there was considerable emphasis on how Quebec's cultural values differed from those of the rest of North America. Paquet and Wallot, by contrast, came to maturity during the Quiet Revolution of the 1960s, when Quebec asserted cultural values in harmony with those dominant throughout North America and sought to catch up economically so its people could participate more fully in North American consumerism. According to Rudin, historians who grew up in this environment were more likely than their predecessors to mine the Quebec past for its similarities with other North American societies at various periods.[25]

•Notes

[1] Peter A. Russell, "Forest Into Farmland: Upper Canadian Clearing Rates, 1822–1839," in *Historical Essays on Upper Canada: New Perspectives*, ed. J.K. Johnson and Bruce G. Wilson (Ottawa: Carleton University Press, 1989), 132.

[2] Ibid., 143.

[3] *The Correspondence of Lieutenant Governor John Graves Simcoe*, ed. Brigadier General E.A. Cruickshank (Toronto: Ontario Historical Society, 1923), 27.

[4] *Lord Durham's Report: An Abridgement of Report on the Affairs of British North America by Lord Durham*, ed. Gerald M. Craig (Toronto: McClelland and Stewart, 1963), 119.

[5] Allan Greer, *Peasant, Lord, and Merchant: Rural Society in Three Quebec Parishes, 1740–1840* (Toronto: University of Toronto Press, 1985), 159.

[6] J.M. Bumsted, *The People's Clearance: Highland Emigration to British North America* (Edinburgh: Edinburgh University Press, 1982), 217.

[7] Anna Brownell Jameson, *Winter Studies and Summer Rambles in Canada: Selections* (Toronto: McClelland and Stewart, 1965), 167.

[8] Quoted in Chris Raible, "In Sable Garments of Mourning . . . Cholera Devastates Upper Canada, 1832," *The Beaver*, April/May 1992: 44.

[9] Ibid., 43, 48.

[10] Marjorie Griffin Cohen, *Women's Work, Markets, and Economic Development in Nineteenth-Century Ontario* (Toronto: University of Toronto Press, 1988), 24.

[11] W.H. Graham, *The Tiger of Canada West* (Toronto: Clarke, Irwin, 1962), 92–93.

[12] Catharine Parr Traill, *The Backwoods of Canada* (1836; rprt. Toronto: McClelland and Stewart, 1959), 185.

[13] Quoted in Paul Craven, "The Law of Master and Servant in Mid-Nineteenth-Century Ontario," in *Essays in the History of Canadian Law*, Vol. 1, ed. David H. Flaherty (Toronto: University of Toronto Press, 1981), 177.

[14] Quoted in *Upper Canada in the 1830's*, ed. Virginia R. Robeson (Toronto: OISE, 1977), 14.

[15] William T.N. Wylie, "Labour and the Construction of the Rideau Canal, 1826–1832," *Labour/Le Travail* 11 (Spring 1983): 29.

[16] Susan E. Houston and Alison Prentice, *Schooling and Scholars in Nineteenth Century Ontario* (Toronto: University of Toronto Press, 1988), 308.

[17] The Clio Collective, *Quebec Women: A History* (Toronto: The Women's Press, 1987), 131.

[18] Quoted in Judith Fingard, "The Winter's Tale: The Seasonal Contours of Pre-Industrial Poverty in British North America, 1815–1860," Canadian Historical Association *Historical Papers* (1974): 72.

[19] Fernand Ouellet, *Lower Canada, 1791–1840: Social Change and Nationalism* (Toronto: McClelland and Stewart, 1980), 260.

[20] Gilles Paquet and Jean-Pierre Wallot, "The Agricultural Crisis in Lower Canada, 1802–12: mise au point. A Response to T.J.A. LeGoff," *Canadian Historical Review* 56 (June 1975): 133–61.

[21] T.J.A. LeGoff, "The Agricultural Crisis in Lower Canada 1802–12: A Review of a Controversy," *Canadian Historical Review* 55 (March 1974): 1–31.

[22] John McCallum, *Unequal Beginnings: Agriculture and Economic Development in Quebec and Ontario until 1870* (Toronto: University of Toronto Press, 1980).

[23] Greer, *Peasant, Lord and Merchant*, 205.

[24] Allan Greer, "Wage Labour and the Transition to Capitalism," *Labour/Le Travail* 15 (Spring 1985): 22.

[25] Ronald Rudin, "Revisionism and the Search for a Normal Society: A Critique of Recent Quebec Historical Writing," *Canadian Historical Review* 73, 1 (March 1992): 30–61.

•Selected Reading

See also Selected Reading for chapter 10.

The early history of male Europeans in Ontario is surveyed in two general works: Randall White, *Ontario 1610–1985: A Political and Economic History* (Toronto: Dundurn Press, 1985); and Robert Bothwell, *A Short History of Ontario* (Edmonton: Hurtig, 1986). An excellent history of female Europeans in Ontario is Marjorie Griffin Cohen, *Women's Work, Markets and Economic Development in Nineteenth-Century Ontario* (Toronto: University of Toronto Press, 1988).

The social history of early Ontario is examined in a variety of excellent essays in J.K. Johnson and B. Wilson, eds., *Historical Essays on Upper Canada: New Perspectives* (Ottawa: Carleton University Press, 1989); and an earlier volume, *Historical Essays on Upper Canada* (Ottawa: Carleton University Press, 1975). Another important study is Peter A. Russell, *Attitudes to Social Structure and Mobility in Upper Canada, 1815–1840: "Here We Are Laird Ourselves"* (Lewiston, NY: Edwin Mellen Press, 1990). On elite formation in the colony, see Johnson's *Becoming Prominent: Regional Leadership in Upper Canada 1791–1841* (Montreal: McGill-Queen's University Press, 1989); and Bruce Wilson, *The Enterprises of Robert Hamilton: A Study of Wealth and Influence in Early Upper Canada* (Ottawa: Carleton University Press, 1983). Also useful in revealing the social history of the colony are the contemporary observations by Susanna Moodie, *Roughing It in the Bush* (Ottawa: Carleton University Press, 1970) and by Catharine Parr Traill, *The Backwoods of Canada* (Toronto: McClelland and Stewart, 1959). On women in Upper Canada, see Marjorie Griffin Cohen's work, and Rosemary R. Ball, "A Perfect Farmer's Wife: Women in Nineteenth Century Rural Ontario," *Canada: An Historical Magazine* 3, 2 (Dec. 1975): 2–21.

There are several excellent works on Irish immigrants, including Donald Harmon Akenson, *The Irish in Ontario: A Study in Rural History* (Montreal: McGill-Queen's University Press, 1984); and Bruce S. Elliott, *Irish Migrants in the Canadas: A New Approach* (Montreal: McGill-Queen's University Press, 1988). Robin Winks, *The Blacks in Canadian History* (Montreal: McGill-Queen's University Press, 1971) contains information on a smaller but more immediately visible group of immigrants. On Scottish immigrants, see Marianne Maclean, "Achd an Righ: A Highland Response to the Assisted Emigration of 1815," *Canadian Papers in Rural History* 5 (1986): 181–97. Irish conflict with other groups is the subject of Michael S. Cross, "The Shiners' War: Social Violence in the Ottawa Valley in the 1830s," *Canadian Historical Review* 54, 1 (1973): 1–26, while the article by Ruth Bleasdale in Johnson, *Historical Essays on Upper Canada* (1989) deals with the importance of ethnic solidarity among Irish workers in responding to harsh employment conditions. Working conditions generally are the subject of William T.N. Wylie, "Labour and the Construction of the Rideau Canal, 1826–1832," *Labour/Le Travail* 11 (Spring 1983): 7–29.

Two good community studies with information regarding landholding patterns that is suggestive for the entire province are David Gagan, *Hopeful Travellers: Families, Land, and Social Change in Mid-Victorian Peel County, Canada West* (Toronto: University of Toronto Press, 1981); and Leo A. Johnson, "Land Policy, Population Growth and Social Structure in the Home District, 1793–1851," *Ontario History* 69 (1977): 151–68. The most detailed urban study is Michael Katz, *The People of Hamilton, Canada West: Family and Class in a Mid-Nineteenth Century City* (Cambridge, MA: Harvard University Press, 1975).

On religion, see William Westfall, *Two Worlds: The Protestant Culture of Nineteenth Century Ontario* (Montreal: McGill-Queen's University Press, 1989); Curtis Fahey, *In His Name: The Anglican Experience in Upper Canada, 1791–1854* (Ottawa: Carleton University Press, 1991); J.W. Grant, *A Profusion of Spires: Religion in Nineteenth-Century Ontario* (Toronto: University of Toronto Press, 1988); and J.L.H. Henderson, ed., *John Strachan: Documents and Opinions* (Toronto: McClelland and Stewart, 1969).

For Lower Canada, Brian Young and John A. Dickinson, *A Short History of Quebec: A Socio-Economic Perspective* (Toronto: Copp Clark Pitman, 1988), ch. 4, 5, provides a vivid account of life in nineteenth-century Quebec. The Clio Collective, *Quebec Women: A History* (Toronto: Women's Press, 1987), ch. 3–7, summarizes much of the literature on women in Lower Canada.

Fernand Ouellet, *Lower Canada 1791–1840: Social Change and Nationalism* (Toronto: McClelland and Stewart, 1980), and his *Economic and Social History of Quebec* (Toronto: Macmillan, 1981) provide abundant information as well as suggestive interpretations of the economic, social, and political history of Quebec during this period. Jean-Pierre Wallot, *Un Québec qui bougeait: trame socio-politique au tournant du XIXe siècle* (Trois-Rivières: Boréal Express, 1973), offers a view of Lower Canada's economy and society before 1815 at variance with Ouellet's. Closer to Ouellet's views but far more sympathetic to the British merchants is Donald Creighton, *The Empire of the St Lawrence* (Toronto: Macmillan, 1956).

Case studies of rural life are found in Allan Greer, *Peasant, Lord and Merchant: Rural Society in Three Quebec Parishes, 1740–1840* (Toronto: University of Toronto Press, 1985); Claude Baribeau, *La Seigneurie de la Petite Nation 1801–1854: Le rôle économique et social du seigneur* (Hull, PQ: Éditions Asticou, 1983); and Normand Seguin, *La Conquête du Sol au 19e Siècle* (Montreal: Boréal Express, 1977). The reasons for Quebec's slow agricultural development relative to Ontario's are explored in John McCallum, *Unequal Beginnings: Agriculture and Economic Development in Quebec and Ontario until 1870* (Toronto: University of Toronto Press, 1980). The changing economy of Canada East after the rebellion is discussed in Gerald J.J. Tulchinsky, *The River Barons: Montreal Businessmen and the Growth of Industry and Transportation, 1837–1853* (Toronto: University of Toronto Press, 1977). On the English-speaking minority, see Ronald Rudin, *The Forgotten Quebecers: A History of English-Speaking Quebec 1759–1980* (Quebec: Institut québécois de recherche sur la culture, 1985).

The impact of epidemic disease on British North America, particularly Lower Canada, is assessed in Geoffrey Bilson, *A Darkened House: Cholera in Nineteenth-Century Canada* (Toronto: University of Toronto Press, 1980). The dismal conditions of urban life that aided in the spread of disease are the subject of David-Thiery Ruddel and Marie La France, "Québec, 1785–1840: problèmes de croissance d'une ville coloniale," *Histoire sociale/Social History* 18, 36 (1985): 315–33.

CHAPTER 10

REBELLIONS AND RESPONSIBLE GOVERNMENT: Politics in the Canadas, 1800–1850s

While the poverty of Lower Canada's habitants and the hardships faced by English-speaking settlers in both Canadas had a variety of causes, the people affected often blamed government action and inaction. One typical complainant, a farmer in the New Glasgow settlement in Lower Canada, wrote to the editor of the Montreal *Gazette* in 1824:

> We are in a pitiful predicament, although possessing lands of the first quality as to soil, although the settlers are quiet industrious people. . . . From the wretched state of our roads, we are for a considerable part of the year completely locked out from all communication with our neighbouring settlements. We were induced to fix upon this settlement, having understood that government had liberally granted money to make a road to our door. This road has never been completed. The swamps are not wooded; the bridges rock like cradles. The raveens are so steep in the banks that a horse might as well ascend the side of a house as climb them. In the months of May and June the water in many places is three feet deep, on what is called the road. Would you Mr. Editor believe, although our roads are left in this state, the person who contracted to make them is said to have received £1000 of the public money for this job.[1]

From the turn of the century, governments in the Canadas faced growing opposition to their policies—especially land policies—and eventually to their legitimacy. Opposition politicians in elected assemblies increasingly questioned the Constitutional Act's provision that the executive council, or cabinet, be named by the lieutenant-governor and answerable to him rather than to the elected members. Although some lieutenant-governors made policy concessions to the opposition, they defended the basic political system outlined in the Act. Making the lieutenant-governor a figurehead, they charged, would cut colonial ties to Britain, leaving the colonies autonomous and paving the way for their absorption into the United States. Still, the American example of democratic rule, although denounced by the ruling elite and at times regarded suspiciously by reformers, exerted considerable influence among colonists. Many of them believed that their concerns were being ignored and that the government was in the grip of a small, self-perpetuating oligarchy.

•Opposition Before 1812

A substantial opposition to the government soon developed in the popularly elected houses of assembly in the two Canadas. Although disciplined party organizations were slow to develop, opposition blocs of legislators in the two assemblies co-operated to pressure the government to change course on various issues. By 1812, members generally opposed to the thrust of government policy formed a majority in the Lower Canadian Assembly and held about half of the seats in the Upper Canadian Assembly.

In Lower Canada the Parti canadien emerged as the voice of the *Canadien* middle class. Before the 1820s this "party" was simply a collection of legislators, primarily but not exclusively French-speaking, who had been elected on anti-government platforms; they did not as yet have an organization outside the House of Assembly to unite people who wanted fundamental political reforms. The Parti canadien first flexed its political muscles in 1805 when it successfully prevented the executive council from implementing a land tax to pay for the establishment of jails. To the howls of the wealthy merchants involved in the import-export business, the group proposed an alternative: an increase in the tariff on goods entering and leaving the colony. A year later the French-speaking nationalists had their own newspaper, *Le Canadien*, edited by Pierre Bedard and François Blanchet, which denounced the administration of Governor James Craig and asserted the right of the Assembly to shape policy for the colony. Craig retaliated in 1810 by imprisoning the editors and dissolving the Assembly for a second straight year, which forced new elections. Earlier the Assembly had twice attempted to expel from its midst a French-Canadian judge and a Jewish merchant who were regarded as supporters of Craig.

Some historians have dismissed the Parti canadien leaders as frustrated office-seekers whose interests were separate from those of the habitants.

EZEKIEL HART

Ezekiel Hart was born in Trois-Rivières in 1770, the son of a Jewish merchant. There were fewer than one hundred Jews in the Canadas before 1800, but their number included enterprising and prosperous individuals. Hart and his two brothers had run a successful brewery and potashery before Ezekiel established his own import-export business and a general store and began to purchase a great deal of land. In 1807 Hart won a by-election in Trois-Rivières, but the Parti canadien, regarding him as a supporter of the government, declared him ineligible to serve. The following year Hart was re-elected and took the Christian oath of office required of members; but the Assembly majority argued that his adhesion to the Jewish faith invalidated his oath. Although Governor Craig supported Hart's right to take his seat in the Assembly, the colonial secretary confirmed that Jews were unable to serve in British legislatures. Catholics in Britain suffered from the same legal restrictions as Jews, so it was ironic that the mainly Catholic assemblymen of Lower Canada embraced the British ban on Jews in government. In 1832, with religious toleration established in British law, Ezekiel Hart's son Samuel won a seat in the Lower Canadian Assembly and became the first Jew to hold a seat in a British legislature.

The Parti canadien's rejection of Hart may suggest that the *Canadiens* were anti-semitic. Anti-semitism was indeed widespread in Christian societies in the nineteenth century, as it had been earlier. But Hart had been elected on both occasions by an electorate that was predominantly French-speaking. The Parti canadien, in turn, was most likely using Hart's Jewishness as a pretext to exclude a rich merchant likely to be a supporter of the governor. The judge rejected by the same Assembly was, after all, a *Canadien*. Nevertheless, the Parti canadien's willingness to use a man's religion as an excuse to ban him from its midst demonstrates that the party was not a liberal grouping that would defend individual freedom of conscience.

Certainly, early leaders of the Parti canadien such as Pierre Bédard, who was given a judgeship, and Austin Cuvillier, who became a director of the Bank of Montreal, eventually joined forces with the government against the nationalists. But such behaviour on the part of a few leaders does not destroy the Parti canadien's case: the state was orchestrating an assault on the social customs of the French-speaking population.

In the Upper Canadian Assembly, challenges to the government's authority before 1812 were usually identified closely with three Irish-born men: William Weekes, Robert Thorpe, and Joseph Willcocks. While misgivings about Britain's brutal suppression of an Irish uprising in 1798 may have initially kindled these men's critical appraisal of colonial governance, their focus was on the denial of democracy in Upper Canada; their supporters were united by a sense of grievance rather than by ethnicity. Weekes, a York lawyer, made the first assault on the government's privileges in 1805 when he called for all executive expenditures to receive Assembly approval. The government argued that it required Assembly approval only for monies raised through property taxes; money raised from land sales belonged to the government and could be spent as the government wished. A year later Thorpe, a judge influenced by Weekes's ideas, enunciated the principle that the Executive Council should be responsible to the Assembly rather than the governor. The British connection, he claimed, would last only if the colonial legislature enjoyed independence.

Thorpe influenced Willcocks, a minor government official, who subsequently joined him in opposing proposals for increased fees on land grants and tightened eligibility requirements for Loyalists seeking free land. As a former sheriff, Willcocks was aware of the problem of people being forced to auction off land to pay debts. The lieutenant-governor dismissed Thorpe and Willcocks from their positions. Thorpe left Upper Canada for a judgeship in Sierra Leone, but Willcocks stayed in the colony, won election to the Assembly, and founded the colony's first opposition newspaper, *Upper Canada Guardian or Freeman's Journal*. Although on one occasion the Assembly had him jailed for contempt, by 1812 Willcocks had emerged as the Assembly's leading spokesman for dissent, the unofficial leader of about half its members. Opposition demands included control of the civil list (the list of government appointments) by the legislature rather than the lieutenant-governor; reduction in the salaries of public officials; an easing of regulations for Loyalists and military personnel seeking land; and tighter controls over jury practices and electoral procedures. The colonial administration rejected these demands and, as war with the Americans loomed, demanded that the Assembly approve emergency powers for prosecution of the war. Willcocks, initially supportive of efforts to resist the American invasion of the colony, changed sides in 1813 when he became convinced that the lieutenant-governor was using the war as a pretext to increase his powers. Defecting to the Americans, he commanded a unit of about 120 expatriate Upper Canadians, including several of his former colleagues in the Assembly. The Conservatives of Upper Canada cited his actions as proof that opposition led to treason.

• The War of 1812

The causes of the War of 1812 were external to the Canadas, and British troops aided by their Native allies living in American territory did most of the fighting. Recognizing a stalemate, Britain and the United States agreed to peace in December 1814 without taking British North America's interests into consideration. Nevertheless, the war created powerful mythologies in the two Canadas that strengthened anti-democratic ideology among the elite in Upper Canada and reinforced nationalism among the French-speaking middle class in the lower province.

The main goal of the United States in the war was to seize Britain's thinly populated North American colonies, particularly the Canadas. In this it had the support of a small group of Upper Canadian expatriates, including some prominent figures. Several hundred more Upper Canadian settlers moved back to the United States to avoid being called upon to fight their former homeland, and many more settlers sat on the fence. But the threat of invasion also caused thousands to flock to the British colours. Many were active in the 11 000-strong militia—poorly trained and equipped as it was. Members of the elite received officer commissions.

Still, both the governor, Sir George Prevost, and the military commander, Major-General Isaac Brock, regarded the population as defeatist. To demonstrate that Britain could win a war with the Americans, the British executed a victorious assault on Michilimackinac on Lake Huron. This aggressive posture won the British the support of the Native peoples of the Ohio valley, who united under the Shawnee chief Tecumseh after receiving false promises that Britain would seek to win the return of this vast area to Native control. With Native help, Brock went on to seize Detroit, but then his luck ran out. At a battle in October 1812 on the heights above the village of Queenston, in the Niagara region, Brock and one hundred of his men were slain along with 1300 American attackers. In the following year the Americans recaptured Detroit and took temporary control over the western part of Upper Canada, burning Niagara to the ground and killing Tecumseh. They proved unable to capture York for more than a few days, although they did manage to torch its parliament buildings. The British in turn razed sections of Buffalo in New York state as well as the city of Washington, D.C.

In 1814 battles in the Niagara peninsula exhausted both sides. The bloodiest occurred in pitch darkness at Lundy's Lane, not far from Queenston Heights, on 25 July 1814. British regulars, assisted by the militia, confronted American troops who could barely be seen in the dark. By morning the casualties on both sides were enormous. While the Upper Canadian authorities touted Lundy's Lane as a glorious victory, it actually confirmed the pattern of rough equivalence between the two sides and deepened war-weariness in both Washington and London.

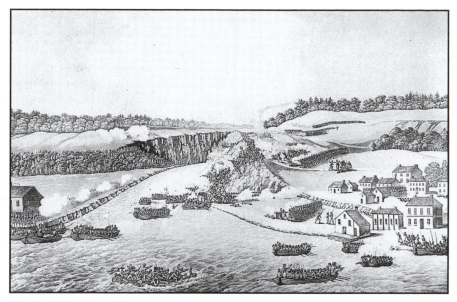

Battle of Queenston Heights (Metropolitan Toronto Reference Library/J. Ross Robertson Collection/T14987)

In Lower Canada, meanwhile, the squabbles between the Parti canadien and the governor were set aside as both factions united to defend the colony. Britain made matters easier by recalling James Craig and appointing the more conciliatory Sir George Prevost in his stead. The Lower Canadian Assembly authorized Prevost to conscript manpower and to keep as many as six thousand men in the field for a full year. The Parti canadien was not as enamoured of the Americans as it would be later, in the 1830s, and its leaders decried American republicanism. The Roman Catholic Church, grateful that Britain had allowed it to retain its religious privileges, joined the attack. Bishop Joseph-Octave Plessis of Quebec denounced the United States as a godless republic akin to revolutionary France, from which providence had detached Quebec as a result of the British conquest. Following a French military defeat several years earlier, Plessis had proclaimed: "Anything that weakens France tends to put her farther from us. Anything that puts France farther from us means security for our lives, our liberty, our peace of mind, our property, our religion and our happiness."[2] For the church, the upstart republic to the south threatened to undo the good effects of what God had decreed in 1760.

Under native-born Charles-Michel de Salaberry, 1600 French Canadians fended off 4200 undisciplined, poorly trained American recruits who crossed the river Châteauguay en route to Montreal in October 1813. Although de Salaberry was an opponent of the nationalists, the Battle of

Châteauguay became part of nationalist lore. *Canadiens* rather than British troops had kept the American interlopers at bay and, by implication, the local inhabitants, should they ever choose to rise against their British conquerors, might also hope to win a victory.

Yet it was the Roman Catholic Church, not the Parti canadien, that won governmental support for its behaviour during the War of 1812. Bishop Plessis, whom the British regarded before the war only as "superintendent" of the church, was officially recognized as bishop shortly after the conflict and named to the Legislative Council in 1817 as a reward for his stalwart support of British rule.

In Upper Canada, Queenston Heights became the centrepiece of a new mythology. The War of 1812 joined the American Revolution as a rationale in Tory thought for rule by appointed officials rather than the elected assembly and for a hierarchical, class-stratified society rather than an egalitarian one. The alternative to British rule and British class structures was a slide into Americanism and eventually into the allegedly atheist republic itself. For John Strachan, who became archdeacon of York in 1827 and served as the chief intellectual of the "high Tories" of Upper Canada for several decades, the lesson of the War of 1812 was clear: "No great and decided amelioration of the lower classes of society can be reasonably expected. . . . That foolish perfectability with which they have been deluded can never be realized."[3]

Strachan and other Conservatives used the war to justify control of public offices at all levels by an elite loyal to British institutions and values. He and many of his influential students, such as John Beverley Robinson, sometime attorney-general and long-time chief justice of Upper Canada (1829–63), rejected John Grave Simcoe's optimistic assumption that American immigrants would embrace the British political system because they would see that it provided stability while guaranteeing their right to property. In the 1820s opponents of Strachan's views would accuse his supporters of constituting a Family Compact. The term implied somewhat misleadingly that the leading members of the oligarchy were interrelated and located in one geographical area. In practice they had formed small cliques throughout the province and were not, at least initially, related by blood. But there was indeed a colonial oligarchy that was favoured by most of the lieutenant-governors and monopolized government positions, government contracts, and large land grants. Its members saw themselves as the gentlemen of the colony, a class akin to the British aristocracy. To their opponents, they were pretentious and corrupt beneficiaries of undeserved patronage.

The American thrust, exemplified by the War of 1812, offered government in the postwar period a pretext to suppress dissent. Anyone who railed against land speculators and Crown and clergy reserves was held to be sowing disunity, which could weaken Upper Canada's ability to resist future American attacks. So, for example, the government jailed and eventually deported Robert Gourlay, a recent Scottish immigrant who in 1817 published a survey of settler complaints and began to rally the population behind a campaign for major land reforms. After 1814 the government also actively discouraged American immigration to Upper Canada and, for a time, placed the political and property rights of Americans in the colony in doubt. Most new settlers who arrived in the Canadas after the War of 1812 would come from Britain, not the United States.

THE DEFENDED BORDER

The War of 1812 was the last official war between Britain and the United States. By the Treaty of Ghent, signed 24 December 1814, both sides agreed to return any enemy territory that they had occupied. Both sides hoped for much more: the United States wanted Britain to recognize its rights on the high seas, while Britain hoped to modify the boundary settlement of 1783, in particular the area west of New Brunswick and in the upper Great Lakes region.

In the aftermath of the war, two agreements helped to establish peaceful relations between the United States and Britain in North America. The Rush-Bagot agreement of 1817 limited the number of armed vessels on the Great Lakes and Lake Champlain to those required to control smuggling. By the Anglo-American Convention of 1818, the 49th parallel was recognized as the boundary between the Lake of the Woods and the Rockies, and the disputed territory on the Pacific coast was to be subject to joint occupation until an agreement could be reached. American rights to the inshore fisheries of the Atlantic region were also restricted.

Although the United States and Britain never again declared war on each other, both sides continued to see the other as a potential enemy. Military bases were constructed and strengthened on both sides of the border over the next century. Between 1826 and 1832, the British built the Rideau Canal linking Kingston and Ottawa as an alternative water route to the vulnerable international section of the St Lawrence River between Montreal and Kingston, and the route of the Intercolonial Railway was chosen with military considerations in mind. As late as the 1920s Canadian defence plans still focussed on warding off an American invasion.

•The Road to Rebellion
Lower Canada

The agricultural crisis in Lower Canada, coupled with the frustration of a *Canadien* middle class excluded from the executive and legislative councils, provided a backdrop to the rebellions in that province in 1837 and 1838. The Parti canadien, created by the middle class, won the support of the habitants because it campaigned for the opening of new seigneuries in the twenty-five million hectares outside the seigneurial belt. The habitants felt betrayed as, from 1795 to 1840, almost seven million hectares of land in the Eastern Townships passed into the hands of speculators. Some historians have labelled the rebellion as a "feudal reaction" because the Parti canadien supported the seigneurial system over freehold tenure. Many habitants no doubt would have preferred freehold tenure. Still, they were in no position to accumulate the cash required both to pay a speculator for land and to acquire the materials necessary to start a farm. They blamed the government for condemning them to landlessness and supported the Parti canadien because that party promised them land if it could get hold of the levers of power.

The Parti canadien and its successor, the Parti patriote, handily won all elections for the House of Assembly. For example, in 1827 it won 90 percent of the Assembly seats. Its stature had been raised significantly in 1822 when it joined with the clergy to fend off a proposal by the British government to unite Lower Canada and Upper Canada into one province. English-speaking merchants in Lower Canada and their allies in London had been responsible for pressing for a union of the two provinces to reduce the influence of *Canadien* representatives in the Assembly.

To the merchants, the members of the Assembly majority were opponents of commerce, because they balked at several proposals for state-funded canal construction on the St Lawrence and demanded grants of new seigneuries before they would approve road-building expenditures for the Eastern Townships. With the completion of the Erie Canal in 1825, a development that gave New York state an advantage over Montreal in shipping, the clamour of the Montreal merchants for canal expenditures grew louder, and their resolve to oppose Assembly demands for a greater say stiffened. The leading English-speaking merchants, along with the French-speaking merchants favoured by the governors, were labelled the Château Clique because they could often be found at the Château St-Louis, the governor's residence. As in Upper Canada, a small merchant-dominated group appeared to monopolize government appointments at all levels except the elected Assembly. This privileged group, it seemed, received all the Crown land grants and government contracts.

Although their relations with the church were at times strained because of Bishop Plessis's coziness with the governing clique, Louis-Joseph

Papineau and his colleagues initially stressed that the Catholic Church, the seigneurial system, and the French language and culture were fundamental aspects of the nationality of their people. They defended these three elements against all perceived attacks. In the 1830s, perhaps as a result of the governors' failure to listen to the Assembly, the Parti patriote program began to change. While Papineau remained a defender of the seigneurial system—a feature so at odds with North American landholding practices—he and other leaders were increasingly drawn to American republicanism and the democratic ideal of a government controlled by the people.

The change in Patriote views was reflected in their educational policies. The government had set up a small number of state schools after creating a Royal Institute for the Advancement of Education in 1801. Bishop Plessis, correctly believing that the goal of such schools was the inculcation of Protestant values, won legislative support in 1824 for placing control of education in the hands of *curés* and churchwardens. But in 1829 the Assembly voted to establish schools that it would itself control, supervise, and partly finance. By 1836 there were 1530 such schools, and Bishop Jean-Jacques Lartigue was horrified by the direction that the politics of the nationalists in the Assembly was taking.

In 1834 Papineau put forward in the Assembly a set of ninety-two resolutions designed to make the authority of an electoral majority supreme. The resolutions demanded an executive council chosen by the Assembly, an elected legislative council, and the approval of civil service appointments and salaries by the Assembly. The resolutions made thinly veiled

Louis-Joseph Papineau, his wife, Julie Bruneau, and their daughter Eliza   (National Archives of Canada/C21005; Antoine Plamandon, National Gallery of Canada/17920)

threats that if Britain did not agree to a figurehead role in running the colony, independence would become the option of the *Canadiens*. While the Assembly passed the resolutions by a vote of fifty-six to twenty-three, seventeen of the nay votes came from Patriotes who refused to embrace the radicalism of their leader. During the Assembly elections that year, the Patriote leadership ensured that none of these moderates—or backsliders as the radicals perceived them—was renominated as a Patriote. The new Assembly, with seventy-eight Patriotes in an elected group of eighty-eight, was adamant in its calls for an end to government by an appointed British colonial clique in the executive and legislative councils.

The Patriotes, while drawing most of their support from the French-speaking population, were not ethnically exclusive. Irish settlers, angry with land speculators, and English-speaking democrats joined their ranks, and in 1834 Dr Edmund O'Callaghan and Dr Wolfred Nelson won election in French-Canadian ridings under the Patriote banner. The party's growing radicalism, however, also prompted the defection of some of its earlier English-speaking supporters. John Neilson, editor of the Quebec *Gazette*, for example, had supported Papineau's party and served as an assembly-man during the period when the party concentrated its attention on defence of traditional Quebec institutions and the British connection. The new emphasis on republican virtues repelled this monarchist.

Lord Matthew Whitworth-Aylmer, the governor from 1830 to 1835, attempted to reduce Assembly influence by selling over 2.1 million hectares to the British American Land Company. This would provide the executive with the revenue it needed to meet the costs of the civil list without requiring Assembly approval. His action appalled Patriote supporters and crystallized the popular view that the government wished to deny ordinary people both land and democracy.

In August 1837, tired of continued obstructionism by the Lower Canadian Assembly, Colonial Secretary Lord John Russell instructed the new Lower Canadian governor, Lord Gosford, via ten resolutions approved by the British Parliament, to appropriate provincial revenue without the authority of the elected Assembly. Russell also rejected calls for an elected legislative council and confirmed the title of the British American Land Company to the lands it had acquired fairly cheaply and was selling at prohibitive prices. In the minds of the major Patriote leaders, there was no longer any possibility of peacefully achieved reforms. Louis-Joseph Papineau became determined to overthrow British rule by a campaign of civil disobedience and economic boycotts leading finally to armed rebellion.

Papineau was an unlikely rebel. After purchasing his father's seigneury in 1817 he had become the lord of the manor to about three hundred people, a number that swelled as a result of both migration and births to 1290 in 1842 and 3289 in 1852. He was not an ideal master. In an analysis of Petite Nation, Papineau's seigneury, Claude Baribeau concludes: "On the one hand, he took part in a feudal type of exploitation that he condemned elsewhere; on the other, he gave to anglophone capitalists the responsibility of exploiting the forestry resources of his seigneury, commercializing agriculture and to an extent proletarianizing his people, activities that he reproached elsewhere as an agrarian, anti-capitalist nationalist."[4] Yet, the contradictions in Papineau's personal life aside, there is little doubt that he spoke for a Lower Canadian majority in rejecting the notion of land as simply capitalist real estate to be bought and sold for whatever price speculators believed it could fetch.

In the 1830s Papineau and the Patriotes organized economic boycotts and petition campaigns to pressure the British government to transfer real power to the French-speaking majority in the assembly. By 1837 an atmosphere of violence pervaded Lower Canadian political life. English-speaking defenders of the government formed paramilitary loyalist associations in 1835 and 1836 in Montreal, Quebec, Trois-Rivières, and the Eastern Townships to defend their own and government property against any disloyal attackers. These associations, such as the Doric Club in Montreal, tried to break up Patriote meetings. The Patriotes responded with the creation of a paramilitary organization of their own, the Fils de la liberté.

In the summer of 1837 Lord Gosford, following Russell's orders, dismissed the Assembly for refusing to vote support for long-term funding of civil servants appointed by the governor. The Patriote central committee responded with a call for a constitutional convention for Lower Canada in December 1837, to be preceded by an economic boycott, large rallies, and petitions. Preparations were also made secretly for an armed uprising. The Patriote women's associations led the boycott movement, organizing women to replace bought clothing with homespun and encouraging co-operative production of goods and the purchase of other goods only from merchants known to be Patriote supporters. The women also made bullets and cartridges.

The government was determined to stop what it regarded as Patriote subversion. A street battle in Montreal between the Doric Club and the Fils de la liberté on 6 November became Gosford's pretext for calling for the assistance of troops from the other British American colonies to suppress the protest movement. Gosford ordered the arrest of Papineau and other Patriote leaders. When Papineau fled to the United States, many of his supporters lost some of their patriotic zeal.

On 23 November a mainly habitant Patriote army under Wolfred Nelson defeated British troops at Saint-Denis on the Richelieu River. Two days later the British defeated another band of Patriotes at Saint-Charles farther south on the Richelieu. They destroyed Saint-Denis on 1 December and two weeks later sacked Saint-Eustache, leaving fifty-eight Patriotes dead and sixty homes burned. Two days afterwards British forces burned and looted the village of Saint-Benôit, and the first rebellion was over. Martial law was declared and Patriote leaders fled south of the border.

Saint-Denis insurgents   (Henri Julien/National Archives of Canada/C18294)

THE BATTLE OF SAINT-CHARLES

Sydney Bellingham was second-in-command of the British forces that suppressed the rebels of the area and provided a first-hand though partisan account of the battle of Saint-Charles.

> Colonel Wetherall's 300 men were soon in battle array. Their appearance, near the battlefield of St. Charles, was greeted by the rebels with bravado and loud cries of defiance. The rebels, about 2 p.m. on the 22nd, commenced the battle by firing at our men.
>
> A timber and mud wall, which was frozen solid, confronted us. It covered the front of St. Charles. Five old cannon were mounted behind the mud wall near the road.
>
> The north side of St. Charles rested on the Richelieu River. The south side rested on a dense wood of heavy timber.

Colonel Wetherall ranged his force about one hundred and fifty yards from the defensive four-foot mud wall, behind which the rebel marksmen sheltered themselves.

Our Artillery tried the range of their gun. The first shot sent a ball through the steeple of the Church of St. Charles.

The five guns of the rebels were contemptible, and inflicted no serious loss. They were almost useless. . . .

After about two hours' fighting, during which the enemy fought bravely, but fired too high, Colonel Wetherall ordered a charge, and it was responded to in true British style. Cheer after cheer arose—then came a rush.

Major Ward hastened from his position at the breastworks, where, several times during the fight, he dyed his trusty sword in the blood of any unfortunate rebel daring to hold his head above the breastworks. By this time his noble charger had several balls in his body, yet he still carried his master. The Major's military frock-coat was so pierced with balls as to make it a cloth riddle. He was at once at the head of a company of the Royals, and led them to a small gate in the breastworks, immediately facing the highway. He rode through it, his brave soldiers following with all speed to face three mounted cannon and two dismounted, but no cannoniers to handle them.

On proceeding to the top of the rising ground, the Major saw a large number of rebels lying on their face and hands, but, on seeing the soldiers, they were instantly on their feet. They received the soldiers with a few bayonets, old muskets, old fowling pieces, pikes, and long poles, and fought with wonderful courage as long as there was hope, but the English bayonets cowed them and made short work of them.

After some of the rebels had fallen, several of their comrades threw down their arms and fled in all directions. The Major did not fire on the fleeing foe. The moment he saw the rebels had given up the fight and were running away, he called a halt of his men.[5]

In the United States a core of exiles led by Robert Nelson organized the Frères Chasseurs and proposed a more militant program to gather popular support for another uprising. It included an end to all seigneurial dues, with lands to be handed freely to the habitants, a promise that alienated

British troops on the march from Fredericton to Quebec, 1837   (Metropolitan Toronto Reference Library/J. Ross Robertson Collection/2238)

Papineau. The rebels entered Lower Canada in November 1838 and gathered about four thousand insurgents, but they were no match for the British troops. Determined to prevent future attempts at rebellion, the British forces went on a rampage of looting and burning of farms and houses in Patriote strongholds in the Montreal area and on the Richelieu. The government also arrested 850 Patriotes; twelve of them were hanged, fifty-eight deported to Australian penal colonies, and two banished. The Australian exiles produced the haunting folksong, *"Un canadien errant,"* which described the pain of banishment and would inspire generations of Quebec nationalists.

The military failure and the absence of revolts in the Quebec district, the Ottawa valley, and the Gaspé have caused some historians to question the extent of support for the rebels. The church, long estranged from the Patriotes, who had become supporters of the separation of church and state and of democracy generally, condemned the rebellions and ordered its flock to be obedient to the British. The strength of British arms along with church authority helped to limit the spread of the rebellions.

Fernand Ouellet observes that the active rebels included 186 professionals (76 notaries, 43 lawyers, and 67 physicians) and 388 mainly small-scale merchants along with 700 to 800 tradesmen and labourers in Montreal and 4000 to 7000 farmers, tradesmen, and labourers in the rural regions close to Montreal. Although he is a critic of the rebels' leaders and program, Ouellet states: "Those actively involved in the events of the rebellions revealed a rancour that was in a sense the voice of the rural masses everywhere; it was not merely personal or restricted to the Montreal region."[6] Others, however, are skeptical of this assessment. The habitants, like the farmers of Upper Canada, wanted economic changes that would limit the depredations of rentiers and speculators. For them, a political struggle between the Assembly and the governor was not worth risking their lives. The same logic prevailed in Upper Canada.

Upper Canada

The Family Compact in Upper Canada resisted growing opposition demands after 1815 for land reforms, secularization of clergy reserves or at least their distribution among all religious denominations, and greater power for the elected Assembly. The oligarchy could count on significant support from British immigrants in Assembly elections against the allegedly pro-American Reformers, and by the 1830s had an uneasy electoral alliance with the Orange order, the Roman Catholic hierarchy, and some moderate reformers. It was a delicate balancing act to court the monarchist but anti-Catholic Orangemen while maintaining the support of Catholics who feared the consequences for a religious minority in the system of majoritarian rule espoused by the Reformers.

The Reformers, for their part, did not achieve the degree of unity characteristic of the Patriotes. Several Reform factions were represented in the Assembly, and by the 1830s their differences were as pronounced as their common objectives. In the 1820s, however, several issues united opponents of the oligarchy in control of the colony. One was a defence of the civil rights of Upper Canada's American-born population. Bishop Strachan and his supporters called into question the property rights of "aliens" and, by inference, the voting rights for American émigrés of the post-Loyalist period. Only British intervention in 1828 settled this issue in the immigrants' favour. The clergy reserves issue also united Reformers, causing conservatives such as Egerton Ryerson, a leader of one of the Methodist churches, to make common cause with more radical figures. But indications in the early 1830s that Britain would move to resolve the reserves question caused Ryerson, who rejected popular democracy in terms similar to those used by the Tories, to break with his former allies.

In the 1830s two poles of reform were to be found in the assembly. One, associated with Dr W.W. Baldwin and his son Robert, called for a continued role for Britain in colonial government but also for a guarantee that the executive council appointed by the lieutenant-governor would have support from a majority in the elected Assembly. Radical Reformers also supported this notion of a cabinet drawn from the majority group, party, or set of parties in the legislature—a notion that later would be termed "responsible government"—but said its achievement would be only a half-measure of reform. Led by William Lyon Mackenzie, Marshall Spring Bidwell, and Dr John Rolph, the radicals opposed the continuation of a legislative council with life-long British appointees that could veto legislative initiatives from the Assembly. They wanted the council, like the Assembly, to be an elected body with the lieutenant-governor reduced to a figurehead. They also wanted many appointed positions in government to be filled by elections. As in Lower Canada, when the Reformers controlled the Upper Canadian Assembly, they refused to vote the civil list provided by the lieutenant-governor except for short periods. The administration demanded that the list be voted for long periods such as the reign of a particular sovereign so that its patronage efforts would not be continuously thwarted by elected Assembly members. Periods when the Reformers held large majorities in the Assembly—1828–30 and 1834–36—witnessed a stalemate between the Compact and the elected members.

With the support of a large percentage of new British immigrants, the governing clique had no need to fear, as it did in Lower Canada, the continuing dominance of the Assembly by reformers. The squabbling Reformers lost their majority in 1830, regained it in 1834, and lost it again in 1836. The win by the Tories in 1836 was controversial. Sir Francis Bond Head, a gentleman-adventurer who became governor in late 1835, was less willing than some of his predecessors to attempt to reconcile the competing claims of Tories and Reformers. Faced with a truculent Assembly in 1836, he dissolved it and called new elections. Head made a mockery of the election. He blackmailed voters who wished their constituencies to receive roads and other government expenditures, and he condoned bullying tactics by Orangemen at the polls and dubious procedures by government-appointed returning officers. Only seventeen Reformers held their seats in the sixty-three-member Assembly, and they were convinced that Head's tactics had deprived them of another majority. There was also great bitterness at Head's simple-minded claim throughout the election that a vote for the Reformers was a vote for annexation to the United States.

Moderate Reformers such as Robert Baldwin, while appalled by Head, believed that they would eventually achieve political change in Upper Canada if they bided their time and continued to apply pressure in London. The radicals were less sanguine. They took particular aim at

Head's announcement of the endowment of fifty-seven Anglican rectories, a decision made but not announced by his predecessor in his last days of office. They also attacked Head's dismissals of government officials with apparent sympathy to the Reform cause. Mackenzie became convinced of the need for a break between Upper Canada and Britain and concluded that this should be achieved by the use of violence if necessary.

A fiery Scot who arrived in York in 1820, Mackenzie had established himself as a newspaper publisher. His *Advocate* became the leading voice of the radicals in the colony, particularly after several younger members of the elite destroyed his printing press in 1826. Although his tirades against the Compact leaders were often intensely personal, his differences with the self-appointed colonial aristocracy were mainly ideological. They regarded themselves as the natural leaders of the colony, men of education and refinement whose ancestry and record of service qualified them to run the colony without interference from elected demagogues in an unruly assembly. Mackenzie, for his part, regarded the Compact as a collection of corrupt, conceited individuals whose public high-mindedness concealed an attachment to the public trough. Against their assertions of the need for a hierarchical society where each person knew his or her place, Mackenzie extolled a society of small farmers and small businessmen of relatively equal wealth and equal opportunities for education. Influenced like Papineau by romanticized notions of what the United States represented, Mackenzie railed against land speculators, special privileges for the Church of England, corporate entities such as the Compact-controlled Bank of Upper Canada, and a myriad of policies that he blamed for the creation of a system of social classes in Upper Canada.

William Lyon Mackenzie   (National Archives of Canada/C1993, detail)

After 1832 Mackenzie and other Reformers had reason to criticize the British government not only for appointing lieutenant-governors who prevented reform but for instituting reactionary policies of their own for the colonies. When Lord Goderich, the colonial secretary, ordered Lieutenant-Governor Sir John Colborne to begin charging all immigrants for land, the reasoning demonstrated Britain's distaste for the egalitarian principles espoused by Mackenzie and his associates. Goderich wrote:

> I know not how to propound in plainer terms than I have already done . . . the necessity that there should be in every society a class of laborers as well as a class of capitalists or land-owners. The high rate of wages and the scarcity of labour is the complaint of every growing Society. To force that condition artificially, by tempting into the class of Landowners those who would naturally remain laborers, appears to me a course opposed to the dearest interests of the Colony . . . because, as I have stated, to the good of every society a supply of Labour and a division of employment must be indispensable.[7]

While new settlers would increasingly be forced to buy land, speculators were able to purchase more land cheaply. In 1826 the government, anxious to have sources of revenue beyond the reach of the Assembly so it could fund the civil list, sold 3.5 million hectares of Crown reserves at a low price to the Canada Land Company, headed by John Galt. Later Galt's company bought another 2.8 million hectares along Lake Huron, the so-called Huron Tract. To the Reformers, already riled by the grants of land to government figures and their supporters, the sale of land to a new group of speculators added insult to injury.

For many British immigrants, however, the prospect of being able to buy land after a few years as farm labourers in the colony did not seem outrageous. In England four thousand landholders owned 60 percent of the land. There were perhaps 60 000 owner-occupiers, 240 000 tenant farmers, and 1.5 million agricultural labourers. Most Irish families eked out a living on less than two and a half hectares of land. In Scotland destitute crofters watched as their former clan leaders, now outright capitalist landowners, pushed them onto tiny infertile plots while saving most land for sheep. While British immigrants may not have liked Upper Canada's class system, it seemed mild compared to what they had known. Few proved willing to resort to arms to achieve greater equality.

By the fall of 1837 Mackenzie believed that an armed uprising would be necessary to bring his vision of a frontier agrarian democracy into being. His newspaper, now called *The Constitution*, presented a constitution for the state of Upper Canada that was modelled on the American constitution. However, the planning for a rebellion, undertaken mainly in the taverns of republican publicans in the Home District, was amateurish and confused. Convinced by his oratory that the government was planning to confiscate their land, many Reformers joined Mackenzie's cause out of sheer desperation. Mackenzie and his confederates hoped to take advantage of the departure of troops from Upper Canada to Lower Canada after the Lower Canadian rebellion erupted, but their plans were foiled.

Problems began when Head learned of an insurgency scheduled for Thursday, 7 December: on that day Mackenzie's forces had planned to seize a large cache of government arms in York. Mackenzie then pushed the rebellion date ahead to the 4th and gathered men at Montgomery's Tavern north of Toronto for the assault on the capital. But when news of the changed date did not reach all the rebels, Mackenzie decided to wait until the 7th after all. The gathering on the 4th, however, tipped off loyalists in the area, and they warned Head. Head had assembled fifteen hundred volunteers and reports of the size of this force caused many of the rebels to abandon Mackenzie. On the fateful Thursday his rag-tag army therefore numbered only about four hundred men.

Word of the Home District rebellion spread to the London District where, as in the Toronto area, American-born settlers proved to be the most willing to take up arms. The news arrived in distorted form. It was believed that Mackenzie and company were in control in the capital. Rumours spread that the London-area oligarchy, aided by the violence-prone Orangemen, were planning to arrest local Reformers. To forestall this event, Dr Charles Duncombe hurriedly organized local Reformers to make a stand, but pro-government volunteers, better armed than their opponents, carried the day.

The rebellion in Upper Canada resulted in 885 arrests, with 422 of them in the Home District, 163 in the London District, 90 in Gore (which included Hamilton, Guelph, Kitchener, and Brantford), and 75 in Midland (which included Kingston). Most of those arrested were established farmers or tradesmen, men neither wealthy nor poor. For their part in the rebellion, two men were hanged: Samuel Lount, a blacksmith, and Peter Matthews, a farmer. While Lount hailed from Pennsylvania, Matthews was a veteran of the War of 1812 on the British side. Another rebel, Colonel A.G.W. Van Egmond, a veteran of the Napoleonic Wars, had settled in the Huron Tract and complained bitterly that the Canada Company provided no services to settlers. Cajoled by Mackenzie to serve as military leader of the rebels, the disillusioned sixty-five-year-old colonel died in his prison cell.

Mackenzie and other rebel leaders fled to the United States. With the help of sympathetic Americans, the exiles formed "Hunters' Lodges" and conducted border raids on Upper Canada in hopes of fomenting a new insurgency. But a combination of British troops, lack of popular enthusiasm, and American unwillingness to alienate Britain by supporting the rebels doomed these efforts at a new rebellion. During 1838 in Upper Canada 156 men were imprisoned, 99 deported, and 18 hanged. At least thirty people were killed in an attack on a militia barracks in Windsor.

•The Struggle for Responsible Government

Traditionally in English-Canadian historical writing, the achievement of "responsible government" in the United Province of Canada in 1848—that is, acceptance of the principle that the cabinet must have and retain the support of the majority in the elected legislative branch—is regarded as a watershed. The principle had been conceded earlier in Nova Scotia and would soon be conceded in the other Atlantic colonies as well. It meant that Britain accepted the right of the colonies to a large degree of internal self-rule and would allow the party system, which had in any case been active in the Canadas before the rebellions, to achieve legitimacy. For many nationalists in Canada East, however, the main political objective was not the achievement of responsible government but the dissolution of the union of Upper and Lower Canada decreed by Britain in 1840.

The forced union of Lower Canada and Upper Canada, along with the granting of responsible government, had been the two main recommendations of the Durham Report of 1839. John George Lambton, Earl of Durham since 1832, was an heir to collieries in Newcastle. Like many British capitalists, he was suspicious of aristocratic landowners who were widely blamed for high food costs that in turn led to high labour costs in factories. The son-in-law of a former British prime minister, Durham was named governor-general of the Canadas in 1838 and asked to prepare a report on the causes of the rebellions and to suggest ways of avoiding recurrences.

Durham was impressed with the moderate Reformers of Upper Canada, who shared his vision of a society organized not on the Compact's principles of rigid social hierarchy but on the basis of the individual's pursuit of profit unhindered by unnecessary monopolies. He blamed the Family Compact for the colony's slow development, accepting the Reformers' view that undeveloped land held for speculative purposes hindered the progress of the colony. Responsible government, Durham felt, would weaken the power of the landholding, office-holding oligarchy and allow market forces to prevail in Upper Canada. To ensure that an elected government in the Canadas would not harm British interests, he recommended that Britain retain control over foreign relations, trade, and the distribution of public lands.

Durham's partial embrace of the Upper Canadian reform perspective, or at least its more moderate version, was not matched by sympathy for Lower Canadian reformers. After spending a mere eight days in Lower Canada, Durham concluded that the rebellion there had been purely ethnic-based. He claimed to have found "two nations warring in the bosom of a single state."[8] Ignoring the conservatism of colonial policy and the extent to which the Patriotes had embraced liberal ideology, Durham blamed Lower Canada's economic problems on the reactionary prejudices of the *Canadiens*. An ethnocentric Englishman, Durham regarded the French Canadians as backwards and priest-ridden. He believed that anything that tended to assimilate them to British Protestant values would be for their benefit as individuals. Indeed, as a supporter of individual liberties he placed no value on the protection of the collective liberties of a subordinate group. From his point of view, an amalgamation of the two Canadas and the granting of official status to only the English language constituted no attack on liberty. Instead it would be a step along the road to material advancement for the *Canadiens*.

Durham's report was followed in 1840 by the Act of Union, which created a shotgun marriage of the two Canadas to form the United Province of Canada—although Durham's call for responsible government was rejected. The governor would continue to name an executive council and a legislative council according to his own perception of which individuals could best be counted upon to reflect British colonial interests. The elected Assembly would continue to be a relatively powerless body. The pre-1837 status quo had been restored, except that where there had been two governors, two executive councils, two legislative councils, and two assemblies, there would now be only one of each.

The union was unpopular in both Canadas. Although Assembly seats were divided equally between the two Canadas, so that Upper Canada would not suffer because of its smaller population, Upper Canadians generally feared French and Catholic domination. Lower Canadians, for their part, were convinced that union was a plot to achieve their assimilation—a goal that Durham had openly recommended. Nonetheless, with the radical agrarians routed by the defeat of the rebellions, moderate reformers in the two Canadas supportive of Durham's vision of a progressive capitalist society joined forces. The Upper Canadian Reformers were led by Robert

Baldwin, a Toronto lawyer, and railway promoter Francis Hincks. In Lower Canada, or Canada East as it was now known, Louis-Hippolyte La Fontaine, a lawyer and former Patriote who had not taken part in the rebellions, was the major proponent of an alliance with Upper Canadian Reformers. He argued that by winning responsible government and ensuring the formation of a progressive administration requiring *Canadien* co-operation, the French culture of Lower Canada could be preserved despite Durham's wishes. Initially regarded as a traitor for proposing these views, La Fontaine failed to win a Lower Canadian riding in the Assembly elections of 1841. Later, once it became clear that Britain would not allow Lower Canada to exist as a separate province, La Fontaine's option began to appear realistic, if not palatable, to his compatriots.

The Reform alliance demonstrated considerable strength in Assembly elections through the 1840s, but the first several governors proved unwilling to grant the degree of colonial autonomy implied in the phrase "responsible government." Lord Sydenham (1840–41), Sir Charles Bagot (1841–43), and Sir Charles Metcalfe (1843–46) attempted, in varying degrees, to retain the former powers of the lieutenant-governors, although Bagot in particular was prepared to go a long way to meet the Reformers' demands for some degree of power sharing.

Metcalfe's successor, Lord Elgin, arrived at a time when British trade and colonial policy were in the process of a significant transformation, most notably in the economic realm, with the abandonment of imperial protectionism in favour of free trade. This alteration in trade policy reflected a fundamental change in attitude towards the white-settler colonies. Britain no longer considered it necessary to control their internal political processes. Elgin became the agent of this new British attitude in the Canadas. After elections held in 1848 returned a large Reform majority in the two sections of the United Canadas, Elgin called upon La Fontaine and Robert Baldwin to form a ministry. The power of patronage, once in the hands of the governor, was handed over to a cabinet that enjoyed a majority in the elected Assembly.

•Responsible Government in Action

The government of La Fontaine and Baldwin, unlike its predecessors in both the pre-union and union periods, could claim to have a mandate from the electors. How faithfully it fulfilled that mandate is debatable. As apostles of economic progress, La Fontaine and Baldwin had supported the undertaking, at taxpayers' expense, of the completion of the St Lawrence canals from 1842 to 1848. In office they showed their eagerness for the state to play a positive role in the transportation revolution. In 1849 they placed the Guarantee Act before the legislature, pledging the government's credit for half the bonds of any railroad over 120 kilometres in length after half the line was built. While the provisions of this act were restricted in 1851 to the three railways then under construction, later guarantees were also given to the Grand Trunk Railway, the most ambitious of the pre-Confederation railway schemes. The boards of the favoured railway companies and the membership of Canadian cabinets in the 1850s bore striking resemblances. Cynics claimed that the unelected cliques who had previously handed themselves free or cheap land had now been replaced by an elected clique who used their offices to support pet railway projects and other industrial and commercial endeavours.

The old oligarchy, believing that it had been abandoned by Britain, was livid. First the trade laws that gave protected markets to Canadian products and encouraged Americans to ship through Canadian ports had been abandoned. Then the political power of the oligarchy had been destroyed. In 1849 Lord Elgin agreed to sign into law a legislative motion called the Rebellion Losses Bill, which provided compensation for Lower Canadians, including rebels, whose property had been damaged in 1837 or 1838 (an earlier bill gave similar compensation to Upper Canadians). This caused the conservative forces to explode in anger. A Tory mob in Montreal attacked the Parliament building, then located in that city, and burned it to the ground. These erstwhile exponents of law, order, and Britishness then called for annexation of the Province of Canada to the United States.

By 1854 the old oligarchy and the upstarts of 1848 found they had more in common than they once believed. Agrarian reformers known as the Clear Grits—a faction including William Lyon Mackenzie, who had been allowed to return from exile—had won several seats in Canada West in 1851. This group denounced the moderate Reformers for their support of big business interests and extolled free trade and inexpensive government. A new Reform alliance gradually emerged around George Brown, editor of the *Globe*, a businessman and land speculator in the Toronto area. Brown embraced the Clear Grits' calls for cheaper government and free trade, but he rejected their anti-business bias. His denunciations of the legislature's attempts to impose publicly supported Catholic schools on Canada West helped him gain a dominant position among English-speaking Reformers by the end of the 1850s.

The emergence of the new Reform coalition in Canada West exposed the Baldwin–Hincks alliance as Tories in disguise. Hincks replaced Baldwin as head of the Canada West half of the coalition government in 1851, but by 1854 Brown's Reformers and Clear Grits held the majority of Canada West seats, with a new group of moderate Conservatives constituting a respectable minority and the Hincksites reduced to a rump. The La Fontaine group, now led by A.N. Morin and E.P. Taché and generally referred to as the *bleus* to distinguish them from the radical reformers, who were labelled the *rouges*, held an overwhelming number of seats in Canada East. But the Hincksites provided too small a group of partners from Canada West to form a stable government.

The *bleus* agreed to join a coalition with the Conservatives led by Allan MacNab. MacNab was a charter member of the old Family Compact and had extensive land, railroad, and other business interests. Referred to as the "laird of Hamilton," he had played an active role in crushing the rebellions in Canada West and he strongly opposed the march towards responsible government. Over time he begrudgingly accepted the need to implement political change. "Railways are my politics," he allegedly responded when asked how he could join forces with his old political enemies. On the whole, economic development was creating new political alliances, and out of these alliances embryonic political parties emerged: the Conservatives wanted the state to help underwrite private economic development, while the Liberals favoured more modest state involve-

Dundurn Castle, Allan MacNab's home   (courtesy of Dundurn Castle, Department of Culture and Recreation, Corporation of City of Hamilton)

ment. Appropriately, the new administration assumed the label Liberal-Conservative.

The Conservatives of the 1840s and 1850s consisted partly of the old Compact politicians. They also included other strong supporters of the British tie, people who after the granting of responsible government were difficult to distinguish from the Baldwin-Hincks group of Reformers. They, too, were involved in the new manufacturing firms, railways, and insurance companies that began to spring up in the 1840s and 1850s in Canada West. A rising star in their ranks after his election to the Assembly for the constituency of Kingston in 1844 was John A. Macdonald, a young lawyer-businessman. In 1857 Macdonald replaced MacNab as the leader from Canada West in the governing Liberal-Conservative coalition.

Macdonald's opposite number was George-Étienne Cartier, a former Patriote turned wealthy lawyer whose corporate links typified the dramatic change from feudal to capitalist connections among the leading French-Canadian politicians. Historians Brian Young and John A. Dickinson note: "As a lawyer, his corporate clients included the government of France, the Seminary of Montreal, the Grand Trunk Railway, and various mining, railway and insurance companies. He supplemented his law and political income with property investments that returned substantial rents. By the 1860s he was investing his surplus capital in banks and, to a lesser extent, industrial stocks."[9]

George-Étienne Cartier   (National Archives of Canada/C2728)

Industrial capitalists and their lawyers in Canada East were predominantly English-speaking, and the French-speaking element of this group formed a miniscule proportion of the Quebec population. Their dominance in Canada East politics was the result of the shrewd informal alliance their leaders made with the hierarchy of the Catholic Church. The *bleus* militantly defended church control of both Catholic education in the United Province of Canada and social services, marriage, and the family life of Catholics in Canada East. In return the clergy thundered against the *rouges* and other political opponents of the *bleus* who defended separation of church and state. According to the church, these misfits were nothing more than supporters of the anti-Christ. For Cartier, the leading *bleu*, the alliance with Quebec's dour clergymen appears to have been opportunistic. While as a politician he stressed the need to confirm the church's right to govern the moral lives of its adherents, he did not submit his own private life to church control—he had an opulent lifestyle and lived common-law with his wife's cousin. The church, in turn, was pleased with Cartier's political services and did not intrude upon his private affairs.

The *rouges* were the spiritual heirs of the radicals of 1837 and 1838. Supporters of free trade and of a property-owning democracy, they joined the Reformers of Canada West in attacking the governing coalition's decisions that granted government monies to special interests. The *rouges* favoured low taxes and complete separation of church and state, including an end to public support of church-controlled schools. Strongest in Montreal, the *rouges* had important allies in the *violettes*, based in Quebec City. The *violettes* were moderate liberals who shared the *rouges'* economic policies but trod gently on issues involving the church. The church's resurgence in the countryside in the period after the rebellions limited Reform penetration outside the cities, and the combined strength of the *rouges* and *violettes*, while impressive in vote totals, was not enough to prevent the *bleus* from winning the lion's share of the seats in Canada East in the pre-Confederation period.

•Education and the Changing Political Order

One area in which the role of the state changed significantly in the mid-nineteenth century was education. Before the 1840s, only a minority of children had formal schooling. The state had no control over the curriculum and had no right to tell parents how their children should be educated. In the era of responsible government, education became the focus of public debate and political action. With literacy increasingly a factor in economic development, the state assumed greater control over who should be educated and what they should learn.

From the earliest days of European settlement, the elite made an effort to see that their children received formal instruction. They either sent their children, at considerable cost, to private schools or hired tutors for home instruction. By the nineteenth century, locally run classical colleges, such as the Collège de Montreal, and grammar schools, such as Upper Canada College in Toronto, provided education for the sons of the elite. The curriculum in these institutions included Greek, Latin, and rhetoric, the "basics" for the professions of theology, law, and medicine. Although Upper Canada's grammar schools received state subsidies, they served only a tiny minority of the population. In 1839 there were only 300 pupils enrolled in grammar schools in a colony that had over 200 000 people under the age of sixteen. A further 14 776 Upper Canadian children attended common schools, which were sustained with the help of grants from the state.

Both Tories and Reformers favoured the expansion of the common school system, but they differed on how public education should be financed. Conservatives called for a special property tax to fund education while liberals favoured using the proceeds from the sale of clergy reserves, which, after 1840 were divided among the various denominations with the Church of England receiving a disproportionate share. In Lower Canada the Roman Catholic Church struggled to retain control over education, but it was hampered in its efforts to expand educational facilities by a lack of funds.

Politics also played a role in the way higher education developed in the United Canadas. As in the Atlantic region, the Church of England attempted to establish a university—King's College—under its exclusive control. This plan, associated in Upper Canada with Bishop John Strachan, was roundly attacked by other denominations, which insisted upon establishing their own colleges and upon having access to any public monies made available for higher education. In the 1840s, the Methodists established Victoria College in Coburg and the Church of Scotland founded Queen's College in Kingston. As early as 1843, Robert Baldwin introduced a University Bill, which would transform the Anglican-controlled King's College into a non-sectarian arts college known as the University of Toronto, with which other denominational colleges might affiliate. Baldwin finally saw his bill passed in 1849. According to historian J.M.S. Careless, "it represented an entire victory for the forces of secularization and centralism in Upper Canada higher education."[10] Contrary to Baldwin's wishes, denominationalism survived in the affiliated colleges of the University of Toronto and reasserted itself later in the century when Queen's went its separate way and the Baptists established McMaster University. In Canada East, linguistic and religious differences were responsible for the emergence of three universities: Université Laval in Quebec City, McGill University in Montreal, and Bishops University in the Eastern Townships.

A SCHOOL LESSON IN THE 1840s

Every Boy's Own Book, a school text in use in Canada West in the 1840s, provides clues about the particular social values that educational authorities hoped children would absorb. The text attempted to convey to young people definite views about monarchy, imperialism, patriarchy, and democracy.

> "Great Britain—a power to which Rome in the height of her glory is not to be compared, which had dotted the whole earth with her possessions and military posts—whose morning drum follows the Sun, and keeping company with his beams, circles the globe daily with one continuous and unbroken strain of the martial airs of England."—Daniel Webster.

> LESSON 1ST.

> Adam, the first King, as well as the first man, was the father of his own subjects, and when the eldest son succeeded to his father's authority, he succeeded also to his title of father, and hence the style of father is given to this day to all Kings, which points remarkably to the origin of Government, or Kingship, in the time of man's innocency in Eden, which God first instituted there, both in nature and by positive command. And therefore we owe to our Sovereign the same obedience, which Adam's children or subjects paid to him, for God's commands and institutions descend through all ages to the end of time, and Government is of the same

necessity and obligation now, as it was when it was first imposed by God, and it is equally "his ordinance" now, as it was then.

If Government and its succession was ordained by God himself,—then it is as natural that it should succeed in the same track as for the sun to proceed in his diurnal course.

There are but three kinds of Government. When the sovereign power is vested in one person it is called a Monarchy: if in all the nobles it is called an Aristocracy, or an Oligarchy if confined to a few of these: if an assembly of the people have the chief authority, it is called a Democracy or a Republic.*

Of all the different species of Governments, the Monarchical is the most ancient and natural, originating at first in parental authority, hence Kings are called the fathers of their people.

The Assyrian and Egyptian Monarchies are the most ancient that we read of, but, there are several Kings mentioned in the Scriptures, in the early history of the Patriarch Abraham. The Jews were governed by God himself 'till Sauls' [sic] time, from whence it has been called a Theocracy— taken from the Greek word signifying GOD. After his elevation to the Throne of Israel by Gods' [sic] appointment, the Government continued Monarchical till the destruction of the temple.

Democracy on the other hand, is that form of Government, which irrespective of the obligation of law and custom, places the present will of the populace above all restraint, and of course leaves the general weal entirely at the mercy of that, which is more fickle and capricious, than the winds of heaven.

The ancient Lacedamonian Republic was likewise provided with hereditary Monarchs, who reigned in a direct line for 700 years.[11]

* Note. In strictness of language, a great difference exists between a Republic and a Democracy. Properly speaking, the term Republic, is more justly applicable to Great Britain than to any other nation on earth, for although it may be objected, that one of its pillars is Monarchy, yet it is very evident, that the whole tendency and practice of the British system is Republican, that is impartially respective of the general good.

King Street East, Toronto, 1835   (Metropolitan Toronto Reference Library/J. Ross
Robertson Collection/T10248)

•Conclusion

The rebellions of the 1830s can be explained in several ways: as class struggles, ethnic struggles, and ideological conflicts. The rebellions pitted social
classes against one another and had economic roots in the complaints of
farmers, labourers, and the landless against the entrenched oligarchies of
Upper and Lower Canada. In Lower Canada the class struggle had an ethnic character, because most of the elite were of British descent and most of
the rebels of French descent. But the prominent presence of English
speakers on the rebel side and French speakers on the government side
suggests the need for caution in employing an ethnic explanation for the
Lower Canadian rebellions. The importance of middle-class leadership in
the rebellions of both provinces, as well as the role of the prominent
seigneur Papineau in Lower Canada, suggests that explanations stressing
only the oppression of the majority may partly miss the mark. Elements of
the middle class and even of the wealthy who were excluded from the privileges bestowed by the ruling oligarchy had their own interests in changing
the political system.

Although material interests motivated the various actors in the rebellion drama, ideas were also important. The rebels were influenced by both

the example of American democracy and British notions of parliamentary rule; the ruling elites followed the model of British society in which social classes were rigidly stratified and order and stability went hand in hand.

By the late 1840s parliamentary democracy had been established in the Canadas, but it did not live up to expectations held by radicals in the 1830s. While most radical theorists believed in a society of virtually equal property-holders whose political representatives would fight against privileges for the few, the legislature of the 1850s was dominated by wealthy capitalists and lawyers, tiny groups within the general population—the people with the time and money to spend in Parliament. Yet the need to win election guaranteed that they could not operate as the oligarchies before 1837 did. They might use their positions in the legislature to aid their own business projects, but they also had to be attentive to voter concerns. Measures such as greater state aid to schools and the abolition of clergy reserves and the seigneurial system in 1854, while serving the interests of a nascent capitalism, were also attempts to respond to popular grievances. The rebels of the 1830s might regard the legislature of the 1850s as a travesty of the democratic ideal, but they could rightly be proud that they had forced Britain to take an important step in granting popular control over government.

•Social Mobility in Canada West:
A Historiographical Debate

The old American stock and the early British settlers in "the bush" had created a rural economy and society of farm and market town into which the new-comers were soon incorporated and became, with the sons of pioneers, fresh assault troops in carrying the frontier of blazed forest trail and squared field on squared field back towards the granite shoulders of the Shield and westward across the Ontario peninsula towards the waters of Huron, Champlain's Freshwater Sea. Upper Canada in the 1840's entered on a surge of growth which made it by 1850 a wealthy, a populous and a British province.[12]

This optimistic view of mid-nineteenth-century Canada West, presented in a Canadian history textbook in 1969, is widely disputed. Subsequent research suggests that social mobility both in towns and rural areas was limited and that only newcomers of certain ethnic groups were "incorporated."

Historian Judith Fingard's studies of the poor in British North American cities before 1860, including the cities of Canada West, suggest that the urban labouring classes were caught in a poverty trap: "If the cold climate produced the nineteenth-century myth of ruggedness, independence, and self-reliance, it was a myth in which the urban poor played no part and from which they drew no inspiration."[13] The exhaustive studies of mid-century Hamilton by urban sociologist/historian Michael Katz confirm this analysis. Katz, writing in 1969, estimated that about 40 percent of the city's population were poor and about 20 percent well-to-do. Life for the poor was "a constant struggle for existence that offered only a slim chance of advancement into the relatively small middle ranks of society."[14] Although some of Katz's early work paid close attention to those middle ranks, by 1982 he had concluded that mid-century urban British North America was best understood using a two-class model: capital and labour. The entry of labour into the ranks of capital was restricted not only by lack of capital but also by discrimination on the basis of ethnicity within the society, which tended to lock out the Irish and Catholics.[15]

Some historians believe this view of a rigidly stratified urban society applies better to the late nineteenth century than to mid-century. In a labour history text, for example, Desmond Morton and Terry Copp maintain that the lack of an organized labour movement at mid-century owed much to a frontier mentality that suggested to a working man: "If he were not an independent farmer, businessman, or craftsman, he should either be on the way to become one or he was a failure. If he had missed the opportunities offered by the new country, a worker must accept his fate with a decent servility."[16] But historian David Gagan notes that it was precisely the lack of "decent servility" on the part of the urban poor that caused the middle class to promote programs of social reform meant to "minimise the potential for social disorder."[17]

Rural studies do suggest that although settlers needed some capital to begin farming in Canada West at mid-century, many immigrants were still able to establish themselves on farms. Some of those who became successful farmers in the province were Irish Catholics, notes historian Donald Akenson, who suggests that over-emphasis on the Irish element among the urban poor disguises the fact that most Irish immigrants became farmers.[18] But according to historian David Gagan, there was little new land to be settled after the early 1850s. In Peel County, which Gagan has studied closely, "The assimilation of new farm families into the economy . . . was possible only through the death or displacement of established farmers, or the subdivision of existing farms."[19] Instead of subdividing land, prosperous farmers attempted to expand their holdings, reducing the total number of farms and farmers in the county. This process, although it moved quickly in the 1860s, was only in its early stages in the 1850s.

The debate on social mobility lacks a sufficient data base to indicate clearly what percentage of the population was experiencing either a climb or a descent on the socio-economic ladder. As David Gagan states, perhaps exaggerating the point: "We know virtually nothing about the nature of wealth and the process of acquiring and keeping it and, hence, about the nature and extent of social mobility in nineteenth century Canada."[20]

•Notes

[1] Montreal Gazette, 10 November 1824, rprt. in *The Workingman in the Nineteenth Century*, ed. Michael S. Cross. (Toronto: Oxford University Press, 1974), 17.

[2] Quoted in Denis Monière, *Ideologies in Quebec: The Historical Development* (Toronto: University of Toronto Press, 1981), 79.

[3] S.F. Wise, "Sermon Literature and Canadian Intellectual History," *The Bulletin*, Committee on Archives, United Church of Canada (1965): 14.

[4] Translated from Claude Baribeau, *La Seigneurie de la Petite-Nation 1801–1859: Le rôle économique et social du seigneur* (Hull, PQ: Éditions Asticou, 1983), 112.

[5] Sydney Bellingham, *Some Personal Recollections of the Rebellion of 1837 in Canada* (1901, rprt. Toronto: Canadiana House, 1970), 17–18.

[6] Fernand Ouellet, *Lower Canada 1791–1840: Social Change and Nationalism* (Toronto: McClelland and Stewart, 1980), 340.

[7] Quoted in Leo Johnson, "Land Policy, Population Growth and Social Structure in the Home District, 1793-1851," *Ontario History* 63, 1 (March 1971): 57–58.

[8] *Lord Durham's Report: An Abridgement of Report on the Affairs of British North America*, ed. Gerald M. Craig (Toronto: McClelland and Stewart, 1963), 23.

[9] Brian Young and John A. Dickinson, *A Short History of Quebec: A Socio-Economic Perspective* (Toronto: Copp Clark Pitman, 1988), 121.

[10] J.M.S. Careless, *The Union of the Canadas: The Growth of Canadian Institutions, 1841–1857* (Toronto: McClelland and Stewart, 1967), 123.

[11] From John George Bridges, *The Every Boy's Own Book, or a Digest of the British Constitution, Compiled and Arranged for the Use of Schools and Private Families* (Ottawa, 1842), rprt. in *Family School and Society in Nineteenth-Century Canada*, ed. Alison L. Prentice and Susan E. Houston (Toronto: Oxford University Press, l975), 23–24.

[12] W.L. Morton, *The Kingdom of Canada: A General History from Earliest Times*, 2nd ed. (Toronto: McClelland and Stewart, 1969), 262–63.

[13] Judith Fingard, "The Winter's Tale: The Seasonal Contours of Pre-Industrial Poverty in British North America, 1815–1860," in Canadian Historical Association, *Historical Papers* (Ottawa: 1974), 86.

[14] Michael B. Katz, "Social Structure in Hamilton, Ontario," in *Nineteenth-Century Cities: Essays in the New Urban History*, ed. Stephan Thernstrom and Richard Sennett (New Haven, CT: Yale University Press, 1969), 240.

[15] Michael Katz, Michael Doucet, and Mark J. Stern, *The Social Organization of Early Industrial Capitalism* (Cambridge, MA: Harvard University Press, 1982), ch. 1, 2.

[16] Desmond Morton and Terry Copp, *Working People* (Ottawa: Deneau and Greenberg, 1980), 4.

[17] David P. Gagan, "Class and Society in Victorian English Canada: An Historiographical Reassessment," *British Journal of Canadian Studies* 4, 1 (1989): 78.

[18] Donald Harman Akenson, *The Irish in Ontario: A Study in Rural History* (Montreal and Kingston: McGill-Queen's University Press, 1984).

[19] David Gagan, *Hopeful Travellers: Families, Land, and Social Change in Mid-Victorian Peel County, Canada West* (Toronto: University of Toronto Press, 1981), 42.

[20] Gagan, "Class and Society in Victorian English Canada," 75.

•Selected Reading

See also Selected Reading for chapter 9.

The causes of the war of 1812 are assessed in Harry L. Coles, *The War of 1812* (Chicago: University of Chicago Press, 1965). Military aspects of the war are dealt with both in Coles and G.F.G. Stanley, *The War of 1812: Land Operations* (Toronto: Macmillan, 1983). A two-volume popular history of the war is Pierre Berton, *The Invasion of Canada, 1812–1813* and *Flames Across the Border, 1813–1814* (Toronto: McClelland and Stewart, 1980; 1984).

On Upper Canadian politics, Gerald Craig's *Upper Canada: The Formative Years* (Toronto: McClelland and Stewart, 1963) is informative but conservative. The rebel view is presented forcefully in Stanley Ryerson, *Unequal Union: Confederation and the Roots of Conflict in the Canadas, 1815–1873*, 2nd ed. (Toronto: Progress Books, 1983). The ideological battles of the period are discussed in David Mills, *The Idea of Loyalty in Upper Canada 1784–1850* (Montreal: McGill-Queen's University Press, 1988); and Jane Errington, *The Lion, the Eagle and Upper Canada: A Developing Colonial Ideology* (Montreal: McGill-Queen's University Press, 1987). Their impact on "loyalist" literature is evaluated in Dennis Duffy, *Gardens, Covenants, Exiles: Loyalism in the Literature of Upper Canada/Ontario* (Toronto: University of Toronto Press, 1982).

Events leading to the rebellions of 1837 and 1838 and the conduct of the rebellions are outlined in Colin Read and Ronald J. Stagg, eds., *The Rebellion of 1837 in Upper*

Canada: A Collection of Documents (Toronto: Champlain Society, 1985); and Colin Read, *The Rising in Western Upper Canada, 1837–38* (Toronto: University of Toronto Press, 1982).

The causes and character of educational changes are treated somewhat differently in Susan Houston and Alison Prentice, *Schooling and Scholars in Nineteenth Century Ontario* (Toronto: University of Toronto Press, 1988); and Bruce Curtis, *Building the Educational State: Canada West, 1836–1871* (London, ON: Althouse, 1988).

For Lower Canada, the causes of the 1837–38 rebellions are explored in Jean-Paul Bernard, *Les rébellions de 1837–1838* (Montreal: Boréal Express, 1983), and in the works by Ouellet and Creighton cited in chapter 9. Ryerson, *Unequal Union*, provides a more favourable treatment of the nationalists. Ouellet's *Louis-Joseph Papineau: A Divided Soul* (Ottawa: Canadian Historical Association, 1964) provides a brief biography of the key Patriote. Events of the rebellions are outlined in Elinor Kyte Senior, *Redcoats and Patriotes: the Rebellions in Lower Canada* (Montreal: McGill-Queen's University Press, 1981).

The politics of the 1840s and 1850s are discussed in J.M.S. Careless, *The Union of the Canadas: The Growth of Canadian Institutions 1841–1857* (Toronto: McClelland and Stewart, 1967); and Jacques Monet, *The Last Cannon Shot: A Study of French-Canadian Nationalism 1837–1850* (Toronto: University of Toronto Press, 1969). Monet's positive assessment of the post-rebellion political elite contrasts with Brian Young's critical evaluation of a key member, *George Étienne Cartier: Montreal Bourgeois* (Montreal: McGill-Queen's University Press, 1981). A continuing rebel tradition is discussed in Jean-Paul Bernard, *Les Rouges: libéralisme, nationalisme et anticléricalisme au milieu du X1Xe siècle* (Montreal: Les Presses de l'Université du Québec, 1971). On Lord Durham, see Janet Ajzenstat, *The Political Thought of Lord Durham* (Montreal: McGill-Queen's University Press, 1988).

CHAPTER 11

THE WEST, 1763–1850s

In 1830 Governor George Simpson of the Hudson's Bay Company brought his British bride to live at Red River. Simpson had been chief administrator for the HBC on the frontier of British North America since the early 1820s. Like other fur traders, he had initially found it expedient to develop relationships with mixed-blood women. In 1829 he had gone back to England and found a wife. Now, as the couple settled into married life, it became clear that the Simpson household, a centre of activity in the pioneer community, no longer welcomed fur traders' non-white wives—in fact the Simpsons treated them with disdain.

In Rupert's Land, over time, it was becoming increasingly common for fur company officers to marry women of European origin who came from the Canadas or abroad. These women, following a behavioural pattern common to upper-class Victorian women who went to live in non-white colonies in the age of British imperialism, tended to adopt an air of superiority over the local women, who were hard-working, strong, and brash rather than ladylike in the prescribed Victorian manner.

This new pattern marked a distinct change in marriage practices, a change symbolizing the wider transformation that had occurred in the European–Native partnership within the western fur trade. Initially the fur traders, dependent on Native knowledge and skills, gladly married Native women, who knew the country and participated in the trade alongside their new husbands. For the white fur trader a liaison with a Native woman had the additional advantage of cementing a relationship with a Native community. The traders depended on firm relationships for a continuing supply of furs and provisions. But as time passed a new generation of fur traders made the female offspring of these European–Native alliances their preferred choices as wives; or, if at all possible, they married white women.

Underlying this transition was a new attitude towards Native people. As the traders became more confident of their ability to dictate the terms of trade with Indians and Métis, their positive views of Native people gradually gave way to increasingly racist attitudes. The arrival in Western Canada of white settlers who were not involved in the fur trade and who saw Native peoples as competitors for resources hardened that racism.

Once partners in a great commercial enterprise, the first nations were increasingly marginalized and their lands threatened with conquest. Beginning around 1763 there was a gradual but continuous growth in European occupation of the western territories from the Great Lakes to the Pacific coast. Changes in the fur trade and its extension to new areas were responsible for much of this growth before the 1850s. Eventually, agricultural settlement and, on the Pacific coast, mining would displace the fur trade's economic importance and pose new challenges to Native people.

When British railway interests purchased a controlling interest in the Hudson's Bay Company in 1863, the event signified the end of an era for a region that, in European eyes, had become part of British North America a hundred years earlier with the conquest of Quebec. In the 1760s, Native peoples had undisputed rule over British Columbia and the Northwest. A century later they had neither undisputed control over the region nor even a large degree of manoeuvrability in their dealings with the Europeans.

• HBC–NWC Rivalry and Native People

In the winter of 1783–84, in response to the new aggressiveness on the part of the rival Hudson's Bay Company, the leading Anglo-American traders in the western territories pooled their resources with the Montreal merchants who marketed their furs abroad. Together they formed the North West Company to supply trade goods to "wintering partners"—the leaders of the trade in the interior—as well as market the furs shipped from the trading posts to Montreal. The main Montreal partners, Benjamin and Joseph Frobisher and Simon McTavish, held more shares than did the "wintering partners." In the years that followed, the western fur trade would make fortunes for these and other Montreal businessmen—fortunes invested in land, the timber trade, and other ventures in Lower Canada.

The new company's main advantages over the Hudson's Bay Company were its experienced French-Canadian voyageurs, its Native-style birchbark canoes, and its wintering partners. In a short time, however, the HBC had built and put into operation large numbers of York boats, flat-bottomed vessels made of spruce and rowed by eight men with long oars. The experienced boatmen hired for the purpose were found mainly in the Orkney Isles north of the Scottish coast. To match the wintering partners of the "Nor'Westers," the HBC placed its posts in the hands of inland masters. Although these traders, unlike the wintering Nor'Westers, did not initially share in profits, they were permanently stationed in the interior. The two rival companies, pitting London against Montreal capital, continuously expanded their operations until they finally merged in 1821 to deal with declines in markets, fur supplies, and profits.

For Native peoples it mattered little whether their furs went to London or Montreal merchants. Their goal remained the receipt of as many high-quality goods as possible for their furs at a conveniently located post. During the period of HBC–NWC competition, this goal was often met. Economic advantages as well as aggressive attempts by the companies to enlist new groups of Natives to their respective sides drew an ever-expanding number of nations into the trade. Although they depended upon the Natives as trappers and providers of local food, and lived in proximity to them and often married Native women, most traders were sufficiently Protestant in outlook to decry the "want of industry" among the Natives. They tended to champion a work ethic and materialist ethos that suggested Native life would be ennobled and enriched by involvement in the fur trade. Any other viewpoint, of course, would have deprived the trade of its main work force.

THE IMPACT OF THE FUR TRADE ON NATIVES: A TRADER'S VIEW

In 1774 Samuel Hearne, a former officer in the Royal Navy, was placed in charge of Cumberland House, a post set up by the Hudson's Bay Company to compete with the Montreal traders for customers among the first nations. He had proved his mettle by surviving in the Canadian interior and dealing on a friendly basis with the aboriginals during a 1900-kilometre journey in 1771–72 that led him as far as the Arctic Ocean. His description of the Chipewyan in the early 1770s reflects the views of a trader who admired the Indians and had few illusions about the impact of the fur trade on Native society:

> The real wants of these people are few, and easily supplied; a hatchet, an ice-chisel, a file, and a knife, are all that is required to enable them, with a little industry, to procure a comfortable livelihood, and those who endeavour to possess

more, are always the most unhappy, and may, in fact, be said to be only slaves and carriers to the rest, whose ambition never leads them to anything beyond the means of procuring food and clothing. It is true, the carriers pride themselves much on the respect which is shown to them at the Factory; to obtain which they frequently run great risques of being starved to death in their way thither and back; and all they can possibly get for the furrs they procure after a year's toil, seldom amounts to more than is sufficient to yield a bare subsistence, and a few furrs for the ensuing year's market; while those whom they call indolent and mean-spirited live generally in a state of plenty, without trouble or risque; and consequently must be the most happy, and, in truth, the most independent also. It must be allowed that they are by far the greatest philosophers, as they never give themselves the trouble to acquire what they can do well enough without. The deer they kill, furnishes them with food, and a variety of warm and comfortable clothing, either with or without the hair, according as the seasons require; and it must be very hard indeed, if they cannot get furrs enough in the course of two or three years, to purchase a hatchet, and such other edge-tools as are necessary for their purpose. Indeed, those who take no concern at all about procuring furrs, have generally an opportunity of providing themselves with all their real wants from their more industrious countrymen, in exchange for provisions, and ready-dressed skins for clothing.

It is undoubtedly the duty of every one of the company's servants [employees] to encourage a spirit of industry among the natives, and to use every means in their power to induce them to procure furrs and other commodities for trade, by assuring them of a ready purchase and good payment for every thing they bring to the Factory; and I can truly say that this has ever been the grand object of my intention. But I must at the same time confess, that such conduct is by no means for the real benefit of the poor Indians; it being well known that those who have the least intercourse with the Factories, are by far the happiest. As their whole aim is to procure a comfortable subsistence, they take the most prudent methods to accomplish it, and by always following the lead of the deer, are seldom exposed to the gripping hand of famine, so frequently felt by those who are called the annual traders.[1]

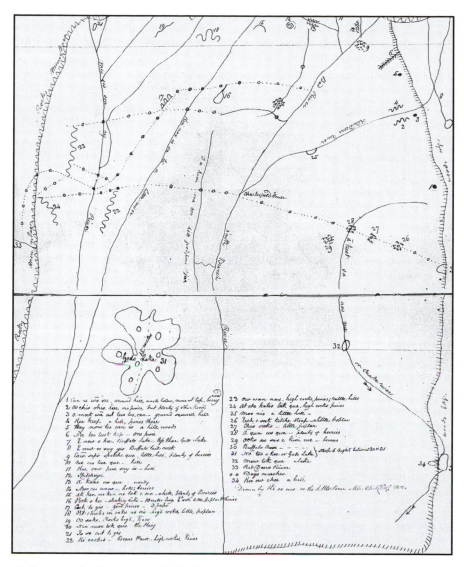

Indian map by Ki oo cus, or Little Bear, a Blackfoot chief, 1802, showing the Missouri and South Saskatchewan rivers   (Hudson's Bay Company Archives/Provincial Archives of Manitoba/N4346)

The impact of the early trade varied from nation to nation and region to region. The Ojibwa of what is now northwestern Ontario, for example, had experienced a cycle that would be repeated for many tribes on the parklands and plains of the Northwest in the era of the HBC's monopoly. In the late eighteenth century the Ojibwa were indispensable to the traders north and west of Lake Superior not only as trappers but also as guides to the many superficially similar rivers of the area, as providers of venison, and as labourers on the supply boats. They were able to command good prices for their furs and to influence the location of the companies' posts. Continuing as ever to hunt big game and to provide themselves with most of the necessities of life, the Ojibwa valued the fur trade for the firearms and metal utensils that made their lives easier. But from 1804 onwards there were reports that beaver were becoming scarce in the region trapped by the Ojibwa. In the 1810s it became clear that big game in the area was also disappearing.

Reports of death from starvation and rumours of cannibalism under-lined the gravity of the situation. With few furs to sell and food supplies low, it was necessary to spend more time and to travel further in search of game, an ironic circumstance considering that European goods had once been attractive because they reduced the amount of work necessary for survival. Overtrapping and overhunting had jeopardized Ojibwa independence. Many of them moved west to areas where they could continue to hunt and trap, while those who remained behind were increasingly dependent upon the fur trade companies to tide them over until they could manage to feed themselves. Debt also trapped many of them; they could not afford snow-shoes and proper footwear for the increasingly long and less remunerative journeys to hunt and trap, but if they did not carry out these activities they could not pay existing debts. Although their communities maintained co-operative patterns and traditional religious customs, there were signs of cul-tural erosion. The young who were reared in poverty often showed little respect for elders, whom they saw as poor providers.

Some of the Ojibwa adapted to the new circumstances by turning to the cultivation of corn and potatoes, both for subsistence and for exchange with the fur traders. At Lake of the Woods and Red Lake, substantial Native gardens had been established by the 1820s. Agriculture had not been prac-tised in the western interior in the early fur trade period, and it was not the traders but the Ottawa nation moving westward with the trade who intro-duced it into the region. But growing food provided a livelihood only for a minority of the aboriginal population; most Natives continued to rely on hunting, fishing, and trapping even as local resources diminished. They tended to see agriculture as at best a supplementary source of food and income.

The experience of the Blackfoot was different from that of the Ojibwa. About 1730 the Blackfoot had come into indirect contact with the European presence when they received their first horses from the Shoshoni, another western plains nation, and firearms and iron from the

INDIAN AGRICULTURE IN THE NORTHWEST

While archaeological research suggests that agriculture was practised in the Northwest as far north as today's Lockport, Manitoba, in the pre-contact period, it had ceased during the early fur-trading period, probably because corn, tobacco, and other cultivated products had become available through trade. Trade goods received from the Europeans in exchange for furs were, in turn, traded with agricultural nations further south, including the Mandan, Hidatsa, and Arikara of the upper Missouri River region. As the availability of both fur-bearing animals and game declined in areas under Ojibwa control, many Native peoples tried to adapt to the new circumstances by taking up agriculture. The Ottawa resident on the Red River in the village of Netley Creek reintroduced agriculture to the Northwest in 1805 after receiving seed from trader Alexander Henry. They planted Indian corn, potatoes, and other crops. In turn the Ottawa taught the Ojibwa, migrants from parklands areas with no farming tradition, how to plant corn. Initially the HBC and the NWC discouraged Indians from planting crops, fearing it would diminish their participation in the fur trade. Later, as game became more scarce in the region, it was accepted that Native farmers could contribute to the traders' food requirements. Agriculture spread among the Ojibwa despite the early lack of enthusiasm on the part of fur traders. South of Lake Manitoba corn was the major crop; north of the lake it was potatoes. While no group gave up the hunt and became completely sedentary, for the Ojibwa agricultural sites often became the centre of ceremonial gatherings. A description by HBC trader William Brown in 1819 indicates the impact of agriculture on Ojibwa life, including the gender division of labour:

> A considerable number of the Indians particularly those of Fort Dauphin, and the Manitoba, have ground under cultivation, and raise a great many Potatoes, but that is their only crop. . . . Those of the Manitoba . . . [cultivate] on an Island towards the North end of the Lake, they have erected there what they call a Big Tent, where they all assemble in spring, hold Councils and go thro' their Religious Ceremonies—The soil here is excellent and each family has a portion of it under cultivation, which the women and old men remain, and take care of during the summer—while the young men go a hunting—In the fall of the year when they are going to abandon

the place, they secure that part of the produce, under ground till spring, which they cannot carry along with them—During favourable years, they generally make a considerable quantity of maple sugar, part of which they also put in Cache—The Big Tent is constructed in the form of an arch, and consists of a slight frame of wood covered on the outside with the bark of the pine tree, and lined in the inside with bulrush mats. It is 60 ft. long—15 ft. wide—and 10 ft. high.[2]

There was commercial corn production in the region between Lake Superior and Lake of the Woods, where big game supplies had dwindled dramatically, leaving both Natives and traders with a diminished food supply. The Ottawa were innovators in this region, as they had been on the Red River. In 1812 they began growing crops on Garden Island, their first agricultural site in the Lake of the Woods area, and by 1819 the women were growing corn, potatoes, pumpkins, onions, and carrots. Ojibwa agricultural sites soon followed.

Later, in the period of rapid European settlement beginning in the 1850s, missionaries believed that turning the Native peoples towards agriculture could speed up their process of becoming "civilized" and "Christianized." Ironically, agriculture in the early nineteenth century had proved a means by which the Ojibwa and Ottawa of the Northwest retained their culture in the face of threats to their independence resulting from a declining resource base.

Cree and Assiniboine. At the time the Blackfoot lived on the northern plains of Saskatchewan, but their new weapons and a fortuitous outbreak of smallpox among the Shoshoni allowed them to expand south and west and eventually to dominate southern Alberta as well as Montana. As the Peigan, followed by the Blood and Blackfoot, pushed west to the foothills of the Rockies, the Shoshoni and Kutenai were forced across the mountains.

Anthony Henday, sent inland in 1754 by the HBC to induce the more remote tribes to come to York Factory on Hudson Bay to trade, encountered the Blood, one of the groups that made up the Blackfoot Confederacy. They made clear their disinterest in journeying from their territory to trade in furs. Their livelihood, they noted, was the buffalo hunt, and their territorial expansion was focussed on areas where buffalo were plentiful. In 1787 David Thompson was sent by the HBC to persuade the Blackfoot to bring furs to company posts on the South Saskatchewan River, but he met with the same response. In the 1790s the Blackfoot apparently had a change

Indians hunting buffalo   (Peter Rindisbacker/National Archives of Canada/C114467)

of heart. As the HBC and NWC built posts on the northern fringe of Blackfoot country, this once aloof nation began to bring wolf and fox skins to trading posts, although they still refused to trap beaver. The major item in Blackfoot trade with the Europeans quickly became pemmican, a mixture of dried buffalo and berries that became the mainstay of officers and employees at fur trade posts as other game became less plentiful.

The Blackfoot, unlike the Ojibwa, did not become dependent on the Europeans during the fur-trading period because the large number of buffalo in their territory continued to provide them with self-sufficiency in food, clothing, and much else besides. They were not interested in either the Europeans' food or, for a long period, clothing—the women in particular refused to respond to the traders' blandishments to purchase their woollens—so the Blackfoot traded for guns, powder, awls, iron, beads, tobacco, and liquor.

To some extent the trade was profitable for the Blackfoot. It allowed them to expand their territory, increase the size of their tipis and buffalo corrals, and generally to prosper. But their self-sufficient economy was slowly transformed into an increasingly commercial one, and tendencies towards inequality dating from the pre-contact period were reinforced. The traders from the two companies, wooing the Blackfoot tipi by tipi, encouraged a degree of individualism that eroded the unity of the tribes. At the same time the scale of warfare increased dramatically, with the result that the relative balance in numbers of men and women evident at the time of David Thompson's 1787 visit gave way in two generations to a three-to-one preponderance of women over men. While the men who survived were often able to marry four or even eight wives and live in huge tipis, the women were not as fortunate. A sorority of wives had characterized polygamy in an earlier period when most men had one or two wives, but that tendency broke down in cases where there was an extended number of wives, because wives beyond a third or fourth were regarded almost as slaves. They were usually excluded from the sun dance and otherwise discriminated against.

Still, by the 1820s the Blackfoot remained in control of their destiny and regarded the fur trade as beneficial. Other tribes of the parklands and plains, unlike the Ojibwa of Northern Ontario, felt the same way. The major groups in this area, apart from the Blackfoot, were Cree, Ojibwa, and Assiniboine, many of them immigrants during the fur-trade period. All had experienced a degree of cultural change after moving onto the plains, mainly through the adoption of a number of the beliefs and rituals of the original plains nations. The sun dance, for example, was adopted by all the new residents of the northern plains. While missionaries settled among these nations and attempted to convert them to Christianity, the Natives were as yet under little compulsion to accept beliefs and practices that they found unconvincing. For one Native group, however, the question of cultural identity was inevitably complicated. This was the Métis, whose heritage was both Indian and European.

Blackfoot camp   (Provincial Archives of Alberta/E. Brown Collection/A284)

•The Birth of the Métis Nation

The term Métis theoretically refers to "mixed-blood" people, that is, people whose known ancestral heritage is a mixture of European and Native Indian. In practice, only a fraction of mixed-blood individuals ever identified themselves as Métis. During the French regime intermarriage between white men involved in the fur trade and Indian women was so common that one demographer suggests that as many as 40 percent of French-Canadians in Quebec today have at least one Indian ancestor. Children of part-Native descent who integrated into Quebec society did not develop a sense of being part of a separate nation, nor did the offspring of trader–Indian liaisons who rejoined the tribes of their mothers. The term Métis, then, is probably most usefully applied to persons who were members of mixed-blood communities and whose sense of corporate identity was with other mixed-bloods rather than with a particular Indian or European group. Before the end of the French regime, sizable Métis communities had sprung up in the territory of the upper Great Lakes, and more such communities developed in the area of the modern-day Prairie provinces during the years that followed. The large number of mixed-bloods and their treatment by the traders reveal a great deal about the contradictory attitudes of both the fur trade companies and their employees to Native peoples. Métis anxieties about their status led to a violent clash with the first European agricultural settlers on the Prairies. It was a reaction to the beginnings of settlement by outsiders in their territory that created a sufficient degree of corporate identity for the Métis of the Red River valley to speak of themselves as the "Métis nation."

Liaisons between fur traders and Native women were frowned upon by the Catholic Church and forbidden by the HBC. The church could have little impact upon young men who lived much of their lives in Indian country, but the HBC was somewhat more successful in restraining its employees—at least until competition from the North West Company forced it to relax its regulation that only officers of posts could have sexual relations with Indian women. This was an enforceable policy while the HBC restricted its operations to a small number of forts along Hudson Bay, but it later became a detriment in attracting employees to winter at inland posts.

Native society approved of marriages between its women and European traders, because such unions were consistent with pre-contact practices in which intertribal marriages cemented trade and military relationships between groups. Both in the French regime and afterwards, the traders often proved fickle marriage partners. When it came time to retire they would abandon long-term relationships that had produced many children. In the French period most of the abandoned Native wives and their children were reintegrated into their former communities. Later, as it became common both for the traders and first nations to move frequently, Native women could no longer easily return home, and many of them and their children became dependent upon the fur trade posts for their survival.

As the numbers of mixed-blood women increased, they became the preferred marriage partners for white fur traders. Meanwhile, the Métis men played a special role in the plans of the two fur trade companies. For the most part the sons of British employees, whether officers or clerks, were hired as labourers at the posts. The French-speaking Métis, who had started their own settlements, were valued as providers of pemmican, as boatmen, and as guides. Significantly, all the jobs reserved for Métis were low in status and low-paying. Even the Métis sons of officers or partners were blocked from advancement in both rival companies before 1821 and in the new HBC monopoly afterwards.

The Métis communities developed cultural patterns that set them apart from both Indian and Euro-Canadian culture. The offspring of the French developed their own language, Michif, which combined French and the plains Cree language in almost equal quantities. English-speaking Métis also developed their own language, Bungi, a combination of Cree with the Scots dialect of the Orkneys. The dances of the Métis combined the intricate footwork of aboriginals with Scottish and French forms, including reels and jigs. In the Red River area Métis travelled in carts with

Red River Cart   (National Archives of Canada/C61689)

"dished" wheels—saucer-shaped—to avoid getting stuck in the Prairie mud. The carts were made entirely of wood, the parts bound together by wet rawhide that shrank after drying and proved particularly sturdy. The Métis women, maintaining the leather-work skills of their aboriginal ancestors, used beads rather than porcupine quills to decorate the coats, belts, and moccasins they produced. Later the women of the plains nations also adopted this practice.

• The Founding of the Red River Settlement

Although the Métis played a crucial role in the life of the two rival fur trade companies, they were not consulted by the HBC when it established the Red River settlement near present-day Winnipeg in 1812. Lord Selkirk, a Scottish landowner and peer in the British House of Lords, regarded with concern the fate of Scots Highlanders turfed off their land by his fellow landowners who wanted land for sheep enclosures. He also had sympathy for impoverished Irishmen whose revolt against British rule in 1798 had been bloodily suppressed. In 1808 and 1809 Selkirk and a group of associates purchased a third of the HBC's shares and used their voting power within the company to promote an agricultural settlement in the Red River valley. Selkirk's partner, Andrew Colvile, argued that the settlement could help provision the western fur trade, reducing the costs associated with getting supplies from Britain.

That settlement began modestly in 1812 with thirty-five people, whose numbers were reduced by scurvy the first winter. Although the settlers were able to survive with the help of local Saulteaux (Ojibwa), their early attempts at farming were disastrous. They did not begin to sow viable crops until the late 1820s.

While the experienced HBC fur traders viewed Selkirk's settlement derisively, the Nor'Westers suspected that it was a ploy to create a strategic outpost that could disrupt their company's river links between Montreal and the interior. The Métis, with several large settlements in the area, also believed that the Red River colony threatened their future, and NWC traders encouraged them in this view. As it turned out, the actions of the colony's governor, Miles Macdonnell, suggested that the Nor'Wester and Métis paranoia was justified. With poor crops and more settlers arriving annually, the fledgling colony was dependent on pemmican supplies for its survival. So in January 1814 Macdonnell issued a proclamation against the export of pemmican from the vast region known as Assiniboia that had been placed under his control as a potential area of settlement. This proclamation threatened the NWC's supplies and confirmed fears about the real purposes of the colony. It was also a blow to the Métis, who were the main producers and exporters of pemmican.

The Métis had another reason to dislike Macdonnell. Emulating the plains nations, the Métis hunted the buffalo by running them on horse-back, a practice that was gradually driving the animals away from the lower Red River. Wanting to avoid a situation in which the colony would depend on Indians and Métis for provisions, Macdonnell issued a proclamation in July 1814 forbidding the running of buffalo. This confirmed the Métis view that the settlement would not recognize their rights in the region.

The NWC encouraged the Métis to respond belligerently to these provocations. Nor'Wester Duncan Cameron named three prominent Métis "captains" and in 1816 made one of them, Cuthbert Grant, "Captain-General of the Métis." The militia led by these captains solidified the sense of corporate identity among the Métis of the Prairies.

In 1815 the NWC's intrigues forced Macdonnell to leave the settle-ment, which was then besieged by Métis attackers. His interim replace-ment, Peter Fidler, a long-time fur trader and father to a large Métis family, capitulated to Métis demands to disband the colony, but the colonists had only been gone a few months before they returned under new leadership and with reinforcements. Governor Robert Semple, like his predecessor, was insensitive to Métis interests and belligerent towards the NWC. He rein-stated the pemmican ban and, to make it last, ordered the seizure of Fort Gibraltar, the NWC's post in the Red River area, in March 1816. In retalia-tion, the Métis under Grant seized pemmican from HBC posts on the Qu'Appelle River to provision the Nor'Westers on Lake Winnipeg. On their way to the Nor'Westers, Grant's Métis militia was surprised by Semple and a group of armed colonists at a place called Seven Oaks. Semple, mis-judging the numbers under Grant's direction, demanded that the Métis disarm. In the ensuing confrontation Semple and twenty of his men were killed; on Grant's side, there were only two casualties. Lord Selkirk, deter-mined to punish the Métis as well as the Nor'Westers, whom he blamed for the Métis aggressiveness, hired Swiss mercenaries to improve the colony's defences and had Grant and other Métis leaders charged with murder and forced to appear before Canadian courts. None was convicted. Selkirk's actions against several NWC officials were similarly unsuccessful.

The court rulings confirmed the finding of a British-appointed com-mission that no premeditated Métis massacre of Selkirk settlers had occurred at Seven Oaks. William Bachelor Coltman, the principal commis-sioner, concluded in his report that the Selkirk party had fired the first shot. While Coltman believed that the Métis had subsequently killed wounded men rather than taking prisoners, he suggested that the heavy casualties of the HBC men were the result of their "standing together in a crowd, unaccustomed to the use, of fire-arms, or any of the practices of irregular warfare" while they faced "excellent marksmen, advantageously posted in superior numbers around their opponents."[3]

The conclusions of Coltman and the courts did not prevent most Manitoba historians from treating the Seven Oaks incident as a massacre. The discrediting of the Métis formed part of the narrative of the conquest of "savagery" by "civilization" and could be used to mask the reality of dispossession of Native lands.

The merger of the HBC and NWC in 1821 resulted in massive layoffs as rival posts in the interior were merged. The Selkirk settlement, where a poor crop record, floods, and locusts were driving away many settlers, received a much-needed boost from the arrival of many of these discharged employees. Henceforth large numbers of retired HBC men, usually the fathers of Métis families, would choose to spend their declining years with their families as farmers in the Red River settlement. The strengthening of the settlement was only one of the far-reaching consequences for Western Canada of the amalgamation of the two rival fur-trading companies.

• The Fur-Trade Monopoly Period, 1821–49

The establishment of a nominal monopoly in the fur trade of Rupert's Land—nominal because of the illegal competition from American traders within the HBC's territory—allowed the HBC to streamline its operations, institute conservation measures, and rewrite the terms of trade with the Native peoples. The impact on the various Native groups of the new power of the European traders in their midst varied according to their degree of dependence upon the fur trade.

The new company followed an NWC practice, belatedly introduced in the pre-merger HBC as well, of making field officers partners in the company. Under the new system, the company divided 40 percent of its profits among twenty-five chief factors and twenty-eight chief traders, with the factors receiving twice as much as the traders. The factors supervised trade districts, while the traders supervised large posts. These men were at the top of a status-and-pay hierarchy within a company that attempted to control all aspects of the lives of its servants. From 1821 to 1833, chief factors earned average profits of £800 a year while traders received £400 a year.

Clerks, just below field officers in the hierarchy, earned £100 a year, although many of them were in charge of posts and expeditions. Apprentice clerks kept the posts' accounts and earned half the salary of full clerks. A variety of *engagés* were next to the bottom of the hierarchy and held posts that included postmaster, interpreter, voyageur, and labourer. At the very bottom were apprentice labourers. Although Métis held an increasing number of company jobs, none was ever named chief factor or trader and few were ever given the position of clerk. All employees of the company were expected to attend church, deal with the Indians in a prescribed manner,

---

LIFE AT A FUR-TRADING POST

Both the Hudson's Bay Company hierarchy and its concessions to frontier realities were evident in Fort Edmonton. The fort, built in 1795 on the North Saskatchewan River near today's Edmonton and originally named Fort Augustus, was an HBC response to Fort George, a nearby post built by the NWC in 1792. After the merger of the two companies, Fort Edmonton became the headquarters for the fur trade of the western prairies. The large two-storey residence where the chief factor lived, with its spacious dining and entertainment areas, provided a marked contrast both to the crowded and cold ramshackle huts where the labourers bunked and the Native tents set up outside the fort's walls.

Each fall, when the fur brigade arrived from York Factory with trade goods, the "Big House" of the chief factor became the scene of an all-night party with dancing and free rum for everyone at the post. Meanwhile, the Natives were kept outside of the fort, its gates locked. When the time came to take care of business, the Natives were allowed to enter, and during an all-day ceremony that followed Native traditions of trade, gifts were exchanged and the peace pipe passed around. Only on the next day could the real trading begin.

After celebrating the completion of their journey from Hudson Bay to the main regional fort, the company employees set off on horseback and by boat to take supplies to the smaller posts in the area. During the winter these men hunted buffalo, moose, and deer while their Native wives prepared snowshoes, shirts, and pemmican for the brigades that would leave in May to carry furs to York Factory. In the spring, voyageurs brought furs from other posts to be inspected at Fort Edmonton and loaded onto boats along with the furs received by Fort Edmonton's traders. During the summer, employees who were not part of the brigade hunted or joined the women in planting crops and tending livestock.

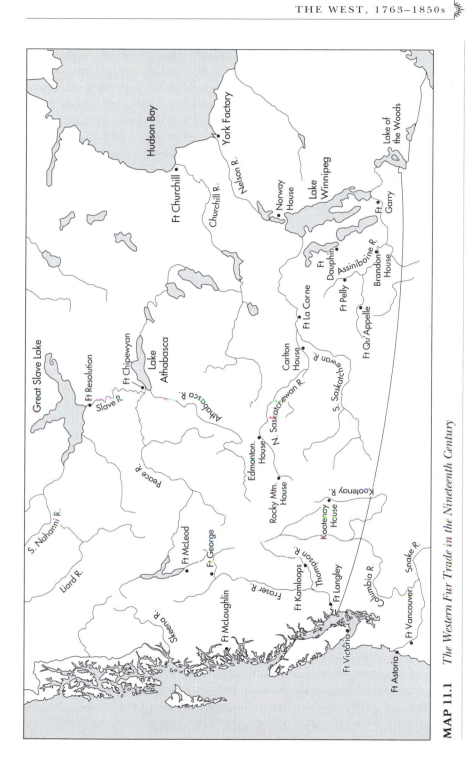

MAP 11.1 *The Western Fur Trade in the Nineteenth Century*

avoid drunkenness and adultery, and submit their letters to responsible officials for censorship before sending them.

In charge of company operations in Western Canada for most of the monopoly period was George Simpson, one of two field governors from 1822 to 1826 and sole governor-in-chief of all HBC territories in North America from 1826 to 1860. Although his authority could be counter-manded by the governor and board of the company in London, Simpson in practice made company policy in the field. An annual council meeting of all chief factors and traders assisted him in his work, but Simpson ran the council and set his stamp upon company operations in Rupert's Land. Born in Scotland, Simpson had little prior involvement with the trade when Andrew Colvile used his connections to put his friend in charge of the Northern Department of Rupert's Land one year after Simpson had joined the company. He headed the austerity campaign that reduced the HBC's full-time staff from 1983 in 1821 to 827 in 1825; and those workers remaining in the company's employment had their wages cut.

Monopoly and the Indians

Simpson implemented a policy of substantially reducing the goods exchanged with the Indians for beaver pelts. In doing so, however, he rec-ognized that the company's ability to impose its will on the Native peoples was directly proportional to the degree of dependence of specific Native groups on the company. In 1822, after having visited the posts within his district and hearing Indian complaints about lowered prices, he described the situation for Andrew Colvile:

> Their immediate wants have been fully supplied, but of course the scenes of extravagance are at an end, and it will be a work of time to reconcile them to the new order of things. I have made it my study to examine the nature and character of the Indians and however repug-nant it may be to our feelings, I am convinced they must be ruled with a rod of iron, to bring, and keep them in a proper state of subordina-tion, and the most certain way to effect this is by letting them feel their dependence upon us. In the Woods and Northern barren grounds this measure ought to be pursued rigidly next year if they do not improve, and no credit, not so much as a load of ammunition given them until they exhibit an inclination to renew their habits of industry. In the plains however this system will not do, as they can live independent of us, and by withholding ammunition, tobacco and spirits, the staple arti-cles of trade, for one year they will recover the use of their Bows and spears and lose sight of their smoking and Drinking habits; it will there-

fore be necessary to bring those Tribes round by mild and cautious measures which may soon be effected.[4]

The Ojibwa in the area north of the Great Lakes were particularly affected by the new toughness of the monopoly fur trader. The company implemented conservation policies in the area to try and increase the supplies of beaver. Outposts with low volumes of trade were abandoned; steel traps, which made trapping easier, were proscribed; and quotas on pelts were imposed at the very moment when the price of trade goods was rising. With game in the region already scarce, the Indians found their dependence on the company heightened at the same time that the company appeared to want their services less and at a cheaper rate. Many Ojibwa, like many Cree and Assiniboine from the northern parklands, simply moved to the plains where, as Simpson observed, the company felt obliged to remain more magnanimous.

Yet increasing population pressures soon reduced the number of beaver and buffalo on the plains and resulted in conservation measures and higher prices for trade goods in that region as well. As Arthur Ray observes:

> In spite of the fact that necessity for cooperation prevented any deliberate attempts to destroy the Indians and their cultures by hostile actions, their traditional life ways were transformed nonetheless. The fur trade favoured economic specialization. . . . Ultimately, the resource bases upon which these specialized economies developed were destroyed due to over-exploitation. Significantly for Western Canada, this occurred before extensive European settlement began.[5]

Tragically, the Indians of the West faced not only growing dependence on the Europeans but the continued scourge of European diseases. From 1818 to 1820 whooping cough and measles cut a huge swath through Native populations on the plains. Smallpox in 1837–38 proved even more devastating, wiping out, for example, six thousand of the nine thousand members of the Assiniboine nation.

Overexploitation of resources during the fur trade period assumed non-Native demand, but it also required Native willingness and ability to supply. In the case of the buffalo, the Blackfoot, with their growing emphasis on commercial values, gladly filled all orders for pemmican given them by the HBC. From the 1830s they also took advantage of the growing American market for buffalo robes and in the 1840s for buffalo tongues. The buffalo still roamed in the millions in Blackfoot country, and few people in the area suspected that the buffalo hunt in Blackfoot country would sustain only one more generation.

Monopoly and the Métis

An expansion of the buffalo hunt also characterized the Métis settlements within and near the Red River settlement. While 500 Métis participated in the hunt in 1820, 1210 participated in 1840, and twenty years later 2690 Métis reportedly took part. The buffalo hunt contributed to Métis self-identity. Various rules for the hunt—from a prohibition against the running of buffalo on Sunday to a requirement to wait for the assigned command before running the buffalo—were enforced by threats of public censure of offenders. Like the Indians, the Métis seemed able to maintain order through community pressure without resort to formal legal mechanisms.

European influences upon the Métis during this period were almost as strong as Indian ones. Beginning in 1818, Catholic missionaries arrived in Red River, led by Bishop Joseph-Norbert Provencher, and Protestant ministers, particularly Anglicans, soon followed. The Church of England persuaded many English-speaking Métis to practise full-time farming and set up schools to educate their children. Yet many educated English-speaking Métis, who had accepted the church's attempts to assimilate them to Euro-Canadian culture, were frustrated when it became clear that the HBC had no intention of discarding racial barriers in its hiring policy.

Many French-speaking Métis began to farm on river lots. Generally, however, they remained more aloof from the HBC than their English-speaking counterparts. As company orders for pemmican and furs fell along with the prices for these products, many Métis, particularly French-speaking ones, began to do business with American traders in direct violation of the HBC rule that only the company could act as a buyer of furs or pemmican within its claimed territories. In 1849 the company charged a Métis trader named Pierre-Guillaume Sayer with infringing the company's trade monopoly by selling furs to American traders. Some two hundred armed and furious Métis milled menacingly outside the courthouse as Sayer's trial proceeded. The jury, aware of what was going on outside, found Sayer guilty but recommended mercy on the grounds that he truly believed he had the right to sell furs freely. The HBC then avoided a possible confrontation by dropping charges. The crowd outside was jubilant: the company monopoly had been broken and trade was now free. It would prove a pyrrhic victory, because both the fur-bearing animals and the buffalo declined drastically over the next thirty years.

The history of the Métis community in the monopoly period was intertwined with the history of the Red River colony, which had developed slowly following the debacle of Seven Oaks. Locusts, drought, and floods took turns and sometimes combined to ruin crops from 1812 to 1826, causing many settlers to leave. Good crops from 1827 to 1835 offered encouragement, but they were followed by several more poor years. Attempts by George Simpson to diversify the colony's economy through an experimental farm, a buffalo-wool company, and the cultivation of hemp and flax all fizzled. Nonetheless, by 1850 the colony's population was estimated at five thousand. A majority were Métis; most non-Métis were retired company servants.

Relations among the various groups in the colony were strained by religious, linguistic, and racial divisions. White English-speakers tended to be the most prosperous group and more likely to be included by the HBC in political decision-making. When the free-trade movement of the Métis began to gain strength in the late 1840s, many English-speaking Métis pulled away from the movement after it was denounced by the Anglican clergy as an Oblate plot to increase papal power in Assiniboia. Still, English- and French-speaking Métis managed to co-operate in the buffalo hunt, and intermarriages occurred between the two groups.

Initially, membership in the Council of Assiniboia, which served as the governing authority within Rupert's Land, was restricted to former company officers, that is, chief factors and traders, all of them of British or Anglo-Canadian origin. That year Cuthbert Grant was named to the council. In 1828 Grant had become "Warden of the Plains" for the company he had once fought, charged with preventing the illicit trade of furs in Assiniboia. He was also the founder of Grantown (now Saint-François Xavier), a Métis settlement of several hundred families along the Assiniboine River. Grant's enforcement of the HBC's monopoly did not make him popular among the Métis.

The French-speaking Métis developed a strong sense of "national-ism," a sense of being a distinctive community. Their language and religion separated them from the Indians, while their Indian heritage separated them from the French. Although their economic activities parallelled those of the English-speaking Métis, many of the English speakers desperately sought respectability in European eyes; the French-speaking Métis largely sought autonomy. Their sense of community was enhanced not only by the Sayer victory but also by successful battles with the Sioux to the south for control of major hunting grounds.

Among the English-speaking group, racism was becoming more apparent in daily life. The refusal of upper-class white women to associate with the Métis and Indian women was a major symptom of the racial antag-onism rampant in the colony. Court cases of the period testify to a harden-ing of social divisions. In 1850 Mrs Ballenden, Métis wife of the officer in charge of Upper Fort Garry, sued members of the elite for defamatory con-spiracy. Charging that these men and women, including judges, sheriffs, clergymen, and doctors, had falsely spread word that she was an adulteress, Mrs Ballenden convinced a jury to award her a substantial sum for damage to her reputation.

The English-speaking colonists were bitterly divided throughout the trial, largely along Métis–white lines, with clergymen and their wives being particularly strident in their denunciations of Mrs Ballenden and her supporters. That same year Adam Thom, recorder of Rupert's Land and Assiniboia, who was being sued for failure to pay a bill, objected to French-speaking jurors, including bilingual ones, hearing his case, claiming that they would not understand the nuances of British law. Thom had been editor of the francophobic *Montreal Herald* in the 1830s and brought his anti-French, anti-Catholic views with him when he came to Red River in 1839. Asked by the HBC to prepare a legal code for the colony, he later acted as a judge and refused to allow the use of French in his court.

By 1850 the Red River colony was showing signs of becoming a tension-ridden outpost of empire rather than simply a fur traders' retirement home. The same kind of evolution was evident in another infant settlement in western British North America—Victoria on Vancouver Island. Its establishment marked the beginning of changes to come in the area west of the Rockies.

•British Columbia: The European Phase
Coastal Trade

In 1778, when Captain James Cook surveyed the northwest coast and landed on what is now Vancouver Island, he recorded the first European observations of life among the coastal Pacific aboriginals. He was repulsed by what he regarded as the filthiness of the Nuu'chah'nulth—or Nootka, as the Englishman mistakenly called them. He was also puzzled by the elaborate rituals that seemed to govern every activity, including trade, and intrigued by the large, extended-family cedar homes that made up the villages. Nevertheless, Cook's arrival among these people quickly led to a rush for fur trade wealth, with sea-otter pelts as the main prize. British, French, Spanish, and American traders participated in the exchange of goods—usually iron tools—for pelts collected by the Nuu'chah'nulth and other coastal peoples, including the Haida of the Queen Charlotte Islands area. The trade soon narrowed down to the Americans (the "Boston men") and the British ("King George men").

Generally relations between the traders and the coastal nations were courteous. The Natives were hard bargainers who were not dependent on European goods and refused to trade except on their own terms. Like the woodland and parkland nations in the late eighteenth century and the plains

Nuu'chah'nulth village drawn by John Webber during Captain Cook's 1778 voyage
(John Webber/National Archives of Canada/C6641)

nations well beyond that time, the coastal Natives held the upper hand in the transactions. The maritime trade and the new trade goods it brought into their territories did not appear to have an adverse effect on their institutions; on the contrary, labour-saving devices and metal tools gave the original peoples more time and scope to develop their much-cherished crafts, such as the making of totem poles and face masks. The end result was an enhancement of the existing culture rather than an adaptation to the culture of the traders. Indeed, the shipbound traders made no attempt to impose cultural change upon the Indians—their only interest was in acquiring pelts. By the late 1820s, however, sea otters were rare and the maritime trade was starting to wind down. The Nuu'chah'nulth appear to have adjusted poorly to the changed circumstances, but the Haida, anxious to maintain the flow of European goods into their villages, began to cultivate potatoes to sell to mainland Natives and later to the HBC at Fort Simpson. They also successfully found markets for their wood and argillite carvings and cedar canoes.

Inland Trade

While the coastal trade declined, the trade in the British Columbia interior was expanding. The first trader to reach this region was Alexander Mackenzie of the North West Company. The NWC was at a disadvantage in supplying its posts because, unlike the HBC, which could deliver supplies by ships to its posts on Hudson and James Bay in the heart of the continent, the Nor'Westers relied on long and expensive overland journeys. Mackenzie, hoping to find a river link between the northern posts and the Pacific, made two voyages, one in 1789 and one in 1793, in search of the elusive route. On the second voyage he arrived in what is now British Columbia.

As beaver in the western interior became more scarce, the Nor'Westers began to seriously pursue the idea of trading in the British Columbia interior. The first steps were made with the explorations of David Thompson and Simon Fraser, who, aided by the Natives of the region, provided the NWC with critical knowledge of the area's river system. Fraser established posts across the Rockies during a journey from 1806 to 1808, and Thompson descended the Columbia to its mouth in 1811, discovering that it offered a satisfactory connection to the coast. Within the central interior of British Columbia, called New Caledonia by the fur traders, posts such as Fort Fraser, Fort St James, and Fort George became year-round homes to some Nor'Westers. Like their counterparts further east, most of these men formed liaisons with Native women. Although some of them abandoned their Native families when they left the posts, many did remain and retired with their families to Red River or, after its founding in 1843, Fort Victoria.

After the merger of the NWC and the HBC, the company increased the number of posts in the British Columbia interior and also established coastal posts that formed part of the land-based trade. In 1834 Fort Simpson was established on the northern Pacific coast near today's city of Prince Rupert. The local Tsimshian people were so anxious to participate in the trade that all nine of their villages on the lower Skeena River moved to the vicinity of the fort.

In the land trade, as in the maritime trade, the fur-company men made no attempt to alter Native cultures, and the Native interest in the trade lay in the possibilities for enriching their own cultures rather than in adopting foreign ways. But European diseases limited the extent to which the coastal nations could control their own destiny. A smallpox epidemic had spread to many communities as early as the brief period of trade with the Spanish in the 1770s. In 1835 and 1836 another smallpox epidemic ravaged the coast, and during that same decade influenza also decimated many villages. According to some estimates, the Native population of the Pacific coast between what is now Alaska and Oregon declined from about 50 000 to 13 000 in the period 1835–43. While the population appeared to recover swiftly, to about double that number by the early 1860s, another smallpox epidemic in that decade wiped out many communities. The

Haida village of Skiddegate   (Provincial Archives of British Columbia/HP33784)

Haida, whose cultural florescence during the maritime trade had been a positive example of how the first nations could control the process of change in their interaction with Europeans, failed to master European bacilli. From a population of six thousand in 1835 the Haida count fell to only eight hundred persons in 1885.

So many deaths interfered with the coastal Natives' elaborate kinship-based social relations. Everyone in these societies had titles and positions, rights and responsibilities, which were marked out from birth. But the inheritance of rights and titles presumed that most people remained alive long enough to claim their inherited honours. Inevitably, with so many heirs in their graves, new claimants for their titles and property appeared, and a stratification system that had developed over a long period gave way to turmoil. There was a large increase in the number of potlatches as contenders for honours tried to establish the legitimacy of their claims.

Yet the resource base of most of the coastal nations remained intact, and the fur trade itself, because it brought a comparatively small number of outsiders to their region, did not produce as significant a breakdown of Native society as would be seen in the subsequent settlement period. Before the 1840s the HBC had no intention of settling the region. Urged on by George Simpson, the HBC sought to create a coastal fur trade empire from Alaska to Oregon. Such an empire could only survive if European settlement stayed away. Simpson's imperial goal produced conflicts in British–American and British–Russian relations. The Russians were mollified in 1825 when the British agreed that all territory north of "54 40" would belong to their country. But the southward push continued until the Oregon Treaty of 1846 established the current boundary between the United States and Canada along the 49th parallel. By that time the HBC had established total control of the fur trade in the "Oregon territory" (today's states of Washington and Oregon), mainly by overtrapping the region south of the Columbia.

Sir George Simpson and Sir James Douglas (William Notman/National Archives of Canada/C44702 and PA611930)

The Oregon treaty was signed two years after James K. Polk had successfully contested the American presidency on the belligerent pledge, "Fifty-four Forty or Fight"—a promise, in short, to win for the United States the entire coastal region south of Russian-held territory. Polk proved willing to compromise the American claims, however, and Britain's corresponding willingness to compromise indicated that there were clear limits to the power of the fur trade monopoly to dictate imperial politics.

The Close of the Fur Trade Era

The British government had long viewed the HBC as a guarantor of imperial control over the Northwest and the Pacific Coast. But the rapid rate of settlement in the American west in the 1840s and 1850s raised concerns that the thinly populated fur trade empire of the HBC would eventually be seized by the Americans. Furthermore, a vocal minority in Canada West was promoting the idea of westward expansion. For these expansionists, the HBC and its fur trade were an anachronism. The "primitive" Indian territories, they argued, must inexorably give way to the progress of "civilization." Under such conditions British authorities began to question both the fur trade and the company that had become synonymous with that industry in British North America.

British fears regarding the fur-trading territories centred initially on Vancouver Island. In January 1848 shipping magnate Samuel Cunard alerted the Admiralty that action must be taken to protect Vancouver Island coal from the Americans. The British government was receptive to this argument, and it soon came to the view that an agriculturally based colony must be established on the island to shore up British control in the area. While the HBC field governor George Simpson argued that colonization and the fur trade did not mix, he was overruled by the London governor of the HBC, John Henry Pelly. Pelly indicated to the government that the HBC was willing to colonize Vancouver Island and extract its coal.

The company sent instructions on to James Douglas, the chief factor at Fort Victoria, founded in 1843 partly as a retirement home for west-coast traders and their Native families. Douglas was directed to purchase Indian land on Vancouver Island. Under British laws of rights of possession of territory, Indian land was deemed to include only places where permanent structures had been built and land placed under cultivation, so the treaties negotiated with the Native peoples on Vancouver Island excluded most of the fishing and hunting territories that provided them with their livelihood. Douglas, a veteran HBC employee and head of a large Métis family, encouraged the Indians to become farmers—a radical move, because the company had not previously interfered with the way of life of the Natives.

He also welcomed missionaries who would convert and re-educate the Indians, and he began to employ the Indians as coal miners. About eight hundred Native miners, mainly Kwagiulth (Kwakiutl), worked the coal deposits of Fort Rupert, where mining started in 1849 (and proved unsuccessful). They continued to work when Scottish miners, imported by the HBC, struck for better pay and food. When a mine at Nanaimo began operations in 1852, Native men and women were hired to haul coal to the harbour. The women carried the coal by canoe to ships, which were headed for the most part to San Francisco. Native people, once lords of the fur trade, were becoming wage labourers.

Britain gave the HBC a ten-year lease of Vancouver Island in 1849 but named a governor for the colony and required that the HBC recruit permanent settlers of British descent within five years or forfeit its lease. Land sales were to be used to finance roads, churches, schools, and other necessary services. The first governor, Richard Blanshard, a British lawyer, quit after nine months in the position, charging obstruction by the HBC hierarchy. James Douglas, the top man in that hierarchy on the island, was named the second governor in 1851 and was not asked to relinquish his company position. Although he established schools, roads, and a courthouse, Douglas opposed democratic institutions, believing that only a small number of men in any society were fit to rule. Instructed by Britain in 1856 to have an assembly elected, Douglas subverted this request by setting a stiff property qualification for voting and holding office, a move that restricted political participation to a fraction of the population. Meanwhile the HBC continued to run the mainland as it saw fit.

In 1858 reports of company discoveries of gold on the shores of the Fraser and Thompson rivers created a gold rush. That year over 27 000 men left San Francisco ports alone for British Columbia. Most were transient adventurers who had come to the west coast in search of gold during the San Francisco rush of 1849. Douglas attempted to control this invasion with decrees forbidding, for example, the entry of foreign vessels on the Fraser River. But the miners questioned the right of an HBC officer to make this kind of regulation. Britain, now recognizing the need for imperial rather than company control over both the mainland and the island, cancelled the company's lease on Vancouver Island and made the mainland a formal Crown colony. Douglas, after agreeing to resign his HBC posts, was named governor of British Columbia (which then referred only to the mainland) in November 1858, while retaining his position as governor of Vancouver Island.

New Westminster, now a suburb of Vancouver, was named the capital of the mainland colony. Douglas made use of mining licences and judges to control the behaviour of the miners. His main aim was to establish firmly that the territory was under British control and fend off any sentiment on the part of American immigrants to reverse the boundary treaty of 1846. Part of the plan included construction of about six hundred kilometres of highway connecting settlements and gold-mining territories with the capital.

Meanwhile, the HBC, having overtrapped the region, turned to other profit-making ventures. In the central interior company officials formed the Puget's Sound Agricultural Company, established farms along the Columbia River, and secured a contract in 1841 with the Russian fur traders in the region north of HBC territory for exclusive provisioning of their posts. By 1850 Fort Victoria housed several sawmills that sold lumber to California miners. Both the fort and Esquimalt, a few kilometres away, sold supplies to Royal Navy ships that docked there and benefited from increasing demands for lumber during the Crimean War from 1854 to 1856. The coal mines at Nanaimo had a steady market in the United States. Four manorial farms had been established near Fort Victoria, although it proved difficult to attract labourers on the five-year contracts that were offered. While independent businesses were slowly established in the 1850s, it was the gold rush that challenged the HBC's commercial dominance of the island. A six-week period in 1858 saw over two hundred buildings, mainly businesses, erected. These ramshackle structures, surrounded by a tent town created by the gold-seekers en route to imagined riches, transformed the fort from a tidy, compact village of three hundred people to an overcrowded town of six thousand. The population would decline by half in a few years as the gold rush ended, leaving empty buildings.

The European population on both the mainland and the island was overwhelmingly male. Most settlers and miners were young, single males seeking their fortune and satisfying their sexual desires by visiting the white and Chinese prostitutes who came to work in the area. By 1860 Governor Douglas, anxious to create permanent, family-based settlements, was advertising in Britain for marriage-minded women to come to the colony as domestics. The fur traders who preceded these settlers had generally married Native women, but most settlers had little desire to mingle with, much less marry, Native women.

Settlers and Race Relations

The HBC had a certain respect for the Natives of the coast, but this was not the case with the settlers. Like agricultural settlers in other overseas colonies, ranging from South Africa to the early American colonies, the Vancouver Island settlers regarded the Indians as a lower form of life.

Unlike the fur traders they had no need of the Indians' services and regarded them as competitors for land. For their part, the Native peoples were stunned by the Europeans' penchant for building fences around everything and the viciousness of the settlers' response to anyone who scaled fences in a search for food. As historian Robin Fisher notes: "For the settler concerned to establish and defend a beachhead of civilization in the wilderness the Indian was the symbol of something that he must not allow himself to become. The British colonist established a line of cleavage based on race and would not permit any crossing of that barrier by admitting that the Indian was in any way comparable to western man."[6]

The Natives often resorted to violence in their attempts to prevent their lands from being taken by settlers. In 1844, Cowichan, Songhee, and Klallum destroyed livestock belonging to Fort Victoria and attacked the fort. Beginning in the 1850s, warships were used when Indian revolts occurred. For example, when the Newitty Indians killed three runaway sailors on Vancouver Island in 1850, two warships were sent, each to destroy a village.

By 1860 the first inhabitants of British Columbia, their numbers already weakened by European diseases, were being quickly dispossessed. Settlers and transients grabbed their land or established mining operations on it. Many Natives were demoralized as their intricate societies collapsed around them. Others, accustomed after a fashion by the fur trade to notions of trading their labour in exchange for goods, did integrate themselves into the resource-based economy that the European settlers established. From the 1850s onward, many Natives worked at commercial fishing, canning, sailing, coal mining, farming, and lumbering.

The Amerindians were not the only British Columbia residents to suffer from racism in the mid-nineteenth century. The province's first black residents arrived in Vancouver Island in 1858, escaping restrictive legislation in California. Some farmed or ranched, others found employment as miners, bakers, restaurateurs, merchants, or barbers. Discouraged by prejudice and the harsh conditions of life on Vancouver Island, most of them returned to the United States after the Northern victory in the Civil War appeared to herald a new era of race relations in that country.

The gold mines of the Fraser valley and the Cariboo Mountains region attracted between six and seven thousand Chinese, mainly men, from both California and Hong Kong in 1858 and 1859. The men worked as prospectors for gold and jade, importers, fishers, gardeners, labourers, restaurateurs, and handymen. A small number of wives also came—women who were generally married to merchants and worked alongside their husbands. Most of the other Chinese women who came were either female servants or prostitutes imported by Chinese merchants. Like the blacks, the

NATIVE VIEWS OF EUROPEAN LAND CLAIMS

In 1860 Gilbert Sproat purchased land in the Alberni district of Vancouver Island, although he needed the aid of two armed vessels to take possession. With loaded cannons aimed at their village, the Nuu'chah'nulth agreed to surrender their village site to Sproat, but they made clear to him that his title to the land was illegitimate in their eyes. Sproat wrote an account of his impression of the confrontation:

"We see your ships, and hear things that make our hearts grow faint. They say that more King-George-men will soon be here, and will take our land, our firewood, our fishing grounds; that we shall be placed on a little spot, and shall have to do everything according to the fancies of the King-George-men."

"Do you believe all this?" I asked.

"We want your information," said the speaker.

"Then," answered I, "it is true that more King-George-men (as they call the English) are coming: they will soon be here; but your land will be bought at a fair price."

"We do not wish to sell our land nor our water; let your friends stay in their own country." To which I rejoined: "My great chief, the high chief of the King-George-men, seeing that you do not work your land, orders that you shall sell it. It is of no use to you. The trees you do not need; you will fish and hunt as you do now, and collect firewood, planks for your houses, and cedar for your canoes. The white man will give you work, and buy your fish and oil."

"Ah, but we don't care to do as the white men wish."

"Whether or not," said I, "the white men will come. All your people know that they are your superiors; they make the things you value. You cannot make muskets, blankets, or bread. The white men will teach your children to read printing, and to be like themselves."

"We do not want the white man. He steals what we have. We wish to live as we are."[7]

Chinese learned that economic success did not lead to acceptance by the whites: the norm was segregation in churches, saloons, theatres, and residential areas. As the gold rush ended in the 1860s, most of this first wave of Chinese immigrants departed.

• Visions of the Northwest

The migration of whites to British Columbia in the 1850s was not matched by a parallel migration to the Northwest. But there the writing was on the wall for the fur trade by the end of the decade. The rapid agricultural settlement of the American frontier caused first British expansionists and then Canada West expansionists to proclaim the possibility and the necessity of "civilizing" the northern plains. American expansion also raised fears that the United States would seize control of the HBC's territories before the Canadas had a chance to do so. The legislature of the state of Minnesota, whose population had grown from 6000 in 1850 to 172 000 in 1860, staked a claim on Assiniboia in 1858 and it seemed that only warfare with the Sioux, lasting from 1857 to 1865, had slowed down Minnesota's northward advance.

In 1857 John Palliser, a scion of wealthy Irish landowners, convinced the Royal Geographic Society to sponsor a fact-finding expedition through HBC territories east of the Rockies. The Society, in turn, convinced the British government to foot the bill. The expedition, which lasted from May 1857 to October 1859, included a botanical collector, a magnetical observer, an astronomical observer, and a geologist-naturalist-medical man.

In 1862 Palliser produced a report that confirmed what he had suspected before setting out: much of today's Prairie region, particularly the Red River and North Saskatchewan valleys, was suitable for agricultural settlement. He did, however, identify a fairly large area, stretching from present-day Brandon to the Rocky Mountains and from the 49th to the 52nd parallel, that he believed to be too dry for successful farming. Henry Youle Hind, a University of Toronto professor of chemistry and geology and the head of an expedition sponsored by the Canadian government in 1857, reached much the same conclusions. Hind, writing of a "fertile belt" within the HBC territories, stated in his 1860 report:

> It is a physical reality of the highest importance to the interests of British North America that this continuous belt can be settled and cultivated from a few miles west of the Lake of The Woods to the passes of the Rocky Mountains, and any line of communication, whether by waggon road or railroad, passing through it, will eventually enjoy the great advantage of being fed by an agricultural population from one extremity to another.[8]

The Hind and Palliser reports confirmed the view of Canada West expansionists that Rupert's Land could become an agricultural paradise. Toronto's merchant community, anxious about their future as the city's western hinterland filled up, regarded the far-flung territories further west as an extension of that hinterland. The American cities of the eastern seaboard had profited by supplying the needs for manufactured products of the farmers of the new western states and territories, and the Toronto businessmen hoped to imitate their success. They were led in this by the most powerful Reformer in Canada West, George Brown, the editor of the *Globe* and a businessman with a variety of speculative investments whose future returns were tied to Toronto's prosperity. The expansionists found sympathetic ears in the British government and financial circles of the 1850s. They also gradually won over the colony's farmers, who were anxious because land for their children could not be found closer to home.

In 1857, a select committee of the British House of Commons accepted in principle Canada West's "just and reasonable wishes" to annex Rupert's Land. As historian Doug Owram notes, "By the end of the decade, the debate on the Hudson's Bay Company had ended, because everyone, including its own officials, accepted the impending end of the fur trade empire."[9] Of course, that empire was not about to collapse altogether; rather, its southern section was about to be lost. The northern fur trade would continue to operate for more than a century.

Hind expedition, 1858   (National Archives of Canada/C4572)

The HBC remained profitable in the years leading up to the shrinkage of its territory. Despite a doubling of company stocks from 1821 to 1857, which halved the value of single shares, company profits during that period averaged 12 percent of invested capital, and profits from 1846 to 1856 never fell below 10 percent. But once it became clear that the HBC's lands would soon be sought after by farmers and presumably railway interests, speculators with little interest in the fur trade began to buy shares in the company. In 1863 London bankers closely associated with the Grand Trunk Railway bought control of the HBC. In one year the share value of the company rose from £500 000 to £2 000 000. The character of both Western Canada and the HBC was about to change forever.

• The Northern Fur Trade

In the Mackenzie valley and the Yukon, the changes affecting the fur-trading regions to the south had no parallel before 1860. Here, as yet, resources had not been significantly depleted, and Europeans had shown no interest in replacing fur trading with economic ventures that would bring new settlement into the area. The fur trade reached the Mackenzie valley in the 1790s during the period of intense competition between the NWC and the HBC. In the period following the HBC–NWC merger, the HBC regarded the region as of little importance. While furs remained readily available in southern regions, the company allocated only a modest quantity of trade goods for the north. The Natives traded both furs and food to the poorly supplied remote posts and in return received flour, tea, sugar, metal implements, beads, blankets, tobacco, and alcohol. Like the early encounters of aboriginal groups throughout British North America with whites, the Natives of the Mackenzie valley retained their cultural values and practices in the early period of the fur trade. Anthropologist Michael Asch, writing about the Slavey in the period from 1790 to 1870, concludes: "The only significant changes in Native economic life during this time were the adoption of certain trade good items that made life a little easier and a shift in seasonal rounds to include both occasional trips to the trading posts for supplies at various times in the year, and, especially later in the period, the occasional use of the trading posts rather than the major lakes as places for encampment during the summer."[10]

Still, the impact of European diseases on the northern peoples was no less devastating than it was on the southern Natives. Infection spread rapidly among Native groups. In the Yukon, for example, epidemics of mumps and scarlet fever occurred even before contact with non-Natives began in the 1840s: Native groups from outside the region, trading with Yukon nations, carried diseases contracted by contact with Europeans. The Native population of the Yukon, estimated to have been between 7000 and 9000 in the immediate pre-contact period, had fallen to about 2600 by the end of the nineteenth century. The Natives remained largely self-sufficient, acquiring mainly luxury goods—knives, guns, iron goods, alcohol—from the Europeans living among them. Despite the ravages of disease, the first nations of the Yukon would not face a real challenge to the control of their territory before the Klondike gold rush at the close of the century.

•Conclusion

By the 1850s the period in which British Columbia and the Northwest were significant to Europeans solely as outposts of the fur trade was coming to a close. The fur trade era witnessed the arrival of only small numbers of Europeans into these regions, leaving the Native peoples in control of most of the territory. Native groups drawn into the trade derived material benefits that allowed them, at least for a period, to enrich both their material and spiritual lives. Depending on the impact of the trade on the general resource base of a region, the aboriginal peoples might retain relative independence from the Europeans they traded with, or over time they might become reliant on them to varying degrees.

The first nations' retention of lands and access to resources became more problematic as the fur trade began to give way to agricultural settlement and mining. In the mid-century period and the following few decades, the spread of these activities to the western half of present-day Canada would occur within the context of sweeping changes in the economic organization of Western Europe and North America.

•Native Women and the Fur Trade:
A Historiographical Debate

Before 1980 historians studied the fur trade as a virtually all-male affair. That year saw the publication of two books high-lighting the role of Native women in the trade. The books, by Sylvia Van Kirk and Jennifer Brown, not only filled in an impor-tant gap but also reshaped historical perspectives on the fur trade itself.

Discussion of relations between European men and Native women in earlier histories often reflected traditional European race and gender biases. E.E. Rich's authoritative three-volume history of the Hudson's Bay Company, which appeared from 1958 to 1960, devoted scarcely two out of over 1500 pages of text to the subject. Repeating misunderstandings common since the writings of the Jesuits in the seventeenth century, Rich asserted that Native women were promiscuous and Native men were willing to prostitute their wives and daughters for a bottle of brandy. Despite the HBC's prohibitions against sexual inter-course with Native women, Rich said, "Such behaviour was almost inevitable when active men were quartered for long peri-ods among those with the concepts and habits of the Indians."[11]

While Rich appeared to believe that sexual availability was the only attraction of Native women, he also recognized that "domestic ties to some extent explained the willingness with which men spent year after year at the posts, willingly renewed their engagements, and volunteered to settle there if the Company's Charter were overthrown."[12] For Rich, like other early historians of the fur trade, this incidental observation mer-ited little further exploration. The real focus of his and similar studies of the fur trade was the leading European male figures in the trade: HBC officials in Canada, partners in the North West Company, explorers, and the like. Family life received scant concern in accounts centred on the public sphere of com-pany life.

Brown and Van Kirk, in contrast, focussed on the domestic realm and thereby demonstrated the danger of separating fam-ily life from the overall operation of the fur trade. Native women provided their fur-trading husbands with far more than sex, companionship, and babies, although all of these were important. Their unpaid labour was crucial to the fur trade— the women made moccasins and snowshoes, prepared pemmican, fished, collected food supplies such as wild rice and berries, snared small game, tended crops at company posts, and assisted in making and powering canoes. Their knowledge of local language and geography also made them invaluable as interpreters, guides, and diplomats.

The story of Thanadelthur, a Chipewyan captured by Cree in 1713, provides an example of the Native woman's diplomatic role. Escaping her captors, Thanadelthur stumbled upon HBC servants and subsequently became the fur company's prime agent in persuading the Cree and Chipewyan of the Churchill River area to cease their hostilities. While Thanadelthur's aim was most likely to bring peace to her own people, she served the HBC's aim of ending a conflict that was reducing the supplies of furs brought to the post.

Van Kirk, relying on fur traders' accounts, concludes that many Native women actively sought alliances with the traders. Many of these women believed that the Europeans offered an easier life with more material goods. Furthermore, their new husbands quickly learned that Native women, more so than European women, enjoyed autonomy within their domestic sphere and brooked no interference from men. Even the trading of furs, often viewed as a male-only activity, tended to be a shared husband-and-wife venture. The Native women, knowing the people who were supplying the furs and often having excellent business acumen, became indispensable to many traders. Madame Lamallice, the wife of the brigade guide at an HBC fort on Lake Athabasca, was the only interpreter in the area and could demand extra rations for her family. She also carried on "her own private trade in pounded meat, beaver tails and moose skins, with a hoarded stock of trade goods, including cloth and ribbons."[13] She threatened that if the HBC tried to stop her trade, she would turn the Indians against it.

Van Kirk emphasizes that while many Indian women were abandoned by fur traders whom they had married *à la façon du pays*, fur trade society on the whole was characterized by stable interracial marriages. Yet over time the female progeny of these marriages, rather than Native women, became the favoured marriage partners of fur traders: "The replacement of the Indian wife by the mixed-blood wife resulted in a widespread and complex pattern of intermarriage among fur-trade families. It produced a close-knit society in which family life was highly valued. James Douglas echoed the sentiments of many of his colleagues when he declared that without 'the many tender ties' of family, the monotonous life of a fur trader would be unbearable."[14]

Although Native wives tried to pass on their wilderness skills to their children, daughters were often encouraged by their fathers to emulate European examples of what was considered to be ladylike behaviour. Compounding the resultant crisis of identity was the fact that, after the 1820s, the gradual arrival of European women in fur trade society provoked an unfavourable re-evaluation of Métis wives. Officers began to marry European women, and these new wives snubbed the Métis wives of traders as racially inferior and unladylike, making the Métis women victims of racist and sexist stereotypes. By then, the fur trade itself was in decline and the white wife in the Red River settlement, like the missionary, "symbolized the coming of a settled agrarian order" where "native women would have little role to play."[15]

The insights of Van Kirk and Brown had a negligible effect on Peter C. Newman, who in the 1980s wrote a lively popular history of the Hudson's Bay Company. In the first volume of his work Newman gave scant attention to the role of women in the trade and presented a traditional image of larger-than-life male adventurers rather than the family men portrayed by Van Kirk and Brown. The fur traders, he claimed, saw the women as "bits of brown," and he added: "Love-making on the frontier did not carry much emotional baggage, being routinely offered and casually accepted."[16] Academic historians, unlike journalists, largely rejected Newman's approach and conclusions and the second volume of his study gave more credence to the Van Kirk–Brown thesis. Nevertheless, his first volume, set against the studies of Van Kirk and Brown, demonstrates how different perspectives of a society can be depending on whether the categories of family life and gender are included or excluded from historical analysis.

•Notes

[1] Samuel Hearne, *A Journey from Prince of Wales's Fort in Hudson's Bay, to the Northern Ocean* (London, 1795), 51–52.

[2] D. Wayne Moody and Barry Kaye, "Indian Agriculture in the Fur Trade Northwest," *Prairie Forum* 11, 2 (Fall 1986): 176.

[3] Lyle Dick, "The Seven Oaks Incident and the Construction of a Historical Tradition, 1816 to 1970" *Journal of the Canadian Historical Association* (new series) 2: 97.

[4] *Fur Trade and Empire: George Simpson's Journal*, ed. Frederick Merk (Cambridge, MA: Harvard University Press, 1968), 179.

[5] Arthur J. Ray, *Indians in the Fur Trade: Their Role as Trappers, Hunters, and Middlemen in the Lands Southwest of Hudson Bay, 1660–1870* (Toronto: University of Toronto Press, 1974), 228.

[6] Robin Fisher, *Contact and Conflict: Indian–European Relations in British Columbia, 1774–1890* (Vancouver: University of British Columbia Press, 1977), 93.

[7] Quoted in Peter A. Cumming and Neil H. Mickenberg, eds., *Native Rights in Canada* (Toronto: General Publishing, 1972), 175.

[8] Henry Youle Hind, *Narrative of the Canadian Red River Exploring Expedition of 1857 and of the Assiniboine and Saskatchewan Exploring Expedition of 1858*, Vol. 1 (London, 1860), 234.

[9] Doug Owram, *Promise of Eden: The Canadian Expansionist Movement and the Idea of the West 1856–1900* (Toronto: University of Toronto Press, 1980), 38.

[10] "Summary of Evidence of Michael Asch, Department of Anthropology, University of Alberta, before the Mackenzie Valley Pipeline Inquiry, Yellowknife, N.W.T.," 1 April 1976.

[11] E.E. Rich, *The History of the Hudson's Bay Company 1670–1870*, Vol. 1, *1670–1763* (London: Hudson's Bay Records Society, 1958), 605.

[12] Ibid.

[13] Sylvia Van Kirk, *"Many Tender Ties": Women in Fur Trade Society in Western Canada, 1670–1870* (Winnipeg: Watson and Dwyer, 1980), 84–85.

[14] Ibid.

[15] Ibid.

[16] Peter C. Newman, *Company of Adventurers*, Vol. 1 (Markham, ON: Viking, 1985), 205.

•Selected Reading

For the Prairies and northern Ontario, the period covered in this chapter is surveyed in the first seven chapters of Gerald Friesen, *The Canadian Prairies: A History* (Toronto: University of Toronto Press, 1984). Also see the opening chapters of the major provincial histories: Howard Palmer with Tamara Palmer, *Alberta: A New History* (Edmonton: Hurtig, 1990); John Archer, *Saskatchewan: A History* (Saskatoon: Western Producer Prairie Books, 1980); and W.L. Morton, *Manitoba: A History* (Toronto: University of Toronto Press, 1957). The early history of British Columbia is the subject of the opening chapters of Margaret Ormsby, *British Columbia: A History* (Toronto: Macmillan, 1976); and Jean Barman, *The West Beyond the West: A History of British Columbia* (Toronto: University of Toronto Press, 1991).

For Native peoples, two textbooks are a useful place to start: Olive Patricia Dickason, *Canada's First Nations: A History of Founding Peoples from Earliest Times* (Toronto: McClelland and Stewart, 1992); and J.R. Miller, *Skyscrapers Hide the Heavens* (Toronto: University of Toronto Press, 1989). Several essay collections focus on Prairie and Northern Canadian Native peoples, particularly R. Bruce Morrison and C. Roderick Wilson, eds., *Native Peoples: the Canadian Experience* (Toronto: McClelland and Stewart, 1986). Philip Drucker, *Cultures of the North Pacific Coast* (San Francisco: Chander Publishing, 1965), outlines the pre-contact history of Pacific coast Natives. A popular history of British Columbia Natives is George Woodcock, *Peoples of the Coast: The Indians of the Pacific Northwest* (Edmonton: Hurtig, 1977).

Among excellent studies of the religious and cultural life of Native peoples are Jennifer Brown, Robert Brightman, and George Nelson, *The Orders of the Dreamed: George Nelson on Cree and Northern Ojibwa Religion and Myth* (Winnipeg: University of Manitoba Press, 1988), and David G. Mandelbaum, *The Plains Cree: An Ethnographic, Historical and Comparative Study* (Regina: Canadian Plains Research Centre, 1979).

Studies of the impact of the fur trade on major Native societies include: Robin Fisher, *Contact and Conflict: Indian–European Relations in British Columbia, 1774–1890* (Vancouver: University of British Columbia Press, 1979); Arthur J. Ray, *Indians in the Fur Trade: Their Role as Trappers, Hunters, and Middlemen in the Lands Southwest of Hudson Bay, 1660–1870* (Toronto: University of Toronto Press, 1974); Charles A. Bishop, *The Northern Ojibwa and the Fur Trade: An Historical and Ecological Study* (Toronto: Holt, Rinehart and Winston, 1974); Oscar Lewis, *The Effects of White Contact Upon Blackfoot Culture with Special Reference to the Role of the Fur Trade* (Seattle: American Ethnological Society, 1942); John S. Milloy, *The Plains Cree: Trade, Diplomacy and War* (Winnipeg: University of Manitoba Press, 1990); and Paul C. Thistle, *Indian–European Trade Relations in the Lower Saskatchewan River Region to 1840* (Winnipeg: University of Manitoba Press, 1986). On the North, see Ken S. Coates,

Best Left as Indians: Native–White Relations in the Yukon Territory, 1840–1973 (Montreal: McGill-Queen's University Press, 1991); and his *Canada's Colonies: A History of the Yukon and Northwest Territories* (Toronto: Lorimer, 1985). On the work of missionaries among the Native peoples, see John Webster Grant, *Moon of Wintertime: Missionaries and the Indians of Canada in Encounter Since 1534* (Toronto: University of Toronto Press, 1984).

On Native peoples in the early period of settlement in British Columbia, see Fisher, *Contact and Conflict;* Barry M. Gough, *Gunboat Frontier: British Maritime Authority and Northwest Coast Indians, 1846–1890* (Vancouver: University of British Columbia Press, 1983); and Paul Tennant, *Aboriginal Peoples and Politics: The Indian Land Question in British Columbia 1849–1989* (Vancouver: University of British Columbia Press, 1990).

A good short introduction to the fur trade is Frits Pannekoek, *The Fur Trade and Western Canadian Society, 1670–1870* (Ottawa: Canadian Historical Association, 1987). A lengthier but highly readable account is Daniel Francis, *Battle for the West: Fur Traders and the Birth of Western Canada* (Edmonton: Hurtig, 1982). An earlier overview is E.E. Rich, *The Fur Trade and the Northwest to 1857* (Toronto: McClelland and Stewart, 1967). On the west coast trade, see James Gibson, *Otter Skins, Boston Ships and China Goods: The Maritime Fur Trade of the Northwest Coast, 1785–1841* (Montreal: McGill-Queen's University Press, 1992). On the northern trade, see James Parker, *Emporium of the North: Fort Chipewyan and the Fur Trade to 1835* (Regina: Canadian Plains Research Centre, 1987). The Hudson's Bay Company's history to 1870 is surveyed in Glyndwr Williams, "Highlights of the First 200 Years of the Hudson's Bay Company," *The Beaver,* special issue (Autumn 1970). A detailed account of the company's history is E.E. Rich, *The Hudson's Bay Company,* 3 vols. (Toronto: Hudson's Bay Records Society, 1960).

Accounts of traders and company officials abound. Among the better are J.B. Tyrrell, ed., *David Thompson's Narrative of His Explorations in Western America, 1784–1812* (New York: Greenwood Press, 1968); and Frederick Merk, ed., *Fur Trade and Empire: George Simpson's Journal* (Cambridge: Harvard University Press, 1968). Merk's introduction is an excellent source of information regarding Hudson's Bay Company organization. Useful biographies include: J.S. Galbraith, *The Little Emperor: Governor Simpson of the Hudson's Bay Company* (Toronto: Macmillan, 1976); and J.G. McGregor, *John Rowand: Czar of the Prairies* (Saskatoon: Western Producer Prairie Books, 1979).

Two excellent accounts of women in the fur trade are Sylvia Van Kirk, *Many Tender Ties: Women in Fur Trade Society in Western Canada, 1670–1870* (Winnipeg: Watson and Dwyer, 1980); and Jennifer S.H. Brown, *Strangers in Blood: Fur Trade Company Families in the Indian Country* (Vancouver: University of British Columbia Press, 1980).

The social history of the Red River colony is related in Frits Pannekoek, *A Snug Little Flock: The Social Origins of the Riel Resistance of 1869–70* (Winnipeg: Watson and Dwyer, 1991). Barry Kaye, "The Red River Settlement: Lord Selkirk's Isolated Colony in the Wilderness," *Prairie Forum* 11, 1 (Spring 1986): 1–20, outlines how a decision was made to establish a colony at the forks of the Red and Assiniboine rivers. The confrontation between the settlement and the Métis is detailed in Margaret Macleod and W.L. Morton, *Cuthbert Grant of Grantown: Warden of the Plains of Red River* (Toronto: McClelland and Stewart, 1974). A critique of their account and the historical tradition within which it was written is in Lyle Dick, "The Seven Oaks Incident and the Construction of a Historical Tradition, 1816 to 1870," *Journal of the Canadian Historical Association* (new series) 2 (1992): 91–113.

On the early history of Métis communities in Canada, see Jennifer Brown and Jacqueline Petersen, eds., *The New Peoples: Being and Becoming Métis in North America* (Winnipeg: University of Manitoba Press, 1985). On Red River, W.L. Morton's introduction to *Alexander Begg's Red River Journal* (Toronto: Champlain Society, 1956) is useful, if dated in its notions of "civilization" and "primitivism." D. Bruce Sealey and Antoine Lussier, in *The Métis: Canada's Forgotten People* (Winnipeg: Pemmican, 1983), present an unabashedly partisan account of Métis life. Conflicts at Red River between French and English speakers, Métis and white, are the subject of Kathryn M. Bindon, "Hudson's Bay Company Law: Adam Thom and the Institution of Order in Rupert's Land 1839–1854," in *Essays in the History of Canadian Law*, vol. 1, ed. David H. Flaherty (Toronto: University of Toronto Press, 1981), 43–87. Barry Cooper's biography, *Alexander Kennedy Isbister: A Respectable Critic of the Honourable Company* (Ottawa: Carleton University Press, 1988), elaborates the conflicts in Red River. On the Métis outside Red River in this period, see J.E. Foster, "The Plains Métis," in Morrison and Wilson, *Native Peoples*, 375–403; and his "End of the Plains Buffalo," *Alberta* 3, 1 (1992): 61–77.

The goals and attitudes of Canadian expansionists with eyes on the west are detailed in Doug Owram, *Promise of Eden: The Canadian Expansionist Movement and the Idea of the West 1856–1900* (Toronto: University of Toronto Press, 1980); and Douglas Francis, *Images of the West: Changing Perceptions of the Prairies, 1690–1960* (Saskatoon: Western Producer Prairie Books, 1989). Their American rivals are the subject of Alvin Gluek, *Minnesota and the Manifest Destiny of the Canadian Northwest* (Toronto: University of Toronto Press, 1965). British expansionists are discussed in Irene M. Spry, *The Palliser Expedition: An Account of John Palliser's British North American Expedition 1857–1860* (Toronto: Macmillan, 1963), and the opening chapters of Vernon Fowke, *The National Policy and the Wheat Economy* (Toronto: University of Toronto Press, 1957). On early settlement in British Columbia, see Fisher, *Contact and Conflict*, and Gough, *Gunboat Frontier*.

CHAPTER 12

BRITISH NORTH AMERICA AT MID-CENTURY

Wilson Benson was born in Belfast, Ireland, in December 1821. Within a year his mother died. His father moved the family out of Belfast and eventually remarried, to a widow with several children of her own. They lived on the new wife's property—until the wife's children by her first marriage claimed possession and ejected all of the Benson family. Forced to rely on his own resources, Wilson Benson at the age of twelve began a series of jobs that took him to Scotland, back to Ireland, and finally to Canada West in 1841 with his eighteen-year-old wife Jemima Hewitt, who had worked as a dressmaker.

In Canada, with only a few months of formal schooling, Benson had difficulty finding work. He failed miserably as a farm hand and survived by taking a variety of seasonal jobs. Despite a series of misfortunes, the Bensons saved enough money to buy a farm by 1849. They lived in Orangeville for two years and then moved to Artemesia, Grey County. Jemima Benson died in 1860 and Wilson Benson remarried a year later. In 1873 he was badly mauled by a threshing machine and moved to Markdale, where he made a modest living as a storekeeper. Benson's motive in becoming a farmer was, in his own words, to gain "a livelihood without having to work for, or have to take orders from, anyone, be he employer or landlord."[1]

While not everyone experienced Benson's degree of occupational variety, most immigrants to British North America sought security in a world fraught with uncertainty. Many people lived life on the margins, even during periods when the North Atlantic economy was buoyant. The British North American colonies and territories themselves claimed a marginal existence as isolated commercial outposts of the vast and expanding British empire. Yet, in less than a quarter of a century all British North America except Newfoundland would be swept into a political partnership called Confederation.

Emigrants   (National Archives of Canada/C4986)

The speed with which British North Americans became Canadians reflects the dramatic changes taking place in mid-nineteenth-century colonial society. Spurred by the Industrial Revolution, economic and social change penetrated to the core of pre-industrial British North American cultures and transformed them beyond recognition. It was in this highly uncertain and changing world that immigrants like Wilson Benson endeavoured to earn a living for themselves and their families and to provide security for their old age.

• Small Worlds

In 1850 the British North American colonies and territories were a study in contrasts. On the west coast the Crown colony of Vancouver Island had only a handful of white settlers and was ruled without an elected assembly. Its seat of government, Victoria, was, in the words of its unhappy first governor, Richard Blanshard, "nothing more than a fur trading post." Like the vast northern area that stretched from the Pacific to the Atlantic oceans, Vancouver Island was part of the fur trade empire of the Hudson's Bay Company. Most of the 100 000 aboriginal peoples in the great Northwest were tied to the market economy through the company's trading posts. The heart of the Northwest was the sprawling district of Assiniboia, where a growing Métis population was rapidly emerging to challenge the hegemony of HBC officialdom.

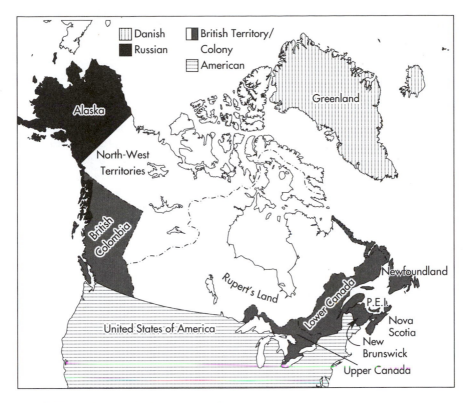

MAP 12.1 *British North America, 1866*

Over 10 000 Inuit lived in the far north but they were loosely, if at all, integrated into European trade networks. Effectively isolated from European culture by climate and terrain, the Inuit lived by hunting and fishing. Their co-operative kinship and community structures were dictated by an unyielding environment. Whites ventured into the land of the midnight sun only at their peril. As late as the 1840s the "true north" had claimed the life of British explorer Sir John Franklin during his third expedition in search of the elusive Northwest Passage.

Decimated by disease and loss of traditional habitat, fewer than 20 000 aboriginal peoples lived in the whole of eastern British North America, which by 1850 was home to 2.5 million people of European background. The eastern colonies, with their now predominantly white population, were characterized by diversity. Divided between English- and French-speaking inhabitants, the United Canadas contained two distinct cultures. Canada West was a rough and ready frontier society where nearly half of

THE FRANKLIN EXPEDITION

Many navigators tried to find a Northwest Passage, but none sparked as much continuing interest as John Franklin. In 1819 and again in 1825 Franklin's attempts to penetrate the northern wilderness ended in failure. Franklin set out again in 1845, but failed to return. Between 1848 and 1859 some thirty rescue missions attempted to find the missing Franklin expedition. One group, headed by the resourceful Captain Robert McClure, actually traversed the Northwest Passage by foot and sled in a desperate attempt to escape the Arctic ice. Finally in 1857 Lady Franklin sent her own expedition under Captain Leopold McClintock to solve the mystery of her husband's disappearance. Acting on information supplied by the Inuit to Dr John Rae, a fur trader working for the Hudson's Bay Company, McClintock searched the shores of King William Island. There he found a stone cairn with a message, dated April 1848, indicating that twenty-four men, including Franklin, were dead, and that the survivors were heading overland. We now know that they all perished.

Interest in the fate of Franklin and his men did not end with McClintock's discovery. Explorers and scholars continued to search for more clues relating to Franklin's expedition and to debate why these seasoned explorers had failed to survive the rigours of the North. In the early 1980s anthropologists from the University of Alberta undertook a scientific and systematic approach to the problem. Their archaeological investigations on King William Island unearthed the remains of seven unidentified crew members. Analysis of the bodies seemed to confirm that the survivors had resorted to cannibalism, a controversial issue that the fur trader Rae had first raised in 1854.

Between 1984 and 1986 the remains of three of Franklin's crew members found on Beechy Island, where the expedition had wintered in 1846, were temporarily exhumed and examined. One of them was identified as the body of the twenty-year-old officer John Torrington. Buried in the permafrost, the corpse was almost perfectly preserved. Torrington had apparently died of pneumonia, but the high levels of lead in his blood suggested that he and the others in the expedition may have been slowly poisoned by the containers that held their food supplies.

More recently, David C. Woodman, relying on Inuit legend, argues that while Franklin's men may have been suffering from lead poisoning, they were more likely killed by a disease common to earlier explorers. According to the Inuit, the bodies of Franklin and his men were found with hard black mouths and emaciated limbs, symptoms of the dreaded scurvy.[2]

the people were immigrants, primarily from the British Isles. As in most frontier societies, men outnumbered women and the proportion of people over seventy years of age was relatively low. In Canada East most of the people were Canadian-born, sharing a common heritage with its roots in the French migrations of the seventeenth century. In the Atlantic colonies three out of four people were native-born, and like Canada East the region had a population profile more balanced in age and gender. Nearly half of the population was under seventeen years of age, making youth a dominant characteristic of all colonial societies. While Prince Edward Island was the most densely populated colony by virtue of its small size, over three-quarters of white British North Americans were concentrated in the St Lawrence and Great Lakes basin, an area that the aboriginal peoples in the pre-contact period had also favoured as a place to live.

Sprawled over 7 percent of the earth's surface, the British colonies and territories in 1850 remained isolated from each other. Although people in the Atlantic region might brave the harsh winter seas of the Cabot and Northumberland straits or the Bay of Fundy to reach their closest neighbours, the Canadian ports were frozen for nearly half the year to ocean transport. Overland communication between the United Canadas and territories east or west was confined to ill-marked trails that could be negotiated only by the most intrepid travellers.

By 1850 telegraph and railway communication promised an end to colonial isolation, but the cost of building intercolonial lines was prohibitive for a population of less than three million. A telegraph line linking Canada to the American system was completed in 1847, and in the following year New Brunswick was linked with Calais, Maine. In a roundabout way Maritimers could thus communicate telegraphically with Canadians. Underwater cable connected Prince Edward Island to the mainland in 1851 and Newfoundland in 1856. In 1850 a twenty-three-kilometre railway connecting La Prairie on the St Lawrence with St Jean on the Richelieu was the longest railway in the colonies. Great plans were afoot to run rails from the Maritimes to Canada, but everything hinged on financial assistance from Britain.

While stagecoach service carried passengers and mail to and from major colonial cities, the trunk roads left much to be desired. Stumps, rocks, and potholes commonly threatened to overturn carriages. In spring, raging torrents removed bridges, roadbeds, and even travellers. Road construction depended largely on statute labour, which men were required to perform every year. As a result, road repair varied according to the density and the enthusiasm of the population in any given area. British North Americans experimented with corduroy roads (made from tree trunks), plank roads (subject to rot), and macadamized roads (crushed rock and

The Atlantic Telegraph. *In 1866 the Great Eastern managed to successfully lay an underwater cable between Great Britain and British North America* (Confederation Life Gallery of Canadian History)

gravel), but each had its disadvantages and all were in need of constant repair. Anna Jamieson's experience in the "backwoods" of Canada at mid-century was typical: "The road was scarcely passable; there were no longer cheerful farms and clearings, but the dark pine forests and the rank swamp, crossed by those terrific corduroy paths (my bones ache at the mere recollection), and deep holes and pools of rotted vegetable matter with black, bottomless, sloughs of despond." Such conditions explain why roads were a primary concern of colonial legislatures and why isolation remained a condition of life in British North America.

Despite their isolation, most British North Americans had moved beyond the pioneer stage by mid-century. Each region produced a staple that helped to shape its domestic economy: furs in the Northwest; wheat and timber in the Canadas; fish and timber in the Atlantic colonies. On the west coast, whaling fleets had all but hunted the right whale to extinction and were moving further north in pursuit of the bowhead. Notwithstanding Britain's adoption of a free-trade policy in the 1840s, the expanding empire continued to absorb most of the staples produced in the colonies. The United States was also emerging as a significant market for colonial primary products. The potential would be realized between 1854 and 1866 when a Reciprocity Treaty was in effect between the United States and British North America. By mid-century, too, secondary producers—shipbuilders and fish processors in the Atlantic and St Lawrence regions, and Canadian millers and distillers—were beginning to develop a reputation for quality beyond the boundaries of British North America.

The eastern colonies also sustained a vibrant domestic economy that revolved around the family farm and artisan shops. From the countryside came the wool, flax, and foodstuffs that kept colonials clothed and fed. Most of the furniture, footwear, clothing, and hardware used by British North Americans was crafted in private homes or in shops employing fewer than five people. In every town and village local blacksmiths forged shoes for horses and nails for carpenters from their stocks of pig iron, while tailors and seamstresses fashioned custom-made suits and dresses, and at least one or two cobblers produced the footwear needed to protect colonial feet from the intractable terrain and cold climate. By 1850 a number of shops had expanded to serve the growing urban market, but only a few had adopted industrial techniques of division of labour. Generally artisans still made each item, such as a dress or shoe, from start to finish and developed a reputation based on the quality of the product.

Commercial activity kept goods and services moving in colonial British North America, but only in the major cities was there any specialization in the wholesale and retail trades. Merchants in towns and villages sold a variety of products, often including farm surpluses, and might also serve as the local postmaster, hotel operator, and political representative. General stores were exactly what the name implies, selling everything from tea and sugar to glassware and crockery. Prices were bargained, and purchases were made through barter or on long-term credit to established customers. Depending on location, merchants sometimes became involved in farming, milling, distilling, lumbering, or fishing.

Most mercantile firms operated on a twelve-month cycle, reflecting the rhythms of primary pursuits. Credit radiated out of the British cities of London, Glasgow, and Liverpool, binding backwoods producers, local merchants, and giant wholesalers and export dealers in a complex network of economic dependency. Because merchants operated individually or in partnerships, businesses rarely survived the death of an owner, and bankruptcy meant disaster not only for the business but also for the merchant personally. Most British North Americans, it seems, lived not only in small worlds, but also in uncertain ones.

•Town and Country

In 1851 over 85 percent of British North Americans lived in unincorporated communities, most of them decidedly rural by twentieth-century standards. The work of country folk was regulated by the sun and seasons and characterized by occupational pluralism.

For men, the rhythm of the rural farm included hunting wild animals in the fall, followed by clearing land, cutting firewood, and perhaps working for a timber company in the winter. Many farmers also possessed artisan skills and served their families and communities as blacksmiths, carpenters, cobblers, tanners, and wheelwrights. In settlements bordering the oceans and inland waterways, fishing preceded and followed spring planting. Fishing was the main occupation in parts of the Atlantic region where the rocky soil restricted agriculture to the cultivation of a kitchen garden and raising a few hens and sheep. On the fringes of the timber frontier, gangs of men lived in bunkhouses during the winter and returned to towns in the spring with the timber drive. In widely dispersed areas from Sydney to Nanaimo, miners extracted minerals—gypsum, coal, iron, copper—from the bowels of the earth.

Colonial women were responsible for bearing and raising children, preserving and preparing food, weaving cloth, and making clothing for the family. Indeed, the term "spinster" was derived from the custom whereby single daughters in the family spun yarn from wool. Women cared for the sick and elderly and, in wealthier households, managed the servants. Farm women also took charge of the orchard, dairy, and chicken coop and, in many cultures, performed outdoor work during peak periods of planting and harvest. In fishing communities women assumed more of the farm chores than did most of their inland counterparts, and during the fishing season women cleaned and dried the fish caught by the men. Farm women whose husbands were away part of the year working in the timber trade also took greater responsibility for farm management than did women in families where the farm supplied all of the household income. Women in hunting and gathering societies were often adept at fishing, trapping, and guiding as well as their traditional skills of cooking, preparing hides, and gathering roots, berries, and herbs.

While the family and tribal economies displayed varying degrees of self-sufficiency, economic independence eluded most British North Americans. There were some farming families who subsisted without buying much in the way of imported products and some Native peoples for whom economic contact with the marketplace involved only barter for luxuries rather than necessities, but most British North Americans in 1850 were caught in a vast web of economic dependence.

The "truck" system served as the link between the rural staples trade and international commerce. While HBC factors and British fish and timber merchants prospered, trappers, fishers, and lumberjacks lived modest and sometimes precarious lives. As historian A.R.M. Lower observes with regard to the timber trade, "The Canadian forests contributed to the prosperity of the British timber importer and the enrichment of the American lumberman. Canadians got some crumbs from their own rich table."[3]

The increased presence of truck between 1800 and 1850 demonstrated the erosion of subsistence as the dominant experience of British North American families. So, too, did the increase in the number of landless labourers available for employment for wages in cash or kind on farms and in towns and villages. In Canada West many of these primarily itinerant labourers, like Wilson Benson, would eventually save enough money to buy a farm, but many of the rural dispossessed of 1850 would never become landowners. Their fate was to travel from place to place and job to job, most of them gravitating to cities in the hope that there the family could collectively eke out a living.

The frontier of farm, forest, and fishery contrasted dramatically with the colonial cities, where variety, activity, and congestion prevailed. In 1851 the largest city in British North America was Montreal, with 57 000 people. Quebec City had 42 000 inhabitants and Toronto 30 000. Saint John, with a population of nearly 30 000, was the largest city in the Atlantic region.

Most cities in 1850 were little more than overgrown villages. Even Montreal was a "walking" city, its commercial section crowded near the port. Markets were the centre of urban life. There farm families hawked their produce, and in the nearby streets merchants and artisans sold specialized goods and services that were unavailable in the rural areas. At mid-century cities in British North America were building imposing new structures to house their markets and other activities of urban civic life. Bonsecours market in Montreal was, not surprisingly, the biggest of them all.

Unlike their twentieth-century counterparts, colonial cities were not planned around business and residential activities. Merchants, artisans, and apprentices usually lived and worked in the same building, and the "seedy" side of town was often a block away from elite business and residential areas. The colonial elites were inclined to build their "estates" on the edge of the city, and working people were clustered according to ethnicity and occupation. Census records indicate that widows and single women gravitated to urban areas, where they could get work as domestics. A few women made livings as schoolteachers, inn- and tavern-keepers, seamstresses, and prostitutes.

Despite the excitement of cities, they were not entirely pleasant places to live. Early nineteenth-century cities were larger versions of their eighteenth-century counterparts and filled with sights and smells that would offend most people in the twentieth century. Decaying garbage and the excrement of thousands of horses, cows, and pigs filled the streets. Market squares were awash with animal carcasses, fish heads, and rotting vegetables. In the lower regions of the town noxious cesspools accumulated to become a breeding place of foul odours, enormous rats, and dreaded disease. Outdoor toilets still graced the backyards of many urban homes along with pigs, chickens, and even cattle.

By 1850 city councils were beginning to install rudimentary water and sewer systems and street lighting, but even in the most advanced cities, such as Montreal, Quebec, and Saint John, only a few wealthy wards had access to such services. The lack of water systems and the wooden construction that still characterized British North American cities made fires a common colonial tragedy. For those unable to afford the cost of indoor plumbing, public wells and private carters provided water. The condition of the water that actually reached urban dwellers helped to account for a higher death rate in cities than in rural areas.

Major British North American cities boasted a military presence to protect citizens against invasion from without and civil strife from within. Over ten thousand British soldiers were scattered from St John's to Victoria, with Halifax, Montreal, and Kingston serving as the major garrison towns. As well as infusing money into the colonial economy, the military made a substantial contribution to urban social life. Amateur theatre, sports events, and libraries were sponsored by the military, while grog shops, taverns, and prostitution inevitably flourished in the vicinity of the barracks. Civilian British North Americans also shouldered a responsibility for defence. Every able-bodied man between sixteen and sixty (except for judges, Quakers, and "lunatics") could be called out for militia duty, theoretically providing an impressive force of over 300 000. In practice the militia were unarmed, untrained, and unenthusiastic—not to be relied upon in time of crisis.

Town and country in British North America were bound together by commercial exchange, which extended to the frontiers of settlement. In the Canadas, Montreal and Toronto were emerging as the focus for road, water, and eventually rail transportation networks to their economic hinterlands, but no city had assumed metropolitan dominance over the whole colony. In the Atlantic region the ocean gave many communities direct communication with the great commercial capitals of the world. Boston, New York, Liverpool, and London therefore competed directly with Halifax, Saint John, Charlottetown, and St John's for economic control over the regional economy. Victoria's closest links were with San Francisco, which was growing by leaps and bounds following the California gold rush of 1849. As the American frontier moved steadily westward, inhabitants of Red River and other centres in the Northwest felt the inexorable pull of their southern neighbour.

•Gender and Society

The old adage "women to the hearth and men to the plough" was firmly rooted in the pre-industrial division of labour. No distinction in colonial society was more fundamental than that between the sexes. Boys and girls were socialized to separate roles and taught different subjects in colonial schools. Men and women performed distinct tasks in the colonial economy and were treated differently under the law. Ultimately separate gender roles, believed to be complementary, were brought together in the family, the basic unit of production in colonial society.

While men and women contributed different skills to the family economy, women were placed in a subordinate position by laws that recognized men as household heads and wives and children as their property. In this patriarchal system, women's sexuality and reproductive powers were carefully controlled. In pre-industrial society girls and women were supervised within families, while church, state, and collective community pressure encouraged strict conformity to acceptable sexual behaviour. Women considered to be of easy sexual virtue were publicly ridiculed and socially ostracized.

Although there was often great sympathy expressed for single mothers, their lot was not an easy one. In a curious twist of legal logic, a woman could not sue a man for the support of their child, but her own father could sue the man for the loss of his daughter's services, as well as his personal distress and dishonour. Denied any recourse under the law, children without legal fathers were called "illegitimate" and carried that stigma for life. According to historian Peter Ward, fewer than 5 percent of all colonial births were deemed illegitimate, although a considerably higher percentage of first children were born less than nine months after the wedding day.[4]

Under the British laws that prevailed in the colonies in the early nineteenth century, anyone convicted of infanticide, abortion, or rape was subject to the death penalty. Although lighter sentences for these crimes were gradually adopted, colonial law remained highly patriarchal in intent. Married women were particularly vulnerable. Upon marriage all personal property belonging to the wife and any wages she earned were placed under the absolute control of her husband. Husband and wife were declared to be one under British common law, which made it impossible for a wife to sign a contract, sue or be sued in her own name, or take her husband to court if he mistreated her. Nor could a married woman engage in business separate from her husband without his consent.

The injustice of such laws was most glaring in cases where wives were deserted by their husbands. In 1853, for example, James Whibby in Newfoundland abandoned his wife Mary and four children. Over the next thirteen years Mary Whibby worked at various menial jobs to provide for her family. After she died in 1868, James Whibby returned to claim his wife's estate, which included savings of $1000. When a son contested his father's claim, Chief Justice Sir W.H. Hoyles concluded that although the common-law rule worked "in this case very hardly," James Whibby was entitled to his wife's wages.[5]

Upon the death of her husband a woman in English Canada was entitled to "dower rights," usually one-third of her husband's estate, but she received no assistance if the marriage broke down. In Canada East, marriage contracts and the "community of goods" provision of the Custom of Paris theoretically provided more protection to the married woman's property interests. But this traditional protection of women's economic interests was undermined by pressure on women to legally renounce their community rights so that husbands could be free to manage the family economy.

Throughout British North America divorces were difficult to obtain, frowned upon by both the church and state as a threat to social stability. Laws required women to live with their husbands, permitted men to inflict physical "discipline" on their wives, and gave fathers exclusive custody over the children of the marriage. In the Maritime colonies the divorce laws, rooted in New England practice, were less rigid than in Canada West, where only five divorces were granted before Confederation. The Custom of Paris was even more stringent and did not recognize divorce at all.

The pre-industrial social structure was predicated on the ideal of male-headed households in which women, children, apprentices, and servants were provided for and protected. While there is no question that families were the basic social unit, they often varied widely from the ideal. A significant proportion of British North Americans at any given time (more than 25 percent in most regions) inhabited households extended by the presence of another family, a relative, or boarders. At least 5 percent of British North Americans never married, while a growing proportion of families were headed by women who had been widowed or abandoned by their husbands. Step-parents were common in many family units. Despite biblical and legal injunctions to the contrary, marriage between cousins was considered a positive match in families attempting to retain control of property or other forms of wealth. Throughout British North America, most marriages were endogamous, that is, within the same cultural group.

For young women who found themselves pregnant outside marriage, the alternatives could be grim. On 2 February 1850 the *Acadian Recorder* of Halifax reported:

> INFANTICIDE—This unnatural crime, we are sorry to say, seems to be on the increase in our city. A few evenings ago a Bayman on board his shallop was about to weigh anchor when his attention was directed to a sudden splash, and it being moonlight, he discovered something as if cast into the water from the wharf near which his craft was lying. The sudden disappearance of a person who had apparently caused the object to be thrown into the water, excited his surprise, and he boldly rushed to the rescue. Upon recovering it to his surprise and horror it proved to be a healthy newborn infant, wrapped up, loaded with weights to sink it. The child was immediately cared for and is doing well.[6]

Infanticide was the desperate resort of many unwed mothers in the mid-nineteenth century. According to legal historian Constance Backhouse, the bodies of newborn infants were found buried in the snow, inside hollow trees, at the bottoms of wells, under floor boards, in privies and stovepipes, and floating down rivers. The mothers who were caught were usually destitute, unmarried, working-class women with no family to share the burden of their shame or help them raise a child.[7] Unwanted children were often placed in charitable institutions, where many of them died.

• Class and Culture

In British North America, class, religion, and ethnicity were major sources of identity and, together with gender, determined individual identity. Class in colonial society was based on kinship, wealth, and relationship to production. Although hereditary privileges were largely absent in North America, access to sources of wealth and power was narrowly restricted. Most people lived in the middle and lower ranks of society and faced a lifetime of unrelenting toil.

Tight little cliques of merchants, professionals, and politicians dominated all aspects of life in the settled colonies. While individual members of the colonial elite might experience failure, as a group they were growing more powerful. Michael Katz's studies show that at mid-century less than

10 percent of the adult men in Hamilton, Canada West, held "virtually all of the resources necessary to the health, well-being, and prosperity" of the rest of the community. "The rulers, the owners, and the rich were by and large the same people."[8]

A middle class of farmers and artisans constituted the "bone and sinew" of colonial society. A term first used in England in 1811, "middle class" was beginning to take on a new, more complex meaning in the nineteenth century as some "producers" in colonial society expanded their operations beyond the family farm and the artisan's shop to emerge as successful entrepreneurs. Respectable artisans in British North America joined Mechanics Institutes and fraternal organizations and were elected to city councils. On the lower end of the middle-class spectrum, subsistence-farming, fishing, and artisan families struggled to survive, their fate never far removed from the uncertainty of wage dependency.

In both town and country a class of propertyless labour survived by doing manual work, often on a seasonal basis. Skilled labourers such as printers and ship pilots earned a living wage while unskilled labourers were subject to cycles of boom and bust, the rhythms of the seasons, and payment in kind rather than cash. For some British North Americans, wage labour was only a stage in their life cycle, a chance to earn a little money before returning to the family farm or setting up in business. But for most labourers, these possibilities were receding in a society where class lines had become increasingly rigid.

Religion was a significant source of identity in nineteenth-century British North America. Four out of ten British North Americans were Roman Catholics, but only in Assiniboia and Quebec were Roman Catholics in the majority. Over 40 percent of the population of Newfoundland and Prince Edward Island, a third of New Brunswickers, and one-quarter of Nova Scotians subscribed to the Roman Catholic faith. Canada West, where Roman Catholics accounted for only 20 percent of the population, was the most Protestant region in British North America. Methodists, Presbyterians, and Anglicans were the largest Protestant denominations. In the western portions of Nova Scotia and New Brunswick, Baptist churches attracted a significant following.

While religious affiliation was closely tied to ethnic origin, it also had a bearing on class. The Methodists and Baptists, for instance, were particularly adept at winning converts among farmers and artisans. Although Methodists and Baptists could be found among those who had already acquired wealth and status in mid-nineteenth-century British North America, members of the Church of England and the Church of Scotland were over-represented among colonial elites. Outside Canada East, Roman Catholics were excluded from the corridors of wealth and power, and throughout British North America Roman Catholics were heavily concentrated in the labouring class.

The impact of cultural differences varied. Nowhere in British North America was there a closer correlation between class, ethnicity, and religion than in Newfoundland, where an overwhelmingly Protestant mercantile elite stood apart from a predominantly (though not exclusively) labouring class of Irish Roman Catholics who caught and cured the fish and did manual work in the mercantile centre of St John's. Similarly, T.W. Acheson has found in his study of Saint John that in 1851 only 2 percent of the New Brunswick-born inhabitants and 3 percent of the Scots were labourers, while over 90 percent of the Irish-born inhabitants fell into that category.[9] In contrast the native-born, English, and Scots made up four-fifths of the people in high-status occupations. Conversely, historian Donald Akenson has found that immigrant Irish Catholics in Leeds and Landsdowne townships in Canada West were among the most successful farmers and no more likely to be found among the ranks of the labouring class than their Canadian-born neighbours.[10] Ethnicity, unlike race, was an invisible identity that could be modified by time, marriage, and deliberate choice. In Charlotte County, New Brunswick, Irish Protestants in the late nineteenth century escaped any negative implications of their ethnic identity in a "Loyalist province" by adopting the more general "English" designation.

• Race and Racism

People whose skin was not white suffered most from the smug, small worlds of class and culture in British North America. At mid-century, Indians, Inuit, and blacks made up the majority of people of colour. People of Chinese origin began arriving on the west coast only during the gold rush of 1858. Although few in number outside of Rupert's Land, people of colour were pushed to the margins of colonial society and held at the bottom of the social scale.

In the eighteenth century the fur trade and strategic considerations required Europeans in the eastern colonies to treat Natives with some respect. Decline in the region's fur trade limited the economic importance of Native peoples. Until 1814, the British military authorities, like their French predecessors, recognized the importance of Indian allies in dealing with the threat of American invasion. Afterwards, improved British–American relations reduced the military role of aboriginal people. Civilian rather than military officials began to frame aboriginal policy.

That policy was based on segregation and paternalism. Once they no longer posed a threat to European settlement, aboriginal peoples became a cause for concern among administrators and humanitarians. At the same time, early nineteenth-century anthropological theories supported a belief in the common origin of human life and the possibility of "improving" primitive people through education in Christian principles and civilized behaviour. Efforts to encourage aboriginal peoples to abandon their nomadic existence and to become farmers, "like everybody else," informed both imperial and colonial policy by the mid-nineteenth century. In practice Native policy was constrained by racial biases—at best, well-meaning but condescending; at worst, exploitative, fraudulent, and negligent.

The lives of aboriginal people in the colonies varied considerably. At Grand River in Canada West the Six Nations lived a settled agricultural existence and were reasonably successful in resisting white encroachment on their lands. Nevertheless, the superintendent of Indian affairs invested $38 000 of band money in the failing Grand River Navigation Company (of which the superintendent was a director) without their consultation. Like the Mohawk of Caughnawaga (Kahnawaké) near Lachine, most aboriginal peoples trapped within the confines of white settlement found the world around them changing rapidly in the mid-nineteenth century. They were not only isolated on reserves but also had to contend with constant interference by white bureaucracies.

Aboriginal peoples still dependent upon the hunt moved north and west with the receding fur trade frontier, but the white bureaucracies followed them there as well. Manitoulin Island in Lake Huron became a centre of Ojibwa settlement in the late 1830s. By 1848 armed skirmishes between Ojibwa and the Quebec Mining Company resulted in a new series of treaties on the boundary separating Canada from the HBC territory, a sign that the fur trade frontier and a way of life originally identified with the first nations in eastern British North America was virtually gone.

As in the past, white policy was based on the willingness of aboriginal peoples to surrender claims to land in return for reserves, annual gifts, and the right to hunt and fish on unoccupied land. The treaties arranged by W.B. Robinson with the Ojibwa in the upper Great Lakes region in 1850 included several new provisions, reflecting the changing circumstances. Among them were the rights to royalties on any minerals found on their reserves and an "escalator" clause providing for an increase in the annuity payments should the value of the surrendered land increase dramatically.

In the Atlantic colonies by 1850 the fur trade frontier was little more than a memory. The aboriginal economy was based on seasonal labour—men worked as woodsmen, guides for white hunters, and casual labourers—and artisan production, including the quill boxes and woven baskets fashioned by Native women and the axe handles, brooms, butter tubs, and barrels made by the men. Each summer the Mi'kmaq and Maliseet emerged from their winter retreats to peddle their wares in markets and

Mary Christianne Paul Morris made a living from her sale of traditional Mi'kmaq crafts. (Public Archives of Nova Scotia)

from door to door in white communities. Sought by collectors throughout the world, Native crafts were prominent among colonial exhibits appearing at the Industrial Exhibition in London in 1851, but cheap manufactured goods were beginning to undermine crafts as a mainstay of the aboriginal economy.

Despite valiant efforts to live on the margins of white culture, most aboriginal peoples had a difficult time just surviving. Their numbers declined precipitously in the first half of the nineteenth century, and by all accounts they suffered terribly from tuberculosis, typhus, smallpox, measles, scarlet fever, and whooping cough. Sickness attacked families and whole bands and drained the energy from survivors. Language barriers made it difficult for aboriginal peoples to express their concerns and to use the court system effectively. Although alcohol took its toll among whites, its effects were particularly noticeable among the Natives, whose lives were more open to public scrutiny. According to an October 1833 issue of the *Acadian Recorder*, each summer "small groups of wretched Indian men and women, in various stages of intoxication, bearing unfortunate squalid infants, and followed by half-starved dogs, were continually to be met with in our streets." Brawling between drunken Natives was relished as a spectator sport among crude and unthinking colonials.

Only treaties gave aboriginal peoples some legal grounds to use against the relentless encroachment of white settlement on reserve lands. Yet even land guaranteed by treaty had to be defended against the public policy of selling off portions of reserves to make Native administration self-sustaining. "More than once I have seen the tears trickle down the furrowed cheeks of aged Indians as they recounted the losses of their Tribe by what they always call an impolitic Treaty," Nova Scotia's Indian commissioner Abraham Gesner noted in 1847.

Aboriginal people who managed to play the white man's game had difficulty functioning within the context of the reserve system. Miramichi chief Barnaby Julien, for instance, leased reserve lands amounting to $2000 and consequently was deposed by the band on the grounds that he was personally profiting from a communal resource. The likelihood of securing the consent of a whole tribe for commercial transactions was extremely remote.

By mid-century responsibility for Indian policy was gradually being transferred from British to colonial governments. The colonies were even more reluctant than Britain to spend public money on aboriginal people. In Nova Scotia Joseph Howe was appointed first Indian commissioner under colonial legislation of 1842, but the position carried no salary and his enthusiasm soon flagged. In 1857 the colony ceased special relief payments to the Mi'kmaq and insisted that they be included under the general municipal poor laws. On Prince Edward Island, where aboriginal people had never been granted reserves, no Indian commissioner was appointed until 1856. It was only through the financial assistance of philanthropic organizations such as the Aborigines' Protection Society and the persistent efforts of Indian commissioner Theophilus Stewart that Lennox Island was finally purchased as a reserve for the island's Mi'kmaq population in 1870.

Church and philanthropic agencies frequently filled the vacuum left by sluggish colonial administrations. In 1845, Methodist minister Peter Jones, son of a white surveyor father and a Mississauga mother, established the Mount Elgin Industrial Institution at Munceytown Reserve, Canada West. The objective of the institution was to "Christianize and elevate the Indian youth of our country, to teach the boys useful trades, viz. shoe-making, carpentering and cabinet-making, as well as correct principles of farming; the girls, sewing, knitting, spinning and general house work." The Natives were also to be taught the "habits of industry and frugality," which, it was felt, were "essential to the future prosperity and happiness of our Indians."

In the Maritimes, Baptist Missionary Silas Rand compiled a Mi'kmaq dictionary, collected Indian legends, and urged evangelical beliefs upon his Roman Catholic charges. In general, the promotion of mission schools, evangelical religion, and useful skills in an environment segregated from the corrupting influences of white society testified to the paternalism of whites and the barriers preventing aboriginal peoples from full participation in North American society.

Discrimination against blacks in British North America was less formal but equally crippling in its impact. Compared with the United States, where slavery was still practised, British North America appeared to be a mecca, and refugees from the United States arrived in substantial numbers throughout the first half of the nineteenth century. They soon separated themselves both from white settlement and from the descendants of the black Loyalists. Blacks had their historical and cultural differences, but in the eyes of whites these were often blurred by the overriding factor of colour.

Notwithstanding strong anti-slavery sentiment in the colonies, the treatment of blacks was characterized by little Christian charity. Some twenty years after the arrival of the black refugees following the War of 1812, land title in Nova Scotia and New Brunswick was still uncertain. When their complaints were eventually addressed, blacks were given small allocations. The grants to their white neighbours were both larger and more efficiently registered. Following the abolition of slavery in the British empire in 1833, the Nova Scotia Assembly finally passed "An Act to prevent the Clandestine Landing of Liberated Slaves . . . from Vessels arriving in the Province."

In every area of public life blacks faced discrimination. Although black men who owned land could vote in British North America, they complained in Nova Scotia in 1841 that they could not do so "without being at every Election questioned, browbeaten and sworn." They were also denied equal access to public schooling. Only through the initiative of religious and philanthropic societies such as the Society for the Propagation of the Gospel, Dr Bray's Associates, and the Society for Promoting Christian Knowledge were schools provided for blacks.[11]

By the 1830s Canada West was the preferred destination of refugee slaves who crossed the border to settle near Windsor and Niagara Falls. Increasingly the refugees organized themselves into group settlements; a pioneering community was established at Wilberforce, near London. The most famous attempt to plant a black colony in Canada was initiated in 1842 under the auspices of the British–American Institute. Josiah Henson, a slave who escaped to Upper Canada in 1830, was the moving spirit behind the settlement, located near Chatham. Christened Dawn, the community attracted over five hundred settlers who raised tobacco, wheat, and coarse grains and engaged in lumbering activities. Believing that separation was the best means of preparing slaves for freedom, the Dawn settlers were served by their own school, church, gristmill, sawmill, and brickyard. The publication of Harriet Beecher Stowe's novel *Uncle Tom's Cabin* in 1851 brought immediate fame to Dawn, because Henson was reputedly the prototype for the character of Uncle Tom. Although there were other black refugee communities in Canada West, none received such widespread publicity.

Following the passage of the Fugitive Slave Law in the United States in 1850, permitting slave owners to pursue their "property" in non-slave states, Canada West became the terminal of the "underground railroad"— an informal network that helped blacks escape to British North America. As many as 40 000 "fugitives" made British North America their home. It was not long before they felt the cold shoulder of racial prejudice. In London, for example, whites insisted that blacks be taught in separate schools because of "the inbred feeling of repugnance in the breast of almost every white person at hybridism, which must to some extent be the result of a commingling of the races." Segregated schools were officially sanctioned in Canada West in 1850, and communities near black settlements petitioned against further black immigrants. In 1860 two blacks were hanged in Brantford, and even the most liberal of whites often assumed that black people were especially prone to thievery and violence.

Mary Ann Shadd, who in the 1850s edited a newspaper for her people called the *Provincial Freeman,* argued against the separatist tendencies of both whites and blacks, but to little avail. When John Anderson, a fugitive slave accused of killing his master, was tried in Toronto in 1860, two of the three judges, including Sir John Beverley Robinson, argued that by killing a man Anderson had made himself liable to extradition to the United States to stand trial for his crime. Following massive protests from the international abolitionist community and a threat of intervention by Britain, the case was dismissed on a technicality. Meanwhile, Anderson was taken to Britain by his abolitionist friends and he eventually settled in the West African state of Liberia.

• Contours of Colonial Society

Inequality, insecurity, and mobility characterized the lives of British North Americans in the mid-nineteenth century. Everywhere people were on the move—to the cities, to farm and timber frontiers, to new canal and railway

MARY ANN SHADD

Born in Wilmington, Delaware, in 1823, Mary Ann Shadd was the eldest child of a free black abolitionist family. She was educated at a Quaker boarding school in Pennsylvania and from 1839 to 1850 worked as a teacher in the United States. Following the passage of the Fugitive Slave Law in 1850, Shadd moved to Windsor, Canada West, where she opened a school with funds provided by the American Missionary Association. She soon became involved in anti-slavery societies and in 1852 published *A Plea for Emigration*, an information manual for African-Americans who were interested in moving to Canada West. She was the driving force behind the founding of the *Provincial Freeman*, an anti-slavery weekly newspaper, which published more or less regularly between 1854 and 1858.

An ardent integrationist, Shadd opposed the founding of segregated black communities and schools. After the death of her husband, Thomas Cary, in 1860, she supported herself and her two children by teaching at an interracial school in Chatham. Shadd moved to the United States in 1863 to help recruit volunteers for the Union Army during the American Civil War. Although she returned briefly to Canada West in 1866, she spent most of the rest of her life in the United States. She taught school to support herself while studying law at Harvard, and after graduating in 1883 she set up a practice in Washington, D.C. In 1881 she visited Canada to help organize a suffrage campaign. She died in 1893.[12]

Mary Ann Shadd   (National Archives of Canada/C29977)

construction projects, to American industrial towns, to refugee havens, to reserves, and to the seven seas of trade. Perceived by many people as a land of opportunity, British North America was, in reality, a place where as many people seemed to descend the social ladder as rise from poverty to riches.

As many unfortunate British North Americans realized, economic recessions, illnesses, and bad luck could wipe out a lifetime of hard work in an instant. The labouring class and people dependent on public charity were often close to destitution. Death and disaster threatened both young and old, rich and poor. Given the realities of colonial life, it is not surprising that community was a more abstract and idealized concept than a practical reality. Violence as much as accommodation characterized social interaction, and social control rather than consensus motivated much of public policy.

For most British North Americans a strong family unit was the best insurance policy against disaster. A few colonials married at astonishingly young ages, but most men remained unmarried until they were twenty-five years old. The majority of women were over twenty-three when they married. Protestant Scots tended to marry late and have smaller families, while French-speaking Roman Catholics married earlier and had larger families. Indeed, French-speaking women on the average could expect to bear nearly twice as many children as English-speaking women. Completed families—that is, families in which both parents lived for the mother's entire childbearing years—were large, averaging seven children in 1851. Married women of normal fertility could expect to have a child every two to three years. Urban women had fewer children than rural women. Aboriginal women also had low fecundity, as did those who suffered from extreme poverty and malnutrition.

At mid-century the average family size was beginning to decrease. For the rich, too many children brought complicated claims on their estates; for the poor they brought additional stress on the family economy. Although late marriage was the most acceptable form of family limitation, artificial methods of birth control were practised. Douches, condoms, and diaphragms were available by mid-century but not widely used. The rhythm method was inadequately understood, and patent medicines to "regulate" menstruation were highly unreliable and sometimes dangerous to a woman's health. Most married women who wanted to limit the size of their families either abstained from sexual intercourse or practised extended breast-feeding to reduce their fertility.

Social factors determined who went to school and what they learned once there. For a fur trapper, farmer, fisher, or housewife, formal schooling was far less important than practical experience. The skills of the artisan were acquired through apprenticeship. Girls learned domestic skills from their mothers and female relatives and perhaps practised them for a brief period in domestic service before setting up their own households.

Although over 60 percent of British North American youngsters received formal schooling at mid-century, most of these children attended irregularly and for only a few years. Regular and extended school attendance was difficult for the poor, especially in rural areas where children's labour was required on the farm. Historian Chad Gaffield has discovered that only 7 percent of French-speaking and 17 percent of English-speaking children between the ages of five and sixteen in Alfred Township, Canada West, were enrolled in school in 1851. While children of both ethnic groups in this frontier region had little time for school, formal education was a particularly daunting experience for those whose first language was French, because both schools in the township catered to students who spoke English. As more schools in each language were added over the following two decades, the proportion of children who went to school rose substantially, reaching about one-half for both groups in 1871.[13]

Despite the uneven educational picture, a majority of British North Americans seem to have been literate. Many of them were taught at home or in the shop. While publicly supported schools increasingly became the choice of parents for educating their children, some families continued to rely on privately operated schools. The elite wanted their children educated separately from the riff-raff, and ordinary folk often had misgivings about the public-school curriculum or the local public-school teacher. In Kingston in 1849 there were 738 children in common schools and 826 in private schools of one kind or another.

Notwithstanding the patchwork of educational institutions, it was clear to the middle class by 1850 that formal education was a valuable asset. Protestants, particularly Scots and Americans, sent their children to school more regularly than did French and Irish Catholics. Boys tended to receive more formal education than girls, and they learned different subjects. Especially in the elite private schools, emphasis was placed on Latin, science, mathematics, and philosophy for boys destined for business and the professions, while girls were taught the "ornamental skills" of sewing, music, painting, and polite manners. The growing number of common schools taught the "three r's" to both boys and girls but offered few of the "frills" found in the private schools.

Even death was forced to respect the rigid prescriptions of class, ethnicity, and religion. Members of the colonial elite could expect to live longer than the workers whose labour they hired. Thus, HBC officials outlived the aboriginal people who brought them their furs, and merchants born in British North America outlived the farmers, fishers, and timber drivers who mined the land's resources. The poor were more likely to be the victims of the periodic plagues than their wealthier and better-fed neighbours. In Native communities, "white man's" diseases continued to take their toll. French Canadians, more susceptible to fatal diseases than wealthier English Canadians, felt that the influx of plague-carrying immigrants in the early 1830s was part of a deliberate policy of ethnic genocide.

Despite its selectivity, death was a constant companion in British North America. One in five children died before reaching one year of age and the rate of infant mortality was higher in crowded, disease-ridden cities. Life expectancy was less than fifty years for both men and women and even those who managed to survive to the age of twenty could on the average expect to live only to sixty years of age. Among the poor, malnutrition was a problem, and the rich often ate such poorly balanced diets that they contracted gout and rickets.

Given the high incidence of death in colonial society, it is not surprising that much attention was paid to the rituals relating to death and dying. Wakes, funeral processions, and elaborate church services were turned into social occasions where people came together to comfort relatives and friends. In middle-class families, extended periods of mourning were observed, special mourning clothes purchased for the occasion, and separate rooms set aside for experiencing grief.

A healthy constitution was an asset in pre-industrial British North America. Most illnesses were treated by home remedies that were often more successful than the bleeding, blistering, and poisonous purges of medical doctors. Doctors commonly prescribed calomel, a derivative of mercury, and opium for stomach ailments and continued to believe in the value of bleeding their patients to cure them of their "bad humours."

By 1850 the Hippocratic theory that illness was the result of an imbalance among the four humours present in the body—black bile, phlegm, blood, and yellow bile—was gradually being abandoned, but most people still subscribed to the miasmatic theory of disease that held that "miasma," or the poisonous atmosphere from swamps, sewers, and cellars, caused plagues. It was only during the cholera epidemic of 1854 that the connection between illness and polluted drinking water was established, and it was much longer before the germ theory of disease was accepted by medical practitioners.

In 1850 university-trained doctors were on the defensive against "root doctors," homeopaths and patent-medicine dealers who were gaining wide popularity in the nineteenth century. Medical books such as John Wesley's *Primitive Physic* or Samuel Thompson's *The New Guide to Health* were particularly popular among ordinary people who found the "heroic" treatment of the medical profession less than inspiring. Armed with new therapeutic techniques, anaesthetics, and antiseptic methods, and the widespread desire to impose some control over "regular" and "irregular" practitioners, trained medical doctors in the second half of the nineteenth century moved quickly to professionalize their trade and exclude midwives, home-opaths, herbalists, and "quacks" who threatened their ascendancy. But in 1850 the medical practices of British North American physicians were, for good reasons, widely suspected. Doctors of any kind had little ability to cure a disease once it was contracted and their interventionist practices often had disastrous consequences.

British North Americans suffered from periodic epidemics of cholera, typhoid, smallpox, diphtheria, and other contagious diseases. The most dreaded scourge was cholera, a disease that struck its victims suddenly with cramps, diarrhoea, vomiting, and, in over half the cases, death.

In northern New Brunswick an outbreak of leprosy among a few Acadian families resulted in government legislation to isolate the victims from their communities. Eighteen lepers were sent to an island in the Miramichi River in 1844. Five years later they were moved to Tracadie, where the colonial Board of Health had constructed a walled lazaretto for their confinement. The angry inmates burned their building to the ground in 1852, but it was rebuilt and after Confederation Tracadie became the home of other Canadians suffering from the dread disease.

Nurses in colonial society and elsewhere were little more than poorly paid domestic servants. During the Crimean War (1854–56) British reformer Florence Nightingale began her long crusade to make nursing a profession. Hospitals in 1850 were places where the poor were incarcerated and given medicine and morality in equal doses. As late as 1861 in the Kingston General Hospital, 45 percent of the admissions were reported to be suffering from alcohol-related diseases and most of the babies born in hospitals were the children of single mothers.

Home was the place where most women had their children, aided by the services of an experienced midwife. Only affluent colonials could afford the services of a doctor. In Red River, British-born Letitia Hargrave had a doctor to assist at the birth of her first child, a procedure that intrigued the Native women of the area:

> I have good reason to be grateful to him as he had his own trouble with me neither Margaret nor Mrs Gladman knowing anything, he had everything to do, even to making my bed. I likewise got well whenever baby was born, and Mrs. Gladman said I would have died had he not

been there. The ladies here never have a doctor, nor do they go to
their bed, but sit on their knees, and she was clear for my bestirring
myself. I never will forget the look of astonishment and incredulity that
she stared at him when he congratulated me on my good behaviour.
She must have thought him easily pleased.[15]

Given the dangers associated with childbirth, middle-class British North
Americans medicalized the experience in the hope of reducing the incidence of infant and maternal mortality.

Alcohol was a widely used remedy for both physical and psychological
ailments. Home-made beer, cider, wine, and distilled liquor were supplemented by almost universal access to commercially produced rum, rye, and
beer, the preferred drinks of British North Americans. Nearly all hotels,
inns, and general stores sold alcohol, as did the ubiquitous taverns and
saloons designed especially for the purpose. For many British North
Americans, it was common to begin the day with a glass of hard liquor.
Alcohol and beer were quaffed to quench thirst, to ward off winter's chill,
to treat illness, to drown troubling thoughts, and to celebrate social occasions. A stiff swig of alcohol was often administered to a patient before
surgery. Women as well as men sought the soothing effects of alcohol, and
even children were introduced to liquor at an early age. The yearly per
capita consumption of alcohol by British North Americans was about
twenty-seven litres of liquor and beer for every man, woman, and child.
Given the growing success of the temperance movement and the fact that
half the population was under seventeen, the consumption of some British
North Americans must have been very high indeed.

•Poverty in a Cold Climate

By modern standards, British North Americans in 1850 were materially
poor. The comforts of life were difficult to acquire and even more difficult
to keep. Michael Katz has estimated that in Hamilton the bottom 40 percent
on the social scale earned only 1 percent of the income of the city and controlled only 6 percent of the city's wealth. In contrast, the top 10 percent of
the population held 88 percent of the property and 60 percent of the
wealth. While such extremes of wealth and poverty were confined to urban
centres, rural areas had their own patterns of inequality, based on control of
land and ability to work. Economic disparity naturally led to social tensions
as well as efforts to ameliorate the most obvious cases of human suffering.

The poor in British North America lived a precarious existence.
Family life, indeed survival itself, was often at stake when unemployment,
illness, death, or other disaster struck. Cases of death from hunger and

exposure were uncommon enough to warrant coverage by colonial newspapers, but it is impossible to estimate the hours of human suffering or the shortened life expectancy brought on by the ravages of poverty. The poor immigrants who flooded the colonies as a result of the famine migration of the 1840s were particularly vulnerable. In Newfoundland the seasonal nature of the fishing industry brought annual demands for massive relief, both in St John's and the outports. While the poor were sometimes blamed for their own misfortunes, it was widely recognized that poverty was often the result of circumstances beyond the control of the poor themselves. Sir Richard Bonnycastle, who served as commanding officer of the Royal Engineers in Newfoundland, noted in 1842, "If the fishery was unproductive, or the winter very rainy, the solitary settler had no means of answering the cries and wants of his family, however industrious."

When the potato blight, which devastated Ireland, also invaded British North America in the 1840s, families living on the margin of subsistence were forced back on relief for survival. "It is a well known fact that the potatoe is the only article on which a poor man and his family have to live upon for years on new back farm lands in the island of Cape Breton," one petitioner noted. Described as the "Ireland of Nova Scotia," Cape Breton was the scene of widespread famine between 1845 and 1851. Historian Robert Morgan cites the account of one woman from Loch Lomand:

> A group of men and women started from L'Ardoise by foot over blazed roads, following the lake and river down as far as Grand River then taking a blazed trail over l'Ardoise Highlands, for some of us were over thirty miles from our homes. The poor women were barefooted and each woman took her knitting along with her and knitted away as they walked over and around the hills, by waterfalls and swamps until they reached the shore, hungry and tired. Each man and woman was supplied with half a barrel of Indian meal, then they cried for something to eat. Mr. Bremner rolled out a barrel of meal and they rolled it to a brook, opened it and poured the water from the brook into the barrel and made raw cakes and passed it around to each person. All ate heartily then each man and woman took their half-barrel on their backs and sang "Ben Dorian" as they left for their homes over the blazed roads.[16]

Although most people responded generously to the plight of famine victims, some Presbyterians were quick to see God's hand in events. The *Presbyterian Witness* in August 1851 pronounced the famine as "a punishment inflicted upon man for his presumption in attempting to introduce disorder into the economy of Nature by giving undue prominence to the Potato."

Winter was an especially difficult season for the poor, who were often thrown out of work at the very time that the cost of life's necessities—food and fuel—were prohibitively expensive. Judith Fingard cites the remarks of G.E. Fenety in the 23 December 1850 edition of the Saint John *Morning News*:

> Winter is a terrible enemy to the destitute in this most rigorous climate. None but those who experience it, can tell the amount of suffering there is in this City, during five months of the year, among women and children. We see the pauper in the streets, in tattered garb and attenuated form, and he passes by and out of mind in a moment. Could we follow him to his inhospitable abode, and see his little ones crouching around a single brand of fire, to keep themselves warm, and witness the scanty meal of which they are to partake, we should soon begin to learn something of the dark shades of human life and incline towards charity.[17]

The chronically poor often lived in substandard housing, sometimes with several families to one room. Malnutrition and illness made it difficult to find and keep a wage-paying job. For very old people, pregnant mothers, and dependent children, poverty reduced them to begging on city streets or from door to door. Even the poor person's best friend and only beast of burden, the dog, showed evidence of the poverty-stricken state of its master.

Social policy relating to the poor was a haphazard mixture of public and private initiatives. Although colonial cities maintained jails, almshouses, hospitals, and asylums where the poor could take refuge, attitudes towards poverty restricted those eligible for public assistance. Only the disabled, the old, and the very young were considered "deserving" of charity. The able-bodied poor, victims of seasonal-employment patterns, the absence of kinship networks, crude exploitation, or their own human weaknesses, were given little public assistance and even less sympathy.

In rural areas, local assessment for the poor was levied on the ratepayers, a policy that led naturally to parsimony. "Outdoor" relief was handed out begrudgingly. The recipients were often required to do community work—perhaps breaking rock for roads—in return for assistance. It was common in some localities to auction the poor as labourers to the bidder who would agree to provide room and board at the lowest price. Because the poor laws permitted municipalities to "warn out" vagrants from their jurisdiction, poor immigrants often lived a peripatetic existence wandering from place to place in search of food and shelter.

Private charity dispensed by church, ethnic, and labour organizations was at once more generous and less accessible than that provided by the state. With the rapid growth of organized churches in nineteenth-century British North America, the poor could turn to the local priest or parson when all else failed. The Roman Catholic Church had a long history of involvement in charity and by 1850 was moving quickly to develop institutions to meet the needs of its rapidly growing constituency. In Protestant areas, the emergence of church-sponsored benevolent societies, staffed by the volunteer services of middle-class women, ministered to the poor. Ethnic societies also helped to take care of their own. As early as 1786 the Charitable Irish Society was founded in Halifax. The Orange Order included charity among its many activities. Labour unions often began as charitable organizations designed to help the families of members threatened by death, illness, or unemployment. A few fire and life insurance companies operated in British North America by 1850, but they offered "assurance" only to those who could afford to pay the premiums.

The poor, of course, made up the majority of those who appeared in colonial courts. While it was no longer a crime to be poor, desperation frequently led to infractions of the law and subsequent conviction. Minor offences were punished by fines, branding, or the stocks; major offences, such as theft, murder, treason, and mutiny, brought the death penalty or banishment to a penal colony. Although long prison sentences were rare, prisons outside major colonial cities were usually crowded with the poor, criminal, and insane because there were few specialized institutions to house the casualties of pre-industrial life.

The role of prisons is well illustrated by a report on prison conditions in Canada East produced by Dr. Wolfred Nelson in 1852. The report noted that women constituted 47 percent of those in Montreal's prisons at that time. According to the sheriff of Montreal, "it is very often the case that people who are simply homeless or devoid of funds are incarcerated. The old, the sick, the infirm and the mad are often sent to prison on the very vague charge of being idle and debauched and for having disturbed the peace." The doctor in the Montreal prison claimed that, "The Montreal prison is improperly referred to as simply a prison. . . . One could almost call it a maternity hospital, because so many of the women who go there are pregnant and give birth there. . . . One could call it a children's home since very large numbers of very young children are taken in there."[18]

• Social Control

Violence was a last—and for some a first—resort for expressing frustration with a society based on inequality and uncertainty. Labour disputes, along with an increased incidence of highway robbery and theft in rural areas, testified to the growing complexity and conflict in British North American communities.

Those on the margins of organized society frequently used rough justice to challenge the constituted public order. The charivari could be used not just to control private morality and public virtue but also to forge communal solidarity. Historian Bryan Palmer cites the statement of a Swiss-born missionary, Madam Feller, during the rebellion of 1837 in Lower Canada:

> The movements of the rebels always took place at night. They met in companies of one hundred, two hundred, and sometimes more. They were all masked, and they were furnished with instruments of every kind imaginable, to get up a *charivari*. They went from house to house mingling with their infernal music shouts and imprecations still more infernal. Those who did not come out immediately and join them were pelted with stones and threatened with fire. Some houses were entirely destroyed. . . . I could hardly believe they were men.[19]

In Newfoundland, *mumming* sometimes served a similar purpose to the charivari. During the period between Christmas and Twelfth Night, people donned masks and bizarre clothing, disguised their voices, and paraded throughout the community, performing strange antics in the homes of their neighbours. A typical folk ritual to shake off the restraints of everyday identity and obligations, it sometimes became an occasion for expressing hostile class and cultural feelings among the "lower orders." This was especially the case in mid-nineteenth-century St John's, where social tensions ran higher than in most outport communities. In 1861 it was made illegal to appear as a mummer, masked or otherwise disguised, in the public streets, but the custom of "visits" by mummers still prevails in many areas of Newfoundland.

Class and culture proved a potent mixture in colonial cities. Orange Orders and Ribbon societies clashed on 17 March and the "glorious 12th," bringing regular activities to a standstill. Authorities often resorted to reading the Riot Act as a means of dispersing a potentially volatile mob. Sometimes harsher measures were used. In 1853, when Italian patriot Alessandro Gavazzi gave anti-papal lectures in Montreal, the military were called out to prevent a confrontation between the city's Protestant and Roman Catholic communities. During the confusion following one of Gavazzi's public performances, the police opened fire, killing ten and wounding fifty people. The military in British North America was more often called out to put down civil disturbances and potential threats to property than to deal with threats from foreign invasion.

Mummers, as depicted in **The Evening of the Twelfth Day Fifty Years Ago—Prescott Stret** *[sic]* **by** *J.W. Hayward*   (Courtesy of Harold Hayward, great grandson. Photo courtesy University Relations Photographic Services, Memorial University of Newfoundland)

Violence punctuated all aspects of colonial life. Because voting was conducted openly, rather than by secret ballot, polling stations at election time were scenes of violence and intimidation. Although it was illegal to do so, colonial men still occasionally challenged each other to duels, and killed their opponents. Wife-beating, though increasingly considered socially unacceptable, was still legally sanctioned. Adults did not confine their aggressive behaviour to each other. Children were sometimes the victims of their anxiety-ridden elders and "spare the rod and spoil the child" informed disciplinary policy at both home and school. Even animals bore the brunt of human anger and frustration. The fate of horses, oxen, and dogs, the "beasts of burden" in colonial society, was to work to exhaustion and be shot or abandoned when no longer useful. In the late 1820s old circus animals were packed into leaky boats and sent over Niagara Falls, while callous onlookers took bets to see which ones and how many would survive.

Seaport towns were noted for their violent and illegal activities. Areas such as Lower Town in Quebec and Water Street in Halifax were separate worlds of crimps, prostitutes, and boarding-house keepers who traded in the labour of sailors and defied sea captains, shipping masters, and local constables who tried to enforce the law. Drunken and disorderly behaviour often brought seamen to colonial courts. Injured victims went to special hospitals established for sailors.

Like raftsmen and soldiers, sailors lived in an all-male environment under repressive and often violent regimes. Judith Fingard has determined that green hands, cabin boys, stewards, cooks, and blacks were most likely to be victimized by hard-bitten captains, and all sailors were the victims of the unscrupulous shore-based underworld.[20] Desertion, absence without leave, insubordination, mutiny, and other forms of resistance were common reactions among men for whom extra-legal action was as effective as colonial courts in securing justice. Until the mid-nineteenth century, vice-admiralty courts and local magistrates had often favoured sailors in their battles with captains and shipowners over wages, contracts, and working conditions. With the tightening of marine law and the appointment of stipendiary magistrates in the 1850s, the sailor had little chance of success without the help of an able—and expensive—lawyer.

The elite were equally prepared to use violence as a means of achieving their ends, throwing rocks at the governor and burning the parliament buildings when public policy failed to meet their approval. Because elite interests were expressed in both the legislatures and the law courts, there was usually little need for "respectable" citizens to resort directly to violence. In cities, councils representing property owners appointed marshals and constables to keep the peace, swore in special deputies during emergencies, and in extreme cases could call on the military for assistance. By mid-century, city fathers were beginning to establish full-time police forces and installing street lights to protect the lives and property of the respectable city folk.

Police and troops were also used to impose labour discipline on workers who believed they could use strikes or other shows of force to improve wages and working conditions. As economist H.C. Pentland observes, "The state sought by force to suppress any resistance to the unilateral determination of wages by employers."[21] For example, the Board of Works, in charge of awarding canal contracts in Canada in the 1840s, flatly rejected notions of wage negotiations and used police intervention as required to protect the profits of the contractors.

•Leisure, Sports, and Creative Arts

Most British North Americans had little time for what in the twentieth century is called leisure activity. Yet weekly and seasonal rhythms incorporated social activity as a break from the monotony of daily toil. The "sabbath" was rigorously observed among those of evangelical persuasion, and church services were important community occasions for all Christians. In rural areas, "bees" brought people together for quilting, building, planting, and harvest activities. Priests and parsons often complained of the drunkenness and immorality that prevailed at rural "frolics" that were popular among those of Scottish and Irish background.

In urban centres the military and social elite engaged in organized sports. Colonial cities also sprouted theatres where local amateur players and professional travelling troupes delighted audiences, and appalled evangelicals, with their performances. During winter months, enforced relaxation provided a good opportunity for sleighing parties, weddings, and extended visits with friends and relatives. Winter travel over well-packed snow or ice was often a welcome alternative to muddy and uncom-fortably rough roads in other seasons of the year. Diaries and letters of the colonial middle class often tell of family members reading and writing let-ters around a flickering candle or oil lamp on a chilly winter's evening.

In 1850 religious holidays had yet to take on the crass materialism that developed later in the century, but most cultural groups formally marked Christmas and Easter as well as the passing of the old year and the arrival of spring. For aboriginal peoples in the Maritime colonies, the feast of Saint Anne on 26 July was a time to meet at Shubenacadie, Chapel Island, Lennox Island, and Burnt Church to reaffirm their culture. Days devoted to St George, St Patrick, and St Andrew were celebrated by the English, Irish, and Scots respectively. Irish Protestants, and increasingly Protestants generally, remembered the anniversary of the Battle of the Boyne. Many of these cultural events preserved limited identities and made a sense of a larger community identity difficult to establish.

Games, sports, and competitions were part of the festive and commu-nal occasions of all pre-industrial cultures, but they were unorganized, unsophisticated, and accompanied by drinking and brawling. In rural areas of British North America, cock fighting, bearbaiting, horse races, wrestling, and fisticuffs were popular. The colonial elite participated in organized sports, copied, for the most part, from events held among the British aris-tocracy. Clubs devoted to racing, yachting, rowing, and curling could be found from St John's to Toronto by the mid-nineteenth century and would soon take root in Victoria. Sports developed by aboriginal peoples, most notably lacrosse and snow-shoeing, were also popular in elite circles.

As the largest British North American city, and one with a significant military presence, Montreal emerged as the centre of organized sports. It boasted the first organized club—the Montreal Curling Club—in 1807; the first cricket, lacrosse, hunt, and snow-shoeing clubs, the first Olympic Games in 1844, and the first specialized sports facilities.

The Caughnawaga Lacrosse Club, 1867   (McCord Museum of Canadian History, Notman Photographic Archives, 29,099-BI)

Cricket was the game of champions in mid-nineteenth century British North America. Historian Alan Metcalfe has identified Toronto as the cricket capital of British North America, in part because of the influence of the first headmaster of Upper Canada College, which was founded in 1829.[22] Considered a vehicle for teaching elite values, cricket was initially the sport of British immigrants and others who aped British sporting ideology. On 13 July 1836 the editor of the *Toronto Patriot* even claimed that a "cricketer as a matter of course, detests democracy and is staunch in his allegiance to his King." By the 1850s cricket enjoyed a wide popularity and cricket clubs had mushroomed all over British North America. International matches with American teams began in 1844 and became annual events after 1853.

British North Americans consumed literature produced abroad and generated some of their own. In 1850 Thomas Chandler Haliburton and Susanna Moodie had gained an international reputation for their work, which consisted primarily of humorous sketches of colonial life. Moodie's sister, Catharine Parr Traill, was one of several British writers who wrote guides for fellow immigrants. Traill's *Backwoods of Canada* (1836) and *The Canadian Settler's Guide* (1855) presented a mixture of sound advice and pious homilies that reflected the literary taste of the time.

An intellectual awakening in French Canada was one of the noteworthy cultural developments of the mid-nineteenth century. Following Durham's cruel comment that the French Canadians were a people with no literature and no culture, histories and creative writing appeared to prove the British lord wrong. François-Xavier Garneau's *Histoire du Canada*, which appeared in several volumes between 1845 and 1852, was an inspired piece of scholarship. In the Maritimes Peter Fisher and Haliburton had turned their hands to writing history and in Canada John Richardson published the *War of 1812* in 1842. Robert Christie's *History of the Late Province of Lower Canada*, published in six ponderous volumes, began appearing in 1848.

Magazines published in British North America had a difficult time competing with American publications and colonial newspapers that contained popular works of British and American writers. *The Literary Garland*, based in Montreal, expired in 1851 after a valiant effort to provide a forum for colonial writers. In the same year, Halifax-born poet Mary Eliza Herbert began publishing the *Mayflower, or Ladies Acadian Newspaper*. Devoted to literature for those who wished "to roam a while in the flowery field of romance,—to hold communion with the Muses," it survived for only nine issues and most of the contributions came from Herbert herself.

Despite the paucity of colonial contributors, the reading audience was growing and the pace of intellectual life quickening noticeably. Mechanics Institutes served as vehicles for literary and scientific dissemination among the middle classes in major colonial cities, while branches of the Institut Canadien in Canada East were hotbeds of intellectual debate and literary creativity.

Circuses and travelling shows were popular in British North America in the mid-nineteenth century. Even John A. Macdonald was reputed to have briefly joined a travelling troupe in his younger days. A "mud show," so called because of the conditions of the roads, could get around in a horse and wagon convoy, making perhaps little more than fifteen or twenty kilometres a day. With the advent of the train, travelling troupes and circuses became grander affairs, with long parades of jugglers, exotic animals, and other weird and wonderful sights parading down the village street from the railway station.

The sublime, exotic, quaint, and unusual were considered appropriate subjects in the romantic age, and British North America, in the eyes of outsiders at least, was a fertile field for the creative imagination. In 1847 New England poet Henry Wadsworth Longfellow—who never visited the

The Burning of the Parliament Building, c. 1849, by Joseph Légaré   (McCord Museum of Canadian History/M11588)

Interior of a French Canadian Farm House, by Cornelius Krieghoff   (Metropolitan Toronto Reference Library/JRR1659)

LANDSCAPE PAINTING IN A COLONIAL SETTING

As in the eighteenth century, artists in early nineteenth-century British North America were influenced by conventions defined in Europe and increasingly also in the United States. Romantic notions of the rural countryside led city-trained artists to produce idealized landscapes to grace the homes of people who could afford to buy artwork. In British North America this trend was reflected in panoramic views of the rugged colonial terrain and romantic renderings of the supposedly quaint and exotic peoples who lived there.

In their pursuit of subjects that would not offend the buying public, colonial artists often ignored reality. Thus, the Dutch-born artist Cornelius Krieghoff painted happy habitants in colourful costumes at a time when political and economic pressures were eroding seigneurial society. Similarly, the Toronto-based painter Paul Kane, who made his artistic reputation painting the aboriginal peoples of the western plains, failed to capture the dark side of a world that was being rapidly transformed by outside forces. The work of both men displays a preoccupation with light and colour typical of artists in the romantic era.

One of the most accomplished of colonial artists was Quebec-born Joseph Légaré. His use of light and colour was exceptional, and he turned out landscapes, portraits, and religious subjects to suit the most conventional tastes. At the same time, Légaré was an ardent Patriote who was arrested during the rebellions of 1837–38. Such paintings as the *Cholera Plague, Quebec* (c. 1837) and *After the Fire at Saint-Roch* (1845) testify to his political sensibility and the less romantic side of colonial life.

By the mid-nineteenth century colonial artists were being forced to adjust to the impact of photography. While the growing middle class continued to buy landscape paintings for their walls, they were now less inclined to have their portraits painted. Instead, people of all classes visited "photographic studios" where they sat motionless in front of a big, bulky mechanical device that "shot" their photographic images. The most successful photographic studio in pre-Confederation British North America was founded by William Notman, in Montreal, in 1856. Over the next thirty-five years, Notman established fourteen branch studios in Canada and the United States, all managed by his trainees, including three of his sons who followed him into the trade. The 400 000 pictures in the Notman Archives in the McCord Museum at McGill University constitute a national treasure of incalculable value.[14]

Maritimes—immortalized the deportation of the Acadians with his poem *Evangeline*. Two Cape Breton "giants," Angus McAskill and Anna Swan, became well-known attractions throughout North America and were courted by American promoter P.T. Barnum, who specialized in the bizarre and unusual. In June 1859, Blondin, the famous French funambulist, walked a tightrope over the even more famous Niagara Falls. Already a favourite haunt of tourists, especially honeymooners, the falls was becoming ringed with stalls, hawkers, and pickpockets anxious to profit from the breathtaking natural attraction.

Colonial theatres hosted a variety of functions, including live plays, music concerts, and dramatic readings. Toronto's much-praised St Lawrence Hall was opened in 1851 to accommodate, among other things, the increasing variety of local and international artists. In 1846 Haligonians converted a hay barn into the Theatre Royal, which in the following decade became the Sothern Lyceum, named after E.A. Sothern whose troupe was located briefly in the city. No British North American writer made a living from producing plays, but a few actors did well on the theatre circuit. Most plays had conventional themes that appealed to the relatively unsophisticated tastes of the colonial middle class. On occasion sparks flew, as in 1845 when a play entitled *The Provincial Association* by Thomas Hill provoked a riot among the hired hands of the satirized protectionist merchants and politicians of Saint John. Although art was still confined primarily to polite drawing-room sketches—nudes were the source of much head-shaking—a few art teachers survived in the colonies, and art shows were no longer a rare event.

In the mid-nineteenth century, music appealed to a wider audience than most artistic forms. Regimental bands, operas, operettas, symphonies, and choral recitals were well attended. Even in the backwoods, itinerant teachers inspired the formation of singing schools—all the rage in the 1850s—in which the basics of hymn and psalm singing were taught. Of course any Victorian parlour worthy of the name was incomplete without a pump organ, the perfect accompaniment to hymns and popular tunes. With its elite Grenadier and Cold Stream guards, Quebec City boasted the best band concerts in the colonies. Those British North Americans too poor or in regions too remote to attend gala performances made their own music, using their own voices and whatever musical instrument happened to be at hand. Combs, spoons, saws, and stepping feet would serve as reasonable accompaniment if nothing else was available. Many families treasured a violin or harpsichord brought from their homelands, and the very talented could often fashion instruments from local resources.

French Canadians had a rich musical heritage, which was enhanced by European immigrants such as Charles-Wugk Sabatier, who arrived from Paris in 1848. A student of the famous Conservatoire de Paris, Sabatier taught Calixa Lavallée, the future composer of *O Canada*. By 1850 Joseph Casavant, who had installed his first church organ in 1840, was already well on his way to establishing a worldwide reputation as an organ manufacturer. British North Americans were also beginning to develop careers that took them outside of their homeland. Emma (Lajeunesse) Albani, the child prodigy destined to become an international singing star, made her debut at the Mechanics' Hall in Montreal in 1856.

• Conclusion

In 1850 a hierarchical class system, the unequal distribution of wealth and status, and the carefully prescribed roles of men and women were increasingly being called into question. Although religious prescription and the ever-present threat of death and disaster tended to encourage fatalism and discourage long-range planning, "free will" was becoming increasingly accepted among the middle class as the basis for making personal decisions. For the poor and powerless, Providence, God's will, or Lady Luck were still acknowledged to have as much influence in shaping destiny as human motivation, but their social superiors would no longer tolerate such a rationalization for their pitiful state. As the values of the new industrial order settled upon the colonial landscape, everyone was called upon to rise to the occasion, and there would be no place for slackers.

• Religion and Culture:
New Historiographical Approaches

Despite the abundance of documentary evidence, the new social historians were slow to focus attention on the significance of Christian religion in Canadian development. Marxist scholars had a tendency to dismiss religion as a manifestation of "false consciousness," while early feminist writers either ignored or treated unsympathetically the impact of religion on women's culture. A few intrepid scholars, such as George Rawlyk and his students at Queen's in the 1970s, treated religion seriously enough, but they initially emphasized its conservative rather than revolutionary potential.

Recent studies, including several by George Rawlyk himself, offer a new interpretation of the role of religion in colonial society. Instead of serving as a reactionary force, evangelicalism, it is argued, struck at the roots of the divine-right ideology that justified the old aristocratic order.[23]

Historian Michael Gauvreau maintains that the several waves of evangelical fervour that occurred in the North Atlantic world in the nineteenth century "touched and transformed the religion of all social classes." In addition to empowering individuals to shoulder tremendous burdens and make great changes in their lives, evangelicalism had a significant impact on Canadian public life. Evangelicalism, Gauvreau argues, coincided exactly with the seven decades in which society, ideologies, and institutions took shape in English Canada, and it helped mould new ideologies and institutions in a way impossible in the older societies of Britain and France, and even of the United States.

Gauvreau maintains that evangelicalism was one of the key cultural forces leading to the emergence of the complex of ideas and attitudes that we designate as "modern." "For those who lived through the cataclysmic social and cultural changes of the decades between 1800 and 1870," he argues, evangelicalism "was expressive of their participation in a transatlantic movement of religious revival, which transformed not only personal piety but also values, institutional life and the relationship of the Christian churches to state and society."[24]

Like Gauvreau, John Webster Grant, in *A Profusion of Spires: Religion in Nineteenth-Century Ontario*, interprets evangelicalism as a "new age" religion that supplied the language, values, and goals for people immersed in the culture of commercial capitalism. The evangelical emphasis on "individual" religious experience and the voluntary association of free individuals prepared people for participation in a variety of voluntary associations, including temperance groups, missionary societies, fraternal groups, and Sunday Schools, as well as business enterprises and democratically elected political institutions.

By approaching religions as belief-systems rather than institutions, William Westfall in his book *Two Worlds: The Protestant Culture of Nineteenth-Century Ontario* shows that people in the nineteenth century were beginning to draw distinctions between the Old World view based on order and the new one based on experience. Anglicans such as Bishop John Strachan feared the political implications of the religious "experience" promoted by the Methodists because it led to rejection of received religion and the leadership of one's social superiors.

Gradually, over the course of the first half of the nineteenth century, the evangelical perspective prevailed and a "Protestant consensus" emerged about how the world worked. Rather than being divinely constructed, as conservative Anglicans and Roman Catholics maintained, or preordained as argued in the Calvinist tradition, the basic elements of human life were now defined as being created through the personal actions of individuals. Ultimately, the state, the economy, and society itself took shape around this consensus. "Responsible" government, "free" enterprise, and "voluntary" association became basic tools that British North Americans used to enter the second half of the nineteenth century.

•Notes

[1] Michael B. Katz, *The People of Hamilton, Canada West: Family and Class in a Mid-Nineteenth Century City* (Cambridge, MA: Harvard University Press, 1975), 103, 106.

[2] David C. Woodman, *Unravelling the Franklin Mystery: Inuit Testimony* (Montreal: McGill-Queen's University Press, 1991); Leslie H. Neatby, *The Search for the Franklin Expedition* (Edmonton: Hurtig, 1970); Owen Beattie, *Frozen in Time: Unlocking the Secrets of the Franklin Expedition* (New York: Dutton, 1988).

[3] A.R.M. Lower, *Great Britain's Woodyard: British America and the Timber Trade, 1763–1867* (Montreal: McGill-Queen's University Press, 1973), 250.

[4] Peter Ward, *Courtship, Love, and Marriage in Nineteenth-Century English Canada* (Montreal: McGill-Queen's University Press, 1990), 33.

[5] Constance B. Backhouse, "Married Women's Property Law in Nineteenth Century Canada," in *Canadian Family History: Selected Readings*, ed. Bettina Bradbury (Toronto: Copp Clark Pitman, 1992), 322.

[6] Mary Ellen Wright, "Unnatural Mothers: Infanticide in Halifax, 1850–1875," *Nova Scotia Historical Review* 7, 2 (1987): 13–30.

[7] Constance Backhouse, *Petticoats and Prejudice: Women and Law in Nineteenth-Century Canada* (Toronto: Women's Press, 1991), 113.

[8] Katz, *People of Hamilton*, 43.

[9] T.W. Acheson, *Saint John: The Making of a Colonial Urban Society* (Toronto: University of Toronto Press, 1985), 232–33.

[10] Donald Harman Akenson, *The Irish in Ontario: A Study in Rural History* (Montreal: McGill-Queen's University Press, 1984), 242.

[11] Robin Winks, *The Blacks in Canada: A History* (New Haven, CT: Yale University Press, 1971).

[12] Jason H. Silverman, "Mary Ann Camberton (Cary) Shadd," *Dictionary of Canadian Biography*, vol. 12, *1891 to 1900* (Toronto: University of Toronto Press, 1990), 960–61.

[13] Chad Gaffield, *Language, Schooling and Cultural Conflict: The Origins of the French-Language Controversy in Ontario* (Montreal: McGill-Queen's University Press, 1987), 103.

[14] See Sandra Paikowsky, "Landscape Painting in Canada," in *Profiles of Canada*, ed. Kenneth G. Pryke and Walter C. Soderlund (Toronto: Copp Clark Pitman, 1992), 336–45.

15 Cited in Linda Siegal, "Child Health and Development in English Canada," in *Health, Disease and Medicine: Essays in Canadian History*, ed. Charles G. Roland (Toronto: The Hannah Institute for the History of Medicine, 1984), 364.

16 R.J. Morgan, "'Poverty, Wretchedness and Misery': The Great Famine in Cape Breton, 1845–1851," *Nova Scotia Historical Review* 6, 1 (1986): 93.

17 Judith Fingard, "The Winter's Tale: The Seasonal Contours of Pre-Industrial Poverty in British North America, 1815–1860," Canadian Historical Association *Historical Papers* (1974): 66.

18 Raymond Boyer, *Les crimes et les châtiments au Canada français* (Montreal: Le Cercle du livre de France), 477, 482, cited in the Clio Collective, *Quebec Women: A History* (Toronto: The Women's Press, 1987), 172.

19 Bryan D. Palmer, *Working-Class Experience: The Rise and Reconstitution of Canadian Labour, 1800–1980* (Toronto: Butterworths, 1983), 44.

20 Judith Fingard, *Jack in Port: Sailortowns of Eastern Canada* (Toronto: University of Toronto Press, 1982).

21 H.C. Pentland, *Labour and Capital in Canada* (Toronto: Lorimer, 1981), 196.

22 Alan Metcalfe, *Canada Learns to Play: The Emergence of Organized Sport, 1807–1914* (Toronto: McClelland and Stewart, 1987), 17.

23 See, for example, G.A. Rawlyk, *Ravished by the Spirit: Religious Revivals, Baptists, and Henry Alline* (Montreal: McGill-Queen's University Press, 1984).

24 Michael Gauvreau, "Beyond the Half-Way House: Evangelicalism and the Shaping of English Canadian Culture," *Acadiensis* 20, 2 (Spring 1991): 158–77; "Protestantism Transformed: Personal Piety and the Evangelical Social Vision, 1815–1867," in *The Canadian Protestant Experience, 1760–1990*, ed. George A. Rawlyk (Burlington, ON: G.R. Welch, 1990), 48–97; and *The Evangelical Century: College and Creed in English Canada from the Great Revival to the Great Depression* (Montreal: McGill-Queen's University Press, 1991).

• Selected Reading

Several of the books in McClelland and Stewart's Centenary Series provide a context for the society and culture of British North America in the mid-nineteenth century: W.S. MacNutt, *The Atlantic Provinces: The Emergence of Colonial Society, 1712–1857* (Toronto: McClelland and Stewart, 1965); J.M.S. Careless, *The Union of the Canadas:*

The Growth of Canadian Institutions, 1841–1857 (Toronto: McClelland and Stewart, 1967); and E.E. Rich, *The Fur Trade and the North West to 1857* (Toronto: McClelland and Stewart, 1967). R.C. Harris and J. Warkentin, *Canada Before Confederation* (Toronto: Oxford University Press, 1974) is still the most comprehensive source of social history for the period before 1867. Also useful is Fernand Ouellet, *Economic and Social History of Quebec 1760–1850* (Toronto: Macmillan, 1981), and Brian Young and John A. Dickinson, *A Short History of Quebec: A Socio-Economic Perspective* (Toronto: Copp Clark Pitman, 1988). For the West, see the early chapters of Gerald Friesen, *The Canadian Prairies: A History* (Toronto: University of Toronto Press, 1987); Margaret Ormsby, *British Columbia: A History* (Toronto: Macmillan, 1958); and Jean Barman, *The West Beyond the West: A History of British Columbia* (Toronto: University of Toronto Press, 1991). Raw data on the population and production from pre-Confederation censuses is contained in the *Census of Canada, 1871*, Vol. 4, and analysed in M.C. Urquhart and K.A.H. Buckley, eds., *Historical Statistics of Canada* (Cambridge: Cambridge University Press, 1965); F.H. Lacey, ed., *Historical Statistics of Canada*, 2nd ed. (Ottawa: Statistics Canada, 1983); Jacques Henripin, *Tendances et facteurs de fécondité au Canada* (Ottawa: Ministry of Supply and Services, 1968).

Nineteenth-century conditions leading to improvements in transportation and urban amenities are described in Norman R. Ball, ed., *Building Canada: A History of Public Works* (Toronto: University of Toronto Press, 1988). The role of the military is the subject of Elinor Kyte Senior, *British Regulars in Montreal: An Imperial Garrison, 1832–1854* (Montreal: McGill-Queen's University Press, 1981); and the early chapters of Desmond Morton, *Canada and War: A Military and Political History* (Toronto: Butterworths, 1981). Several detailed studies have contributed much to our understanding of social history in the pre-Confederation period: T.W. Acheson's *Saint John: The Making of a Colonial Urban Community* (Toronto: University of Toronto Press, 1985); Donald Akenson, *The Irish in Ontario: A Study in Rural History* (Montreal: McGill-Queen's University Press, 1984); David Gagan, *Hopeful Travellers: Families, Land and Social Change in Mid-Victorian Peel County, Canada West* (Toronto: Ontario Historical Studies Series, 1981); Michael Katz, *The People of Hamilton, Canada West: Family and Class in a Mid-Nineteenth Century City* (Cambridge, MA: Harvard University Press, 1976); Claude Baribeau, *La Seigneurie de la Petite Nation, 1801–1854: Le role économique et social du seigneur* (Hull, PQ: Asticou, 1983); Normand Séguin, *La Conquête du sol au 19è Siècle* (Montreal: Boréal Express, 1977); and J.I. Little, *Crofters and Habitants: Settler Society, Economy and Culture in a Quebec Township, 1848–1881* (Montreal: McGill-Queen's University Press, 1991). More general studies of rural life include John McCallum, *Unequal Beginnings: Agriculture and Economic Development in Quebec and Ontario to 1870* (Toronto: University of Toronto Press, 1980); and Marjorie Griffen Cohen, *Women's Work, Markets, and Economic Development in Nineteenth-Century Ontario* (Toronto: University of Toronto Press, 1988).

The working class in the nineteenth century has received considerable attention, most notably in Bryan D. Palmer's *The Working Class Experience: Rethinking the History of Canadian Labour, 1800–1991*, 2nd ed. (Toronto: McClelland and Stewart, 1992); M.S. Cross, ed., *The Workingman in the Nineteenth Century* (Toronto: Oxford University Press, 1975); and Steven Langdon, *The Emergence of the Working-Class Movement, 1845–1875* (Toronto: New Hogtown, 1975). Class and culture are the subjects of J.I. Cooper, "The Social Structure in Montreal in the 1850s," Canadian Historical Association, *Report* (1956); and Fernand Ouellet, "Liberté ou exploité: le paysan québécois d'avant 1850," *Histoire sociale/Social History* 13, 26 (Nov. 1980): 339–68. The plight of poor and easily exploited groups in Victorian society is a major theme in Judith Fingard's *The Dark Side of Life in Victorian Halifax* (Porters Lake, NS: Pottersfield, 1989), and *Jack in Port: Sailortowns of Eastern Canada* (Toronto: University of Toronto Press, 1982), and in her much-quoted article, "The Winter's Tale: The Seasonal Contours of Pre-Industrial Poverty in British North America, 1815–1860," Canadian Historical Association *Historical Papers* (1974): 65–94. See also Richard B. Splane, *Social Welfare in Ontario, 1791–1893: A Study of Public Welfare Administration* (Toronto: University of Toronto Press, 1965).

Women's experience is summarized in Alison Prentice, Paula Bourne, Gail Cuthbert Brandt, Beth Light, Wendy Mitchinson, and Naomi Black, eds., *Canadian Women: A History* (Toronto: Harcourt Brace Jovanovich, 1988); and the Clio Collective, *Quebec Women: A History* (Toronto: Women's Press, 1986). See also Peter Ward, *Courtship, Love and Marriage in Nineteenth Century English Canada* (Montreal: McGill-Queen's University Press, 1990). The social implications of legal reform in the period are discussed in several collections of articles: four volumes of *Essays in the History of Canadian Law* (Toronto: University of Toronto Press, 1981, 1983, and 1990); Peter Waite et al., *Law in a Colonial Society: The Nova Scotia Experience* (Toronto: Carswell, 1984); W. Wesley Pue and Barry Wright, *Canadian Perspectives on Law and Society: Issues in Legal History* (Ottawa: Carleton University Press, 1988); and R.C. Macleod, ed., *Lawful Authority: Readings on the History of Criminal Justice in Canada* (Toronto: Copp Clark Pitman, 1988). On the same subject, see Constance Backhouse, *Petticoats and Prejudice: Women and Law in Nineteenth-Century Canada* (Toronto: Women's Press, 1991), and "Married Women's Property Law in Nineteenth-Century Canada," in *Canadian Family History: Selected Readings*, ed. Bettina Bradbury (Toronto: Copp Clark Pitman, 1992), 320–59.

Religion in the mid-nineteenth century is the focus of work by Michael Gauvreau, *The Evangelical Century: College and Creed in English Canada from the Great Revival to the Great Depression* (Montreal: McGill-Queen's University Press, 1991); William Westfall, *Two Worlds: The Protestant Culture of Nineteenth-Century Ontario* (Montreal: McGill-Queen's University Press, 1989); John Webster Grant, *A Profusion of Spires: Religion in Nineteenth-Century Ontario* (Toronto: University of Toronto Press, 1988); Jacques Monet, *The Last Cannon Shot: A Study of French-Canadian Nationalism*

(Toronto: University of Toronto Press, 1969); Nire Voisine and Jean Hamelin, eds., *Les Ultramontaines Canadiens-français* (Montreal: Boréal Express, 1985); Goldwin French, *Parsons and Politics: The Role of the Wesleyan Methodists in Upper Canada and the Maritimes from 1780–1855* (Toronto: Ryerson Press, 1962); George Rawlyk, *Ravished by the Spirit: Religious Revivals, Baptists, and Henry Alline* (Montreal: McGill-Queen's University Press, 1984) and *Canadian Baptists and Christian Higher Education* (Montreal: McGill-Queen's University Press, 1988); and John S. Moir, *The Church in the British Era: From Conquest to Confederation* (Toronto: McGraw-Hill Ryerson, 1972). For a discussion of current thinking on the evangelical tradition, see Michael Gauvreau, "Beyond the Half-Way House: Evangelicalism and the Shaping of English Canadian Culture," *Acadiensis* 20, 2 (Spring 1991): 158–77.

For education in this period see Susan Houston and Alison Prentice, *Schooling and Scholars in Nineteenth Century Ontario* (Toronto: University of Toronto Press, 1988); Bruce Curtis, *Building the Educational State: Canada West, 1836–1871* (London, ON: Althouse Press, 1988); Alison Prentice, *The School Promoters: Education and Social Class in Mid-Nineteenth Century Upper Canada* (Toronto: McClelland and Stewart, 1977); J.D. Wilson et al., *Canadian Education: A History* (Toronto: Prentice-Hall, 1970); and Claude Galarneau, *Les collèges classiques au Canada français* (Montreal: Fides, 1978).

The experience of aboriginal peoples is discussed by L.S.F. Upton, *Micmacs and Colonists: Indian–White Relations in the Maritimes, 1713–1867* (Vancouver: University of British Columbia Press, 1979); Donald Smith, *The Reverend Peter Jones (Kahkewaquonaby) and the Mississauga Indians* (Toronto: University of Toronto Press, 1987); Robin Fisher, *Contact and Conflict: Indian–European Relations in British Columbia, 1774–1890* (Vancouver: University of British Columbia Press, 1977); Ian A.L. Getty and Antoine S. Lussier, eds., *As Long as the Sun Shines and the Rivers Flow: A Reader in Canadian Native Studies* (Vancouver: University of British Columbia Press, 1983); Robin Fisher and Kenneth Coates, eds., *Out of the Background: Readings in Canadian Native History* (Toronto: Copp Clark Pitman, 1988); and Kenneth Coates and William R. Morrison, eds., *Interpreting Canada's North* (Toronto: Copp Clark Pitman, 1989).

Blacks are the subject of Robin Winks, *The Blacks in Canada: A History* (Montreal: McGill-Queen's University Press, 1971); and Daniel Hill, *The Blacks in Early Canada: The Freedom-Seekers* (Agincourt, ON: Book Society, 1981). See also Jason H. Silverman, "Mary Ann Camberton (Cary) Shadd," *Dictionary of Canadian Biography*, Vol. 12, *1891 to 1900* (Toronto: University of Toronto Press, 1990), 960–61.

Sickness and health are discussed in Geoffrey Bilson, *A Darkened House: Cholera in Nineteenth-Century Canada* (Toronto: University of Toronto Press, 1980); Wendy Mitchinson, *The Nature of Their Bodies: Women and Their Doctors in Victorian Canada*

(Toronto: University of Toronto Press, 1991); and Charles G. Roland, ed., *Health, Disease and Medicine: Essays in Canadian History* (Toronto: Irwin, 1984). Sports in the nineteenth century is the focus of Alan Metcalfe, *Canada Learns to Play: The Emergence of Organized Sport, 1807–1914* (Toronto: McClelland and Stewart, 1987); Morris Mott, *Sports in Canada: Historical Readings* (Toronto: Copp Clark Pitman, 1989); and Don Morrow et al., *A Concise History of Sports in Canada* (Toronto: Oxford University Press, 1989).

Literature in the mid-nineteenth century is discussed in Carl Klinck, *Literary History of Canada* (Toronto: University of Toronto Press, 1976). Historiographical developments are the subject of M. Brook Taylor, *Promoters, Patriots and Partisans: Historiography in Nineteenth-Century English Canada* (Toronto: University of Toronto Press, 1989); and Serge Gagnon, *Quebec and Its Historians* (Montreal: Harvest House, 1982). The folk custom of mumming is explored in Herbert Halpert and G.M. Storey, eds., *Christmas Mumming in Newfoundland* (Toronto: University of Toronto Press, 1969). J. Russell Harper has written extensively on nineteenth-century art and artists. A good place to start is his *Painting in Canada: A History* (Toronto: University of Toronto Press, 1977). *The Historical Atlas of Canada*, the *Horizon* series, *The Dictionary of Canadian Biography*, and *Canada's Visual History Series* each offer valuable perspectives on aspects of Canadian social and cultural history. See also Sandra Paikowsky, "Landscape Painting in Canada," in *Profiles of Canada*, ed. Kenneth G. Pryke and Walter R. Soderlund (Toronto: Copp Clark Pitman, 1992), 336–45.

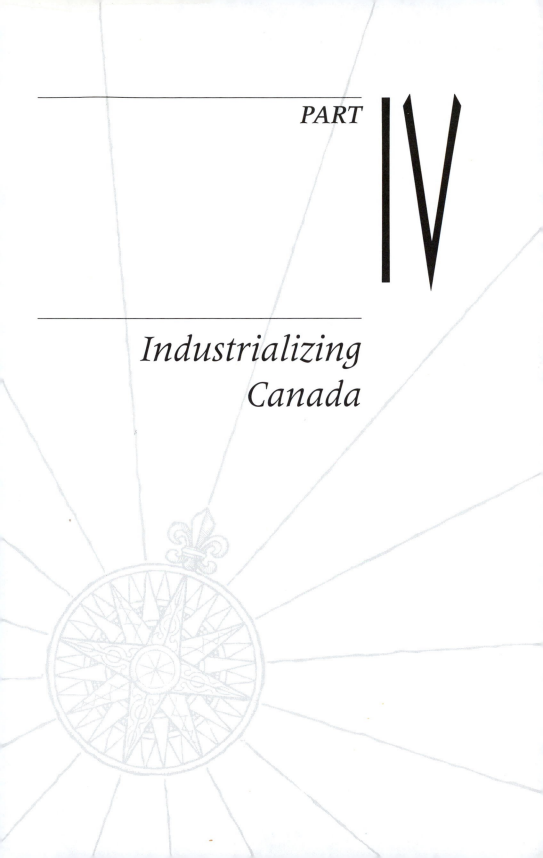

PART **IV**

Industrializing
Canada

Time Line

1844	–	Provincial association in New Brunwick calls for higher tariffs
1844–76	–	Egerton Ryerson is superintendant of education in Canada West/Ontario
1849	–	Joseph Howe proposes Intercolonial Railway; Annexation Manifesto; British North America League calls for union of British North American colonies
1854	–	Reciprocity agreement signed
1854–56	–	Crimean War
1858	–	Association for the Protection of Canadian Industry established; A.T. Galt proposes confederation of British North American colonies
1859	–	Grand Trunk Railway completed; Darwin's *The Origin of Species* published
1861–65	–	American Civil War

1862	–	Reform ministry formed in United Province of Canada
1863	–	Conservatives win majority in Nova Scotia; election in United Province of Canada produces an impasse
1864	–	Pro-confederation coalition government formed in United Province of Canada; Charlottetown conference; Quebec City conference
1865	–	New Brunswick elects anti-confederate majority; legislature of United Province approves confederation
1866	–	Fenian raids; New Brunswick elects pro-confederate majority; Nova Scotia legislature approves further negotiations on confederation; London conference; Reciprocity ends
1867	–	Confederation of New Brunswick, Nova Scotia, Quebec, and Ontario

CHAPTER 13

BRITISH NORTH AMERICA'S REVOLUTIONARY AGE

At noon-hour on a fine July day in 1836, some three hundred guests arrived by ferry in the town of La Prairie on the south shore of the St Lawrence, just across from Montreal. The new wood-burning locomotive the *Dorchester*, recently delivered from Newcastle-upon-Tyne in England, was set to take its first trip for the Champlain and Saint Lawrence Railroad, travelling south to St-Jean on the Richelieu. The directors of the railway company were nervous: they didn't know if the great machine would work or not.

> It was a beautiful summer day. . . . The governor of British North America, the Earl of Gosford, got on board. Other government officials, British military officers and the directors of the company and their wives climbed in. In all, 32 passengers boarded. The last door slammed and they puffed off on their first ride on a steam train.
>
> The rest of the dignitaries got into the other ten cars and were towed along the line by teams of horses. . . . At the station in Saint-Jean a cold buffet was served with champagne. Peter McGill, chairman of the board, presided at the ceremony. He proposed two toasts: the first to the king of England, the other to the President of the United States. Without the Americans, he said . . . the railway would not have been built.
>
> "Too much praise cannot be bestowed," wrote Thomas Storrow Brown reporting the event in Montreal's radical newspaper *The Vindicator*. "We in Canada are so accustomed to see things done ill, that a work well done is a miracle."[1]

Little did Thomas Storrow Brown realize on 26 July 1836 that less than two weeks earlier, the *Dorchester* had been reported out of order. The engineer, also imported from England, had forgot to put out the fire before draining the boiler on the trial run. No wonder company directors were apprehensive. Despite some anxious moments, the *Dorchester* managed to impress excited onlookers and made its run. The age of the iron horse had dawned in British North America.

•Industrial Revolution

In the mid-nineteenth century, British North Americans were conscious of living in an era of rapid change. New ideas, new methods of transportation, and new ways of doing things were quickening the pace of life and requiring people to adapt to new challenges. Sweeping all before it, the Industrial Revolution was transforming the economy and society of the North Atlantic world.

The impact of the Industrial Revolution on British North America was distinctive in two respects. First, the colonies experienced the effects of industrialism long before they were industrialized themselves. Second, the timing of British North America's Industrial Revolution coincided with a revolution in communications and values that made its advent all the more "revolutionary." Initially restricted to a few industries and locations, industrial growth inspired dreams of confederation from the Atlantic to the Pacific and the fruits of industrialism—most notably the railway—helped to make those dreams a reality.

The Industrial Revolution takes its name from fundamental changes in technology and the organization of production that gradually transformed how people lived. The world's first industrial nation was Great Britain, which pioneered in the application of machines to production, and steam power to machines, in key sectors of the economy: agriculture, manufacturing, and transportation. In the eighteenth century, developments in mining and metallurgy made Great Britain a leader in the production of pig iron in large quantities and at low costs. British "mechanics," inspired by the possibilities of iron and steam power, experimented with machinery that transformed the labour process. By the end of the eighteenth century, spinning machines and power looms had multiplied textile output in Britain far beyond anything that could be done by human hands. Within a remarkably short time machines were developed to perform a wide range of tasks, and the volume of manufactured products exploded.

Mechanization also changed how people related to each other. In pre-industrial society artisans had retained control of the production process, making a product from start to finish and determining standards and prices through organizations called guilds. Now, machines encouraged the division of labour into repetitive tasks; they also encouraged centralization—work was centralized at factories where the machines were located, and control of the factory system was centralized in the hands of a few capitalists who could finance such extensive operations. Under the factory system labourers lost control over their work. Factory owners, if they were competitive and shrewd, became wealthy from their entrepreneurial activities.

There was nothing particularly inevitable about this process, except that commercial societies in Britain and North America had a well-developed exchange system that adapted easily to industrialism. Since the fifteenth century, successful merchants, artisans, and farmers in the North Atlantic world had gradually adopted a capitalist perspective. They worked for profit instead of subsistence; they translated all transactions into monetary value; they established structures such as joint-stock companies and banks to accumulate capital; they experimented with new ways of performing traditional tasks; and they developed laws to protect their property and the market system from fraud, piracy, and theft. As they grew in numbers and wealth, capitalists had little difficulty incorporating people and resources into their exchange processes or in convincing governments to pass legislation to protect their new interests. Under the pressure from this new entrepreneurial class, the communal management of land in the countryside, the guild control of industry in the towns, and the privilege of monopoly were all eventually pushed aside to facilitate the new industrial order.

Industrial capitalism transformed Britain and eventually the whole world. It introduced a new materialism that challenged traditional spiritual values, encouraged the growth of cities at the expense of the countryside, and created a new class structure based on relationship to production rather than heredity. It redistributed wealth geographically as well as socially and drove a wedge between the public world of work and the private realm of the family. It altered the relationship among men, women, and children and the relationship of human beings to their natural environment.

British North Americans were no strangers to this revolutionary process. They read about the new machines in their newspapers, purchased the products of Britain's factories with their hard-earned cash, and sent an increasing volume of their own raw resources to sustain Britain's expanding industrial economy. The impact of the changing British economy was also felt on colonial policy. As the output of British factories began to dominate world markets, formal colonies became less important to imperial strategy. The rising middle class of industrialists in Britain wanted a policy of *laissez-faire*, which meant fewer taxes and less government intervention in the market economy. Colonies, they argued, were an expensive luxury, at least those colonies controlled by white settlers who could be safely left alone to govern themselves. Let the invisible hand of supply and demand be allowed to operate freely and Britain would soon conquer the whole world economically rather than militarily. These industrial interests prevailed, which for the colonies meant free trade and responsible government. The onus was now on British North Americans to decide what economic strategy to pursue.

• Free Trade, Reciprocity, and Protection

"We are in the same condition as a man suddenly precipitated from a lofty eminence. We are labouring under concussion of the brain." This remark came from George S. Workman, president of the Toronto Board of Trade, after Britain's adoption of free trade. The mercantile community in the colony of Canada was thrown into a tailspin by the commercial revolution of the 1840s. Its members were equally nonplussed by the temporary loss of political power signalled by the introduction of responsible government. In their frustration they lashed out against the governor and the British Parliament and even considered severing all ties with the British empire.

It was, nevertheless, a good time to experience economic crisis. The British economy was entering a boom period that would last for over two decades. With typical enthusiasm and success, the Americans had also embarked on the road to industrialization and were gobbling up resources at an amazing rate. The discovery of gold in California, Australia, British Columbia, and New Zealand and the expansion of credit through the growing bank and insurance businesses fuelled the global economy. In addition the Crimean War (1854–56) in Europe and the Civil War in the United States (1861–65) increased the demand for colonial products. If circumstances had thrust the colonies back on their own devices, the context was favourable for developing economic strategies appropriate for the industrial age.

While a few merchants, especially those closely tied to the timber and wheat trade, saw annexation to the United States as the solution to their temporarily failing fortunes, others, in particular those involved in the production side of the trading process, advocated a protectionist strategy to develop internal markets. The British–American League, which was formed

ANNEXATION MANIFESTO

In October 1849 a number of leading Montreal merchants issued a manifesto calling for annexation to the United States. The first paragraph read, in part: "Of all the remedies that have been suggested for the acknowledged and insufferable ills with which our country is afflicted, there remains but one to be considered. . . . THIS REMEDY CONSISTS IN A FRIENDLY AND PEACEFUL SEPARATION FROM THE BRITISH CONNECTION AND A UNION UPON EQUITABLE TERMS WITH THE GREAT NORTH AMERICAN CONFEDERACY OF SOVEREIGN STATES." The manifesto also outlined the advantages that the merchants felt would come from such a union:

> The proposed union would render Canada a field for American capital, into which it would enter as freely for the prosecution of public works and private enterprise as into any of the present States. It would equalise the value of real estate upon both sides of the boundary, thereby probably doubling at once the entire present value of property in Canada, whilst, by giving stability to our institutions, and introducing prosperity, it would raise our public corporate and private credit. It would increase our commerce, both with the United States and foreign countries, and would not necessarily diminish to any great extent our intercourse with Great Britain, into which our products would for the most part enter on the same terms as present. It would render our rivers and canals the highway for the immigration to and exports from, the West, to the incalculable benefit of our country. It would also introduce manufacturers into Canada as rapidly as they have been introduced into the northern states; and to Lower Canada especially, where water privileges and labour are abundant and cheap, it would attract manufacturing capital, enhancing the value of property and agricultural produce and giving remunerative employment to what is at present a comparatively non-producing population. Nor would the United States merely furnish the capital for our manufacturers. They would also supply them the most extensive market in the world, without the intervention of a custom house officer. Railways would forthwith be constructed by American capital as feeders for all the great lines now approaching the frontiers; and railway enterprise in general would doubtless

be as active and prosperous among us as among our neighbours. The value of our agricultural produce would be raised
at once to a par with that of the United States, whilst agricultural implements and many of the necessities of life, such as
tea, coffee and sugar, would be greatly reduced in price.

Among those who signed the manifesto were John Abbott, who would one
day be a Canadian prime minister, and Alexander Galt, who would serve
as finance minister for the colony of Canada in the 1850s.

in 1849 to challenge annexationist sentiment, included tariff protection as
a plank in its platform and called for a union of all British North America
as a means of "creating large home markets for the consumption of agricultural products and domestic manufactures." Still others, eyeing the nearest
booming industrial economy, suggested free trade with the United States
as the best policy for sustaining British North America's primary industries.
Annexation was quickly abandoned by all but the most principled republicans, and a union of British North America still seemed highly impractical.
Tariff protection was perceived as an inadequate measure by a business
community dominated by mercantile interests. Free trade, perhaps, was an
idea whose time had come.

In 1851 the eastern British North American colonies agreed to free
trade among themselves in natural products. Three years later Britain
negotiated a reciprocity, or free-trade, treaty that provided for the free
exchange of natural products between the British North American colonies
and the United States. Under the Reciprocity Treaty, which remained in
effect from 1855 to 1866, colonial staples such as foodstuffs, wheat, timber,
fish, and coal found American markets to supplement their imperial ones,
while Americans enjoyed access to the inshore fisheries of the Atlantic
region and access to the Great Lakes–St Lawrence canal system.

Economists disagree about the exact impact of the reciprocity agreement on the British North American economy. Even without free trade the
American market was looming ever larger on the British North American
horizon. Moreover, the outbreak of the Civil War between the northern
and southern states in 1861 stimulated the southern movement of commodities essential for the war effort. The disruption of the American economy resulting from the war would have stimulated British North American
trade no matter what policy was in place. What is clear is that the
Reciprocity Treaty coupled with the Civil War reinforced north–south lines
of trade and gave British North Americans another option in a world of
expanding markets.

Protectionists did manage to win small victories. In Saint John, local producers had established a Provincial Association in 1844 to lobby the government for a protective tariff policy. Following the introduction of free trade, the New Brunswick legislature raised the tariffs on imported manufactures. In Canada, the tariff was set at 12.5 percent of the value of imports in 1849 and raised even higher in 1858 and 1859. Although the goal was still to raise revenue, or so Finance Minister Alexander Galt argued in 1859, it clearly served to protect local producers from cheaper imports. The Association for the Protection of Canadian Industry, established in 1858, included among its ranks agricultural-implements manufacturer Hart Massey, furniture manufacturer Robert Hay, and drug manufacturer William Lyman. Behind a tariff wall these and other entrepreneurs could develop a "Home Industry" and perhaps become strong enough to compete effectively in other regions of British North America. Countering the free traders who argued that tariffs raised the costs to colonial consumers, Montreal-based journalist D'Arcy McGee maintained that the effect of judicious protection would "not be to make them dear, but to make them here."

• Transportation

In addition to revolutionizing production techniques, mechanization also inspired new methods of transportation. Steam applied to sea and land transport offered a stronger and more reliable power than wind, water, and animal power. Steamboats became commercially viable in the first decade of the nineteenth century; railways in the 1820s and 1830s. In Britain industrialization was under way before the transportation revolution wrought by steam, but in British North America the steamboat and the railway accompanied and accelerated the industrialization process.

In 1809, two years after the world's first steamship navigated up the Hudson River in New York State, John Molson, an ambitious Montreal brewer, launched the steamship *Accommodation* in partnership with two Englishmen. Its six-horse-power engine was made at the Saint-Maurice forges. Although the *Accommodation* was a commercial failure, its successors did a roaring trade on the Great Lakes and St Lawrence, and competition for traffic among the "river barons" was keen. Halifax native Samuel Cunard was the merchant prince of steam service throughout the Atlantic region. In 1830 he joined forces with other merchants in Halifax and Quebec City to run a mail service between the two port cities. This group also sponsored the *Royal William*, which in 1833 made one of the first

*The **Royal William** was the first Canadian ship to cross the Atlantic almost continuously under steam. In 1833, it took twenty-five days to make the trip from Pictou, Nova Scotia, to Gravesend, England*   (J.P. Cockburn/National Archives of Canada/C12649)

Atlantic crossings under steam. In 1840, when Cunard succeeded in capturing the contract for mail delivery between Britain and North America, steam had come of age in British North America.

By that time colonials were all agog with the potential of the iron horse. Only space travel in the twentieth century compares with the railway in the degree of public excitement it induced. Although American engineers supervised the construction of the twenty-four-kilometre line from St-Jean on the Richelieu River to La Prairie on the St Lawrence, Montrealers provided the financing. A great chunk of it came from the Molson family. Railways promised to liberate British North Americans from the problems of climate and isolation and fully launch them on the road to progress. Canadian engineer T.C. Keefer, who wrote a book entitled *Philosophy of Railroads* in 1850, waxed positively lyrical about their potential, indicating that they would form a "powerful antidote" to the "state of primitive" existence in the colonies:

> Poverty, indifference, the bigotry or jealousy of religious denominations, local dissensions or political demagogueism may stifle or neutralize the influence of the best intended efforts of an educational system; but that invisible power which has waged successful war with the material elements, will assuredly overcome the prejudices of mental weakness or the designs of mental tyrants. It calls for no cooperation, it waits for

no convenient season, but with a restless, rushing, roaring assiduity, it keeps up a constant and unavoidable spirit of enquiry or comparison; and while ministering to the material wants, and appealing to the covetousness of the multitude, it unconsciously, irresistibly, impels them to a more intimate union with their fellow men.[2]

While the reality of the railway never quite matched the grand promise prophesied by Keefer, the mid-nineteenth-century railway boom generated industry in British North America and inspired dreams of bigger and better lines and bigger and better political organizations to sustain them. Among the many supporters of Confederation were railway promoters and politicians, the heroes and villains of British North America's early age of industry.

In the years between 1852 and 1867 the British North American colonies built over 3200 kilometres of track and sank over $100 million into railways. Much of the capital came from Britain, as did the expertise required to build the new transportation systems. Colonial governments, whatever their political stripe, were obliging in their efforts to support railway development. Joseph Howe was a great railway booster, and the Liberal government in which he served sponsored lines from Halifax to Windsor and Pictou. His Conservative nemesis Charles Tupper was equally enthusiastic about the potential of railways in his native province, especially a railroad that would make his Cumberland County constituency the link between Nova Scotia and points north and west. New Brunswickers sank money into a railway, grandly labelled the European and North American, which ran between Shediac on the Northumberland Strait and Saint John on the Bay of Fundy. A line connecting St Andrews with Quebec was abandoned in the backwoods of New Brunswick when its promoters ran out of money in 1863.

The Canadians were among the world's great railway builders in the 1850s. One of the first acts of the Baldwin–La Fontaine administration was to guarantee the interest on half the bonded debt of railways over 120 kilometres long. Municipalities were also given legislative authority to invest in railway company shares, and in 1852 local investment in railways was further encouraged by a provincially backed Municipal Loan Fund. In the initial flush of railway enthusiasm, British North American politicians made plans for an intercolonial railway that would link Canadians to an ice-free Atlantic port. Failure to agree on a route or to secure imperial backing caused the expensive project to be abandoned. In the meantime, a Montreal–Portland line, completed in 1853, gave the colony of Canada its much-desired winter port. By the end of the decade railways crisscrossed the colony, reaching northward to the timber stands of the Ottawa Valley and Lake Huron and linking the market towns of the Ontario peninsula.

Canada's most ambitious project was the Grand Trunk Railway. Completed in 1859, it was one of the longest railways in the world, stretching from Quebec City to Sarnia and on American lines to Chicago.

Despite the enthusiasm of their promoters, the Grand Trunk and other government-sponsored railways proved a burden to colonial taxpayers. The decision to raise tariffs in both New Brunswick and Canada in the 1850s had as much to do with the need to raise revenue to finance the growing railway debt as it did with the protection of colonial producers. In a curious feat of convoluted logic, colonial politicians and promoters argued that the solution to failing railways was more railways—to link the colonies with each other and with American lines, and even with the Pacific Ocean. Only by expanding could railways tap new frontiers and secure the traffic that would make them pay.

The close link between railway promoters and politicians in the colony of Canada inevitably led to scandals. Politicians bought shares in railway companies and sat on their boards. Although the line between public and private interests was not then as carefully drawn as it would be later on, the prospect of government leader Francis Hincks making £10 000 on the Great Northern Railway contract in 1854 raised more than a few eyebrows. Hincks was forced to resign over the "Ten Thousand Pound Job" but he did not go to jail, nor was he made to give back the money.

If railways were sometimes a failing and scandalous proposition, they nevertheless fulfilled many of the expectations outlined by their promoters. Areas where the railway ran invariably experienced a quickening of economic pace. In the cities where railway-repair shops were located, heavy industry was given a tremendous boost.

Historians Paul Craven and Tom Traves have noted that large railway companies such as the Grand Trunk were Canada's first "large scale integrated corporations." Not only were they transportation companies, but they also had the capacity to rebuild and repair lines, to manufacture locomotives and industrial machinery, to store and forward freight, to operate grain elevators and steamships, and to maintain large administrative offices. They were among the largest employers in the colony. Through their practices relating to management, division of labour, accounting, quality control, and even waste recycling, they introduced advanced capitalist practices into British North American society.

A journalist's 1857 description of the Great Western's locomotive shop in Hamilton suggests the awe inspired by the magnitude of the site:

> The first room we entered seemed to be the general hospital, in which the sick giants were disposed in long rows and supported at consider-

able height, on wooden blocks and beams. Passing in we came to two rows of ponderous machines. There were drilling machines, boring holes of various sizes through any thickness of metal. There were planing machines which dealt with iron and brass as if they were soft wood, and rapidly reduced the blocks of metal to the necessary form— machines which cut iron as if it were paper, and punched holes through quarter inch plates as easily as you would punch a gun-wad from a piece of pasteboard. Lathes of all imaginable shapes and sizes, for doing all imaginable things, and in short, the complete furniture of a first class establishment.[3]

In Montreal the Grand Trunk which eventually employed nearly two thousand people and included a wide range of metal-producing shops, was a monument to the industrial era.

British North America's industrial revolution came of age with the railway, but its origins can be found in earlier transportation developments. Historian Gerald Tulchinsky has shown that in the 1840s industries located along the Lachine Canal were near transportation routes and potential hydraulic power. Between 1847 and 1854 $500 000 was invested in thirty industries in Lachine by entrepreneurs from Canada, Britain, and the United States. Mills and factories producing flour, beer, iron, furniture, sewing machines, steam engines, heating and ventilating equipment, paints, rubber, footwear, clothes, and drugs employed nearly two thousand people who crowded into the nearby suburbs of Saint-Ann's, Point Saint-Charles, and Verdun. By 1856 Montrealers boasted that their city was "the best site for a manufacturing city in Canada, perhaps on the Continent."

• Mobilizing Labour and Capital

Money was the lifeblood of capitalism, and channelling money into enterprises with the greatest potential for profit was at the heart of the industrial capitalist system. In pre-industrial British North America, colonial governments, military commissariats, banks, and successful merchants often accumulated large pools of capital, but most major projects, such as Canadian canals and railways, relied on capital from Britain. As late as the 1840s the Bank of Montreal's paid-up capital stock was smaller than that of the city's military commissariat.[4] Commentators complained about how easily capital was drained out of the colonies to purchase British and American products. If the colonies could substitute their own manufactures for imports, they reasoned, more capital could be invested in colonial enterprises.

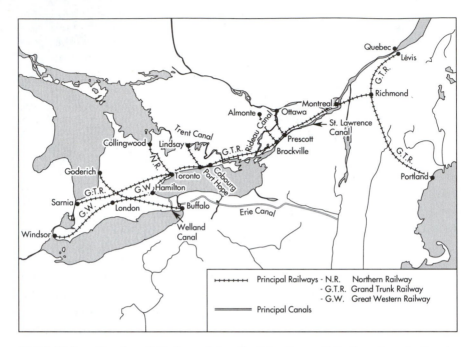

MAP 13.1 *Canals and Railways before Confederation* (P.G. Cornell, et al., *Canada: Unity in Diversity* (Toronto: Holt, Rinehart, and Winston, 1967), 239)

Transportation injected large infusions of capital into the colonies, especially in the United Canadas, which led the way in canal and railway building. It was no coincidence that the 1850s saw the rapid development of banks and insurance companies in the colony, and the appearance of a fledgling stock market. Financial institutions also expanded in the Atlantic colonies, where shipbuilding, another transportation industry, helped to fuel economic growth. The output of wooden vessels grew dramatically after 1850 and brought steady returns on capital investment in the major shipping ports of Saint John, Yarmouth, Windsor, Halifax, Charlottetown, and St John's well into the 1870s. Shipbuilders and owners often invested their money in industrial concerns, their ships supplying the raw products—cotton, tobacco, flax, wheat, and molasses—required in their mills to produce textiles, sails, rope, spices, biscuits, sugar, and candy.

Financial activities also benefited from currency legislation that reduced confusion over exchange. The variety of coins and notes in circulation, including British, Spanish, and American currencies, made transactions cumbersome if not impossible. Consider, for instance, the impediment to

In the early 1860s, Father George-Antoine Belcourt helped his fellow Prince Edward Island Acadians to establish a banking co-operative, the Farmer's Bank of Rustico (Public Archives of Prince Edward Island)

exchange caused by the "haggis" of currencies and barter transactions that occurred in the busy port city of Halifax in 1820:

> This morning, I went to the green market to buy a bunch of carrots, one of turnips, a squash, and two cabbages, and I carried with me a province note for 20s.—after I had made my bargain I offered my note in payment. First, one said he could not change it; another shook his head and shrugged his shoulders, uttering with a foreign accent "me no small money, will keep my cabbage till you pay them"; a third who had the squash, began to fumble with his waistcoat pocket, and emptied out of it, coppers, ragged bits of paper and one solitary seven-pence-half-penny in silver; "my squash, sir, if I change the note is 6d. but only 3d. if you give me the coppers—change the note, said I, and the d——l take it; for I am tormented. . . ." I had thus 8 paper notes, 1 silver piece, and 84 coppers—in all 93 separate things before I could get vegetables for my family's dinner. . . . Our currency is like a scotch

haggis, made up of contradictions, of good things and bad, oatmeal, onions, hog's lard, butter, crumbs of bread, salt, pepper, garlic, leeks, parsley, etc., etc.[5]

In the 1850s and 1860s British North Americans adopted decimal currency, which was both easier to calculate than British pounds and shillings and increasingly popular in the age of reciprocity with the United States.

Without a supply of cheap and willing labour to work in the new factories, the Industrial Revolution would have been stillborn. Two developments, one demographic and the other economic, interacted with each other to guarantee the labour supply needed both in Britain and North America. Over the course of the eighteenth century the population of Europe in general and Britain in particular grew dramatically. From a population of five million in 1700, Britain grew to nine million a century later. Demographers do not know exactly the reasons for this phenomenon: higher birth rates, lower death rates, better living standards, more efficient exchange networks, and even improved psychological conditions seem to account for some of the growth. At the same time overcrowding in the countryside and the commercialization of agriculture pushed people off the land and into the cities to find work. Factory towns, like the colonies, became magnets for the rural dispossessed. Indeed, factory towns and colonies, considered frontiers of opportunity, attracted people whose rural lives were reasonably stable. In 1700, 80 percent of people in Britain made their living in agriculture; by 1800 only 40 percent did so.

Those fleeing the economic dislocation of the Industrial Revolution in Britain also found the land frontier disappearing in British North America. By the nineteenth century overcrowding on the seigneuries had reached crisis proportions, and in the Atlantic colonies most of the best agricultural land had been occupied in the eighteenth century. Even in Canada West immigrants were confronting the rugged Canadian Shield, which proved an inhospitable barrier to the farmer's plough. It took a lifetime for a pioneer without capital or a large family to make a farm out of tree-covered wilderness. With the free land virtually gone and the cost of labour in British North America relatively high, the capital requirements of farming were steadily mounting. Although a prosperous farm was still the goal of most immigrants and native-born British North Americans, it was beyond the reach of many people, and they found themselves forced into other occupations. Railway, canal, and shipbuilding projects also attracted large construction crews and skilled labour to British North America, while Irish famine immigration in the late 1840s added to the pool of available labour.

Many immigrant labourers brought with them traditions of resistance against unfair labour practices. Craftsmen, whose skills were often rendered obsolete by the new machines, and work crews, whose livelihood was jeopardized by attempts to lower wages, protested efforts by employers to exploit them. The state assisted the interests of capital by creating conditions conducive to managerial control over labour. As early as 1816 the Nova Scotia legislature passed an act to curb the behaviour of journeymen and workmen who "by unlawful meetings and combinations are endeavouring to regulate the rate of wages." Various master and servant acts passed in the colonies included provisions for punishing craftsmen, labourers, and servants who left their jobs. Couched in the language of pre-industrial labour relations, these acts were designed primarily to control servants, timber workers, and ship crews. Nevertheless, they reveal the bias in favour of employers that would continue to prevail in industrial settings and would make labour's lot a difficult one.

•Law and Industry

The law was a vital instrument in capitalist accumulation during the Industrial Revolution. In the colonies, however, legal principles and practices were quickly rendered dated by the pace of economic change. Based on a belief in eternal principles and natural law, colonial legal systems lacked the extensive laws and trained personnel required to deal with the complexities of commercial transactions. In most colonies executive councillors sat in judicial capacities, and their lack of specialized legal knowledge coupled with their busy schedules was a growing cause for complaint.

Legal reform followed hard on the heels of responsible government. In most colonial jurisdictions, new laws relating to contracts, partnerships, patents, and property were introduced, while the courts were reorganized to separate executive and judicial functions, to increase efficiency, and to incorporate change into legal decisions. Reform extended beyond commercial law and court procedures to the fundamental basis of law itself. No longer paternalistic and protective in its thrust, the law became an instrument for individual accumulation and economic development.

Nowhere in British North America was legal reform more at issue than in the rapidly developing colony of Canada. In 1849 William Hume Blake, solicitor-general in the Baldwin–La Fontaine administration, introduced legislation to establish a Court of Common Pleas and a Court of Error and Appeals as well as to reform the Court of Queen's Bench and

Court of Chancery. As chancellor from 1849 to 1862, Blake attempted to inject the principles of freedom and progress into his legal decisions. In the case of O'Keefe v. Taylor (1850), for example, Blake made the following argument concerning the purchase of land under instalment:

> We are about to define the position of multitudes by whom a country is being peopled—by whose enterprise and labour the wastes of this vast province are rendered subservient to the purposes of civilization with unexampled rapidity. . . . It is of vital importance, not only to the attainment of justice in particular cases, but to the general welfare, that in this court, the numerous titles which depend exclusively upon this jurisdiction for their validity, should not be shaken by the introduction of doctrines, which however suited to other states of society, have no application to our present social condition. . . . But were we to apply the rule to be deduced from some of the English cases which were cited, especially some of the latter cases, upon the subject of delay, without reference to the totally different social condition of the country, we should not only produce great practical evil and injustice, but should also, in my opinion, very much misapply a doctrine which in England would never have been laid down under circumstances in which we are placed.[6]

Blake's declaration of legal independence from Britain brought incremental changes, introducing capitalistic values of individualism and progress, which were incorporated into the legal system.

Legal reform was not confined solely to English jurisdictions. As early as 1846 the *Revue de législation et de jurisprudence* in Canada East published this revealing statement:

> The conquests which modern society has made in politics, science, the arts, agriculture, industry and commerce necessitate the reform of the old codes which directed the ancient societies. Everywhere, one feels the inadequacy of laws made for an order of ideas and things which no longer exists, and the need to remodel ancient systems and of promulgating new ones, in order to put ourselves at the level of society's progress.[7]

In 1857 George-Étienne Cartier, lawyer and leader of the *bleus* in Canada East, introduced bills to make the legal system more centralized and uniform. He also chaired the committee that produced a new Civil Code to replace the antiquated Custom of Paris. The code brought major revisions to contract and labour law. It also introduced changes in the property provisions of family law, abolishing dower rights except in cases where they were formally registered. In practice this freed husbands from any claims held by their wives and children on family property. Although the Civil Code retained the principle of patriarchy in requiring a husband's permission for a married woman to engage in business, once this permission was granted she was free to conduct her activities as she saw fit.

• The Structure of Industrial Capitalism

The Industrial Revolution proceeded unevenly, its impact varying from sector to sector and from one region to another. Only a few colonial industries, following the precedents set in Britain and the United States, initially lent themselves to large-scale production: metal trades, locomotives, textiles, boots and shoes, furniture, agricultural implements, tobacco, beer and ale, biscuits, bread and candies, carriages, and sails and rope. While most factories adopted techniques for division of labour (as in the shoe industry) or included a number of skills under one roof (as in carriage-making), not all industries relied on steam-powered machinery. Cheap hand labour remained central to the Industrial Revolution and in certain sectors, such as textiles and cigar-making, guaranteed its success against foreign competitors.

Manufacturing in British North America, as elsewhere, tended to be geographically concentrated. Saint John, Montreal, Toronto, and Hamilton led the way in the industrial process. Montreal, with its large domestic market, low-wage structure, and pivotal location in the St Lawrence trading system was British North America's leading industrial city before Confederation. Hamilton never recovered from the recession of the late 1850s and was gradually eclipsed by Toronto as the major industrial city in Canada West. Between 1851 and 1871 Toronto was transformed from a city of artisans to one where over 70 percent of the labour force worked in units of over thirty people. In Atlantic Canada Saint John emerged as the major manufacturing centre, holding sway over the whole Bay of Fundy basin, which, with over 300 000 people, contained nearly half the region's population. By the 1860s the foundry, footwear, and clothing industries in Saint John each exceeded shipbuilding in the value of their output.

In some cases demand inspired large-scale production—an example being Moirs in Halifax, which had the bread contract for the military stationed in the city. When new technological developments occurred, whole industries were transformed. For instance, the shoe industry in Montreal and Toronto was reorganized within a decade of the introduction of the sewing machine in the early 1850s. External factors also figured prominently in the

Taylor Safe Works, Toronto   (E.C. Guillet/National Archives of Canada/C18540)

encouragement of industry. Disruptions caused by the American Civil War, for example, led to tobacco companies locating in Montreal and Toronto.

Entrepreneurs came from every class and culture, although hardly in equal proportions. A few, like John Molson of Montreal, had a long tradition of capitalist investment in everything from beer to railroads. Many "captains of industry" emerged from the ranks of the merchant class that had accumulated capital in its commercial ventures to invest in new frontiers of opportunity. Successful primary producers and artisans were also in a good position to expand their operations in such areas as milling, tanning, or carriage-making when demand, technology, or sheer luck made it possible to reap a profit. Most of British North America's entrepreneurs were English-speaking, many of them recent immigrants from Britain or the United States. One French-Canadian exception was Austin Cantin, Montreal's major steamboat builder and the first person to integrate ship construction and marine engineering. By 1856 Cantin's shipyards on the Lachine Canal covered five and a half hectares and included two harbours, a sawmill, and an engine foundry.

British North America's industrial work force was overwhelmingly male. Men were hired almost exclusively in the milling, woodworking, and

Young women sorting ore at the Huntington Copper Mining Company Works, Quebec, 1867 (McCord Museum of Canadian History/Notman Photographic Archives, 28, 901-MISC-I)

metal industries and held supervisory positions throughout the industrial structure. Women, both married and single, and children, some as young as eight or nine years of age, were employed in the clothing and tobacco industries and made up a significant proportion of the people hired in printing, footwear, and confectionery. Women and children also formed the bulk of workers employed in the "sweated trades," the term used to describe industrial tasks performed at home at appallingly low rates. The exploitation of women and children in the industrial process was already a cause of concern in Britain when the industrial system was adopted in British North America. Nevertheless, pre-industrial relationships based on the patriarchal authority of adult males in the family remained part of the industrial structure in British North America.

The impact of industrial production was soon felt throughout British North America. Artisans in industries where the new processes prevailed were either thrown out of work or found their jobs radically altered. In 1863 in the *Report* of the Toronto Board of Trade, Erastus Wiman described the transformation in the shoe industry: "Eight years ago there was only one regular traveller from Montreal and one from Toronto who solicited orders from the country trade, and these seldom left the line of the railroad. Now it is no uncommon thing to meet from fifteen to eighteen in a single season—all keenly alive to business, and pushing into all sections of the country, remote or otherwise." Wiman remarked that where shoes had once been made in over a thousand workshops scattered across the colony, now manufacture was concentrated in "eighteen or twenty establishments of the five cities of the provinces."[8]

As Wiman correctly observed, British North Americans had witnessed an economic revolution in the decade of the 1850s. Factories, railways, and new values were now part of the colonial scene. By 1859 even Red River had a steamboat, and on the west coast fur trade society was rapidly receding in the wake of the gold rush of 1858. Perhaps no one was more conscious of the changes wrought by the industrial revolution than eighty-five-year-old Mi'kmaq Peter Paul, who remarked in 1865 that steamboats scared the fish and polluted the water and added to the pressures that made Mi'kmaq strangers in their own lands.

• Intellectual Revolutions

The Industrial Revolution was a child of the Age of Enlightenment, a term applied to the dramatic shift in the tenor of European intellectual life in the eighteenth century. Building on developments in science and philosophy that had been gaining momentum since the Renaissance, intellectuals in the eighteenth century called into question the claims of revealed religion and a divinely sanctioned social order. They argued that societies could be studied rationally and scientifically, and that social conditions could be improved by human planning and purposeful action. With enlightened rulers and educated citizens, people could move progressively toward a better society in this world instead of only dreaming of ascending to a heavenly city after they died.

Such ideas, once held by a tiny minority, gradually gained wide acceptance, especially among members of the rising middle class. Scientific innovation was the source of much of their new-found wealth, and their desire to change antiquated laws and institutions that restricted their advancement was reinforced by the reforming spirit of the age. Since middle-class people were in the vanguard of progressive developments, they saw their values as the only appropriate ones for a vastly improved social order in which they held the reins of power. Separation of church and state, the distinction between public and private lives, equality of opportunity, and social reform would usher in a new era of progress from which all would benefit.

Science, Technology, and Progress

Nothing excited British North Americans as much as the promise and practice of science. It stimulated industry, advanced civilization, filled hours of leisure time, and somehow even, it was said, brought people closer to God. Just as God had revealed Himself in the written word, it was argued, He was also manifested in the natural world. Natural history, a comprehensive term applied to the general study of science, was popular in educated circles, and natural scientists combed the colonies classifying the flora and fauna, studying geological formations, and finding evidence of God's wisdom, power, and goodness.

Practical scientists, most of them amateur tinkerers, were inspired by the applications of their discoveries, which if successful promised to bring them both wealth and fame. Historian Carl Berger has noted that the advancement of science was the most noteworthy intellectual achievement of British North Americans in the nineteenth century, one befitting a new country with a short history and a shallow literary tradition.[9]

Early in the nineteenth century only a few educated immigrants, such as Thomas McCulloch in Nova Scotia and Charles Fothergill in Upper Canada, had systematically pursued their interest in natural history. By mid-century science had become a popular movement. Societies devoted to the study of science were founded in most colonial cities, and large audiences turned out to hear lectures on scientific topics and participate in field trips. Mechanics Institutes devoted attention to scientific matters, while any university worthy of the name hired a professor of science. Such a professor was required to be an accomplished generalist, teaching subjects that today would include everything from chemistry and physics to biology and geology.

People in the rural areas learned about the latest scientific discoveries through newspapers, books, and travelling lecturers. In August 1849 Margaret Dickie of the seaport town of Hantsport, Nova Scotia, noted in her diary that a Mr Giffin from the United States had lectured to packed houses on "Electricity, Galvanism and Magnetism" as well as "Animal Physiology." Not only that, he had also "explained how the telegraph worked." During the time that Dickie was not teaching school or attending to domestic duties, she was reading books on navigation, geography, and the new psychology of phrenology. The practical applications of science were not lost on Dickie—she later became the telegraph operator in Hantsport.

British North Americans not only gobbled up scientific knowledge; but they also helped to advance it. Andrew Downs, creator of a zoological garden in Halifax in 1847, supplied specimens to museums in Europe and the United States. William Logan, director of the Geological Survey of the Province of Canada, was knighted in 1856 for his pioneer work on the geology of Canada. In the 1860s Hudson's Bay Company fur traders, at the behest of scientists from the Smithsonian Institution in Washington, D.C., began collecting information on everything from birds' eggs to the weather. Scientists such as James Robb at the University of New Brunswick, William Dawson at McGill, and George Lawson at Queen's remained in close contact with the larger scientific community for whom they published their findings.

British North American inventors also had a wide impact. Abraham Gesner, a medical doctor, geologist, and museum curator in the Maritimes,

The Exhibition Palace in Fredericton   (G.T. Taylor, New Brunswick Provincial Archives/ T-43)

developed a process for making kerosene oil in 1847 and promptly established a factory on Long Island, New York, to market his product. Ironically, Gesner's process was eclipsed by drilled oil, with the first well dug by James Williams in Enniskillen Township in the late 1850s. In turn, Canada West's boom town, Petrolia, was superseded by oil fields in Ohio and Pennsylvania.

Practical inventions were the stock and trade of British North Americans who, like their southern neighbours, were obsessed with finding better ways of doing things. The timber-crib slide was developed on the Ottawa River in 1829. Robert Foulis, an engineer from New Brunswick, produced the world's first steam fog-whistle, installed in the Partridge Island lighthouse in 1860. Given the abundance of timber in Canada, it is not surprising that the first plank roads were built east of Toronto in the mid-1830s. A variety of patents for steam engines were filed by the "river barons" of the St Lawrence. The failure of Nova Scotia native Charles Fenerty to secure a patent for his method of making paper out of pulverized wood in 1838–39 meant that the credit went to others. In any event the new process heralded the decline of a brisk trade in cotton and linen rags that had hitherto been the major ingredient in paper.

By the mid-nineteenth century most British North Americans had adjusted to the "age of progress," accepting the new science as part of the larger movement toward a better society. Scientific pronouncements concerning the age of the earth or aggressive tendencies in the animal kingdom remained consistent with God's purpose for human beings. But when Charles Darwin published *The Origin of Species* in 1859, this complacency was undermined. Darwin's view that all living things had evolved from a single, primitive form of life and had developed by a process of natural selection and survival of the fittest flew in the face of Christianity's human-centred view of creation and the notion of a benevolent God.

As the long debate over "Darwinism" dragged its weary way through the second half of the nineteenth century, most Christians simply accepted the discrepancy between Darwin's findings and divine revelation as a mystery that would be revealed in God's good time. Others became more sceptical about religion, and a few deserted the church for the cold comfort of atheism. Still others attempted to refute Darwin's theories on a scientific basis. Geologist William Dawson of McGill, renowned for his study of fossilized plants and animals in the rock formations of the Cumberland Basin, became one of the world's foremost apologists for the creationist view. Although millions of years old, these fossils showed no evidence of evolutionary development, he argued, a view which, both then and now, offered comfort to the creationists.

The Hamilton pumping station opened in 1859   (Courtesy Special Collections, Hamilton Public Library)

Religion and Reform

The divisions created by Darwinism were restricted to a small minority of intellectuals and did little to alter the fundamentally Christian world view of most British North Americans. Nor did the separation of church and state in British North America halt the growing power of colonial churches as agents of intellectual and social influence. By the mid-nineteenth century colonial churches were advocating a variety of reforms and taking institutional initiatives to achieve their goals. Attention was focussed on ignorance, alcoholism, crime, poverty, disease, and racial discrimination. Initially inspired by the evangelical movement, with its strong roots in the rural-farming and urban-artisan communities, the reform impulse soon spread to embrace a wide spectrum of colonial society, including the Roman Catholic Church. While often divided on the means, reformers were united in the common goal of achieving a transformed and much improved British North American society.

Promoting spiritual rebirth as the vehicle for transforming individuals and society, the evangelical movement was a sharp reaction to the cold rationalism of the Enlightenment. Nevertheless, evangelicals were heirs of the Enlightenment in their commitment to social improvement. In addition to urging personal piety and perfection, evangelicals attempted to create an environment in which spiritual salvation would be more readily accepted. In the name of religion, evangelicals formed missionary societies, fought slavery, encouraged education, founded hospitals for the sick and asylums for the insane, and urged temperance and civic reform.

The evangelical impulse was strongest among Methodists, Presbyterians, and Baptists, but it touched all Protestant denominations and was complemented by a revitalized spirituality in the Roman Catholic Church at mid-century. At its height the evangelical movement organized alliances for direct political action, but intense anti-Catholicism and internal factionalism prevented the emergence of stable political parties based on religious affiliation.

No reform effort enlisted more support or caused greater controversy than the temperance movement. Initiated by various evangelical churches in the late 1820s, the temperance movement was soon embraced by all classes and cultures. While the temperate use of alcohol was encouraged by evangelicals as a means of self-help, it also offered a solution to what seemed to be the social effects of intemperance: crime, insanity, poverty, violence, and the abuse of women and children. Even the Roman Catholic Church in British North America, following the Irish example, threw its support behind the temperate use of alcohol in the 1840s. C.P.T. Chiniquy, a colourful and controversial preacher, led the temperance crusade in the Catholic parishes of Canada East.

In the late 1840s a secular organization called the Sons of Temperance made its appearance in British North America. With its elaborate rites and rituals, Cadets of Temperance and Cold Water Armies, and divisions for women and children as well as men, the Sons of Temperance drew its members from all denominations and became a potent political force in the era of responsible government. By mid-century the temperance crusade was so successful that it seemed possible to go one step further—state prohibition of the manufacture and sale of intoxicating beverages. The call for prohibition split the movement between those for and against greater state intervention in the lives of individuals and drew fierce opposition from brewers, distillers, sellers, and drinkers of alcoholic beverages.

In New Brunswick the prohibition movement was temporarily successful. There, political timing and the influence of the state of Maine, which passed prohibition legislation in 1851, were crucial to events. In 1855, fresh from their success in achieving responsible government, the Liberals, known as "Smashers" because of their views on alcohol, passed a prohibition bill. The outcry was so great that Lieutenant-Governor Manners-Sutton dissolved the legislature and called another election. The Smasher faction in the Liberal Party, including Samuel Leonard Tilley, Most Worthy Patriarch of the Sons of Temperance in North America, was roundly defeated and the offensive legislation was repealed. Other colonies avoided the New Brunswick experience by letting individuals and municipal corporations make the difficult decision on the thorny temperance question.

Education Reform

It was not so easy to delegate responsibility for education to individuals and local communities. Acts by colonial legislatures encouraging local initiative in education had led to a "hodge-podge" of schools. Some were privately sponsored, many church-affiliated, and the whole system lacked the efficiency and uniformity so dear to the hearts of educational reformers. Like temperance, education was expected to accomplish many purposes. Egerton Ryerson, the Methodist superintendent of education for Canada West from 1844 to 1876, defined education in 1846 as "not the mere acquisition of certain arts, or of certain branches of knowledge, but that instruction and discipline which qualify and dispose the subjects of it for their appropriate duties and employments of life, as Christians, as persons of business, and also as members of the civil community in which they live." Programs in Prussia, Ireland, and the United States to establish systems of non-denominational state-supported schools offered models for colonial reformers to follow. Only three obstacles stood in the way of success: class, race, and religion.

The notion of state-supported schools open to all classes and cultures was, like prohibition, one that struck terror into the hearts of many British North Americans. The supporters of the idea, again a loose alliance of Protestant middle-class reformers, hoped to establish social harmony through a universal curriculum and a "common" school experience. They also saw obvious benefits for their own children in the implementation of such a system, especially one that they had a hand in designing. In contrast, working-class families feared that schools would take children away from productive labour at home and in the work force and impose taxes they were ill-equipped to pay. At the other end of the social scale, the colonial elite opposed the "levelling" impact of common schools and the low standards that would surely prevail in such a system. Anglican Bishop John Strachan, determined to stop the colony of Canada from "imitating the irreligious scheme of our [American] neighbours," fought long and hard for a system of publicly funded Church of England schools.

The question that concerned many British North Americans was the role of religion in a common-school system. While education reformers left little doubt that Christian morality would have a high priority in their classrooms, opponents of the system charged that morality could not be divorced from religious instruction. Roman Catholics were particularly wary of state-supported schools, which with their daily Bible readings and prayers seemed little more than Protestant schools in disguise.

Between 1856 and 1860 Prince Edward Island's advanced "free" school system was rocked by the question of Bible reading in the schools, which was demanded by the "Protestant Combination" and staunchly opposed by Roman Catholics. A compromise was effected: Bible reading in the common schools was to be mandatory by law, but children who found it offensive could be excused. In addition to fuelling denominational tensions, the controversy altered the political alignment on the island. A coalition of Tories and evangelicals led by Edward Palmer swept the Liberals and their Roman Catholic supporters from office, in the process creating a party system dangerously divided by religion.

Common-school legislation was so controversial that most colonial administrations championed its cause only at their peril. Nevertheless, Egerton Ryerson managed to achieve most of his objectives during his long tenure in office. Under Ryerson's careful guidance, Canada West adopted general assessment for schools, uniform textbooks, a system of graded subjects, the bureaucratization of administration, and the centralization of power at the expense of local school boards. He also pointed teachers on the path to professionalization through his encouragement of normal-school training, teachers' institutes and associations, and the publication of the *Journal of Education for Upper Canada*. Theodore Harding Rand, a Nova Scotia Baptist who served as superintendent of education in both Nova Scotia and New Brunswick, followed Ryerson's lead. Despite their opposition to separate schools, both men were forced to accept compromises as the politically powerful Roman Catholics insisted that confessional schools be eligible for state support. In contrast, Canada East and Newfoundland, where the Roman Catholic Church and Church of England were strong, made denominational schools the basis for public education.

Racial and linguistic differences were also reflected in the public school systems. Both Nova Scotia and Canada West had "Negro Separate Schools," which black children were obliged to attend. Canada West also administered separate schools after 1860 for Algonkian children. In addition, there were bilingual schools where instruction was given in French, German, or Gaelic.

The education revolution that occurred during the middle decades of the nineteenth century had a profound effect on the course of British North American childhood. Since that time most children have left home for a significant portion of the day during the school year to receive moral and academic training at the hands of a trained teacher, rather than from their parents. Increasingly that teacher was drawn from the ranks of young women between the ages of sixteen and twenty-five—women prepared to work long hours for low wages. In this way British North Americans avoided paying higher taxes for their new educational institutions and, while preparing women for their later roles as mothers, also offered them an alternative to marriage and motherhood. The overall effect of this schooling experience on children was to prepare them for the vastly different ways in which they would make their living in a rapidly industrializing British North America.

• The Discovery of the Asylum

By 1850 the notion that poverty, criminal behaviour, and mental illness should be cured rather than endured was beginning to gain currency. Emphasis was therefore placed on providing the needy with skills and values necessary for them to become self-supporting citizens. By helping unfortunate people to help themselves, it was argued, society in general and the taxpayer in particular would benefit. Reformers also argued that specialized institutions designed to focus on specific problems would be

more effective than the family in achieving the desired results. With appropriate treatment there was even hope for the rehabilitation of the criminal
and the insane, two groups hitherto considered beyond redemption.

Following the lead of Britain, which had instituted a new Poor Law in
1834, urban British North Americans erected Houses of Industry where the
poor would not only find shelter but also be taught habits of industry and
self-discipline. These institutions were designed to reduce the cost of outdoor relief and avoid the practice of committing the poor to common jails.
At the same time they would offer an ideal setting for moral uplift. In
Toronto, for instance, private subscriptions led to the construction of a
House of Industry in 1836. Since social services were the responsibility of
local authorities and continued to remain so after the achievement of
responsible government, the reach of reform was limited. Only affluent
municipalities, which in practice meant cities, could sustain such asylums
for their poor.

Asylums were also built especially for the treatment of the insane. In
1836 the citizens of Saint John established British North America's first
"lunatic asylum," but it housed both the poor and the insane until 1848.
The spate of new asylums in colonial cities at mid-century was inspired by
the view motivating the commissioners of the Beauport Asylum near
Quebec. They argued that their new institution was a place where the
insane could "exchange their chains, gloom and filth for liberty, cheerful-
ness and cleanliness, where they are subject to the remedial powers and
moral influences, and to the mode of treatment in accordance with the
most improved principles of the present day." Institutional treatment of
the insane was so significant on the reform agenda in Canada West that
when the Lunatic Asylum opened its doors in Toronto in 1850 it was the
largest building in the colony.

Under the reform impulse, prisons, too, became institutions of
reform rather than punishment. The Kingston Penitentiary, opened in
1835, was designed "to correct" deviant behaviour by imposing rigid discipline in a closely controlled environment. Like many of the new asylums,
Kingston Penitentiary soon came under severe criticism for the harsh treatment of its inmates. Prisoners, who included men, women, and children,
were flogged for minor infractions, confined for days to a dark cell, and fed
on diets of bread and water. In 1848–49 George Brown chaired a commission of inquiry into conditions at the Kingston Penitentiary that laid bare
the cruel and corrupt regime of warden Henry Smith. Brown's charges
earned him the undying enmity of John A. Macdonald, in whose constituency the penitentiary was located. They also resulted in the appointment of a paid inspector to investigate prison operations.

Provincial Lunatic Asylum, designed by John G. Howard   (City of Toronto Archives, A75–77)

By the 1850s, social reform had run aground on the shoals of denominational rivalry. The high incidence of Roman Catholics among those committed to institutional care prompted Protestants to complain about the costs of treating Roman Catholics and to conclude that social problems were associated with religious belief. In an effort to avoid the proselytizing tendencies of custodians in public institutions, a reinvigorated Roman Catholic Church expanded its social services to assist its own people. Protestants, not to be outdone, established separate institutions for themselves. Most British North American cities in mid-century spawned church-sponsored asylums, hospitals, and hostels, thus creating a patchwork of state, church, and privately supported efforts, vastly uneven in quality and accessible to only a fraction of the potential clients.

Reformers of all denominations placed a special emphasis on saving the child, who, it was believed, was the most receptive to socialization. Orphanages, workhouses, and industrial schools were targeted as special agents of social reform because they focussed on dependent mothers and their children. As early as 1832 a group of reform-minded women in St John's set up a factory to teach carding, spinning, and net-making to the children of the poor. Saint John established a House of Female Industry in 1834. In the wake of the Irish famine migration of the 1840s, orphanages were established in colonial cities to care for homeless children. Reformers also promoted "reformatories" as alternatives to prisons for juveniles in trouble with the law. It was argued that by separating impressionable youths from hard-bitten criminals and by teaching them appropriate behaviour, they might be "saved" from a life of crime. E.A. Meredith, reporting on Canada's penal institutions in 1862, also suggested an intermediary institution for the "great proportion of the children of the lower classes" who "are utterly destitute and neglected, and grow up in our midst without receiving any education or training to fit them to act their part in life as honest and useful citizens." Meredith's solution was the creation of special "Homes" for children of the poor in order to "'stand between the living and the dead and stay the plague' of immorality and vice around us." Compulsory school attendance, implemented later in the century, would solve some of Meredith's concerns, but the class bias so evident in reform programs compromised the success of their policies.

The rage for reform among the colonial middle classes in the mid-nineteenth century was motivated by altruism and by the example of their counterparts in Britain and the United States. It also served to disguise the growing disparity between rich and poor that increasingly characterized colonial society. Operating on the democratic belief that self-discipline and education would enable everyone to benefit from the new economic and political order, middle-class reformers made life even more difficult for those excluded from the race for success. Once merely perceived as the world's unfortunates, the poor were increasingly attacked for their lack of character and moral fibre. By placing the blame on individuals rather than on the system that created and tolerated inequality, reformers avoided any wholesale critique of the social order that sustained their own affluence.

•Public and Private Worlds

New social values and production processes had a profound effect on how people organized their lives. Home in the pre-industrial world was, in the words of historian John Demos, "a little commonwealth," the centre of work and play, business and politics, religion and education. By the mid-nineteenth century British North Americans were increasingly making a distinction between their public and private lives. Apprenticeship and work, once done in the home, began to move into physically separate shops and factories. The public world of business, paid labour, and politics contrasted sharply with the domestic realm of the family, which was becoming, as American historian Christopher Lasch puts it, "a haven in the heartless world."

The impact of these changes was felt first in urban middle-class families where marriages were based on sentimental as well as economic considerations and fewer children were raised. In these families the work performed by women in the home changed with the introduction of manufactured goods such as textiles, the increasing number of servants, and the

tendency to send children to public schools. As the productive and reproductive roles of women decreased, more emphasis was placed on motherhood and household management. Women's special spiritual qualities and
their capacity for charitable works were also singled out for approval. In
Protestant cultures middle-class women functioned as the unpaid staff of
church-sponsored charitable organizations, while Roman Catholic women
entered convents in unprecedented numbers. The careful delineation of
separate spheres for men and women that had prevailed in the pre-industrial world was thus maintained: men dominated the public sphere with all
its attendant opportunities while women were relegated to the private
sphere of domesticity and good works.

Life-cycle choices were also being gradually altered to accommodate
the new social reality. Both men and women married later, and they spent
more time in the paid labour force before they married. Although the
work of unmarried women was largely confined to domestic service, new
professions such as school teaching gave educated women experience in
the public sphere and the possibility of economic independence outside
the institution of marriage. With the delaying of marriage, adolescence—a
word coined only in the late nineteenth century—was emerging as a stage
in the life cycle of British North Americans. Childhood was also becoming
distinct from infancy and adulthood, and children were perceived as innocent and angelic rather than primitive creatures to be socialized to adult
behaviour as quickly as possible. The increased emphasis on childhood and
adolescence complemented the emergence of motherhood, which was taking on new meaning in the privatized world of the family.

By the mid-nineteenth century, separate spheres for women and men
began to take on the status of a prescriptive doctrine. The Reverend Robert
Sedgewick's lecture to the Young Men's Christian Association in Halifax in
1856 was typical of the patriarchal concern voiced over women's "proper"
sphere in colonial society: "The errors and blunders which are interwoven
with the subject of women's rights and women's place in modern society
are . . . to be traced either to the ignoring of the fact or the omission of the
fact that in the economy of nature or rather in the design of God, *woman is
the complement of man.* In defining her sphere and describing her influence,
that fact is fundamental." Predictably, for Sedgewick women's "proper
sphere" was "the home and whatever is co-relative with the home in the
social economy."

Sedgewick's outburst was a calculated response to the emergence of
the women's rights movement in the United States. There women involved
in the anti-slavery movement soon recognized their own lack of civil rights
and began organizing to remove the legal and attitudinal barriers that made
women subordinate to men. In 1848 American abolitionist women, led by

Elizabeth Cady Stanton and Lucretia Mott, held a convention at Seneca Falls, New York, where a Declaration of the Rights of Women was adopted. Using the language of the earlier Declaration of Independence, the advocates of women's rights maintained "that all men and women are created equal; that they are endowed by the Creator with certain inalienable rights; that among these are life, liberty and the pursuit of happiness." They also charged that "the history of mankind is a history of repeated injuries and usurpations of men toward women having its direct object the establishment of an absolute tyranny over her." Such views were certain to draw the fire of men whose power was directly challenged by women's rights advocates.

Lacking the spur that the anti-slavery crusade provided for women in the United States, British North American women were slow to organize. Nevertheless, they were aware of their inequality under the law. Between 1852 and 1857, three groups of women petitioned the legislature in Canada West for reform of laws relating to married women's property. In 1852 a landmark statute passed by the Prince Edward Island legislature permitted cases of seduction to be brought in the name of the woman seduced rather than in the name of the father. A Nova Scotia law of 1857 made divorce easier to obtain on the grounds of desertion or adultery. In Canada West an 1855 law gave the court discretion to permit access to or custody of infant children in cases where judges "saw fit." Subsequent decisions rendered by the courts recognized the enhanced status of motherhood in British North American society. Changes in colonial laws reflected the new middle-class notions of family emerging in the mid-nineteenth century.

The accelerated pace of change in their public and private worlds was a source of growing anxiety for middle-class British North Americans. Businessmen complained of "distress," while women often took to their beds with mysterious illnesses diagnosed as neurasthenia or "nerves." The extent of Robert Baldwin's lifetime of repressed anxiety was revealed only upon his death in 1858. In his will he asked that a doctor make "an incision . . . into the cavity of the Abdomen extending through the upper two thirds of the Linea alba." The motivation behind such a strange request was to ensure that his body would bear the same surgical wound as that of his beloved wife, Eliza, who had died in 1836 after childbirth by Caesarean section. The silence surrounding the private sphere of public men has been carefully respected by historians. It was not until the 1980s that Michael Cross and Robert Fraser revealed the close connection between Baldwin's private life and his public career.[10]

Working-class family life was far removed from concerns for privacy and sentimentality. In her study of families in the working-class district of Saint-Jacques in Montreal, historian Bettina Bradbury has outlined the difficulties experienced by families dependent on wage labour for survival.

EMILY JENNINGS STOWE

British North American women were close observers of the women's movement in the United States. Although there was no colonial equivalent to the Seneca Falls declaration, many British North American women opposed laws and practices that discriminated against them, and they often travelled to the United States to take advantage of educational opportunities denied them at home.

The experience of Emily Jennings reveals the obstacles placed in the path of women seeking equality in the professional sphere. Born in 1831 in Norwich, Upper Canada, Emily was the eldest of six daughters. She and her sisters were raised in the Quaker tradition, which emphasized the freedom and equality of women. A clever student, Emily began teaching school at the age of fifteen and saved her income to further her education. Denied admission to the University of Toronto, she took a teaching degree at the Normal School in Toronto in 1854. At the age of twenty-three, she was appointed principal of the Brantford Public School, the first woman to hold such a position in the public school system.

In 1856 she married Howard Stowe. When her husband became ill with tuberculosis, she decided to become a doctor. Since the University of Toronto's Medical School was closed to women, Emily Jennings Stowe studied at the New York Medical College for Women, which two of her sisters had already attended. Upon graduation in 1867, Stowe returned to Canada, where she set up a medical practice.

Stowe's difficulties were not yet over. The College of Physicians and Surgeons of Ontario refused to grant her a licence to practise because she had not attended lectures in an Ontario medical school. Since she was barred from doing so because of her gender, there was little Stowe could do other than practise illegally and fight for fairer laws. She finally received a licence to practise in 1880. By that time, women were being grudgingly permitted to attend classes in Canadian medical schools, but they still faced ridicule and hostility from male professors and students. Stowe was the moving spirit behind the founding of the Women's Medical College of Toronto in 1883, and in the same year another medical college was opened in Kingston.

In 1876 Stowe also helped to organize the Toronto Women's Literary Club, a polite euphemism for a women's rights organization. Seven years later, the group's name was changed to the Toronto Women's Suffrage Association.

Faced with unemployment, illness, death, and unplanned pregnancy, families were often forced to commit their younger children to the Saint-Alexis Orphanage run by the Sisters of Providence. The lot of the working-class widow and her children was particularly difficult. Josephine Brousseau, for instance, shared a dwelling with a married couple and a twenty-four-year-old widower and his one-year-old child, while she worked as a washerwoman. She placed her eight-year-old daughter Clara in Saint-Alexis in 1868. By the time she was twelve Clara and her brothers, aged ten and fourteen, were working in Macdonald's tobacco factory. Bradbury has found that the majority of children at Saint-Alexis in the mid-nineteenth century were not technically orphans but had lived in families who were too poor to care for them at home.

Despite objections of middle-class moralists to "working wives," a working-class family could often survive only if all of its members engaged in paid labour. Middle-class families might live very well on the income of the male head of household and hire servants to attend to household chores. For the working class, the whole family was the economic unit and the work of wives was crucial to family survival. Although a wife's work in the home was not calculated in monetary terms, the family could not survive without her labour at home and, when necessary, in the paid work force. By the same token, children who were not old enough to work threatened the delicately balanced economy of the working-class family.

Nationalism and Colonial Identities

Among the forces unleashed by the intellectual developments of the late eighteenth century was a militant nationalism that infected peoples all over the world. Following the French Revolution and Napoleonic Wars, periodic nationalist uprisings, most notably in 1830 and 1848, rocked European empires. Nationalism fuelled movements to unify the Italian and German states, and in the name of nationalism Irish patriots demanded an end to the hated union between Britain and Ireland. Nationalist rhetoric inspired the "rebels of '37," especially among French Canadians, whose common language, religion, and history provided the basis for a cohesive national identity.

British immigrants brought their cultural identities with them, a confusing mixture of the ethnic, national, and imperial sentiment that prevailed in Great Britain itself. By the mid-nineteenth century there were voices calling for a larger British North American nationalism to mute class and cultural cleavages. The concept of a united British North America was not new to the mid-nineteenth century. In the late eighteenth century, Loyalists had voiced such sentiments and Lord Durham had been a recent proponent of the idea. But developments in communication and transportation, coupled with expanded horizons, made a larger national outlook possible, though not, it must be conceded, inevitable.

Outside French Canada, British North American patriotism was an expression of colonial identity. Thus Joseph Howe could say that he was a "dear lover of old England, and to save her would blow Nova Scotia into the air or scuttle her like an old Ship," while at the same time he would pay tribute to his native "Acadia" in romantic poetry. He also was enthusiastic about the potential of British North American unity. In his efforts to garner support for an intercolonial railroad in 1851 he asked his constituents to "stand by me now in this last effort to improve our country, elevate these noble Provinces, and form them into a Nation."

Colonial poets, politicians, and newspapermen—Howe was all three—were the first to voice lofty national sentiments. Indeed, by the mid-nineteenth century British North American literature had moved beyond travel accounts and vignettes of colonial life to the exploration of colonial environment and history and to expressions of native pride. As the British North American contribution to the age of sentiment, colonial writers penned romantic tributes to the land and its people, especially the noble Natives, Acadians, and military heroes. Charles Sangster, for instance, in his poem *The St Lawrence and the Saguenay*, tried to praise Wolfe and Montcalm equally:

> Wolf and Montcalm! Two nobler names ne'er graced
> The page of history, or the hostile plain;
> No braver souls the storm of battle faced,
> Regardless of the danger or the pain.
> They pass'd unto their rest without a stain
> Upon their nature or their generous hearts.
> One graceful column to the noble twain
> Speaks of a nation's gratitude, and starts
> The tear that Valour claims, and Feeling's self imparts.

Nevertheless, Sangster's attitude toward the "courteous, gentle race," expressed later in the poem, was clearly patronizing and condescending.

The nationalist theme grew dramatically in strength in French Canada, gathering religious overtones as the century progressed. François-Xavier Garneau actually tailored later editions of his *Histoire* to meet clerical criticism of his overt liberalism. Romantic nationalism typical of the French empire under Napoleon III also found echoes in poems by Octave Crémazie, Antoine Gérin-Lajoie, and Philippe Aubert de Gaspé. Crémazie's "Le Canada," written in 1859, is one of the earliest expressions of French Canada's love for the "fatherland":

Greetings, O Heaven of my fatherland!
Greetings, O noble St Lawrence!
In my softened soul your name
Flows as an intoxicating perfume.
O Canada, you son of France,
Who covered you with her blessings
You our love, our hope,
Who will ever forget you?

One of British North America's most passionate nationalists was Thomas D'Arcy McGee. An Irish patriot who had participated in the Irish rebellion of 1848, McGee fled to the United States and in 1857 moved to Montreal. As a newspaperman and later a member of the legislature in the colony of Canada, McGee became a supporter of a "new Northern nationality" within the larger British imperial context. For McGee, nationalism offered a solution to the ethnic and sectional conflicts that he felt impeded the progress of British North America just as they had poisoned the potential of his native Ireland.

As in Ireland, nationalist sentiment posed problems for British North Americans because one patriot's nationalism often proved to be another patriot's bigotry. Safer ground for the new nationalism was the economic potential of the northern half of the continent, which stirred the hearts and imagination of both the romantic idealist and the practical businessman. The alternative vision of national destiny came not from across the Atlantic but from south of the border. By mid-century the Americans were advancing across the continent, dazzling the world with the speed and scope of their economic achievement. British North Americans had their own western frontier and, like the United States, began to see it as their "manifest destiny" to develop it. Eyeing Rupert's Land as their next resource frontier, empire builders in Montreal and Toronto dreamed of railways that would link them to their economic hinterland. In 1857 the colony of Canada sent delegates to the commission of inquiry into the Hudson's Bay Company monopoly, where they laid claim to Rupert's Land by virtue of French exploration.

With dramatic suddenness, the notion of a formidable and inaccessible western territory gave way to glowing reports of agricultural potential and unlimited opportunity. In 1857 Canada sponsored a scientific expedition led by S.J. Dawson, a civil engineer, and geologist H.Y. Hind. Their report, together with that of a British scientific team led by Captain John Palliser, served, in the words of historian Gerald Friesen, as "the point of transition from fur trade to agriculture in the thinking of outside observers."[11] Another 1857 report, this time by American climatologist Lorin Blodget, dispelled long-held views about the harsh climate of the west and confirmed what everyone wanted to hear: that the "commercial and industrial potential" of the region was "gigantic." With the Fraser valley gold rush of 1858, the potential of the west seemed endless. Alexander Morris, who published the *Hudson's Bay and Pacific Territories* in 1859, expressed the optimism of many British North Americans when he described the possibilities offered by westward expansion:

> With two powerful colonies on the Pacific, with another or more in the region between Canada and the Rocky Mountains, with a railway and a telegraph linking the Atlantic and the Pacific and absorbing the newly-opened and fast-developing trade with China and Japan . . . who can doubt of the reality and accuracy of the vision which rises distinctly and clearly before us, as the Great Britannic Empire of the North stands out in all its grandeur.[12]

•Educational Reform:
A Historiographical Debate

The educational reforms of the mid-nineteenth century put in place a state-supported education system that is still part of the Canadian social fabric. In recent years a lively debate has developed over the goals of Canada's early education reformers, such as Egerton Ryerson and his supporters in Canada West. Were they really inspired by the potential of education for improving the lives of the common people, as they said, or were they only resorting to desperate measures to impose social control over an increasingly anarchistic industrial society? If the latter, what form did the control take, and how did it succeed?

Before 1970 most education histories chronicled the growth and development of schools and rarely, if ever, raised larger questions. Charles E. Phillips perhaps best summed up the progressive view of education by noting that he saw past developments as leading to a present that "is the best kind of life we know."[13] By 1970 most historians had abandoned such an approach to the history of education and argued, as did J. Donald Wilson, Robert M. Stamp, and Louis-Philippe Audet, that education must be viewed in a broader context. Although they still believed that reforms had improved education and that Canadians as a whole had benefited from the reformed system, the "moderate revisionists," as they became known, were more critical of the methods and motives of early reformers such as Ryerson.[14]

Meanwhile, at the Ontario Institute for Studies in Education (OISE) in the 1970s, historian Michael Katz trained a generation of so-called "radical" scholars who abandoned narrative history for hard-hitting analysis. Drawing upon the example of revisionist historians in the United States, they tried to see education in the larger context of the socialization of children and explored the new social-history categories of class, gender, and ethnicity. They asked questions about who went to school, who controlled schools, and who benefited from formal educational systems. Their answers raised questions about the fundamental nature of formal education.

In a pioneering study of the Ontario school system, Alison Prentice concluded that in the nineteenth century the middle class benefited most from schools sustained by public taxes. She also argued that Ryerson imposed his stamp on the school system, systematically eroding the power of local school trustees and the families who sent their children to the schools. By bureaucratizing and centralizing school administration, Ryerson put in place an instrument for social control, not a vehicle for upward mobility of the lower orders.[15]

As Prentice and other scholars from OISE pursued their research, they continued to make startling revelations about Ryerson's much-vaunted school system. In most cultures boys, they discovered, were more likely to attend school than girls. Indeed, in the early years girls were "worth" only half as much as boys in determining education grants from the government. The state further encouraged a distinction between boys and girls by creating a different curriculum and establishing gendered entrances and spaces to play. For ethnic and racial minorities, schools served as little more than arenas for systematically destroying their culture.

OISE scholars were instrumental in demonstrating that the structure of school life was as significant as what went on in the classroom. Schools, they argued, subtly transformed family life as the school day, week, and year dictated domestic routines such as meal times and holidays. Moreover, in the classroom children learned more than the basics of how to read, write, and cipher. They were also instilled with the work ethic and moral discipline. Ryerson's own *First Lessons in Christian Morals: For Canadian Families and Schools*, published in 1871, was little more than a tract advocating middle-class Victorian values.

Bruce Curtis, a Marxist sociologist working at Wilfrid Laurier University, moved beyond the work of Prentice and others to look at the larger impact of schools on Canadian society. He argued that schools in the nineteenth century were repressive instruments of social control designed to protect middle-class society against the "dangerous" classes emerging in a rapidly industrializing Ontario. He saw teachers as the main agents of repression and the classrooms as the main arena for their repressive actions.[16]

According to Curtis, the school system put in place in Canada West in the mid-nineteenth century bore no relation to the educational practices that preceded it. All of the diversity of the voluntary system prior to 1850 was swept away and in its place was an institution whose primary aim was thought control. "School knowledge," he concluded, "became state knowledge, uniform and specified from the centre."

For Curtis state control was the most significant feature of nineteenth-century educational reform:

> The School Acts put new forms of political governance in place. They abolished the power of school meetings in the locality to directly govern the local school. The direct and regular participation of parents in pedagogical practice was suppressed. Measures were taken to differentiate teachers from the community. Legal penalties were applied to effective opponents of pedagogical activity. The state came to specify the curriculum and the nature of the school books. The direct participatory democracy of communal schooling was replaced in state administration by limited forms of representative democracy.[17]

If students benefited from the "learning" that took place in school, it was because they found ways of using the experience that was not anticipated by those who taught them. Although students might feel liberated by their new knowledge, schooling had succeeded in its intended purpose: to teach students to control themselves. New concepts such as "delinquent" and "truant" were invented to signify those who failed to conform, and angry parents found the laws ranged against them when they complained about high-handed teachers and excessive corporal punishment.

Curtis's important insights are perhaps best used in conjunction with detailed case studies. For instance, in his work on Prescott County, Ontario, historian Chad Gaffield used quantitative methodology to explore the impact of Ryerson's education system on children and families in rural farming and lumbering communities of mixed English and French ethnicity. By approaching his research from "the bottom up," and from the periphery to the centre, he was able to show that bureaucratic structures had a different impact upon French and English, farming and lumber families, boys and girls. In Prescott County, Ryerson's public education system was not imposed overnight, nor was it left entirely unchanged by those who used it. Human agency and self-control took different forms depending upon the social fabric on which the new bureaucratic structures were imposed.[18]

Because formal educational structures have been such an important and controversial feature of Canadian society over the past 150 years, it is unlikely that we have heard the last of this debate. As Canadians continue to reinvent their educational institutions to meet the demands of changing times, scholars will no doubt find new perspectives on what happened in Egerton Ryerson's Ontario.

•Notes

[1] John Thompson, "The First Last Spike," *Horizon Canada*, vol. 4, 1031–32.

[2] Thomas C. Keefer, "Philosophy of Railroads" (1850), in *Philosophy of Railroads and Other Essays*, ed. T.C. Keefer (Toronto: University of Toronto Press, 1972), 10–11.

[3] Paul Craven and Tom Traves, "Canadian Railways As Manufacturers, 1850–1880," Canadian Historical Association *Historical Papers* (1983): 268.

[4] Elinor Kyte Senior, *British Regulars in Montreal: An Imperial Garrison, 1832–1854* (Montreal: McGill-Queen's University Press, 1981), 191.

[5] Cited in Michael Bliss, *Northern Enterprise: Five Centuries of Canadian Business* (Toronto: McClelland and Stewart, 1987), 141–42.

[6] R.C.B. Risk, "The Law and the Economy in Mid-Nineteenth Century Ontario: A Perspective," in *Essays in the History of Canadian Law*, ed. David H. Flaherty (Toronto: University of Toronto Press, 1981), 117.

[7] Jean-Marie Fecteau, "Prolégomènes à une étude historique des rapports entre l'État et le droit dans la société québécoise, de la fin du XVIIIe siècle à la crise de 1929," *Sociologie et sociétés* 18, 1 (April 1986): 129–38.

[8] Cited in Greg Kealey, *Toronto Workers Respond to Industrial Capitalism, 1867–1892* (Toronto: University of Toronto Press, 1980), 23.

[9] Carl Berger, *Science, God, and Nature in Victorian Canada* (Toronto: University of Toronto Press, 1983), xiii–iv.

[10] Michael Cross and Robert Fraser, "'The Waste That Lies before Me': The Public and Private Worlds of Robert Baldwin," Canadian Historical Association *Historical Papers* (1983): 164–83.

[11] Gerald Friesen, *The Canadian Prairies: A History* (Toronto: University of Toronto Press, 1984), 108.

[12] Alexander Morris, *The Hudson's Bay and Pacific Territories* (Montreal: John Lovell, 1959).

[13] Charles E. Phillips, *The Development of Public Education in Canada* (Toronto: Gage, 1957).

[14] J. Donald Wilson, Robert M. Stamp, and Louis-Philippe Audet, *Canadian Education: A History* (Toronto: Prentice-Hall, 1970).

[15] Alison Prentice, *The School Promoters: Education and Social Class in Mid-Nineteenth Century Upper Canada* (Toronto: McClelland and Stewart, 1977).

[16] Bruce Curtis, *Building the Educational System: Canada West, 1836–1871* (London, ON: Althouse Press, 1988). See also Susan Houston and Alison Prentice, *Schooling and Scholars in Nineteenth-Century Ontario* (Toronto: University of Toronto Press, 1988).

[17] Bruce Curtis, "Policing Pedagogical Space: 'Voluntary' School Reform and Moral Regulation," *Canadian Journal of Sociology* 13, 3 (1988): 283–304.

[18] Chad Gaffield, *Language, Schooling, and Cultural Conflict: The Origins of the French Language Controversy in Ontario* (Montreal: McGill-Queen's University Press, 1987).

•Selected Reading

The classic discussion of the impact of industrialism is Karl Polanyi, *The Great Transformation: The Political and Economic Origins of Our Time* (Boston: Beacon Press, 1957). Canadian studies include Donald Creighton, *The Commercial Empire of the Saint Lawrence, 1760–1850* (Toronto: Macmillan, 1937) and Stanley Ryerson, *Unequal Union: Confederation and the Roots of Conflict in the Canadas, 1815–1873* (Toronto: Progress Books, 1968). The "great transformation" in the British North American context is also the subject of Gerald Tulchinsky, *The River Barons: Montreal Businessmen and the Growth of Industry and Transportation, 1837–1853* (Toronto: University of Toronto Press, 1977); Douglas McCalla, *The Upper Canada Trade, 1834–1872, A Study of Buchanan's Business* (Toronto: University of Toronto Press, 1979); and T.W. Acheson, *Saint John: The Making of a Colonial Urban Community* (Toronto: University of Toronto Press, 1985). Michael Bliss usefully summarizes the general trends in *Northern Enterprise: Five Centuries of Canadian Business* (Toronto: McClelland and Stewart, 1987). Other general studies include Kenneth Norrie and Douglas Owram, *A History of the Canadian Economy* (Toronto: Harcourt Brace Jovanovich, 1991); W.L. Marr and D.G. Patterson, *Canada: An Economic History* (Toronto: Macmillan, 1980); and W.T. Easterbrook and H.G.J. Aitken, *Canadian Economic History* (Toronto: Macmillan, 1963). A valuable perspective on the industrializing process is offered in the introductory chapters to R.T. Naylor, *The History of Canadian Business, 1867–1914*, Vol. 1 (Toronto: Lorimer, 1975); Bryan Palmer, *A Culture in Conflict: Skilled Workers and Industrial Capitalism in Hamilton, Ontario, 1860–1914* (Montreal: McGill-Queen's University Press, 1979); and Gregory S. Kealey, *Toronto Responds to Industrial Capitalism, 1867–1892* (Toronto: University of Toronto Press, 1980). See also Ian McKay, "Capital and Labour in the Halifax Baking and Confectionary Industry During the Last Half of the Nineteenth Century," in *Essays in Canadian Business History*, ed. Tom Traves (Toronto: McClelland and Stewart, 1984), 47–81; Paul Craven and Tom Traves, "Canadian Railways as Manufacturers, 1850–1880," Canadian Historical Association *Historical Papers* (1983): 254–81; R.C.B. Risk, "The Law and the Economy in Mid-Nineteenth Century Ontario: A Perspective," in *Essays in the History of Canadian Law*, vol. 1, ed. David H. Flaherty (Toronto: University of Toronto Press, 1981), 88–131.

Other studies on nineteenth-century economic development include T.C. Keefer, *Philosophy of Railroads* (1850; rprt. Toronto: University of Toronto Press, 1972); S.A. Saunders, *The Economic History of the Maritime Provinces* (1939; rprt. Fredericton: Acadiensis Press, 1984); G.N. Tucker, *The Canadian Commercial Revolution, 1845–1851* (Ottawa: Carleton University Press, 1964); D.C. Masters, *The Reciprocity Treaty of 1854* (Toronto: McClelland and Stewart, 1963); John McCallum, *Unequal Beginnings: Agriculture and Economic Development in Quebec and Ontario Until 1870*

(Toronto: University of Toronto Press, 1980); A.R.M. Lower, *Great Britain's Woodyard: British America and the Timber Trade, 1763–1867* (Montreal: McGill-Queen's University Press, 1973); G.P. de T. Glazebrook, *A History of Transportation in Canada*, Vol. 1 (Ottawa: Carleton University Press, 1964); Brian Young, *Promoters and Politicians: The North-Shore Railways in the History of Quebec* (Toronto: University of Toronto Press, 1978); Jacob Spelt, *Urban Development in South Central Ontario* (Ottawa: Carleton University Press, 1972).

In addition to the sources on religion, education, law, and society cited in chapter 12, the following sources on nineteenth-century intellectual history are useful: Carl Berger, *Science, God, and Nature in Victorian Canada* (Toronto: University of Toronto Press, 1983); A.B. McKillop, *A Disciplined Intelligence: Critical Inquiry and Canadian Thought in the Victorian Era* (Montreal: McGill-Queen's University Press, 1979); *Contours of Canadian Thought* (Toronto: University of Toronto Press, 1987); and "Culture, Intellect and Context," *Journal of Canadian Studies* 24 (Fall 1989): 7–31.

For education in this period see Susan Houston and Alison Prentice, *Schooling and Scholars in Nineteenth Century Ontario* (Toronto: University of Toronto Press, 1988); Bruce Curtis, *Building the Educational State: Canada West, 1836–1871* (London, ON: Althouse Press, 1988); Alison Prentice, *The School Promoters: Education and Social Class in Mid-Nineteenth Century Upper Canada* (Toronto: McClelland and Stewart, 1977); J.D. Wilson et al., *Canadian Education: A History* (Toronto: Prentice-Hall, 1970); Claude Galarneau, *Les collèges classiques au Canada français* (Montreal: Fides, 1978); and Chad Gaffield, *Language, Schooling and Cultural Conflict: The Origins of the French Language Conflict in Ontario* (Montreal: McGill-Queen's University Press, 1987). The historiographical issues are usefully discussed in J. Donald Wilson's introduction to *An Imperfect Past: Education and Society in Canadian History* (Vancouver: University of British Columbia, 1984), 7–24, and "The New Diversity in Canadian Educational History," *Acadiensis* 19, 2 (Spring 1990): 148–69; and Chad Gaffield, "Children, Schooling, and Family Reproduction in Nineteenth-Century Ontario," *Canadian Historical Review* 72, 2 (June 1991): 157–91.

CHAPTER 14

THE ROAD TO CONFEDERATION

The year before the British North America Act was passed by the British Parliament, Joseph Howe, a leader of the anti-confederate movement in Nova Scotia, proclaimed:

> Let us see what these Canadians desire to do. They are not . . . a very harmonious or homogeneous community. Two-fifths of the population are French and three-fifths are English. They are therefore perplexed with an internal antagonism. . . . The wisdom of Solomon and the energy and strategy of Frederick the Great would seem to be required to preserve and strengthen such a people, if formed, as it appears they desire to form themselves into "a new nationality.". . . A more unpromising nucleus of a new nation could hardly be found on the face of the earth.[1]

Many British North Americans, especially those in the colonies' political and economic elites, disagreed with Howe's assessment, and three colonial legislatures—the United Province of Canada, New Brunswick, and Nova Scotia—agreed to a federal union that took effect 1 July 1867. The decision came after years of debate pitting supporters of the creation of the new nation-state of Canada against opponents of the confederation scheme. Not surprisingly the debate emphasized the special conditions and needs of British North America, but it also took place in the context of a global movement that promoted the formation of nation-states.

• The Nation-State in the Nineteenth Century

The nineteenth century has often been described as a century of nationalism. Encouraged by improved communications and greater mobility, populations that shared a common language, history, and popular mythologies began to demand national self-determination. In such places as Italy and Germany, this meant carving a new, larger state out of territories either ruled by local potentates or controlled by outsiders. Elsewhere, as in modern Norway and Romania, it meant demands for smaller nation-states to replace empires headed by people of different languages and cultures.

The American and French revolutions provided the catalysts and the models for much of the nationalism of the nineteenth century. Nationalists were not always democrats, as the leaders of the American Revolution were; nor were they always opponents of aristocracy, in the tradition of the main leaders of the French Revolution. When, for example, Prussian statesman Otto von Bismarck created the German Confederacy in 1871, he was backed by feudal aristocrats, known as the Junkers.

The nationalists of the nineteenth century, including the Junkers, were all apostles of industrial progress. They regarded the nation-state not only as the cultural expression of a people but also as a force for industrial development. In pursuing their nationalistic goals, they were inspired by the eradication of barriers to national commerce achieved in the French Revolution and the more recent use of national tariffs and public works to sponsor industrial advance in the United States.

For the peoples who embraced it, nationalism was not an unmitigated blessing. Wars were often necessary to achieve national unification, as was the case in Italy. Furthermore, cultural minorities sometimes found themselves better protected within culturally diverse empires than in ethnically conscious nation-states; indeed, for minorities, the notions of cultural superiority that informed nationalism frequently led to oppression. Meanwhile, the dominant ethnic group often embarked upon dubious military adventures that benefited only the upper and middle classes and invariably used workers and peasants as cannon fodder.

Within this atmosphere of increased national sentiment in Europe, the United States, and Latin America, British North Americans began to ponder their fate in the late 1850s—to consider whether they had a grander future than that of citizens of isolated outposts of the British empire. The discussion cut several ways. For some British North Americans it seemed only natural that the colonies form a new, large nation to rival their giant southern neighbour. In their eyes this new political unity would loosen, though not sever, the link with the mother country. For other British North Americans it seemed equally natural that their particular colony—because it had its own history and its own economy separate from those of the neighbouring colonies—become a nation unto itself. This small nation could, perhaps, remain within the British empire, but it would be a sovereign state and not a subordinate part of an artificial entity composed of disparate colonies united only by the fact of British rule.

Like their European counterparts, supporters of British North American unity were often inspired by dreams of economic development. Although a depression from 1846 to 1849 followed the dismantling of imperial preferences, the 1850s and 1860s witnessed dramatic economic growth in most of the British American colonies. With Britain and the United States experiencing an industrial boom, the demand for wheat, lumber, minerals, and ships from Britain's overseas colonies soared. Two very specific factors added to the prosperity of these years: the Crimean War of 1854–56 and the 1854 reciprocity agreement in natural products between British North America and the United States. The Crimean War, matching Britain against Russia, deprived the mother country of an important source of grain and so gave an additional boost to an already expanding demand for Canadian

Bytown (later Ottawa) and the Rideau Canal   (Willis, *Canadian Scenery*, vol. 2, p. 7, Metropolitan Toronto Library Board)

wheat and flour. During the Civil War that raged in the United States from 1861 to 1865, colonial produce found steady markets, reinforcing the trends already encouraged by the Reciprocity Treaty of 1854.

Responsible government had given power to elected representatives in the various colonies; but wealthy men—women had as yet neither voice nor vote—tended to dominate political office. Believers in material progress and often speculators in the various economic ventures of their colonies, these men risked tremendous sums of public money to build railroads, roads, and canals to ensure the advancement of both their colony and their own private welfare. They were increasingly convinced that the most direct route to economic growth was British North American union.

•The Canadas: Economic Success and Political Impasse

During its brief existence as a political entity, the United Province of Canada experienced steady economic and population growth. Economic development did not guarantee political stability. Unable to find a political formula that would convince Lower Canadians and Upper Canadians alike that their interests were represented within the union, politicians had difficulty governing the unwieldy union.

Part of the problem was the unequal population growth of Canada West and Canada East. At the time of the union Lower Canada had a popula-

Table 14.1: POPULATION OF BRITISH NORTH AMERICA

	1851	1861	1871
Ontario	952 004	1 396 091	1 620 851
Quebec	890 261	1 111 566	1 191 516
Nova Scotia	276 854	330 857	387 800
New Brunswick	193 800	252 047	285 594
Prince Edward Island	62 678 (1848)	80 857	94 021
Newfoundland	—	122 638 (1857)	158 958 (1874)
British Columbia	55 000	51 524	36 247*
Manitoba	—	—	25 228
Northwest Territories	—	—	48 000

*This figure probably understates the Native population of the province by about 15 000.

Sources: "Series A 2-14. Population of Canada by province, census dates, 1851 to 1976," in *Historical Statistics of Canada*, 2nd ed., ed. F.H. Leacy (Ottawa: Minister of Supply and Services, 1983); James Hiller, "Confederation Defeated: The Newfoundland Election of 1869," in *Newfoundland in the Nineteenth and Twentieth Centuries: Essays in Interpretation*, ed. James Hiller and Peter Neary (Toronto: University of Toronto Press, 1980).

tion of 650 000, compared to 450 000 in the upper province. By 1851, owing particularly to the large-scale influx of Irish immigrants, Canada West's population had more than doubled, to 952 000. The population of Canada East, by contrast, had risen only to 890 000. Many of the Upper Canadian politicians who in 1840 had decried Lower Canadian complaints about under-representation now believed that representation by population in the legislature of the United Province must replace the equal division of seats provided for in the Act of Union. By 1861, when the population of Canada West had reached 1.4 million, compared to just over 1.1 million in Canada East, "rep by pop" had become the rallying cry of George Brown's Reformers. Unsurprisingly, opposition to this principle in Canada East matched support for it in Canada West. The claim that democracy demanded representation proportional to population was met by the charge that the undemocratic union of 1840 provided no protection of French Catholic rights other than the presence of a large bloc of French seats in Canada East.

Capitalizing on sectional tensions, George Brown, the major leader of the Reform movement in Canada West, shaped an organization that resembled in embryo a modern political party. Apart from the goal of representation by population, the glue bonding Reformers together was opposition to public monies for separate schools and for subsidies to the Grand Trunk Railway, as well as support for annexation of the Northwest to Canada.

John A. Macdonald emerged as the leader of an equally organized bloc of Conservative politicians who resisted the Reformers' demands as impediments to an alliance with the majority *bleu* group of Canada East. Macdonald could rely on skilful use of patronage, traditional sentimental ties to Britain, and the importance of the economic link to the St Lawrence River to convince many voters in Canada West of the folly of support for a program of reforms that would alienate the French-speaking majority of Canada East. Increasingly, however, the majority in Canada West liked what the Reformers had to say more than they liked Macdonald or his programs. In 1863, in the last general election for the Legislative Assembly of the United Province of Canada, only twenty of the sixty-five seats in Canada West went to John A. Macdonald and his supporters.

In Canada East the opponents of the *bleus* never won more than twenty-five of the sixty-five seats allocated for their province. Divided between the liberal *rouges* and independents, the reformist element in Canada East formed neither a coherent party nor an easy ally of the Canada West Reformers. A Reform ministry created in 1862 under the leadership of John Sandfield Macdonald, Brown's chief rival among Canada West Reformers, survived for merely a year and a half and did so by abandoning principles of "rep by pop" and opposition to public support of denominational schools. No French-speaking politician could afford politically to support either the

JOHN A. MACDONALD: THE CHANGING FACE OF TORYISM IN CANADA WEST

When John A. Macdonald was first elected as a Conservative to the Assembly of the United Province of Canada in 1844, he opposed responsible government, the secularization of clergy reserves, the abolition of primogeniture, and the broadening of the franchise. He argued that the democratic changes favoured by Reformers would lead to a weakening of both the British connection to the colony and of property rights. Although his support of the British connection and of the propertied classes never waned, he adapted quickly to the introduction of responsible government in the Province of Canada in 1848. He recognized that pragmatism, patronage, and party organization could keep conservatism alive in an age of democratic competition.

Macdonald was born in Glasgow, Scotland, in 1815 and immigrated to Upper Canada with his parents five years later. The family moved to Kingston, and his father's merchant activities were sufficiently successful for young John A. to attend private and grammar schools. At age fifteen he began to article in a Kingston law office, and he was called to the bar in 1836. An active Presbyterian and Kingston clubman, Macdonald became the solicitor for several major financial concerns by the early 1840s. His entry into politics in 1843 began with a successful run for Kingston town council, followed by election to the Assembly in 1844.

Appointed to the cabinet in 1847, by 1856 he was Canada West's first minister, chief Conservative strategist, fund raiser, and campaign organizer. No candidate could be elected by a Conservative riding in Canada West without Macdonald's approval. He developed a centralized system of government patronage that guaranteed the personal loyalty of many state employees and recipients of government contracts. Attempting to create a mass base for conservatism, he appealed for support to leaders of disparate groups such as the Orange Order and the Catholic and Methodist churches. He not only dropped his opposition to secularization of clergy reserves but also, as attorney-general, steered the government's legislation on the subject through the Assembly in 1854. Such a pragmatic change of heart would be repeated ten years later, in the interests of retaining office, when he agreed to lead the fight for a confederation agreement—a project he had denounced just days before becoming one of the leaders of a coalition government formed for the sole end of achieving confederation of the British North American colonies.

reduction of *Canadien* legislative representation or the abandonment of their co-religionists in Canada West; and no government, Conservative or Reform, was thinkable without *Canadien* representation. By 1864, the chances of forming a government acceptable to both halves of the United Province seemed remote. A "double majority"—majority support in each of the two sections of the province—was not constitutionally necessary, but most politicians accepted it as a practical necessity for commanding legitimacy throughout a province created by a shotgun wedding.

The schools issue demonstrated the difficulties facing supporters of a "double majority." In 1841, well before responsible government had been granted, the Common School Act for Canada West had established the right of religious minorities to share in the provincial grant for schools. In 1853 the Hincks-Morin ministry, relying mainly on the vote of Canada East politicians, strengthened the government's commitment to separate schools in Canada West by explicitly exempting separate-school ratepayers from property taxes for the support of common schools. A majority in Canada West opposed the bill and railed against Canada East politicians who thought they could impose the principle of separate schools upon the United Canadas. Canada West seemed no more reconciled to separate schools ten years later, when John Sandfield Macdonald was forced to rely on votes from francophone members in Canada East to allow separate schools to license their own teachers.

The political impasse resulting from sectional differences on key issues was not the only problem facing the administration of the Canadas by the early 1860s. Three railways—the Northern, Great Western, and St Lawrence and Atlantic—received bond guarantees under the Guarantee Act of 1849 from an Assembly filled with railway investors. Three years later the Assembly chartered and began providing guarantees for the Grand Trunk Railway, whose investors included both major British banking concerns and the usual crew of Canadian politicians. In 1853 the Grand Trunk, which initially sought only to build lines from Montreal to Hamilton, recognized the need for an Atlantic link and bought, at inflated prices, the assets of the St Lawrence and Atlantic Railway, in which A.T. Galt was a leading figure. By 1859 the Grand Trunk ran from Sarnia to Lévis, with a winter port in Portland, Maine, but it was a huge money loser and a nest of corruption.

Only the wealthy could afford to participate in a political life, which offered no salary for an elected member of the Assembly. Furthermore, responsible government had placed the running of public affairs in the hands of elected officials who barely recognized a boundary between their

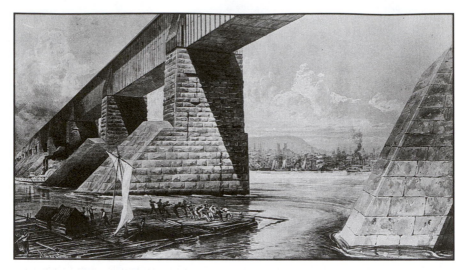

The Victoria Bridge, opened in 1859, gave the Grand Trunk Railway access to Portland, Maine (National Archives of Canada/C3590)

own and the public's interests. Answering critics within the British American Land Company who thought his foray into politics in 1849 reduced the time he could spend on company matters, Galt answered: "I consider the interests of the Company and the country to be identical."[2] By the early 1860s crushing public debts had been incurred because the politicians believed that public revenues should stand behind their railway projects.

The province's main source of revenue was a tariff on imported goods. As finance minister, A.T. Galt had raised that tariff to a record 15 percent in 1859 to protect Canadian manufacturers and raise money to pay the growing public debt. Nonetheless, the revenues of the Canadas could not meet the expenditures necessary to pay interest on existing debts and, at the same time, begin other public works. Increasingly, Canada's British creditors balked at making loans to a tiny colony that could not live within its own means and appeared to have no plans to expand its revenue base.

By 1864, the political and economic impasse caused a coterie of leading Canadian politicians to look to a confederation of the British North American colonies as a solution. At George Brown's instigation, the Assembly appointed a constitutional committee to examine options for the Canadas. In June 1864, the committee issued a report in which twelve of its fifteen members called for consideration of a federal union of the British North American colonies.

The idea was not new. Lord Durham had proposed a union of the colonies in his 1840 report, and Galt had made the same suggestion to the legislature in 1858. Brown had been pushing since 1857 for reform of the political system imposed on Upper and Lower Canada in 1840. In 1860 he introduced a motion into the Assembly favouring the adoption of a federal union: a central government with specific responsibilities for legislation would continue to exist, but provincial governments with their own responsibilities would also be created. Brown hoped that by making the provincial governments powerful enough—for example, by giving them complete control over education—Canada East's ability to impose legislation on Canada West would be greatly reduced. In 1860 no member from Canada East was willing to support a federal union of the Canadas, but the continuing impasse in the legislature gave Brown another chance to achieve his goals.

Brown, as editor of the Toronto *Globe*, had been one of the bitterest foes of the conservative regimes that predominated in the 1850s. A booster of his home city, Brown had invested in a variety of mercantile and manufacturing ventures in Toronto. He regarded the Cartier–Macdonald coalition as supporters of the imperial ambitions of Montreal and particularly resented the Grand Trunk as an agent of Montreal interests. Toronto's imperial ambitions, according to Brown and like-minded business people, required less public spending on railway projects centred on Montreal and more attention paid to acquiring the Northwest. As fertile land for settlers disappeared, Toronto merchants seeking new markets began to cry all the louder for acquisition of the Northwest. Farmers echoed the call. The monoculture of wheat had led to soil exhaustion, and while diversification in the 1860s staved off a decline in farm incomes, most farmers believed that more land was the key to preventing an agricultural crisis. Interestingly, Galt, in his call for confederation in 1858, had also supported expansion into the Northwest. But personality differences between Brown and Galt made it difficult for these men to make common cause at that time.

After the release of the Assembly committee's report in June 1864, it was Brown who took the decisive political move that made the first round of negotiations for confederation possible. He approached George-Étienne Cartier and John A. Macdonald, who were having great difficulty establishing a functioning majority in the Assembly, with the idea of a "Great Coalition" whose goal would be the achievement of confederation. The coalition would include the supporters of Cartier, Macdonald, and Brown and would thus command a strong majority in both sections of Canada. Only the recalcitrant *rouges* would be excluded. Macdonald would remain the government leader for Canada West, but half of the cabinet posts from that section would be filled by Brown and his Reform associates.

John A. Macdonald had been one of the three members of the constitutional committee who opposed confederation, partly because he favoured a legislative union over a federal union. He was also lukewarm to the proposal for annexing the Hudson's Bay Company territories to Canada. But he wanted to remain in office and build a broader base for Toryism in Canada West. He and Cartier quickly came to terms with Brown, and a new ministry dedicated to the idea of a confederation of the British American colonies was sworn in.

It was a strange first step in the creation of a new nation-state. A ministry in one of the colonies of the state-to-be had been formed with the objective of nation-building without a single member having received an electoral mandate for the undertaking. Although E.P. Taché was its figurehead, the leader of this ministry was a man who only days before had rejected the idea of the new nation as at best premature.

Macdonald was, however, a consummate political organizer whose persuasive skills could only be an asset in promoting his new-found project. Like most leading Canadian politicians of the period, Macdonald was a businessman-politician. Both a workaholic and an alcoholic, he was a lawyer with directorships in bank, insurance, railway, and utility companies in his home constituency of Kingston. His land speculations were spread over a dozen counties of Canada West. Like Brown, he came to view the Northwest as a vast territory awaiting Upper Canadian settlement and the Maritimes as another potential market for Upper Canadian manufactures.

As it happened, the premiers of the Maritime colonies had committed their ministries to consider Maritime union. Happily for Macdonald

Joseph Howe and George Brown   (Public Archives of Nova Scotia; National Archives of Canada/C9553)

and the other pro-confederates, the lieutenant-governors of the Maritime colonies were easily persuaded to broaden the scope of their constitutional deliberations to include consideration of a complete British North American union.

•Great Expectations in the Maritimes

In the Atlantic region, Nova Scotia and New Brunswick were the most receptive to the idea of British North American union. The healthy state of the coastal trade, shipbuilding, and the fisheries as well as increased demand for Nova Scotia coal and New Brunswick lumber fattened the treasuries of these two colonies in the 1850s and 1860s. Elected governments, following the Canadian lead, chose to spend much of this money on the building of railways and soon found themselves with revenue shortfalls.

Reformers dominated the Nova Scotia legislature until 1863, when the electorate gave a clear majority to their Conservative opponents. Joseph Howe, although serving as premier only from 1860 to 1863, played a towering role in the Nova Scotia cabinets of the period, always promoting railway projects as the key to increased colonial prosperity. He was largely responsible for the government's decision in the 1850s to place railways built with provincial money under public ownership, in contrast to the other colonies' practice of giving grants and loan guarantees without demanding a direct return to the public purse.

Howe's railway projects were the main culprit in a $4.5-million provincial debt accumulated by 1863. His favourite venture was a line linking Halifax to the St Lawrence, generally referred to as the Intercolonial Railway. Howe had proposed the Intercolonial as early as 1849 at a conference held in Halifax to discuss the Atlantic colonies' future as Britain embarked on free trade. Howe believed the railway line would provide a valuable military highway for Britain in time of war as well as stimulate British North American trade. But despite a number of false starts the project always failed to attract the necessary investment from British financiers, and in 1863 the line was far from being completed.

The Conservatives continued the Reformers' commitment to public works in Nova Scotia. Particularly after Charles Tupper became premier in early 1864, expenditures began to climb and the provincial debt rose to over $8 million by 1866. Tupper, a medical doctor, had represented Cumberland County since 1855. With substantial investments in the county's coal mines, the Nova Scotia premier believed that the region's future in both coal and iron was assured as long as secure markets for its products could be found. Rumours that the Americans, angry at Britain's support of the South during the Civil War, would abrogate the Reciprocity Treaty caused him grave concern about whether Cumberland County would achieve its potential. The Intercolonial might provide Nova Scotia with new markets in New Brunswick and Canada, but the province was in no position financially to proceed with it. With only 235 kilometres of track laid down by 1867, Nova Scotia had invested $7.5 million in railways and was too deeply in debt to build more.

The Intercolonial was also on the minds of leading New Brunswick politicians. For a time in the 1850s the temperance issue became the focal point of New Brunswick politics as supporters of prohibition campaigned to have the Assembly stop the importation of "demon rum." Led by Baptists and Wesleyan Methodists, the temperance forces succeeded in 1854 and again in 1855 in bending the legislature to their wishes. But prohibition proved unenforceable and died with the election of a wet majority in 1856. The "Smashers," the name the prohibitionists were given derisively by their "Rummy" opponents, took power again in 1857. They stayed in office until 1870, but railways, not prohibition, were now their passion.

Unable to secure the funds for the Intercolonial, New Brunswick's politicians began to follow a pied piper from Maine named John Alfred Poor, who was promoting a railway to link Maine with New Brunswick and Nova Scotia. When Poor declared bankruptcy in 1855, the colony pressed ahead with a line linking Shediac to Saint John and continued to plan its extension into the United States. A labour shortage had forced the province to import British navvies to build its railway lines, and labour costs plus a variety of technical problems resulted in huge cost overruns. Smasher patronage in the awarding of contracts also pushed up costs.

In 1861 the Smasher premier Charles Fisher had his political career smashed when it was revealed that he had acquired vast areas of Crown land despite a Crown Lands Office regulation forbidding elected officials and civil servants from making such purchases. He was hardly the only legislator to take advantage of the increased market for New Brunswick timber, but he proved a convenient sacrificial lamb.

Fisher's replacement was Samuel Leonard Tilley of Gagetown, son of a Loyalist and the leader of the temperance forces in the 1850s. Tilley had been an apothecary, and his patent medicines and pills had made him one of the wealthiest men in the colony. He wanted to press forward with the Intercolonial, but with a $5-million railway debt and an annual revenue of only $600 000, the legislature voted in 1862 not to undertake any new railway construction.

Prince Edward Island built no railways until 1871 and for a time its Assembly had greater revenues at its disposal, chiefly because reciprocity increased demand for the island's potatoes and fish. Indeed, in the years 1855 to 1865, exports to the United States as a proportion of all island exports grew from 22 percent to 42 percent. One year later, with reciprocity a thing of the past, the figure fell to 9 percent. The land question still nagged at successive island administrations. In the 1850s Liberal premier George Coles used provincial revenues to buy out some of the absentee landlords so that tenants could become landowners. Although the landowners and the Colonial Office resisted his efforts, by 1861 about 40 percent of the island's residents were freeholders.

In 1864, when the Conservative Protestant-dominated government proved dilatory in pressing for more land reform, a Tenant League was formed. The league crossed denominational barriers, and its members, who supported a tenant takeover of rented land with rates of compensation to landlords to be set by townships, vowed to pay no further rents. Their collective action to resist the rent collectors resulted in the government using soldiers to serve writs on tenants in arrears and to repress the league.

There was less militancy in Newfoundland politics in the 1850s and 1860s, although party loyalties there, as in Prince Edward Island, had a strong denominational flavour, with the Liberals mainly Catholic and the Conservatives exclusively Protestant. Nonetheless, the politicians agreed in the 1860s to provide public support to school systems for each of the two sides of the religious divide and to split civil-service positions in proportion to the numbers of Catholics and Protestants. The election of Hugh Hoyles's Conservatives in 1861 was greeted with angry riots among Catholics in St John's and Conception Bay; but Hoyles proved conciliatory to the Catholics, and open hostility, if not suspicion, between the two groups subsided. Newfoundland's flagging economy caused Hoyles to take an interest in the idea of a union of the Atlantic colonies, although Newfoundland was not invited to the conference on Maritime union planned for Charlottetown in 1864.

• The External Pressure for Confederation

Politicians in Nova Scotia were most receptive to the idea of restoring "greater Nova Scotia" through some kind of Maritime union, and they took the initiative in suggesting a conference on the issue early in 1864.

Although resolutions to send delegates to a Maritime union conference passed easily in both the Nova Scotia and New Brunswick legislatures, the proposal was less enthusiastically received in Prince Edward Island and no action was taken to set a time and place for the meeting. The proposal might well have been shelved completely had the Canadians not intervened with their request late in June to attend any conference that the Maritimers were planning.

By the 1860s both Liberal and Conservative administrations in Britain were in favour of reducing the costs of the colonies. The Colonial Office urged representatives in the colonies to support political unions that could take more responsibility for their own military and administrative needs. Nova Scotia's lieutenant-governor, Richard Graves Macdonnell, and his counterpart, Arthur Gordon, in New Brunswick supported Maritime union. From their upper-class British perspective, colonial assemblies were dominated by pretentious, corrupt politicians. When the Canadians asked to attend a conference on Maritime union, Macdonnell and Gordon did

Prelude to Confederation. *William Henry Pope welcomes delegates to the Charlottetown conference* (Confederation Life Gallery of Canadian History)

everything in their power to ensure that the event went ahead. In an effort to get the support of the Prince Edward Islanders, as well as to make it easier for the Canadians who would come down the St Lawrence by ship, Charlottetown was chosen as the site of the proposed meeting to be held on 1 September 1864.

Edward Cardwell, who became colonial secretary in March 1864, supported the Canadian initiative for the larger union of the British North American colonies. Like his immediate predecessors, he regarded Britain's white-settler colonies as unnecessary financial burdens on the British treasury. The Colonial Office had for some time encouraged its North American colonies, particularly the United Province of Canada, to shoulder a greater share of defence costs. Saddled with railway debts, the Canadian Assembly had made only token gestures to improve the quality and quantity of members in the local militia and to upgrade the equipment that they used.

The defence issue was driven home to British North Americans by the American Civil War, which pitted the slave-holding South against the industrial North. Although many British North Americans were sympathetic to the Northern cause, the Southern Confederates also had their supporters in the colonies, especially among elite circles in cities such as Halifax and Montreal. Public opinion in Britain was also divided over the conflict. There were important interests in Britain, especially those involved in the importation of such southern products as cotton and tobacco, who would have been happy to see the Confederacy gain independence. As the war dragged on, a number of incidents on the high seas and along the border helped to increase tensions between Britain and the North and exposed the vulnerability of the British North American colonies.

In late 1861 a Northern naval ship seized the *Trent*, a British steamer en route from Cuba to Britain, and arrested two Confederate agents aboard. Although the North eventually yielded to Britain's protests and released the two agents, the British responded to the threat of an eventual war with the United States by reinforcing the existing 3000 troops in British North America with an additional 15 000 men.

During the war British-built destroyers purchased by the Confederacy, including the *Alabama*, the *Florida*, and the *Shenandoah*, sank over one hundred vessels. The North in turn pursued Confederate ships into British waters: in December 1863 they chased the *Chesapeake* into Nova Scotia waters and arrested the men aboard. Border raids also increased tensions. The government was livid in 1864 when a Montreal magistrate set free Confederate agents who had robbed three banks in St Albans, Vermont, and then crossed back into Canada.

While military goals dominated Colonial Office policy in the period when the colonies debated confederation, there were also vested economic interests pressing for British North American union. The British financiers who bought the Hudson's Bay Company in 1863 hoped to make a fortune when the expansion-minded Canadians bought the lands of Assiniboia for settlement. But the political impasse in the United Province of Canada and the railway debt were impediments to fast action by Canada on the Northwest. A new union with a strong central government might be more efficient. Other British businessmen, under pressure to lend money to the Intercolonial project, likewise believed that their investments would be safer if British North America were politically united. Otherwise any one of three colonial governments could take actions harmful to investors' interests. Such British support for confederation would prove a great asset to the pro-confederates in British North America in overcoming opposition within the various colonies.

•Planning Confederation

The Charlottetown conference in September 1864 quickly shelved its discussion regarding a union of the Maritime colonies in favour of a focus on Canada's proposal for a British North American federation. The delegates agreed to reassemble in Quebec City one month later to produce a detailed proposal that could be presented to their respective legislatures. Representatives from Newfoundland attended the Quebec conference where the basis of union was hammered out.

As subsequent events indicate, it was only by chance that the five colonies (six, if the two sections of the United Province of Canada are considered separately) happened to be led by pro-confederate premiers. Two premiers would prove unable to bring the colonies they led into confederation in 1867; a third lost an election over confederation in 1865 before imperial intervention allowed him to return to power in 1866; and the others refused to submit confederation to a vote in their colonies.

John A. Macdonald favoured a legislative union of the colonies with the former provincial legislatures simply disappearing. From his point of view, federal unions such as that which prevailed in the United States inevitably fell prey to internal discord of the type that had produced the American Civil War. But a legislative union was politically impossible to sell to the Maritime leaders or to the political parties of Canada East.

With a legislative union out of the question, Macdonald sought to ensure the primacy of the federal government in any federal union. All important economic and diplomatic matters, he argued, ought to be in federal hands, leaving matters of purely local concern, such as education and care of the indigent, to the provinces. For this position, he had the support of George-Étienne Cartier and George Brown, who represented respectively the interests of the business elites of Montreal and Toronto. Brown, once a supporter of a loose federal union, had come to accept the view that the federal government required the greatest powers if it was to be able to carry out national objectives such as the acquisition of the Northwest. The leaders of the Atlantic colonies were generally warier about centralization of power and the motives of the Canadians. When the delegates from Nova Scotia and New Brunswick met with their counterparts from the United Canadas in London in 1866 for the third and final conference on Confederation, they pushed for modifications to the Quebec resolutions. Their most significant achievement was the inclusion in the British North America Act of a clause guaranteeing that the Intercolonial Railroad would be constructed "by the Government of Canada." By including the railroad in the constitution, Canadians would not be able to back out of their promise to bind the union together by ties of steel rails.

The plan for confederation created both a federal government and provincial governments and gave each level of government specified powers.

FESTIVITIES IN QUEBEC

The Quebec conference stretched over sixteen days in October 1864. Judging by the news accounts that appeared in papers supportive of the political leaders taking part, it was a solemn event dominated by discussions of high principle and a search for reasoned compromises among the participating parties. Part of the time, however, was consumed in more carefree festivities, and the lavishness of various balls and banquets received much attention in newspapers opposed to the plans laid in Quebec City. Opponents of confederation even suggested that the fathers of confederation were rather drunk as they approached agreement on the constitution for the new Canadian nation-state. Particularly amusing was the fictional re-creation of the conference meetings serialized in the *Halifax Citizen* and later published as *Barney Rooney's Letters on Confederation, Botheration and Political Transmogrification* (1865). A typical excerpt involves John A. Macdonald, George Brown, and Thomas D'Arcy McGee from the United Province of Canada, Samuel Leonard Tilley of New Brunswick, and Charles Tupper and Jonathan McCully of Nova Scotia.

John A. ". . . but hand us the tipple iv ye iver stop suppin' to see iv it's strong enough; and toss a lemon to Tilley, the sowl, iv he must do penance like a patriarch."

"I'll hae whuskey," sez Jarge [Brown]. . . . "My certie, ye're richt though, Darcie lad, aboot the danger o' gangin' ower early tae the polls. . . . Dinna ye think sae, Mister Crupper?"

"Sir," sez Tupper, as he dried the bottom iv his tumbler, and held it handy to D'Arcy's ladle, "the well understood wishes iv the people are so notoriously in favor iv this scheme that it would be a reckless and infamous policy to put them to the trouble of expressing themselves. . . ."

. . . the whole set staggered on to the Confrince omnibus, in the top of good humour, Brown droning out "Soggarth Aroon" to plaze D'Arcy, and Darcy blarneying the Scotch to plase Brown, and McCully and Tupper swearin' etarnal friendship on Confederashun.[3]

The existing colonies would become provinces, with the important exception of the United Province of Canada: each of its two sections would have a separate provincial administration under the new names of Quebec and Ontario. Representation in the federal assembly (House of Commons) would be proportional to population, and all members in the House of Commons would be elected. To appease complaints from the Maritimes that the smaller provinces would not have their voices heard in such an assembly, the plan also called for an appointed Senate that gave Quebec, Ontario, and the Maritimes equal representation.

The division of powers finalized in 1866 and confirmed in the British North America Act passed by the British House of Commons in March 1867 gave the federal government control over a number of areas, including international and interprovincial trade; foreign policy and defence; criminal law; Indian affairs; currency and banking; fisheries; and interprovincial transportation. The provinces in turn would control commerce within their borders, natural resources and public lands, civil law, municipal administration, and education. Federal and provincial governments would split authority in the areas of agriculture and immigration. Both levels of government would have taxing powers; however, while the federal government's powers in this area were unrestricted, the provinces were restricted to direct taxation. Tariffs and excise duties, at the time the source of most income for the various colonies, could be collected only by the federal government. Loss of such revenues would be compensated by a federal per capita grant to the provinces. The federal government would also take over responsibility for paying off principal and interest payments on debts accumulated by the colonies before confederation, up to a specified limit based on a per capita formula.

A caveat on provincial powers regarding education was a provision that enshrined, in perpetuity, educational rights acquired by law or custom before confederation. This would protect the tax-supported separate schools of Canada West and the Protestant schools of Canada East. Attempts by Catholic minorities in the Maritimes to achieve guarantees for equality between secular and confessional schools failed, but provision was made that groups that believed their rights had been violated by a province could ask the federal government for "remedial" legislation.

Like any constitution that divides power between separate levels of government, the British North America Act contained ambiguities. For example, the centralizers managed to include a general clause that allowed the federal level of government to make whatever laws were necessary for maintaining "peace, order and good government" in the new nation, even though that clause seemed to contradict the provinces' right to legislate freely on matters concerning "civil rights and property."

One area given little thought was language. French and English were made official languages in the House of Commons and federal courts, and Quebec was to be recognized as bilingual, but the status of French outside Quebec was ignored. The French-Canadian *bleu* leaders believed that the new Quebec government would act as the guarantor of the French language in Quebec and gave little thought to French-speaking people outside Quebec and those who might move out of Quebec after confederation.

• The Selling of Confederation

None of the colonial leaders present at Quebec City had an electoral mandate to support a confederation of the British North American colonies. Given the growing emphasis on "responsible" government and democratic principles, the premiers would have to seek either a new electoral mandate to allow their respective provinces to enter confederation or, at a minimum, a majority vote from their legislatures.

For Premier John Hamilton Gray of Prince Edward Island, a majority vote in the legislature was impossible because his own Conservative party was divided on the issue. His attorney-general, Edward Palmer, a former premier, flatly rejected the confederation idea. To submit the proposal to the electorate would most likely result in electoral defeat and disarray in his party. Gray wisely chose to shelve the idea of confederation.

Premier Hoyles of Newfoundland was also unable to muster the votes for confederation in his province's legislature, and the issue was resolved only in 1869 when the electorate decisively rejected a surrender of independence. Newfoundland supporters of union argued that it would provide new markets for local products as well as grants that would allow them to build roads and other public works. The importance of federal subsidies, however, had to be balanced against the likely costs to Newfoundlanders of paying taxes to build mainland railroads. Also, most St John's and Conception Bay merchants believed that confederation would mean Canadian competition for the island's home market. They argued that Newfoundland's economy would continue to depend on the sea and on trade with Britain, and they discounted trade possibilities with the rest of British North America—at the time, only 5 percent of Newfoundland's exports went to the other colonies. Irish Catholics, led by the church leaders in Newfoundland, feared that newly won Catholic rights would be threatened within the proposed union. Many of the leaders of the confederation movement, including John A. Macdonald, had Orange affiliations, which contributed to fears that confederation was an anti-Catholic plot.

For manufacturers and merchants in Nova Scotia and New Brunswick, the agreement to transfer the right to impose tariffs to the federal government was a major cause for concern. They feared loss of protection and the competition from goods from the United Province of Canada. Politicians and merchants, including many who did not reject the notion of a confederation of the colonies out of hand, were appalled at the Quebec City resolutions that granted all monetary and most fiscal powers to the federal government, which would be dominated by Quebec and Ontario. The argument that the colonies together could muster the defence forces to fend off American invaders struck opponents of confederation as spurious: in their view it was the bellicose Canadians who had courted American hostility. Now, via their crushing majority in the House of Commons, the Canadians were about to drag Maritimers into their disputes. In any case, each Atlantic colony had far more trade with the Americans than with the Canadians, and they valued continuing good relations with their southern neighbours more than manufacturing a cosy arrangement with the haughty Canadians.

Premier Tilley, leader of a divided party, agreed to face the New Brunswick electorate in March 1865. The anti-confederates, led by Albert J. Smith, a long-time Smasher politician who had turned against the government even before confederation became the major political issue, won three-quarters of the legislative seats.

ALBERT JAMES SMITH AND OPPOSITION TO CONFEDERATION IN NEW BRUNSWICK

When Albert James Smith set about to form a cabinet after elections to the Assembly of New Brunswick in 1865, he knew that it would be impossible to choose a harmonious group. Although twenty-six declared opponents of the confederation agreement had been elected in an Assembly of forty-one, they were a diverse bunch. Some were outright opponents of confederation who wanted New Brunswick to remain a separate colony; others supported the notion of confederation but wanted the terms renegotiated to strengthen the powers of the provinces and the representation of smaller colonies in the proposed House of Commons and Senate; still others wanted a stronger central government than the agreement provided. Among the Assembly members were Conservatives and Liberals unaccustomed to working with their ideological opponents.

Smith proved unequal to the task. A grandson of Massachusetts Loyalists and the son of a successful timber merchant in Shediac, Smith was a part-time politician. After attending private and Church of England schools, he had articled in a Dorchester law office and was called to the bar in 1847. Although he was elected to the provincial Assembly as a Reformer in 1852, Smith spent much of the time during his political career focussing on his law practice and business investments. Despite his own privileged background, he supported electoral reforms to limit the powers of the colonial elite, whom he accused of intimidating voters (because there was no secret ballot) and using public funds to promote their private interests. A member of Reform governments from 1854 onwards, Smith, like A.A. Dorion in Canada East, had broken with his Liberal colleagues over the use of government funds for developing private railways. In 1862 Smith left Tilley's cabinet to protest increased grants to railway developers. For Tilley the Intercolonial Railway promised in the Quebec agreements was New Brunswick's prize from confederation. For Smith it was another example of public risk in an area where the private sector should do the risk-taking if it expected the profits.

Smith's "anti-confederation" government soon broke up into warring factions. In the following election of 1866, with the lieutenant-governor and the Roman Catholic Church supporting confederation, Smith was unable to carry more than a handful of seats. He did, however, win personal re-election and became a spokesperson for revising the agreement. His proposed changes included equal representation for provinces in the upper house (Senate), a guarantee of a cabinet minister for each Atlantic province, strict control over taxation, and establishment of an independent court to arbitrate federal–provincial disputes. The pro-confederation Tilley government largely dismissed these demands as unattainable.

In spring 1865 the American government gave notice of the abrogation of the Reciprocity Treaty—putting an end to the hopes of New Brunswick anti-confederates, as expressed in the 1865 election, of expanding trade with the United States. In December another problem appeared in the form of the American wing of the Fenian Brotherhood, a group dedicated to Irish independence. One section of the American Fenians believed that a takeover of Britain's North American possessions could force Britain to negotiate freedom for Ireland. Fenian raids and rumours of impending raids sowed fear among all British North Americans and emphasized their dependence on British protection—protection that the British were loudly indicating could not continue indefinitely. In New Brunswick Protestant pro-confederates, all the while seeking the support of the Catholic hierarchy for their cause, sowed suspicion among their co-religionists that Irish Catholics in the colony and American Fenians were in league, thus fostering the belief that loyal Protestants should support confederation.

British backing for confederation played the major role in unravelling popular opposition to the project in New Brunswick. Lieutenant-governor Arthur Gordon succeeded in winning support for the union from the Catholic bishops of the province as well as from the timber merchants. He also forced a second confederation election in May 1866 and left little

Fenian raid near Fort Erie, Ontario, 1866   (National Archives of Canada/C18737)

doubt in the electorate's mind about what the mother country expected from loyal voters. In that election Tilley and his confederates carried thirty-three of the forty-one legislative seats.

Like his counterparts in the other Maritime provinces, Premier Tupper of Nova Scotia soon found that he lacked the legislative majority to back Nova Scotia's entry into confederation on the terms arrived at in Quebec City, and perhaps on any terms. One of his principal arguments was that confederation would allow the province to use its coal and iron to build a heavy-industry sector, but this carried little weight with people who depended upon a mercantile economy for their profits or wages. While Tupper had powerful supporters, including the colony's Anglican bishop and Roman Catholic archbishop along with three judges of its Supreme Court, he faced almost universal opposition from the merchants. This group soon aligned itself with former premier Joseph Howe. They had once hated Howe for building publicly owned railways, but now together they worked to create the public pressure needed to block confederation.

If Tupper had been left to his own devices, the anti-confederates might have carried the day. By March 1865 he had retreated from confederation to the less-radical ground of Maritime union. But the new lieutenant-governor of Nova Scotia, Sir William Fenwick Williams, a Nova Scotia native and British military officer, revived Tupper's resolve. He made clear Britain's rejection of any half-measure and twisted the arms of enough politicians to convince the cautious Tupper to risk a legislative showdown on confederation in April 1866. His task had been aided by John A. Macdonald's assurance in September 1865 that the building of the Intercolonial would be guaranteed in the act of union of the colonies.

The confederation resolution introduced into the Nova Scotia legislature in April 1866 tactfully made no reference to the Quebec City plan or any other specific terms of union. Authorizing only continued negotiation on the issue of British North American union, Tupper's resolution won the support of thirty-one of fifty legislators. The same number also defeated a call for a referendum on the confederation issue.

There was also to be neither a referendum nor an election in the Canadas. None of the leaders of the Great Coalition was a radical democrat and even George Brown, the Reform leader, opposed electoral reforms that would expand the voting base from the approximately one-quarter of all adults over twenty-one years of age who met the property and gender qualification in Canada West. Macdonald, Cartier, and Brown collectively controlled enough votes to win passage of a motion supporting confederation both in the Legislative Assembly and in the Legislative Council. Only the size of their victory was in doubt.

The anti-confederate opposition in the United Province was led by A.A. Dorion, the *rouge* leader, and John Sandfield Macdonald, the leader of moderate reformers in Canada West. They had different reasons for rejecting the Quebec City resolutions. John Sandfield Macdonald was a lawyer and businessman who had established a political fiefdom among the Scottish Highlanders of Stormont and Glengarry counties. For him, the proposed confederation was unacceptable because it detached the Ottawa valley from the upper St Lawrence by dividing the United Province of Canada into two provinces. The region would exchange the political hegemony of Montreal for that of Toronto, to Macdonald's chagrin.

A.A. Dorion, by contrast, supported the division of the United Province of Canada into two provinces. Like many *Canadiens* he regretted the loss of a separate Lower Canada that had resulted from the Act of Union in 1840. Although he recognized that Britain was still unlikely to grant Lower Canada independent status, he hoped that something approaching sovereignty might be achieved if a loose federal union between the two sections of the United Province replaced the union. Only the degree of centralization implied in proposals from English-Canadian politicians had prevented the *rouges* from supporting earlier plans for a federal union of two provinces.

Now, however, not only was a federal union with a strong central government being proposed, but the union was to include the largely English-speaking Atlantic colonies. Fears that Canada East would be drowned in an English sea aroused Quebec nationalism and allowed the *rouges* to get signatures for monster petitions against the confederation project. In a speech to the Legislative Assembly during the debate on the confederation motion in February 1865, Dorion made a last-ditch attempt to have the political impasse in the Canadas resolved via a loose federal union. Among other things Dorion invoked a popular theme of anti-confederate spokesmen: the allegedly overweening influence of the Grand Trunk in the project. With a large number of cabinet members involved in the Grand Trunk—including Cartier, the railway's chief solicitor—there is no doubt that the company's prospects played some role in the thinking of the fathers of confederation. Dorion said, in part:

> I never hesitated to say that something ought to be done to meet the just claims of Upper Canada, and that representation based on population was in the abstract a just and correct principle. I held, at the same time, there were reasons why Lower Canada could not grant it; I entreated Lower Canadian representatives to show themselves disposed to meet the views of Upper Canada by making, at any rate, a counter proposition; and in 1856 when Parliament was sitting in Toronto, I, for the first time, suggested that one means of getting over the difficulty would be to substitute for the present Legislative union a Confederation

A.A. DORION: THE CHANGING FACE OF QUEBEC LIBERALISM

While Antoine-Aimé Dorion led the anti-confederation forces in Canada East in the 1860s, he was no radical nationalist in the mould of the Patriotes of 1837. Rather, he was a moderate liberal who recognized the political realities of the post-rebellion period and thus distanced himself from the anticlericalism of the early *rouge* leadership and ignored campaigns for complete dissolution of the union of the Canadas. He won considerable support from Montreal's English-speaking electors because he fought for development of the port of Montreal and improved trade with the United States. He had worked with the annexationists of 1849 and, over time, his close association with English speakers showed in a loss of facility in his first language.

As the son and grandson of Patriote assemblymen, Dorion had received an education in the classics at the Séminaire de Nicolet in the 1830s before articling in a law firm. Called to the bar in 1844, he

Sir Antoine-Aimé Dorion   (National Archives of Canada/C23599)

became well known in liberal circles in Montreal and in 1849 helped found the Club National Démocratique, an organization committed to universal male suffrage and extensive state support for education. After his election as a *rouge* in 1854, Dorion, a practising Catholic, attempted to alleviate church concerns about his party's goals. Nevertheless, the church became alarmed about his attempts to establish a working understanding with the Reformers of Canada West, led by George Brown, who was hated by the Catholic hierarchy for his attacks on public subsidies for Catholic schools.

Dorion served in the short-lived pre-confederation Liberal ministries. In October 1862, however, he resigned from the Liberal cabinet, accusing its members of being too uncritical of Edward Watkin's proposal for an intercolonial railway. From the late 1850s onwards Dorion had proposed schemes for a federal union of the two sections of the United Province, in all cases granting jurisdiction in most domestic areas to the provinces. This would give Canada East a great deal of autonomy while recognizing its economic links with Canada West. For Dorion, the confederation agreement of 1864 represented a repudiation of his notions of a loose federation and of private capital developing privately owned railways without government funds.

of the two Canadas, by means of which all local questions could be consigned to the deliberations of local legislatures, with a central government having control of commercial and other questions of common or general interest. I stated that, considering the different religious faith, the different language, the different laws that prevailed in the two sections of the country, this was the best way to meet the difficulty. . . .

But the Confederation I advocated was a real Confederation, giving the largest powers to the local governments and merely a delegated authority to the General Government—in that respect differing *in toto* from the one now proposed which gives all the powers to the Central Government, and reserves for the local governments the smallest possible amount of freedom of action. . . . There was then another cause for this Confederation scheme of which representation by population was made the pretext. . . . The Confederation of all the British North American Provinces naturally suggested itself to the Grand Trunk officials as the surest means of bringing with it the construction of the Intercolonial Railway. . . . Such was the origin of their Confederation scheme. The Grand Trunk people are at the bottom of it; and I find that at the last meeting of the Grand Trunk Railway Company, Mr.

Watkin did in advance congratulate the shareholders and bondholders on the bright prospects opening before them, by the enhanced value which will be given to their shares and bonds, by the adoption of the Confederation scheme and the construction of the Intercolonial as part of the scheme.[4]

Dorion, no doubt, overstated the influence of the Grand Trunk in initiating the confederation scheme. At the same time, economic arguments were as important as political issues such as "rep by pop" in influencing the Canadian supporters of confederation. In the Assembly the confederates argued forcefully that the two Canadas would be the major economic benefactors of confederation. Galt prophesied that the acquisition and settlement of the western territories would stimulate both manufacturing and mercantile activity in Quebec and Ontario, just as the settlement of the American West had enriched the Atlantic seaboard states and New York. The Maritimers, too, would provide new markets for what would, after 1867, be Central Canada. Only 3 or 4 percent of New Brunswick's trade was with the Canadas, but the completion of the Intercolonial would, it was predicted, dramatically alter this figure. Ontario farmers, long under George Brown's influence, were particularly receptive to the economic arguments for confederation because their eyes were fixed westwards: Assiniboia would become the first frontier for the new province of Ontario, providing agricultural opportunities for the farmers and farmers' sons who faced hard times in Ontario now that the most fertile lands were occupied and much of the soil had been exhausted.

In Canada East, outside of the business circles of the Grand Trunk and the Bank of Montreal, both of which saw Montreal as the metropolitan centre serving a developing west, there was virtually no interest in the Northwest. Not only was it far away, but the Catholic missionaries there had insisted for some time that its soil was inimical to agriculture. The missionaries were perhaps motivated by a desire to keep worldly white *Canadiens* away from their recent Indian and Métis converts, who were undoubtedly often puzzled by the contradiction between Christian teachings and the behaviour of Christians.

The confederation scheme was sold in Canada East on political grounds as much as on its economic potential. To the *rouge* claim that confederation meant centralization, Cartier and the *bleus* countered by focussing on the re-establishment of a separate province of Quebec. That province, because of the powers granted provincial governments, would be able to assure its continued French and Catholic character. The supporters of confederation emphasized the separation of Canada East from Canada West rather than its union with the Atlantic colonies within a confederation that

Grand Trunk offices, Montreal   (Canadian National Railways)

also aimed to embrace the Northwest. The confederate cause was also supported by the Catholic Church. Prompted by British encouragement and more particularly by guarantees in the Quebec City resolutions for continued public support of the separate school system in the new province of Ontario, the church put its substantial weight behind the push for confederation.

In the end a majority of the elected members from each of the two sections of the Province of Canada voted in favour of confederation. Even among the French-Canadian members, a small majority supported it. But popular enthusiasm for confederation was largely confined to Canada West. In Canada East, as in New Brunswick, the acceptance of confederation seemed to amount more to resignation than to a wholehearted embrace of the concept. The church, the British government, and the dominant political party in Canada East were steadfast in their resolve to see confederation come about. The nationalist forces in Canada East, humiliated in 1837 and divided over socio-economic policies, no longer had the élan to rally the masses against such formidable foes.

•Conclusion

The British North America Act was introduced in the British parliament in March 1867 and passed with little debate. On 1 July 1867, the Dominion of Canada officially came into being. "With the first dawn of this gladsome midsummer morn," trumpeted the Toronto *Globe*, "we hail this birthday of

---

CLOSING A HISTORICAL DEBATE

The debate in the Assembly of the United Province of Canada on the confederation proposals stretched from 2 February 1865 to 11 March 1865
and featured long, often raucous sittings as elected members cheered or
hooted for speakers. The *Stratford Beacon* gave a vivid account of the last
hours of that debate:

> The House was in an unmistakeably seedy condition, having,
> as it was positively declared, eaten the saloon keeper clean
> out, drunk him entirely dry, and got all the fitful naps of sleep
> that the benches along the passages could be made to yield.
> For who cared at one, two, three, and four in the morning, to
> sit in the House, to hear the stale talk of Mr. Ferguson, of
> South Simcoe, or to listen even to the polished and pointed
> sentences of Mr. Huntingdon? Men with the strongest constitu-
> tions for Parliamentary twaddle were sick of the debate, and
> the great bulk of the members were scattered about the build-
> ing, with an up-all-night, get-tight-in-the-morning air, impa-
> tient for the sound of the division bell. It rang at last, at
> quarter past four, and the jaded representatives of the people
> swarmed in to the discharge of the most important duty of all
> their lives.[5]

---

a new nationality. A united British America . . . takes its place among the
nations of the world."[6]

What was the character of this new nationality? Focussing on railways
that would link the former colonies, the supporters of confederation evoked
the progressive spirit of the age. Theirs was a vision of ever-expanding factories, whose goods would move by rail to every corner of the new dominion
along with the products of farm, forest, sea, and mines, linking once-separate
peoples with bonds of prosperity. Continuing ties with Britain would cement
these bonds.

Opponents of the confederation proposals approved at Quebec City
in 1864 usually embraced similar nineteenth-century capitalist notions of
progress, and many of them were not averse to a federation on different
terms. For them, the vision embodied in the British North America Act was
a centralizing force, ignoring regional and linguistic communities.
Confederation's supporters retorted that the federation proposals carefully
balanced provincial needs with the efficiencies that could be achieved in
some areas by central authority. They derided the argument that thinly
populated colonies hugging the northern boundaries of the United States

had a future as semi-independent entities in an era of capitalist expansion-ism. In their view, material progress was to be achieved only through the efforts of entrepreneurs acting with the support of the governments of strong nation-states.

Confederation was essentially a top-down exercise. The failure to hold referenda or elections (except in New Brunswick) on the issue or to follow the American example and hold a constitutional convention of elected dele-gates suggested a continuity with British North America's tradition of lim-ited democracy. In the era of responsible government the old oligarchies were forced to accept a degree of openness both in government and in the economy, but government remained in the hands of a small group of wealthy white men. Women played no role in the deliberations regarding the new constitution, and the document, not surprisingly, was silent on issues related to gender; in keeping with the times, patriarchy was an assumed part of the "new nationality." First nations peoples were similarly excluded from participation. The BNA Act recognized their existence only to the extent of giving the federal authorities responsibility for their welfare.

The debates about confederation in the British American colonies in the 1860s indicated that community identity was as important to many peo-ple as the elusive search for prosperity through the creation of a new framework. In the years that followed 1867, there would be echoes of the same debate. Could Quebec's French-speaking majority preserve a national existence within a confederal framework? Could the Atlantic provinces and later the western territories have enough say in the deliberations of the fed-eral government to protect the interests of their regions? Would provinces have enough powers and financial resources to promote economic devel-opment and the social well-being of their people? As time went by these issues would be joined by the concerns of Natives, women, working people, and non-British immigrants regarding the social values underlying the pact devised by the political leaders of the 1860s.

From the beginnings of human occupation of what is now Canada, the peoples of the area had shaped a multitude of societies, sometimes in harmony with nature, sometimes in blind disregard of nature's limits. Collectively they would also shape the "new nationality"—in reality a gath-ering of nationalities within a single nation-state. The sun that shone bril-liantly in clear blue skies over most of the new nation-state on 1 July 1867 seemed to announce new beginnings; but the people who, on that day, became citizens of Canada were not marked out for a particular destiny. Rather they would continue to shape their own destinies, both in concert and in conflict with others. Confederation on 1 July 1867 was simply a doc-ument and a territorial map; in the days and years following the peoples of the new nation-state would define, through their struggles, the real shape of the new nation.

•Economic Elites and Confederation:
A Historiographical Debate

The emergence of Canada as a modern state is inevitably a part of the spread of industrialism and capitalism. Confederation became an effective credit institution with the demands for long-term securities which accompanied the spread of industrialism especially as shown in transportation. The rise of Canada was in a sense the result of the demand for adequate imperial cost accounting which arose with Gladstonian Liberalism.[7]

This unlovely account of the Canadian confederation movement was provided in 1933 by Harold Innis, the dean of Canada's economic historians. In short, he suggests that British financial interests required the creation of the Canadian state to ensure that railway investments in British North America would be protected. While much of the historical work on confederation focusses on political arguments and personalities, many scholars argue that economic elites and economic arguments provided the real impetus for the confederation movement. They differ, however, on whether British or Canadian capitalists had the greatest impact on the Confederation movement.

The economic historian Vernon Fowke, while acknowledging the role of Canadian and Maritime economic interests in pursuing a confederation agreement, also stresses the role of British capitalists in promoting the project. According to Fowke, the British politician-businessman E.W. Watkin exemplified imperial attitudes to the economic potential of confederation. Watkin "accepted the task of salvaging the finances of the newly constructed Grand Trunk Railway for its British owners," but only after "exacting the pledge that the Imperial government would give consideration to a scheme for the union of the British American colonies to be followed eventually by a railway from coast to coast."[8] Fowke says that Watkin's influence was evident in the Quebec City round of negotiations on confederation, which devised the terms of the new constitution. Watkin also led the groups that bought controlling interest in the Hudson's Bay Company in 1863, removing that firm as a possible obstacle to a takeover of the territories north and west of the United Province of Canada.

For Watkin, a railway across Canada would be simply a means of linking British trade with China, Japan, India, and California and a stimulus to natural development (mainly resource extraction). Above all, he foresaw the Grand Trunk Railway surviving because of the international commerce that this company would come to handle.

Railway investors within Canada and the Maritimes, generally men with important political connections, also saw economic merit in the notion of a British North American federation. In Canada the impending end of reciprocity and the prospect of having to rely on the tiny population base of British North America caused many businessmen to look to confederation to produce a viable alternative to existing economic arrangements. But what alternative did they seek?

Economic historian R.T. Naylor argues that the Canadian promoters of confederation, much as their British counterparts, envisioned profitable exploitation of resources rather than the development of manufacturing as the aim of the new nation:

> *Far from being the response of a rising industrial capitalism striving to break down intercolonial tariff walls, Confederation and the national policy were the work of the descendants of the mercantile class which had aligned itself with the Colonial Office in 1837 to crush the indigenous petite bourgeoisie and nascent industrialists. . . . The direct line of descent runs from merchant capital, not to industrial capital but to banking and finance, railways, utilities, land speculation, and so on.*[9]

This characterization of the Canadian business interests supporting confederation has been contested. The railway companies were vertically integrated operations involved not only in moving goods but also in a great deal of manufacturing activities. The Grand Trunk and the Great Western built rail cars and locomotives as well as the machinery required in railway construction.

Apart from the railway executives, whose interests appear to have been *both* industrial and commercial, there were many businessmen prominent in the confederation movement whose interests seemed to straddle mercantile and manufacturing activity. George Brown and Charles Tupper, as businessmen, were certainly in this category. As for those whose main field of activity was manufacturing, key elements favoured the project for British American unity. In Saint John, for example, most of the principal manufacturers as well as the master tradesmen signed a pro-confederation address, which a local newspaper reproduced before the confederation election in the colony in 1865. The signatories believed that the railway construction promised in the Quebec resolutions would "enable our rising manufacturers to take a firm stand, and instead of the periodical stagnation of trade caused by the fluctuations of our only articles of export—Lumber and Ships—we shall have manufactures that will be a continual source of prosperity, not affected by the changes in the European Market, and giving our working people employment all the year round."[10] By contrast, small manufacturers in Prince Edward Island and parts of Nova Scotia resisted plans for a common British North American market as a threat to local tariffs and therefore local and international markets.

It is difficult to draw a clear dividing line between business supporters and opponents of confederation. Each side of the debate contained both small and big businessmen as well as manufacturers and mercantilists. Attitudes to publicly subsidized railway projects, however, based on the perceived usefulness of such projects to a particular business, were often pivotal in the positions taken on confederation: those who believed that railway extension held the key to their economic futures were usually supporters of confederation, while advocates of *laissez-faire* railway development usually opposed union of the colonies, at least on the terms proposed in the Quebec City resolutions.

•Notes

[1] Quoted in James L. Sturgis, "The Opposition to Confederation in Nova Scotia, 1864–1868," in *The Causes of Canadian Confederation*, ed. Ged Martin (Fredericton: Acadiensis Press, 1990), 125.

[2] A.A. den Otter, *Civilizing the West: The Galts and the Development of Western Canada* (Edmonton: University of Alberta Press, 1982), 15.

[3] P.B. Waite, *The Life and Times of Confederation 1864–1867: Politics, Newspapers, and the Union of British North America* (Toronto: University of Toronto Press, 1962), 98.

[4] P.B. Waite, ed., *The Confederation Debates in the Province of Canada, 1865* (Toronto: McClelland and Stewart, 1963), 86–90.

[5] Waite, *The Life and Times of Confederation*, 156.

[6] Ibid., 322.

[7] Quoted in Tom Traves, "Business–Government Relations in Canadian History," in *Government and Enterprise in Canada*, ed. K.J. Rea and Nelson Wiseman (Toronto: Methuen, 1985), 13–14.

[8] Vernon C. Fowke, *The National Policy and the Wheat Economy* (Toronto: University of Toronto Press, 1973), 31.

[9] R.T. Naylor, "The Rise and Fall of the Third Commercial Empire of the St Lawrence," in *Capitalism and the National Question in Canada*, ed. Gary Teeple (Toronto: University of Toronto Press, 1972), 16.

[10] Quoted in Rosemarie Langhout, "About Face," *Horizons Canada* 53 (1986):1252.

•Selected Readings

The political and economic history of the pre-confederation and early post-confederation years is surveyed in W.L. Morton, *The Critical Years: The Union of British North America 1857–1873* (Toronto: McClelland and Stewart, 1964). Stanley Ryerson's *Unequal Union: Roots of Crisis in the Canadas* (Toronto: Progress Books, 1968) provides a Marxist perspective on the period. The years immediately preceding confederation are examined closely in P.B. Waite, *The Life and Times of Confederation 1864–1867* (Toronto: University of Toronto Press, 1962); and Donald Creighton, *The Road to Confederation: The Emergence of Canada 1863–1867* (Toronto: Macmillan, 1964). Several important essays on confederation itself appear in Ramsay Cook, ed., *Confederation* (Toronto: University of Toronto Press, 1967); and Ged Martin, ed., *The Causes of Canadian Confederation* (Fredericton: Acadiensis Press, 1990). On the early post-confederation years see also P.B. Waite, *Canada, 1874–1896: Arduous Destiny* (Toronto: McClelland and Stewart, 1971).

Quebec attitudes to confederation are discussed in A.I. Silver, *The French-Canadian Idea of Confederation, 1864–1900* (Toronto: University of Toronto Press, 1982). Quebec society at the time of confederation is analysed in Paul-André Linteau, René Durocher, and Jean-Claude Robert, *Quebec: A History 1867–1929* (Toronto: James Lorimer, 1983). The key Quebec pro-confederate politicians are the subjects of critical biographies: Brian Young, *George-Étienne Cartier: Montreal Bourgeois*

(Montreal: McGill-Queen's University Press, 1981); and A.A. den Otter, *Civilizing the West: The Galts and the Development of Western Canada* (Edmonton: University of Alberta Press, 1982).

Ontario's key confederation politicians are also the subjects of biographies. The major biography of John A. Macdonald is D.G. Creighton's laudatory two-volume *John A. Macdonald* (Toronto: Macmillan, 1965), much of which is cast into question by other works in this bibliography. Other biographies of the first Canadian prime minister are, however, lightweight. George Brown's political and journalistic career is traced in a two-part biography, *Brown of the Globe* (Toronto: Macmillan, 1959), by J.M.S. Careless. The politics of Canada West more generally are outlined in J.M.S. Careless, ed., *The Pre-Confederation Premiers: Ontario Government Leaders 1841–1867* (Toronto: University of Toronto Press, 1980).

Two books edited by George Rawlyk, *The Atlantic Provinces and the Problem of Confederation* (St John's: Breakwater, 1980) and *Historical Essays on the Atlantic Provinces* (Ottawa: Carleton University Press, 1967) contain articles on the confederation period. Economic conditions in the region are treated in S.A. Saunders, *The Economic History of the Maritime Provinces* (Fredericton: Acadiensis Press, 1984).

Nova Scotia and Confederation 1864–74 by Kenneth G. Pryke (Toronto: University of Toronto Press, 1979) provides detail on Nova Scotia politics in the 1860s and 1870s. The leading anti-confederate is portrayed in J. Murray Beck, *Joseph Howe*, Vol. II, *The Briton Becomes Canadian, 1848–1873* (Montreal: McGill-Queen's University Press, 1983).

New Brunswick politics during this period are discussed in W.S. MacNutt, *New Brunswick: A History 1784–1867* (Toronto: Macmillan, 1984); William M. Baker, "Squelching the Disloyal, Fenian-Sympathizing Brood: T.W. Anglin and Confederation in New Brunswick, 1865–1866," *Canadian Historical Review* 55, 2 (June 1974): 141–58; William M. Baker, *Timothy Warren Anglin 1822–1896: Irish Catholic Canadian* (Toronto: University of Toronto Press, 1977); and Alfred G. Bailey, "The Basis and Persistence of Opposition to Confederation in New Brunswick," *Canadian Historical Review* 23, 4 (December 1942): 374–97.

Prince Edward Island politics are discussed in Ian Ross Robertson, "Prince Edward Island Politics in the 1860s," *Acadiensis* 15, 1 (Autumn 1985): 35–58; David Weale and Harry Baglole, *The Island and Confederation: The End of an Era* (Summerside: Williams and Crue, 1973); and F.W.P. Bolger, *Prince Edward Island and Confederation* (Charlottetown: St Dunstan's University Press, 1964).

On Newfoundland's rejection of confederation, see James Hiller, "Confederation Defeated: The Newfoundland Election of 1869," in *Newfoundland in the Nineteenth and Twentieth Centuries: Essays in Interpretation*, ed. James Hiller and Peter Neary (Toronto: University of Toronto Press, 1980), 67–94. Newfoundland politics in the period are discussed in S.J. Noel, *Politics of Newfoundland* (Toronto: University of Toronto Press, 1971).

I N D E X

Abbott, John, 540
Abenaki, 138
Aboriginal land claims, 5
Aboriginal rights, 218–19
Absolutism, 130–32
   in New France, 133, 136, 138–39
Acadia, 96, 118, 138, 166, 198, 221
   in the 18th century (map), 223
Acadian forest, 7
Acadians, 177, 178, 224–26, 232, 244, 273
   expulsion of, 235–38
   in Nova Scotia following expulsion,
      275–76
Accommodation (steamship), 541
Acheson, T.W., 340, 497
Act of Union (U.K., 1801), 321, 326, 344
African Canadians
   immigration to Atlantic colonies, 329
   in the colonies, mid-19th century,
      501–502
   Loyalists, 291–93
   in Nova Scotia, 293, 354
Age of Enlightenment, 173, 554
Agriculture, 7
   agricultural crisis in Lower Canada,
      373–74, 390–91, 397–99, 412
   in early modern Europe, 58, 59
   in New France, 195–96
Aix-la-Chapelle, Treaty of (1748), 231, 232
Akenson, Donald, 437
Albanel, Charles, 160
Albani, Emma (Lajeunesse), 521
Alcohol
   consumption in mid-19th century, 508
   effects on Native people, 500
   as a trade item, 161
Algonkian, 112
Algonkin, 138, 298
Allan, John, 288
Alline, Henry, 288, 289, 351, 352
American Revolution, 255–58. *See also*
      Loyalists
   Declaration of Independence, 258
   impact on colonies outside U.S.,
      287–90
   and Quebec, 256–59
Amherst, Jeffrey, 240, 241, 244, 249
Amundsen, Roald, 87
Anderson, John, 502
Anglo-American Convention (1818), 336,
      411
Animals, destruction by immigrants, 338
Annapolis Royal, 227, 228
Annexation to U.S., 538, 539–40

Anse-aux-Meadows, Newfoundland, 84
Anti-Semitism, 406
Appalachia, 6–7
Arctic, 8
Arnold, Benedict, 256, 257
Art, 283–87, 518, 519
Arrêts de Marly, 156
Articles of Capitulation (1760), 219
Artisans, 489, 496, 553–54
   in the Atlantic colonies, 340
   effect of Industrial Revolution on, 321,
      340
Asch, Michael, 474
Asian travel in the Americas, 83
Assemblies
   in the Atlantic colonies, 344
   in the Canadas, 404–405, 406, 407
   granted by the Constitutional Act, 303,
      304
   Upper Canada, 419, 420
Assiniboia, 484
Assiniboine, 306, 307, 450
Associations in cities of Lower Canada,
      394–95
Asylums, 562–63, 564
Athapaskans, 38–39, 41
Atlantic and Gulf Region, 6–7
Atlantic colonies
   in 1850, 487
   in 1850s and 1860s, 589–91
   beginnings of British rule, 221–24
   boundaries, 320
   class distinctions in, 340
   colonial economy in: a historiographi-
      cal debate, 358–60
   cultural diversity, 329
   culture, 356–57
   domestic economy, 337–42
   economic adjustment (1785–1849),
      330–37
   economic growth after 1850, 546
   emigration from (mid-19th century),
      330
   geographic and political region, 318,
      320
   immigration to (1749–1850), 271–75,
      278–81, 290, 291, 293, 294, 321–30
   Native people in, 318, 319, 320, 498–99
   politics in (1758–1849), 343–50
   religion, 350–56
   social relations, 342–43
Atlantic Region, 1871 (map), 349
Austrian Succession, War of (1744–48),
      174, 227–29, 231

Axtell, James, 10
Aylen, Peter, 377
Aztecs, 75

Backhouse, Constance, 495
Bagot, Sir Charles, 426
Bailey, A.G., 11
Baillie, Thomas, 346
Baldwin, Robert, 420–21, 425–26, 427–28,
    431, 567
Ball, John, 292
Ballenden, Mrs, 461–62
Baptists, 292–93, 351
Barbel, Marie-Anne, 188
Baribeau, Claude, 415
Barkley, Murray, 312
Basques, 88
Bauge, Anne, 145
Beauharnois, Charles de, 208, 231
Beavan, Frances, 339
Beckwith, Julia Catherine, 356
Bédard, Pierre, 406
"Bees," 515
Bégon, Marie-Élisabeth, 193, 199–200
Bégon, Michel, 199, 200
Bégon de la Cour, Claude-Michel,
    199–200
Belcher, Jonathan, 246–48
Bellingham, Sydney, 416–17
Benson, Wilson, 483, 484, 491
Beothuk, 19, 85, 87, 278, 283, 318, 319,
    320
Berczy, William, 284, 285
Berger, Carl, 555
Bering, Vitus, 308
Bernon, Gabriel, 146
Berthelet, Pierre, 394
Bidwell, Marshall Spring, 420
Bigot, François, 131–32, 181, 189–90, 196,
    206, 242
Birchtown, 292
Birth control, 24, 392
Black Death, 52
Blackfoot, 16, 31, 32, 33–34, 307, 446,
    448–50, 459
Blacks. See African Canadians
Blainville, Pierre-Joseph Cloron de, 233
Blake, William Hume, 549–50
Blanshard, Richard, 468, 484
Bleus, 428, 430, 583, 605
Blodget, Lorin, 571–72
Bodega y Quadra, Juan Francisco de la,
    308
Bonnycastle, Sir Richard, 509

Boreal forest, 6, 7
Boscawen, Edward, 241
Boullé, Hélène, 100, 167
Bourgeoys, Marguerite, 109, 110
Bourget, Bishop Ignace, 395
Bradbury, Bettina, 567, 569
Braddock, Edward, 234, 235
Bradstreet, John, 226, 241
Brant, Joseph, 258, 296, 297
Brant, Molly, 296–97
Braudel, Fernand, 64–65, 73
Brébeuf, Jean de, 105
Brendan, Saint, 84
Briand, Jean-Olivier, 250, 257
Brightman, Robert, 16
British American Land Company, 414
British–American League, 538, 540
British Columbia
    coastal trade (1778–1820s), 462–63
    inland trade (to 1840s), 463–67
British North America Act (1867), 595,
    596–97, 606
British North America in 1800, 310–11
British North America in 1866 (map), 485
Brock, Sir Isaac, 408
Brooke, Frances, 301–302
Brown, George, 427, 428, 473, 563, 583,
    586, 587, 595, 601, 604, 610–11
Brown, Jennifer, 16, 476
Brown, William, 447–48
Brûlé, Étienne, 101–102
Brunet, Michel, 261–62
Bubonic plague, 52
Buffalo, 33, 307, 454, 459, 460
Buffalo pound, 16
Bumsted, J.M., 281
Bungi, 452
Burke, Bishop Edmund, 355
Byles, Rebecca, 295
Bytown, 386, 387

Cabot, John, 76, 85
Cadet, Joseph, 189
Cadillac, Lamothe, 165
Cajuns, 238
Callbeck, Phillips, 290
Calvert, George, 89
Cameron, Duncan, 454
Campbell, Agathe, 222
Campeau, Lucien, 121
Canada East
    created (1840), 366
    in 1850, 487
Canada Land Company, 422

Canada West
    created (1840), 366
    frontier society in 1850, 485, 487
Canadian Shield, 7–8
Canadiens, 375, 377
    emigration to U.S., 390
Canal construction, 387, 388, 411, 412,
    426–27, 545, 546
Cantin, Austin, 552
Cape Breton, 290, 320
    famine (1845–51), 509
Capitalism, 343, 537–38, 544, 545
    structure of industrial capitalism,
    551–54
Cardwell, Edward, 593
Careless, J.M.S., 431
Carignan-Salières regiment, 136
Carillon (Ticonderoga), 239
Carleton, Sir Guy, 252, 253, 254, 257, 258,
    300
Carrying trade, 334, 336
Carson, William, 345
Cartier, George-Étienne, 429, 430, 550,
    587, 588, 595, 605
Cartier, Jacques, 91–93, 338
Cartwright, George, 283
Casavant, Joseph, 521
Censitaires, 155, 208–209
Champlain, Samuel de, 94, 99–101, 114,
    117
Charitable institutions, 328, 353, 510–11
    in Lower Canada, 395–96
Charivari, 380–81, 512
Charlottetown, 280
Charlottetown Conference (1864), 593,
    594
Château Clique, 412
Châteauguay, Battle of, 409–410
Chesapeake (ship), 593
Childbirth by 1850, 507–508
Children. *See also* Education
    in mid-19th century, 564–65, 566
    in New France, 201–202
    in Upper Canada, 383, 384, 387, 389
Chinese immigrants, 470–71
Chiniquy, C.P.T., 559–60
Chipewyan, 306, 443–44
Chipman, Eliza, 350
Chirikov, Aleksei, 308
Cholera epidemics, 377–78, 379, 506, 507
Christie, Robert, 517
Church of England, 67
    in Upper Canada, 367, 369, 370
Cipolla, Carlo, 58

Cities and towns, 551. *See also* Urban life
    in Europe, 50, 60
Civil Code in Canada East, 550–51
Civil War (U.S.; 1861–65), 538, 540, 582,
    593
Class and society
    in colonial society, 495–96
    in New France, 115–16, 156–58,
    202–206
    in Upper Canada, 387
Classical colleges, 431
Clear Grits, 427, 428
Clearing land, 337
Clergy reserves, 304, 368, 419
Coal
    in Nova Scotia, 336
    on Vancouver Island, 467, 468
Cochran, William, 294
Code Noir, 207, 208
Cod fishery, 85–86, 90, 158, 281–82
    growth (1785–1815), 332
    importance to Newfoundland
    economy, 332, 333, 335, 342
Cohen, Marjorie Griffin, 382
Colbert, Jean-Baptiste, 119, 131–32, 139,
    140, 146, 151, 158, 160
Colbert family, 132
Colborne, Sir John, 422
Coles, George, 591
Collins, Enos, 341
Colonies, appeal to Europeans, 65
Coltman, William Bachelor, 454–55
Columbus, Christopher, 48, 74–75
Colvile, Andrew, 453, 458
Comingo, Joseph Brown, 284, 287
Common-law relationships in New France,
    200
Common schools, 431, 561–62
Communauté des Habitants, 114
Communication, in 1850, 487. *See also*
    Canal construction; Railways;
    Roads; Transportation
Compagnie de la Colonie, 180
Compagnie de la Nouvelle France,
    113–14, 115, 119
Compagnie des Indes, 173–74, 175, 182, 183
Compagnie des Indes Occidentales, 140
Compagnie du Saint-Sacrement, 114
Confederation
    British support, 593, 594
    concepts of the new nation, 607–608
    defence issue, 593
    development of ideas, 579, 580–82,
    586–87

economic elites and, 609–611
"Great Coalition," 587–88
proposals for Maritime union replaced, 588–89, 593, 594
"selling" Confederation, 597–606
Confréries, 186
Congés (trading permits), 162, 180
Congrégation de Notre Dame, 110
Conquest of New France
    capture of Quebec, 241, 242–43
    civilian rule following, 252–54
    impact on Canadians, 260–62
    military occupation, 249–52
    Native policy, 246–49
    surrender to the British, 244
Conquistadores, 75, 78
Conservatism, 344
Constitutional Act (1791), 302–305
    structure of government under, 303, 304
Continental shelf, 7
Cook, Captain James, 282, 307, 308, 462
Cooper, William, 345–46
Copernicus, Nicolaus, 69
Copp, Terry, 437
Cormack, William Epps, 318
Corn Laws, 327, 337
Cornwallis, Edward, 232, 272, 273, 274
Cortés, Hernán, 75
Corvée, 209
Cottnam, Deborah Howe, 295
Council of Assiniboia, 461
Counter-Reformation, 68
Courcelles, Rémy de, 218
Coureurs de bois, 116–17, 159, 161–62, 164, 165, 180, 198
Coyne, Henry, 311
Craig, Governor James, 405, 406
Craven, Paul, 544
Creationists, 557
Creation myths
    Cree–Ojibwa, 43–44
    Iroquoian, 23
    Sioux, 32
Cree, 16, 29–31, 306, 307, 450
    dreams and Cree culture, 30–31
Crémazie, Octave, 570–71
Cricket matches, 516
Crimean War (1854–56), 581–82
Crosby, Alfred W., 77–78
Crowe, Keith J., 39
Crowley, Terence, 212
Crown Reserves, 368, 422
Crusades, 68, 77

Cugnet, François-Étienne, 186
Culture
    in the Atlantic colonies, 356–57
    cultural development of French Canada, 517
    distinctive culture in New France, 172
    in early modern Europe, 69–70
    religion and, 496–97, 522–23
Cumberland House, 306, 443
Cunard, Samuel, 341, 467, 541–42
Cupid's Cove, Newfoundland, 88
Currency, 546–48
    after the Conquest, 251
    card money, 153, 154
    in New France, 153
Curtis, Bruce, 574–75
Custom of Paris (legal code), 141, 143, 197, 494
Cuvillier, Austin, 406

Dalhousie, George Ramsay, 328, 339, 353
Dalhousie College, 353
Darwin, Charles, 557
Davies, Thomas, 284, 286
Davis, John, 87
Davis, Ralph, 62, 78
Dawson, S.J., 571
Dawson, William, 556, 557
Death rate in New France, 200–201
De la Roche, Troilus, 88
Democracy, 344, 372, 435. *See also* Representative government; Responsible government
    assemblies granted by the Constitutional Act, 303
    example of U.S., 405
Demos, John, 565
Denonville, Marquis de, 163
Dependency, colonial, 359–60
De Salaberry, Charles Michel, 409
DesBarres, Joseph Frederick Wallet, 284, 345
Descartes, René, 70
Detroit, 175–76, 180, 249
De Villiers, Louis Coulon, 231
Diaz, Bartolomeu, 73
Diblee, Filer, 271
Dick, John, 273
Dickason, Olive, 14, 17
Dickie, Margaret, 555–56
Dieskau, Baron de, 235
Dinwiddie, Robert, 234
Disease
    cholera epidemics, 377–78, 379, 506, 507

effect of European diseases on Native peoples, 77–79, 110, 111, 121, 210, 307, 459, 464–65, 474–75, 499
epidemics in Europe, 52
medical practices by 1850, 506–507
in New France, 200–201
Divine right of kings, 130, 344
Divorce, 494, 567
in Upper Canada, 383–84
Doane, Edmund, 276
Doane, Elizabeth, 276
Dollard des Ormeaux, Adam, 117–18
Donnacona, 92, 93
D'Alonne, Madeleine de Roybon, 136
Donovan, Kenneth, 177, 203
Doric Club, 415
Dorion, Antoine-Aimé, 602, 603–605
Dosquet, Bishop, 191
"Double majority" in the United Canadas, 585
Douglas, James, 467–69, 478
Dower rights, 494, 550–51
Downs, Andrew, 556
Duchambon, Louis Du Pont, 228
Dumont, Micheline, 167–68
Duncombe, Dr Charles, 423
Dupuy, Claude-Thomas, 192
Duquesne, Marquis de, 233, 234
Duquesnel, Le Prévost, 228
Durham, John, Earl of, 346–47, 368, 424–25, 517, 569–70, 586–87
D'Youville, Marie Marguerite, 193
Duvivier, François Du Pont, 228

Eastern Townships, 303, 372, 373, 377, 390, 412
Eccles, William J., 138, 206, 211–12
Economic boom of the 1850s and 1860s, 551–54, 581–82
Economy of New France, 178–89
Eddy, Jonathan, 288
Edict of Nantes (1598), 67
revocation (1685), 145–146
Education. See also Universities
in the Atlantic colonies, 352–53
educational institutions, 294–95, 323
for farm families in Upper Canada, 384
in mid-19th century, 505
reform, 560–62, 572–75
and state role, 413, 430–33, 561–62, 572–75
Elections, 513
in Atlantic colonies, 350
Elgin, Lord, 426, 427

Emigration
from Britain to Atlantic colonies (1785–1850), 321–29
of French-Canadians to U.S., 390
Engagés, 180, 209
English immigrants to the Atlantic colonies, 88–90, 322, 329
Erie Canal, 412
Escheat Movement, 345
Ethnohistorians, 10
Europe. See also Exploration and expansion
culture and ideas, 69–70
economic life, 58–62
life cycle, 56–57, 58
life expectancy, 53–55
population changes, 52–55, 59
social order, 49–51
technology, 71–72
Western Europe in 1500 (map), 51
Evangelicalism, 351–52, 356, 522–23
and social reform, 559
Executive councils
in the Atlantic colonies, 344–45, 346, 347
under the Constitutional Act, 304
in Upper Canada, 404–405, 407, 420
Exploration and expansion by European countries, 72, 73–76
England and France, 75–76
Portugal, 73–74
Spain, 74–75
Ex-votos, 194

Factory system, 321, 332, 537
in Upper Canada, 387
Family Compact, 410, 419
Family life
middle-class, 565–66, 569
in mid-19th century, 494–95, 504
in New France, 198, 200–202
working-class, 567, 569
Farm life
in Lower Canada, 389–93, 397–99
in mid-19th century, 490
in Upper Canada, 382–85
Fenerty, Charles, 357, 557
Fenians, 327, 600
Ferryland, Newfoundland, 89–90
Feudal system, 50–51
Fidler, Peter, 454
Filles du roi, 133, 136
Fils de la liberté, 415
Financial institutions, 545, 546

Fingard, Judith, 436, 510, 514
Fires
    in cities, 394, 492
    land clearing, 337
First Continental Congress (1774), 256
First Nations
    agriculture in Northwest, 447–48
    aid French exploration of interior, 176
    alliances with European settlers,
        217–19, 221
    and American Revolution, 258
    appeals for redress of grievances, 348,
        350
    artists, 283, 285
    Atlantic and Gulf Region, 18–20
    attacks on British settlements, 226–27,
        248–49
    British policy following Seven Years'
        War, 246–49
    in Canadian Shield, 24–31
    denied voting rights in Nova Scotia
        (1854), 348
    dependence on European settlers, 343
    displacement by Europeans, 297, 298,
        442
    effect of European diseases, 77–79,
        110, 111, 121, 210, 307, 459,
        464–65, 474–75, 499
    effects of contact with Europeans, 82,
        99, 219, 221, 318, 462–63, 464–66
    excluded from participation in confed-
        eration, 608
    farming, 7, 14, 15, 20–21
    fishing, 14, 15, 19, 35, 36
    and fur trade, 181, 441–52, 458–59,
        476–78
    governmental structures, 20, 23, 30
    Great Lakes–St Lawrence Lowlands,
        20–24
    hunting, 12, 15, 16, 19, 26, 30, 32, 33,
        38, 39
    impact on French settlers, 116, 1202
    Interior Plains, 31–34
    inventions, 16
    involvement in colonial wars, 233, 235,
        239
    knowledge of environment, 16–17
    in Labrador, 283
    language groupings, 12
    life in mid-19th century, 497–501
    Loyalists, 296–98
    in the Northwest, 38–40, 474–75
    origins, 42–43
    on Pacific coast, 462–71

    paternalistic attitudes towards, 500–501
    peacemaking among (1700–1701), 164
    plains Indians, 305–306
    recreation, 27–29, 36, 39
    relationships between fur traders and
        Native women, 117, 441–42, 451–52,
        476–78
    relationship to the land, 30
    relations with New France, 138, 164
    religious beliefs, 16, 19, 23, 26–27,
        30–31, 32, 33, 37–38, 38–39, 40–41,
        43–44
    reserves, 498, 500
    revolt against British, 216, 227, 248–49
    in Rupert's Land, impact of
        Europeans, 305–306, 307
    self-government, 218–19
    sexual and childrearing practices, 18,
        24, 29
    size of Native populations, 14
    slaughter and exploitation by
        Europeans, 73–74, 78
    slaves, 35, 207
    trade, 17
    treaties, 500
    treatment following conquest of New
        France, 244, 245
    tribes at time of European contact
        (map), 13
    views of Europeans, 105, 108–109, 110,
        471
    warfare among, 17–18, 24, 27, 110–113,
        120
    in warfare between colonies, 184
    Western Cordillera, 34–38
    women and the fur trade, 441–42,
        451–52, 476–78
    writing Native history, 9–11
Fisher, Charles, 590
Fisher, Peter, 338, 358, 517
Fisher, Robin, 470
Fisheries
    French, 139
    in Labrador waters, 320
Fishing, 222, 224, 490
Fiske, Joanne, 11
Five Nations Confederacy, 23
Forbes, George, 365
Forests, destroyed by settlers, 337
Fort Beauséjour, 232, 235, 236
Fort Cumberland (formerly Fort
        Beauséjour), 288
Fort Duquesne, 234, 235, 241
Fort Edmonton, 456

Fort Frontenac, 241
Fort Lawrence, 232
Forts and trading posts, 305, 306–307
    in British Columbia, 464
    in New France, 174, 176, 180, 232, 233,
        234, 241
Fort William Henry, 239
Fothergill, Charles, 555
Foulis, Robert, 557
Fowke, Vernon, 609
Fox nation, 174
France. *See also* New France
    early colonies in North America, 90–98
    France in America, 1663–1755 (map),
        220
Francheville, François Poulin de, 186
Francklin, Michael, 279
Franklin, Benjamin, 274
Franklin, Sir John, 485, 486
Franquet, Louis, 183
Fraser, Simon, 464
Free ports, 334
Free trade, 426, 538, 540, 541
    replaces mercantilist policies (1840s),
        327, 331, 337, 347, 426
Frégault, Guy, 211, 261
French Revolution, 302
Frères Chasseurs, 417
Friesen, Gerald, 571
Frobisher, Martin, 87
Frontenac, Louis de Buade, Comte de,
    160, 163, 164
Frost, Sarah, 294
Fur trade, 86, 91, 94, 151, 158–62, 209
    administration of, in New France,
        180–81
    alcohol as trade item, 161
    competition between Bay men and St
        Lawrence traders, 159–60, 253,
        306–307, 442–43
    and explorations of the interior,
        158–60, 305, 306
    factor in military strategy, 158, 165,
        174, 217
    impact on Natives, 97, 98–99, 110–11,
        120, 161
    importance to Canadian economy
        (18th century), 178–79, 370
    life at fur-trading post, 456
    loss of agricultural labour to, 162, 374
    marriage practices of traders, 117,
        441–42, 451–52, 476–78
    merger of HBC and NWC (1821), 455
    monopoly period (1821–49), 455–62
    in the Northwest, 474–75

on Pacific coast, 462–67
western fur trade in 19th century
    (map), 457

Gaffield, Chad, 505, 575
Gagan, David, 437
Galeano, Eduardo, 78
Galileo, 69–70
Gallicanism, 145
Galt, Alexander T., 540, 541, 585, 586–87,
    605
Galt, John, 422
Gama, Vasco da, 73
Garneau, François-Xavier, 260, 517, 570
Garnier, Charles, 104–105
Gaspé, 374
Gaulin, Antoine, 227
Gauvreau, Michael, 522
Gavazzi, Alessandro, 512
George, David, 292, 293
George III, 255
Gesner, Abraham, 357, 500, 556–57
Ghent, Treaty of (1814), 411
Giffard, Robert, 116
Gilbert, Sir Humphrey, 87
Ginseng, 182–83
Goderich, Lord, 422
Gold rushes
    Fraser Valley (1858), 468, 469, 572
    Klondike (1896–99), 475
Gordon, Arthur, 592–93, 600–601
Gosford, Lord, 414, 415
Gourlay, Robert, 411
Governor, powers under Constitutional
    Act, 304
Governor-general in New France, 139, 140
Gowan, Ogle R., 378
Graham, W.H., 382–83
Grammar schools, 431
Grandfontaine, Hector d'Andigne de, 138
Grand River valley reserve, 297
Grand Trunk Railway, 393, 427, 544, 545,
    585, 602, 604–605, 609, 610
Grant, Cuthbert, 454, 461
Grant, John Webster, 523
Gray, John Hamilton, 597–98
Great auk, extinction of, 338
Great Lakes–St Lawrence Lowlands (phys-
    iographic region), 7
Greer, Allan, 374, 398–99
Grenville, William, 302, 303
Grey Nuns, 193
Groseilliers, Médard Chouart des, 159
Groulx, Canon Lionel, 211, 261
Guarantee Act (1849), 427, 585

Gubbins, Joseph, 358
Guercheville, Madame de, 96, 167
Guilds, 60, 63
    in New France, 186–87

Habitants, 155, 172
    agricultural crisis, 373–74, 390–92, 397–99
    attitude to 1837–38 rebellions, 419
    life by mid-18th century, 194–98, 206
    reaction to American Revolution, 257
    views of historians, 261, 397–99
Haida, 308, 462, 463, 465
Haldimand, Sir Frederick, 257, 297, 298, 299, 367
Haliburton, Thomas Chandler, 330, 343, 356, 516, 517
Halifax, 232, 272–73, 288, 295, 334, 513
    in 1800, 310
Hamelin, Jean, 262
Hamilton, 387, 436, 508, 551
    pumping station, 558
Hargrave, Letitia, 507–508
Harris, Moses, 284
Hart, Ezekiel, 406
Harvey, Sir John, 347
Haszard, William, 345
Haven, Jens, 283
Havy, François, 188
Head, Sir Francis Bond, 420, 421, 423
Hearne, Samuel, 306, 443–44
Heidenreich, Conrad, 22, 120–21
Henday, Anthony, 175, 305, 448
Henripin, Jacques, 117
Henson, Josiah, 502
Herbert, Mary Eliza, 517
Hincks, Francis, 426, 427–28, 544
Hind, Henry Youle, 472, 571
Hobson, Peregrine, 233
Hocquart, Gilles, 184
Holland, Samuel, 280
Homosexuality, 18, 381
Honorat, Jean-Baptiste, 391–92
Horses, imported by Europeans, 305–306
Hospitals in 1850, 507
Hôtel Dieu, 109
Houses of Industry, 389, 563
Houston, Susan, 389
Howe, John, 294
Howe, Joseph, 341, 346–47, 353, 357, 500, 543, 570, 579, 589, 601
Hoyles, Hugh, 591, 598
Hudson, Henry, 87
Hudson's Bay Company, 159, 175, 283, 305, 484

British Columbia trade, 463, 464, 466, 467–69
    control bought by British financiers (1863), 442, 474, 609
    merger with NWC (1821), 455
    monopoly period (1821–49), 455–62
    rivalry with the St Lawrence traders, 159–60, 253, 306–307, 442–43
    traders gather scientific information, 556
Huguenots, 145–46
Hull, 371
Hundred Years War, 53
Hunt, George, 120
"Hunters' Lodges," 423–24
Huntingdonians, 292
Huron, 21, 22–23, 24, 102, 103, 306
    destruction of Huronia, 112–13, 118, 119, 120–21
    and French, 100–102, 103–106, 112, 113
    wars with Iroquois, 110–13, 118
Huron Tract, 422

Iberville, Pierre Le Moyne d', 162, 163, 165, 205
Ice Ages, 6, 7
Igloos, 39
Île Royale, 185
Illegitimate children, 493
Illinois country, 174
Immigration
    to Atlantic colonies, 271–75, 278–81, 290, 291, 293, 294, 321–30
    to Lower Canada, 371–72, 377–78
    to New France, 136, 137–38, 155
    to Quebec, 295, 297–300
    to Upper Canada, 366, 375–76, 377
Industrial Revolution, 261, 262, 484
    effect on artisans and gentry, 321–22
    impact on British North America, 536–38
Infanticide, 495
Infant mortality, 506
Inglis, Bishop John, 351
Inglis, Charles, 294
Innis, Harold, 358–59, 360, 609
Innu, 11
Instituts Canadiens, 395, 517
Insurance companies by 1850, 511
Intellectual life in New France, 193–94
Intendant in New France, 139–40, 142, 151
Intercolonial Railway, 411, 589, 590
Interior Plains, 8

Interracial marriages, 117, 441, 451–52, 476–78
"Intolerable" acts, 255, 256
Inuit, 8, 39, 43, 310, 485
Inventions
  in British North America, 556–57
  in Europe, 71–72
Ireland
  emigration from, to Atlantic colonies, 321, 326–28
  famine in, 326–27, 337
Irish immigrants
  to the Atlantic colonies, 327–29, 355
  to the Canadas, 387–88
  Irish–French confrontations, 377
  religious feuds among, 378, 379
  to Upper Canada, 377
Ironworks at St-Maurice, 186, 541
Iroquoian peoples, 20–24, 99
Iroquois, 221, 258
  battle at Long Sault rapids, 117–18
  Five Nations, 101, 110–11, 112, 120–21
  relations with French settlers, 133, 162–63, 164
  wars with Hurons, 110–13, 118

Jaenen, Cornelius, 120, 212
James Bay hydro-electric project, 9
Jameson, Anna Brownell, 377
Jamieson, Anna, 488
Jarvis, Samuel, 368
Jarvis, William, 368
Jay's Treaty (1794), 298, 334
Jefferson, Thomas, 334
Jesuits, 68–69, 73, 74, 82, 94, 96, 103, 117, 121, 129, 149, 176
  changing approach to missionary work, 104–106
  Native views of, 105, 106, 110
Jews, 67
Johnson, Guy, 249, 258
Johnson, Sir John, 298, 299
Johnson, Sir William, 249, 296
Johnstone, Walter, 337
Jolliet, Louis, 160
Jones, Peter, 500–501
Julien, Barnaby, 500
Jumonville, Joseph de, 234

Kah-Ge-Gah-Bowh, 27–28, 29
Kalm, Peter, 172, 192
Kane, Paul, 519
Katz, Michael, 436, 495–96, 508, 573
Kavanagh, Lawrence, 355
Keefer, T.C., 542–43

Kelsey, Henry, 160
Kent, Edward Augustus, Duke of, 355
King, Boston, 292
Kingston, 368, 386
Kingston Penitentiary, 563
Kirke, David, 89, 114
Krieghoff, Cornelius, 518, 519
Kwagiulth (Kwakiutl), 468

La Barre, Joseph-Antoine de, 162–63
Labour, 551, 552–53. See also Slavery
  effect of mechanization on, 537
  immigrant labourers, 548–49
  itinerant labourers in mid-19th century, 491
  labour disputes, 511–12, 514
  loss of agricultural labour to fur trade, 162, 374
  in mid-19th century, 437, 496
  in New France, 206, 208–209
  unions, 511
Labrador, 283, 320
Lachine Canal, 545
Lafitau, Joseph-François, 202
La Fontaine, Louis-Hippolyte, 426–27
La Galissonière, Roland-Michel Barrin de, 172, 200, 233
Laissez-faire, 537–38
Lalémant, Jérôme, 105
Lamallice, Madame, 477
Land bridges, 12, 42
Land clearance, 337
Land grants
  in Eastern Townships, 372, 373
  in Upper Canada, 367–68
Land speculation, 412, 414, 422
Lane, Michael, 282
La Ronde, Denys, 185
La Roque, Marguerite de, 94
Lartigue, Bishop Jean-Jacques, 395, 413
La Salle, René Robert de, 160
Lasch, Christopher, 565
La Tour, Agathe Saint-Étienne de, 226
La Tour, Charles de, 96, 97
La Tour, Marie de, 97, 168
Lauson, Jean de, 203
Laval, Bishop François de, 110, 114–15, 146–47, 208
Lavalle, Calixa, 521
La Vérendrye, Pierre Gaultier de, 175, 176
Law, John, 173–74
Law and order
  community regulation of behaviour, 380–81, 512
  laws in early 19th century, 493–94

legal reform, 549–51
in Lower Canada, 303
in New France, 141–45
Lawrence, Charles, 236, 237, 238, 253–54, 274
L'Incarnation, Marie de, 107–108, 150–51
Leacock, Eleanor, 25
"Leader and associate" system, 371–72
League of Augsburg, 163
Le Borgne, Emmanuel, 96
Le Canadien (newspaper), 405
Le Caron, Joseph, 103
Lefebvre, Jean, 188
Légaré, Joseph, 518, 519
LeGoff, T.J.A., 398
Leisure activities in mid-19th century, 514–21
Le Jeune, Paul, 25, 106
Le Loutre, Abbé Jean-Louis, 227, 228, 232, 233
Le Moyne, Charles, 205
Le Moyne, Charles, Baron de Longueil, 205, 208
Leprosy, 507
Lesslie, James, 379
Lévis, Chevalier de, 243, 244
Liberalism, 344
Libraries in the Atlantic colonies, 356
Lieutenant-governors in the Atlantic colonies, 344, 345
Life expectancy, 505–506
Literature, 294–95, 301–302, 356, 516–17, 520, 570
Liverpool Packet (ship), 335, 341
Local government in Upper Canada, 370
Logan, William, 556
London, 387
Longfellow, Henry Wadsworth, 517, 520
Longhouse, 21
Long Sault, Battle of the, 117–18
Louisbourg, 174, 177–78, 193, 225, 228, 229, 231, 232, 240–41
Louisiana, 174–75, 244
Louis XIV, 130, 141, 145, 162, 163, 218
Louis XV, 173
Lount, Samuel, 423
Lower, A.R.M., 491
Lower Canada, 370–75
    agricultural crisis, 373–74, 390–92, 397–99
    cities and towns, 374, 393–96
    country life, 389–93, 397–99
    English-speaking merchant elite in, 370–72, 412
    immigration to, 371–72, 377–78

laws, 303
party system in, 405–406. See also Parti canadien; Patriotes
population, 1800, 310
rebellions in, 405–408, 412–19, 434–35
Roman Catholic Church in, 372, 395, 431
shipbuilding in, 371, 394
timber trade in, 370–71, 393, 394
Loyal Electors (Prince Edward Island), 345
Loyalists
    churches and schools, 292–93, 294, 295
    class and culture divisions, 291, 293, 295
    free blacks, 291–93
    in the "Great Lakes heartland," 298–99
    historical interpretations, 311–13
    "late Loyalists," 298
    Natives, 296–98
    in Nova Scotia, 271, 290–95
    political concerns, 295, 300
    in Quebec, 259, 295–300
    religious views, 292–93, 294
    women and children, 293–94, 295
    writings, 294–95
Lundy's Lane, battle at, 408
Lunenburg, Nova Scotia, 273
Luther, Martin, 67

Macdonald, John A., 429, 517, 563, 583, 584, 587–88, 594–95, 598
Macdonald, John Sandfield, 583, 585, 602
MacDonnell, Margaret, 323
Macdonnell, Miles, 453–54
Macdonnell, Richard Graves, 592–93
Mackenzie, Alexander, 306, 463–64
Mackenzie, William Lyon, 420, 421, 422–23, 427
Mackenzie valley, 474
MacLean from Raasay, 325
MacMhannain, Calum Bàn, 324–25
MacNab, Allan, 428
MacNutt, W.S., 335
Mactaggart, John, 387–88
Madras school system, 352
Magazines by 1850, 517
Magdalen Islands, 320
Maillard, Abbé Pierre-Antoine-Simon, 227, 247
Maisonneuve, Paul Chomedey de, 114
Maliseet, 20, 138, 226, 232, 246, 277, 278, 498–99
Malthus, Thomas, 375
Mance, Jeanne, 109
Mandan, 307

Manufacturing in British North America, 551–54
Marin, Pierre-Paul de, 234
Maritimes. *See* Atlantic colonies
Maritime union, 588, 591–93, 594
Marquette, Jacques, 160
Marriage
    in New France, 198, 200, 201
    interracial marriages, 117, 441, 451–52, 476–78
Martínez, Esteban José, 308
Mascarene, Paul, 228
Massachusetts, 255
"Massacre of Grand Pré," 231
Matthews, Peter, 423
Mauger, Joshua, 273, 275
McCallum, John, 398
McClintock, Captain Leopold, 486
McClure, Captain Robert, 486
McCulloch, Thomas, 323, 555
McDougall, John, 33
McGee, Thomas D'Arcy, 541, 571
McNutt, Alexander, 279
Mechanics' Institutes, 356, 517, 555
Membertou, 96
Menou d'Aulnay, Charles de, 96, 97
Mercantilism, 119, 151–53, 393
    and development of Atlantic colonies, 331–32, 333, 336–37, 358–60
    replaced by free trade policies (1840s), 327, 331, 337, 347
    varying historical opinions on, 358–60
Merchants
    in Atlantic colonies, 331
    after the Conquest, 251, 252–253, 300
    English-speaking, in Lower Canada, 371–72, 412
    in mid-19th century British North America, 489
    in New France, 187, 188–89
Meredith, E.A., 564–65
Metcalfe, Alan, 516
Metcalfe, Sir Charles, 426
Methodist churches, 351, 369
Métis, 198, 208, 307, 450, 451–53, 454–55, 484
    development of distinct communities, 452–53, 454, 461
    in fur-trade monopoly period, 452, 456, 460–62
    wives of fur traders, 441, 452, 478
Meulles, Jacques de, 153
Mi'kmaq, 18–20, 84
    culture, 19, 20

effects of contact with Europeans, 96–98, 277–78, 348, 350, 554
efforts to adapt to white culture, 498–99, 500
relations with Europeans, 94, 138, 226, 227, 232–33, 238, 246, 247–48, 273
Michif, 452
Michilimackinac, 159, 176, 180
Middle class
    in New France, 205–206
    rise of, 344, 496, 554–55
    urban life for, 565–67, 569
Migration to Canada. *See* Immigration
Military establishment, 492
    in British North America, 512
    in New France, 184
Militia, 492
    in New France, 141, 184, 229–30
Mining, 336, 490
    in New France, 185–86
Missionaries, 82, 83, 94, 96, 102–106, 118–19, 448, 460, 605
    effects on Native people, 98, 102, 104–105, 110, 450
    impressions of Native people, 20, 24, 25, 102, 103, 104, 105
    in Labrador, 283
"Mississippi bubble," 174
Mobility in mid-19th century, 502, 504
"Moderate revisionists," 572–73
Mohawk, 296, 297, 310, 498
Molson, John, 371, 541, 552
Monckton, Robert, 235
Montagnais, 24–25, 82, 138
Montcalm, Marquis de, 239–40, 242, 243
Montezuma, 75
Montgomery, Richard, 256, 257
Montreal, 114, 180, 191–92, 393–95, 491, 492, 515, 551
Montreal *Gazette*, 302, 394, 404
"Montreal School" of historians, 261–62
Monts, Pierre du Gua de, 93, 94, 99, 100
Moodie, Susanna, 380–81, 516
Moogk, Peter, 204
Moose, 338
"Moral missionaries," 389
Morgan, Robert, 509
Morin, A.N., 428
Morris, Alexander, 572
Morton, Desmond, 437
Morton, W.L., 436
Mumming, 512
Murrant, John, 292

Murray, James, 243, 250, 251, 252, 253, 254
Music, 520–21

Napoleon, 305
Napoleonic Wars (1793–1815), 332, 333, 334
Nationalism, 580–82
and colonial identity, 569–72
Nation-states, 64–65
in the 19th century, 580–82
Native people. *See* First Nations
Natural selection, 557
Navigation, 72
Navigation Acts, 331, 337, 359
Naylor, R.T., 610
Neilson, John, 414
Nelson, Dr Wolfred, 414, 415, 511
Nelson, Robert, 417
Nepotism in New France, 132
New Brunswick, 345
in 1850s and 1860s, 589, 590
confederation debates, 598, 599, 600–601, 611
created (1784), 290
effects of timber trade, 333, 335, 346, 358, 359, 360
prohibition movement in, 560
New England
warfare with New France, 163, 165
Newfoundland, 7, 222, 224, 254, 281–83, 348
in the 1850s and 1860s, 591
during the American Revolution, 288
Confederation, 598
early British colonization, 88–90
English immigrants to, 329
growth (early 19th century), 332–33
importance of fishery to economy, 332, 333, 335, 342
political structure in, 345
social divisions in mid-19th century, 497
Viking settlement on, 84
New France
absolutism in, 133, 136, 138–39
agriculture in, 195–96
class and society in, 115–16, 156–58, 202–206
colonial administration in, 139–41, 142, 143, 144, 151
conquest of, *see* Conquest of New France
distinctive culture, 172

economy of, 178–89
family life in, 198, 200–202
France in America, 1663–1755 (map), 220
fur trade in, *see* Fur trade
habitants in, *see* Habitants
immigration to, 136, 137–38, 155
intellectual life in, 193–94
labour in, 162, 206, 208–209
law and order in, 141–45
map of New France in the 17th century, 95
marriage in, 198, 200, 201
merchants in, 187, 188–89
militia in, 141, 184, 229–30
population growth, 136, 155, 210
relations between Natives and French settlers, 138, 164
religious establishment in, 118–19, 145–51, 206, 211, 212
seigneurial system in, *see* Seigneurial system
slavery in, 174, 175, 206–208
territorial expansion of, 160
town life in, 190–94
trade in, 152–53, 187, 188–89
wars and alliances, 162–66
women in, 133, 136, 167–69, 188
Newman, Peter C., 478
Newspapers, 273, 302, 346, 353–54, 356–57, 502, 503, 517
in Lower Canada, 394, 405
in Upper Canada, 407, 421, 422
New Westminster, 468
Niagara Falls, 520
Nightingale, Florence, 507
Ninety-Two Resolutions (1834), 413–14
Noblesse in New France, 205, 206
Noel, Jan, 167
Nonsuch (ship), 159
Nootka Sound Convention (1790), 308
North America, 1697 (map), 134
North America, 1713 (map), 135
North America, 1763 (map), 247
North America, 1783 (map), 259
North physiographic region, 8
North West Company, 301, 306, 307, 374
merger with HBC, 455
on Pacific coast, 463–64
rivalry with Hudson's Bay Company, 442–43
Northwest Passage, 83, 87, 485, 486
Notman, William, 519
Nova Scotia, 222, 223, 224–27, 272–79

in 1850s and 1860s, 589–90, 591
during the American Revolution, 288, 290
Blacks in, 278
Confederation, 601
court system, 344
culture, 356, 357
economy following 1815, 336
German- and French-speaking immigrants, 273
home-based production in (1851), 339–40
Irish in, 278–79
Loyalists in, 290–95
Native peoples, 277–78. *See also* Maliseet; Mi'kmaq
New England Planters, 274–75, 276
politics in, 346–47
reaction to American Revolution, 258
religious revival in, 289
representative government, 344
Scots in, 279, 322–23
settlers from Yorkshire, 279
Nova Scotia Magazine, 295
Novascotian (newspaper), 346, 357
Nuu'chah'nulth (Nootka), 308, 309, 462–63, 471

Ohio Company, 233
Ohio territory, 234, 249, 254
   granted to Quebec in Quebec Act, 254, 255
Ojibwa, 16, 25–29, 113, 298, 306, 307, 445–46, 447–48, 450, 459, 498
O'Donel, Bishop James Louis, 355
Oral history, 10–11, 323–25
Orange Order, 328, 378, 419, 511
Oregon Treaty (1846), 466, 467
Orléans, Philip, Duc de (regent), 173
Orphanages, 564, 569
Osborn, Captain Henry, 222
Oswego, 239
Ottawa people, 298, 447, 448
Ouellet, Fernand, 262, 397, 398, 399, 419
Overpopulation in Lower Canada, 373, 374
Owram, Doug, 473

Pacific Coast. *See also* British Columbia
   European exploration of, 307–309
Palliser, Hugh, 282–83
Palliser, John, 472, 571
Palliser's Act (1775), 254–55, 283
Palmer, Bryan, 512

Palmer, Edward, 561
Palmer, James, 345
Panting, Gerald, 359
Papacy, 65, 66, 344
Papineau, Louis-Joseph, 372, 391, 412–15, 417–18
Paquet, Gilles, 397–98, 399
Parish system in New France, 146, 147
Parkman, Francis, 211, 260
Parr, John, 290
Parti canadien, 372, 405–406, 409, 412
Passamaquoddy, 232, 246
Paternalism, 141, 211, 213, 343
Patriarchy, 343, 493, 566
Patriotes, 395, 412–14, 415, 418
Patronage, 370, 410, 420, 426, 584
Patterson, Walter, 280
Paul, Peter, 554
Pawnee, 207
Peasant revolts in early modern Europe, 53
Peel, Sir Robert, 327
Pelly, John Henry, 467
Pemmeenauweet, Paussamigh, 348, 350
Pemmican, 449, 453–54, 459, 460
Pentland, H.C., 514
Pepperell, William, 228
Pérez, Juan, 308
Perkins, Simeon, 278
Peterloo Massacre, 375
Philipps, Colonel Richard, 222
Phillips, Charles E., 572
Phips, Sir William, 163
Photography, 519
Physiographic regions of Canada, 6–9
Pichon, Thomas, 235
Picquet, Abbé, 233
Pictou Academy, 323
Pitt, William, 239
Placentia, 139, 158
Plains of Abraham, Battle of, 243
"Planters" from New England, 274–75, 276, 289
Plessis, Bishop Joseph-Octave, 409, 410, 412, 413
Police forces, 514
Political system in New France, 140–41
Politics in the Canadas, 404–405, 428–30
   before 1812, 405–408
   War of 1812, 408–11
Polk, James K., 467
Pond, Peter, 258, 306
Pontchartrain, Jérôme Phélypeaux de, 177, 226–27

Pontchartrain family, 132
Pontiac, 216–17, 248, 249
Poor, John Alfred, 590
Portland, Duke of, 367
Port Royal, 94, 96, 165, 221
Potlatch, 34–35
Poutrincourt, Jean de, 94
Poverty, 389, 436, 504, 565. *See also* Houses
    of Industry
    by 1850, 508–511
    in the Canadas, 366, 376
    dependent poor in the Atlantic
        colonies, 342
    in Lower Canada, 375, 396
Powell, William, 369
Prentice, Alison, 389, 573
Preston, Rev. Richard, 354
Prevost, Sir George, 408, 409
Prince Edward Island, 288, 342–43, 348,
    500
    in the 1850s and 1860s, 591
    Confederation, 597–98, 611
    economy following 1815, 335–36
    given new name, 320
    Irish immigrants to, 328
    land question, 345–46
    land speculation in, 279–80
    Loyalists on, 290–91
    Scottish settlement in, 280–81, 322
Prisons, 511, 563
Privateering, 290, 335, 341
Professional class in Lower Canada, 372
Prohibition movement, 560, 590
Proprietorial system, 345–46
Prostitution, 374, 469
    in New France, 145, 198
Protectionism, 541
Protestant churches, 67
    in the Atlantic colonies, 355–56. *See
        also* Evangelicalism
Provencher, Bishop Joseph-Norbert, 460
Puritans, 76

Quebec
    and American Revolution, 256–59
    boundaries extended, 254, 255
    English-speaking settlers in, 300–302
    Loyalists in, 295–300
    social life after Conquest, 301–302
Quebec Act (1774), 254–55, 259, 300
Quebec City, 99–100, 116, 118, 394–95,
    491
    in 1800, 310
    attacks on, 163, 165, 241, 242–43
    capture of (1759), 243
    cholera in, 378
    town life under French rule, 190–91,
        192
Quebec Conference (1864), 594, 595–96
Queen Charlotte Islands, 308
Queenston Heights, Battle of, 408, 409,
    410

Racism, 441, 442, 461, 470–71, 478,
    497–98, 501, 502
Radisson, Pierre-Esprit, 159
Rae, Dr John, 486
Railways, 393, 411, 427, 487, 517, 535–36,
    542–45, 546, 585, 589, 590, 595,
    609, 610, 611
Ramezay, Sieur de, 231
Rand, Silas, 501
Rand, Theodore Harding, 562
Raudot, Jacques, 207
Rawlyk, George, 352, 522
Ray, Arthur, 459
Raynal, Abbé, 183
Rebellion Losses Bill (1849), 427
Rebellions of 1837 and 1838
    in Lower Canada, 405–408, 412–19,
        434–35
    sources of rebellion, 396, 405–408,
        412–14, 419, 434
    in Upper Canada, 419–24, 434–35
Reciprocity Treaty (1854), 489, 540, 581,
    582
    cancelled, 600
Récollets, 102
Red River cart, 452–53
Red River settlement, 453–55, 460–62
Reformation, 67
Reformatories, 564
Reform Bill (U.K., 1832), 345
Reformers
    in Lower Canada, 405–406, 412–15
    in Upper Canada, 419–23, 424,
        425–26
Reform spirit in early 19th century, 356
Religion. *See also* Evangelicalism; Roman
        Catholic Church
    in Atlantic colonies, 289, 350–56
    and culture (19th century), 496–97,
        522–23
    debate over Darwinism, 557, 559
    in early modern Europe, 67, 69
    in Europe during the Middle Ages,
        65–66, 68
    and reform, 559–60

religious establishment in New France, 118–19, 145–51, 206, 211, 212
in Upper Canada, 367, 369–70, 419
Religious orders, 68–69, 102, 118, 146, 147, 395
after the Conquest, 250
Religious revival in Nova Scotia, 289
Renaissance, 69, 70, 71, 72
"Rep by pop," 583
Repentigny, Madame de, 153
Representative government
in Atlantic colonies, 344, 348
Reserves for Native people, 498, 500
Responsible government, 585–86
achievement of, 424–26
in action, 426–30
in Atlantic colonies, 346, 347–48
Rich, E.E., 476
Richardson, John, 517
Richelieu, Cardinal, 113–14
Rideau Canal, 387, 388, 411
Ripsin, Thomas, 339
Roads, 404, 487–88
Roberval, Jean-François de, 93, 94, 218
Robinson, John, 339
Robinson, Sir John Beverley, 383, 410, 502
Robinson, W.B., 498
Rolph, Dr John, 420
Roma, Jean-Pierre, 178
Roman Catholic Church, 65–66, 67, 130
in Canada East, 430
after Conquest, 250, 254
and Irish immigrants to Atlantic colonies, 328
in Lower Canada, 372, 395, 431
in New France, 118–19, 146–51, 206, 211, 212
opposition to rebellions, 418
religious orders, see Religious orders
social concerns, 511, 559–60, 564
support for confederation, 606
in Upper Canada, 419
in War of 1812, 409, 410
Roman Catholics
civil rights for, 303–304, 355
in mid-19th century, 496–97
Rouges, 428, 430, 583, 602, 605
Royal government in New France, 119
Royal Proclamation of 1763, 219, 248, 252
Royal William (steamship), 541–42
Rudin, Ronald, 399
Rupert's Land, 159, 272, 305–309
claimed by Canada, 571
wishes of Canada West to annex, 472–73

Rural population in Upper Canada, 369
Rush-Bagot Agreement (1817), 411
Russell, Lord John, 346, 347, 414
Ryan, Shannon, 333
Ryerson, Egerton, 369, 419, 560, 561–62, 572, 573, 574, 575

Sabatier, Charles-Wugk, 521
Sable Island, early settlement on, 88
Sagard, Gabriel, 103, 105
Sager, Eric W., 359
Saint-Charles, Battle of (1837), 415, 416–17
Saint-Denis, Battle of (1837), 415
Sainte-Foy, Battle at (1760), 243–44
Sainte-Hélène, Mère, 149
Sainte-Marie Among the Hurons, 104, 105–106
Saint-Jean Baptiste Society, 395
Saint John, 336, 491, 551
Saint-Pierre and Miquelon, 282, 332
Saint-Vallier, Jean-Baptiste de la Croix de, 147, 148, 149
Salt smugglers, immigrants to New France, 209
Sangster, Charles, 570
Saunders, Charles, 241, 243
Sawmills in Lower Canada, 393
Sayer, Pierre-Guillaume, 460
Scammell, G.V., 74, 78
Schools, see Education
Scientific development, 555–57
Scottish immigrants
to Nova Scotia, 322–23
to Upper Canada, 376
Scurvy, 93, 94, 100, 116, 486
Second Continental Congress (1775), 256
Sedgewick, Rev. Robert, 566
Séguin, Maurice, 261
Seignelay, Marquis de, 132
Seigneurial system, 115, 154–58, 195, 197, 365–66, 372–73
after the Conquest, 252, 253, 254
Selkirk, Earl of, 322, 453, 454
Semple, Robert, 454
Seneca, 163
Separate schools, 562, 585, 597
Serfs, 50
Servants, 387
Seven Oaks incident, 454–55
Seven Years' War (1756–63), 174, 238–45
Shadd, Mary Ann, 502, 503
Shamans, 25, 37–38
Shawnadithit, 318, 319, 320
Shelburne, Nova Scotia, 291, 292

Sherbrooke, Sir John, 334
Shiners' War, 377, 388
Shipbuilding, 546, 552
    in the Atlantic colonies, 323, 333, 336,
        359–60
    in Lower Canada, 371, 394
    in New France, 184–85
Shirley, William, 235
Short, Richard, 284
Sierra Leone, emigration of black Loyalists
    to, 293
Simcoe, John Graves, 366–67, 368, 369,
    370, 410
Simonds, Charles, 346
Simpson, Sir George, 441, 458–59, 461,
    466, 467
Sioui, Georges, 121
Sioux, 16, 31, 32, 307
Six Nations, 296–97, 498
Slavery, 48, 60–61, 74, 278
    in New France, 174, 175, 206–208
    refugee slaves from U.S., 329, 501–502
    slave trade abolished in British Empire
        (1807), 329
Smallpox, 464
"Smashers," 590
Smith, Adam, 331
Smith, Albert James, 598, 599
Smith, William, 295, 300
Smuggling, 334
Social divisions in colonial society, 508,
    565
Socialism, 344
Social mobility in Canada West, 436–37
Social services
    in Lower Canada, 395
    in mid-19th century, 510
Société de Notre Dame, 109, 114
Sons of Temperance, 560
Sovereign Council (later Superior
    Council), New France, 140, 141,
    143, 144
Spanish Succession, War of the,
    (1702–13), 165
Speculation in land, 412, 414, 422
Sports, 515–16
Sproat, Gilbert, 471
St John's, 332, 342
St John's Island. See Prince Edward Island
Stadaconans, 92–93
Staples-based economy, 488–89
    Atlantic colonies, 331–32, 333, 336–37,
        358–60
    the Canadas, 396
Steamships, 541–42, 554

Stone, Lawrence, 57
Stowe, Emily Jennings, 568
Stowe, Harriet Beecher, 502
Strachan, Bishop John, 410, 419, 431, 523,
    561
Strikes, 388, 389, 514
Stuard, Susan, 62
St Vincent de Paul societies, 395
Sulpicians, 146
Sulte, Benjamin, 260
Sun dance, 33, 450
Sunday school movement, 352
Survey system in New France, 156
Sydenham, Lord, 426

Taché, E.P., 428, 588
Talon, Jean, 151–52, 159, 160
Taxation
    in New France, 173
    "no taxation without representation",
        303
Technological developments, 551
Tecumseh, 408
Telegraph, 487
Temperance movement, 353, 389, 559–60,
    590
Tenant League in P.E.I., 591
Territorial expansion of New France, 160
Thanadelthur, 477
Theatres in colonial cities, 515, 520
Thirteen Colonies, 239, 244
Thirty Years War, 53
Thom, Adam, 462
Thompson, David, 33–34, 448, 464
Thorpe, Robert, 407
Thule, 39
Tilley, Samuel Leonard, 560, 590, 598, 601
Timber trade, 491
    in Atlantic colonies, 332, 333, 358, 359
    effects on politics in New Brunswick,
        346
    in Lower Canada, 370–71, 393, 394
Tithe, 147
Toronto, 233, 491, 492, 551
Towns. See Cities and towns; Urban life
Tracy, Marquis de, 133
Trade, 334, 336
    American–Canadian, 393
    change from protectionism to free
        trade, 327, 331, 337, 347, 426
    in early modern Europe, 64, 65
    in New France, 152–53, 187, 188–89
    triangular trade with West Indies, 332,
        334, 336
Trade unions, 389

Traill, Catharine Parr, 516–17
Transportation, 541–45, 546. *See also* Canal
    construction; Railways; Roads;
    Steamships
Travelling lecturers, 555
Travelling shows, 517, 520
Traves, Tom, 544
Treaty of Montreal (1701), 164
Treaty of Paris (1763), 244
Treaty of Versailles (1783), 258, 297
Trent (ship), 593
Trigger, Bruce, 121
Trofimenkoff, Susan Mann, 260
Troupes de la Marine, 193, 205–206
"Truck system," 342, 491
Tsudaike, 5
Tulchinsky, Gerald, 545
Tupi-Guarani, 73–74
Tupper, Charles, 543, 589–90, 601, 610–11
Typhus epidemic, 378

"Underground railroad" for refugee
    slaves, 502
Uniacke, James Boyle, 347
Union Act (1840), 366, 425
Unions, 389, 511
United Province of Canada
    debates on confederation, 601–606,
        607
    political impasse, 583–86
    population growth, 582–83
United States of America. *See also*
    American Revolution; New England
    annexation to, 538, 539–40
    Civil War (1861–65), 538, 540, 582, 593
    emigration of *Canadiens* to, 390
    Loyalists from, *see* Loyalists
    as a market for primary products, 489
    migration to the Atlantic colonies
        from, 329
    refugee slaves from, 329, 501–502
    temporarily excluded from Britain's
        imperial trade, 331–32
Universities
    in the Atlantic colonies, 352–53
University of Toronto, 431–32
Upper Canada, 366–70
    children in, 383, 384, 387, 389
    cities and towns in, 379, 386–89
    country life in, 382–85
    "Family Compact" in, 410, 419
    farm life in, 369, 382–85
    government in, 370, 404–405, 407, 419,
        420

immigration to, 366, 375–76, 377
land grants in, 367–68
laws, 303
Loyalists in, 298
newspapers in, 407, 421, 422
population, 1800, 310
population growth, 366, 377
rebellions in, 419–24, 434–35
religion in, 367, 369–70, 419
varying conditions for settlers, 365, 366
Upper Canada College, 516
Urban life, 565–67
    in the Canadas, 366, 376
    in Lower Canada, 374, 393–96
    in mid-19th century, 491–93
    in New France, 190–94
    in Upper Canada, 379, 386–89
Ursulines, 69, 107, 108
Utrecht, Treaty of (1713), 165–66, 217,
    221, 224, 226

Vancouver, George, 308
Vancouver Island, 467–68, 469–70, 484
Van Egmond, Col. A.G.W., 423
Van Kirk, Sylvia, 476, 477, 478
Vaudreuil, Governor, 165, 201, 209
Vaudreuil, Pierre de Rigaud de (Governor
    Vaudreuil the Younger), 189, 235,
    239, 240, 244
Verchères, Madeleine de, 164, 168
Versailles, 130
Victoria, B.C., 484, 492
Victoria, Queen, 350
Viger, Denis-Benjamin, 394
Viking settlements in the Americas, 84
Ville Marie, 109
Violence in colonial life, 511–14
Violettes, 430
Virginia, 76
Voltaire, 244
Voting rights
    in Atlantic colonies, 348
    under Constitutional Act, 303
    in Upper Canada, 365
    for women, 303, 348, 566–67, 568
Voyageurs, 209, 306

Walker, Sir Hovenden, 165
Wallis, Provo, 341
Wallot, Jean-Pierre, 397–98, 399
Walrus hunting, 87–88
Ward, Peter, 493
Warfare in Europe, 52–53
War of 1812, 329, 334–35, 408–411